D0387816

THE CONNOISSEUR'S
HANDBOOK OF

Antique Collecting

THE CONNOISSEUR'S HANDBOOK OF

Antique Collecting

A DICTIONARY OF FURNITURE, SILVER,
CERAMICS, GLASS, FINE ART, ETC.

Edited by
HELENA HAYWARD

With an introduction by L. G. G. Ramsey
Editor of *The Connoisseur*

GALAHAD BOOKS · NEW YORK CITY

Published by Galahad Books, a division of A & W Promotional Book Corporation, 95 Madison Avenue, New York, N.Y. 10016, by arrangement with Hawthorn Books, Inc., 260 Madison Ave., New York, N.Y. 10016.

Library of Congress Catalog Card No.: 73-85505

ISBN: 0-88365-125-4

Copyright © 1960 by The Connoisseur

All rights reserved, including the right to reproduce this book, or portions thereof, in any form.

Manufactured in the United States of America.

Preface

The purpose of this book is to provide a glossary of terms used by connoisseurs and collectors of antiques. Interest in works of art, whether furniture or faience, porcelain, prints or pistols, is so widespread that more and more books devoted to them are appearing. Specialized studies in each field are available but many collectors and newcomers to the art world must often be confused by the volume of information and the terminology used. Sometimes the names of the objects themselves are unfamiliar, while terms describing the material of which they are made or the varying styles of decorative ornament are often obscure. In particular, auction sale catalogues make no concessions to the less experienced. What, for example, is a chiffonier or a fuddling-cup, of what is paktong made and when were chinoiseries popular? It is intended in this book to provide answers to such questions and to include, where appropriate, a brief historical outline. The names of some of the more famous craftsmen, such as cabinet-makers or porcelain decorators, have been included as they are frequently quoted, without further explanation, in catalogues. But with a vast field to cover, no attempt is made to provide exhaustive information. The book is conceived as a work of reference and a select bibliography is included to encourage further reading.

Helena Hayward

Introduction

Collecting antiques is no longer the privilege of kings or the perquisite of the rich. Today, an inestimable number of private collectors are active all over the world. The wealthy eighteenth-century patron of the arts has been replaced by foundations, industrial concerns, civic corporations, private societies and colleges. These bodies, fortunately, now commission the contemporary work of art. The whole pattern of collecting and patronage has thus completely changed. Yet this new twentieth-century source of patronage not only nurtures the antiques of the future but is immensely welcome and vitally necessary in all countries of the Western world. The survival of a particular craft and individual craftsmen depend upon it.

The high prices which have been obtained in the art auction rooms of London, Paris and New York during the last few years may give the impression that any from of collecting is now a highly competitive and expensive pastime. So it is, if a French Impressionist painting, a piece of silver by Paul de Lamerie, a rare Chippendale bookcase, or a commode by a leading American cabinet-maker like Duncan Phyfe is sought. Indeed, it must often seem that beautiful and interesting objects are vanishing so swiftly from the market that it may soon be impossible to find anything worth collecting. Museums are buying on a larger scale than ever before, thus making themselves formidable rivals to the private collector. Every work of art, too, that enters a museum is, in theory, lost to the collector and the antique trade for ever.

It is still possible, with the exercise of shrewdness and care, to collect in a less exalted way and pay a modest price for so doing. Few today could afford as Andrew W. Mellon did, to acquire thirty-three paintings from the Hermitage for nineteen million dollars or to pay the £275,000 for which the Rubens' *Adoration of the Magi* was purchased in London in 1959. But discerning collectors can be in advance of official taste and acquire for comparatively small sums the objects which may be the museum pieces of tomorrow. One instance of this was seen in the paintings of Charles François Daubigny, one of the earliest *plein air* painters in France in the 1850s and a leading member of the Barbizon School. His first successes outside France were in America; and to a great extent this was due to the Boston picture dealer Seth Morton Vose, who imported his first Corots in 1852 and his first Daubignys in 1857. It was undoubtedly due to Vose's perspicacity that some of the finest Barbizon School pictures are now in American museums.

Clearly it is not possible to forecast what objects are likely to go out of taste with collectors and what are likely suddenly to find favour. But there is more than one field which lies open to the discriminating collector; that of European prints, for example. Fine impressions of incunabula, or Dürer woodcuts may be rare, but the print collector can assemble a group of exquisite etchings and, engravings for a relatively modest outlay. Many of the finest graphic artists of the sixteenth, seventeenth, and eighteenth centuries are unaccountably neglected and their works may be acquired for small sums.

Another interesting field, especially for young collectors, is "Victoriana," or, as it is more broadly labelled in America "nineteenth century". The American interest is in the international quality of nineteenth-century art objects. Of particular interest are furniture and other objects made of *papier mâché*, which for some reason, was never produced in America.

In short, the type of collecting enjoyed by real enthusiasts is still feasible and will continue to be. It is these enthusiasts, invariably with limited means, who probably have the greatest enjoyment and eventually become true connoisseurs. How exciting it must have been for that great connoisseur, Sir Clare Ford, when, as a boy, he saw his father bring home a hundred and fifty superb specimens of fifteenth and sixteenth-century Italian maiolica. These were unpacked on the lawn and were washed "like a variegated bed of flowers, by means of a watering can." All these important specimens from Urbino, Castel Durante, Faenza and Gubbio are still in the Brinsley Ford Collection in London.

There are now many people in America and England with small collections of furniture, glass, silver, porcelain and so forth. This is an encouraging fact. The American antique collector pursues his interest in much the same way as his English counterpart, but he takes his collecting much more seriously. He is much more conscious of "values", which can usually be obtained from dealers or from the art press. He prefers to acquire an American piece of furniture, if he can afford it, rather than an English piece, which some American dealers will often consider to be overcarved. He keeps meticulous records of art prices and provenances, and he is also deeply conscious and wary of pitfalls. This is primarily because attendance at museum and historic house lectures and a constant study of art books and magazines have provided a useful theoretical knowledge.

As a further aid to the collector, a number of important American public collections of furniture are now being methodically analysed. A detailed study is being made of the woods used in every piece; provenances are being carefully determined; information is being collated which will throw light on methods of construction and usage in relation to the social customs and manners of the period. The latter is of particular importance, since in any country works of art mirror the society for which they were originally produced. These scholarly statistics will be made available to the public and will prove of wide interest to the student of art history. They will be an immense aid to collecting: an aid which was never available when George Watson Taylor was acquiring French furniture in the 1820s; to Consul Smith when he was buying pictures in Venice in the eighteenth century; to Cadwalader and Chew when they were establishing their collections of works of art in Philadelphia in the eighteenth century; or to Swan in Boston in the early nineteenth century. There was no literature of antiques available for the young Grand Tourist to study while having his portrait painted by Batoni in Rome; or to Robert and James Adam when they were engaged in purchasing works of art in Italy. There were no lavishly illustrated art books, especially on period furniture designs, as there are today, available to the Vanderbilts and the Astors when they were furnishing their new homes on Fifth Avenue after the Civil War.

In the collecting of antiques there are many complexities to be mastered. An understanding of the language of antiques is essential and as a reference work this book will provide much information needed by the connoisseur. It is only by close study both of the literature of the subject and the subjects themselves that the collector and student can train the eye to distinguish between works of good and indifferent quality; between the genuine article and the fake; between the piece of furniture which has the essential qualities of good colour, patination and proportions and that which lacks these features. It is certain, also, that a trained and expert eye is an infinitely more valuable possession than an expansive bank balance.

It becomes clearer to me each year, from the enquiries which reach my desk, that many of my correspondents have little conception of how to evaluate a work of art, or of what features to look for when considering a purchase. To decide, for instance, whether a piece of porcelain is genuine or whether it was made by Samson in Paris within the last hundred years is difficult, particularly as Samson's products are cleverly made. Only constant examination of the quality of genuine pieces will eventually train the eye. Much can also be learned from knowledgeable antique dealers.

What should be looked for, broadly speaking, for example, in the initial stages of collecting armour or silver? In the former, the Rothschild phase of armour collecting, which favoured embossed pieces in the taste of the High Renaissance, gave scope to the faker. Parts of armours, as distinct from complete suits, swords and firearms produced by highly skilled Milanese fakers in the last quarter of the nineteenth century are still occasionally to be encountered on the art market. In collecting silver the mark may show signs of being false or of having been transposed. Obviously, immediate doubts should be raised if a false mark, struck with a soft metal punch, has been made to give the appearance of wear when it has been struck in such a position which would normally be protected from rubbing. Fakers usually make a simple mistake somewhere. The trained eye and the retentive memory will in time detect it.

The collector today has never been better served in the pursuit of his chosen interests. There are great public and private collections everywhere, and, more than ever before, connoisseurs ready to share experience and impart knowledge. The literature of the subject is detailed and scholarly and The Connoisseur's Handbook of Antique Collecting will help to make it more intelligible and will be a useful background for all enthusiasts of the art world.

L. G. G. Ramsey
Editor of *The Connoisseur*

Absolon, William: (1751–1815), pottery decorator and china and glass dealer at Yarmouth. About 1790 he set up a pottery decorating business at a place on the Denes known as "The Ovens" where he enamelled earthenware and porcelain bought "in the white" from Staffordshire and Leeds. Absolon's mark, "Absolon Yarme No 25" painted in red, occurs on wares bought from Turner, Wedgwood, Shorthose and Leeds and impressed with their marks. In 1808 Absolon purchased a shop at the corner of Market Row (Row No 63) Yarmouth, and he died in Yarmouth in 1815. A painted arrow is also said to be Absolon's mark. There are examples of Absolon's decorated pottery and glass in Norwich Castle Museum.

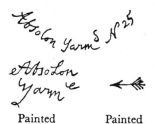

Painted   Painted

Acanthus: conventional foliage adapted from the capitals of Corinthian columns, used extensively as a decorative form throughout the Renaissance(q.v.) period and again in the late 18th cent. on furniture, silver, ormolu, etc.

Acid gilding: a process of decorating china with patterns etched into the ware and covered with gold. The design, usually in the form of a narrow border is transfer-printed to the ware in an acid "resist". The rest of the plate is then stopped out, both back and front, and dipped in acid which corrodes away the exposed parts of the design to a certain depth. When the etching is completed, the ware is removed from the acid, the resist and "stopping" dissolved and washed off and the etched border banded over in gold. After firing the ware is burnished, yielding a polished relief pattern against a duller matt gold background. First introduced by Mintons, 1863. A process which appears similar was invented by the Austrians and acquired, improved and worked by Powell & Bishop of Hanley.

Acorn clock: shelf or mantel clock, generally about two feet high, with the upper portion shaped somewhat like an acorn. An American type, popular in New England about 1825.

Acorn knop: a knop or protuberance on the stem of a drinking glass, tooled in the form of an acorn and sometimes inverted.

Acoustic jars: the name is given to pottery vessels found embedded in the fabrics of many medieval churches, usually upon the top of the walls of the chancels.

Acqua Fresca, Matteo: see Chiselled and cut steel.

Act of Parliament clock: a misnomer applied to a timepiece, usually weight-driven, with seconds pendulum, having a large unglazed dial and a small trunk. According to legend, these clocks were first put into inns and post taverns for use of the general public, many of whom had sold their clocks and watches when Pitt introduced his Act in 1797 levying 5s per annum on all clocks and watches. Such distress was caused in the trade that the Act was repealed next year.

A.d. and **a.d.s.:** autograph document, and autograph document signed, as distinguished from an a.l. or a.l.s. (q.v.), is likely to have relatively less collector's value; thus ship's papers, commissions, and land grants made out to or signed by famous men would be described as a.d. or a.d.s.

Adam, Robert: (1728–92), an eminent architect who, in common with his predecessor, William Kent, paid much attention to the interior decoration of his buildings. He was responsible for the classical revival initiated in the 1760s that ousted the furnishings made popular by Chippendale (q.v.). Adam designed the furniture for the houses he built or remodelled and a great number of original designs are in Sir John Soane's Museum, Lincoln's Inn Fields, London.

Adhesive book bindings: many illustrated books and, in particular, illuminated books made between 1840 and 1870 were composed of leaves of thick cardboard. These were very difficult to bind, since the weight of the cardboard tended to tear the stitches out. Hancock patented a process first used in 1839 for sticking the leaves to the spine of the binding case by a solution of caoutchouc. This solution was temporarily very popular, and many illustrated books, even when ordinary paper was used, were so secured. But the solution was perishable, and so a very large number of the books, and particularly the larger books of this period, fall to pieces when they are opened. The remedies are: (one) to have the leaves stuck in again, when, after another period, the process will repeat itself; (two) to have the rear edges of the leaves shaved and mounted on guards, since if this were not done the stitches would burst the binding, and then sew them in in the usual way. This is expensive. For books of no great value, therefore, the only practicable course is to allow the leaves to remain loose.

"Admiral Lord Howe" jug: a variety of toby jug (q.v.) known as "Admiral Lord Howe" or "Admiral Vernon", representing a seated naval figure. Admiral Howe had destroyed Cherbourg in 1758 and in 1794 won a famous victory over the French off Brest.

Adze-surfaced wood: some late medieval and early Tudor chests of heavy, strong construction show a pleasing irregularity of surface under the metal bindings, due to the fact that they have been faced with an adze. This tool, resembling a hatchet but with the blade at right angles to the shaft, inevitably left the surface faintly patterned with ridges and saucer-shaped hollows.

Aes: the term used for Roman coinages in copper and bronze.

Aes grave: the heavy cast bronze coinage of the Roman Republic in the 3rd cent. B.C. The unit was the as with its fractional parts.

Aesop's Fables: scenes illustrating the Fables occur on Chelsea porcelain table wares, c. 1753, derived from Francis Barlow's folio edition of *Aesop's Fables*, 1687.

Aes signatum: earliest Roman coinage. Large rectangular bronze blocks stamped with a design on each side.

Affleck, Thomas: an American cabinet-maker. Born in Aberdeen, Scotland, he learned his trade in London where, as a young man in 1763, he was chosen by John Penn, commissioned governor of Pennsylvania, to go with him to Philadelphia as resident cabinet-maker. Affleck died there in 1795, a prominent citizen who counted among his friends eminent persons such as Benjamin Franklin. He is generally reckoned the most skilful cabinet-maker in 18th cent. Pennsylvania.

Afghan rugs: rugs woven in Turkestan of coarser texture and design, and following the tradition of the other Turkoman types, looking rather like a coarse Bokhara rug (q.v.).

After-cast: a bronze figure or article produced not by the *cire-perdue* (q.v.) process but by making moulds from an existing model. After-casts can date from any time between the original production of the article and the present day.

"Agate" glass: a glass of several colours which have been allowed to mingle before the vessel is formed, in imitation of agate. This type of glass was popular during the Renaissance (q.v.), particularly in Venice and Germany, and is sometimes known as *Schmelzglas*.

Agate ware: salt-glazed stoneware or lead-glazed earthenware made in imitation of variegated natural stones, such as agate, by wedging together different coloured clays (early 18th cent.): more refined wares imitating semi-precious stones were made by Josiah Wedgwood (q.v.). A surface agate, known as marbled ware, was produced by combining various coloured slips in the manner of marbled papers.

Agon or **Queen's Guard:** a game played on a hexagonal board, divided into 91 equal hexagonal compartments, arranged in concentric bands of two contrasting colours, such as ivory and ebony or mahogany and satinwood. The numbers of hexagons contained in the bands were 30, 24, 18, 12, 6 and one in the centre. Each of the two players had seven men, a queen and six guards. Card tables combining boards for playing games such as agon, backgammon, etc. became fashionable during the Restoration period.

Aigrette: jewel supporting a feather or imitating it in form, worn in hair or cap since the end of the 16th cent.

Aiguillette: a knot, worn on the shoulder in the 19th cent., often jewelled.

Air-twist stem: a type of stem familiar on 18th cent. drinking glasses which is found in several forms between 1740–65: (a) single-twist air spirals in a drawn stem formed by the extension of air bubbles: multiple spirals were common throughout the period, and from 1745 two or four corkscrews; not until about 1750 do we encounter threads of uniform thickness spaced regularly; (b) single-twist in a three-piece glass: between 1740–65 the shank was cut from long lengths made by an extension of air bubbles; from 1750 spirals were made by a mould process, the filaments being finely drawn and coiled with precision in some thirty variations; (c) compound-twist in three-piece glass: between 1760–65 this type is found in a dozen variations.

Akce: Turkish silver coin issued between the 14th and 17th cent. with inscription types on both sides.

A.l. and **a.l.s.:** autograph letter, and autograph letter signed; these, as opposed to l.s. and t.l.s., mean that the letter, in the one case without, in the other with, a signature, is in the hand of the writer, that the letter is not typed, not a copy (unless the writer's own), and not in the hand of a secretary.

Albarello: a word of obscure derivation used to describe the nearly cylindrical form of the maiolica drugpot which was introduced into Italy from Spain, and later copied by English makers of tin-glazed earthenware. Possibly derived from *el Barani*, a vase for drugs. Albarelli were used for ointments and dry medicines.

Albert: a 19th cent. gold chain intended to hold a watch at one end and fitted with a bar at the other.

Albertin: gold coin named after its issuer, Albert, Archduke of Austria, governor of Spanish Netherlands (1598–1621). Types, busts of Albert and wife Elizabeth with reverse cross and date.

Alcora maiolica: tin-glazed earthenware made at Alcora in the province of Valencia at a factory founded in 1727 by the Count of Aranda, with the help of French potters from Moustiers (q.v.). The early wares are closely akin to those of Moustiers. They achieved a fine quality white enamel.

Ale-glass: long, narrow flute for serving strong ale, a highly alcoholic drink; from 1740 ale-glasses were sometimes engraved with the hop and barley motif.

Alençon lace: needlepoint lace was made at Alençon, where the craft was established in 1665 under Venetian tutelage. The early Venetian influence, however, soon became less important than the lighter, fine-threaded Flemish pillow lace notions, but like Argentan lace (q.v.), Alençon was regarded as a heavier Winter lace. By 1700 or 1720 the famous grounded point d'Alençon was evolved with rich fillings (q.v.) and a stiff cordonnet and picots (q.v.). This was mainly a narrow lace for borders and caps and was reintroduced in the 19th cent., more flimsy and often on a spotted ground. A softly looped hexagonal mesh was made first and the pattern put in, worked in close buttonhole stitch. (See Point de France and Grounded laces.)

Alentours: (*Fr.*) a term used to describe the borders surrounding tapestries. Except in German examples, these are rarely seen on tapestries until the beginning of the 16th cent. They then began to play a very important part in the general effect, and the best artists of the day were called in to design them. Very beautiful and varied effects were produced, especially in the 16th and 17th cent. In the 18th frame-borders became general, but the *alentours* which surround a subject inset in the main field, and enliven it with rococo displays of drapery and flowers, create an effect which is really that of an enlarged border. The style of a tapestry border is very important in determining questions of date and workshop and is sometimes a certain indication of this. Normally, borders were woven in one piece with the main field, and it is important to see whether a border has been re-applied. (See also Galloons.)

Allgood family: operated the Pontypool (q.v.) japan works from 1730 until 1818, and Usk (q.v.) from 1761 until early in the 19th cent. They had agents throughout the country and an average turnover of £5,000 a year in the 1760s. Few records of prices exist, but "a basket for cakes" sold for 5 guineas and an oval tray painted with a landscape for 15 guineas. (See also Pontypool).

Allison, Michael: New York cabinet-maker who flourished about 1800–20.

Some of his furniture is stamp punched; many of his other pieces have been attributed to Duncan Phyfe (q.v.).

"All-over" design: a pattern of close character which, conventional or abstract, and of large or small repeat, gives an all-over coverage on textiles or wallpapers. All-over book-bindings have the same motif repeated at equal intervals all over the covers.

Alloy: a composition of two or more metals intimately mixed by fusion, or a base metal mixed with precious metal to harden it or make it easier to work.

Alma: a chain, worn in the 19th cent., consisting of wide, ribbed links.

Almsdish: circular dish with broad, flat rim, plain or decorated in prevailing style of period. Single examples of 17th cent. domestic plates sometimes mistaken for almsdishes.

Alphin: (chess-man), the old name for the bishop, derived from the Italian *alfieri* or standard-bearers who administered the king's laws. English players eventually altered these pieces into cross-bearing bishops, supporting the king as immediate upholders of law and order.

Altun: Turkish gold coin introduced by Muhamad II in 1454. Obverse type, Sultan's name with mint and date; reverse, titles.

"A" mark: see Ansbach porcelain and Fulda porcelain.

Ambrosino: (1) gold coin of Milan of 13th cent. with type of St Ambrosius; (2) silver coin of 13th to 15th cent. with types, cross and St Ambrosius.

Ambry (aumbry, almery; armoire): (*Fr.*) enclosed compartment or recess in a wall or in a piece of furniture, the original sense of the term having been usurped by cupboard, which originally had a different connotation. "Cuppbordes wyth ambries" are mentioned in inventories of Henry VIII's furniture. Today aumbry, etc., is principally used architecturally and ecclesiastically, as of the doored compartments or recesses for the Reservation of the Blessed Sacrament, this usage perpetuating the original sense. The French form armoire is often applied to large presses or press-cupboards.

"Amen glasses": drinking glasses, mostly of the drawn-stem or baluster type, dating from about 1720 to 1745, with one or two verses of a Jacobite hymn engraved upon the bowls, ending with the word "Amen", and the cipher of James, the Old Pretender.

Amorini: cupids, which were frequently used as a decorative motif on late 17th cent. furniture, such as mirrors, chair-backs and day-beds.

Amulet: an ornament worn as a charm or talisman. (See also Pilgrim's badges.)

A.n. or **a.n.s.:** autograph note or autograph note signed. The expression refers to ms. memoranda, fragments, etc.

Ana: a collective noun meaning a compilation of sayings, table talk, anecdotes, etc. Its most familiar use is, however, the original one (from which the noun was made) in the form of a Latin suffix meaning material related to as distinct from material by; e.g. Boswelliana, Railroadiana, Etoniana.

Anatolian rugs: see under Turkish rugs.

Anchor mark: see Chelsea, Bow, Derby, Davenport, Sceaux and Venice porcelain. Also Holdship, Richard.

Anchor escapement: a type of clock escapement (q.v.) invented about 1670 by William Clement. It revolutionized timekeeping. With it the pallets are in the same plane as the escape wheel, instead of being at right angles to it, as in the verge escapement (q.v.). It largely eliminated circular error and also made practical the use of long pendulums swinging more slowly, hence with a lesser cumulative error. It is still used to-day for most domestic clocks and particularly in longcase

clocks with pendulums beating one second. It is also known as the recoil escapement, in which recoil is seen in the slight shudder at each beat in the seconds hand of long-case clocks so equipped. The vastly improved timekeeping of this escapement made really practical the use of clocks for astronomical purposes. Flamsteed, the first Astronomer Royal at Greenwich in 1675, used clocks made by Thomas Tompion, equipped with the anchor escapement. This largely accounted for the far greater accuracy of his observations as compared with those of his contemporaries. From this invention followed, either directly or indirectly, practically all the subsequent improvements in timekeeping.

Andirons: the iron fire-dog or andiron dates back to Roman times, but the earliest known examples date from the 15th cent. As long as the fireplace occupied the central position in the hall, the fire-dog was of purely utilitarian design, but when the former was transferred to a side wall, becoming an important decorative feature, the fire-dog also received ornamental treatment. The earliest surviving fire-dogs conform to a standard type, whether of English, French, German, or Flemish origin, namely an arched base enriched with Gothic cusping, supporting a pilaster, the front of which is decorated with running scrolls (Fig. A). 16th and 17th cent. fire-dogs were made to the same design but with Renaissance instead of Gothic ornament (Fig. B). Fire-dogs of this type were made of cast iron, the English ones being produced by the Sussex iron-masters. There seems from an early date to have been a distinction between andirons and fire-dogs. The former term was used for the large dogs, standing three feet or more high, which were intended to decorate the fire-place. Though these andirons could also be used, they were usually accompanied by a smaller pair of fire-dogs proper, which stood closer into the hearth and supported the burning logs.

The earlier andirons were of wrought iron, but as early as the 16th cent. they were garnished with silver. In the 17th cent. andirons entirely of silver were produced and there was a fashion for them in England after the Restoration. The Restoration andiron had a particularly handsome baroque form, consisting of a pedestal on volute or claw feet supporting either a flaming vase or a figure. The finest examples are of great magnificence and weight of silver. Similar designs were also produced for the less wealthy in gilt brass. The introduction of the grate in the 18th cent. rendered the fire-dog superfluous.

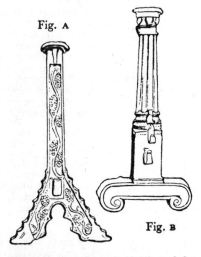

Fig. A

Fig. B

Ange d'or: gold coin instituted by Philip IV of France in 1341 with types of St Michael and the dragon and an elaborate cross with four crowns. Imitated with variations in the Low Countries.

Angel: gold coin of value 6s 8d, introduced by Edward IV in 1465 with types of St Michael slaying dragon and ship bearing shield with cross above. The angel was struck up to the reign of Charles I.

"Anglo-Japanese" style: Japanese craftmanship displayed at the International Exhibitions of 1862 in London and 1867 in Paris excited the interest of Victorian designers. This hitherto unknown culture inspired a vogue for what was taken to be the Japanese manner and designs in this spirit between the 1860s and the 1880s became familiar on wallpapers, textiles and in book illustrations. The furniture of the period also betrayed this new influence.

Anglo-Venetian glass: glass vessels of fine soda-glass made in London from about 1570 until the last quarter of the 17th cent. These glasses were made in the Venetian manner by immigrant Italian workmen. The number of examples to which an English origin can definitely be attributed is limited, but many vessels probably made in London are mistakenly thought to be Venetian in origin or to have been made in the Netherlands by Venetian workmen. (See also Verzelini, Jacopo.)

Angular knop: a knop or protuberance on the stem of a drinking vessel, of rounded-edge flattened form.

An hua ("secret") decoration: faint engraving or painting in white slip, visible only against the light; found on Chinese porcelain especially on early Ming and 18th cent. white porcelain.

Anna: a coin; a copper sub-division of the silver rupee in India. Types, badge of East India Company and balance.

Annealing: (1) a process of toughening flint-glass by raising it to a high temperature and then cooling it gradually. (a) Annealing oven: an oven known as the tower, built above the melting chamber and operated on waste heat from below; (b) annealing tunnel, or leer: a tunnel five or six yards in length through which newly-made glass passes slowly to cool, toughen, and acquire increased brilliance. (2) Similarly a process of tempering metals. Silver, for example, becomes brittle under hammering during the process of raising from a flat street and requires heating to soften it.

Annulated knop: a knop or protuberance on the stem of a drinking glass, of flattened form, sandwiched between two, four or six thinner flattened knops, each pair progressively less in size.

Annuals, drawing-room scrapbooks, keepsakes, etc.: annuals of all kinds are timeless, but the particular type of annual which developed into a book to leave on the drawing-room table has its origin in the period just before Victoria. In 1825 the first annual in this sense appeared in England, a volume bound in watered silk with contributions by well-known authors and illustrated by leading artists. Charles Heath produced, in 1832, as an Annual *The Drawing Room Scrap Book* and the *Book of Beauty* a year later. With Lady Blessington as editress until 1849, the *Book of Beauty* was a great success, and she also edited the *Keepsake* from 1841 till 1850 and contributed to other similar works. Many other books, though not annuals, made their appearance with a view to being glanced at in the drawing-room, such as Andrews's *Flower Book Gems for the Drawing Room*, Paul Jerrard's books, e.g. *The Floral Offering*, and Miss Giraud's *Flowers of Shakespeare, of Milton, and of Scott*. They represent a particular side of Victorian taste, and are not to be found at any other time.

Anon.: anonymous; i.e. published without the name of the author.

Ansbach porcelain: porcelain was made at a factory set up at Ansbach, Germany, under the protection of the Margrave Alexander of Brandenburg from 1757. The factory was transferred to the castle of the Margrave at Bruckberg in 1762, and although it ceased to have State protection soon after the death of the Margrave in 1791, it actually continued to exist until 1860. Ansbach porcelain is hard-paste and of fine quality. Many of the figures modelled were taken from

Meissen (q.v.) examples, while the tables wares were largely influenced by Berlin and Nymphenburg (q.v.). The mark used from about 1758 to 1762 was a shield surmounted by an A in blue, while an A alone was used from about 1762 to 1785 and later. The figures are often unmarked or bear an impressed shield.

Anthemion: (or honeysuckle), a formal ornament of Greek derivation based on the honeysuckle flower or the branch of a date palm and sometimes also described as a palmette. It was much used as a  decorative motif on Classical architecture, and for this reason became a favourite ornament in England in the second half of the 18th cent. and during the Regency, when it appears as a motif on furniture, silver, etc.

Antoninianus: a Roman coin, being the double denarius (q.v.), instituted by the emperor Caracalla in A.D. 215. The obverse bears an Imperial portrait wearing a radiate crown. The piece was originally issued in silver, but through successive debasements it became by mid-3rd cent. a copper piece with a surface wash of silver, and disappeared in Diocletian's reform of A.D. 296.

Antwerp lace: pillow lace, strong and heavy looking, the patterns outlined in a *cordonnet* (q.v.) of thick untwisted thread and made at the same time as the *fond chant* (q.v.) ground. The style of pattern has given this the name of pot lace or potten kant, from the substantial two-handled vase usually prominent in it. This motif was very popular in 18th cent. embroideries. It appeared also in Normandy laces.

Aogai: Japanese lacquer-work technique in which mother-of-pearl, made from Haliotis shell, is inlaid into the surface of the lacquered wood.

"Apostle" jug: a straight-sided jug modelled in relief with figures of the Apostles under an elaborate gothic arcading, made by Charles Meigh in porcellanous stoneware, c. 1845.

Apostle spoon: early type of spoon with full-length figure of an apostle or Christ (The Master) as finial. Extant examples date from late 15th cent. till Charles II period. Complete sets of thirteen are of very rare occurrence.

"Apple-green" ground: a trade name for a ground colour used extensively in the decoration of porcelain at Worcester (q.v.) during the Wall period from about 1770 when Sèvres (q.v.) influence was felt. The colour was introduced at Sèvres in 1757. W. B. Honey describes it as "pea-green" (*Old English Porcelain*, 1928, new ed. 1948).

Applied ornament: a term used to describe ornament which is separately applied to an object. Carved decoration was sometimes applied to furniture, while decorative motifs were also chased and applied to silverware.

Applied work: the sewing of patches on to the surface of a material so that they form a pattern. The edges of the pattern are usually outlined by embroidery. In the Middle Ages applied work was used as a cheaper substitute for tapestry, and during the Renaissance, figured brocades and velvets were imitated by this method. In the

16th and 17th cent. applied work was widely used for altar-frontals and vestments, for hangings, chair-covers, and horse-trappings. In England during the 16th and 17th cent. motifs of animals, floral sprigs and insects were worked in tent stitch on canvas and then cut out and applied to cushion-covers and hangings. Needle-point lace motifs, in silk and metal thread, were similarly applied to work-boxes and embroidered pictures.

Appliques: see Wall-lights.

Apron-piece: an ornamental member, either carved or simply shaped, sometimes used below the seat rail of a chair or settle or below the frieze of cabinet stands and dressers.

Aquamanile: this term is used to describe the bronze ewers used in the Middle Ages for pouring water over the hands of guests after each course of a meal. As forks were not normally employed for conveying food to the mouth, frequent washing of the hands was indispensable. Though originally referring to all kinds of ewer, the term is now confined to a particular type of medieval ewer of naturalistic form, the most popular being a lion on whose back crouches a dragon, serving as a handle. Other forms include a monster, a knight on horseback wearing a great helm, etc. Medieval aquamaniles of this type were cast by the *cire-perdue* process (q.v.) and no two were exactly alike; many reproductions have, however, been cast from moulds in recent times. The earliest examples date from the 13th cent., but they continued in use until the 16th cent., when they were replaced by the more convenient ewer of helmet shape. They are now objects of extreme rarity, and few authentic examples are to be found in private ownership.

Aquatint: the name of a process by which the plates, from which many coloured prints were produced, came into being. It is an indirect method in that, unlike the etching, where the engraving tool scratches the lines directly on to the plate, an upper surface formed of resin or other substance is placed over the plate, and this is worked on, leaving room for acid to come down on to the plate and eat its way in, thus producing the desired effect. Aquatint is therefore not a line process but one which produces a more general effect on the plate, and is softer than a line engraving. The aquatint flourished before the Victorian age, e.g. Acker-mann's *Microcosm of London*, Dr Thornton's *Temple of Flora 1867*, and thousands of other examples, both as separate prints and in books. None the less, a number of aquatints appeared after 1837, notably the sporting prints of Herring and Dean Wolstenholme Junior (see Sporting prints). (See S. Prideaux, *Aquatint Engraving*, 1909.)

Aquilino: silver coin of gros (q.v.) class, struck in Tyrol and North Italy in the 13th cent. with types of eagle and double cross.

Arabesques: ornament used for borders or panels, derived from the true mauresque ornament which was, however, of abstract form, composed of naturalistic elements both foliate and figural. The term is sometimes loosely used to apply to mauresques.

Arbor: the shaft of a clock which carries wheels and pinions.

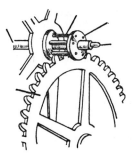

Arbour group: lovers seated within an alcove or a leafy arbour, made in Staffordshire white salt-glazed stone-ware (q.v.) or Whieldon (q.v.) ware.

Arcaded decoration: a form of ornament in which a series of arches are represented, supported on columns or pilasters, and frequently found on furniture between 1600 and 1670.

Arcanist: a person knowing the secret of pottery-making in general, and of porcelain-making in particular.

Arcanum: chemical composition and technique of porcelain-making.

Architectural clock: a clock in which the hood, in long-case, and the top in mantel clocks, is in the style of a classical pediment, with or without supporting columns. Usually a sign of work in the third quarter of the 17th cent., although these pediment tops were revived for a short period early in the 19th cent.

Arch-top clock case, plain: a case, usually in bracket clocks, where the arch rises directly from the sides of the case.

Argentan lace: needlepoint lace made at a workshop established in 1665. Resembled Alençon lace made ten miles away until they developed meshed grounds. The so-called Argentan lace was made also at Alençon, the work tending to be larger and more perfect than so-called Alençon, with bold patterns and a hexagonal ground, sometimes *picotée*, worked over in tiny buttonhole stitches. (See *Point de France*).

Argentella lace: a needlepoint lace, being a variant of *point d'Alençon*, with a large dotted mesh. (See *Œil de perdrix*).

Argenteus: the larger silver Roman coins issued from the reform of 296 throughout the 4th cent.

Argil: clay, especially potters' clay, hence the trade name Mason's Cambrian Argil used for earthenware allegedly made from Welsh clay by the firm of G. M. and C. J. Mason, c. 1820. "Cambria Clay" occurs in sale notices and means Welsh clay.

Argyle: a silver, plate or pottery gravy container, cylindrical or vase-shaped, resembling a small coffee-pot, with either outer lining or central container (sometimes detachable) for hot water. Introduced about 1770; in favour until about 1820.

Arita porcelain: Japanese porcelain made at Arita, where the first Japanese porcelain kilns were established. Two styles of decoration were developed at Arita, both much copied in the West: the Kakiemon style, so called from the Kakiemon family of potters, and the "Imari", this being the neighbouring port from which the wares were shipped to Europe. (See also Kakiemon and Imari.)

Ark: term frequently encountered in medieval inventories, seemingly meaning (1) a chest with a coped or gabled lid; (2) perhaps a structure resembling a reliquary (*Fr.* chasse), as exemplified by the 16th cent. almery in Coity Church, Glamorganshire. That ark was a distinct term is shown by such entries as the following from an inventory of the contents of St Mary's, Warwick, 1464:
"It: in the Vestrye i gret olde arke to put in vestyments etc.
"It: in the Sextry above the Vestrye, i olde arke at the auters ende, i olde coofre irebonde having a long lok of the olde facion, and i lasse new coofre having iii loks called the tresory cofre and certeyn almaries." (Quoted by Philip Mainwaring Johnston,. FR.I.B.A.: *Church Chests of the Twelfth and Thirteenth Centuries in England;* 1908, p. 60.)

Armada chest: the heavy iron or iron-bound coffers of German manufacture, used in England and elsewhere until the invention of the modern safe in the 19th cent., have acquired the name of Armada chests on the romantic assumption that they were survivals from the wrecked ships of the Armada. Most of them date from the 17th or 18th cent. and were imported for practical use.

"AR" mark: see Meissen porcelain.

Armet: a term used in 15th and early 16th cent. texts, apparently to denote a close-helmet (q.v.). Modern writers generally confine it to the early form of this helmet with hinged cheek-pieces overlapping and fastening at the chin, and having at the back a steel disc (roundel) on a short stem.

Armillary sphere: a construction of rings showing the path of the heavenly bodies, similar in appearance to a skeleton globe.

Arming chest: chest for the housing of armours and weapons. Arming chests might be fitted with compartments of varying size to accommodate breast-plate, etc. (In navigation an arming box contains tallow for the "lead".)

Armoire: French term for wardrobe. In France this item of furniture developed out of the cupboard and the cabinet in the late 17th cent. and was treated monumentally by Boulle and his workshop, many examples being made for the Crown and very sumptuously decorated.
    From the constructional point of view it consists of a straight, upright cupboard closed by two doors and with one or more shelves in the undecorated interior. It survived into the early Regency, sometimes of plain carved wood, but as rooms became smaller it seems to have disappeared. A number were made in the Boulle technique in the Louis XVI period from earlier designs. Some also were made of plain wood under the Empire.

Armorial binding: (1) a bookbinding stamped with the coat-of-arms, usually in gilt, of its original or a subsequent owner, and (2) armorial book-plates are based on, or incorporate, the owner's arms.

Armorial fan: an ivory or tortoiseshell *brisé* fan (q.v.) enriched with a coat of arms or crest in a floral cartouche. Fashionable during the third quarter of the 18th cent.

Armorial china: services of porcelain with coats-of-arms and crests were popular in the 18th cent., but until 1755 all were made in China at Chingte-Chen and ordered through merchants at Canton or through the East India Co. The decoration was done from bookplates, engravings or sketches specially sent to China.
    After 1755 some English Armorial services were made, notably at the Worcester factory (q.v.) during the Dr Wall period and also later. Champion produced armorial porcelain at Bristol (q.v.), and most of the factories made pieces as replacements of broken Chinese examples. Some armorial wares were

made by Josiah Wedgwood and the Leeds factory (qq.v.).

Arquebus: a term occurring as early as the 14th cent. referring to some type of hand-gun. In the late 15th and early 16th cent. it was applied to the earliest type of portable gun, fitted with a shoulder-butt and a match-lock (q.v.). In the late 16th and early 17th cent. it was applied loosely to almost any type of light wheel- or match-lock gun.

Arrasene embroidery: a variation of chenille embroidery used mainly for curtain borders, mantel borders and screens where the pile of the arrasene (a fine wool or silk chenille thread) was not injured by friction. It was worked on canvas, silk, velvet or serge, in tent-stitch, stem or crewel stitch and couching.

Arras lace: pillow lace, sometimes spelt orris in old records. Usually associated with a coarser version of Lille (q.v.), but with scalloped edges. George I had 354 yards of it for his coronation. (See *Point de France*.)

Arras tapestry: under the Dukes of Burgundy in the 14th to 15th cent. Arras became a synonym for tapestry (as did Gobelins later) and "thread of Arras" denoted the highest quality. Only one hanging has survived which can with absolute certainty be attributed to Arras: this is the story of SS Piat and Eleuthère in Tournai Cathedral, dated 1404. Throughout the 14th and 15th cent. Arras, with its great rival Tournai, produced enormous quantities of tapestry besides famous pieces of special quality. The city was razed in 1477, never recovered its position, and was a Habsburg possession from 1493–1640. (See also Franco-Burgundian tapestry.)

Arrow mark: see Worcester and Pinxton porcelain.

Arts and Crafts Movement: in the latter years of Queen Victoria's reign a number of Guilds and Societies were formed with the purpose of fostering a revival of interest in the craftsmanship of the 18th cent. and of developing a greater co-operation between the various crafts. The Arts and Crafts Exhibition Society, formed in 1888, arranged a series of exhibitions between that date and 1899 which illustrated the many contrasting tendencies of the age. The activities of these groups have come to be known as the Arts and Crafts Movement.

As: the unit of the early Roman Republican bronze coinage, with, obverse, head of Janus and, reverse, the prow of a galley and sign of value. After the reorganization of the coinage by the emperor Augustus in 27 B.C. the as was struck as a quarter of the large bronze sestertius. On the Imperial as, which continued to be struck till the late 3rd cent. A.D., the types are, on obverse, the Imperial portrait and titles and, on reverse, a personification or scene.

Asparagus tongs: silver and plate asparagus tongs were introduced in the late 18th cent. Derived from fish-slice with spring-hinged upper jaw. Later type of spring-bow form with pierced flat grips. Handle patterns conform to table-services.

Aspergill: the orb-ended rod or brush used for sprinkling holy water; the handle is often of silver and made to match a holy-water bucket (q.v.).

Assay-groove: the wriggled groove by which metal was taken for purposes of assay. Occurs on Scottish silver usually in proximity to hall-marks up to the late 17th cent. This method was practised also on the Continent, and is an interesting minor reflection of close historical links between Scotland and certain European countries.

Assisi-work: a type of embroidery (so called from the modern embroidery made in Assisi) in which the ground is covered in long-armed cross-stitch, leaving the pattern reserved in plain linen. It is usually found in borders or strips, and the earliest examples date from the 16th cent. The patterns include formal designs in typical Renaissance style, figure subjects, including hunting scenes, and stylized birds and animals. Red silk is most commonly used, but green and brown are also found. A similar type of embroidery comes from Azemmour in Morocco, but the designs are more geometric, often of birds, and some-what bolder in style.

Association copy: this term is applied to a book which once belonged to, or was annotated by, the author; which once belonged to someone connected with the author or someone of interest in his own right; or again, and perhaps most interestingly, belonged to someone peculiarly associated with its contents.

Astbury, John: (1688–1743), John Astbury is almost a legendary figure in Staffordshire pottery history, though little can be stated with certainty about him. Simeon Shaw's stories that he introduced the use of Devonshire white-firing clays and calcined flints into the earthenware body may be true but contemporary evidence in support is lacking. On the strength of tradition John Astbury is credited with the manufacture of red earthenware tea-pots and other articles with applied white relief decorations, and image toys of musicians, soldiers etc. made in red and white clays under a lead glaze, sometimes crudely stained with colouring oxides. Both types were made by other Staffordshire potters.

Astbury's name does not occur in Wedgwood's list of early Staffordshire potters; nor are there any authentic examples marked with his name, although the impressed mark ASTBURY is recorded on productions by later members of the Astbury family potting at the Foley, Fenton.

"Astbury" type ware: a classifi-cation of Staffordshire pottery, pro-duced about 1730–40, in which red and white clays are combined under a transparent lead glaze. Similar wares, in which the glaze is splashed or dabbed with metallic oxides, are generally called "Astbury-Whieldon".

Astbury-Whieldon ware: see Ast-bury type ware.

Astragal: a plain semi-circular moulding. The term is used also to

describe the glazing bars of cabinet furniture, such as book-cases and secretaires, made from about 1750.

Astrolabe: instrument formerly used to ascertain the position of the heavenly bodies. Early examples are Arabian and those made in Europe in the Middle Ages emulate the earlier types. Usually made of brass or gilt bronze, finely engraved and pierced.

Astrological dials: these are embod-ied in many early clocks and watches and reflect the important part that astrology played in the everyday life of the people. They show the relation or aspect of the planets to one another at any time. They are usually shown as related to the moon, whose phases are to be seen through an aperture in the dial for this purpose. The distances in degrees are shown by the Trines △ (120°), Quartiles □ (90°), Sextiles * (60°), Conjunction ♂ (0°), and Oppo-sition ♂ (180°).

Atlanta: a sculptured male figure or half-figure, used as a support, in place of a column, and found on Classical architecture. A motif adopted as a decorative form on oak furniture such as chests, cupboard fronts and beds in the early 17th cent., it regained popularity in the late 18th and early 19th cent. being used by architects, metalworkers, furniture makers, etc. (See also Caryatid.)

Aubusson and Felletin tapestry: it is rare to see tapestries from these workshops in La Marche on the road between Bordeaux and Lyon, which date from earlier than the 18th cent. But they also flourished in the 16th and 17th cent.; although they lost many workmen abroad in 1685 (Revocation of the Edict of Nantes). Aubusson tapestry is generally less fine than that of Beauvais and was made for the less pretentious houses of the aristocracy and bourgeoisie. Felletin tapestries tend to be coarser, and at Bellegarde, nearby, where the weavers only worked in the winter months, the most rustic of French hangings were produced. Aubusson copied the *Verdure*, animal, and *Fable* designs of Oudry, Boucher's *Chinoiseries*, and Huet's pastorals, interpreting them very effectively in their somewhat coarser texture. In the late 18th and 19th cent. much tapestry for upholstery was woven.

Aubusson carpets: knotted pile carpets were made at Aubusson from 1742 and at nearby Felletin from 1786. An upright loom was used as at the Savonnerie, but the carpets were considerably cheaper. Women, who were not allowed to work at the *basse-lisse*, and children were employed for low wages. 18th cent. Aubusson carpets were designed by the Court painters and were of excellent quality. Tapestry or smooth-faced carpets were also made, especially in the 19th cent. With the Revolution the production of moquette carpets (q.v.) was introduced.

Augustalis: gold coin of Frederik II of Sicily (c. 1231), with profile portrait type in Roman manner on obverse and eagle on reverse.

Aureus: the chief Roman gold coin. Little issued in the Republic except by the contenders for power in the civil wars at the end of the 1st cent. B.C. Under the emperors the aureus became a regular issue and was struck at varying standards till its replacement by a new piece in A.D. 312.

Automata: mechanically operated figures; the first maker of actual automata as distinct from jacks, and of whom there is a full record, was

Jacques de Vaucanson, who exhibited his three mechanical figures before the *Académie des Sciences* in Paris, in 1738. The success that greeted their appearance when they were later shown in London, St Petersburg and in Germany encouraged the making of more automata. The displaying of them became a common feature of the scene in any big city, and the fame of Spring Gardens in London, where Cox showed his pieces, was duplicated in other capitals. (See also Miniature automata and Automata watches.)

Automata watches: not content with following the hours and sounding them, adding a repeater and, perhaps, music, the Swiss craftsmen found space for automata; from a dog that barked quietly, but with realism, at each hour to jousting knights complete with trumpeter, and see-sawing children enjoying themselves before a playing (glass) fountain. Mostly they were cased in gold, and the tiny figures and landscapes made of the same precious metal in different colours.

Automatic winding watch: a pocket watch which is wound up by means of a weight actuated by the motion of the body. A patent was taken out in London in 1780 by Louis Recordon, but prior claim is made for Abraham Louis Perrelet, of Le Locle.

Ave Maria lace: pillow lace made at Dieppe until the mid-19th cent. in long strips with a plaited lozenge ground.

Aventail: see Bascinet.

Aventurine glass: glass rendered opaque, usually of a brown hue, the substance spangled by the addition of metallic particles. Copper oxide and forge-scales are included in the mixture to create this effect. It is said to have been first introduced at Venice in the early 17th cent. by the glass-making family Miotti.

Axminster carpets: Thomas Whitty began the weaving of knotted pile carpets, at first inspired by Turkish models and then learning from Parisot at Fulham (q.v.) (1750–55). In 1757–59

he won three awards from the Royal Society of Arts, submitting six carpets for the 1759 competition. His prices were more moderate than Moore or Passavant (see under Moorfields and Exeter carpets) and his industry thrived and was continued by his son. The Axminster workshops closed down in 1835, when the looms were taken over by Wilton (q.v.).

Azured: descriptive of tooling on book-bindings consisting of a series of slanting parallel lines. (From the method of depicting azure in heraldic engraving.)

Baby-cage: see Go-cart.

Baccarat glassworks: one of the most eminent in France during the 19th cent. All types of paperweights were made there, including encrusted (sulphide), millefiori, mushroom, flowers, fruit and butterfly. No dated weight from the Baccarat factory is known marked earlier than 1846 and, as elsewhere, none later than 1849. The numerals are in red, blue or green in white canes set in a line, and there is often a letter "B", similarly coloured, above and between the figures "8" and "4". The glassworks, which takes its name from the town, Baccarat, in which it is situated, is still working.

Back-board: the back section of a long-case clock.

Backgammon board: a square board painted or inlaid to mark 24 points, 12 on each side. The pieces were draughtsmen moved in accordance with the throw of dice. (See also Tric-trac.)

Backless bindings: a whimsical style of book-binding in the 16th and 17th cent. in which the spine of a binding is replaced by a fabric which is covered with gilt paper, so that the book appears to have four gilt edges.

Back-painting: the art of mounting prints on to the back of glass, making them transparent, and colouring them in from behind. This art, which probably originated in England, dates

back to the second half of the 17th cent. It is not known how it originated. There were several variants of the principal method used for making these prints, described in full in the chapter entitled *Process or Art of Making a Glass Picture* in the book *Polygraphice* (1700) by William Salmon.

The print itself was first soaked in water for four or five hours to remove the size from the paper. A sheet of fine Bristol glass was then covered with an adhesive (usually Venice turpentine) and the print, when dry, laid face down upon it. When it had set the back of the print was again damped, and the paper rubbed away with a sponge or the finger-tips, leaving only a thin tissue with the impression of the print adhering to the glass. After it had again dried out it was coloured in.

The earlier and more beautiful back-paintings owe their clarity to the fact that only the smallest quantity of paper was allowed to remain on the print. Later examples made by amateurs or less skilled professionals have a much more opaque and stodgy appearance, owing to a greater thickness of paper being allowed to remain, the required transparency being partially produced by a white varnish. Back-painting was an anonymous art, although in its earliest days it is almost certain that the engraver of the print himself produced them.

Back-stool: by the end of Queen Elizabeth I's reign it had become fashionable to take meals on joined stools which could be placed round the dining table more conveniently than the medieval wall benches. To increase comfort a back was added and the stool became known as a back-stool. In the 17th and 18th cent. this term was used to describe an upholstered single chair.

Backsword: a sword having a blade with a back on one side and a single cutting edge on the other.

Bacon, John: (1740–99), sculptor and porcelain modeller. Apprenticed to Crispe of Bow Churchyard, "an eminent maker of porcelain", in 1754. Tradition ascribes to him porcelain figures of Quin as Falstaff, Garrick as Richard III, figures of cooks, and John Wilkes. He is known to have worked for Wedgwood, for Duesbury, who paid his account in 1769, possibly for Champion's Bristol factory and for Enoch Wood of Burslem. He certainly worked, after leaving Crispe, at Coade's Artificial Stone manufactory, of which he eventually became manager.

Baguettes: gemstones of small dimensions cut in narrow rectangles.

Bail: an American term for a half-loop metal handle, usually brass, secured by metal bolts. First used in America about 1700 it became the most popular form of drawer handle between 1720 and 1780.

Baiocco: Papal copper coin of 18th and early 19th cent. Usual types, Papal arms with reverse, word Baiocco.

Bale handle: a hoop or semicircle hinged on a pair of pivots or looped ears on hollow-ware, such as a basket or cream-pail.

Ball and claw foot (or **claw and ball**): terminal to a cabriole leg, representing a dragon's claw or a bird's claw holding a ball. It is said to be an adaptation from the Chinese of a dragon's claw grasping a pearl. In use on English furniture from the early until the late years of the 18th cent. and very popular as the foot of American cabriole leg furniture in the Queen Anne and Chippendale styles.

Ball clay: a very plastic clay from Devonshire and Dorsetshire used in the manufacture of earthenware so called from the manner of its excavation.

Ball foot: a round foot in the shape of a ball used as a terminal to cabinets or table legs in the late 17th cent. (See also Bun foot.)

Ball knop: a knop or protuberance on the stem of a drinking glass or other vessel of large spherical form, often found immediately above a shouldered stem. (See Moulded pedestal stem.)

Ballock-knife: see Kidney-dagger.

Balloon clock: a type of waisted clock popular in the late 18th and early 19th cent.

Balloon seat: see Bell seat.

Ballot box: see Salt kit.

Baluster measure: a pewter tavern measure, bulging below, concave above.

Baluster stem: a type of stem, resembling a baluster, familiar on glass drinking vessels between 1685 and 1760 and made in a variety of forms: a stem consisting of a pure baluster form which might be inverted: also a baluster associated with various knopped motifs; (a) 1685–1725: heavy inverted baluster with solid bowl-base, the depth of the bowl being almost invariably less than stem length; (b) 1700–25: simple knop such as an angular, annulated, cushioned or drop knop (q.v.), with or without a baluster; from 1710 acorn, cylinder, or mushroom knops were usual; from 1715 true baluster alone or with various knops and a pair of balusters placed head to head between a pair of knops; (c) 1725–65: light balusters, true or inverted, supporting bowls with thin bases; illustrated on trade cards of the 1760s. Between 1725 and 1740 the stem and collar baluster is found in which a merese separated bowl from stem. Baluster stems were familiar on silver, wooden, and pewter cups at a much earlier date, while candlesticks of baluster form in a variety of materials were made throughout the 17th and 18th cent.

Baluster turning: a variety of wood turning carried out on the pole lathe in which a number of shapes are achieved by the turner holding the chisel himself and varying the pressure accordingly. A familiar form was the vase-shaped turned support, found particularly on stools and tables of the first half of the 17th cent.

Bamboo turning: furniture made in the Chinese taste in the latter half of the 18th cent. and during the Regency was often constructed of soft wood and painted or japanned, the legs being turned to resemble bamboo.

"Bamboo" ware: a dark shade of cane-coloured stoneware, made by Josiah Wedgwood (q.v.) in 1770, in imitation of bamboo.

Banding: a decorative inlaid border, used on late 17th and 18th cent. furniture, made of a wood contrasting in colour or grain with that of the surface of the piece. (See also Cross-banded veneer and Herring-bone banding.)

Bands: horizontal projections on the spine of a book, where the leather crosses the cords on which it is sewn. On a hollow-backed book or one with sewn-in cords the same effect can be obtained with false bands.

Bandurria: see Mandoline.

Banford, James: a porcelain painter who first worked at Bristol although the work that he did then cannot now be identified. He worked for the Derby factory from 1790 until 1795, having also done some work at Wedgwood's decoration workshop at Chelsea. He excelled as a figure painter but did also flowers, landscapes and birds, turning his hand, in fact, to everything. Most of his painting was done to a small scale with miniature-like delicacy, often upon coffee-cans.

Banister-back chair: a chair with a tall back consisting of several splats of split-banister form made in America and widely used there in the early 18th cent. It is usually of maple and often ebonized.

Banjo barometer: barometer with a case resembling a banjo.

Banjo clock: modern name for an American wall clock with a longish pendulum, the whole housed in a case shaped somewhat like a banjo. Invented in the 1790s by Simon Willard, and patented by him about 1800.

Bannock-rack: resembles an outsize in toast-racks, the silver tray secured to a wooden base. Few examples known date from the second half of the 18th cent. Bannock is a flat home-baked cake made from oatmeal, barley or peasemeal, generally the first, broken into pieces when removed from the girdle and served hot.

Bantam work: a name given to incised lacquer, from the trading station of the Dutch East India Company in Java whence it was exported. (See also Japan work.)

Bar-and-heart thumbpiece: a plain, wide thumbpiece (q.v.), pierced by a heart and surmounted by a thick bar found on pewter flagons and tankards.

Barberini vase: see Portland vase.

Barber's dish: a wide-rimmed circular dish with a segment notch in the rim to fit the neck, part of the barber-surgeon's equipment.

Barbute: a 15th cent. open helmet of Italian origin, one of the forms of the sallet (q.v.). It was tall, at first with a pointed apex, later becoming rounded, and extended over the cheeks, leaving only the eyes, nose and mouth exposed. Some examples closely resemble the classical Greek Corinthian helmet, on which they may perhaps have been directly based.

Baren: the burnisher or rubbing instrument used in Japan in hand-printing from blocks.

"Bargeman" jug: a late and very rare variety of toby jug (q.v.).

Bargueño or **vargueño:** Spanish cabinet with fall-front enclosing drawers and often mounted on a stand. Made of various woods.

Barker of Bath: an artist in sporting scenes, Benjamin Barker was engaged by William Allgood (q.v.) as foreman decorator at the Pontypool Japan works in the late 1770s. He was the father of the celebrated artists, Thomas and Benjamin Barker of Bath, both of whom were born at Pontypool and decorated trays for Allgood. Thomas specialized in rustic groups and figures of shepherds and woodsmen; Benjamin was celebrated for his landscapes. (See Pontypool ware.)

Barley-sugar turning: see Twist turning.

Barm pot: pot for storing barm or yeast (see also Salt kit).

Barograph: a self-recording barometer actuated by clockwork.

Baroque: the word appears to derive from the Spanish Barucca, meaning a deformed pearl, and describes a style which lasted, in general terms, though the 17th cent. Ostensibly based on classical ideals, baroque, originating in Italy, is ebullient in spirit and is characterised by rich, decorative effects and the use of prolific foliage, rounded contours and heavy symmetrical volutes. Dynamic movement replaces the restraint of classic order, plastic form is fully exploited and light and shade are used for dramatic effect. A wide range of individual schools falls under the term, whether of architecture, painting or sculpture while the minor arts too reflect the baroque spirit. In England the sumptuously carved late Stuart woodwork and richly embossed silver of the period are manifestations of the Baroque style.

Barrel-organ: the barrel-and-pin technique applied to the operation of an organ. Many such instruments were supplied for use in churches during the last years of the 18th cent. and in the early part of the cent. following. A few still remain in their original situations.

Basaltes: unglazed fine-grained black stoneware perfected by Wedgwood. "A black porcelain biscuit of nearly the same properties with the natural stone, striking fire from steel, receiving a high polish, serving as a touchstone for metals, resisting all acids and bearing without injury a strong fire – stronger indeed than the basaltes itself." (Wedgwood *Catalogue*, 1787.) Basaltes was a refinement of the

"dry" black stoneware originally made by Elers (q.v.). Its black colour was due to the presence of iron and manganese in the "body". In addition to Wedgwood it was made by Adams, Neale & Co., Palmer, Turner, Birch, Mayer, Hollins, Walton and others.

Bascinet: the characteristic light helmet of the 14th and early 15th cent. It was conical in shape and usually had a mail curtain (aventail) laced to its lower edge, protecting the throat and neck. In the second half of the 14th cent. it was often worn with an acutely pointed "pig-faced" visor, a form for which the rare Medieval term "hounskull" is now generally used.

In the 15th cent. the helmet became more rounded, and the eventail was replaced by a plate gorget; in this form it remained in use for fighting on foot in the lists until the beginning of the 16th cent.

Basin-stand: see Washing-stand.

Basket-hilted sword: a sword with a hilt in the form of a basket, usually with a broad blade. Introduced at the end of the 16th cent. Much used by the cavalry in the 17th cent. (See Broadsword and Schiavona.)

Basket-top clock case: a pierced metallic and roughly dome-shaped case top, current at the end of the 17th and early in the 18th cent.

Bason: the usual spelling in the 17th and 18th cent. for a large vessel.

Bas relief: a term used in sculpture to describe a modelled decoration in low relief, in which the design is only slightly raised from the surface.

Basse-taille enamel: see Enamel.

Basting spoon: long-handled, with nearly oval bowl, early examples rat-tailed (q.v.) presumed to have been used for basting. Similar in form to early punch-ladles and probably of general domestic use.

"Batavian ware": Chinese porcelains with lustrous brown-glazed ground and panels of *famille rose* (q.v.) decoration; named after the Dutch trading station in Java through which they reached Europe in the early 18th cent.

Bateman, Hester: she registered her mark as a goldsmith in 1774–76. Popularly regarded as a woman goldsmith. It is, in fact, more likely that she was only concerned with the office side of the business. Her firm turned out good quality but not outstanding work in the neo-classical style.

Baton-cut stones: stones cut in a long narrow rectangle.

Bat-printing: process of transfer-printing from engraved copper-plates in which a bat of gelatine takes the place of transfer tissue. Used on enamels from about 1780, twenty years after its introduction to England by William Wynn Ryland. Because of its sensitiveness to fine engraving the process was extensively used in the first decade of the 19th cent. at Minton's, Copeland's, etc., for transfer-printing vignettes of shells and flowers.

Bat's-wing fluting: graduated gadrooning curved to resemble the

outline of a bat's wing and encircling hollow-ware.

Battersea enamel: a painted enamel produced at York House, Battersea, London (q.v.), while this factory was controlled by Stephen Theodore Janssen (q.v.), 1753–56, the firm at first being styled Janssen, Delamain and Brooks. It appears obvious that this association was based on a common belief in the possibilities of decorating the enamels with transfer-prints taken on transfer-papers from engraved copper plates. But Janssen's position in the art world enabled him to call on the services of such exceptionally skilled craftsmen as Ravenet (q.v.). The enterprise was discontinued in 1756, the year in which Janssen was declared bankrupt; the notices of sales, of Janssen's household goods and of the York House stock-in-trade, are the main source of information regarding the types of enamel the firm produced, though engraved copper plates bought at the sale were subsequently used elsewhere. The list included snuff-boxes, pictures, wine-labels, watch-cases, toothpick-cases, coat and sleeve buttons, crosses and "other Curiosities".

"Battle for the Breeches": theme of popular imagery concerning marriage occurring on 17th cent. slipware (q.v.) and as a subject for 19th cent. spill vases. Possibly made by Obadiah Sherratt (q.v.).

Bawbee: billon coin issued in 16th and 17th cent. in Scotland with types of thistle and cross. Later, royal portrait on obverse.

Baxter licensees: George Baxter (see Baxter prints) granted licences to work his process of colour printing to a number of firms between 1849 and 1854, when the patent expired. The firms were all known as Baxter licensees, and this name seems to have clung to them even after the expiry of the patent. The licensees were Le Blond & Co., J. M. Kronheim, Bradshaw and Blacklock, William Dickens, Joseph Mansell, Myers & Co. The work of all these firms, both in the form of individual prints and in books, has been collected by many. The best-known series, at one time eagerly sought after, were the Le

Blond ovals, country scenes, whose shape, of course, gives them the name.

Baxter prints: a process of printing in colours patented by George Baxter (1804–67) in 1835 and used by him with considerable success for a number of years. The method is very simply as follows: an uncoloured impression was taken from a key block and the colour was added by successive impressions from wood blocks, one block for each colour, using oil inks. The process was known as Oil Colour Picture Printing, but the oil is a reference to the inks and does not imply that Baxter prints are like paintings in oils. Many hundreds of Baxter prints appeared up to 1860, in particular in the early fifties. The first use of Baxter's work was in Mudie's *Feathered Tribes of the British Isles 1834;* the first complete book of Baxter's was *The Pictorial Album or Cabinet of Paintings 1837.* Baxter prints cover almost every possible subject, including some interesting illustrations of the Great Exhibition. They are of all sizes, from folio down to that of a postage stamp.

Baxter, Thomas: (b. 1782), a china painter. His father was the proprietor of an outside decorating business in London, and he worked for the Worcester porcelain factory. Baxter removed to Worcester in 1814, working as an instructor of apprentices and as an outside artist until 1816 when he went to Swansea. He returned, however, to Worcester, in 1818. He was a painter of landscapes, flowers and figures, subjects which he executed with careful regard to finish and detail. He was particularly successful with shells and feathers.

Bay-leaf garland: a crown of bay-leaves or laurels traditionally worn by classical poets or heroes. Border ornaments composed of stylized leaves, bound with ribbon were used particularly by goldsmiths both in the late 17th cent. and during the neo-classical revival.

Bayonet: a dagger, or short sword, fitted to a musket to convert it into a pike. Known early in the 17th cent., it

was not generally adopted for military purposes until the second half of that cent. At first simply a dagger with round grip, tapered to fit into the musket muzzle, a form which remained in use until well into the 18th cent., but this was gradually superseded by the socket-bayonet introduced in the late 17th cent. This had a tubular hilt fitting over the muzzle, the blade being set to one side so that the musket could be fired with the bayonet fixed. It was superseded in the 19th cent. by the sword-bayonet, attached to a lug on the barrel by a spring-catch and with a hilt like that of a sword.

Bead: a term used to describe a plain moulding of semi-circular section used as a decorative motif on furniture.

Bead moulding: a moulding made to simulate a string of beads. Bead mouldings are familiar on 18th cent. furniture and metalwork.

Bead-work: the earliest surviving English bead-work dates from the 17th cent. Particularly interesting are the shallow baskets, almost tray-shaped, with a flat bottom and sloping sides, decorated entirely with small coloured glass beads sewn on linen canvas. Pictorial subjects, similar to those of the contemporary embroidered pictures, are most common. Looking-glass frames were decorated in this manner, and also caskets, some of which have miniature gardens inside the lid with free-standing flowers made of glass beads mounted on wire. Bead-work purses are also found during the 17th, 18th and early 19th cent. Bead-work was commonly used to decorate garters.

Beaker: handle-less drinking vessel of all periods, usually of tapering cylindrical form. Early examples in silver have engraved or repoussé decoration, but later are usually plain.

Bear jug: a jug in the form of a bear hugging a dog, illustrating the sport of bear-baiting. The detachable head was used as a cup. Made in white salt-glazed stoneware in Staffordshire and brown stoneware at Nottingham and in Derbyshire in the 18th cent. Enamelled bear jugs were made in Staffordshire and Yorkshire in the late 18th and early 19th cent.

Beauvais carpets: knotted pile carpets in the Savonnerie manner were made between 1780–92 and again for a few years under Napoleon.

Beauvais tapestry: the factory was founded in 1664 as a private enterprise supported by the State (Colbert). It was to Beauvais that foreign princes and lords had recourse to obtain tapestry in the French taste and by the best designers of the Courts of Louis XIV, XV and XVI (see Gobelins). Béhagle (who came from Tournai) created the first successful Beauvais period (1684–1705). Particularly popular were the *Grotesques* after Bérain's designs, which are still frequently met with; also the first *Tenture Chinoise*, after Bernansal. An even more prosperous period followed under Oudry, painter at Beauvais from 1726 and inspector from 1734. His own designs included, besides landscape & animal scenes, the famous *Fables de la Fontaine* series, which were particularly popular as an ensemble of hangings and upholstery. Tapestry covers for suites of chairs and *canapés* (q.v.) remained a special feature of Beauvais throughout the 18th and 19th cent. In the 1730s and '40s Boucher's designs attained a preeminence which they have never lost, i.e. the *Italian Comedy*, the *Amours des Dieux*, the *Chinese set* (Second *Tenture Chinoise*). The weaving at Beauvais achieved a very fine texture at this time; much silk and finely-tinted dyes were used. But it should be remembered that not all Beauvais tapestry is of this excessively fine quality; good but less expensive furnishing tapestry was always produced there. Also, many 18th cent. designs were reproduced throughout the 19th cent., but as the dyes had been over-refined and an excessive number of tones were used,

they easily fade to a rather dull and lifeless uniformity. The last triumph at Beauvais was the *Pastorals* designed by Huet and woven in the decade before the Revolution.

Bedwarmers: Covered metal containers, normally of brass, with big wooden handles, into which hot charcoal could be placed. They were occasionally made in silver, but few have survived.

Beefeater flagon: a pewter flagon having a lid somewhat resembling the head-dress of the Yeomen of the Tower of London.

Beefsteak-dish: similar to an entrée dish, and described in a 1797 catalogue of Sheffield plate by John Cadman of Sheffield as fitted with "the handle to screw off to make a pair of dishes occasionally".

Beehive clock: a form of small Connecticut shelf clock, also called "flatiron" clock; so named because of the resemblance of the shape to an old-time beehive or flatiron. c. 1859–60. Common.

Beer-wagon: see Coaster.

Beilby, William: (1740–1819) a celebrated enameller of flint-glass vessels who worked with his sister Mary in Newcastle-upon-Tyne from about 1760 to 1776 signing his best work by name and with a lifelike butterfly.

Belcher chain: a chain, worn in the 19th cent., consisting of broad, equally sized links.

Belcher ring: a ring worn in the 19th cent., for securing a neckerchief.

Bellarmine: a stoneware ale-house bottle, big-bellied, narrow-necked, with a bearded mask opposite the handle. It was named after Cardinal Robert Bellarmine (1542–1621). First imported to this country from the Rhineland and Holland, it was later, in the 17th cent., made in England by John Dwight (c.1633–1703) of Fulham and others.

The bellarmine is frequently mentioned or referred to in English 17th cent. literature, notably by Ben Jonson, Thomas Shadwell and Thomas D'Urfey; and Hogarth figures a bellarmine in the sixth plate of *The Harlot's Progress* (published 1733–34).

It was also known as a Grey Beard or Long Beard.

For its use in witchcraft and magic see under Witch bottles.

Belleek: a light, fragile feldspathic porcelain cast in moulds, with lustrous pearly glaze. Invented c. 1860 by William Goss of Stoke, improved by William Bromley at the Irish factory of David McBirney & Co. (founded 1857 at Belleek, Co. Fermanagh) which by 1865 won a medal at the Dublin Exhibition. Produced at many American factories 1882–1900 and called Lotus Ware by Knowles of East Liverpool.

Bell flower ornament: an American term for a conventionalized hanging ("belle") flower-bud of three, occasionally five, petals carved or, more often, inlaid one below the other in diminishing size down the legs of a table or chair or, sometimes, a chair splat. Seen in American, notably Maryland, furniture of the late 18th cent. It is practically the same as the English "husk" motive. (See also Husk ornament.)

Bell form bowl: the bowl of a drinking glass of a deep, waisted form with incurved profile and wide mouth popular during the 18th cent.

Bell horse brass: the lower brass or brasses on a martingale might contain a small swinging bell cast from bell metal. In some of these the brass itself might follow the silhouette of a bell, with a tiny loose bell set in a bell-shaped perforation. In others a lavishly patterned brass contained a loose bell in the centre.

A set of bells might rise vertically above the horse's collar. In the 18th cent. these were of latten (q.v.), and those of rolled brass in the 19th cent. were further toughened by hammer-

ing. The bells were hung in three or four rows, each row ringing its own chord. Each set hung within a shallow rectangular cover of leather-lined brass, the leather preventing the bells striking a discord upon the metal hood. Four-row sets were most unusual: in these the lowest row containing five bells was known as the lead; the next, of four bells, the lash; the third and fourth rows each containing three bells were termed body and trill. A single bell might hang in the terret (q.v.).

Bellows: contrivances for making a draught artificially, dating from very early times. Mention is made of bellows in wills from 1500 onwards, but as they suffered hard usage, survivors are seldom earlier than the 17th cent.; and any of that date are a great rarity. They received their due share of attention and were decorated in many styles. Carved and inlaid wood, wood overlaid with leather or silver, and even finely stitched needlework were used to ornament them. Lacquered examples were made in the first quarter of the 18th cent. Apart from the small hand-bellows, which were often decorative rather than useful, more business-like machines were made; doubtless for the use of those servants on whom the warmth of the house depended. These standing-bellows were in heavy wooden frames, and rested on the ground firmly, to be worked by means of a lever. Another type, lighter in weight, was operated by turning a wheel which was linked to the mechanism by a cord. This last type dates from the early 19th cent.

The construction of the bellows has not changed in the course of the centuries. It comprises two shaped boards with a spring to keep them apart, held together by a loose leather hinge. One of the boards is pierced in the centre and fitted with a flap of leather on the inside, which acts as a valve, letting air enter but not allowing it to escape except by way of the nozzle.

Bell ringers' jugs: jugs for serving ale to bell ringers, kept either in the church tower, as at Macclesfield, Cheshire; or in the home of one of the ringers.

Bell seat: an American term describing the rounded, somewhat bell-shaped, seat often found in late Philadelphia mid-18th cent. side chairs. These are sometimes now known as balloon seats.

Bell-top clock case: the top of a clock case where the lower portion is shaped like the bell of a turret clock with concave sides.

Belouchistan rugs: early Turkoman rugs often in prayer designs, the use of blue and lustrous yarn, combining with the coppery red, giving an iridescent effect to otherwise heavy colours.

Belper pottery: a manufacture of coarse brown ware existed here from about 1750. The incised mark "Belper" is recorded on a mug dated 1775. William Bourne took over the factory about 1800. It was closed down in 1834.

Bended-back chair: name given to the early 18th cent. walnut chairs with hooped backs and solid splats, on account of the curved shape of the splat which allowed for the sitter to lean back comfortably.

Beneman, Jean Guillaume: French cabinet-maker, German by birth. Came to Paris c. 1784 but trained prior to this date, when he is first mentioned as being employed by the *Garde Meuble de la Couronne* (q.v.). In 1785 he became a *maître-ébéniste* (See *Menuisiers-Ebénistes, Corporation des*) but without the normal formalities. His employment by the Crown coincides with the disfavour into which Riesener (q.v.) fell owing to his high charges. Beneman made a large amount of furniture for Queen Marie Antoinette and the Court, and was employed also to repair earlier furniture in the possession of the Crown. He collaborated with all the leading craftsmen of the time, including Boizot and Thomire, but his furniture retains usually a rather heavy Teutonic appearance. He seems to have specialized in making commodes and *meubles d'entre deux* (q.v.). He was officially employed under the Directoire and Consulate,

but his name disappears about 1804. He used the stamp:

G·BENEMAN

Beni: a pink or red pigment used in Japanese prints and obtained from saffron flowers.

Beni-ye: (Japanese print), pink picture: generally applied to two-colour prints, in which the *beni* (q.v.) was used with one other colour, usually green.

Beni-zuri-ye: Japanese pink-printed pictures, a more correct term for the two-colour prints. (See also Beni-ye.)

Bergama rugs: Turkish rugs usually with a Mihrab on each end, giving a balanced design. These rugs, woven entirely of very lustrous wool, though not fine in texture, have pleasing colours, the borders bearing a marked affinity to the Caucasian weaves. (See also Turkish rugs.)

Bergère: a type of armchair with upholstered sides, frequently with a lose cushion, much favoured in France in the mid- and late 18th cent.

Berlin porcelain: a porcelain factory was started in Berlin in 1752 by Wilhelm Kasper Wegely, a wool-merchant, with the encouragement of Frederick the Great, who had long wished to own a porcelain factory. Frederick, however, soon became dissatisfied with Wegely's porcelain and withdrew his patronage in 1757, when the venture was abandoned. Wegely's porcelain was hard-paste and in form and decoration much influenced by Meissen (q.v.). The mark used was a "W" in blue, sometimes with numerals. A second factory was started in Berlin in 1761 by Johann Ernst Gotzkowsky, which was subsequently purchased by Frederick the Great in 1763 and became the Royal Porcelain Manufactory. After the first World War the title was changed to the State Porcelain Manufactury which exists to the present day. The most important Berlin wares are those made between 1763 and the death of

Frederick the Great in 1786. Dinner services with flower painting and mosaic borders are notable, while after 1770 pierced borders were popular and flower-painting in a camaieu (see En camaieu) of two colours. Figure modelling in the best period was in the hands of the brothers Friedrich Elias Meyer, who had previously worked at Meissen, and Wilhelm Christian Meyer. The mark of a G was used from 1761–63, after which a sceptre in blue was introduced.

Berlin wool-work: a type of embroidery in coloured worsteds on canvas in which designs printed on squared paper were copied by counting the squares of the canvas. The designs were published in Berlin and were first imported into England about 1810 but did not reach the country in large numbers until after 1830, the fashion reaching its height about the middle of the cent. The first designs were often worked in silk or glass beads, but the garishly coloured worsteds imported from Berlin (which gave the work its name) became the general medium, and tent- or cross-stitch the usual method of execution. The designs were usually of flowers, depicted with great naturalism, but pictorial subjects, frequently biblical, were also popular. Samplers on long strips of canvas showing various patterns worked in Berlin wools are also found.

Beshire or **Bushire carpets:** Turkoman carpets actually made in Bokhara City, and providing a variation in the design strongly reminiscent of the Herat (q.v.) "fish" design, but the colouring is the usual red, often on dark blue; a strong yellow outlines the design.

Bevelled edges or **bevelled boards:** a style of book-binding in which the edges of the boards – usually extra thick boards – have been bevelled, i.e. cut to an oblique or slanting angle, before being covered.

Bevelled glass: the angular shaping of the surface at the edges of a mirror-

plate performed by grinding and then polishing the glass. A patent for a method of doing this with the aid of water-power was granted in 1678. Much glass for mirrors had the edges bevelled, but the finish was not always employed for large plates after the middle years of the 18th cent.

Bevor: see Sallet.

Bezant: general name given to gold coins of the Byzantine Empire and their imitations (see Nomisma and Solidus).

Bezel: (1) the metallic framing of a clock or watch glass; (2) the inside rim of the cover or lid of an object; (3) originally the part of a ring which holds the stone, and now generally used to describe the setting of the ring, including the stone.

Bezoar: the gall-stone of an animal, usually an ox or a cow, mounted in precious metal and thought to have magical powers.

"BFB" mark impressed: see Worcester porcelain.

Bianco sopra bianco: a type of earthenware decoration meaning literally, white on white, but used as a form of white decoration upon a pale grey or blue ground at the Lambeth, Bristol, and Liverpool delftware factories from about 1750.

Bible-box: popular term for a variety of box, generally of small size. That some such boxes were used to hold the family Bible, or average meagre domestic library, is probable, though they doubtless served other purposes. Lace-boxes enter this category.

Bibliography: the word has two main meanings, really quite different, despite the fact that they may shade into each other in some cases. One (the more familiar to the general public) is a reading list, a guide for further study or a list of works which have been consulted by the author; and this will not normally give any detailed description of the books listed. The other, familiar to collectors, is a book about books as physical objects. Bibliograph in this sense is the systematic description of books according to subject, class, period, author, country or district; or of the products of a particular press or publishing house. Bibliography may be enumerative, analytical or descriptive: ranging in method from a hand-list to a heavily annotated catalogue.

Bibliothèque-basse: (*Fr.*) a low cupboard fitted with shelves for books, and doors often of glass but sometimes fitted with grilles.

Bidjar rugs: see Kurdish rugs.

Biggin: a form of cylindrical silver coffee-pot with short spout, often with stand and spirit-lamp.

Bijin-ye: a Japanese term meaning pictures of beautiful girls.

Bilbao or **"Bilboa":** an American term for a wall mirror framed in coloured marbles or marble and wood with a scrollwork headpiece and gilded mouldings. American cabinet-makers working in the Adam or Hepplewhite style may have designed them, yet they are believed to have originated in the Spanish seaport Bilbao. Stylish in New England seaport towns 1780–1800.

Bill: see Pole-arms.

Billet: see Thumbpiece.

"Billies and Charlies": a notorious class of fake lead medallions and amulets (q.v.), made in London about the end of the 19th cent. and commonly known after their inventors as "Billies and Charlies".

Billingsley, William: (1760–1828), a china painter and wandering arcanist (q.v.) who discovered the secret of a white and exceedingly translucent porcelain paste which could be produced only at an incredible loss. His career was therefore dogged by disappointment and failure.

Born at Derby and apprenticed as a china painter at the Derby works in 1774; influenced by Boreman (q.v.); became celebrated as a painter of flowers in a new naturalistic style marked by the illusion of depth, and the use of longish sprays of flowers spreading from a central bloom. He left Derby in 1796, entered into association with Coke at Pinxton as an arcanist, then went to Mansfield in 1799 and later to Torksey, Lincolnshire, where he decorated white china bought in Staffordshire. He found employment at Worcester in his trade in 1808 but left once more to become a china-maker at Nantgarw in 1813. His association with Dillwyn at Swansea in 1814 broke down in 1816, and he returned to Nantgarw. In 1819 Rose of Coalport bought his moulds and made use of his ideas.

He died in 1828 in greatly reduced circumstances.

"Billy Waters": a celebrated early 19th cent. London black fiddler, with a wooden leg, who became the subject of popular pottery imagery. Edward Keys modelled a figure of him for Derby before 1826. A puppet of Billy Waters appeared in Chandler's *Fantoccini* in 1825.

Bilston: early South Staffordshire centre of the enamelling trade, where snuff-boxes and similar goods of japanned metal had been produced from the beginning of the cent. The rare japanned snuff-boxes with enamel decoration on their lids are considered to date to 1740–50. During the 1760s to 1790s Bilston produced great numbers of fine painted enamels.

Binche lace: pillow lace made with very fine thread and such a close texture that the pattern was almost lost. Gradually it became more open and eventually lost its delicacy.

Binder's blanks: see Blank leaves.

Binder's cloth: any cloth bookbinding, whether old or new, which is individual to the copy, i.e. not edition-binding.

Binder's ticket: see Signed binding.

Binding variants: a general term for the variations, whether of colour, fabric, lettering or decoration, between different copies of the same edition of a book bound (cased) in publisher's cloth. They are usually the result of the publisher's practice of binding up an edition, not all in one operation, but in batches as required; sometimes of his selling copies wholesale in quires for binding to another's order.

Bin label: large-sized pottery label, usually pierced with a hole for suspension from a hook or nail, for hanging beside a wine bin. Some date from the late 17th cent. and it has been suggested that they were made at one of the Lambeth potteries. Later examples originated in Staffordshire.

Bird call: pottery whistle in the form of a bird. Sometimes built into old chimneys as a charm against evil spirits.

Bird fountain: wall bracket with a projecting socket for water, made in blue-printed, lustred, or enamelled earthenware, 18th and 19th cent.

Bird-organ: also known as a Serinette (*Fr.*: canary). A small mechanical instrument, with both barrel and bellows, for teaching a bird to sing. Larger and louder was the Merline, for teaching a blackbird. There was also a Turlutaine (Turlu: curlew), probably used as a lure.

Bird's-eye veneer: a veneer patterned with small spots, supposed to resemble birds' eyes, often found in the wood of the sugar maple. Used and much prized in America from the earliest to present times.

Biscuit: a fired but unglazed pottery or porcelain, usually the latter. In porcelain, used as a modelling medium to resemble marble (see Derby porcelain).

Bismuth: a metal added to harden pewter. Also called tinglass.

Bisque: see Biscuit.

"Black and White" wall paper: modern name given to the 16th and 17th cent. letterpress-printed wall-

paper, much of which was designed in imitation of the black-thread embroideries of the Tudor period.

Black Egyptian ware: see under Basaltes.

Black-glazed pottery: red earthenware covered with a lustrous black or brownish-black glaze made in Staffordshire at Fenton Low by Whieldon and others; at Burslem by Thomas Holland (1748–1807), often erroneously stated as the "first" maker of "shining black" ware, and his widow, Ann Holland; and in Shropshire at Jackfield.

Blackjack: leather tankard occasionally mounted with silver rim, of 17th and 18th cent. date. Certain examples bearing pretentious historical inscriptions should be viewed with scepticism.

Black-printing: described by William Evand in *The Art and History of the Potting Business* in 1846 as "a term for applying impressions to glazed vessels, whether the colour be black, red or gold", it was extensively used by outside decorators in Staffordshire and the potteries of Liverpool, Yorkshire and the Tyne in the second half of the 18th cent. and first three decades of the 19th cent. Black was more extensively used than other colours, hence the term. (See also Transfer-printing.)

Black-work: the name given to a type of Elizabethan embroidery worked in black silk on linen. It was used widely for both household articles and cos-

tume, particularly on long pillow-covers, bodices, coifs and nightcaps. Gold thread is often found in conjunction with black-work and coiling stem designs were most frequently used.

Elaborate diaper filling patterns, worked in back-stitch, are a feature of this work, and the effect is often similar to the wood-block-printed lining papers of the period. Black-work is also found in Spain.

Bladed knop: a knop or protuberance on the stem of a drinking glass or other vessel of thin, sharp-edged flattened form, placed horizontally.

Blanc-de-Chine: the porcelain known as *blanc de Chine* was made at Tê-Hua in the Province of Fukien. This china, in which the white varies in colour from a deep ivory to the starkest bluish white, was first manufactured some time during the Ming dynasty (1368–1644). The factory specialized in figures of the numerous deities and sages of the Buddhist faith.

From about 1650 this factory began to make pieces that show European influence. A soldier, perhaps Dutch, dates from this time; another well-known figure of a man wearing a tri-corn hat is probably rather later. It has been pointed out that the inhabitants of Fukien Province are extremely superstitious, and it has been suggested that this may explain why there exist *blanc de Chine* groups and figures of Europeans placed in typically Chinese settings and attitudes. For example, there is a group in which a European is seen standing on the head of a dragon, which symbolizes the attain-ment of the highest literary honours.

Tê-Hua porcelain was occasionally painted in China, but when coloured is found to have been decorated more often in Holland or Germany during the 18th cent.

Blank leaves, blanks: blank pages which may be an integral part of a book as completed by the printer, in which case the fastidious collector will insist on their presence, though he may make allowances in the case of a very rare book. Blanks sometimes occur at the beginning of a book, sometimes at the end of a clearly marked division, more often at the end of the last gathering. In 17th cent. or earlier books, an initial blank may carry a signature letter (q.v.). In a leather-bound book it is necessary to distin-guish these printer's blanks from any extra leaves which the binder may have used in the front or back – conveniently called binder's blanks.

Blazes: pattern formed on a glass vessel by cutting in deep relief a series of upright or slanting lines.

Bleeding bowl: see Cupping bowl.

Bleu celeste: a turquoise blue ground used on Sèvres porcelain (q.v.) and introduced in 1752. Also known as *bleu turquin.*

Bleu-de-roi: Sèvres porcelain ground colour imitated at Worcester (q.v.) and contemporaneously at Derby (q.v.) at the end of the Chelsea-Derby period, consisting of a bright lapis-lazuli opaque enamel.

Bleu persan: semi-oriental type of decoration on pottery in which the design is painted in opaque white over a dark blue ground colour. Used in France at the Hevers factory, and copied in England.

Blind printing: see Gauffrage.

Blind-tooled binding: when deco-ration or lettering on a book-binding is said to be blind or in blind, this means that a plain impression has been made in the leather or cloth by the tool, die-stamp or roll, without any addition of gold or colour.

Blister: American term to describe the marking, thought to resemble a blister, found in various woods, such as cedar, mahogany, pine, poplar and especially maple.

Blister pearls: unevenly shaped and sometimes hollow "pearls" obtained from a nacreous deposit within an oyster shell.

Block: a piece of wood or metal, without a handle, bearing an engraved design for decorating the cover of a book or for printing illustrations, and intended to be used in a printing press.

Block book: a type of book produced before the invention of movable type in which each page was printed from a single block (q.v.) on which both text and illustration had been cut. The recto and verso (qq.v.) of each page were printed on separate sheets which were stuck together.

Block-front: various types of American furniture – chests of drawers, chests-on-chests, knee-hole dressing-tables, slant-front desks, secretaries, etc. – were made with block fronts in the late 18th cent. Thick boards, usually mahogany, for the fronts of the drawers and cabinets, are cut so that the centres recede in a flattened curve while the ends outcurve in a flattened bulge. At the top of the three curves, one concave and two convex, a shell is often carved or glued on. Should the piece be in two sections, often only the lower section is block-fronted. The origin of block-fronting is unknown; the development is believed to be American, evolved about 1760–80, by John Goddard of Newport, Rhode Island, perhaps with the aid of his associate, John Townsend (q.v.). They may have arrived at it by straightening the curves of the Dutch cabinet. The late American authority Wallace Nutting called block fronts "the aristocrats of furniture". The English antique furniture authority Cescinsky described them, especially the secretaries, as "the finest examples of American furniture". They are much sought after.

Block-printed wallpaper: most early wallpapers were printed by wood block, the engraving of which was a skilled craft owing its origin to the wood engravers of medieval times. The size of block varied according to the size of design, but was usually governed by the ease with which the operator could handle the block. Hand-printed wallpaper is produced today according to traditional methods.

Block printing: a method of printing textiles. The colour is applied by means of wood upon which the design is cut in relief. A "coppered" block is one in which the design is outlined with brass or copper strips driven edgewise into the block, the areas intended to print solid colour being filled with felt.

Blonde lace: a French pillow lace, silk, made in the Arras, Lille and Chantilly regions from the 1740s, first in unbleached Chinese silk but soon in white and black. Had a ground of the Lille type, loosely twisted.

Bloom: an all-over film of opaque dullness occasionally found on the surface of flint glass both of English and Irish origin, although it is frequently associated with Irish glass. The effect is caused by the use of high-sulphur fuels in the lehr (q.v.). Bands of bloom may be found encircling hollow-ware a little distance below the rim; these are the results of re-heating at the furnace mouth. This bloom is not to be confused with the milkiness found inside old decanters.

Blowhole: a small hole pierced in hollow castings or seamed hollow members as handles, finials, etc., to allow escape of the air expanded by heat when soldering to the main body. Silver tankards with this feature have long been mistakenly known as "whistle" tankards, to be used for calling for another drink. This fantasy dies hard.

Blowing-tube: forerunner of, and contemporary with, the bellows was a long metal tube widening from a mouthpiece and with a short projection at the base to raise it from the ground. The tube was placed where the draught was needed, and the user simply blew down the mouthpiece.

Blown glass: see Free-blown glass.

Blown-moulded glass: see Mould-blown glass.

Blowpipe: long, hollow, iron tube used to hold a gather of molten glass.

"Blue-and-white" Chinese porcelain: decoration with painting in cobalt blue under the glaze has continued ever since its introduction. It is both attractive and economical, requiring one firing only. Some 14th cent. wares depict plants and animals within floral scroll borders. The classic 15th cent. Ming reigns of Hsüan Tê and Ch'êng Hua produced perhaps the finest of all "blue-and-white", with perfect forms, superb glaze, rich colour, and lively yet restrained painting of dragons and floral scrolls. A deep violet-blue was used in the Chia Ching period, and 16th cent. painting is freely executed in "outline and wash" technique. As well as the traditional subjects, ladies on garden terraces, playing boys, and animals in landscapes are now depicted. Much Ming porcelain now in European collections comes from the Near East or South-East Asia, whither it was exported in many styles and qualities. From about 1600 the East India Companies imported into Europe thin porcelain plates and bowls with indented edges, painted with emblems and figures in wide panelled borders. The "Transitional" period wares of the mid-17th cent., e.g. cylindrical vases and bottles with tulip designs, bold landscapes and figure subjects, are often finely painted. The paste of K'ang Hsi period wares is fine and white, and for the best pieces a brilliant sapphire blue was used, applied in overlapping flat strokes, as on the famous "prunus jars", with sprays of plum-blossom reserved in white. Decorative vases and "useful" wares are extremely various in shape and decoration. Landscapes and scenes from literature, with elegant ladies or huntsmen, are common, and a great variety of panelled, brocaded and bordered designs with flowers (aster and tiger-lily patterns, lotus, chrysanthemum, etc.), as well as the traditional animals and emblems. Ming reign-marks were often used; that of K'ang Hsi rarely. The Yung Chêng and Ch'ien Lung periods produced little besides revivals of early Ming styles, and export wares of declining quality. Later 18th cent. services made to European order ("Nankin china") are rather coarse, with thick glazes, and crowded designs of the "willow-pattern" type.

Blue clay: more commonly known as ball clay (q.v.). A plastic clay quarried in Devon and Dorset, forming the basis of most earthenware bodies.

Blue-dash chargers: circular Delft-ware (q.v.) dishes painted with various figural or floral subjects with blue strokes or dashes at the edge, ranging in date from 1614 to 1740 or later. The archaistic word "charger" was applied to this purely decorative class of tin-glazed earthenware by E. A. Downman who collected them.

Blue glass: glass vessels tinted blue, which could be achieved by the addition of cobalt. In England blue glass scent-bottles, snuff-boxes and similar small articles were popular about 1770 and later, inspired by Sèvres porcelain (q.v.). These blue glass wares were made not only at Bristol but also in South Staffordshire and Birmingham among other centres, and the boxes, etc., were decorated in enamellers' workshops. Blue finger-bowls were favoured about 1800. (See also Coloured glass.)

Blue John: also known as Derbyshire spar. A fluorspar of violet-blue colour, much used in the second half of the 18th and in the 19th cent. for decorative purposes, such as vases, urns, sometimes mounted in ormolu (q.v.), candlestick bases, etc.

Blue tint: the faint bluish hue present in the texture of some late Georgian flint-glass. This has often been taken as a characteristic of Waterford glass (q.v.), but it is apparent not only in examples from Waterford but also in the productions of Stourbridge, Birmingham, Bristol, Scotland and elsewhere.

This peculiar depth of tone shows the glass to contain lead oxide prepared from Derbyshire mined lead, preferred at many glasshouses because of the superior manipulative properties it gave to the molten metal. The Derby lead contained an impurity which caused the bluish tint. The Irish glass-houses for the most part used lead oxide made by Wilson Patten, Bank Quay, Warrington, from Derbyshire lead. Not every consignment contained the blue-tingeing impurity, then known as Derby blue, so there was no consistency in the presence of Derby blue in flint-glass during the period concerned and depth and tone of tint varied.

Blunderbuss: a short musket with large bore widening at the muzzle, designed to fire shot. Apparently introduced into England from the Continent in the middle of the 17th cent., it was used principally by civilians as a protection against thieves until well into the 19th. Many blunderbusses are equipped with a hinged spring-bayonet, which is thrown forward into the fixed position when a catch is released.

"B" mark: see Bristol and Worcester porcelain.

Boarded chest: early, poor alternative to the framed or joined chest, the horizontal planks of wood forming the front and back being hammered to the vertical end-pieces or flush with heavy corner stiles, and frequently reinforced with corner-pieces of iron. As wood tends to shrink across the grain, the result was never satisfactory, and the horizontal planks usually show signs of splitting. Oak might be used, or planks of elm, large and comparatively little given to warping. The flush construction as contrasted with the loose panels of the mortice and tenon jointed (q.v.) chest offered a smooth surface for covering with leather or hair cloth.

Boards: a term to describe (1) in the widest sense, the wood, paste-board, strawboard or other base for the sides of any bound or cased book, i.e. any book in hard covers. As commonly used, the term includes the covering of the actual board; (2) also used in a specialized sense, to mean the original boards, backed with paper, in which most books were temporarily encased for distribution between about 1780 and the 1830s, when edition-binding in cloth became popular among the book-reading public.

Boat bed: an American Empire style bed shaped somewhat like a gondola. A variant of the sleigh bed.

Bobbin lace: alternative term for pillow lace (q.v.), but distinguished from bone lace (q.v.) in early inventories as being coarser, of thicker thread requiring large bobbins.

Bobbins: spools wound with thread for pillow laces (q.v.), a separate bobbin for each thread. English bobbins are distinctively ornamental, light and dainty for Honiton and Buckinghamshire lace, but often weighted with spangles, or beads, for the coarser laces.

Bobbin turning: one of the many varieties of wood turning popular in the 17th cent. Table legs, turned on a pole lathe to resemble a bobbin, were in fashion during the Commonwealth but the result was rather too severe in form to suit the lavish taste of the Restoration period.

Bob clock pendulum: the earliest form of pendulum invented by Christiaan Huygens in 1657 and used with the verge escapement (q.v.). In England the pendulum rod was usually fixed to the end of the escape pallet arbor, but on the Continent suspension was generally from a silk cord, the pendulum being actuated by a crutch. Regulation was by means of a fine thread cut on the lower end of the pendulum rod. The hole in the bob had a softwood core which "took up" the threads of the rod.

"Bocage": foliage or tree backgrounds to porcelain or earthenware figures or groups, 18th and 19th cent.

"Boccaro" ware: a misnomer for Yi-hsing stoneware (q.v.).

Body: the composite materials of which potter's clay is made – the ware itself, usually pottery or stoneware; for porcelains the word paste is preferred (as hard-paste, soft-paste).

Boettger, Johann Friedrich: (1682–1719), an alchemist in the service of Augustus the Strong, Elector of Saxony and King of Poland, whose early researches were concerned with a means of manufacturing gold. His efforts in this direction proving fruitless, he was employed on the problem of making porcelain. In fact, he discovered in 1710 a red stoneware "which surpasses the hardness of porphyry". Shortly afterwards he succeeded in replacing the red clay with white kaolin (see China clay). Thus he produced the first real porcelain to be made in Europe. As a result of his discovery the Royal Saxon Porcelain Manufacture was established at Meissen in 1710. (See also Meissen porcelain.)

Bokhara or **Bokara rugs:** these rugs, known as "Bokara", have long been popular in England. They are made by Turkestan tribes of which the Tekke is the most esteemed, the gules being well balanced and the side borders following variations of the same motif. The end borders are usually latch hook in diamond formation, and conventional tree or life forms. The yarns are very fine, often knotted 300 to 400 to the square inch on a weft and warp usually of wool, but sometimes of fine hair. (See also Turkoman rugs.)

"Bokhara-work": the term generally applied to the bright-coloured embroideries of Western Turkestan. Large floral sprays or a diapered ground filled with flowers are the most common patterns and diagonally laid Oriental-stitch and chain-stitch are most frequently used. Large coverlets and divan covers are most common and the finest date from the 18th cent.

Bolection moulding: a moulding of ogee section used as a projecting surround to door or wall panels.

Bolognino: silver coin originally issued by Bologna from the 12th cent. with types, Imperial title and word BONONI. Widely copied throughout Italy.

Bolt and shutter device: a form of maintaining power in clocks. The shutters cover the winding squares so that the clock cannot be wound without pushing them aside. This action brings into play a small subsidiary force that keeps the clock going during the period of winding.

Bombé form: a term adopted from the French to describe a curved or swelling form. Late 18th cent. commodes were frequently of bombé form.

Bonbonnières: small shaped boxes intented for sweetmeats made of gold, silver, porcelain or enamelled copper and made in various forms according to the fantasy of the designer.

Bone china: the standard English porcelain since 1800. It is basically hard-paste, modified by the addition of bone ash which may be as much as 40 % of the ingredients of the bone china body. Josiah Spode is credited with stabilising the proportions, although bone as an ingredient of porcelain was used at Bow from 1749, Lowestoft, Chelsea and Derby in the 18th cent. and is stated by Church to have been common knowledge among potters in Staffordshire in Spode's time.

Bone lace: a term sometimes specifically applied to gold and silver lace (q.v.) but more often also to all good quality pillow lace (q.v.), as distinct from needlepoints (q.v.). It has been variously argued that the name referred to the sheep's trotter bones sometimes used as early bobbins (q.v.) and to the bone pins used in place of metal pins to shape the pattern – fish bones on occasion. Metal pins were priced in 1543 at as much as 6s 8d a thousand. The term has been applied also to the ivory effects of Venetian raised point lace (q.v.). It was the accepted term until the early 18th cent. for much pillow lace and there are many records of its cost: such as 1s 4d a yard for narrow bone lace edging in 1594, and 2s 4d a yard in 1685.

Bonheur-du-jour: (*Fr.*) a small writing-table usually on tall legs, and sometimes fitted to hold toilet accessories and bibelots. It first appeared c. 1760, but remained in fashion for a comparatively short time.

Bonnet-piece: Scottish gold coin of James V with profile portrait of king wearing bonnet and Scottish arms on reverse.

Bonnet top: an American term to describe the top of a piece of case furniture where the broken-arch pediment covers the entire top from front to back. The bonnet top is usually cut in the same curves as the arch but is sometimes left uncut, a solid block of wood behind the arched fronting. It is a form found in America between 1730 and 1785, and sometimes referred to as a "Hood".

Bookcloth: before 1825 ordinary books were issued bound in boards (q.v.), with often a paper label on the spine. In this year, however, Archibald Leighton of London introduced bookcloth, a cotton material to which gum or paste could be applied without harming it. And by 1837 the majority of books published appeared in cloth with the title and embellishments blocked in gold or other colour on to the cloth instead of being printed on to paper labels as before.

Book hinges: found on lids of coffeepots, jugs, and so on. They have a round back resembling a book spine, and the pin-joints, where the base metal is left bare, are concealed beneath slightly ornamented silver caps.

Book of Hours: see Horae.

Book-rest: a stand used in Georgian libraries to support large books, consisting of a square or rectangular framework with cross bars, the upper bar being supported by a strut which was adjusted on a grooved base. This kind of stand was sometimes fitted into the top of a table.

Bookseller's waste: see Waste.

Book sizes and formats: the size of a book depends upon the size of the sheet it was printed on and the way the sheet was folded. A book's format, in turn, depends upon how its sheets were folded and then how these sheets were gathered into quires. Since the two terminologies overlap and are used by professionals in their variant meanings with precision, it is well for the amateur to understand these matters from the beginning. The most common sheet sizes, each of these usually subdivided into large and small are:

Foolscap .	13½	× 17	inches
Post . . .	15	× 19	inches
Crown . .	15	× 20	inches
Demy . .	17½	× 22½	inches
Medium .	18	× 23	inches
Royal . .	20	× 25	inches
Imperial .	22	× 30	inches

If the printed sheets are each folded once, to make two leaves or four pages, then the book is a folio. The Hakluyt folios (printed on sheets of about foolscap size) stand about 13 inches high by about 8 inches wide. But it will be noted from the above table that an Imperial folio would be nearly twice this size. Folios other than chart books are typically gathered into 6 leaves or 3 sheets of 12 pages per quire. Thus, in the bibliographer's annotation, a book described as "fo. A–D⁶" would be made up of four quires (A to D), each made up of 6 leaves of 3 sheets, with A1ʳ: p. 1. A1ᵛ: p. a, A6ʳ: p. 11, A6ᵛ: p. 12. The conjugate pairs of full sheets in the A signature would be A1 and A6, A2 and A5, A3 and A4; and the outer and inner formes would be in the pattern of outer: p. 1 and 12, inner: p. 2 and 11.

If the printed sheet is folded twice, into four leaves of eight pages, the book is quarto. Folded once again, into 8 leaves or 16 pages, the book is an octavo. It should now be clear why a Crown Octavo is 7½ × 5 inches, whereas a Royal Octavo is 10 × 6¼ inches. There are several ways of imposing 12mos, but the most common is a four-leaf cut-off from the top of the sheet inserted into an eight-leaf fold. By the time the 16mo is reached, the book is small enough to be uncommon and the folds so numerous that half-sheet imposition is likely. The quiring in half-sheets of 32mos would be normal.

Boreman, Zachariah: (1738–1810), a landscape painter on porcelain. He worked originally at Chelsea but moved to Derby about 1783, when he renewed a contract with Duesbury for three years at two guineas a week wage. He returned to London in 1794 and worked as an outside decorator at one of the London establishments. His work, executed in quiet tones, possesses a certain sober dignity. It was painted in the 18th cent. water-colour technique of glazing local colours over a monochrome foundation.

Boston rocker: the most popular of all rocking chairs in America. Apparently evolved from the Windsor rocker (see Windsor chair). Usually painted, it has curved arms, a tall spindle back, broad top rail generally showing stencilled designs : a kind of ornamental panel – and a "rolling" seat, curved up at the back and down at the front.

Botanical flowers: a type of floral decoration inspired originally by Meissen porcelain and occurring on Chelsea porcelain, 1750–56 (from engravings in Philip Miller's *The Gardeners Dictionary*, 1724, issued in parts with numerous copperplate engravings from 1755); on Derby porcelain painted by William Pegg (1775–1851), early 19th cent.; on porcelain decorated at Y rmouth by William Absolon (1751–1815); and by Thomas Pardoe (1770–1823) on Swansea porcelain. Pardoe's careful imitations of plants and flowers from Curtis's Botanical Magazine were probably due to the influence of Lewis Weston Dillwyn who was a keen botanist. Decorations from the same source are recorded on earthenware.

Botdrager: silver coin of double *gros* (q.v.) class in 14th cent. in Brabant and Flanders. Name derived from obverse type of helmeted lion, colloquially termed the "pot-carrier".

Bottengruber, Ignaz: an independent porcelain decorator of Breslau in Germany working between about 1720 and 1736, whose painting can be found on Vienna and Meissen (q.v.) porcelain.

"Bottle glass": glass of a greenish or brownish tone caused by an impurity in the silica used in its production.

Bottle-tickets: contemporary term for decanter labels. These labels were intended to be hung by a chain on the neck of a decanter. The engraver Simon-François Ravenet was associated with a series of Battersea enamel (q.v.) bottle tickets depicting putti engaged on tasks associated with the production of the designated liquors. Bottle tickets were also made of silver, engraved or cut with the name of a beverage.

Bouche: a notch cut in the upper edge of a shield to support a lance. The earliest shields seem to have been oval, circular or rectangular, but in the 11th cent. the tall kite-shape appears, remaining in use until the 13th. cent., when the "flat-iron" form was introduced. This survived until well into the 15th cent., when a large variety of shapes appeared, many of which had a notch or bouche cut into the upper edge.

Boulle, André Charles: French cabinet-maker. Born in Paris in 1642, the son of a carpenter, and died there in 1732. His training was very various, and he appears to have worked at different times as a painter, architect, engraver and bronze worker, as well as an *ébéniste* (q.v.) of importance. He worked as an *artisan libre* from 1664 onwards, but in 1672 he was appointed *ébéniste du Roi* through the intervention of Colbert. From this time he worked continually for the Crown and established a workshop in which he employed about twenty assistants, who were constantly at work providing furniture for the new palace at Versailles.

He possessed a large collection of old master drawings from which he may easily have drawn inspiration for his mounts. His ingenuity as a designer was very great, as can be seen from a series of engravings which he published, and from a number of his drawings which exist. But throughout his career his actual style changed very little. He never signed his work and his authenticated productions are very rare. The only pieces which can be said definitely to be by him are two commodes originally made for the Grand Trianon and now in the palace at Versailles. (See also Boulle marquetry.)

Boulle marquetry: the name given to the type of inlay evolved for use on furniture in the late 17th cent. by André Charles Boulle (1642–1732) (q.v.).

The process involves glueing one or more thin layers of tortoiseshell to a similar number of brass. The design of the marquetry is set out on paper, which is pasted on the surface. The pattern is then cut out with a saw. The layers of brass and tortoiseshell are separated and can be made to form two distinct marquetries by combining the materials in opposite ways: either with the design formed by the brass on a ground of shell, known as *première partie* or first part, or the exact opposite, known as *contre-partie*, or counterpart, with the design in shell on a ground of brass. These two types of inlay can be glued on to a carcase in the form of a veneer. Often the two types are found side by side as part of the same design, to give contrast. Again, when pieces are made in pairs one may be veneered with *première partie* and the other with *contre-partie* marquetry.

The brass in the *première-partie* marquetry was often engraved naturalistically, frequently very finely, and was sometimes combined with other substances, such as pewter, copper, mother-of-pearl and stained horn, to give contrasts and naturalistic effects to the design. Additional colour was also given by veneering the shell over coloured foil, usually red or green.

The carcases on to which Boulle marquetry is veneered are usually found to be of oak or deal, and the parts which are not covered are veneered with ebony, coromandel-wood or purple-wood, in order to tone with the shell of the inlay.

Boulle furniture is usually lavishly mounted with ormolu, to protect the corners and the more vulnerable parts of the inlay, but the mounts are frequently also adapted in a decorative manner to form hinges, lock-plates and handles. It will be noticed that the ormolu is sometimes fully gilt, which provides a strong decorative contrast with the inlaid brass; equally, the bronze is sometimes left ungilt, and therefore harmonizes with the metal inlay to a greater extent.

Boulle furniture, so much in demand in the reign of Louis XIV, went out of fashion during most of that of his successor, but did not cease to be made, and the Boulle *atelier* continued to turn out pieces from time to time. They were therefore ready when, under Louis XVI, the taste for this type of furniture returned. At this period a very large number of pieces were made, often using the original designs, mounts and processes as in the former period.

Boulton, Matthew: (1728–1809), a Birmingham manufacturer of small metal objects such as étuis, snuff-boxes, buckles, etc., who combined the functions of manufacturer and merchant. In 1761 he established the firm of Boulton and Fothergill which gradually extended its manufactures to include cut-steel jewellery, Sheffield plate (q.v.), silver and ormolu (q.v.). He was, in fact, the only manufacturer in England of ormolu and achieved a quality rivalling that of the finest Parisian work in this material. Robert Adam (q.v.) supplied designs for his ormolu and Sheffield plate.

Bourg-la-Reine: see Mennecy porcelain.

Bourne & Son: a firm of stoneware manufacturers, which continues to this day, founded by Joseph Bourne in 1812. He was the son of William Bourne, master potter of Belper, and factories at Belper and Denby were carried on by the family simultaneously until 1834 when the Belper works was discontinued and its materials and plant were transferred to Denby. A works at Codnor Park passed into Bourne's control in 1833 but also finally closed down and its plant and workpeople were brought to Denby in 1861. Similarly the Shipley Pottery acquired in 1845 was absorbed in 1856. Marks: The name of the firm J. BOURNE & SON with PATENTEES DENBY POTTERY NEAR DERBY arranged variously, or BOURNE'S POTTERY BELPER & DENBY DERBYSHIRE.

Excellent brown salt-glazed stonewares included hunting jugs with relief ornament and greyhound handles, and other ornamental wares were made.

Boutet, Nicholas: (1761–1833), founder and director of the Royal Arms Factory at Versailles. Established under Louis XVI and continued during the Directorate and Empire. Boutet, who signed himself "Directeur-Artiste", applied the massive Empire style of ornament to the presentation swords and firearms which were the main production of the factory. His finest work, dating from the Napoleonic period, achieves a luxury hardly paralleled in the history of firearms.

Boutique d'Or: a name given to the Paris 17th cent. tapestry factory of De La Planche and Comans. These weavers had been brought from Brussels and Antwerp by Henry IV. The factory was noted for the silken texture of its products and the imposing formality of the borders used. The designers included Simon Vouet and Rubens. The factory was combined with the Gobelins (q.v.) in 1662.

Bow porcelain: the early history of the factory is obscure. In 1744, Edward Heylin, and Thomas Frye took out a patent for the manufacture of "a certain material" equal in beauty and quality to imported porcelain, from a recipe including a material called unaker, "the produce of the Chirokee nation in America". Doubt has been cast upon the workableness of

their specification, and no Bow porcelain of this early date has been identified with certainty.

Another patent was taken out by Frye alone in 1749 for a phosphatic porcelain including a percentage of bone-ash or "Virgin Earth" which accounts for the high phosphorous content of identified early Bow porcelain.

By 1750 the manufactory had been taken over by Weatherby & Crowther, merchants, under the name "New Canton", but Frye remained as manager until 1759. Weatherby died in 1762, and in 1763 Crowther became bankrupt. The factory, however, was continued in operation until 1776 when it was taken over by William Duesbury who closed it down and removed the moulds to Derby.

Numerous factory and workmen's or repairers' marks have been recorded on identified Bow porcelain, but before c. 1760 wares can only be distinguished by qualities other than marks. The most generally recognized Bow marks after 1760 are an anchor and dagger in red or underglaze blue. Chaffers suggests that the dagger was adopted because Weatherby and Crowther were freemen of the City of London.

1750

1760   1770

The manufacture of Bow porcelain may be divided into four periods; (1) before 1749; (2) from 1749 until 1755; (3) from 1755 until 1760, when the most valued and typical Bow qualities appeared; and (4) after 1760, when there was a general lowering of quality apart from modelling, and the work became imitative in character.

(1) The wares made, if made at all, under the patent of 1744 were non-phosphatic. A number of figures, on the evidence of style mannerisms, have been conjecturally attributed to this early period.

(2) From 1749 a creamy bone paste was produced, and wares were rather heavy in weight with an uneven glaze and of variable translucency. Plain white figures were made, and groups attributed on stylistic grounds to the "Muses' modeller", often of women and children with round, doll-like heads and receding chins. These are generally treated with originality and painted sparingly with a limited palette of pigments. Useful wares followed Oriental porcelain shapes or contemporary silver, and were frequently decorated with versions of Chinese *famille rose* patterns; designs reminiscent of Japanese Kakiemon; or with applied prunus sprays in relief on white wares.

(3) The distinctive qualities of Bow porcelain c. 1755–60 are a rather waxy glaze, sometimes slightly iridescent; the irregular spreading of the blue colour used for underglaze painting giving the surface a bluish tinge; and bright clear colouring with delicate flower painting. Figures display a liveliness of modelling and colour, in spite of strong Meissen influence. "General Wolfe" and the "Marquis of Granby" (c. 1759) are examples of the best and most original Bow style. Figures tend to be a little heavy for their size and are sometimes provided with a square hole in which a support for candles could be placed. Mound bases gave place about 1758–60 to 4-footed rococo scroll pedestals tricked out in crimson and purple. Useful wares were decorated in Oriental styles with Kakiemon patterns in red, blue and gold; with floral sprays dominated by two big peonies; or with "botanical" flowers. Mixed decorative styles were sometimes used containing *motifs* from East and West. Transfer-printed decorations in black or brick red are beautiful but uncommon.

(4) Bow figures of the last period retained something of the charms of the earlier work, but the paste was greyer and the decoration tended to become over-elaborate. Useful wares in this phase follow Meissen, Chelsea and Worcester styles and marks.

Bow-back chair: see Windsor chair.

Bow-fronted: in the second half of the 18th cent., case furniture was sometimes designed with a convex front. Sheraton (q.v.) is connected with the bow-fronted chest of drawers, which was used with the serpentine and straight-fronted types.

Boys and crowns: old term for a type of carved ornament on the cresting of late 17th and quite early 18th cent. chairs and day-beds. The motif, a crown, usually, though not necessarily, arched, supported by two flying or sprawling naked boys, derives ultimately from the flying *putti* frequently found in renaissance design. In England, the idea was familiar long before it achieved a vogue on chair-backs.

Box inkstand: a rectangular inkstand of silver, pewter or brass with one or two wells, drawers beneath.

Bozetto: small scale sketch in terracotta, wax or some other suitable material, for sculpture.

Bracket clock: many clocks of the 17th and 18th cent. were provided with their own brackets, usually designed to harmonize with the case. Only rarely have original brackets survived. They frequently contain a drawer to hold the winding key. Portable clocks are known as both mantel and bracket clocks.

Bracket foot: a foot supporting a piece of case furniture and attached directly to the under-framing. It consists of two pieces of wood, joined at the corner. The open side is generally cut out in a simple pattern. The corner end is sometimes straight, at other times curved in an ogee pattern.

Bracteate: thin silver coins with type in relief on one side and incuse on other, widely issued in Germany and Switzerland from 12th to 14th cent.

Types, facing portraits, buildings, and heraldic devices.

Bradwell Wood pottery: the traditional and generally accepted site in Staffordshire of Elers' factory (q.v.). It was situated on a wooded ridge which separates Burslem from Newcastle-under-Lyme and this afforded some element of secrecy. Good red clay was abundant in the area, from which Elers made "red china" teapots which gave him a national reputation.

This site has been frequently investigated but little of any value has ever been discovered. Shaw says that Enoch Wood (q.v.) and John Riley measured the oven in 1808 and came to the conclusion that it was unsuitable for salt-glazed stoneware which Elers was alleged to have introduced into Staffordshire. In a memorandum written in 1814 into Cox's *Magna Britannia and Hibernia*, Enoch Wood recorded his opinion that it had been "built to fire red china only". The site has been frequently explored since Enoch Wood's time by the Rheads, by Thomas Pape, and recently in 1955 by A. R. Mountford who discovered fragments of "red china". The site awaits more through excavation.

Braiding: embroidery executed by means of couched braid chiefly in designs of arabesques (q.v.) or continuous scrolls.

Bramah lock: the first lock to be operated by a small conveniently carried key, invented by Joseph Bramah in 1784. The key did not act directly upon the sliding bolt, but through the medium of the rotating barrel, thus anticipating Yale's cylindrical lock of 1848. Insertion of the key pushed back a number of sliding plates until notches at different positions came into line, allowing the barrel to be turned and the bolt withdrawn.

Brampton stoneware: brown stonewares made from early in the 18th cent. and throughout the 19th cent. The principal potter in 1800 is said to have been William Bromley who was succeeded by Robert Bambrigge & Co.

Six factories existed in Brampton

early in the 19th cent.

The wares made at Brampton were in the 19th cent. classed with and are still when unmarked often mistaken for Nottingham wares. They fall into two categories: one, of a fine chocolate colour similar to Belper wares, decorated with applied ornament; and two, wares varying in colour from buff to red of some brilliancy. This second group included Toby jugs as well as tea and coffee-pots, which were mostly made by Briddon or Oldfield c. 1835. A characteristic feature of Brampton wares is an internal green glaze which occurs on dated specimens from 1820 to 1894.

Marks:

S. & H. BRIDDON
(Samuel & Henry Briddon) c. 1848

OLDFIELD & CO. MAKERS
(Oldfield, Madin Wright, Hewitt & Company, or John Oldfield.)

J. OLDFIELD

OLDFIELD & CO.
CHESTERFIELD

Branch: late in the 17th cent. and during the first half of the 18th, this word was used sometimes to describe a chandelier. That indefatigable traveller Celia Fiennes saw one at Hampton Court Palace early in Queen Anne's reign. She noted: "... thence into the dineing roome where hangs in the middle a chrystall branch for candles..." By the mid-18th cent. the sense of the word would seem to have changed, for Jerom Johnson, the glass-seller, advertised for sale "... brilliant Lustres, Branches...". A confusing statement in view or the fact that "Lustre" was a term used also to describe a chandelier.

Brandenbourgs: jewelled clasps, originally invented for masculine use in the latter half of the 17th cent. and quickly adopted by ladies for the ornamentation of their triangular bodice fronts. A series of these clasps in diminishing size were worn on the bodice, one set below the other. The popularity of this form of jewellery continued into the 18th cent.

Brander: a pierced metal plate, with a half-hoop handle by which it was suspended from a pot-hook. It was used principally in Scotland for the making of brander bannocks (oatmeal cakes).

Brandy-bowls: flat, two-handled silver bowls called *orekovsken* in Denmark, *oreskaal* in Norway and *dopskal* in Sweden, used for serving hot brandy, were popular throughout the Scandinavian countries in the 17th cent.

Bras de lumière: see Wall-lights.

Bratina: a globular, covered cup with a contracted lip (usually decorated with a sententious inscription), peculiar to Russia. It was a form of loving-cup, intimately associated with its owner and used at his funeral feast. Sometimes they were richly enamelled and begemmed; a rare example in gold is in the museum at Vienna.

Brazier: circular bowl with pierced plate in base for burning charcoal as heaters for kettles or dishes. Examples date from late 17th cent. and occasionally from the 18th., but the brazier was then supplanted by spirit-lamp stands (see also Chafing stand).

Breakfast table: a small, four-legged table with hinged flaps which could be extended on brackets. Examples of such tables were illustrated by Thomas Chippendale (q.v.) in the third edition of *The Gentleman and Cabinet-Maker's Director*, published in 1762.

Break-front bookcase or **wing bookcase:** a bookcase in which the central section projects slightly beyond the side sections or "wings", a form popular from the mid-18th cent.

Breast ornament: see Crochet.

Breloque: a small ornament attached to a watch-chain or châtelaine (q.v.).

Brescian steel: see Chiselled and cut steel.

Breton work: a type of embroidery derived from Breton peasant costume worked in coloured silks and gold thread, mainly in chain and satin stitch and used for the borders of garments, neck-tie ends and small articles such as book-markers.

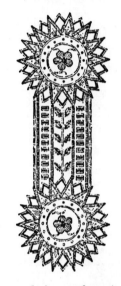

Brewster chair: modern American term for an early 17th cent. Dutch type armchair made of turned posts and spindles. A handsomer variety of the Carver chair (q.v.). It has two tiers of four spindles in the back, a similar tier under the arms and, occasionally, two or more tiers under the seat at the sides. Usually of ash or maple with rush seats. Named after William Brewster, first leader of the Plymouth colony pilgrims, who is said to have brought one to America with him in 1620 in the *Mayflower*. Popular to the end of the 17th cent. Earliest surviving examples perhaps about 1650.

Brewster-shape: oval, straight-sided teapots with lid set into an oval, vertical collar, made at the Wedgwood factory in the 1780s. This shape was popular at all potworks making wares in the neo-classic style.

Briand, Thomas: (d. 1784), a chemist who demonstrated examples of a soft paste porcelain before the Royal Society in 1742–43, and was part-proprietor of the Chelsea porcelain factory on its foundation. Later he worked at Champion's Bristol porcelain manufactory and some plaques in biscuit have been attributed to him.

Bridal fans: date from about 1720 until the end of the 18th cent. At first they were costly, designed and painted by master fanmakers. Souvenir copies by lesser hands were presented to the maids of honour and women guests. Still other fans, with mounts hand-coloured over copies of a specially designed engraving, were sent as mementoes to a wider circle of friends. Marriage fans might be painted with scenes in the lives of the bride and groom, with their miniatures in ivory set into the guards (q.v.).

Brides: French term usually preferred to the English bars or ties, describing those parts of a piece of lace connecting and supporting the pattern where there was no net ground. Found mainly in needlepoints (q.v.) and mixed laces.

Bridge fluting: a decoration applied to drinking glasses, being an extension of faceting from the stem to bridge the junction of the bowl and the stem. This type of decoration was used in the second half of the 18th cent., and in the later examples extends over the lower part of the bowl. Also known as cresting.

Brigandine: a light, flexible body defence (armour), consisting of small, overlapping metal plates riveted to the interior of a canvas or leather jacket. It was usually covered with coloured silk or velvet, the rivet heads on the exterior being gilt to produce a decorative effect. The term first occurs at the end of the 14th cent., but the majority of surviving examples date from the 16th and early 17th cent.

The jack was a cheaper form of the brigandine, its plates, which were often of horn, being held in place by stitching.

Bright-cut engraving: a particular form of engraving on silverware and plate, popular about 1790, in which the metal is removed by bevelled cutting, giving a jewel-like, faceted sparkle to the surface.

Brilliant cut: a form of diamond cutting introduced by Vincenzo Peruzzi at Venice about 1700. Diamonds cut in this way end in points both at the front and the back and have up to 58 facets, visible in open-claw settings.

"Brinjal bowls": K'ang Hsi porcelain bowls with incised flower-sprays coloured yellow and green on an aubergine (Anglo-Indian: *brinjal*) purple ground, in glazes applied "on the biscuit".

Briolettes: drop-shaped stones cut with triangular facets.

Brisé fan: composed solely of sticks of slightly flexible ivory, tortoiseshell or horn, delicately pierced. The sticks were joined by ribbons of closely woven silk, apparently in one continuous length passing through the whole fan, but in reality consisting of many short lengths each separately attached to a fan stick. These leafless fans were introduced in the early 1680s and were fashionable from about 1715 until the end of the cent. The sticks were cut to wafer thinness, the upper part of each being saw-cut with designs so exquisite as to resemble the finest lace and enriched with burnished gilding. In the lower portion might be worked an armorial device. Equal care of craftsmanship was given to both sides of the fan. Another type of brisé fan was made from unperforated sticks which, overlapping, formed a plain field for decoration. Each side might be covered by an all-over painting in oils. The minuet fan is a type of brisé fan. By the end of the 18th cent. ivory and mother-of-pearl sticks were replaced by bone, scented sandal wood, laburnum wood and cut steel.

Brislington: a delftware manufactory flourished here from c. 1650 to 1750. (See under Bristol delftware).

Bristol delftware: a pottery at Brislington, near Bristol, was founded by Southwark potters c. 1650; it in turn colonized a factory in Bristol (Temple Pottery, 1683–1770, when delftware was abandoned). Others were St Mary Redcliffe's (c. 1700–77) and Limekiln Lane (c. 1700–54).

Early Bristol delftware is difficult to distinguish from Lambeth (q.v.) and the later from that of Liverpool (q.v.). The Bristol glaze, however, often had a distinctive lavender-blue tone, and the early red (c. 1700) stands out in appreciable relief. The Bristol *bianco-sopra-bianco* (q.v.) borders usually include a cone motif and curved sprays of leaves. Characteristic Bristol shapes include a plate with straight sides forming an obtuse angle with the bottom; puzzle-jugs (q.v.) with open-work necks formed by intersecting circles; flower-"bricks" pierced with a square hole at the top and mounted on small bracket feet, and (17th cent.) porringers having a circular handle with corrugations radiating from a central hole.

Bristol glass: Glasshouses were in existence in the city and port of Bristol in the 17th cent. By the early 18th cent. some fifteen are recorded, most of them making window-glass or bottles. It was not until the mid-cent. that more sophisticated articles of good quality began to be made. In 1745 the Glass Excise Act placed a duty on glass which was levied by weight and seriously hampered the trade. Forms of decoration suited to lighter glass, such as engraving and enamelling began to flourish and it has been suggested that these circumstances caused the Bristol makers to produce coloured glass, a material with which their name has been linked ever since, although the production of such glass was by no means either wholly or mainly confined to Bristol. A rich deep blue was popular and also purple and green.

Among the articles made were fingerbowls, decanters, etc. and also scent bottles, étuis (q.v.), snuff-boxes and other "toys". Opaque-white glass, made in competition with porcelain, was also produced at Bristol and various glassmakers in the city are recorded as having made it. Again, white glass was also made at other centres and particularly the snuff-boxes and étuis, etc. of opaque glass were most probably made by the box makers of Birmingham and South Staffordshire. Of the larger articles, opaque white glass, not being suitable for tea or coffee services, was employed mainly for ornamental vases and beakers as well as tea caddies and candlesticks, the enamelled decoration resembling that applied to porcelain. (See also Opaque glass and Edkins, Michael.)

Bristol porcelain:

(1) A type of soft-paste porcelain, making use of soapstone quarried in Cornwall, was made between 1749–52 by William Miller and Benjamin Lund at a glasshouse at Redcliffe Backs, Bristol, known, because owned until 1745 by William Lowdin, as Lowdin's China House. A few pieces survive: Chinese-copy figures, and more rarely sauceboats decorated with flowers. They may be marked BRISTOL, or BRISTOL 1750.

In 1752 the factory amalgamated with Worcester, from which its products are no longer distinguishable.

(2) Hard-paste porcelain was made at Bristol for only eleven years between 1770–81, first by William Cookworthy, who moved his factory from Plymouth, later by Richard Champion, his associate, who acquired his patent and bought his business in 1773. Cookworthy's patent soon expired, and when its renewal was contested by Wedgwood, Turner and others in Staffordshire, he retained the sole use of Cornish china clay and china stone in translucent wares, but being

unsuccessful he was compelled to sell his patent and abandon porcelain manufacture in 1781. The patent was acquired by a company of Staffordshire potters who traded from New Hall, Shelton.

Marks: A cross, or a cross and a letter "B" in blue enamel; or crossed swords with a cross in underglaze blue and blue enamel

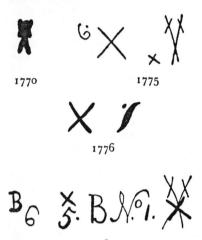

1770   1775

1776

1780

Richard Champion claimed that his hard-paste porcelain rivalled that of Meissen for strength, and Sèvres for elegance. He manufactured with it a variety of useful wares ranging from ungilded cottage china decorated with sprigs of blossom to elaborate services with initials for his friends or to special order. Elegant Sèvres-style cabarets (q.v.) were also made.

Teapots in the form of an inverted pear with double curve handles are characteristic. Tightly bunched floral sprays, or sprays with angular spiky foliage recur. Typical colours are leaf green and clear deep red.

Sets of figures representing the *Seasons*, the *Elements* or *Venus and Adonis* decorated in the Sèvres style of Louis XVI period were made by Champion. Rockwork bases and a touch of sentiment are features of these wares.

Large hexagonal vases were decorated with masks and floral festoons in relief, and painted in colours.

Britannia metal: a trade name given to a tin-antimony-copper alloy, lending itself to mass production by spinning. Although the name was used before 1800 it rightfully should be named "hard metal" until August 10, 1842, when the English patent No. 9441 was granted to Richard Ford Sturges for the name and composition of "Britannia Metal". Plating on Britannia metal was introduced in the early 1820s by Kirby, Smith & Co., Sheffield. A sheet of pure silver was laid on a flat surface and well heated. Molten Britannia metal was poured over this. When cold it was found to have picked up the silver. The two were then rolled into sheets as for plated copper. Owing to difficulties in assembling the method was soon abandoned.

Britannia Standard: the Higher Standard for wrought silver plate introduced in 1697 to prevent the melting down of coinage by silversmiths. It consists of 11 oz 10 dwts fine silver in the Pound Troy (12 oz). So named from the mark of Britannia replacing the Sterling mark of a lion passant. In force till 1720, when Sterling or Old Standard was restored, the Higher being left as optional, which it still is.

"Broad" glass: flat sheet glass made by blowing a long bubble of metal into a cylindrical form, splitting the cylinder and re-heating it for flattening into a sheet.

Broad Street glasshouse: glasshouse set up in London in 1575 by Giacomo Verzelini (q.v.) with the purpose of making glasses in the Venetian manner.

Broadsword: a sword with a straight double-edged blade. The term is applied chiefly to the basket-hilted cavalry sword of the 17th and 18th cent. It survived in the Scottish basket-hilted sword, often erroneously called a claymore.

"Brocaded Imari": see Imari porcelain.

Broderie Anglaise: a type of white-work embroidery (known also as Ayrshire, Eyelet, Madeira or Swiss-work) in which open spaces are cut or punched with a stiletto. The edges of the holes are then overcast. The finest specimens of this type of work, which was used chiefly for sleeve frills, baby clothes and underwear, were produced in the late 18th or early 19th cent.

Broderie Perse: see Cretonne appliqué.

Broken arch clock cases: an arch terminating on either side with a horizontal projection. There are broken arch dials and cases. If a full semicircle, they are known as deep; if less, and this usually applies to the earliest, as shallow arches.

Broken pediment: Georgian cabinet makers frequently made use of architectural motifs in constructing bureau-bookcases and similar pieces. Of these, two forms of broken pediment in which the apex of the triangular cresting was absent, were popular: the angular form in which the two upper sides of the triangle remain straight, and the swan-neck in which these two sides are allowed to curve into an elegant scroll. (See also Pediment.)

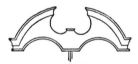

Bronze: an alloy of copper and tin. The earliest metal to be used by man; the ease with which it can be cast, chiselled, chased and engraved and the fine patina (q.v.) it acquires with age have assured its popularity ever since.

Bronze disease: natural patina often of a soft and porous nature, formed on bronzes buried in the soil, tends to retain some saline constituents of the soil. These salts, together with the moisture in the atmosphere, may form bright-green spots, which are sometimes dry or moist, a condition called bronze disease. The disease, if not attended to, spreads quickly and has a destructive corrosive action.

Bronze gilt: see Ormolu.

Bronzes d'ameublement: (*Fr.*), a term, with no exact English equivalent, describing lacquered, patinated or gilt bronze furniture. It embraces such items as candelabra, candlesticks, wall-lights, chandeliers, fire-dogs, clock-cases, mounts for furniture and porcelain, etc. whose manufacture was the particular province of the *fondeurs*, *ciseleurs* and *doreurs*.

Bronzes d'applique: see Ormolu.

Bronzing: the name of the metallic shading on some glass silhouettes. In some cases this was used with beautiful effect, particularly by John Miers, who used real gold. It was usually, though not exclusively, used on painted work.

Brushing slide: some commodes (q.v.) and chests of drawers of the second half of the 18th cent. were equipped with a shelf above the top drawer which could be drawn out when needed for toilet purposes.

Brussels carpets: see Moquette.

Brussels lace: needlepoints and pillow laces. Needlepoint was made from 1720, but took second place to the pillow laces. The ground was a plain looped mesh and late in the century there was a tendency to restrict the slower needlepoint work to the pattern and introduce a pillow lace ground. Pillow laces included bride-linked tape lace of the 17th cent. succeeded by grounded laces, the ground worked after the pattern, its hexagonal mesh consisting of two sides with four threads plaited four times and four sides of two threads twisted. Patterns in the mid-18th cent. included many rococo-Oriental extravagancies. The Brussels point plat appliqué was a pillow lace of the late 18th cent. with a net ground supporting small sprigs worked separately.

Brussels tapestry: capital of Brabant and the Netherlands since 1483, Brussels became Europe's leading centre of tapestry weaving from about 1500, and retained its reputation throughout the 17th and 18th cent., though eclipsed by Louis XIV's Gobelins factory (q.v.) since 1670–80. Brussel's reputation was definitely sealed by Pope Leo X's order for the weaving of tapestries for the Sistine Chapel from Raphael's cartoons (about 1515). But as a tapestry designer Bernard van Orley and his school exercised a far greater influence at Brussels in the first half of the 16th cent. The *History of Jacob*, newly acquired at Brussels, and the *Hunts of Maximilian* at the Louvre are superb examples of his style. Francis I of France, England's Henry VIII, and the Emperor Charles V all had recourse to Brussels for specially fine sets (the *Great Scipio*, *Story of Abraham*, now at Hampton Court, the *Conquest of Tunis*), and it was there also that the Duke of Marlborough ordered his set of *Victories* (c. 1712). Throughout the 16th, 17th and 18th cent. the Habsburgs were Brussel's chief patrons.

Among the many outstanding workshops that of Van Aelst, de Pannemaker and Geubels should be mentioned for the 16th cent. Jan Raes, Martin Reymbouts and the Leyniers family excelled in the 17th. The large and extravagantly designed baroque tapestries of that cent. were probably less popular in England than sets with subjects taken from Roman or Biblical history. Mythological subjects were also in great favour, especially those set in wooded landscapes and surrounded with rich floral borders. So, too, were *genre* and peasant subjects taken from paintings and designs after the second David Teniers. These so-called "Teniers tapestries" were in vogue from the late 17th and all through the 18th cent. J. van der Borcht (senior, who also signed himself in the latinized form "A. Castro"), J. de Vos, and various members of the Leyniers and van den Hecke families are names frequently met with on Brussels tapestries of this period.

$$B \heartsuit B$$

The mark, a red shield between two B's (for Brussels, Brabant) is normally seen in the border of a Brussels tapestry since the Edict of 1528.

Bruting: the grinding into shape of a rough diamond by rubbing it with another – the first step in grinding the precious stone.

Bucket form bowl: bowl of a drinking glass in the form of a straight-sided bucket with horizontal base, a shape which continued in popularity from the 1730s until the early 19th cent.

Buckler: in the 16th cent. the majority of shields were circular, one of the most popular types being the buckler (introduced as early as the 13th cent.), held in the left hand by means of a crossbar on the inside.

Bucks point lace: pillow lace, mainly showing the influence of Lille (q.v.) and with much use of Lille's ground (*fond clair*) (q.v.) although often in company with *fond chant* (q.v.) and the soft Mechlin (q.v.) mesh. The patterns were lightened with attractive fillings and outlined with gimp wide and flat. There was some direct copying of Mechlin.

"Buckwheat" celadon ware: see Tobi seiji.

Bud thumbpiece: a thumbpiece (q.v.) in the shape of two ovoids rising from a common stalk and resembling bursting buds found on 17th and 18th cent. pewter baluster measures, etc.

Buen Retiro porcelain: porcelain was made at Buen Retiro, near Madrid from 1760 until 1808, when the factory closed. The premises at Buen Retiro were set up by Charles III upon his succession to the throne of Spain, the purpose being to house his workmen and artists who had previously worked for him at Capo-di-Monte (q.v.), Naples. Buen Retiro porcelain was soft-paste of a creamy tone, the figure modelling reaching a high level of achievement, although examples are extremely rare.

Buffe: see Burgonet.

Buffet: term variously applied to open, doorless structures, of more than one tier (see also Court cupboard, Livery cupboard).

Bull-baiting group: pottery groups showing a bull goring or tossing a dog, often upon table bases supported by six legs, popular c. 1830–35. They are said to have been made by Obadiah Sherratt (q.v.).

Bullet knop: a knop or protuberance on the stem of a drinking glass or other vessel of small spherical form. Sometimes known as an olive button.

Bull's eye: popular American term for a smallish round mirror of concave or, more often, convex glass in an ornate round frame. With candle brackets attached to the frame, the type is generally known in America as a girandole mirror. Many of these bull's eye mirrors are of English or French rather than American make. They were highly fashionable about 1800–20.

Bun foot: a variation of the ball foot, in which the rounded form is slightly flattened, introduced as a terminal support to cabinets or table legs in the last half of the 17th cent. (See also Ball foot.)

Bureau bookcase: a piece of cabinet furniture which came into use towards the mid-18th cent., consisting of an upper stage with shelves enclosed within doors, sometimes glazed, and below a slope-front desk which opens to reveal small drawers for writing materials in the interior. Below are long drawers.

Bureau-plat: (*Fr.*). a writing-table supported on tall legs with a flat top and drawers beneath. Began to appear in France towards the end of the 17th cent.

Bureau-toilette: (*Fr.*) a piece of furniture intended for the use of ladies, combining the functions of a toilet-and writing-table.

Burgonet: an open helmet, used chiefly by light-horsemen in the 16th and early 17th cent. It usually had a peak (fall) over the eyes and hinged cheek-pieces fastening under the chin. It was sometimes worn with a deep chin-piece (buffe).

Burl: an American term describing a tree knot or protruding growth which shows beautifully patterned grainings when sliced. Used for inlay or veneer. Found in some late 17th and much 18th cent. American furniture, and chiefly in walnut and maple. (See also Burr veneer.)

Burlington, Third Earl of: (1694-1753), a connoisseur of the arts whose devotion to the architectural principles laid down by the Italian architect Palladio in the 16th cent., led him to sponsor their strict observance in England. With a small group of enthusiasts, he occupied himself with architectural designs which, in the interests of harmony, included the layout of gardens and interior decoration and furniture. He worked closely with William Kent (q.v.). (See also Palladian style.)

Burnishing: polishing with a hand tool containing a hard, smooth stone or, in modern times, steel; used to remove planishing marks from the "planishing teast" (q.v.) or hammer.

"Burr" veneer: veneering was the chief decorative feature of walnut furniture. Veneers were thin layers of wood cut by hand-saw and glued to a carefully prepared surface. "Burr" was an intricate figuring from abnormal growths at the base of the trunk.

Bushire carpets: see Beshire carpets.

Bussa: large earthenware pot commonly kept in old Cornish cottages for salting down pilchards.

Busse chests: buscarles' or seamen's chests.

Bustelli, Franz Anton: (1723–63), a porcelain modeller employed at the Nymphenburg factory (q.v.) in Germany from 1754 to his death in 1763. His figures show great affinity of style with those of contemporary Bavarian sculptors. His was perhaps, the greatest creative genius in porcelain of the 18th cent. He recaptured the playful mood of the Rococo period (q.v.) in his figures, often rendered in pure white or in restrained colours. Among the finest of his models are those derived from the Italian comedy.

Butler's tray: a tray mounted on legs or on a folding stand, in use throughout the 18th cent. The X-shaped folding stand was in general use from about 1750, the tray normally being rectangular and fitted with a gallery. Oval trays were sometimes made in the later part of the cent.

Butterfly paperweight: a coloured butterfly occupies the centre of the paperweight. The insect can be poised over a flower, above a latticinio (q.v.), or other filigree, ground.

Butterfly table: drop-leaf table with swinging supports resembling butterfly wings. Believed to be uniquely American. The legs are raked and stretchered so that the "wings" can be pivoted in the stretchers. They were made between 1700–25, the earliest examples being usually of maple.

Butter-pot: cylindrical earthenware vessel made to hold fourteen pounds of butter, made at Burslem in the 17th cent. for use at Uttoxeter market.

Bygones: any objects no longer in use, such as obsolete agricultural implements, old-fashioned spits, fenders, bellows, and so on.

c.: used indiscriminately to mean copyright or *circa*. When anyone wants to be sure of not being misunderstood, the "c" for "copyright" is raised and "ca" is used for "*circa*".

Cabaret set: porcelain tea set for one or two people, provided with a porcelain tray. Sometimes the cups were placed immediately on the tray and the saucers dispensed with.

Cabasset: see under Morion.

Cabbage-leaf jugs: there are two large jugs in Worcester Corporation Museum, moulded with overlapping leaves in relief, dated 1757, which were made at the Worcester porcelain factory. Worcester cabbage-leaf jugs have cylindrical necks, (later ones sometimes with masks), and ovoid relief-ornamented bodies upon which the decoration was superimposed. This type of jug was imitated later at Lowestoft and Caughley usually with the addition of a mask-lip spout.

Cabinet-maker: towards the end of the 17th cent., the joiner was replaced by the cabinet-maker as the supreme furniture craftsman. The new technique of veneering furniture, which was introduced into England at the return of Charles II, was probably taught to the English craftsmen by either Dutch or French cabinet-makers. The new craft found a firm footing and by the mid-18th cent. the work of the English cabinet-makers displayed a great technical excellence.

Cabochon: stones of rounded, natural form, polished but not cut.

Cabochon ornament: a carved ornament found on furniture of the middle years of the 18th cent. and particularly on the knees of chair legs, so named on account of its resemblance to the polished, rounded shape of an uncut gem. It is usually oval and surrounded by a scrolled leaf ornament.

Cabriole fan: fashionable from the 1770s until the 1790s and contemporary with medallion fans (q.v.). The name was derived from a light-weight two-wheeled carriage of the period. The fan consisted not of a single broad leaf, but of two or three narrower, arc-shaped bands of silk or "chicken skin" (q.v.). The upper mount, measuring twice the depth of the others, might be painted with a scene including a cabriole, its occupant being a portrait of the fan's owner. The sticks offered further scope for ornament, such as piercing and gilding, on the spaces visible between the bands. Tiny mirrors might be inset into the blades and a minute telescopic glass inserted into the stick pivot (q.v.).

Cabriole leg: a chair or table leg much favoured in the first half of the 18th cent. The leg curves outward at the knee and in-wards towards the foot in an elongated "s" form and is tapered at the base. Sometimes the knee bears a carved shell or-nament.

Caddy spoon: small spoon with short handle for measuring tea from the caddy. Made in numerous fancy forms, leaf, jockey cap, hand, etc., from about 1780 onwards.

Cadogan teapot: a teapot or jug filled from a hole in the base, said to have been named after the Hon. Mrs Cadogan, who brought to this country an original Chinese teapot of this type. A Cadogan teapot is lidless and shaped like a Chinese peach-shaped wine pot. First made at Swinton, Yorkshire, about 1795, with a purple-brown "Rockingham" glaze, Cadogan tea-pots became popular, and John Mort-lock of Oxford Street, London, whose name, impressed, frequently occurs, bought and sold large quantities of them. In Staffordshire Cadogans were made by Davenport, Copelands and other firms.

Caen lace: pillow lace imitating the silk *blondes* of Chantilly (q.v.) from the mid-18th cent.

Café-au-lait glaze: a warm brown glaze used on Chinese porcelain of the Ch'ing dynasty (q.v.), sometimes over-painted in *famille verte* (q.v.) enamels and sometimes as a monochrome.

Caffaggiolo maiolica: tin-glazed earthenware made after 1500 under the patronage of a branch of the Medici family at their castle of Caffaggiolo, near Florence. During the Renaissance (q.v.), the art of the potter in Italy was encouraged by patronage and maiolica represents one of its supreme achievements.

Caffawa or **caffoys:** English 18th cent. term for flock wallpapers simu-lating damask.

Caffiéri, Jacques: French sculptor, born 1678, son of Philippe Caffiéri, and came from a large family of sculptors. Became one of the chief exponents of the rococo style in France and was employed extensively by the Crown at Versailles, Fontainebleau and else-where. He also occasionally worked as a portrait sculptor. He often signed his bronzes with his surname only, and his chief works are to be found at Versailles, the Louvre, Paris, the Wallace Collection, and elsewhere. Died 1755.

Cake baskets: cake baskets of silver were variously used for bread, cake or fruit. Early examples are rare and usually circular. Oval forms were introduced about 1730, with pierced bodies and swing handles. Wirework bodies with applied foliage, wheat or flowers, were popular about 1770. Later examples have solid bodies, engraved decoration and gadrooned or reeded rims. Circular gilt baskets returned to favour after 1800 for dessert use. (See also Cream, Dessert and Sugar baskets).

Calendar clock: a clock which indicates days, months or years.

Calf binding: leather book-binding made from the hide of a calf: the commonest leather used for this purpose. It is smooth, with no perceptible grain, and its natural colour is brown.

Calf can be treated in a number of ways, and for books full-bound (as distinct from half-bound) it will often be further described as polished, sprinkled, mottled, stained, tree (a special pattern), marbled, diced, scored or grained. There are also special styles, such as rough, reversed, divinity, law and antique.

Calibre cut: gemstones of small dimensions, cut to special requirements.

Callot figures: miniature figures, usually amusing or grotesque, in porcelain or in silver or gold, enamelled or gem-set, are known as Callot figures. This is a reference to the French engraver Jacques Callot (1592–1635), who specialized in vivid drawings of beggars and cut-throats and the swaggering characters of the Italian Comedy.

Caltrop: a three-spiked device so arranged that one spike always projects upwards. Used as a form of defence against cavalry attack as the horses were lamed by these implements placed in their path.

Cam: part of a watch or clock so shaped to turn rotary motion into reciprocal or variable motion.

Cambrian pottery: see Swansea earthenware and porcelain.

Camel back sofa: colloquial term for a sofa, with the top curved somewhat like the hump of a dromedary They date from the late 18th cent.

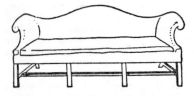

Cameo: a gem or shell carved in relief in such a way that the con-

trasting colours of the material carved are exploited. The cameos cut by the Romans were much admired throughout the Middle Ages and the Renaissance. The neo-classical taste of the late 18th cent. brought a revival of interest in cameos. Cheaper materials began to be used in imitation of gems, such as the paste copies of antique cameos made by James Tassie (see Tassies) or the Wedgwood jasper ware cameos. (See also Wedgwood, Josiah.)

Cameo glass: a relief carved in glass on the lapidary's wheel through a surface layer of white fused on to a darker ground. A Roman technique, it was imitated in England in the late 19th cent. by several Stourbridge firms and others.

"Cameo incrustation": see "Crystallo-Ceramie".

Campana vase: a vase made in the neo-classic style, during the first decades of the 19th cent. Possibly from "campana", a church bell, hence bell-shaped.

Canapé: the ordinary French word for a sofa. Evolved in France in many forms during the Louis XV period.

Cancels: "A cancel is any part of a book substituted for what was originally printed. It may be of any size, from a tiny scrap of paper bearing one or two letters, pasted on over those first printed, to several sheets replacing the original ones. The most common form of cancel is perhaps a single leaf inserted in place of the original leaf" (McKerrow). The original sheet or leaf is called the cancelland (or *cancellandum*). That which is printed to replace it is called the cancel (or *cancellans*). The usual method for indicating to the binder that a certain leaf was to be cancelled was to slit it upwards at the foot. Occasionally a leaf slit in this way, having been overlooked by the binder, will be found bound up in the book (with or without its substitute).

Candelabrum: a standing branched candlestick. Virtually no survivals of silver candelabra before the 18th cent.

but brass examples exist. Stems and base conform to candlestick design, and scroll branches for two or more lights with finials of various forms are either fixed or detachable. Late examples of silver are highly elaborate and many-branched, sometimes with interchangeable epergne dishes (q.v.).

Candle-box: a cylindrical or square box, of metal or wood, widely used in the Georgian period for storing candles.

Candle-stand: a portable stand (known also as a lamp-stand, guéridon and torchère) for a candlestick, candelabrum or lamp. After 1660 the fashion arose of having two candle-stands flanking a side table with a mirror on the wall above; the stands usually took the form of a baluster or twist-turned shaft, with a circular or octagonal top and a tripod base. At the end of the cent. more elaborate kinds, copying French stands, became fashionable, with vase-shaped tops and scrolled feet, all carved and gilded. Other examples were of simpler design, but had rich decoration in gesso or marquetry. In the early Georgian period, when gilt stands followed architectural forms, the vase-shaped tops and baluster shafts were larger, and the feet curved outwards, replacing the scrolled French style. About 1750 stands became lighter and more delicate, many of them being enriched with rococo decoration. There was a distinct change in design in the later 18th cent.: the traditional tripod continued, often in mahogany, with turned shaft and a bowl or vase top in the classical taste; but a new type, which was originated by Adam (q.v.), consisted of three uprights, mounted on feet or a plinth, supporting usually a candelabrum, or with a flat top. Smaller examples of the latter type were made to stand on tables. A smaller candle-stand, popular after 1750, with a circular base and top, and sometimes an adjustable shaft.

Cane: name for the rods of coloured glass from which the patterns were formed in many types of paperweights.

Cane ware: a tan-coloured stoneware "dry" body made by Josiah Wedg-wood in 1770 by refining the red and buff clays used by local potters. Similar bodies were made by John Turner of Lane End, Staffordshire, Elijah Mayer and others. It was sometimes enamelled in blue and other colours. (See also "Bamboo" ware.)

Cann: an American term for a silver drinking vessel, usually of one-pint capacity, like a mug, but always having rounded sides, and standing on a moulded base.

Canopy: strictly a covering forming a roof. Used to describe an umbrella-shaped ornament found at the top and the base of most chandeliers, etc., from 1750 until the end of the cent. The points at the circumference were usually drilled for the attachment of pendent drops. Small canopies were often placed at the top of decorative glass spires, which were stood vertically between the arms.

Canted corner: bevelled or obliquely faced surface. Deriving from an architectural form, 18th cent. case furniture sometimes had canted corners.

Canteen: small individual silver set of knife, fork and spoon with beaker and condiment box, contained in shagreen case, used for travelling, dating from late 17th to early 18th cent.

Canterbury: a term used to describe (1) a small music-stand with partitions for music-books, usually mounted on castors, and sometimes with small drawers, much used in the early 19th cent. Also known as a "Canterbury". (2) was a plate and cutlery stand particularly designed for supper parties in the later 18th cent., with divisions for cutlery and a semicircular end, on four turned legs.

Canton enamel: enamel ware on copper decorated in the *famille rose* (q.v.) style for export to Europe at the Canton enamelling workshops. 18th cent. pieces include teapots, teacaddies, trays, bowls, etc. painted with flowering sprays or fruit and sometimes with European scenes. Examples from the 19th cent. are summararily painted. (See also Canton porcelain.)

Canton porcelain: the familiar name for a type of 19th cent. Chinese porcelain exported to Europe, decorated with butterflies, flowers, etc., on a celadon-green ground. Canton was the principal port on the coast of China for trade with Europe in the 18th and 19th cent. Porcelain was brought to Canton by river from Ching-Tê-Chên. From the middle years of the 18th cent. increasing quantities of porcelain were sent unpainted and were decorated to order by artists in enamelling workshops at the port. (See also Canton enamel.)

"Capacity" mugs: measures: cylindrical mugs of a certified content, stamped with an excise mark, used in ale-houses, or by street hawkers and shopkeepers; and made in salt-glazed stoneware in London, Staffordshire and elsewhere from the end of the 17th cent., and in dipped, mocha, and banded earthenware from the end of the 18th cent.

Capo-di-Monte porcelain: soft-paste porcelain was made at Capo-di-Monte, Naples, at a factory founded by the King of Naples in 1743. Examples are scarce. Decoration in relief and coloured was a characteristic of the factory but as the Doccia factory purchased numbers of the moulds in the early 19th cent. and used them, many reproductions exist, but the copies made at Doccia are of hard-paste porcelain. The factory was moved to Buen Retiro (q.v.), near Madrid in 1759, when the King of Naples also became King of Spain.

Capstan salt: a salt-cellar shaped like a ship's capstan.

Capstan table or **drum table:** a round table with a deep frieze for drawers and a central support in tripod form, the legs having a pronounced curve outwards. Sometimes this table had a solid three-sided pedestal base or monopodium (q.v.), mounted on claw feet. Common in the early 19th cent., it was usually made of rosewood or mahogany.

Caqueteuse: a late 16th cent. chair with tall narrow back and widely splayed arms. This form is thought to have been adopted in Scotland from French examples and was also known in England. As the name implies it was intended as a chair in which ladies could relax for conversation.

Carat: measure of purity of gold. Pure gold is 24 carats.

Carbuncle: a garnet cut en cabochon, that is, rounded and polished but unfaceted.

Carcase: the body of a piece of furniture upon which the veneer (q.v.) is applied.

Cardinal's hat dish: a deep pewter dish with a broad rim.

Carlin, Martin: French cabinetmaker. Very little is known about the life of Carlin. His place and date of birth are unknown. He died in Paris in 1785. He is first mentioned in 1763 and became a *maître-ébéniste* (See *Menuisiers Ebénistes, Corporation des*) in 1766. He worked for Queen Marie Antoinette and the Royal Family, but it is uncertain whether he received an official appointment with the *Garde Meuble* (q.v.).
Carlin was a most refined and delicate craftsman. He worked particularly in lacquer and with plaques of Sevres porcelain (q.v.).

Carlino: gold and silver coins introduced by Charles II of Naples in 1287 with types of angel greeting the Virgin and shield reverse.

Carnet: (*Fr.*), note-book, sometimes mounted with enamels or jewels in the 18th cent.

Carlton House table: a writing table of "D" shape, the flat front containing drawers, the top surmounted by a border containing further drawers, crested by a brass gallery. The term is contemporary and derives from the tradition that tables of this type were first supplied to the Prince of Wales, later George IV, for Carlton House. Many examples exist, dating from c. 1790 to c. 1820, usually of mahogany and sometimes of satinwood,

Carolean: term of convenience strictly applicable to objects made in the reign of Charles I (1625–49), those made under Charles II (1660–85) usually being dissociated. Actually the Carolean style is as much an extension of the Jacobean as the latter was of the later Elizabethan.

Carpet balls: taws or large marbles were used in the Victorian indoor game of carpet bowls. They were made in brown stoneware, agate ware, or earthenware coloured with striped, ringed, flowery or starry designs. A set of bowls comprised one plain or self-coloured taw and six patterned balls.

Carré, Jean: a glass-maker of Arras and Antwerp, who introduced Protestant emigrant glassmakers from Lorraine into England where they settled. He obtained a privilege from Queen Elizabeth I in 1567. In 1570 he set up a glasshouse in Crutched Friars in London, employing Italian workmen and producing glasses in the Venetian manner. He died in 1572. (See also Verzelini, Giacomo.)

Carriage glass: a footless drinking glass for serving travellers or riders.

Carrickmacross appliqué: similar to but not a real lace as the pattern was cut from cambric, applied to net and given needlepoint fillings (q.v.).

Carrickmacross guipure: similar to Carrickmacross appliqué (q.v.) but with needlepoint brides (q.v.) instead of net.

Carron: the Carron Ironworks, Falkirk, Scotland, opened in 1759 and was responsible for the making of much fireside equipment. Small andirons of early 19th cent. pattern are found with the name of the firm cast on the fronts. Many of these have been re-cast from the original moulds, in the present cent., but it is stated that in these instances the name "Carron" appears at the back of each piece.

Cartel clock: a mural clock, usually of somewhat flamboyant design. More often found in France than in England. English are usually of carved wood, whereas the French are usually of cast brass or bronze and gilt.

Cartonnier: (*Fr.*), a piece of furniture, intended to hold paper made in various forms. Usually it stood at one end of a writing-table and was sometimes surmounted by a clock. Also known as a *serre-papier*.

Cartoon: (1) the full-scale painted design according to which a tapestry is woven. The high-warp weaver works with the cartoon on a wall or an easel behind him. For low-warp tapestry it is cut into sections and placed below the horizontal warp. It is therefore designed left-handed, as it is like a mirror image which will be reproduced in reverse. For this reason a cartoon for low-warp tapestry can always be recognized. The original sketches from which the cartoons are enlarged are known as *Petits Patrons*. (2) full scale sketch for decorations to be painted in fresco (q.v.).

Cartouche: a tablet of oval shape sometimes bearing arms or an ornamental device with scrolled or ornate frame. A decorative motif on furniture, frequently the centre of cabinet pediments, or engraved on silver, etc.

Carver chair: modern term for an American early 17th cent. "Dutch"

type arm chair made of turned posts and spindles. It has three rails and three spindles in the back. Such chairs may be seen in 17th cent. paintings of humble Dutch interiors, though the American example was probably derived from an English model. Usually of ash or maple, with rush seats. Named after John Carver, first governor of the Plymouth colony, who is said to have brought one to America with him in the *Mayflower*. Made until the end of the cent. Many examples survive, the earliest dating perhaps about 1650. (See also Brewster chair.)

Caryatid: strictly a female sculptured figure used as a support in place of a column, but frequently used to describe a figure of either sex employed in this manner as a decorative form. The term derives from the legend of the women of Carya, enslaved and immured for their betrayal of the Greeks to the Persians. (See also Atlanta.)

Cased glass: two or more layers of glass differing in colour; called overlay when design is cut through to body colour; popular Bohemian glass technique.

Cash: generic term for many small Oriental copper coins, particularly Chinese (see Ch'ien).

Casing: involves the preparation in quantity of the boards (q.v.) and covering material (usually cloth) needed for binding a book, to form ready-made cases. These are attached by gluing a strip of mull to the back of the book, gluing the overlaps of the mull to the case and pasting down the endpapers (q.v.).

Caskets: the earliest caskets likely to come the way of the collector are those made in Sicily during the 13th to 14th cent. They are constructed of ivory with brass mounts, and are believed to have been the work of Arabic craftsmen. The Near Eastern element in them can be seen, not in any constructional detail but in the painted ornament with which the finer examples were enriched. This ornament

often introduces Cufic characters or amorphous scrollwork of Saracenic origin. Caskets or small coffers of the 15th cent. are far less rare than the earlier examples; there were two main types, those constructed entirely of iron and those of wood, sometimes covered with leather and always furnished with more or less elaborate bands of iron. Such caskets were made in France, the Low Countries, Germany, and Spain, and it is often difficult to be certain of the country of origin, especially of the earlier types. Subsequently, recognized national types emerge. One French type is entirely of iron with arched lid. The earlier examples have applied Gothic tracery ornamentation, the later ones have a plain surface with either etched or damascened ornament (Fig. B). The Spanish type is of almost rectangular section with only slightly curved walls. It is of wood covered with one or more layers of tinned sheet iron, pierced with reticulated ornament. This type is provided with stout bands and an elaborate lock decorated with Gothic pinnacles.

The most common German type dates from the second half of the 16th cent. and shows no trace of the Gothic ornament which persisted so long into the 16th cent. in the locksmiths' workshops. It is rectangular in plan and is constructed of iron sheet sometimes enriched with mounts of gilt brass. The whole of the exterior surface is etched with floral scrolls or with hunting or allegorical subjects. The lock, which is accommodated on the underside of the lid, is of great elaboration, shooting as many as a dozen bolts. These coffers were made in Nürnberg and Augsburg but are never signed (Fig. C). On the other hand, the miniature caskets of gilt brass, sometimes enriched with silver and even enamel, and engraved instead of etched, are usually known as Michael Mann boxes because so many of them bear the signature of a Nürnberg locksmith of that name (Fig. A).

Fine coffers of English manufacture do not appear before the second half of the 17th cent., when we find the very rare but incomparable works of the Bickfords (e.g. the jewel casket of Queen Mary II in the Victoria and

Albert Museum) and the fairly common but extremely attractive caskets with fall fronts veneered with oyster marquetry and furnished with elaborate gilt brass hingework.

Fig. A

Fig. B

Fig. C

Cassel porcelain: table wares and figures of rather simple character were made at a porcelain factory at Cassel between 1766 and 1788, subsidised by the Landgrave of Hesse-Cassel. Between about 1770 and the close of the factory two marks were in use: an "H.C." in blue or a two-tailed heraldic lion from the arms of Hesse.

Cassone: the cassone, an Italian term for chest, was clearly one of the most popular pieces of furniture in 15th and 16th cent. Italy. It was also the most richly decorated, and, for this reason, perhaps, numerous examples have survived. It was used to hold linen or clothes and might also serve as a seat (with or without the upright back which made it into a cassapanca). Cassoni are frequently referred to as dower chests, and although they were often made to hold the supply of linen which a bride took to her new home, there is no reason to suppose that the majority were intended for this purpose.

The earliest cassoni were probably very unpretentious, but a few of the early 15th cent. examples which have survived are decorated with Gothic curvilinear carving or rough paintings of heraldic achievements. In the Renaissance period, great ingenuity was expended on their design and adornment. Some were decorated with gesso (q.v.) friezes of putti sporting on the front and sides and others were fashioned like antique sarcophagi, but most seem to have been painted on the front (some were also painted inside the lid). Several highly able Florentine 15th cent. painters, like the famous Master of the Jarves cassoni, seem to have specialized almost exclusively in the decoration of furniture of this type: and some more important artists, like Bartolomeo Montagna, occasionally turned their hands to this decorative work. In Florence paintings of battles and the triumphs of Roman generals were in particular demand, elsewhere religious and mythological scenes seem to have enjoyed great popularity but in Venice patterns of ornamental motifs were generally preferred. Intarsia (see Tarsia) views of real or imaginary architecture were also employed. In the 16th cent. the painted cassone seems to have gone out of fashion and most surviving examples from this period are simply carved with abstract decorations. A few later 16th cent. cassoni are adorned with figures at the corners and low reliefs in the same style on the front.

Cast: a piece produced by pouring molten metal or plaster into a previously modelled mould.

Castel Durante maiolica: tin-glazed earthenware made at Castel Durante (now Urbania) in Italy. Much Castel Durante ware of the 16th cent. is decorated with figure subjects from classical mythology in rich, full pigments.

Castellani, Fortunato: a Roman jeweller of the mid-19th cent. who rediscovered the Etruscan secret of applying minute grains of gold to a gold base, producing a granulated ground. With his two sons, he produced in his workshop many fine pseudo-Greek pieces of jewellery.

Castelli maiolica: tin-glazed earthenware made near Teramo in the Abruzzi in the 17th and 18th cent. Castelli wares of late 17th cent. date are often decorated with mythological or historical scenes in a subdued range of colours, dominated by a pale, greyish blue.

Caster: found singly or in a set of three, of silver, also occasionally of brass or pewter, for sugar, pepper, and with unpierced cover for mustard. Late 17th cent. form cylindrical. In the 18th cent. pear-shaped and later of vase form, polygonal or circular in outline. Largely replaced in late 18th cent. by cut glass examples with silver covers (see also Cruets, Dredger, Muffineer).

Cast iron: a form of iron containing a relatively high percentage of carbon (approximately 4 per cent) and characterized by hardness and brittleness. Cast iron cannot be worked in a forge but is shaped by being poured into moulds while in a molten state.

Castleford chess-men: chess-men in vitrified stoneware made here between 1795 and 1821 by David Dunderdale. Opposing colours were at first black basaltes and white stoneware, then coloured slips were used and sets might be in chocolate brown and greyish green, or greyish blue and white. The king and queen represent

George III and Queen Charlotte, both in their state robes and crowned; the pawns are kilted Scots Guards, and the rooks are elephants carrying square castellated towers. Both sides were made from the same moulds. These have been widely copied. (See also Chess-men.)

Castleford pottery: at Whitwood Mere, David Dunderdale, an apprentice of the Leeds Pottery, established a factory c. 1790 for the manufacture of cream-coloured earthenware, Egyptian black and felspathic stoneware. From 1793 until 1820 when it closed down, it traded as David Dunderdale and Co. The most typical products were in unglazed stoneware with relief decorations in panels. Similar wares, with or without panels picked out in blue, were made elsewhere. The marks used were:

DD & Co.   DD & Co.   DD & Co.
CASTLEFORD   CASTLEFORD   CASTLEFORD
POTTERY   DD & CO.   POTTERY

In 1825 the factory was partly reopened by Asquith, Wood & Co. and from that time onwards was continued under various ownerships.

Castle Hedingham: pseudo-medieval and Tudor pottery was made here by Edward Bingham (b. 1829). Sometimes mistaken for authentic, 15th, 16th and 17th cent. wares.

Castwork: decoration or parts of a silver vessel cast in a mould and soldered to the main body. Principally used for handles, feet, spouts and finials. Complete castings occur in candlesticks built up in various sections and in some other pieces.

Cat: a stand used after about 1750 to warm plates in front of the fire; it had three arms and three feet of turned wood (or three legs of cabriole form). The turning was well ringed to provide sockets for plates of various sizes.

Catacomb glasses: fragments of gold-engraved glasses found in the Roman catacombs, being the bottoms of shallow bowls decorated with medallions of engraved gold leaf.

Cathedral binding: a term used to describe book-bindings of the period 1810–40, decorated in gold or blind (q.v.) with Gothic architectural motifs, which often include a rose window.

Cat's eye: a type of chrysoberyl displaying a single broad band of light, known as chatoyancy. Some quartz also has this characteristic.

Caucasian rugs: rugs which come from the Caucasian Mountains between the Caspian and Black Seas. The designs show both Persian and Chinese influence, but retain strong characteristics of their own. The employment of the local highland wool, which is unsurpassed, combined with meticulous and regular weaving, has given these rugs lasting quality, and many examples of merit exist.

Among the earliest specimens are the famous Armenian Dragon rugs, woven in the 16th cent. The main motifs consist of conventional upright dragons, forming panels, flowering trees with birds, and often elephants and camels. A pleasing shade of soft rose relieved by dark blue or black are the predominant colours. The dragon design has influenced many later specimens.

A great similarity of design and the knotting, which is almost exclusively Ghiordes (q.v.), through Caucasia renders identifications of each type difficult, if not impossible. It is mainly on quality that the rugs are classified.

The most prevalent motif is of jewel shapes, both diamond and octagonal in form, with use of latch hook in white or cream. The detail is generally of conventional small flowers.

Caudle-cup: an alternative name for porringer (q.v.), derived from its use for caudle, a spiced gruel, also called posset.

Caughley porcelain: Thomas Turner, previously at Worcester (q.v.) became the proprietor of the Caughley works in 1772. These had been worked as an earthenware factory since 1754. Turner manufactured at Caughley a soapstone porcelain similar to that of Worcester but slightly different in colour and less well potted. In 1799

John Rose of Coalport (q.v.) purchased the factory and used it to produce biscuit porcelain which was glazed and decorated at Coalport. The factory closed in 1814. A number of marks were used, some clearly imitating those of other English and foreign factories. The most notable are the letters "S" or "C" in blue, or the word "Salopian" in upper or lower case letters, impressed. The bulk of the factory's output of useful wares was decorated in blue and white, sometimes by transfer printing, in the Worcester manner. Two patterns which were originated here, the "Willow" and "Broseley Dragon", attained great popularity and are known in numerous variations, produced by later Staffordshire and other earthenware factories. Gilding was combined with blue decoration at the end of the cent. A greyish and bright-purplish blue was used for decoration, lighter and brighter than that of Worcester. Shapes and patterns followed Worcester lines. Ambitious coloured decorations were produced.

Cauldron: (Kettle), one of the oldest of all cooking utensils and recorded from the earliest times. They were first made of sheets of bronze, hammered to shape and riveted together; later they were of cast bronze. From the 16th cent. they were made of cast-iron, and formed an important item of equipment. Small-sized cauldrons were known in some regions as "crocks".

"Cauliflower" ware: green and yellow glazed earthenware made in the form of cauliflowers, pineapples and other vegetables, by Whieldon, Wedgwood and others from 1750 onwards: cauliflowers were also made in porcelain.

Causeuse: (*Fr.*) a large chair or small sofa to accommodate two persons. Roughly corresponds to the small English settee. Sometimes referred to colloquially as a love-seat.

Cavetto frieze: see Concave frieze.

"CD" mark: see Coalport porcelain.

Ceiler: the fabric covering hung over the medieval bed, replaced in the 16th cent. by a wooden tester which formed the four-poster bed roof. (See Tester.)

Celadon wares: Chinese porcelain wares with felspathic glaze of characteristic pale greyish or bluish green tone derived from iron; the name was apparently taken from the character Céladon in Honoré D'Urfé's early 17th cent. pastoral romance *L'Astrée*, and not from *Saladin*, as sometimes supposed. Typical are the early Yüeh ware, and the much-exported Lungchüan celadons of the Sung and Ming dynasties. Ch'ing dynasty celadons generally differ from these in their white porcelain body, even glaze and careful finish. But some Sung wares were skilfully copied, and the bluish and lavender-toned Kuan and Ko glazes, their crackle, and even their dark body, were reproduced. In 18th cent. France the later celadons were sometimes mounted in ormolu.

Celestial globe: a spherical model of the heavens. (See Terrestrial globe.)

Cellaret: the name given, generally after 1750 to a case on legs, or stand for wine bottles. Prior to that date, from the end of the 17th cent., the same kind of case was called a cellar. In the early 18th cent. cellarets, lined with lead and containing compartments for bottles, stood under sidetables. They were still made later in the cent. when sideboards, containing drawers fitted to hold bottles, came into general use. Sheraton (q.v.) classified the cellaret with the wine-cistern (q.v.) and sarcophagus, and distinguished them from the bottle-case, which was for square bottles only.

Cellini, Benvenuto: (1500–71), a Renaissance goldsmith and sculptor whose literary work is a guide to the technical background and social standing of the members of his craft in the 16th cent.

Censer: covered bowl with suspension chains for burning incense in liturgical use. Made of precious or base metal, the latter mostly medieval. The most important English example is the Ramsey Abbey silver censer of the 14th cent.

There are earlier continental examples of bronze from the Meuse valley and of enamelled copper from Limoges.

Cent: copper coin of U.S.A., one hundredth part of a dollar. Various types of which the most famous is the Indian head.

Centre-piece: a silver table centre being a late form of epergne, usually with one wirework or pierced central basket on high foliage or figure stem. Centre-pieces are found after 1800 in a wide range of decorative forms, sometimes with separate plinth or mirror plateau. (See also Epergne.)

Centre seconds clock: a clock or watch in which the seconds hand is placed on the same arbor (q.v.) as the hour and minute hands.

Cf.: calf. Used to describe any smooth-finish leather on a book-binding. (See also Hf. cf.).

Chafing-dish: a general term, now extinct, covering various forms of dishes for hot foods.

Chafing-stand: a similar word for brazier or spirit-lamp stand for supporting a chafing-dish.

Chaine de forçat: (*Fr.*), a heavy gold chain, securing perhaps a monocle or a watch, worn by men of fashion over black velvet waistcoats in the earlier part of the 19th cent.

Chain mail: see Mail.

Chaise d'or: large gold coins issued in France in the 14th cent. with type of king enthroned.

Chaise longue: (*Fr.*), an elongated seat intended for rest.

Chalice: cup-shaped vessel used to contain wine in the celebration of the Mass. In England this term should be confined to Communion vessels made before the Reformation and the extension of the cup to the laity in the Church of England. In the 17th cent. the form was revived for a short period and never discontinued in Ireland. The essential form is that of a shallow hemispherical or conical bowl on high knopped stem and circular or polygonal foot (see Communion cup and Paten).

Chalk engraving: an etching technique used for making fascimiles of chalk drawings.

Chamber candlestick: also known as flat candlestick. Usually circular, flat base. Early examples have cast pear-shaped handles, later of scroll or ring form. Extinguishers fit in slots on sockets or handles. Late examples often with snuffers carried in opening in stem. Found from late 17th cent. onwards in silver or brass.

Chamberlain, Robert: in 1783 Robert Chamberlain, a painter at the Worcester porcelain factory, severed his connection and opened a factory of his own in Worcester in rivalry to the old company. It was at first a decorating business, but porcelain of a dense, hard kind was made from 1792, and later in a much improved paste. Robert Chamberlain had for partners his son Humphrey Chamberlain and Richard Nash. In 1840 Chamberlain's factory and the old company were amalgamated. In 1850 W. H. Kerr joined the firm which traded as Kerr & Binns in 1852. In 1862 the firm became the Royal Worcester Porcelain Co. Marks: Various marks were used,

H. Chamberlain
& Sons
Worcester
(incised)

Chamberlains
Wars No 276

Chamberlain
Worcester.

Chamberlains
Worcester
403

Chamberlains

CHAMBERLAINS

HChamberlain & Sons Worcester

Chamberlain's
Regent China
Worcester
& 155
New Bond Street,
London
Printed in red

Elaborately painted wares in a naturalistic style with lavish gilding and striking ground colours. Japans were popular.

Chamber of tapestries: refers to a set of tapestries intended to cover the walls of a living-room. The expression is often met with in medieval and later inventories.

Chambers, Sir William: (1726–96), architect to George III. He visited China in his youth and published in 1757 *Designs for Chinese Buildings, Furniture, Dresses, etc.*

Chamfer: a bevelled edge, or edge which has been smoothed off or cut away from the square.

Champion, Richard: (1743–91), porcelain manufacturer, Bristol; joined forces with Cookworthy (q.v.), c. 1770 and received from him a licence to manufacture under his hard-paste patent when he retired in 1772. In 1774 Cookworthy assigned his patent rights to Champion for a consideration and in 1775 Champion petitioned Parliament for an extension of the patent rights for a further 14 years. In this he was successful (in spite of the opposition of Josiah Wedgwood) but the business crippled him financially. By 1778 Champion's Bristol manu-

factory was in financial difficulties. In 1781 Champion sold the patent for the manufacture of hard-paste porcelain to a company in North Staffordshire (which became known as New Hall) and moved to the Potteries to supervise its manufacture.

Champlevé enamel: see Enamel.

Chandelier: the word was used sometimes in the sense of candelabra or "table-chandelier". One of the first noted uses of it in the modern sense, to describe a centrally placed light-fitting with arms, was in 1725. In that year an inventory of the contents of Canons, near Edgware, Middlesex, listed "four glass chanderleres". The word did not come into general use for some time, and the article was referred to variously for the next twenty-five years as a branch (q.v.), a lustre (q.v.) or as a chandelier. A number of brass chandeliers have survived and a very few examples in silver. From the early 18th cent. glass chandeliers began to appear and grew in popularity with the introduction of cut glass.

Chanfron: the plate defence for a horse's head, introduced early in the 14th cent. and remaining in use until well into the 17th.

Chantilly lace: pillow lace, silk with *fond chant* (q.v.) ground and some use of *fond clair* (q.v.). (See Blonde lace.)

Chantilly porcelain: a porcelain factory was founded at Chantilly in France about 1725, as a result of the financial support and interest of the Prince de Condé, an enthusiastic collector of Arita porcelain (q.v.). The factory was closed in 1800. Soft-paste porcelain was made, and until about 1751 tin oxide was used in the glaze, which rendered it smooth and opaque, as against the usual transparent porcelain glaze. Much early Chantilly is decorated in the Kakiemon style (q.v.) and subsequently first Meissen and then Sèvres (qq.v.) were freely copied. Decoration consisting of small blue flowers, known as the "Chantilly sprig", was popular and much copied in England. The mark used was a hunting horn in red or blue.

Chapbooks: small pamphlets of popular, sensational, juvenile, moral or educational character, originally distributed by chapmen or hawkers, not by booksellers. Not in current use since about 1830, except as a conscious archaism.

Chapter ring: the applied circle, found in earlier clocks, upon which are engraved the hour numerals. Derives its name from the fact that hours are struck on a bell. Originally a clock served to rouse the sexton, who then struck the hour of the chapter, or religious office, on a bell.

Charger: a large circular dish primarily designed for display. Silver examples are usually enriched by finely engraved or embossed armorials.

Chasing: (1) the *cire-perdue* (q.v.) process of casting metal leaves roughness and poor finish as well as often resulting in the loss of detail. It is therefore necessary to work over the rough-cast with steel chisels and gravers. The absence of such evidence of individual treatment of bronzes, for example, may be taken at best as a sign of a poor workshop production, at worst as a sign of modern aftercasting. (2) the term chasing is also used to describe the relief decoration on silver, raised by the surface hammering of the metal. (See also Flat chasing.)

Châtelaine: a clasp or brooch, usually of silver, from which various small objects are suspended by means of a chain. Fastened at the waist, the châtelaine was originally worn by the mistress of the house, and keys, seals, watches, nutmeg-graters, quizzing-glasses and countless other articles are to be found attached to the ends of their chains. In the late 18th cent. Wedgwood (q.v.) jasper cameos were mounted as ornaments to châtelaines.

Chaton: the central ornament of a ring.

Chatoyancy: a characteristic of chrysoberyl and of some quartz, in which a band of light appears in the stone.

Checkers: see Draughts.

Cheese-scoop: introduced in late 18th cent. for serving cheese. Consists of a short, curved blade with silver shaft and ivory or wood handle. Later examples have silver handles conforming to table service patterns.

Cheese warmers: shallow, rectangular trays with rounded corners and projecting handles of turned wood. From second quarter of 18th cent. Attractively simple, but rare.

Chef-d'oeuvre: (*Fr.*), masterpiece.

Chelsea porcelain: the Chelsea Works was probably founded about 1745 or shortly before. Until 1750 it is believed that Charles Gouyn, silversmith, was proprietor and chief manager of the factory. The name of Nicholas Sprimont first appears in connection with Chelsea in 1749 when he managed the factory for Sir Edward Fawkener, and on his death in 1758 became its owner. The factory changed hands in 1769, and again in 1770 when it was bought by William Duesbury and John Heath of Derby. From this time until its closure in 1784 its products followed Derby rather than established Chelsea styles, and so this is known as the Chelsea-Derby period. In 1784 the Chelsea workshops and ovens were demolished and many moulds destroyed. Some were removed to Derby. Marks:

Chelsea 1745 Incised	Incised 1745–49
In applied relief 1750–53	In under- glaze blue 1749
1755 1765	1755 1760

1760   1760   1760   1765

Four clearly defined periods of Chelsea manufacture are recognised: Triangle 1745-49; Raised Anchor 1750-53; Red Anchor 1753-58; and Gold Anchor 1758-70. The earliest Chelsea group bears the mark of an incised triangle.

Work of the "raised" (i.e. embossed) and "red anchor" periods enjoys the highest esteem, in spite of its imperfections. This was made from a very fine soft paste which had the characteristic of forming transparent glass spots or "moons" under firing. These can be seen when the ware is held up to the light. It was eliminated in the gold anchor period (and in occasional perfect red anchor pieces), but the ware also lost its celebrated creamy texture.

During Fawkener's ownership (c. 1749-58), Meissen (q.v.) styles were most often copied, though the colouring and quality of the china give the ware an original beauty. Colour washes were employed to give simple effects in keeping with paste and form. Gilding was little used.

When Sprimont became owner, several changes occurred. Sprimont's is the gold anchor period, the red anchor being rarely used. Bone ash was introduced into the paste; Sèvres became the dominant influence; decoration became richer employing elaborate floral backgrounds; heavy gilding was used. Some fine ground colours were introduced, "mazarine" (an uneven dark blue) and claret, as well as more flamboyant modelling. The resulting quality, though notable, was perhaps inferior to "red anchor" Chelsea.

Under Duesbury the Chelsea and Derby styles gradually blended, the vigour of Chelsea being lost under Derby influence. It becomes difficult to distinguish between wares made at the two factories.

A considerable number of interesting miniature pieces, scent-bottles, flowers, seals, snuff-boxes, known as Chelsea Toys, have survived.

Subjects:

Triangle Period: Silver shapes predominate, with applied ornament, fluting and raised foliage and floral sprays. Painted subjects included Japanese patterns derived from Meissen examples. The apparently haphazard application of tiny flower sprigs or insects concealed imperfections of paste or glaze.

Not many Triangle figures are known. A notable class of uncoloured figures takes its name from the well-known "Girl in a Swing" and is attributed on evidence of paste and style to the earliest Chelsea period.

Raised Anchor Period: Oriental influence via Meissen is strong in this phase of Chelsea. Decorations were applied with regard to the beauty of the paste and glaze. Figures in this period are very uncommon; outstanding are Italian Comedy figures and the tender earthenware-derived "Nurse"; portrait busts, and models of birds.

Red Anchor Period: The finest of the Chelsea porcelains. Meissen, Chinese, and Japanese influences are strong. A version of botanical flowers, some adapted from Philip Miller's *Figures of Plants*, was an outstanding decoration. Fantastic animal and vegetable shapes were used for tureens and dishes, and gaily coloured. Crimson monochrome landscapes and Aesop's Fables again appear. Other subjects of this mature Chelsea phase are naked children at play, birds, moulded scroll borders, Watteau subjects, and bouquets of flowers.

Splendid figures were made, some derived from Meissen.

Gold Anchor Period: Meissen influences yield to Sèvres, and the vigorous playfulness of the earlier phases gives way to a new elegance and sophistication. New colours were adopted including a rich sonorous blue. Elaborate gilding became fashionable, subjects for decoration included groups after Teniers, exotic or naturalistic birds, chinoiseries, flowers and fruits.

Figures with elaborate and fulsome bocages are typical, usually with rococo scroll bases.

Chemise: a prolongation of the covering material at the foot of a bookbinding. Existing examples (in leather and velvet) date from the 15th or early 16th cent. Some pre-Reformation prayer-books were bound in a chemise gathered into a knop or button which could be attached to the owner's girdle. Small folding almanacks were also similarly attached with a cord.

Chenets: (*Fr.*), see Andirons.

Ch'êng Hua period: (1465–87),the rarest Chinese porcelains of this classic reign employ coloured enamels over sparing underglaze blue outlines ("*tou ts'ai*" enamels); and this style was much imitated from the 17th cent. The blue-and-white "palace bowls" were more slightly potted and decorated than previously. The reign-mark is much used on later wares.

Chequer ornament: an inlaid pattern of small squares in light and dark woods, resembling a chess board, used as a decorative border on 16th and 17th cent. furniture.

Chess-boards: at first chess-boards were oblong with ninety-six squares in a single colour, as against the later square board with sixty-four squares in alternating colours. The ninety-six-square chess-board, twelve squares by eight squares, brought into use pieces now unknown to the chess-player – camels, horses and elephants. Caxton in his *Game and Playe of Chesse* noted that the square chess-board was designed "after ye forme of ye citie of Babylon". The squares might be marked on leather, heavy textile, wood or tables of baked clay.

Fashionable chess-boards in England alternated ivory and ebony, or a natural ivory with stained ivory, and each square might be engraved with a pictorial scene. Others were of coloured hardwoods: mother-of-pearl was also used, white nacre alternating with green or other dark-hued shell. For everyday use a wooden board was preferred. This might be inlaid with woods of contrasting colour or a solid board might have the alternate squares coloured with red lead or stained or burned to a dark hue.

After the restoration of the monarchy in 1660 fine chess-boards, exquisitely enriched with parquetry work in exotic woods and ivory, were made. The design might consist of two shallow box-like sections hinged together to contain playing chess-men. The squares were veneered with burr or oyster walnut alternating with holly, lignum vitae or other distinctive wood. Boards set with coloured leathers were also used.

Makers of chess-boards might also turn wooden sets of chess-men: records show that the trade was well-established in Tunbridge Wells by the late 17th cent. Georgian chess-board makers might advertise themselves as turners in ivory, joiners and turners in wood, but more frequently as makers of Tunbridge ware – not to be confused with 19th-cent. wood mosaic work. (See also Chess-men.)

Chess-men: in the Middle Ages the game of chess was considered a noble accomplishment to be played with costly chessmen of ivory, enriched with gold and jewels. By the 15th cent. it had become generally popular. Chess-men for general use were then usually of wood, shaped on a lathe, one side in a natural colour and the other stained or painted, usually red. Cabinet chess-men were highly prized and might be of finely carved ivory enriched with gold and enclosed in an ivory chest. Although ivory, ebony and wooden chess-men have always been preferred, there was a vogue in the 17th cent. for sets cast in metal. These might be in bronze or brass, one side enriched with bright colours and gilding, in burnished pewter or in lead. Records of such sets are frequent, particularly with one side in bronze, the other in pewter. Other contrasting materials include light and dark amber, pink and white alabaster, Scottish pebble and agate, Derbyshire spars and marbles, horn and ivory, the latter being a favourite combination with Stuart chess-players. Silver chess-men were made throughout the 18th cent., while in 1783 Wedgwood (q.v.) commissioned John Flaxman (q.v.) to design a set to be made in blue and white jasper. Porcelain sets had been made even earlier and the Rockingham (q.v.) factory copied a set made at Meissen in the 18th cent. (See also Chess-boards.)

Chesterfield stoneware: brown stonewares characterised by relief decorations of hunting scenes or drinking bouts: J. Aiken (*A Description of the Country round Manchester*, 1795) noted the existence of three potworks making coarse earthenware in Chesterfield in 1795. In 1848 there were several potteries, chiefly for coarse brown and yellow stoneware.

Chestnut servers: these urn-shaped containers might be oval or round, their bodies raised from copper in two halves and vertically joined. From about 1800 to 1820 they were spun from Britannia metal (q.v.), from about 1820 they were spun from a special copper alloy. The vessel was supported on a spreading foot, round or square, and a short, slender stem. It usually had lion mask and ring handles of cast lead gilded and with a domed cover surmounted by a gilt acorn or other simple finial.

Chestnut servers were handed with coffee and contained Spanish chestnuts, boiled and then roasted. They were served hot, and were lifted from the server with a fork; their husks were removed at table and they were eaten with salt.

Chest-on-chest: see Tallboy.

Cheval-glass: a larger type of toilet mirror in a frame with four legs; also

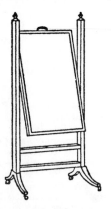

known as a horse dressing-glass; dating from the end of the 18th cent. The rectangular mirror either pivoted on

screws set in the uprights or moved up and down by means of a weight within the frame ("the same as a sash-window" – Sheraton). Turned uprights and stretchers were often found on these pieces about 1800.

Cheveret: see Secretaire bookcase.

Chevron: a zig-zag pattern formed by inlay or a moulding, of architectural derivation, but also used as a decoration on furniture.

Chia Ching period: (1522–66), Ming reign noted for painted blue-and-white porcelain of rich violet tone, and the development of brilliantly coloured enamel painting, chiefly in red, green, yellow and turquoise. Coloured glazes, too, were used, sometimes in combination (e.g. yellow and green), covering incised designs "on the biscuit". Heavily-potted blue-and-white jars and dishes were much exported to the Near East. The reign-mark was used in K'ang Hsi times.

Chia Ch'ing period: (1796–1820), in this period the later Ch'ien Lung (q.v.) porcelain continued to be made, but with poorer glaze and less lively drawing in enamelled wares. Iron-red enamelling was popular, and heavily-potted wares with thick blue or celadon-green glazes may be mentioned.

Chiaroscuro: a term used in painting to describe the arrangement of light and shade in a picture.

Chichi rugs: Caucasian rugs bearing small jewel-like designs in the centre panel.

Chicken skin: fashionable 18th cent. fan mounts were made of fine vellum known to fan makers as chicken skin. Actually it was prepared from the skins of newly born lambs so as to be exceptionally thin and supple. No grain is visible unless held to the light when a slightly mottled appearance may be detected.

Ch'ien: Chinese round copper coin, first introduced in 12th cent. B.C. Earlier type up to 6th cent. B.C. has round hole in centre and characters indicating weight and source. Later types up to 19th cent. have square centre hole. Still later, characters indicating value were added.

Ch'ien Lung porcelain: (1736–95), in the Chinese porcelain made during this period the antiquarian tastes of the Emperor were reflected in continued borrowings from the classical styles and from foreign techniques. The *famille rose* style (q.v.) went on, but often with crowded effects of design and less harmonious combinations of colour. Strong yellow or pink grounds (q.v.) or a celadon ground may surround panels of delicate painting; and the rich effects of *cloisonné* enamel (see Enamel) were sometimes sought. Some of the monochrome wares continue very fine in colour, notably the flambé copper-reds, and the soft, low-temperature enamels were much used as glazes. Shapes such as those in Figs. A and B are certainly not lacking in decided character. But the later wares of the reign undoubtedly show a marked decline in taste, inclining to fussiness and prettiness; and former standards were not to be recovered. Poorer quality materials, slack shapes, uninspired drawing and insipid colour are faults present to a greater or lesser degree in the wares of Ch'ien Lung's successors.

Fig. A   Fig. B

Chien ware: made in Fukien Province, China during the Sung dynasty consisting principally of small conical tea-bowls. A very granular grey-black stoneware, with thick treacly-brown or black glaze, often streaked with fine golden lines ("hare's fur"), or spotted and dappled, and arrested above the foot. These effects result from the varied response of iron to kiln conditions. Known to the Japanese as *"temmoku"* ware. Other brown and black wares from Kiangsi, Honan, or Tz'ŭ Chou, have a lighter body.

Chiffonier: a piece of furniture which has given rise to a certain amount of confusion. The French chiffonier was a tall chest of drawers, but the *chiffonière*, a quite different piece, was a small set of drawers on legs. It was the latter which seems to have been copied in England in the later 18th cent.

Another form of chiffonier was popular in the Regency period – a low cupboard with shelves for books. As this was similar to contemporary commodes, it can be taken that the English version of the *chiffonière* was the only true small piece of furniture.

Chill: earthenware oil lamp shaped like a large candlestick with a lipped cup large enough to hold two cups of "train" (pilchard oil), used in Cornwall before candles. Sometimes known as stonen chill.

Chiming clock: a clock which sounds at the quarters a chime on four or more bells in addition to striking the hour.

Chimney-crane: known in Scotland as a "Swey", this was a bracket of wrought-iron from which a cauldron or tea-kettle was suspended. Cranes were of many types; large and small, simple and complicated. In the case of the latter the pot could be raised or lowered and swung to any position over the fire.

Chimney-glass: a wide mirror above the chimney-piece, usually consisting of three plates, two smaller ones flanking a larger one, introduced in the early 18th cent.

China-clay: a white burning refractory clay produced by the decomposition of felspathic rock, called by the Chinese *kaolin*, and quarried in Cornwall. It is an essential ingredient of hard-paste porcelain, and English bone china. The *unaker* specified in the patent of Heylin and Frye (see under Bow porcelain) in 1744, was American china clay.

Chinaman: an importer of oriental porcelain; a pottery dealer; ("went to see a garden belonging to one Mr Bauldy, a china-man" – *Diary of Sylas Neville*, 20 September 1771.)

China-stand: an ornamental stand for displaying china or flowers, introduced at the end of the 17th cent. and at first taking the form of a low pedestal on carved and scrolled feet, or of a vase on a plinth. In the early 18th cent. the form was sometimes that of a stool with cabriole legs, in mahogany. More fanciful designs, in the rococo taste, were evident after 1750, as in the "Stonds for China Jarrs" presented in Chippendale's *Director*. In the Adam (q.v.) period some attractive stands for flower-bowls resembled the contemporary candle-stands with three uprights. Little four-legged stands with shelves were also made at this time for flower-pots. (See Candle-stand.)

China-stone: a fusible felspathic rock, known to the Chinese as *petuntse*, used in the manufacture of porcelain, and generally known in England as china-stone, or, because quarried in Cornwall, Cornish stone.

Chinese export porcelain: porcelain made in China specially for export to Europe. Although Chinese porcelain had always been eagerly sought after in foreign countries, it was not until the latter part of the 17th cent. that wares were made specifically for exportation. By the 18th cent., trade with the East was flourishing and among the particular types of porcelain made for this trade are plates with wide flat rims, teacups with saucers and sets of vases for the mantelpiece, known as "garniture de cheminée". Sometimes these export pieces bear decorations derived from European sources, such as representations of contemporary European figures in landscapes or scenes from classical mythology. Sometimes dinner services, bearing the coat-of-arms of the European purchaser, were made specially to order, while others bear *famille rose* (q.v.) decoration. The so-called Jesuit porcelain also belongs to the export class. (See also "Jesuit" china and Armorial china.)

Chinese "Imari": imitations of the Japanese export porcelain, with strong decoration in greyish underglaze blue and enamel colours, especially iron-red, and prominent gilding; made in the first half of the 18th cent.

Chinese Lowestoft: an incorrect name sometimes given to Chinese export porcelain (q.v.). (See also Lowestoft porcelain.)

Chinese Turkestan rugs: in these rugs the influence of Chinese art is clearly defined in the use of such motifs as the plate medallion, cloud-bands and lotus, pomegranate and peony, but in subtle manner the rugs show Persian influence.

The stitching generally is not fine and the pile is short. The merit of these rugs is in the extremely varied and unusual colouring, yellows, lacquer red, blues appearing in infinite variety.

The main types are from Khotan and Lashgar, and are often called Samarkand.

Ch'ing dynasty: dynasty of the Chinese Ch'ing Emperors covering the period 1644 to 1912.

Ching-tê-chên: great centre of the porcelain industry, in Kiangsi Province, China. Wares of all kinds have been made here in quantity since the 14th cent.

Chinkinbori: (*Japanese* = sunk gold engraving), a Japanese laquer-work technique in which an incised design is made in the surface of the laquer and gold is rubbed in.

Chinoiserie: a free rendering in western terms of what was thought to represent the Chinese style. Throughout the 17th cent., Chinese lacquered screens and furniture, as well as textiles and porcelain had excited European admiration. Towards the middle of the 18th cent. fashionable taste so concentrated on the Far East that a contemporary comment stated "according to the present prevailing whim everything is Chinese or in the Chinese taste... chairs, tables, chimney-pieces, frames for looking-glasses, and even our most vulgar utensils are all reduced to this new-fangled standard." This vogue resulted in such Chinese motifs as pagodas, latticework and frets and figures of Chinamen appearing as decorative forms on furniture, overmantels and plasterwork, while textiles, porcelain, silver, etc. all bore witness to the enthusiasm. Based largely on romantic fancies, the style was an aspect of Rococo (q.v.) taste and had declined in general favour by 1765.

Chinoiserie wallpapers: known in the 18th cent. as "Mock India", these papers were imitations and variants of the beautiful painted Chinese wallpapers so popular during the 18th cent. A notable English example from Wotton-under-Edge (c. 1740) is to be seen in the Victoria & Albert Museum. France and other European countries also made chinoiserie papers.

Chip-carving: lightly cut ("chipped") surface ornament, mostly of formal character and including whorls, roundels (q.v.), chip-carving appears on woodwork of the Middle Ages. It was done with the aid of a set-square and compass by joiners (q.v.), and did not require great skill. With other forms of carving, it continued as a decoration on oak furniture until a much later date.

Chippendale, Thomas: (1718–79), cabinet-maker and designer. Born at Otley, Yorkshire, it is known that he was in London by 1748, and shortly afterwards was established in St Martin's Lane where, at the sign of "The Chair", he remained until his death. Twice he worked with partners, firstly with James Rannie and later with Thomas Haig. He has attained a world-wide fame from his volume of

designs, *The Gentleman and Cabinet Maker's Director*, which was first issued in 1754. The book was reprinted in 1755, and an enlarged edition appeared in parts between 1759 and 1762. (See Matthias Lock.)

Some of the furniture from Chippendale's workshop has been identified from bills that have been preserved. Two large mirrors at Ken Wood were supplied by Thomas Chippendale in 1769, and were to the design of Robert Adam.

The business in St Martin's Lane was continued on the death of Thomas Chippendale by his eldest son (also named Thomas) in partnership with Haig.

Chippendale, Thomas the Younger: (1749–1822), son of Thomas Chippendale (q.v.). He continued his father's business as a cabinet-maker in St Martin's Lane from 1779 until 1796, during which time he was in partnership with Thomas Haig.

Chiselled and cut steel: the art of steel chiselling is a by-product of the locksmith's and gunsmith's trade. Small articles have been chiselled from iron or steel since the Middle Ages, but from the collector's point of view, four main groups can be recognized. Firstly, the articles made in the northern Italian city of Brescia in the 17th and 18th cent. These include snuff-boxes, scissors, tweezers and thimbles, usually chiselled and pierced with floral scrollwork interspersed with monsters, similar in design to the ornament familiar on Brescian-made firearms (Fig. A). The most distinguished Brescian artist, who usually signed his works, was Matteo Acqua Fresca (Fig. B). The second group was produced in Paris by the same chisellers who decorated sword and gun furniture of the period of Louis XIV and Louis XV. Characteristic of their work are the châtelaines, étuis, shuttles and, more rarely, snuff-boxes, usually chiselled with classical figure subjects against a gilt stippled ground. Similar but somewhat coarser work was also produced in Germany. The third group was produced by the artists of the Imperial Russian small arms factory at Tula. The factory was founded by Peter the Great, and their work dates from the 18th cent. The artisans mastered not only the art of chiselling iron but also of encrusting it with various softer metals and of faceting it (cut-steel). Besides smaller objects, such as candlesticks and caskets, the Tula factory also turned out large pieces of furniture and even mantelpieces entirely constructed of cut and faceted steel. The last group is English and flourished at first about the middle of the 18th cent. in Woodstock in Oxfordshire and subsequently at Birmingham in the Soho works set up by Matthew Boulton. The Woodstock cottage industry produced both chiselled and faceted steel but the Birmingham factory, which eventually put Woodstock out of business, concentrated on cut steel. They made sword hilts, buttons, châtelaines, buckles and cheap jewellery. Cut steel was used as a more durable alternative to marcasite in the late 18th and early 19th cent.

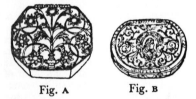

Fig. A　　　　Fig. B

Chocolate-pot: the silver chocolate-pot is of the same basic form as the coffee-pot, from which it can be distinguished by the detachable or sliding cover finial concealing the hole for insertion of the swizzle-stick for stirring the chocolate. Many pieces must have been used indiscriminately for both liquids.

Chop dish: small, flat, two-handled, oblong silver or plate dish made from about 1750 to 1800.

Chopin: a Scottish wine measure (q.v.) containing one and a half Imperial pints. .

Christening goblet: footed four-handled loving cup with whistle attached for calling for replenishment; used for christenings, harvest-homes and other convivial occasions, and specially associated with Wiltshire.

Chromolithograph: lithograph (q.v.) printed in more than two colours.

Chūban: a vertical Japanese print about 11 × 8 inches; medium-sized.

Chün ware: Sung (q.v.) stoneware, more or less porcellanous, usually burnt buff at the foot, with thick, opalescent glaze ranging from pale lavender to deep blue, sometimes with crimson splashes; from Chün Chou (Honan Province). Frequent shapes are spreading bowls, two-handled jars, and flat dishes. There is also a green variety. Large flower-pots and bulb-bowls often have streaked "flambé" glazes. "Soft Chün" wares (Ma Chün) have a sandy buff body and soft crackled glaze. The similar stonewares of Canton and Yi-hsing are seldom earlier than the 17th cent.

Church fans: issued with the sanction of the Bishop of London from about 1730. They were decorated with Biblical subjects pointing a moral rather than illustrating a story. The soft colours of the painted mount were repeated on guards and blades (q.v.). Similar fans for chapel goers date from 1796.

Ciborium: standing bowl and cover used to contain the Host, or in the Protestant church, for Communion bread. Some of the most important examples of Medieval goldsmiths' work take this form (e.g. the ciborium at Kloster Neuburg in Austria). A few silver examples made for the Protestant church in England date from the 17th cent.

Cinq trous: (Fr.), term used to describe the ground found in some Flemish lace in which the threads crossing to form the mesh left five small holes.

Cinquedea: a short sword, or large dagger, with a flat triangular blade some five fingers in width near the hilt (hence the name from the Italian *cinque dei*), and often elaborately etched and gilded. It was essentially a civilian weapon, and was used chiefly in Italy in the late 15th and early 16th cent.

Cire-perdue: the "lost-wax" method of casting, used for all bronze casting of any complication from ancient to modern times. Its processes are, briefly, this: the work is modelled on a clay core in wax of a thickness intended in the final bronze product. The finished wax model, to which vents and pouring channels are added, is then surrounded by an envelope of finely-ground clay mixed with sawdust, chopped straw or some such inflammable material, which will burn out when the mould is fired, giving the envelope the necessary porosity. In the firing process the wax melts and leaves the mould through the vents and pouring channels – and the metal may be poured in to take the place of the wax. The mould is then broken off the bronze and the core removed by breaking it up. It is, of course, obvious that only one bronze can be cast from each wax model by this method. For each of the workshop productions of the Renaissance there must therefore have been a wax model first, and this explains the infinite slight variations in each example made after the master model produced by the head of the workshop. Moulds which may be taken apart in small sections are called piece-moulds, and have perhaps been known since the 16th cent. They were probably never used for bronze sculpture until the 19th cent., and the presence of small ridges, that are the result of the tiny gaps between each section of the mould, may be taken as the surest evidence of modern manufacture.

Ciselé: (*Fr.*), chiselled.

Cistern barometer: a barometer in which the lower open end of the vertical tube is placed below the level of the mercury in open reservoir. The earliest type.

Cistophoros: large silver Greek coin, issued from c. 200 B.C. under the kings of Pergamum and in other cities of western Asia Minor and continuing under Roman proconsuls and emperors. Types, mystic Bacchic *cista* and entwined snakes.

Cittern: see under Mandoline.

Cl.: cloth. Refers to the cloth covering the binder's boards on books.

Claire-de-lune glazes: porcelain glazes of shades of lavender blue obtained by adding small quantities of cobalt to clear glazes. Used on Chinese porcelain and with particular success under Yung Chêng and Ch'ien Lung (qq.v.). At this period also lavender-blue glazes were used in conjunction with crackling in imitation of Sung Kuan and Ko wares (qq.v.).

Claret ground: a ground colour used in porcelain decoration, introduced in England by Sprimont at the Chelsea porcelain factory in 1760; a fine crimson. It was imitated at Derby and Worcester, although the claret ground of Derby tended to a brownish hue and was less attractive in appearance. The fine claret colour of Worcester, was produced, perhaps as suggested by W. B. Honey, with the help of migrant Chelsea craftsmen. Plymouth produced an unsuccessful claret-crimson.

Most of the 19th cent. Staffordshire bone china houses of repute produced a more-or-less successful crimson ground colour, notably Copelands, and Minton's.

Classical style: a style in art based upon the principles of proportion and order practised in ancient Greece and Rome. In England, the influence of the architect Robert Adam in the second half of the 18th cent. did much to encourage a revival of interest in the Classical style. As a result, both in art and architecture, harmony and clarity were sought, while decorative motifs adopted from Classical architecture were employed with unfailing enthusiasm.

Clavichords, pianofortes: the small rectangular instrument called the clavichord, in which the strings are set vibrating by small blades fixed directly into the ends of the keys, survives in England in only a handful of known examples. From the collector's point of view the clavichord is practically non-existent. But while clavichords and, to a lesser degree, the plucked instruments are rare, it is still possible to obtain early pianos. They have in the past been unjustly neglected, but are gradually becoming recognized as instruments in their own right, which in their time have left their mark on the development of keyboard music. Unlike the plucked instruments, whose mechanism has remained unchanged for many centuries, the hammer action has had to be evolved and modified, and the problems were not solved easily or immediately by makers.

The history of the instrument in England commenced about 1760, when pianos first began to be made there, not in the usual "grand" form of the harpsichord but of the small rectangular type known always as the "square" piano. These are the instruments which were erroneously called spinets until a comparatively short while ago. Even now they are often described as "harpsichords". The popularity of the square was at its greatest about 1780–1800 as the ideal domestic keyboard instrument. After that it gradually declined in favour of the "upright" piano, until by 1850 hardly any were being made. Instruments before about 1810 are usually dated on the name-board above the keys. The earliest specimens have a compass of five octaves or less, bicord – that is, two strings per note – throughout the compass. Pre-1780 instruments are rare, but between then and the end of the cent. many were made. They are usually about five feet long by twenty inches wide, with a depth of less than six inches to the bottom board, later increased to over seven inches in instruments with more elaborate actions. The plainest cases are solid mahogany with inlaid stringing, associated with a short trestle stand of mahogany quartering. The better-class instruments show the same fine casework as the contemporary harpsichord, with satinwood bandings, marquetry name-boards, and full-length stands on square taper legs.

Such stands were known as "French stands". The early square had no pedals, but was usually fitted with from one to four hand-stops, housed in the left-hand front corner of the case beside the keyboard. These lifted the dampers (as in the modern "loud pedal") and applied a mute to the strings for soft effects.

Claw and ball foot: see Ball and claw foot.

Claw setting: a means of setting a precious stone whereby the stone is secured by claws. Claw settings are either round or square, whereas coronet settings, in which the stone is similarly held in position, are round in form.

Claymore: from the Gaelic *claidheammor* (great sword). The Scottish two-hand sword introduced in the 16th cent. Of very large proportions, it usually had straight quillons inclining at a sharp angle towards the broad, straight blade. In the 17th cent. the quillons became curved and were supplemented by two (sometimes only one) large solid shells bent towards the hilt. Since the 19th cent. the term has been applied erroneously to the basket-hilted Scottish broadsword.

Clepsydra: a timekeeper motivated by water running either into or out from it. Water clocks are among the earliest forms known; before the discovery of the verge escapement and the weight as a motive power.

Clichy paperweights: Clichy, a suburb of Paris, was the home of a factory that made glass paperweights of most types. They were not dated but are found signed with an initial "C". The presence of a rose in the pattern is an indication that a paper-weight was made there, and the colours are often noticeably vivid.

Clobbering: badly applied fake over-glaze enamel colours on porcelain, only partly obliterating the original underglaze printing or painting.

Clock frets: pierced metallic deco-rative pieces, originally used to hide the balance in lantern clocks. Later, either in wood or metal, inserted into clock cases to facilitate the elimination of sound.

Clock plates, back, front, top and bottom: plates between which are pivoted the trains of a clock or watch. Early back plates in clocks were quite plain, except for the signature; later they began to be decorated, and the decoration became more and more ornate, reaching a peak in the first quarter of the 18th cent. From this point it declined until the last decade of this cent. saw the return of the plain back plate. These back plates are a useful guide to the date of a clock.

Cloisonné enamel: see Enamel.

Close-chairs and **Close-** or **Night-stools:** sometimes chair-shaped, some-times rectangular or drum-shaped boxes (possibly covered and padded), and sometimes rectangular boxes on legs. A type of joined stool with a box-top was so usable, though it does not follow that all stools with this feature were for sanitary use.

Close-helmet: a close-fitting, visored helmet completely enclosing the head.

The term is now usually confined to the type of headpiece introduced early in the 16th cent. with the visor and chin-piece pivoting at the sides, as opposed to the armet (q.v.), which has hinged cheek-pieces fastening at the chin.

Close nailing: brass convex-headed nails of a darkish tint of brass ham-mered with great exactitude by the cofferer, head beside head, were used all around the edges of the leather-covered chest and in sufficient num-bers over the body of the piece to avoid any loose flapping of the in-elastic cover. Similar treatment was given to hair cloth. Brass nails, arranged in one or more lines, or to form a pattern, were used to secure the upholstery on chair seats and backs from a very early date.

Clothwork: see Toilé.

Clous d'or: see Piqué.

Clover-leaf mark: see under Lim-bach porcelain.

Club: see under Pole-arms.

Club foot: the sim-plest terminal to a cabriole leg (q.v.) used on chairs, settees and tables from about 1705 to the late 18th cent., resembling in shape the pad of an animal's foot.

Cluster column leg: a chair leg in the form of pillars clustered together. In the mid-18th cent., a revival of the Gothic taste led to the use among furniture makers of medieval forms such as tracery, clustered columns etc.

"C" mark: see Caughley and Franken-thal porcelain and Clichy paperweights.

"Coaching glass": a 19th cent. drinking cup without a foot which requires to be emptied at one draught.

Coach and post horns: traditionally made in a single straight tube, the coach horn being more conical and funnel-shaped, the post horn having a narrower tube and a more marked "flare" or trumpet bell at the wide end. They are frequently made of copper and possibly look best when made only of that metal. Usually a short section near the mouthpiece is of brass, German silver (see Nickel silver), or silver, and sometimes the bell is also mounted to match. The mouthpiece should be a fixture (i.e. not detachable as in band instruments). Coach horns may vary from thirty inches to fifty-four inches in length, but possibly the finest are those of about four feet, beautiful alike in sound and appearance when in good condition. Apart from the mouthpiece section, they should be in one piece. Two-piece instruments have either been broken at some time and joined together or are common modern replicas made for the "antique" market.

Post or tandem horns are more frequently of brass and may vary between twenty-four inches and forty-eight inches, the most favoured being about midway, known as the "yard of tin". They may be recognized by the narrow tube and wide bell. It is impossible to date either of these instruments closely, for they were still in regular use on the roads before the First World War, and are still made for coaching enthusiasts by Köhler's of Piccadilly.

Coade's stone: moulded architectural stoneware to imitate carved stone made by Batty Langley at Lambeth before 1738. About 1760 the Misses Coade set up a business under the name "Coade's Lithodipyra, Terra Cotta, or Artificial Stone Manufactory". A cousin of the Coades named Sealey joined the business in 1769, and the mark used was COADE & SEALEY, LAMBETH impressed.

Statuary, busts, church monuments and furnishings, and ornamental architectural details were made. Well known artists and sculptors were employed.

The relief upon the pediment over the west portico of Greenwich Hospital, the rood screen of St George's Chapel, Windsor, and the statue of Britannia on the Nelson monument at Yarmouth were said to be the work of this firm.

When Sealey died the business passed through several hands, but continued until about 1840.

Coalbrookdale: see Coalport porcelain.

Coalport or **Coalbrookdale porcelain:** John Rose left the Caughley factory after a difference with Thomas Turner and started on his own first at Jackfield and then at Coalport on the opposite bank of the river, c. 1796. He took over an opposition works started by his brother and then, in an attempt to recover lost business, purchased Turner's Caughley factory, after which biscuit china was made at Caughley and sent to Coalport for glazing and decoration. In 1814 the entire manufactory was removed to Coalport. John Rose bought the Cambrian Pottery at Swansea in 1820.

There have been a number of different proprietors of Coalport since 1862. Coalport china is now made at the Crescent Works, Stoke-on-Trent by Coalport China Ltd.
Marks:

JOHN ROSE & Cº
COALBROOKDALE
SHROPSHIRE

Early Coalport is indistinguishable from Caughley. From 1820 onwards the employment of Billingsley (q.v.) may have led to the use of the Nantgarw and Swansea formula and the product is extremely translucent. Bright flower painting particularly roses, with modelled and applied decoration, is characteristic of the Coalport style up to 1850. At the same time models of Sèvres, Dresden and Chelsea were not only imitated but skilfully faked at the Coalport factory. Less elaborate tea and table ware made from about mid-cent. onwards is lightly decorated and makes use of green and rose coloured grounds.

Coal vases: replaced coal scuttles in wealthy homes from 1840 when the Nasmyth hammer was introduced into japanning factories. They were intended to remain decorating the fireside and be filled from buckets, unlike scuttles which were carried into the cellar. The coal for the first time was concealed beneath an ornamental cover. Fearncombe of Wolverhampton displayed at the Great Exhibition a coal vase in the shape of a nautilus shell resting on coral, the cover handle representing a seahorse. Others were in the shape of miniature Gothic fonts and great tureens which the Jury's Report stated were "ornamented in the Italian style and worthy of being imitated in silver".

Coaster: a receptacle which came into use before 1750 for moving wine, beer and food on the dining-table; also variously known as a slider, decanter stand and beerwagon. For ease of movement, the coaster was normally fitted either with small wheels or with a baize-covered base, and the materials used in good examples included mahogany, papier-mâché and silver. Examples in silver have pierced or solid sides and usually a turned wooden base. They occur in pairs, or sets of four or more. Beer-wagons were sometimes made with special places for the jug and drinking vessels.

Cobb, John: see Vile and Cobb.

Cobirons: these are similar to andirons (q.v.) but are usually quite plain in design and have rows of hooks on the standards on which spits could be placed. Some examples of cobirons have basket-like tops, and it has been suggested that they are "cressets" for holding a light. They may have been intended for a cup used in basting meat.

Cochins: the small cartouches or vignettes (q.v.), named after their inventor, depicting contemporary events. Cochins were used decoratively on boxes and other objects of vertu.

Cock beading: a small moulding of half-round section applied to the edges of drawer fronts from c. 1730 to 1800.

Cockpit Hill pottery: some slipwares were made at Cockpit Hill although the date of origin of this Derby potworks is unknown. Some white cream jugs marked DERBY and dated 1750 were, however, probably made there. From the early 1750s until 1779 the proprietors were W. Butts, Thomas Rivett, John and Christopher Heath. It is likely that the factory closure was due to the Heaths' bankruptcy and that the stock was acquired by William Duesbury (see also Bow, Chelsea, Derby). The ware was of a Staffordshire type and usually unmarked.

Cock's head hinge: twin-plate hinge of curvilinear shape, the finials formed as a cock's head. Frequently found on woodwork of the late 16th and first half of the 17th cent., held in position by handwrought iron nails, never by screws. (See also "H" hinge.)

Coconut cup: standing cup with bowl and sometimes cover formed from the nut with silver straps, lip and foot in the prevailing style of the period. Found from the medieval period down to the 19th cent. In the 18th cent. a low form on small silver feet also occurs.

Codnor Park stoneware: a potworks was established here in 1821 by William Burton for the manufacture of stoneware bottles from local clay, but closed in 1832 when Burton got into financial difficulties. Joseph Bourne of Denby re-opened the factory, which employed about 60 hands, in 1833, and continued to work it until 1861 when the workmen and plant were transferred to Denby.

Coffee, William: porcelain modeller, started in his trade at Coade's factory in Lambeth, but later found employment at the Derby porcelain factory, where he was working in 1794. In 1795 he is said to have gone to another and rather mysterious porcelain factory at Church Gresley, but returned to Derby. Subsequently he entered into partnership with a relative of Duesbury in a small china factory in Derby and, when the partnership was dissolved, commenced to make terra cotta. Finally he emigrated to America. His own productions in terra cotta are said to have been stamped:

W. COFFEE DERBY

Coffer: term freely confused with chest. In strict definition a coffer was a chest or box covered in leather or some other material and banded with metalwork, but it seems likely that the term was not always precisely used. It may not be wrong to class as coffers various stoutly built or heavily ironed strong-chests and -boxes, even though they do not fulfil all the above requirements. Trussing coffers were furnished with lifting rings and shackles or other devices for transportation; but chests and coffers not intended for transport might be chained to the wall for security.

Coffor Bach: the Welsh Bible-box, peculiar to the Principality and an attractive little piece of furniture, suggesting a diminutive mule chest. It was usually made of oak or elm, occasionally inlaid with holly, and most commonly dated from the second half of the 18th cent. onwards, while many 20th-cent. copies exist. The upper chest portion was intended for the Bible, and the two small drawers below for family papers.

Coif: a close-fitting cap formed of one piece of embroidery seamed along the top of the head. These are often found unpicked or not made up, and are therefore difficult to recognize. The Elizabethan coifs were embroidered in coloured silks and metal thread, or in black silk, in patterns of coiling stems or less frequently with diaper patterns.

"Coin glasses": wine glasses in which a coin is enclosed in the knopped stem. Examples exist from the late 17th and the 18th cent

Colfichet: the name given to small embroidered pictures, originating in Italy in the late 18th cent., worked in floss silks on paper so that each side was alike. They were used either as book-markers or placed between two sheets of glass.

Colichemarde: a modern term for a type of small sword blade which is wide near the hilt and narrows abruptly half way down. (See also Smallsword.)

Collar knop: see Merese knop.

Collar lace: early 17th-cent. term for imported Venetian point laces, simple and largely geometrical in vandyke outlines. A few designs are considered identifiable as English. (See also Venetian flat point, grounded point, raised point and rose point laces.)

Collation: a term, used in booksellers' catalogues. In the sentence, "this copy has been collated with the one in the British Museum", the cataloguer is using the word in its simpler sense of "to compare"; and the implication is that the two copies are of the same composition. When he pencils on the back endpaper "collated and perfect" (or simply "c. & p."), he is using it in the special sense of "to examine the sheets of a printed book, so as to verify their number and order".

But collation has acquired a further (and to most collectors more familiar) meaning: the bibliographical description of the contents of a book, expressed in a standardized formula. Thus, "Collation: A-L M" means a book of 92 leaves, gathered in eleven quires of eight and one of four leaves: there is no J (or U or W) in the signature alphabet (see Signature letters).

Collet setting: a method of setting precious stones in which the stone is enclosed in a band or ring of metal, foiled at the back to increase the intensity of the colour. Collet settings were usual until about the close of the 18th cent.

Collier: a broad necklet worn in the 19th cent.

Cologne ware: see Fulham stone-ware.

Colophon: the finishing stroke (from the Greek word meaning summit): a note at the end of a book (sometimes accompanied by a device or mark) giving all or some of the following particulars: name of work, author, printer, place of printing, date. (See also Imprint.) In very early books most of these particulars may not be found elsewhere, and when inspecting the credentials of an incunable (q.v.) it follows that one begins by turning to the last page, not the first.

Coloured aquatint: aquatint (q.v.) with more than one colour applied by hand.

Coloured glass: glass tinted by the addition of natural or prepared metallic oxides. Turquoise-greens and -blues obtained from copper, greens from iron, blues from cobalt, browns and yellows from iron and antimony, purples from manganese were the principle colours used from the very early days of glass-making. Ruby glass was first invented by the German chemist Johann Kunckel in the late 17th cent. by the addition of gold chloride, although pink glass had been produced in the Middle Ages. The 19th cent. increased the range by making black glass with iron and manganese, among others, while new colours from titanium, selenium, nickel, etc. have been produced in modern times.

Coloured lithograph: lithograph (q.v.) printed in one or two neutral colours with other colours applied by hand.

Colour-plate books: a broad category, common in booksellers' catalogues, including any book with plates in colour, whether picturesque, sporting or satirical, and whether these are wholly printed in colour, aquatinted with hand-coloured detail or wholly hand-coloured on an engraved or lithographed base. Many books in the two last-named classes were originally issued in alternative states – coloured and uncoloured.

Colour printing: consists basically in the colouring of a plate from which an impression or print is taken, instead of the application of colour directly on to an otherwise finished print. Hand-colouring was almost universal in 1837, while by the end of the Victorian era everything was in one way or another printed in colours. The principal methods of colour printing until late on in this period were by wood engravings (q.v.) or by stone (lithography and chromolithography, qq.v.). In either case a separate block or stone was prepared for each colour and was applied in turn to the print, usually starting with a key block in black or grey giving the principal outlines. A great many prints were, however, printed in colours, and touched up by hand, and most early chromolithographs were to some extent hand-coloured. Chromolithography was, to start with, more expensive than hand-colouring, and hence the cheaper books between 1840 and 1865 tended to be entirely hand-coloured.

Colour-twist stem: a type of stem found on glass drinking vessels between 1755 and 1775, containing spirals of glass, opaque or transparent, either singly or in combination. The colours favoured were blue, green or ruby, less frequently red, yellow, sapphire, black, and greyish blue.

Colt percussion revolver: a type of percussion revolving pistol, patented in 1836. Numerous attempts had been previously made to produce a revolving pistol but none had hitherto been successful.

Columbine cups: candidates for admission as Masters to the Nuremberg Goldsmiths' Guild were required to produce a standing-cup to a fixed design, based on the form of the columbine flower. The practice was introduced in the second half of the 16th cent. and probably continued until early in the 17th cent.

Comb-back chair: a forerunner of the bent, hoop-back Windsor chair, dating from the mid-18th cent. The cresting rail with its spindles resembles a comb, but the term "comb-back" is not contemporary. They are sometimes known as "stick" chairs. Of good country workmanship, they were usually of beech, elm or ash.

Combed ware: pottery decorated by the application of two or more different coloured slips brushed or combed to produce an effect similar to marbled paper. The finer examples are called feathered wares.

Extensively used by Staffordshire slipware potters, late 17th and early 18th cent.

Comb-morion: see Morion.

Comfit box: see Bonbonnières.

Cominazzò, Lazarino: Italian barrelsmith, working in the small village of Gardone near Brescia about the middle of the 17th cent. His barrels were so strong, in spite of their thin walls, and so highly esteemed that they were exported for mounting all over Europe. The name was widely forged, both at the time and after his death.

Commode: the normal French word for a chest of drawers, which seems to date from the early 18th cent. and was also adopted in England to refer to chests with serpentine fronts.

Communion cup: the Protestant equivalent of the chalice (q.v.). Introduced under Edward VI and continued as a basic form until the end of the 18th cent. Silver examples have a deep, beaker-shaped bowl, spool-shaped stem, with compressed central knop (q.v.) and circular foot. The accompanying paten usually fits the lip to form a cover. (See also Paten.)

Communion table: in churches the Post-Reformation communion table replaced the medieval altar. It was essentially similar to the domestic table of the time, supported on a developed framework with a leg at each corner and possibly others along the sides, and was usually of oak.

"Compagnie des Indes" china: Chinese porcelain imported into

Europe by European trading companies such as the French *Compagnie des Indes* or the English East India Company.

Compagnie dessin: (*Fr.* = Company pattern), the French name for porcelain made to European order in the Far East, and imported by the *Compagnie des Indes*, the French East India Company.

Compensation clock pendulum: a pendulum which provides for the compensation of the effects of heat and cold.

Compound-twist stem: a type of stem found on glass drinking vessels between 1760 and 1800, containing a pair of air or enamel spiral formations, one within the other: a central spiral or (in enamel) a closely knotted central cable with another formation spiralling around it. This type has straight stems only.

Concave frieze or **cavetto:** a hollow moulding or frieze appearing as a feature of the cornice on late 17th cent. case furniture. As a decorative feature, it was contemporary with the convex frieze which it later replaced.

"Concertina" action: a modern term used to describe the way in which the framework of some 18th cent. card tables and side tables are constructed, allowing the hinged top to be opened and to rest at the corners on the two extended legs, drawn into place on a jointed framework.

Confidante: an upholstered settee with additional seats at each end, beyond the arms and at an angle to the settee. This type of settee is illustrated by Hepplewhite (q.v.) in his *Cabinet Maker and Upholsterer's Guide*, and was said to be "of French origin and in pretty general request for large and spacious suits of apartments".

Conical bowl: see Straight-funnel bowl.

Conical clock pendulum: a pendulum that rotates in a circle, the point of suspension being the apex of the cone. Robert Hooke experimented with conical pendulums in 1666. Huygens also made experiments, but it is seldom found in practice.

Connecticut chest: a variety of chest made in the 17th and 18th cent. in Connecticut. Decorative chest, sometimes including one or two drawers, and ornamented with applied bosses and split spindles. The three front panels are carved in low relief with conventionalized flowers – the centre panel containing sunflowers and the side panels, tulips.

Console table: a type of side table permanently standing against a wall and supported by two bracket shaped legs. About 1725, console tables, gesso and gilt, were elaborately ornamented with masks, scrolls and foliage and frequently had marble tops.

Constitution mirror: a term of obscure origin, perhaps a misnomer, widely used in America when referring to a Chippendale-style wall mirror with strings of leaves or flowers at the sides, a scrolled-arch top, and a fanciful finial, generally a bird. The frame is usually in walnut or mahogany and partly gilded.

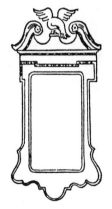

Cont.: a term used in booksellers' catalogues meaning contemporary. As in cont. cf., meaning that the leather binding is contemporary with the printing of the book.

Contorniate: bronze Roman pieces with a distinctive flattened edge issued in the 4th cent. A.D. Types are heroes of mythology, former great emperors and scenes alluding to sports. These were not coins but a kind of token used in connection with the public games.

Contour-framing: a means of decorating pottery in isolating an ornamental feature by means of a white or uncoloured border, being more or less parallel, and following its outline: a feature of near eastern Islamic pottery decoration from which it was derived via Italy and Holland. Recorded on an English late 16th cent. tin-glazed earthenware vase.

Contra-posto: Baroque (q.v.) device for emphasising the dramatic effect of a figure, whether in painting or sculpture, by introducing strongly marked contrasts of rhythm in the composition.

Contre-partie: see Boulle marquetry.

Convex frieze: a frieze or moulding of cushion shaped section; a characteristic feature of the straight cornices of late 17th cent. chests-on-stands and tallboys.

Cookworthy, William: (1705–80), born at Kingsbridge in South Devon, of humble parentage.

Cookworthy was a Quaker. After his wife's death in 1745, Cookworthy developed his researches into the secrets of porcelain-making. He journeyed to Cornwall many times, discovered the Cornish equivalents of kaolin and petuntse (see China-clay and China-stone); and found a partner for his Plymouth hard-paste porcelain venture in Lord Camelford, whom he visited with the object of securing the mineral rights of his land. The first fired experiments in hard-paste were made in 1765, and in 1768 he was sufficiently confident to take out a patent and form a company for its manufacture. The venture was transferred to Bristol in 1770, and in 1774 the patent was bought by Champion.

Copeland: see under Spode.

Copenhagen porcelain: soft-paste porcelain was made at Copenhagen at a factory started by Louis Fournier, a previous modeller at Vincennes and Chantilly (q.v.), between 1759 and 1765, of which examples are rare. The more famous Royal factory, founded in 1774, produced a hard-paste porcelain as a result of the assistance of a previous Fürstenberg (q.v.) modeller and arcanist (q.v.), A. C. Lupau. The most famous production of the factory is the Flora Danica service, upon which work was started in 1789. The service was intended for the Empress Catherine II of Russia and numbered 1,602 pieces, each decorated with a botanical painting of Danish flora. From 1775 onwards Copenhagen porcelain was marked with three horizontal wavy lines. The factory is still in existence.

Copland, H.: see under Lock, Matthias.

Copper blank: paper-thin metal serving as a base or core to every enamel. Only when copper could be refined adequately and also adequate rolling machinery was available did this metal become a practicable, cheaper alternative to gold as a base for enamels. The metal was cut and shaped and, when necessary, jointed before being covered on all sides with enamel and set into metal mounts. Warping was minimized and the general effect improved on plaques and box-lids, etc., by making the blanks slightly convex, but in some scent-bottles, bonbonnières, etc., there was very considerable shaping, the blanks being cut with steel punches.

Copperplate engraving: see Line engraving.

Copperplate printing: a method of printing textiles whereby the colour is applied to the cloth by means of an engraved flat copperplate the full width of the fabric. Used in England c. 1760; introduced a monochrome, pictorial style of printing.

Copper-red porcelain glazes: when successful, the fugitive high-temperature copper-red is one of the most splendid glazes in Chinese porcelain. 14th cent. painted wares were often imperfect in colour, but both painted and colour-glazed wares succeeded brilliantly in the 15th cent. In later Ming times (q.v.) the iron-red enamel is more common. A triumphant revival was however achieved by the K'ang Hsi potters (q.v.). Justly famous are the brilliant *sang-de-boeuf*, or "ox-blood" monochromes (Chinese = lang yao); other shades are the ruby-red and cherry-red, and those of a paler or browner colour, e.g. the "liver-red" and pale "ashes of roses". The apple-red and rare brownish pink "peach-bloom" often show brown or green mottlings. Yung Chêng and Ch'ien Lung (qq.v.) pieces in general show more regular, even glazing and a neatly finished foot. Flambé effects or red streaked with purple or blue, become more common and are imitated in the flambé Canton stone-wares. 19th cent. pieces are distinguishable by poorer shape and finish, especially of the foot. Painting in underglaze red, again popular from the K'ang Hsi period (q.v.), include more or less exact copies of the early Ming, especially in combination with underglaze blue.

Coquillage: from the French coquille, a shell-fish. An ornament in the form of a shell much favoured as an element of Rococo (q.v.) decoration on over-mantels, furniture, silver, etc., in the mid-18th cent.

Coralline point lace: a needlepoint lace, variant of Venetian flat point (q.v.) with confused patterns and very many *brides picotées* (see also Brides and Picot).

Corbould, G.: an outstanding designer and engraver of trade cards, operating in Lombard Street during the 1750s and 1760s. Later work was signed "Corbould & Jeffreys Foster Lane sculp".

"Corded" quilting: see Quilts.

Cordial glass: during the 17th cent. cordials were taken from miniature wine-glasses measuring four inches to six inches in height. A distinct type of glass, its bowl shorter, squarer, and of smaller rim diameter than a wine-glass bowl, it became fashionable from about 1720; (a) 1720–40: straight stem of normal length and diameter; (b) from 1735: the stem was lengthened, of extra thick diameter, and might be centrally knopped; (c) from 1740: the bowl was less capacious; (d) 1740–70: the flute cordial, often termed a ratafia glass.

Cordonnet: French term used in lace-making, usually preferred to the English gimp or trolly thread, to describe the more substantial outline often given to the solid pattern motif on a piece of lace. It might be composed of several threads whipped or buttonholed together, as in Venetian raised point lace (q.v.); or be one thread whipped or buttonholed, as in Alençon (q.v.); or be a different coarser thread as in Mechlin lace (q.v.).

Cords: slight striae discernible to the fingers on the surface of glass.

Cork Glasshouse, later **Cork Glasshouse Company:** established in Hanover Street, Dublin in 1793, as makers of plain and cut flint-glass and black bottles. The firm specialized in light-weight blown-moulded (q.v.) hollow-ware. Although heavily subsidized by the Dublin Society, receiving some £1,600 in 1787 and £2,304 in 1793, throughout its existence the Cork Glasshouse appears to have laboured under financial instability and ever-changing proprietorship. A newly patented Donaldson furnace was installed under a new proprietorship. This gave to flint-glass a clarity and brilliance never before achieved, and some outstanding hand-cut work was produced. The number of hand-cutters employed was such that they founded the Cork Glasscutter's Union.

In 1812 the firm, under the proprietorship of William Smith & Company, became the Cork Glasshouse Company. Pieces marked "Cork Glass Co." date no earlier than this. In 1817 steam-power was installed in a final effort to survive against competition from the newly established Waterloo Glasshouse. A year later, however, the glasshouse was closed.

Cork Terrace Glasshouse: an Irish glasshouse established in 1819 by Edward and Richard Ronayne. The productive capacity was equal to that of Waterford, for when the firm closed in 1841 it was announced that they possessed tools and machines for forty glass-cutters. They made all kinds of table-glass as well as lustres and Grecian lamps, and were specialists in cut and engraved dessert services.

Corkscrew thumbpiece: an American term for a thumbpiece (q.v.) of twisted shape derived from the Dutch form, used especially on New York tankards.

Corner chair: an armchair that could be placed in a corner. The arrangement of the legs is unusual, with one at each side, the third in the centre of the back and the fourth in the centre of the front. The chair back is generally only as high as the arm rest. The shape of the seat varies from a segment of a circle to an almost rectangular shape. Corner chairs were known in the 17th cent. and were sometimes called elbow chairs or roundabout chairs.

Corner cupboard: a triangular structure, fitting a corner, doored or open. The front is diagonal or curved and it is usually fitted with shelving. Small hanging corner cupboards, lacquered or veneered in burr walnut were popular in England in the first half of the 18th cent. and examples in mahogany were made throughout the cent. Known in France as encoignures, standing corner cupboards began to appear during the Louis XV period and were usually in pairs, often en suite with a secretaire or chest of

drawers. They continued to be made right up to the Revolution.

Cornice: the projecting top course of a building or a piece of case furniture.

Cornopean: see under "Crooked" musical instruments.

"Coromandel" lacquer: a variety of Oriental lacquer brought to England in the late 17th cent. in which the design was incised into the surface. Large folding screens or panels were imported and then cut up in England for making into looking-glass frames, door panels etc., so that the designs are often incomplete or appear upside down. Also known as "Bantam" work. (See also Japan work.)

Coronet setting: see Claw setting.

Corrigenda: see Errata.

Costrel: a pilgrim's bottle; a bottle with ears or handles for suspension from a cord or sling.

Coteau enamel: see Enamel.

Cottage clocks: name now given to many small Connecticut spring clocks in wood cases. c. 1850–1900. Common.

Cottages: pottery cottages were used as night-light shields, pastille burners, and mantelpiece ornaments. The latter frequently represent the scenes of sensational crimes, such as the Red Barn at Polstead (Maria Marten) or Stanfield Hall (the Rush murders).

Cottage style (of binding): a style of decoration used in book-bindings, in which the top and bottom of the rectangular panel (which itself will be filled with smaller ornaments in a variety of rich designs) slope away from a broken centre, thus producing a sort of gabled effect. The cottage style was popular with binders of the last forty years of the 17th cent. and was still being used on pocket almanacs and prayer-books as late as the 1770s.

Couched work: embroidery in which the thread is laid on the material and held down by stitching.

Counter: hutch-like structure, sometimes approximating to a table with an under-compartment. The name (surviving in shop-counter, etc.) derives from the use to which the piece of furniture was put, being employed for reckoning accounts with counters or jettons disposed on a marked scale. When not so used the counter was available for a variety of other purposes.

Counter-guard: comprises those parts of a sword in addition to the quillons (q.v.) which are interposed between the hilt and the blade. It may take the form of a solid plate or a network of bars.

Countermark: a symbol, letter or group of letters punched into the face of a coin to extend the validity of the coin in time or space. Commonly found on bronze coins of the early Roman Empire.

Counter-proof: a print made from a damp impression and not a plate. It is much weaker than an ordinary impression and presents the subject in reverse. Artists usually made counterproofs in order to have a print in the same direction as the plate to assist them in making alterations to the plate.

Court cupboard: from the French "court" or "short" cupboard. Introduced early in the 16th cent., probably for use in the dining parlour, existing examples are usually of oak but also of walnut. It consists of a stand in three stages, supported at the back corners by plain posts and at the front by bulbous columns of various forms. A central recessed cupboard with canted sides was sometimes contained in the upper part but it was also made as an open structure. (See also Livery cupboard.)

Courting mirror: small mirror, known in America, framed with mouldings and a cresting, the crested area often containing a painted picture or design. It was traditionally a courting gift in 18th cent. New England. It is said that this type of mirror was derived from a Chinese example made for the export trade.

Couvercle à charnière: (*Fr.*), hinged lid.

Cow-milk jug: model of cow with mouth and tail forming spout and handle. Filled from an aperture in the back. An example, in silver, by John Schuppe, probably a Dutchman, dates from about 1755. Jugs in this form were also made in pottery in Staffordshire, South Wales, Yorkshire, and Scotland.

Cox, James: an 18th cent. London clockmaker and jeweller. He opened an exhibition of clocks, singing birds and automata at Spring Gardens. According to one writer "The charge was half a guinea each person; a regulation providing for the presence of but few visitors at a time was, needless to say, quite unnecessary". Cox made many elaborate and costly clocks for export to the East.

Cozzi porcelain: see under Venice porcelain.

Cr. or **Cr. 8vo:** crown octavo. See Book sizes and formats.

"Cracked ice" pattern: a means of decoration resembling ice cracks, found on Bristol delftware (q.v.), c. 1770.

Crackle: a means of decorating porcelain by intentional or controlled "crazing" (q.v.), used extensively by the Chinese potters but not known in Europe until the 19th cent. Used frequently by modern studio and artist potters.

Cradle pipe-tray: presentation piece of pottery for a newly-married couple. Slipware (q.v.) specimens are recorded from 1673 to 1839.

Cran: an iron trivet fitted over the fire for supporting a kettle, girdle-plate, etc.

Crayon engraving: a process in which etching and engraving were combined to render the lines of a chalk drawing. Roulettes with heads designed to reproduce the grain of a chalk line were used to prepare the plate for biting with acid. After the plate had been etched, burin, dry-point and roulette were used direct on its surface. This process was much employed for the reproduction of Old Master drawings, mainly by artists who otherwise worked in stipple or mezzotint (qq.v.).

Crazing: a fine network of cracks occurring in the glaze of earthenware (sometimes a long time after manufacture) due to the tension set up in the glaze because of unequal shrinkage of glaze and body. In decorative pottery the effect may not be unpleasant. (See also Crackle.)

Cream basket: small silver or plate vase or boat-shaped basket, pierced or plain, introduced about 1760, often matching larger examples for sugar.

Cream-coloured earthenware: a good quality lead-glazed earthenware with light body made of pale clay and usually containing calcined flint, perfected in Staffordshire about 1740–50. It began to oust other tablewares about 1760. It was made extensively in Staffordshire, Yorkshire and elsewhere, and enjoyed a world market in the late 18th and early 19th cent. It could be decorated with pierced, moulded, enamelled or printed designs.

Creamware: see Cream-coloured earthenware.

Credence (*It.* **credenza**): a term sometimes used for a side-table in a church on which the Elements were placed before Consecration. Such tables were sometimes of hutch-like formation, and the term credence has been loosely extended to cover other side-tables of more or less similar construction, although there is no historical justification for this extended use in England. In Italy, the credenza was a type of sideboard or buffet used as a serving-table on which silver might also be displayed. 15th and 16th cent. credenze were either simple tables designed to stand by a wall or else long cupboards, sometimes with canted corners, the height of an ordinary dining-table. As they were normally covered with linen they

were very simple in design and decoration. A recessed top story containing a cupboard was added to many credenze in the 16th cent. and this was usual in subsequent periods.

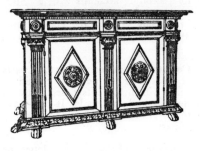

Creepers: these, in pairs, were small irons of similar shape to andirons, between which they were placed in the hearth. Creepers were of very simple design, and they came into use when andirons (q.v.) grew elaborate and costly. A pamphlet of 1642, entitled *Threefold Discourse between Three Neighbours,* speaks of bishops and the lesser clergy, and compares the former to "andirons of state, standing in a chimney but for show; but if a heavy block or red billets are brought to the fire there are poor little creepers or cobirons underneath that must bear all the weight".

Crescent mark: see Caughley and Worcester porcelain.

Cressent, Charles: French cabinet-maker, born at Amiens in 1685, the son of François Cressent, a sculptor, and grandson of a cabinet-maker. He was apprenticed to his father, but probably learned cabinet-making from his grandfather. He became a member of the *Académie de Saint Luc* in Paris in 1714, and in 1719 married the daughter of Joseph Poitou, an *ébéniste* working for the Duc d'Orleans, and he also at this time was given commissions by the Regent. After this he seems officially to have abandoned sculpture for cabinet-making. but he was several times prosecuted by the *Corporations des Fondeurs* and *Doreurs* (qq.v.) for casting and gilding his own mounts. In 1723 he was actually forbidden by law to produce mounts not made by a qualified *fondeur*. This type of litigation was repeated from time to time throughout his life.

The Regent died in 1723 but Crescent continued service with his son Louis, Duc d'Orleans, as late as 1743, on the Duc's retirement from public life. With the profits from the sale of his furniture Crescent formed an impressive collection of works of art, which he three times tried unsuccessfully to sell owing to financial difficulties. Cressent died in 1768.

His best work is never stamped. Towards the end of his life he did use the stamp: C. CRESSENT, but it never appears on pieces of very great quality and should always be treated with suspicion in view of his fame in his lifetime and later. The identification of his work therefore depends almost entirely on documents and tradition.

Cresset: generally an iron basket affixed to a rod and designed to hold wood or other fuel for lighting purposes.

Crested armour: see under "Maximilian" armour.

Cresting: (1) shaped and sometimes perforated ornament on the top of a structure, such as the foliate cresting running round the covers of Medieval silver-silt cups. (See also Cresting rail.) (2) an extension of faceting from the stem of a drinking glass to bridge the junction of the bowl and the stem. Also known as bridge-fluting.

Cresting rail: the top rail or horizontal on the back of a chair variously decorated in the course of the 17th and 18th cent.

Cretonne appliqué or **Broderie perse:** was composed of groups of flowers, leaves, birds, etc., cut out

from printed cotton and applied to a plain ground, usually black. The edges of the motifs were worked round in buttonhole or overcast stitches. Details, such as the veining of the leaves, or the centres of flowers, were picked out with embroidery in coloured silks.

Crewel-work: crewel-work is embroidery in thin worsteds, and is the term usually applied to the curtains and bed hangings of linen and cotton twill embroidered in coloured wools during the second half of the 17th cent. This type of work is often called Jacobean embroidery. The designs were based on the printed cotton "palampores" (chintz hangings) which were imported into England at that time. The "Tree of Life", with waving stems of acanthus-like foliage rising from a hillocked ground, was the most popular pattern. The embroidery was either polychrome or worked entirely in shades of green which has often faded to a dull indigo. Coiling stems and an asparagus pattern are also found.

Crimping: dents or flutes impressed by a tool, usually diagonal, used

round the foot or at the base of the handle of a glass vessel.

Crisselled glass: glass in which the ingredients are not correctly proportioned and an excess of alkali, for example, has resulted in a clouding of the material caused by a network of cracks. Such glass is described as being "diseased" and ultimately crumbles. Some of the early glass vessels made by George Ravenscroft (q.v.) suffered from this defect.

Crochet: a brooch-like jewelled ornament fixed on a vertical pin, worn in the late 17th and 18th cent. and also known as a breast ornament. Contemporary sources refer to "croshetts".

Croft: a small filing cabinet of the late 18th cent. (named after its inventor) specially designed to be moved about easily in the library; it had many small drawers and a writing-top.

Cromwellian: term of convenience applied to English furniture etc., of austere character, actually or supposedly made about the time of the Commonwealth or Interregnum.

Cromwellian chair: a modern term used to describe a chair with a leather seat and back; turned legs and stretchers, occasionally spiral turned. Generally ornamented with brass-headed tacks these chairs were made in the mid-17th cent. and have been much reproduced in modern times.

Cromwellian clock: see Lantern clock.

"Crooked" musical instruments: before the days of valves, which automatically alter the active tube-length of the instrument to obtain chromatic notes, the limited scale of horns and trumpets could only be varied by having separate detachable loops of tubing of different lengths, which the player could change at will. These are the "crooks". Their use survived the change-over to valves and many later instruments – cornopeans, cornets, slide- and valved-trumpets and horns – are found with complete sets of crooks.

Cross-banded veneer or **cross-grained:** a characteristic decoration of a veneered surface in which a border of contrasting wood, cut across the grain, is applied to a piece of furniture. Narrow cross-bandings were frequently employed on walnut furniture, while in the later 18th cent. broad bandings in exotic woods were popular.

Cross-bow: a bow mounted at right-angles upon a stock, which is grooved for the arrow (bolt), and fitted with a trigger-mechanism so that it can be discharged from the shoulder like a gun. The bow was made variously of wood, steel, or a composition of layers of wood, horn and sinew glued together; it could be spanned by hand, a stirrup at the end providing purchase for the foot by a forked lever, or by various forms of windlass. It was known in Europe as early as the 4th cent., but did not become popular until the 10th. Its use against Christians was prohibited by the Church in 1139, but despite this it was used extensively in warfare throughout the remainder of the Middle Ages. As a sporting weapon it has remained in use until the present, especially in Switzerland.

A light version of the cross-bow fitted with a sling to fire bullets or stones, and known as a prodd or stone-bow, was much used from medieval times onwards for shooting small game. It remained popular, particularly in Lancashire and East Anglia, until well into the 19th cent.

Crossed "L"s' mark: see Sèvres porcelain, Limbach porcelain and Longton Hall porcelain.

Crossed swords mark: see Meissen porcelain, Tournai porcelain and Weesp porcelain.

Cross garnet hinge: a type of strap hinge, one leaf of which is a horizontal strap and the other a vertical strap; when in position like a letter T lying on its side.

Cross-grained veneer: see Cross-banded veneer.

Cross mark: see Bristol, Plymouth and Worcester porcelain. Also Mortlake tapestry.

Cross rail: a horizontal rail on a chair back.

Cross-stretcher: X-shaped stretcher in straight or curved lines. Sometimes found on side tables and chairs in the late 17th and early 18th cent.

"Crotch" veneer: see "Curl" veneer.

Crouch ware: the early grey stoneware of Staffordshire with a ferruginous wash is probably the "crouch" ware mentioned by Simeon Shaw (*History of the Staffordshire Potteries*, 1829) as the earliest Staffordshire salt-glazed pottery. The name perhaps came from the Derbyshire Crich clay.

Crown: (a) gold coin of value 5s struck in the reigns of Henry VIII and Edward VI with Tudor rose types, and in reigns of Edward VI, James I and Charles I with various portrait types; (b) large silver coin of same value first struck by Edward VI with equestrian portrait. Continued in all subsequent reigns, usually with profile portrait.

Crown Derby porcelain: see Derby porcelain.

"Crown" glass: flat glass made by a process whereby a blown bubble was spread by rapid rotation on the rod into a flat sheet, leaving a bull's eye in the middle where the rod was attached. (See also "Broad" glass.)

Crown paperweight: a paperweight composed of coloured canes radiating in straight lines from the top.

Crown setting: a means of setting a precious stone whereby the stone is exposed (open setting) and held secure with rebated points.

Crozier: bishop's pastoral staff.

Cruets: (1) the vessels containing the wine and water for use at the Eucharist. Sometimes wholly of silver, they are frequently of glass with silver mounts and follow the patterns prevalent in domestic plate; (2) bottles for condiments, contained in cruet frames. The first examples of silver frames date from Queen Anne. They were made with open rings and central or side handles to hold the sets of casters with or without glass oil and vinegar bottles. Later forms of the frames were oblong or boat-shaped, containing silver-mounted glass bottles, casters and mustard-pot.

Crushed morocco: see Morocco.

Crystal: strictly a clear, transparent variety of quartz, the term also is used to refer to the finest colourless or clear flint glass. The clear Venetian glass, first made perhaps before the 15th cent. was called "cristallo" from its resemblance to rock crystal.

"Crystallo-ceramie": a process of enclosing cameos, moulded in a porcellanous material, representing Classical portraits, figures, etc., in deeply cut glass. The method was adopted by Apsley Pellatt (q.v.) from the French and was also known as "Cameo incrustation".

C-scroll: a term applied usually to the shape of a handle in form like the letter C; also called "single scroll".

Cuirassier armour: armour for the heavy cavalry of the first half of the 17th cent., consisting of a close-helmet and defences covering the whole of the body down to the knees.

Cuir bouilli: (*Fr.*), leather which has been boiled in oil, moulded into shape and allowed to dry hard.

Culet: the point of a brilliant cut (q.v.) diamond at the base of the stone, which is cut to form a horizontal facet.

Cullet: broken glass for remelting, included in the ingredients of the frit used in the manufacture of early soft-paste porcelain. Also used in making new glass, to promote fusion and improve the quality of the metal.

Cup-hilt rapier: in Southern Italy and particularly in Spain, in the second quarter of the 17th cent. the cup-hilt rapier came into fashion, the guard being formed by a circular bowl supplemented by straight quillons (q.v.) and a knuckle-guard. This type of rapier remained in use until the 18th cent.

Cupid's bow cresting: the top rail of a chair or settee in the form of a bow. The typical rococo (q.v.) chair frequently had this form of top-rail, which was introduced about 1730.

Cupping-bowl: this term is popularly but incorrectly used for flat, shallow, circular bowls of silver with one flat, pierced and shaped handle. These

were, in fact, a form of individual porringer, by which name they are always called in America. The covers of early skillets or saucepans are of the same basic form.

Curb pattern: the most usual pattern of 19th cent. gold chain bracelets.

Curfew: a metal cover (*couvre-feu*) used to cover a fire when left un-attended or to enable it to be kept alive during the night. Roughly in the shape of a quarter-sphere with a handle attached, the rare examples which are extant are of brass or copper, with embossed ornament.

"Curl" veneer: a veneer (q.v.) cut from just below a fork in the tree. By using veneers, the cabinet-maker (q.v.) was able to show to the full the beauties of the grain, the pattern obtained from a "curl" or "crotch" veneer resembling an ostrich plume.

Cushion frieze: a frieze of convex or cushion-shaped form appearing as a feature of the cornice on late 17th cent. case furniture.

Cushion knop: a large spherical knop or protuberance, flattened at the top and bottom, on the stem of a drinking glass.

Cut-cardwork: a method of deco-rating silver in which flat sheet metal is cut into foliage and strap outline and soldered to the main surface to produce relief decoration. Of French origin, introduced in late 17th cent. and later built up in various planes to greater relief.

Cut corners: playing cards with cut or rounded corners were illegal prior to 1862.

Cut edges: see under Uncut edges.

Cut glass: glass ground to a required pattern by means of a grindstone equipped with metal or stone disc. These discs are of varying size and can be changed at will according to the requirements of the design. For facet cutting an iron wheel fed with sand or emery is used. Cutting as a form of decoration on English glass was introduced in the early 18th cent. although few examples survive of earlier date than the mid-cent. Excise duties on glass imposed the need for light, thin vessels towards the later years of the cent., hampering the use of cutting as a decoration, but Irish glass of the period, not affected by the duties, was decorated with elaborately cut designs, and decanters, in particular, were treated in this manner.

Cutlass: a term first appearing in the 16th cent., denoting a short, single-edged sword, usually curved, the successor of the medieval falchion (q.v.). In the 18th and early 19th cent. it was a standard naval weapon.

Cutlery stand: see Canterbury (2).

Cut steel: see Chiselled steel.

Cut work embroidery: suggested by drawn work (q.v.) but lighter and more conspicuously ornamental, as part of the fabric was cut away and the holes filled with geometrical patterns worked with needle and thread. At its most advanced, it consisted of buttonhole stitch, double loop, darning and knotting stitch. It was important in Elizabethan England.

"CV" mark: see Kloster Veilsdorf porcelain.

Cycloidal cheeks: curves fitted to a pendulum clock to overcome circular error. It was found, however, that the errors they introduced were greater than those they eliminated, hence they were soon abandoned. Only found in the very earliest pendulum clocks.

Cylinder escapement: a type of watch escapement (q.v.). A form of this escapement was patented by Tompion, Barlow and Haughton in 1695, but it was never developed. It remained for Tompion's successor,

George Graham, to perfect this escapement about 1725. Graham used it very extensively in his watches, and this greatly helped him to gain the reputation of being the best watchmaker of his day. As with the anchor escapement (q.v.), the pallets are in the same plane as the escape wheel. This escapement remained the best for watches until supplanted by the duplex and the lever escapements (qq.v.) about the end of the 18th cent.

Cylinder front: see Tambour front.

Cylinder knop: a knop or protuberance in the form of a cylinder on the stem of a drinking glass, sometimes containing a tear or air bubble.

Cylinder-top desk: (*Fr.* = *bureau à cylindre*), a writing table, incorporating drawers and writing accessories, the functional part of which is closed by means of a curved panel fastened with a lock. It is usually supported on tall legs and differs from a roll-top desk (q.v.) in that the curved panel is in one piece and not slatted.

Cyma recta: a moulding composed of two curves, the upper of concave form.

Cyma reversa: a moulding composed of two curves, the lower of concave form.

Cyst: a round protuberance in the base of a wine-glass bowl.

Daalder: silver coin of the thaler class in the Low Countries. Most common type is a standing mailed figure holding shield and provincial arms.

Dagger mark: (1) see Bow porcelain. (2) mark struck on knife blades made by the members of the Cutlers' Company in London (in addition to the maker's mark).

D'Alva bottles: bellarmines (q.v.). Named after Fernando Alvarez de Toledo, Duke of Alva (1508–83), responsible for a reign of terror in the Netherlands, 1567–73.

Damascening: the art of encrusting the surface of iron, steel, brass, or copper with gold or/and silver has been known and practised since antiquity, especially in the Near East, but at no time in Europe has it flourished more than in Milan during the middle and second half of the 16th cent., where it was a by-product of the thriving armourers' trade. Thin iron sheets were embossed with subjects from Roman history or mythology against landscape backgrounds and damascened with gold and silver. The Milanese damascening of this period is of fine quality and bears comparison with the best Saracenic work. Damascened plaques were made in quantity to more or less standard shapes and were sold to cabinet-makers, who mounted them on ebony caskets, chests of drawers, and even large pieces such as tables and mirrors. Though the majority of the damascened ironwork encountered by the collector is likely to be of Milanese origin, there were highly competent damasceners at work elsewhere in Europe, in Augsburg and Nürnberg, in Paris and in other Italian cities. In the 17th cent. some fine damascening was done on English sword and knife handles, probably by immigrant Italian artists. The art did not survive the 16th cent. in Italy.

Dandies' sticks: walking-sticks flaunted by early 19th-cent. dandies displayed knobs carved with heads of Moors, Turks or Chinese. These have been noted in mahogany, teak, ash, ironwood, snakewood, penang wood, blackthorn. Less expensively the heads might be in cast and gilded brass.

Dangle-spit: a non-mechanical type of spit for roasting meat over a fire which operated in the manner implied by its name. It hung downwards, twisting one way and another on a rope as the latter wound and unwound itself, clockwise and anti-clockwise, sometimes with the aid of two weighted arms.

Dargastan rugs: both Dargastan and Derbend rugs come from the North East Caucasus and resemble Shirvan rugs (q.v.).

Daric: gold coin of the Persian kings, with type of king shooting with bow – incuse reverse. Name derived from Persian king Darius.

"Darkie" toby jug: a late 19th cent. variety of toby jug (q.v.) representing a black man.

Darly, Matthias: designer and engraver of furniture to the trade, produced trade cards of outstanding quality from about 1750 until the 1780s, the finest being in the chinoiserie style in which he was a master designer. His own card, issued from "the Acorn, facing Hungerford, Strand", shows him also to have been a maker of paper hangings. This card also states that he "engraved Shopkeepers' Bills in greater variety and cheaper than any other Shop in Town". The signature "M. Darly Sculp" appears on 81 of the 200 plates in Thomas Chippendale's (q.v.) *Director*.

Date-letter: the specific mark of a letter of the alphabet used on English silver at the various Assay Offices to distinguish the year of hall-marking. There are no date-letters on American silver.

Davenport: a small chest of drawers with a sloping top for writing, popular in the early 19th cent.; said to be named after a client of the firm of Gillow who claimed to have invented it.

Davenport family: John Davenport, took over Brindley's pottery factory at Longport in 1793. In 1801 he added glass manufacture to his other interests. He retired about 1830, the business being continued by his sons.

Marks:

DAVENPORT   DAVENPORT
LONGPORT   LONGPORT
                          STAFFORDSHIRE

DAVENPORT
LONGPORT
STAFFORDSHIRE.
Printed

In the earlier years of the firm earthenware only was made including cream-coloured, painted, and transfer-printed wares. Openwork rims are said to have been typical. Good blue-printed earthenware was made and "flown" blue was extensively used. Wares painted with designs in a peasant style were popular in the period 1815–35. Monochrome painted landscapes over a coloured ground strike a more distinctive note. Stone china with heavy "sumptuous" Imari decorations in colour and gold followed the vogue of the 1830s.

China (which was made from the early years of the 19th cent.) was mostly derivative in character. The paste varied from a translucent and white body reminiscent of Nantgarw to something much more grey in tone. New Hall, or what might be called the "cottage" style of decoration, was used in the early days, but with an influx of Derby artists, heavier ornate wares with lavish gilding and colouring in the Derby styles became general.

Day-bed: a couch which became fashionable during the Restoration, although it had been introduced at an earlier date. Usually made of walnut and sometimes of painted beech, the seat and back rest were often caned, while the uprights, stretchers and legs were turned and carved. The back rest could be adjusted for comfort.

Day of the month clock: a clock with an indication of the date changing daily. Usually the adjustment for the short months has to be made by hand, but some systems provide for this and, in more exceptional cases, for leap year as well (see Perpetual calendar clock).

D.e.: an abbreviation found in booksellers' catalogues to describe deckle edges (q.v.).

Deadbeat escapement: a type of clock escapement (q.v.) invented by George Graham about 1715. Graham was the leading astronomical instrument-maker of his day, and from his close connection with astronomers was, doubtless, aware of their demand for still greater accuracy than could be attained with the anchor escapement (q.v.). The deadbeat escapement is an improvement on the anchor in that it eliminates the recoil, and remains steady at the end of each beat. It held the field for the most accurate escape for astronomical work for nearly two hundred years. It is still used to-day in high-grade clocks, both long-case and mantel.

Deckle edges: the rough, untrimmed edges of a sheet of hand-made paper (the deckle being the frame or band which confines it in manufacture). Much prized by collectors, especially in books before the age of edition-binding in cloth, as tangible evidence that the leaves are uncut; for the deckle edge normally would be – and indeed was meant to be – trimmed off by the binder.

Découpage: until the mid-1670s the mounts (q.v.) of folding fans were cut with open-work lace-like patterns copying the intricate designs of French and Flemish lace. The blades were in tortoiseshell elaborated to harmonize with the lace patterns and trimmed with gold and precious stones; or were in Levantine mother-of-pearl carved and engraved with mythological subjects.

Dedication copy: it is customary for an author to present an early copy of his book to the person (if any) to whom it is dedicated. This is known as the dedication copy; and it will rank very high, in the estimation of most collectors, among presentation or association copies (q.v.) of the book.

Del.: short for delineavit or delineaverunt – Latin for he or they drew. To be seen after the artists' name, usually on the left-hand side of a print.

Delamain, Henry: partner with Janssen and Brooks in the Battersea enamel (q.v.) venture. He left the firm soon after Brooks in 1754 and died in Dublin in 1757.

Delft pottery: Delft became the centre of the Dutch industry about 1650. 17th cent. wares belong to two distinct classes: that produced for country markets, decorated in a rapid technique for cheap sale, and finely shaped pieces, carefully painted in imitation of the Chinese blue and white porcelain. After the mid-18th cent. the general standard sank to a mediocre level. The many factories were known by their signs, "Three Bells", "Peacock", etc. with which the wares are sometimes marked, together with initials of their owners.

Delftware: earthenware coated with a lead-glaze made opaque by the addition of tin ashes, named after the town of Delft in Holland which, in the 17th cent., became an important centre for the manufacture of this type of pottery. It was, of course, manufactured in England much earlier. The industry in fact appears to have been started in Norwich in 1567 by Jasper Andries, and continued there by other potters until 1696 or later. The chief centres of delftware manufacture were:

London	from	1571
Bristol	from c.	1650
Liverpool	from	1710
Glasgow	from	1748
Dublin	from	1737
Limerick	from	1761

Demi-parure: a small matching set of jewellery, consisting of brooch with earrings, or necklace with earrings or other combination. (See also Parure.)

Denarius: the standard silver coin of the Roman Republic and early Empire, first introduced in 187 B.C. Types under the Republic: first, the helmeted head of Roma on observe with mark of value X (ten asses) and Dioscuri on reverse; later, scenes alluding to the family history of the moneying magistrates appeared on the reverse. In the 1st cent. B.C. both obverse and reverse have personal allusions, but portraiture of living persons is not found till the issue of Julius Caesar in 44 B.C. Throughout the Empire the denarius had on obverse the portrait and title of the Emperor or one of his family and on reverse a personification with well-marked attributes as a pictorial shorthand for various qualities and acts of the Emperor. The denarius was ousted by the antoninianus (q.v.) in mid-3rd cent.

Denga: Russian silver coin issued from 14th cent. by Dukes of Moscow and Kiev. Often of irregular shape. Common type, figure on horseback.

Denier: (denar, denaro, etc.), silver coin similar to English penny issued from time of Charlemagne (768–814) and copied all over Western Europe. Variety of types including the inscription type with monogram of Charlemagne, ecclesiastical buildings, portraits, mint names.

Dentelle decoration: a book-binder's term (from the *Fr.* = lace) meaning a border with a lacy pattern on the inner edge, usually gilt. Dentelle decoration may be used on the outside of the covers; but in bindings of the past hundred years or so it has been more often used, in a somewhat emasculated form, on the inside – usually described as inside dentelles.

Dentil moulding: a cornice moulding made up of a row of rectangular, teeth-like forms, used on 18th cent. case furniture.

D'Entrecolles, Père François Xavier: a Jesuit missionary who went out to China in the year 1698. At a time when all the nations of Europe were trying actively to discover the secrets of porcelain manufacture he informed his compatriots of the methods of the Chinese potters. Two long letters, detailing with accuracy all that he had seen and heard, were written by him in 1712 and 1722, and published later in Paris. These documents are still the basis of much of our knowledge of porcelain-making in China. Père D'Entrecolles died in Peking in 1741.

Derband rugs: see under Dargastan rugs.

Derby porcelain: the date when porcelain was first made in Derby is not certainly known. André Planché was making it by 1751 probably at Cockpit Hill, and Duesbury is known to have decorated in London "Darby" or "Darbyshire figures". A cream jug dated 1750 is believed to be the earliest dated specimen.

By 1756 a flourishing business had been built up and the enameller William Duesbury and John Heath had become proprietors. In 1770 the Chelsea factory was acquired.

Heath failed financially in 1779 and in consequence Duesbury became sole owner. He died in 1786, his son of the same name continuing the factory until his death in 1796. In 1795 he had taken as partner Michael Kean who married his widow, and remained in control until 1811.

The works were bought in 1811 by Robert Bloor. He became insane in 1826, and the factory was managed until its closure in 1848 by James Thomason and Thomas Clarke.

The present Royal Crown Derby Porcelain Company was formed in 1876.

Marks:

1750	1780
1795	1830

Chelsea Derby

1760	1770-80	1784	1784-1810

1795-6	Imitation

The paste of the earliest phase of Derby porcelain was non-phosphatic, and the wares produced rather heavy and of a creamy warm white.

The next phase of Derby was characterized by the use of pale delicate colours, large flat flowers and scrolls picked out in colour or mounds with flowery reliefs. The figures themselves were generally of Meissen origin, Derby setting up claims to be "the second Dresden". At this period figures seemed to have had precedence over useful wares.

The third phase of Derby is distinguishable by the dirty patches (three of four) underneath the wares caused by the wads of clay upon which they were rested during firing. Wares of this kind are referred to frequently as belonging to the "Patch" family. Figures become more sophisticated and static, rather larger in size, and tend to over-elaboration.

Useful wares were sometimes decorated with blue-and-white Chinese landscapes upon plates with lattice borders with floral intersections. Other Chinese decorations were in crimson and gold over underglaze blue. Transfer-printing was rarely used.

More importance seems to have been attached to useful wares in the Chelsea-Derby period. A creamy bone paste was used, set off by vigorous shapes, neo-classic in form, and decorations of aristocratic severity, of urns and swags.

Figure groups took on a note of sentiment and tended to fussiness in the leafy backgrounds. The dominant influence was Sèvres. Biscuit-porcelain figures simulating marble statuary are typical of the neo-classic style about 1780.

Ground colours used at Derby did not achieve the beauty of those of Chelsea, but ambitious painting was done by the notable decorators.

Figure painting was done on straight-sided coffee cans intended for display rather than for use. Zachariah Boreman and "Jockey" Hill executed landscapes in a style carried forward into the early 19th cent. by George Robertson and Jesse Mountford, and the two drawing masters, the brothers Brewer.

Showy "Japans" became popular in the Bloor period with heavy colour and lavish gilding. The fruit and flower painting of the Steeles reached a high standard of accomplishment but lacked sensibility. Figures were reissued from earlier moulds.

Derbyshire chair or **Yorkshire chair:** a type of mid-17th cent. oak chair in which the panel back is varied by the use of sturdy hooped rails ornamented with carving or by an arcaded open back.

Derbyshire desks: term for oak writing-boxes, carved and sometimes dated.

Derbyshire pottery: extensive manufactures of pottery and porcelain have flourished in Derbyshire including slipwares at Bolsover and Tickenhall; brown salt-glazed stonewares at Chesterfield, Brampton, Denby, Codnor Park and Belper; cream-colour of Staffordshire type at Cockpit Hill; and porcelain at Derby.

Deruta maiolica: tin-glazed earthenware made at Deruta, near Perugia. Deruta lustred wares of the 16th cent. achieved fame, often employing a pale brassy yellow combined with blue.

Dessert basket: dessert baskets, usually of silver gilt, were introduced in the late 18th cent. and made in sets of various sizes and numbers, the larger often with separate plinths. Usually pierced, they are oval or circular in form.

Deuddarn: a two-tiered cupboard, being a Welsh variety of the press cupboard.

Deutsche blumen: (*Ger.*), see German flowers.

Devonia lace: Honiton (q.v.) product of the 1870s, with flower petals raised in relief by tension on the threads.

Devonshire pottery: several important slipware potteries existed in North Devon working from the early 17th cent. until the end of the Victorian era, notably at Barnstable and Bideford.

Crude pottery made at Honiton gave place in the 20th cent. to "art" pottery. At Bovey, pottery of Staffordshire type was, and is made extensively. Important terra cotta works flourished at Watcombe near Torquay in the second half of the 19th cent.

Diagonal barometer: a type in which the recording part of the tube is at an obtuse angle with the lower upright part, so that the possible variation of the mercury height may be spread over the inclined length of the tube, thus extending the reading scale.

Diamond cutting: glass vessels decorated with cutting in low relief were made in England in the mid-18th cent., a pattern of facets forming diamond shapes being popular. Later in the cent., deep grooves giving high convex raised diamonds were employed, particularly on Irish glass. (See also Hobnail cutting.)

Diamond moulding: see Rib or diamond moulding.

Diamond ornament: the diamond or lozenge motif is frequently found carved on 17th cent. furniture, on the backs of settles, the doors of press cupboards (q.v.) the panels of chests, etc. Much formal ornament was carved on furniture of this period and the diamond motif was particularly suitable, on account of its shape, for the decoration of upright panels.

Diamond-point engraving: engraved designs on glass vessels scratched with the point of a diamond. The technique is of ancient origin and was much practised in Europe from the 16th to the 18th cent., often by independent decorators outside the glasshouses, including amateurs.

Didrachm: Roman silver coin copying the standard and style of Greek silver coins. The earliest Roman silver coins, with their parts and occasional token bronzes, were issued from 269 to 187 B.C.

Die: the metal punch in which the design for a coin or medal is engraved in intaglio. From the die, placed on a piece of metal and struck, a coin is produced.

Dieppe lace: pillow lace suggesting simplified Valenciennes lace (q.v.). (See Antwerp lace, Ave Maria lace).

Dinanderie: small brassware made in or around the Flemish town of Dinant, near Liége. Whereas elsewhere bronze was mostly employed for the manufacture of domestic vessels, the presence of zinc deposits around Liége led the founders of the valley of the Meuse to adopt brass in preference. The town of Dinant became by the late Middle Ages so famous for its brassware that the name Dinanderie was used to describe the production of the whole region. Typical articles made were aquamaniles, basins, jugs, cooking vessels and candlesticks, many of them quite simple objects for domestic purposes. Amongst the more splendid achievements of the Mosan craftsmen may be mentioned lecterns and fonts. In 1466 the town of Dinant was sacked by Philippe le Bon, and as a result the brass-founders emigrated, partly to other towns in the valley of the Meuse but partly to France and England

Dinar: Islamic gold coin. The earliest dinars in later 7th cent. were imitations of Byzantine solidi. From the beginning of 8th cent. the dinar has Arabic inscription types on both sides giving mint, date and religious formulae. Later, ruler's name was added.

Dinara: gold coin of the Kushan kings in North West India and later in 4th and 5th cent. of the Gupta kings in India. Types, commonly standing figure of the king and reverse, a seated god with inscriptions in Sanscrit.

"Dipped" pottery: this class of wares seems to have been first made in Fenton by Thomas Heath from about 1750. In the 19th cent. its manufacture was widespread within and outside the Staffordshire Potteries. William Evans (writing in 1846) described three subdivisions of "dipped" pottery: (1) marbled slipware, (2) "Mocha" and (3) banded wares.

Diptych: a picture on two leaves opening in the manner o a screen.

Dir. or **Direx.:** short for direxit or direxerunt, and means engraved under the supervision of. Occasionally to be seen on bird prints.

Directoire style: style current in France in the last years of the 18th cent., strictly speaking under the Directoire from 1795-99.

Dirhem: Islamic silver coins with types generally similar to those of a dinar.

Discharge printing: a "dyed" style of printing textiles, first used c. 1806, in which the fabric is first dyed a solid colour and then the design is printed as a chemical which bleaches out or discharges the colour, producing a white design on a dyed ground.

Dish: term used for plates upward of twelve inches.

Dish cross: a silver or plated spirit-lamp stand with two adjustable arms revolving around the lamp with sliding feet. The lamp sometimes omitted and replaced by a pierced plate for use with separate lamp below. Found from about 1750-80.

Dish ring: also called "potato ring". Of Irish origin. Circular silver dish or bowl stand with straight or incurved sides usually pierced and chased with pastoral or classical motifs. Found from about 1740 onwards, many dating from about 1770.

Dish strainer: see Mazarine.

Dish-top table: table with the surrounding rim slightly curved up. Rectangular tables on four legs and pedestal tables of the mid-18th cent. are found with dish tops.

Djoshagan rugs: Persian rugs generally of palmette or vase desig- s. They are simpler than those of Ispahan or Tabriz (see also Ispahan and Tabriz carpets), with blue or deep red predominating. (Knot: Ghiordes, q.v.)

"DK" mark: see Derby porcelain.

Doccia porcelain: soft-paste porcelain was made at a factory founded by the Marquis Carlo Ginori in 1735 and towards the end of the cent., a hardpaste body was introduced. The factory specialised in reproducing the work of other factories and especially of Capo-di-Monte (q.v.), while maiolica was also copied. The mark of a star in blue, red, gold and impressed was used in the late 18th cent. and is very similar to the Nove (q.v.) mark.

"Doctor Syntax": fine underglaze blue transfer-prints representing the adventures of Doctor Syntax, used as decorations on tableware by James and Ralph Clews, Cobridge, c. 1821. Pottery figures were also popular. *The Tours of Dr Syntax in Search of the Picturesque* by Dr Combe, with illustrations by Thomas Rowlandson, published 1815-21, was a satire upon the writings of the Rev. William Gilpin.

Dole cupboard: the term strictly applies to hanging or other structures open-shelved, or doored and railed, used in the charitable dispensation of

bread, etc. in churches and other institutions in the 16th and 17th cent.

Dollar: large silver coin of U.S.A. issued from 1785. Name probably derived from thaler. Types, the head of Liberty and American eagle.

Dolphin foot: motifs employing the dolphin's head and scaly body were used decoratively on furniture, and appear to have been adopted from France. Sometimes the dolphin's head forms the foot of a chair or stool leg on mid-18th cent. furniture.

Domed foot: foot of a vessel of glass, silver, etc. rising in the form of a dome to support the stem.

Donaldson, John: (1737–1801), enameller and miniaturist, John Donaldson was born in Edinburgh, and from an early age showed ability as a portratist. When he came to London he became a member of the Incorporated Society of Artists and executed a considerable number of commissions as a miniaturist. In 1760 he was living in London. He became one of the most notable outside porcelain decorators, executing some work for Sprimont at Chelsea, and some extremely fine classical pictures on Worcester porcelain about 1770.

Donegal carpets: Alexander Morton organized the weaving of coarse knotted carpets in Donegal at the request of the Congested Districts Board in 1898. Pile carpets are still woven there.

Don Pottery: John Green, manager of Swinton Old Pottery, started this factory c. 1790, which was probably rebuilt in 1800–01. In 1807 the firm was known as Greens, Clark & Co., and in 1822 as John William Green & Co. It remained with the Greens until the late 1830s when Samuel Barker of Mexborough took over. It traded from 1852 and 1893 when it was finally closed as Samuel Barker and Son. Good quality white and cream-coloured earthenware, green glazed wares, and much painted and transfer-printed pottery, as well as Egyptian black and other stonewares was manufactured. About 1812 some china of good quality is said to have been made.

An engraved pattern book similar to that of Leeds was issued.

Painted   Impressed

Transfer-printed

Door furniture: finger plates, key escutcheons and door handles. The importance attached to harmony of design in the second half of the 18th cent. resulted in attention being paid not only to the decoration and furnishing of rooms, in order that the whole should present a harmonious appearance, but also to the door furniture. Robert Adam (q.v.) designed key escutcheons and door handles for execution in ormolu (q.v.), while door furniture of pottery was made in the 18th cent. by Wedgwood (q.v.) and others. In mid-Victorian times the manufacture of door furniture became a specialist branch of the pottery industry.

Doreurs, Corporation des: (*Fr.*), the craft guild in France responsible for gilding in all its forms. The organization was similar to that of the *menuisiers-ébénistes* (q.v.).

Dos-à-dos: a style of book-binding used mostly for small devotional works in the 16th and 17th cent. in which two volumes are bound back-to-back with a common lower board.

Double-action harp: see Harp.

Double barometer: a type in which the mercury column is divided into approximately two equal halves fixed vertically side by side and connected

by a tube filled with a lighter fluid substance such as oil or air.

Double bob clock pendulum: a spring-suspended type of pendulum appearing towards the latter part of the 18th cent., in which the rod carries two lenticular-shaped bobs.

Double chest: see Tallboy.

Double-headed court cards : playing cards of this type were first used in 1867.

Double rope twist: see Twist turning.

Double-scroll handle: a sinuous line of S-shape, or composed of reverse curves, employed especially in design of handles.

Doublet: a counterfeit gem of which the back consists of glass or paste, covered with a thin layer of gemstone.

Doubloon: more properly dublone, Spanish gold coin of two escudos (q.v.). Introduced in later Middle Ages but struck in quantity from gold of the New World. Types, Spanish arms with value and arms of Leon and Castille. Multiples of four and eight escudos.

Doublure: a book-binder's term, meaning that the paste-down (or inside lining of the covers) is not of paper but of leather, usually decorated.

Doulton porcelain: John Doulton (1793–1873), was a skilled potter who served his time at the Fulham factory. In 1815 with John Watts he acquired an interest in a potworks in Vauxhall Walk, Lambeth, where they made bottles, mugs and jugs in salt-glazed stoneware with relief decorations of topers, windmills, hunting scenes, etc. The firm was known as Doulton & Watts and its business prospered. In 1820 the partners became owners of the factory and in 1826 moved to more spacious premises in Lambeth High Street.

Between 1820 and 1860 new factories were built to answer the requirements of the chemical industry; the demand for salt-glazed drain-pipes which resulted from agitation for healthier living and sanitation; and the demand for insulators, stoneware filters and terra cotta statuary and vases. The Reform Flasks, with demi-effigies of prominent politicians were a popular feature following the Reform Bill of 1832.

John Watts retired from the business in 1854 and the firm became known henceforth as Doulton & Co.

In 1877 the earthenware factory of Pinder, Bourne & Co., Burslem, was acquired for the production of good class domestic pottery, and in 1884 a new wing was added to it for the manufacture of bone china. This factory soon acquired a reputation and made distinctive contributions in the field of ceramic painting and decorative pottery and porcelain.

The subsequent history of Doultons is one of constant development; of the acquisition of fresh factories for special purposes; of plant renewal and factory rebuilding; and finally of reorganisation and regrouping in face of contemporary economic problems. Marks:

Before 1836

Outside the products of chemical, sanitary and other social science industries and the excellent table wares which they make, the important products of Doultons include:
(1) Lambeth: Relief decorated stoneware – toby jugs, bottles, character pieces (Nelson etc.) in style with other contemporary stoneware manufactures of 1810–35, but rather more ambitious in character. These derive from the Fulham tradition. Salt-glazed stonewares with incised decorations by

individual artists and craftsmen who were allowed to sign their pieces, c. 1870 onwards. The Barlow sisters did admirable free sketches on pots of animals and foliage. Painted naturalistic decoration was also popular.

Other types of salt-glazed stonewares, overloaded with carved decoration or ornamental excrescences in blue, purple or grey Rhenish styles. Also figures modelled in naturalistic style by Tinworth, Marshall, Broad etc., ranging from miniatures a few inches in height to monumental statures, altarpieces etc.
(2) Burslem: ordinary type China painting in a free, vignetted, naturalistic style.

Strong colour glaze effects were also used – rouge flambé, sang de boeuf, "Sung" and "veined Sung". The Doulton naturalistic figure, toby jug and character jug were also made at Burslem.

Douters: scissor-like implements with flat, elliptical "blades" for extinguishing candles. Not to be confused with snuffers, which have a cutting edge. Douters are comparatively rare and not always recognized as such (see Snuffers).

Dovetail hinge: a butterfly hinge, the leaves of which resemble two dovetails joined at the narrow part.

Dovetailing: a technique of the cabinet-maker involving a means of interlocking angles on carcases and drawers. The earliest method to be employed was the common or through dovetail. This was strong but had the disadvantage of showing the end grain on both sides of the angle and was consequently not satisfactory for

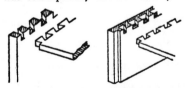

holding a veneer (q.v.). Shortly before 1700 this method was replaced by the lap or stop dovetail which had the end grain on one side only, leaving the front quite clear for veneering.

Dowel: headless pin used in construction. Though, architecturally, dowels may be of other materials, wood is understood when speaking of furniture. Trenail (i.e. treenail) is another term for a wooden dowel.

Down-hearth: a slab of stone or metal raised slightly above the level of the floor of the room, forming the earliest and most simple type of fireplace. The first versions were centrally placed in a room, and smoke rose to escape through a louvre in the roof. The down-hearth built in one side of the room with a flue communicating with the outside has remained in use in cottages to this day.

Dowry chest or **dower chest:** romantic term for any chest reserved for the trousseau and household linen of a bride-to-be.

Drachm: (1) small Greek silver coin struck by many cities and states. The didrachm, the double, is the commoner. Multiple of four, the tetradrachm, was the standard large silver coin, while the ten piece, the decadrachm, was issued only occasionally.

(2) silver coin of the Parthian and Sassanian kings. Parthian types, bust of king with, reverse, seated figure and inscription in Greek. Sassanian types, bust of king with head-dress and, reverse, fire-altar.

Drake foot: see Duck foot.

Dram cup: a small two-handled shallow bowl, similar to a wine taster, (q.v.), seldom made after the second decade of the 18th cent.

Dram glasses: known also as nips, joeys, ginettes, and gin-glasses;

(a) 17th cent.: small tumbler with four tiny feet; (b) 1675–1750: cup-shaped bowl with short, heavy knop or moulded baluster; (c) 1690–1710: straight-sided bowl of thick section on flattened spherical knop; (d) 1710–50: short, plain stem on foot attached directly to bowl; (e) 1720–1850: short, drawn-stemmed, trumpet-bowled: some early examples have folded feet.

Draughts or **Checkers:** the board is the same as for chess with sixty-four squares and each player with twelve men in contrasting colours. The earliest English description of the game dates from 1566, but not until the early 1800s did the game become standardized as played today. Polish draughts was popular in the 18th cent., the board having a hundred squares and each player twenty men.

Drawer-handle tool: an ornament in the shape of an Ionic capital, first used on book-binding tools in the second half of the 17th cent.

Drawing-room scrapbook: see Annuals.

Drawn stem: a type of stem found on glass drinking vessels from the late 17th cent. It consists of a plain knopped or baluster stem drawn directly from a gathering of metal at the base of the bowl.

Drawn work embroidery: forerunner of real lace. Made from linen with some threads drawn out and the remainder grouped and whipped over to form geometrical patterns.

Draw table (drawing table): a type of table with extensions at either end in the form of leaves which could be drawn out when needed to increase the length of the table. This type of table, supported on turned legs with stretchers, was in general use by the late 16th cent. and was made throughout the Stuart period. Most extant examples are of oak, but they were also made of walnut, ash or elm.

Dredger: small, cylindrical pepper-pot with side scroll handle of early 18th cent. date. Also called "kitchen pepper".

Dresden "lace": drawn work (q.v.) on muslin.

Dresden porcelain: see Meissen porcelain.

Dressing-box: a toilet box, fitted with a looking-glass in the lid and compartments for toilet requisites. Small boxes of this type were known in the Elizabethan age, but more elaborate in form were those made with marquetry decoration, probably en suite with a marquetry dressing table, in the late 17th cent.

Dressing glass: see Toilet mirror.

Drop handle: the characteristic handle used on furniture with drawers from about 1690 to 1720. Of brass, solid or hollow, this pendant handle hangs from a brass plate and is attached to the drawer by wire pins. Sometimes known as tear drop or pear drop on account of its shape.

Drop-in seat: a type of upholstered chair seat supported on the seat frame but which can be independently removed. First introduced about 1710.

Drop knop: knop or protuberance on the stem of a drinking glass resembling in shape the frustium of an inverted cone. Usually placed half an inch to an inch above the foot.

Drop-leaf table: a table with one or two hinged leaves which can be raised or dropped by bringing swinging legs or supports into use. Many kinds of drop-leaf tables have special names, such as gate-leg, Pembroke, etc.

Drug jar: pot or jar intended for use on apothecaries' shelves. English 17th cent. examples are of tin-enamelled earthenware, early vessels being squat and cylindrical in shape, either plain or painted with simple designs or stripes in blue or manganese. Later 17th cent. jars are taller and sometimes bear the name of the drug within a cartouche (q.v.). Polychrome designs of sprigs and foliage appear on 18th cent. jars.

Drum: body of a flagon, tankard, etc.

Drum table: see Capstan table.

"Drunken Parson" toby jug: a variety of toby jug (q.v.) representing a parson with his hat askew, his beer mug upturned in his hand and a drunken expression on his face.

Dry-point engraving: a process of engraving on a metal plate with a solid rod of steel shaped like a pencil which is drawn (not pushed like the burin) across the plate and throws up a rich burr. This burr is allowed to remain on the plate, holds the ink and imparts a velvety tone to the print but is soon worn down. Only the first fifty impressions, or even fewer, show the full effect. The first prints scratched in a manner similar to that of dry-point were made by the anonymous German *Master of the Amsterdam Cabinet* in about 1480. Dürer engraved three outstanding dry-point plates, and in Italy Andrea Meldolla (Schiavone) (d. 1582) used dry-point in conjunction with etching. The process was brought to a high pitch of perfection by Rembrandt, who occasionally produced pure dry-points but more often used the dry-point pencil to finish his etchings. In the late 18th cent. dry point was revived in England by Thomas Worlidge (1700–66) and Benjamin Wilson (1721–88): and in the early 19th cent. by David Wilkie (1785–1841), Edward Thomas Daniell (1804–42) and many others. It has been extensively used by modern etchers.

Dubois, Jacques and **Réné:** French cabinet-makers. Jacques Dubois was born in Paris c. 1693, became a *maître-ébéniste* (see *Menuisiers-Ebénistes, Corporation des*) in 1742, and was elected a *juré* (see Stamps on French furniture) of the guild in 1762. He specialized in the use of lacquer both Oriental and European, and died in 1763, the same year as Oeben (q.v.), whose stock he helped to value. He used the stamp:

IDUBOIS

After his death his widow carried on the business with the help of her sons, the most celebrated of whom was

Réné (b. 1757), who always used his father's stamp. He became a *maître* in 1754, was much patronized by Marie Antoinette, both before and after she became Queen, and also by the Court and nobility. He worked mainly in the Louis XVI style and eventually abandoned cabinet-making for selling furniture. He died in 1799.

Ducat: (1) the Medieval gold *zecchino* of Venice, struck from late 13th cent. with types of Christ in oval frame and kneeling Doge receiving standard from St Mark. Name derived from part of the Latin inscription. (2) Venetian gold coin continued from Middle Ages. Name applied to many other similar gold coins throughout Western Europe with varying types. One of the most important was that of the Netherlands with types, mailed figure and inscription reverse.

Duchesse: (*Fr.*), a type of chaise longue (q.v.) in which two bergère chairs face each other, connected by a stool in the middle. An example is illustrated by Hepplewhite in his *Cabinet Maker and Upholsterer's Guide.*

Duck egg porcelain: a much sought after variety of Swansea soft-paste porcelain showing a greenish trans-lucency made about 1816–17.

Duck foot: an American colloquial term for the three-toed club or Dutch foot, mostly found in Delaware River Valley furniture. Also called drake foot and web foot. For some reason the pad foot is often mistakenly called a duck foot.

Duesbury, William: (1725–86), independent porcelain decorator in London 1751–53 (his account book has been preserved and published). He obtained controlling interests in various porcelain factories in England: Derby 1756–86, possibly Longton Hall about 1760, Bow in 1763, and Chelsea 1770–84. His son, William Duesbury II (1763–96/7) owned the Derby factory from 1786 until his death.

Dumb waiter: a dining-room stand. An English invention of the early 18th cent., with normally three circular trays, increasing in size towards the bottom, supported on a shaft with a tripod base. This established design gave way to more elaborate versions at the end of the cent.; four-legged supports and rectangular trays are found and other quite different kinds consisted of square or circular tables with special compartments for bottles, plates, etc. In America a special type, known as the "Lazy Susan", was used for condiments on early 19th cent. dining tables.

Du Paquier porcelain: see Vienna porcelain.

Duplex escapement: a type of escapement (q.v.) of which the in-vention is usually attributed to Pierre LeRoy of Paris, about 1750. The escape wheel has two sets of teeth, one long and pointed, the other short and triangular and rising from the plane of the escape wheel. The long teeth escape through a small notch in the balance staff, which also carries a long arm by which the impulse is given through the short triangular teeth.

Dupondius: Roman coin; two *as* piece in aes (q.v.). In the Empire it was in size and types similar to the *as* (q.v.) but was distinguished from it by the radiate crown worn by the emperor.

Du Paquier, Claudius Innocentius: (d. 1751), founder of the Vienna porcelain factory. He appears to have been conducting experiments in Vienna as early as 1716, and was granted a monopoly in 1718. Success-ful production at the factory does not seem to have begun until 1719, after the arrival of Samuel Stölzel who had been kiln-master at the Meissen factory (q.v.). Du Paquier suffered from recurring financial difficulties and relinquished his factory to the State in 1744. He remained at the factory as manager and died in 1751. (See also Vienna porcelain.)

Dust board: a wooden partition between the drawers on a chest of drawers. This refinement in con-struction was introduced by the cabinet-maker and is not found in pieces made by the joiner in pre-Restoration times. It was a protection against dust and theft. In 18th cent. furniture, the dust board is usually made of deal with a rail of oak or mahogany in front.

Dutch lace: pillow lace made from the 1660s tightly woven and solid looking, often with closely grouped scrolls suggesting heavy flower heads. The grounds included the *cinq trous* (q.v.). Huguenot refugees brought to Dutch lace something of the old Valenciennes (q.v.) style.

Dutch metal: alloy of copper and zinc used in place of gold-leaf in decoration.

Dutch-oven: an open-fronted oven, usually raised on legs, placed before the fire and used for cooking. Dutch-ovens were made of sheet-iron, brass and even of pottery.

Dutch striking clock: one which strikes the repetition of the hour at the half-hour on a different toned bell.

Duty stamps on playing cards: this was levied in August 1712, and from that date until 1862 it was compulsory for every ace of spades to bear a duty mark indicating payment of tax. The changes in the reigning monarchs and in the amount of the tax are shown in a chronological series of aces, making it an accurate guide in the dating of packs:

1712–14: duty 6d. A red stamp with the monogram A.R. (for Queen Anne) crowned.

1714–65: duty 6d until 1756, then 1s. A red stamp as before, but with the letters G.R. (for all three Georges). The red ink used for the stamp has usually faded and is sometimes scarcely visible.

1765–76: duty 1s, half of this being levied by a stamp on the pack's wrapper. The monarch was signified by the letters G. III Rex, and the design on the card consisted of a Garter surrounding the ace of spades, wreaths at the sides, surmounted by a crown, and with DIEU ET MON DROIT on a ribbon below.

1776–89: duty raised to 1s 6d, the previous stamp surmounted by the words SIXPENCE ADD[L] DUTY.

1789–1801: duty raised again, to 2s. This time SIXPFNCE was printed to the left and ADD[L] DUTY to the right.

1801–15: duty 2s 6d. There were now three indications of sixpenny increases, the third – ADD[L] DUTY SIXPENCE – appearing below the design.

C. 1815: duty continued to be half a crown, but the wording was changed on the stamp to DUTY at the top, ONE SHILLING to the left AND SIXPENCE to the right. The other shilling was made up by two embossed sixpenny stamps on the wrapper.

1820–28: duty half a crown, with the stamps as before, but the monarch was changed to G. IIII.

1828–62: duty down to 1s, with a new design of ace, so intricate that it was known as Old Frizzle, surmounted by the words DUTY ONE SHILLING. This ace contained the royal heraldic quarterings and was supported by a lion and unicorn.

1862: duty down to 3d, levied on the wrapper. There was thus no duty ace, but card manufacturers continued to produce elaborate aces of spades, and some late-19th-cent. and early-20th-cent. aces carry the words DUTY THREE PENCE WHEN USED IN GREAT BRITAIN AND IRELAND.

Duty stamp on wall paper: by an Act of Queen Anne (1712) every square yard of wall paper "printed painted or stained" was subject to a tax of 1d, increased two years later to 1½d; the excise officer had to stamp the paper with the appropriate stamp and attended the factories regularly for this purpose. The duty was repealed in 1836.

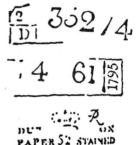

"DV" mark: see Mennecy porcelain.

Dwight, John: (1633–1703), son of an Oxford gentleman of the same name; educated at Oxford and described variously as B.C.L. and M.A. of Christ Church College, 29 June, 1661.

Dwight commenced experiments in the art of pottery (possibly in Lancashire) using local clays found in the Kennel pits at Haigh near Wigan. His first patent for making "transparent earthenware commonly called porcellane or china" was granted for 14 years from April 1671, in which year he probably moved to Fulham. In 1676 he was in partnership in a "Pottworks" at Fulham, with Windsor Sandys of St Martin's-in-the-Fields, and agreed to supply the Glass Sellers Company with bottles. Sandys' name is omitted from the subsequent agreement of 1677. In 1684 he took out a further patent which was the subject of lawsuits in 1693 and 1697 for infringement by potters in London, Southampton, Nottingham and Staffordshire. (See also Fulham stoneware.)

Eagle, American: the Seal of the United States, adopted in 1786, represents the American bald eagle with wings outspread. This emblem quickly became popular as a furniture ornament – carved (free or engaged), inlaid or painted – replacing the fanciful phoenix which had been used since the mid-18th cent.

Ear-dagger: a dagger with a pommel formed by two flattened discs set at an angle and resembling ears. This type of dagger is of Eastern origin and when found in Europe, is usually Venetian or Hispano-Moresque.

Easter egg: see under Fabergé, Peter Carl.

East India Company china: Chinese porcelain imported into Europe by European trading companies such as the East India Company or the French *Compagnie des Indes*.

Ébéniste: the ordinary French term for a cabinet-maker concerned in making veneered furniture as distinct from a *menuisier* (q.v.). The word derives from the ebony (*ébène*) to be found on the earliest veneered furniture in France.

Ebonize: the staining of wood, such as pear wood or, in America, maple, to look like ebony. Much practised in the late 17th cent.

Echinus moulding: a moulding of quarter round section.

Ecuelle: a French form of shallow, circular soup-bowl and cover occasionally also found in English silver. It has flat handles at the sides and a circular dish stand. Late 17th to mid-18th cent.

Edkins, Michael: Michael Edkins was a painter of pottery and of white and coloured glass. He received the freedom of the city of Bristol on 21 February, 1756, but prior to that time is said to have served an apprenticeship in Birmingham. In 1755 he married Elizabeth, daughter of William James, a glass-maker, and it is not unexpected that he should have turned his hand to decorating that ware. He would seem to have started to paint glass soon after 1760, and to have continued at least until 1787.

Edkin's business ledger, now in the Bristol Museum, records that he was employed by the following firms, no doubt in the capacity of a "free-lance" worker:

1763–67 Little and Longman
1767–87 Longman and Vigor, and successors
1765 William Dunbar and Co.
1775–87 Vigor and Stephens
1785–87 Lazarus Jacobs

Michael Edkins was said by his son, William Edkins, senior, to have been "a very good musician and charming counter-tenor singer", and to have performed on the stage both in Bristol and in London. He had a family of thirty-three children, and died about the year 1813. His grandson, also named William, formed a fine collection of pottery and porcelain, which was sold by auction in London in 1874.

The glass decorated by Michael Edkins is unsigned, and much that is claimed as his is the subject of dispute. W. A. Thorpe wrote (*English Glass*, 1949, page 206) that "Edkins is known for his characteristic perched birds and his intense curly flower-bunches".

Egg and dart ornament: a border ornament composed of alternating ovolos (q.v.) and arrowheads. Of Classical origin, this motif was used by furniture makers, goldsmiths, etc. from the late 16th cent. onwards.

Egg and tongue ornament: repeat ornament of alternated ovolo and tongue-like motifs; as much other ornament of classical origin, it was first adopted in England during the Renaissance and was used by architects and craftsmen in the 17th and 18th cent.

Egg, Durs: the first of a family of gunmakers of Swiss extraction, working in London in the late 18th and first half of the 19th cent. He was a noted maker of high quality flint lock duelling pistols and received the Royal Warrant of the Prince Regent, later George IV.

His productions are highly efficient but devoid of ornament.

Egg shell porcelain: porcelain of extreme thinness, first made in China (hard-paste). Thin bodied white bowls of Yung ho (1403–24), with faint incised or slip-painted designs, were copied in the K'ang Hsi (q.v.) period. (See under *famille rose*.) Some modern Japanese porcelains are egg-shell thin. Some English factories in the 19th cent., such as Mintons, Belleek (qq.v.) and others, emulated this Chinese porcelain and produced wares of extreme thinness, finished on the lathe.

Egyptian black: the popular name in Staffordshire for the "dry" black stoneware named by Josiah Wedgwood "basaltes". Also called black Egyptian. (See Basaltes.)

Elbow chair: see Corner chair.

Electro-plate: base metal, usually copper, coated with silver by electrolysis. This process was first used for commercial production by George Richards Elkington and his cousin Henry Elkington of Birmingham, who took out a patent in 1840.

Elers, David (1656–1742), **Elers, John Philip** (1664–1738): the brothers, both potters, are stated to have come to England in 1688 in the wake of William III but there is contemporary evidence that David Elers was already in London in 1686.

David Elers was born in Amsterdam. He is stated to have been a good chemist and widely travelled. Coming to London with his brother he commenced making pottery at Fulham about 1690, and in 1693 he was cited, with others, for an infringement of John Dwight's (q.v.) patent. He appears to have worked a potworks at Vauxhall in Surrey from 1693 until 1700 and kept a shop in the Poultry, London. In 1700 the two Elers became bankrupt. David Elers subsequently continued as a merchant.

John Philip Elers is rather more fully documented. With his brother he was associated in the manufacture of "brown muggs and theapotts" in England from about 1690, and was cited by Dwight for an infringement of his patent and for enticing from his service a workman named John Chandler. The brothers then opened the factory at Vauxhall, Surrey. This factory was in operation until the Elers' bankruptcy in 1700. Many red teapots were made there.

About 1693 one or both of the Elers came to North Staffordshire and started to make red teapots. It is unlikely in view of the continuity of the London factory that both brothers would venture north, and as David Elers is known to have kept a shop in the Poultry it seems likely that it was John Philip Elers who started up in Staffordshire, probably in their joint names. It was at Bradwell Wood that Elers made "Red China". Simeon Shaw mentioned two sites, Bradwell Hall and Dimsdale Hall, which were connected by a speaking tube said to have been used to give warning of approaching people. This Staffordshire venture lasted five years. About this time or shortly after, the factory closed down and David and Philip Elers became bankrupt.

There is no evidence that the Elers made salt-glazed stoneware other than "brown muggs" or that they introduced the salt-glazing technique into Staffordshire. They were justly famous for red stonewares which vary in colour from a rich red-brown to vermilion, are close in texture, and are thinly potted and fine in workmanship. The precision finish of the Elers products was a portent of industrial standards set up by Josiah Wedgwood sixty years later. The Elers decorations comprised beautifully spaced plum blossom springs in relief; countersunk relief chinoiseries, and moulds of merry-andrews and wyverns.
Marks:

None of Elers' ware was marked in an identifiable manner. Imitation Chinese marks were stamped underneath their products, but the square stamps enclosing English initials written pseudo-Chinese fashion occur only on later Elers-type red pottery, some probably by Greatbach for Wedgwood (who produced a jasper cameo medallion of J. P. Elers.)

Elizabethan: term of convenience, strictly applicable to objects, made in the reign of Elizabeth I (1558–1603) though loosely used of pieces of later date displaying Elizabethan characteristics.

Ell: the ell (*Fr. aune*) is the measure used for tapestry. The English ell is 45 inches, the Flemish 27 inches, the French 46¾ inches. Thus 12 Flemish ells are approximately 7 French, or a square French ell equals 3 square Flemish ells.

Ellicott clock pendulum: a type of pendulum invented in 1752, utilizing the principle of the difference in the expansion between steel and brass. The heavy bob is carried on two angular hinged supports. As the length of the pendulum rod changes with the temperature, the vertical arms of the support are raised or depressed, giving a complementary movement to the horizontal arms carrying the heavy bob. Very expensive to make and not materially better than the gridiron, hence not extensively used.

Ellicott, John: London clockmaker of eminence and fellow of the Royal Society. The inventor of the Ellicott pendulum which worked on the principle of the greater expansion of brass over steel. (See also Ellicott clock pendulum). Active between 1731–72.

Email ombrant: an illusionist style of decoration on pottery, like lithophane, but the intaglio decoration was filled with coloured glaze (usually green) which produced a monochrome picture in a variety of tones.

Embossed wallpapers: known in the 18th cent. as "Stamp'd" or "Embost" wallpapers. Description given to an after process involving the use of block or roller under pressure which gives to the paper an embossed finish resembling leather, textiles or plaster. Embossing was practised at an early date although it is not known when it was first introduced (see "Stucco" wallpapers).

Embossing: a general term to describe reliefwork on metal. Strictly applicable only to hammered work (repoussé) but extended to cover any technical method resulting in relief.

Embroidered pictures: a great variety of embroidered pictures is found in England from the mid-17th cent. onwards. Pictorial compositions as part of the decoration of a cushion or valance are not uncommon earlier, but it was not until about 1640 that the fashion for working purely decorative pictures as an end in itself was evolved. Subjects from the Old Testament were most popular, also allegorical figures of the Virtues, Vices or the Senses, or a King and a Queen. Stump-work (q.v.) was the most popular medium for pictures during the second half of the 17th cent., but bead-work (q.v.) was also employed.

The pictures of the early 18th cent. are generally worked on canvas and pastoral or "chinoiserie" subjects are most common. During the second half of the 18th cent. subjects were mostly taken from popular paintings or engravings. The designs were either printed or drawn on the material. Portions of the background and the faces and hands of the figures were painted in water-colours and the rest of the design worked in coloured silks. Other pictures were worked in black silk, or even hair, in fine stitches, to simulate etchings. Simple landscape subjects or portraits of eminent people are most common.

Empire style: style current in France in the early 19th cent., during the period of the first Empire.

Enamel: a form of glass which, when heated, may be applied by fusion to a metallic surface. When colourless this is known as flux. Enamel may be translucent or opaque; opalescent enamel is the term most frequently used to describe the milky semi-transparency which is obtainable by a careful mixture of both.

PAINTED ENAMELS: Opaque enamel on a metal base, fired to achieve a smooth, glossy surface which was then decorated with the brush in variously coloured enamel pastes, each colour being fixed by a separate firing. In England, painted enamel was made at the Battersea factory (q.v.) and in South Staffordshire in the second half of the 18th and in the 19th cent. In the 19th cent. the Swiss perfected the technique of painting extremely highly-finished scenes and pictures in enamel on a prepared *fondant* ground. Very often a coating of counter-enamel is applied on the reverse side of the painted surface to counteract any stress which may be brought about in the firing.

EN PLEIN ENAMELLING: the enamelling most typical of the Louis XV and Louis XVI periods is known as *en plein*, which indicates that the colour has been applied directly on the body of the object and not on *plaquettes* introduced at a later stage. The gold ground or field is prepared by being carved into and engraved to form a sunken bed, sometimes on several levels, to receive the enamel, the top layer of which should be flush with the gold surrounding surface. This operation is also known as *basse-taille* or *sur fond reservé* enamelling.

CLOISONNÉ: one of the most ancient forms of enamelling involving the use of a network of raised metal enclosures, or *cloisons*, which is applied to the object chosen. The enamel is poured into these *cloisons*, the metal tops of which remain exposed, allowing the different colours in each one to be distinctly shown.

CHAMPLEVÉ ENAMELLING: grooves, often in very graceful linear designs, are carved in the metal which is to be treated, and these are filled with enamel, which is polished down so that the top surface is exactly level with the surrounding metal. This inlaid enamel is thus, as the name of this technique implies, a raised field.

PLIQUE À JOUR ENAMELLING: the name given to the vivid stained-glass effects obtained when an object consists of an unbacked honeycomb of cells, each filled with translucent enamel through which the light passes freely.

EN RONDE BOSSE ENAMELLING: the term applied to the opaque enamel, generally white, covering subjects carved in the round.

COTEAU ENAMELLING: a complicated process invented by Jean Coteau, the 18th cent. Geneva craftsman, for which he used different coloured *motifs*, including red and green *paillons* as well as the more conventional gold variety against *bleu de Roi* translucent backgrounds, giving a vivid effect of relief.

EN RÉSILLE SUR VERRE: a technique requiring great skill, practised in France for a very short period in the second quarter of the 17th cent. Miniature cases were enriched in this manner, whereby the design was cut or engraved on a medallion of blue or green glass, the hollows thus formed lined with thin gold and filled with powdered enamel, which would fuse at a low temperature.

Enamel colours: low-firing overglaze ceramic pigments derived from metallic oxides such as copper, manganese, iron or antimony used singly, or combined with an opaque white and lead, zinc or some special flux, were extensively used from the middle of the 18th cent. A fine pink, crimson or crimson-purple was obtained from gold.

Enamelled brassware: copper was used for preference rather than brass for enamelling in the Middle Ages, and apart from a few harness ornaments and the Garter stallplates preserved in St George's Chapel, Windsor Castle, medieval enamelled brass-ware does not exist. During the 17th cent. a cheap form of enamelling was introduced in England and on the Continent in which brass was used as a base. The enamel was of the *champlévé* type, but instead of the depressions for the enamel being cut out by hand they were cast in one with the object. Such a method was unsuited for the production of small or fine objects, but it was applied to quite a variety of brassware, including andirons, candlesticks, stirrups and horse harness, and sword hilts. English enamelled brassware of this type usually goes by the name of "Surrey" enamel, but there are no grounds for thinking that such articles were produced in the county of Surrey. Similar objects were made on the Continent; amongst the Continental items not made in England are small caskets and knife handles. The place of manufacture is not known, but it may have been in the Meuse region. (See also Enamel).

Enamelled glass: glass painted in fusible colours or enamels, being metallic oxides mixed with fluxes and painted on in an oily medium. The painted glass is then fired in a mufflekiln, the colours softening and adhering to the surface. The technique is of ancient origin and was rediscovered by Venetian craftsmen perhaps in the 15th cent. Much German glass of the late 16th and 17th cent. is decorated with vigorous enamelled painting and sometimes with unfired oil or lacquer colours. In England the practice was not adopted before the second half of the 18th cent. (See Beilby, William.)

En arbelette: (*Fr.*), an expression used for shapes and forms which have a double curve similar to that of a stone-bow.

Enarmes: the straps by which a shield was attached to the left arm of the wearer as a defensive weapon.

En camaieu: monochrome painting in several tones on porcelain or pottery.

Encaustic tiles: the word encaustic, meaning baked or burnt is frequently applied to medieval inlaid tiles and the imitations made in the 19th cent.; and in consequence identified not with the firing process but erroneously with the technique of manufacture. Wedgwood decorated some of his black basaltes with white and red "encaustic" enamels after the style of Greek vases, and in 1769 he took out a patent for "ornamenting earthen and porcelaine ware with an encaustic gold bronze, together with a peculiar species of encaustic painting in various colours in imitation of the antient Etruscan and Roman earthenware".

Enclosed overlay paperweight: see Overlay paperweight.

Encoignures: see Corner-cupboards.

Encrusted paperweights: see Sulphides.

End-boards: solid boards, often carved in profile, forming the supports of a Gothic stool or chest. Stools with the seat supported on two vertical end-boards were still made in the middle of the 16th cent. After this date, stools were constructed with joined frames consisting of frieze rail, legs and stretchers.

Endive marquetry: see Seaweed marquetry.

Endpapers: with rare exceptions, endpapers are not part of a book as printed. They are the double leaves added at front and back by the binder, the outer leaf of each being pasted to the inner surface of the cover (known as the paste-down), the inner leaves (or free endpapers) forming the first and last of the volume when bound or cased. Leather-bound and vellum-bound books of the 16th and 17th cent. sometimes had no end-papers. For leather and half-leather bindings marbled endpapers have been used since the late 17th cent. In more elaborate bindings they may be of silk or some other special material, when they are called linings. In really sumptuous bindings the paste-down may be replaced by a doublure (q.v.) of leather.

En esclavage: (*Fr.*), a type of necklace consisting of strands which start and finish together but separate in the centre.

Engine-turning: (1) decorative process involving the turning of an unfired pot in the leather-hard state, upon a specially designed lathe having an eccentric motion to produce geometrical, diced, fluted or similar patterns. Used from c. 1764–65, by Wedgwood and other later potters. (2) the application of similar designs by mechanical means – also on a lathe – to metal articles. Mainly used on gold or silver snuff boxes, étuis and watch-cases.

English plate: a term used by Sheffield platers (see also Sheffield plate), to distinguish ware in which the silver was plated on copper, from that plated on white alloy such as German silver (see Nickel silver).

English guitar: see Mandolines.

Engobe: a thin coating or layer of clay applied to pottery in the liquid form of slip.

Engraved silhouettes: books of printed silhouettes were popular in the 18th and 19th cent., and the collector should be cautious of any such portraits framed up to look like genuine cut or painted examples. The books themselves are well worth collecting. Some silhouettes of celebrities were, however, printed especially for framing.

Engraving: (1) an engraving is a print obtained by a process of incising lines into a metal plate with a burin or graver. (2) Engraving on a metal object, for example, on silverware, involves producing a flat line decoration incised on the surface with a cutting tool. It is the normal method of rendering inscriptions and armorials and has been used at all periods for every variety of ornament. Sometimes combined with flat chasing (q.v.). (See also Bright-cut engraving.)

En plein enamel: see Enamel.

En résille enamel: see Enamel.

En ronde bosse enamel: see Enamel.

Enseigne: see Hat badge.

En suite: (*Fr.*), to match.

Entasis: a slight bulge between base and lip of a flagon, tankard, etc.

Entrée dish: a covered dish of silver or plate, early examples usually circular or polygonal. Later chiefly of oblong form or occasionally oval. The covers may have detachable handles, enabling their use as separate dishes. Later examples have silver or plated heater stands *en suite*.

Epergne: a silver or porcelain table centrepiece of elaborate design incorporating numerous dishes for fruit or sweetmeats. Early examples also fitted with candle-branches, casters and other accessories. Rococo models festooned with floral, pierced and boat-shaped forms, Chinese pagodas, and Classical temples are all recognized examples (see also Centre-piece and Dessert basket).

Equation clock dial: a dial that records both Solar and Mean Time.

Equation kidney device: a kidney-shaped cam (q.v.), invented by Christiaan Huygens in 1695, which made possible the transformation of simple forward rotary motion on a clock into a backward or forward motion, varying daily, both in direction and amount, necessary to indicate the daily difference between Solar and Mean Time.

Erect thumbpiece: a tall, solid thumbpiece (q.v.) found on early 17th cent. pewter flagons. A lighter, curving form is found on certain Scottish measures, notably tappit hens (q.v.).

Errata: mistakes and misprints discovered after a book has been printed; also called *corrigenda*, and in some early books by the homely name of "faults escaped". If the errors are noticed before the preliminary leaves have been completed (these being customarily printed last), there is sometimes a spare page or part of a page to accommodate them. If not, they may be printed on a slip, or on an extra leaf, to be tipped in (q.v.) when the book is bound.

Esari rugs: Turkoman rugs in which the octagonal gule (see Turkoman rugs) is usually enclosed by bands forming a distinct diamond design.

Escapement: the means, or device, by which the power of a time-piece is allowed to escape, and is transmitted to the pendulum or balance. Hundreds of types have been invented, but only a very few are in general use. The anchor or recoil escapement (q.v.) and the dead beat (q.v.) are types used in the majority of pendulum clocks; the lever escapement, the cylinder, duplex and other types were used in watches. Great mechanical ingenuity has been shown by inventors in designing escapements. These technical features are of special importance in the study of watches.

Escape wheel: the final wheel of the time train of a clock or watch which gives impulse to the pendulum or balance. Often shortened to 'scape wheel.

Escritoire: see Scrutoire.

Escudo: Spanish gold coin originally with types of Spanish arms and cross; latterly from Charles III, royal portrait and Spanish arms. Multiples of two, four and eight.

Escutcheon: a shield with a coat of arms.

Espagnolette: (*Fr.*), a decorative motif popularized by the engravings of Gillot and Watteau, consisting of a female head surrounded by a large stiff lace collar of a type worn in Spain in the 17th cent. It was used frequently in the early 18th cent. as a mounted decoration for furniture.

Etagère: (*Fr.*), a small work-table consisting usually of shelves or trays set one above the other. The word is of 19th-cent. origin, the ordinary term used earlier being *table à ouvrage*.

Etched metalwork: the art of etching is believed to have originated in the process of ornamenting armour with acid etching first introduced in the second half of the 15th cent. In the 16th cent. small objects of iron, brass, copper, and even silver, were commonly decorated with etched ornament. This technique of ornament was particularly popular in Germany in the second half of the 16th cent., and was applied to a great variety of objects. In the case of small articles, such as cutlery, tools, watch-cases, locks and scientific instruments, panels of mauresque ornament were used, the larger surfaces available on caskets or clock-cases were decorated with figure subjects. The finest etched ornament is to be found on the various tools, instruments and articles of military equipment made for the Saxon Court. Whether these were produced in Dresden or obtained from Nürnberg or Augsburg, is uncertain. The etched ironwork of Nürnberg and Augsburg had an importance comparable with that of the damascened panels made in Milan. Etched ornament is also found on French and Italian locksmiths' work but it does not approach the quality achieved by the German craftsmen.

Etching: a print made by covering a metal plate of copper or steel with a wax coat, drawing the design with a needle, and "biting" the plate by immersion in a weak acid solution, generally nitric. When inked, the bitten lines hold the ink as the plate is wiped, and when an impression is taken the design is transferred, in reverse, to the paper. (See also Etched metalwork.)

Eternity ring: a ring in the form of a plain circle symbolising eternity, often set with a single row of stones.

Etruria: in 1766 Josiah Wedgwood (q.v.) purchased the Ridge House Estate and planned to build a new pottery, a house for himself, and a village for his workpeople. He appointed Joseph Pickford of Derby as his architect and the factory and Etruria Hall were completed by 1770. He gave the name Etruria to the village because he wished to revive the lost art of the Etruscans.

Etruscan style binding: a bookbinding in calf (c. 1780–1825) decorated by acid staining with classical decoration.

Étui: small case usually of tapering form fitted with scissors, bodkin, snuff-

spoon, etc., for ladies' use, made in a variety of materials, including gold, silver, pinchbeck, enamel, porcelain, etc.

European-style decoration: in the 18th cent. Chinese porcelains were enamelled to order with European heraldic emblems, and with many designs from European prints. K'ang Hsi blue-and-white and *famille verte* (q.v.) examples are uncommon, but subjects skilfully drawn in black or sepia, or with *famille rose* (q.v.) colouring, shortly became popular, and often show an amusing naïvety of interpretation. Large punch-bowls with ships, hunting scenes, etc., were favourites. Later wares exhibit the hybrid style of "mandarin china". There are some close copies of European porcelain; and Chinese porcelain was also decorated in Holland or England, sometimes in Oriental style. (See also Chinese export porcelain.)

Ewer: see Rosewater ewer and basin.

Ewery cupboard: a low oak cupboard upon which stood a ewer and basin for washing, the enclosed portion being used for towels and soap.

Exc. or **Excud.:** short for excudit or excuderunt. Means printed by or engraved and printed by. Sometimes seen on bird prints.

Exergue: the portion of a coin or medal below the ground line of the design. Often contains specific information, such as mint-mark or date.

Exeter carpets: Claude Passavant, a native of Basel, and successful wool merchant and manufacturer at Exeter, started the subsidiary enterprise of making expensive hand-knotted carpets. He bought up Parisot's equipment in 1755 (see under Fulham carpets) and took many of his men to Exeter. In 1758 he was a competitor for the Royal Society of Arts prize and gained an award. A beautifully made and excellently designed carpet by him in the Victoria and Albert Museum is marked "Exon 1757" and may be the prize-winning piece.

Another dated 1758 is at Petworth. Giuseppe Baretti, secretary of the Royal Academy, wrote a favourable account of his factory in 1760 and reported on his success; but his carpets, which were more expensive than Moorfields (q.v.) are extremely rare.

Ex-library: this term is used of a book which has at one time been in a lending library. For cloth books, whether library labels have been left in place, or whether, as often with books of any consequence, they have been removed, their presence or traces are regarded with lively disfavour by most experienced collectors.

Ex libris: a book plate pasted inside the front cover of a book, bearing the name of the owner.

Extended leaf: see Re-margined.

Extra-illustrated books: in 1769 James Granger published a *Biographical History of England* with blank leaves for the addition of portraits, etc., to the taste of the purchaser. Hence grangerizing, for the practice which he formalized and promoted. Grangerized, or extra-illustrated books as they are now more commonly called, are copies which have had added to them, either by a private owner or professionally, engraved portraits, prints, etc., usually cut out of other books, and sometimes also autograph letters, documents or drawings.

Fabergé: born in 1846, Peter Carl Fabergé, a Russian descended from a Huguenot family in Picardy, was a jeweller who brought about an extraordinary revolution in taste in the final decade of the cent. In brief, he declared that valuable materials were of little importance where the craftsmanship was wanting. He delighted in overcoming technical problems and revived the four-colour gold processes of the 18th cent. as well as the forgotten art of translucent enamelling on a prepared *guilloché* field. He often designed, and always scrutinized at every stage, each piece made by his five hundred or so highly-skilled craftsmen working in St Petersburg and Moscow. These pieces were of great variety and ranged from boxes, clocks and miniature frames to automatic toys and bell-pushes.

His work in every type of semi-precious stone remains unsurpassed, and his lively animal studies and miniature flowers, usually in rock crystal pots which are carved to appear as though they are half filled with water, are eagerly collected. Gold and silver cigarette-cases by Fabergé display a seemliness of style and a precision of hinging rarely attained before or since. Apart from his completely original work, he enjoyed designing *pastiches* of earlier manners.

Fabergé is perhaps most celebrated for his fantastic procession of Easter Eggs, each with its own concealed surprise, made annually for the Tzar, his greatest patron, to present to the Tzarina. The House of Fabergé had an elaborate but easily understood system of signing the objects it produced. The firm ceased operating with the Revolution, and in 1920 Carl Fabergé himself died an exile in Switzerland.

"Fable" painter: an unidentified Chelsea artist, working c. 1750-55, who decorated table wares with illustrations derived from the folio edition of *Aesop's Fables* (1687) by Francis Barlow. J. L. Dixon suggests there have been as many as three "Fable" painters of whom one was J. H. O'Neile (q.v.). Landscape subjects are attributed to this artist.

Fabric: a term used to describe the metal from which a coin is made, including the characteristic surface and appearance imparted by production.

Face-piece horse brass: a brass suspended on the forehead of the horse.

Facet: one of the small surfaces of a cut gemstone or of other ground material such as glass, steel, etc. which has been cut into a series of faces set at an angle to each other.

Facet-cut stem: stem of a drinking glass, usually drawn (q.v.), decorated with cutting in the form of diamond or hexagonal facets (q.v.). A type of decoration popular in the second half of the 18th cent.

Faceted steel: see Chiselled and cut steel.

Facs.: facsimile.

Faenza maiolica: tin-glazed earthenware made at Faenza in Italy from the later 15th cent., the early wares often decorated in sombre colours with foliage of pronounced Gothic character. A speciality of Faenza at this period were devotional figures imitating enamelled terra cotta. The Renaissance wares of the 16th cent. show a full range of colour, but towards the end of the cent. slighter painting and more subdued colouring reflects the interest in the cool blue and white Chinese porcelain which was reaching Europe in increased quantities.

Faience: a French word applied to tin-glazed earthenwares, usually of French, German, Italian or Scandinavian origin. Adopted in England in the 19th cent. to describe the larger units employed in architectural ceramics.

Faience fine: fine cream-coloured or white earthenware.

"Fair Hebe" jug: a jug in the form of a tree with spreading base modelled in relief with figures of seated girl to whom a youth is offering a nest full of eggs, above which (on a paper) are the words "FAIR HEBE" on one side; on the other a man holding a glass above which occur the words "A BUMPER". Sometimes signed "Voyez 1788".

A blue-and-white version has also the impressed mark ASTBURY (q.v.). The mark R.M.A. (Richard Meir Astbury) has been recorded. Modelled by John Voyez (q.v.).

Fair Toscophelite: see "Female Archer".

Fake: an object made or assembled in simulation of an authentic antique piece, with deceptive intent. Among the many varieties of fake are (a) wholly modern, although in the case of furniture, possibly made of old wood; (b) the fake incorporating old and authentic parts; (c) an object which is basically genuine but which has been altered to increase its appeal, such as the addition of carving or inlay to furniture or embossing to a piece of silver; (d) the "married" piece of which all, or considerable portions may be authentic but which has been "made up" from more than one source.

Falchion: a short, curved, single-edged sword, known as early as the 12th cent. The medieval form had a broad, cleaver-like blade.

Fall: see under Burgonet.

Fall-front cabinet: a writing cabinet enclosing a system of small drawers first popular in the latter part of the 16th cent. in Italy and Spain. Such cabinets were sometimes furnished with stands, though others were standless, placed on top of a table or chest as needed. Small walnut and marquetry fall-front writing cabinets on chests of drawers or stands became fashionable in England in the late 17th cent. (See also Scrutoire.)

Falling table: see Drop-leaf table.

False bands: see under Bands.

False bob pendulum: see Mock pendulum.

Famille jaune: see *Famille verte.*

Famille noire: Chinese porcelain of the K'ang Hsi period (q.v.) enamelled in *famille verte* (q.v.) style, generally "on the biscuit", with dry black ground colour, made lustrous by a covering of green glaze. The large vases with superb floral designs have fetched great sums, encouraging forgeries and skilful redecoration of old pieces. Cups and bowls are less rare. A few marked examples are of the Yung Chêng period (q.v.).

Famille rose: a class of Chinese enamelled porcelain wares characteristic of the reigns of Yung Chêng and Ch'ien Lung (qq.v.) named after the prominent rose-pink introduced from Europe. The rose, blue and yellow were often thickened with opaque white. A new delicate painting style began to oust that of the *famille verte* (q.v.) about 1720, and was applied especially to plates, bowls and cups and saucers of "egg-shell" thin porcelain. The "ruby-back" variety is coloured deep rose-pink on the reverse. Frequently painted subjects are scenes with ladies and children, birds or flowers, often framed in elaborate diapered borders. Pieces with European figure subjects, often imitated from engravings, were made to order for export. Many Ch'ien Lung and later wares employ the *famille rose* enamels, but with diminishing delicacy and taste.

Famille verte: a large family of Chinese porcelain wares of the K'ang Hsi period (q.v.) painted in a harmonious palette of brilliant green and red, yellow, aubergine-purple and violet-blue enamels, the strong iron-red being almost as characteristic as the green. The blue enamel replaces the underglaze blue of the late Ming (q.v.) and 17th cent. "five-colour" palette. The full range of colours were not always used. To heighten the effect, gilding was sometimes added. The paste of these wares is fine, white and excellently potted, and a great variety of plant, landscape, animal, and romantic or historical figure subjects, as well as emblematic designs and elaborate borders and panel-work, were employed in their decoration. The best examples exhibit superb painting on the finest materials, but others were only sketchily executed. A more delicate style appears towards the end of the reign, e.g. on the Imperial "birthday" plates, foreshadowing the *famille rose* wares. The rarer examples with yellow or black grounds are known as *famille jaune* and *famille noire*, and there are wares with celadon or coffee-brown grounds, or in the "powdered blue" surround. Imitations of Japanese "Imari" porcelains should also be mentioned. (See also *Famille rose* and *Famille noire*.)

Fanam: small gold coin of southern India, Ceylon and Malabar coast, struck with great variety of types from the 10th to the 18th cent. Silver fanams also issued from the 16th cent.

Fan-back chair: see Windsor chair.

Fan blade: the lower ornamental part of an inner stick of a fan. Known also as a brin.

Fancy chair: an American term for almost any variety of decorative occasional chair, generally light in weight, painted, and with a cane seat.

"F" and F reversed mark: see Worcester porcelain, Fürstenberg porcelain, Fulda porcelain and Medici porcelain.

Fanfare style book-binding: originated in Paris, c. 1565. Copied in England from 1620 onwards. Interlacing ribbons, bounded on one side by a double line and on the other by a single line, outline geometrical compartments of varying shapes which (with the exception of a large central one) are filled with conventional floral ornament. The English imitations often have the interlacing ribbon bounded by a single line on each side.

Fan guard: the two outer sticks of a fan between which the mount (q.v.) is folded. The guard consists of three sections, the handle end, the shoulder which extends to the lower edge of the mount, and the guard proper.

Fan mounts: known also as leaves, unite and cover the upper part of the sticks of folding fans, and might consist of vellum, chicken skin (q.v.), silk, lace or paper. The mount was usually double so that each side of the fan could display ornament.

Fan pattern: description of the back of a chair when filled with ribs somewhat resembling the stalks of a half-open fan. Also said of any fan-shaped carving, inlay, or painted decoration.

Fan pivot: a pin or rivet passing through the handle end of the fan sticks joining them together to swing on a pivot. On fine fans the pivot was set with jewels such as diamonds, pearls, rubies, sapphires, opals. Less costly gems were also used. In quizzing fans (q.v.) a tiny spy glass also swung at the pivot. The metal loop for the attachment of a ribbon or cord was introduced after 1816. Such a loop might be added to an earlier fan.

Fan sticks: the principal parts of a fan extending from the pivot (q.v.) to the perimeter of the mount. As a rule early Charles II sticks were deeply shouldered and widely spaced and sparsely decorated: later they touched. In this detail period characteristics overlapped and hybrid varieties are numerous. In the early 18th cent. they became straight without a visible shoulder, with ornament still complete on each stick and never carried over from one stick to another. Several designs might ornament the sticks of a single fan. As the cent. advanced fans became more and more elaborately decorated with carving, painting, staining, gilding and piercing, the design being carried out on two, three or four sticks and finally across the entire fan.

Farthing: a coin struck in silver commonly from time of Edward III in England and Alexander III in Scotland, with types similar to those of the penny. Farthing tokens in copper issued by James I and Charles I. Types with obverse portrait and Britannia reverse first struck in 1672.

Farthingale chair: a type of chair evolved during the reign of James I to accomodate the farthingale or hooped dress, with a comparatively wide and high seat and no arms. It was usually upholstered in Turkey work (q.v.) or velvet.

Fausse-montre: (*Fr.*), a sham watch sometimes worn to balance the real watch on what was known as the Macaroni or hookless châtelaine (q.v.), fashionable at the end of the 18th cent. These hookless châtelaines were of gold, with two ends hanging down, from which a watch and a fausse-montre could be suspended.

Fauteuil: a French arm-chair, less embracing in form than the bergère (q.v.), as the sides are not upholstered.

Fazackerley flowers: delftware decorated with bold floral ornament in polychrome – green, dark blue, brick red and bright yellow – has been identified as of Liverpool origin, on the traditional evidence supplied by a mug with the initials and date "T.F. 1757" said to have been made by Thomas Shaw of Liverpool for Thomas Fazackerley.

"FBB" mark: see Worcester porcelain.

Fcap or **fcp.:** foolscap. A size and quality of writing paper which, when folded once, measures about 13 × 8 inches; formerly identified by its watermark of a fool's cap and bells.

Fe. or **Fec.:** short for fecit or fecerunt. Made by. A less common variant for del (q.v.).

Feather banding: see Herring-bone banding.

Feather edge ornament: decoration of edge of silver spoon and fork handles with chased, slanting lines. (See also Table-service.)

Feathered ware: see Combed ware.

Feather fans: an early Victorian vogue. These fans, painted and embroidered with feathers, with pierced sticks (q.v.) of ivory, were imported from China and sold in England at about twenty shillings each.

Federal style: a term often used in America to describe furniture made in the United States between 1785 and 1830, the early days of the Republic. It includes works showing Hepplewhite, Sheraton, Directoire and early Empire influence. An inexact, therefore unsatisfactory, term – though at times highly convenient.

Fede ring: a ring in the form of a band terminating in joined hands, often holding a heart or a precious stone.

Feeding-cup: small, plain, saucepanlike cup with one or two handles and curved or straight spout designed for child or invalid feeding. Found from mid-17th cent. onwards. Also called "Spout-cup".

Felletin tapestry: see under Aubusson tapestry.

Fels: Islamic copper coin. Earliest were imitations of Byzantine pieces but from begining of 8th cent. have types similar to those of dinar and dirhem.

Felspar china: a felspathic china made by the younger Josiah Spode c. 1820, marked "Felspar Porcelain" within a wreath beneath the name SPODE, transfer-printed in purple.

"Felspathic glazes": those containing felspar rock, an essential ingredient of porcelain glazes; but used also on stonewares.

"Female archer": subject of "Pratt" type (q.v.) jugs and earthenware figures intended as satire upon the smart archery parties popular in "high" society, 1800–50. Sometimes known as the Fair Toscopholite or Toxophilite.

Feraghan carpets: Persian carpets woven with a Sehna knot, which have enjoyed great popularity in this country, and vary slightly in the treatment of the traditional Herat design.

Ferronière: (*Fr.*), a chain worn as an ornament encircling the head with a jewel in the centre.

Ferrule: the cap fitted over the end of a walking-stick to strengthen it and to prevent the wood or cane from splitting. Also the strengthening ring by which the head is attached to the stick.

Fetter chain: a chain worn as an ornament with long-shaped links.

Fiddle pattern spoons: see under Table-services.

Fiddler jug: a rare type of early toby jug (q.v.) representing a seated figure playing the fiddle, probably made by Astbury (q.v.). (See also Midshipmen jugs.)

Field: the flat portion of either side of a coin or any other decorated surface not occupied by the design.

Fielded panel: a raised panel with bevelled edges found on drawer fronts of 17th cent. oak dressers, etc.

Figure: the natural pattern in a wood. The introduction of the use of veneers (q.v.) in cabinet-making made it possible to exploit the full figure and texture of woods such as walnut, mahogany, yew, elm, mulberry, laburnum and many others.

Figure jugs: see Toby jugs.

Filigree: gold wire or pellets of lace-like form, applied to a gold base in ornamental pattern.

Filigree paper work: throughout the 18th cent. filigree was a popular amateur ornament for small cabinets, calling for neat fingers and considerable patience.

The ornament entirely covered the main panels of the cabinet, creating pictorial designs and arabesque patterns in an effect of metal filigree. This was achieved solely with tiny rolls of paper arranged so that they projected edgeways from their background. To complete the effect, they were gilded or coloured on their exposed edges.

Fillet: (1) a narrow strip of wood; (2) a wheel tool used by a bookbinder for impressing one or several parallel straight lines; the term is also used to describe the lines produced by the tool.

Fillings: a term used in lace-making, syn. with the French term *à jours*, to describe the fancy open stitches introduced in the pattern spaces in both needlepoints and pillow laces (qq.v.).

Fine drawings: a term used in lace-making, syn. with French *point de raccroc*, to describe the delicate work of joining lengths of lace net.

Fine paper copy: see Large paper copy.

Finial: an ornamental projection or knob. Found on furniture, sometimes carved in the form of an antique vase with drapery or an acorn, forming a decorative motif on the top of such pieces as knife cases or pole-screens. Similarly used by the goldsmith in a variety of forms such as human figures on covered cups and spoons or in the more familiar urn, acorn or pineapple shape on sugar casters, coffeepots, etc.

Fire-back: a slab of cast-iron, sometimes referred to as a "reredos", standing at the back of the fireplace, protecting the wall and reflecting the heat of the burning fuel. Fire-backs were made by the simple means of pouring the molten metal on to a prepared bed of sand in which a pattern had been impressed. The patterns were carved in wood, and were either of a full-sized design or in the form of single ornaments which were composed into a whole to suit the taste of the maker or his client.

The iron fire-backs of Sussex are the best known. Many were imported from Holland late in the 17th cent. and onwards. It is often difficult to determine the origin of one from another; the fire-backs with scenes from the Bible or mythological subjects are usually said to have been of Dutch make, but these were copied in England and there is no certainty on the point. In Holland the castings were made thinner than in England, but this feature also was adopted here. The earliest English fire-backs were of a wide, low shape, but by the mid-17th cent. tall ones, of "Tombstone" style, were introduced.

Fire-dogs: see Andirons.

Fire-fork: an instrument made of wrought-iron, some 4 feet or more in length in order that the user would be away from the heat when moving burning logs in the hearth. Usually it had two stout prongs, but some examples have a spike at one side about three-quarters of the way down

from the handle. The fire-fork was the forerunner of the poker, and it went out of the general use when coal replaced wood as a fuel.

Fire-polishing: reheating of finished glassware at the furnace mouth to obliterate marks left by tools and produce a smooth, even surface.

Fire-screen: an adjustable screen made from the end of the 17th cent. to give protection from the intense heat of large open fires. Two main kinds were used. (a) Pole screen: with the screen on an upright supported on a tripod base; (b) horse or cheval screen – two uprights, each on two legs, enclosing a panel. Elaborate carving and gilding of the crests was often found until the end of the 18th cent., when lighter and simpler screens were in vogue. Needlework was the popular material for the panel.

Firing-glass: also known as hammering glass. Used for thumping the table as a form of acclamation when drinking toasts, etc. The glass was necessarily heavy with drawn bowl on thick stem and heavy, flat foot.

Fish-tail: an American term to describe the carving, somewhat resembling a fish tail, on the top rail of a banister-back chair.

Five-colour wares: see Wu ts'ai wares.

Fl.: flourished. When the dates of birth and death of an artist or author are unknown, it is common to indicate the period during which he is known to have been working by the use of the abbreviation fl. followed by a date or dates.

Flagon: large vessel for serving wine or other liquors. Pear-shaped and cylindrical bodies occur contemporaneously at most periods and are always closely related in form and decoration to tankards. Except for ecclesiastical use, the flagon is rare after the 18th cent.

Flag seat: an American colloquial term sometimes used to describe a chair seat woven of rush-like material.

Flambé glazes: glazes found on Chinese ceramics in which kiln conditions produce variegated colour effects, e.g. on some Chün porcelain (q.v.) wares of the Sung dynasty, the 18th cent. copper-red wares, and on Canton stonewares.

Flanders chests: more vaguely defined as overseas work in some inventories. They were in great demand by the 16th cent.; as early as 1483 the Cofferers' Guild was protesting at their importation. Inventoried specimens were generally priced at about 5s in the late 16th cent., and were in general use throughout the house. Some remaining specimens may have been preserved because of the exceptional richness of their carving, sometimes applied. In the 17th cent. the ornament associated with Flanders included a range of unambitious applied decoration intended to simulate elaborate constructional work.

Flat chasing: surface decoration in low relief on precious metal, produced by hammering with small blunt tools. The characteristic feature of the process is that no metal is removed.

Flat cutting: see Panel cutting.

Flattened knop: see Annulated knop.

Flaxman, John, R. A.: (1755–1826), born at York, son of a moulder of plaster casts, with premises in Covent Garden, London. He exhibited models at the Free Society of Artists in 1767 and 1769, and in 1770 won a silver medal at the Royal Academy. From 1775 until 1787 he modelled reliefs for Wedgwood's jasper wares such as the well known "Dancing Hours" and "Apotheosis of Homer", and figures. He spent seven years in Italy from 1787, studying art, and while there he executed designs for Dante's *Divina Commedia* (1797) Homer (1793) and Aeschylus (1795), marble groups of "The Fury of Athamas" and "Cephalus and Aurora", and works for Wedgwood. He was elected R. A. in 1800, and Professor of Sculpture to the Royal Academy in 1810.

Flemish scroll: a curving double scroll. Sometimes the front legs and the stretcher connecting the front legs on late 17th cent. chairs are carved with Flemish scrolls.

Flemish tapestry: the term Flemish or Netherlands tapestry, as distinct from French, is only applicable after the fall of the Burgundian dukes in 1477 (for earlier tapestry see Franco-Burgundian). Flanders, Brabant and Hainault, which included the famous tapestry cities of Tournai, the ruined Arras, and the rising Brussels, were then ruled for the Habsburgs by Mary, Governess of the Netherlands, and in 1515 came under Charles V's empire. The Netherlands and France grew further and further apart, and Flemish tapestry became distinct in style and workmanship from French.

Brussels (q.v.) was already in the first decade of the 16th cent. the leading tapestry city, but there was also Bruges, Antwerp, Tournai, Oudenarde and Enghien. The late medieval period was famous for its religious tapestries, finely woven with much silk and lavish use of gold and silver thread; many were made on a very large scale. Brussels was certainly the principal centre for these, but some were probably made at Bruges. Antwerp, a great seaport, was also a principal market, but tapestries were made there, and the 1544 laws prohibited its use of the Brussels mark (though not wholly successfully). Antwerp catered especially for foreign markets in the 17th and 18th cent., England included (see Wauters family). Tournai, with high-warp looms, continued to produce pastoral and other subjects in Late Gothic style, which are often mistaken for French weaving. Its decline in the 16th cent. was rapid, and indeed the terrible religious wars severely affected the Flemish looms. The revival inaugurated by the Archduke Albert and Isabella in 1606 was furthered by the renown of Rubens and Jordaens, who both designed celebrated tapestries, and by the Exhibition Gallery established at Brussels in 1655.

Meanwhile at Oudenarde and Enghien a steady stream of less pretentious tapestries were woven and the former remained famous for its *verdures* (q.v.), adapting its style in the latter part of the 17th cent. to landscape *verdures*, which were popular throughout the 18th cent. During the 16th, 17th and 18th cent. the most widely commercialized tapestry was Flemish. It included many different qualities and never ceased to produce masterpieces under special patronage. From Flemish cities weavers were recruited for the several dozen factories which rose and fell in almost every European country.

Flight and Barr; Flight, Barr and Barr: see Worcester porcelain.

Flint-glass: now termed lead crystal, flint glass was developed by George Ravenscroft (1618–81), who was granted a seven-year patent (No. 176) in May 1674, to make a glass in which the silica was derived from calcined flints. In 1675 he first used lead oxide as a flux in place of vegetable potash. This produced a glass denser, heavier, softer, and with greater refractive brilliance than anything previously made. Flint glass vessels, if flicked with thumb and finger, emit a resonant tone.

Flint-lock gun: a type of gun-lock developed from the snaphaunce (q.v.) in the first quarter of the 17th cent. It is fitted with a pan (holding priming powder round the touch-hole), with a hinged cover from which rises a flat steel. When the gun is discharged, a specially shaped flint, held in the jaws of a spring-operated cock, strikes the steel, throwing it and the pan-cover back, and at the same time sending a shower of sparks into the priming.

In its earliest form this lock had a horizontal scear, the tip of which projected through the lock-plate and engaged with a projection on the heel of the cock, holding the latter back until released by the trigger. There was no half-cock (safety position), although on English locks this was provided by a dog-catch, a small pivoted hook which engaged in a notch at the rear of the cock. The flint-lock proper, with a vertical scear engaging in one of two notches in an internal tumbler, giving respectively half- and

full-cock, appears to have been invented in France about 1610–15, possibly by Marin le Bourgeoys of Lisieux (d. 1634). This form became increasingly popular and virtually superseded all others in the second half of the 17th cent., remaining in use until well into the 19th. A special type of flint-lock used in Spain and Southern Italy was the *miquelet*, which had an external mainspring and a scear operating through the lockplate.

Flitcroft, Henry: (1697–1769), described by George Vertue, the engraver, "Mr Flitcroft was a Joyner – now Architect". He became a protégé of the Earl of Burlington (q.v.) and was among those early 18th cent. Palladian (q.v.) architects who were interested in the furniture in their buildings.

Flock prints: see Samt-teigdrucke.

Flock wallpapers: powdered wool applied to the paper on which the design is first printed, painted or stencilled with a slow-drying adhesive. A process known to antiquity and especially associated with early clothworkers. The drawing illustrates a type of flock box in use during the early Victorian period.

Florin: (1) a coin known as the *fiorino d'oro* struck in Florence from 1252, with types of St John the Baptist and reverse the lily, the arms of Florence. The *fiorino d'argento* of same types also issued; (2) a gold coin of value 6s struck briefly in 1344 by Edward III with obverse type of king enthroned.

Flowered glasses: trade name for wine glasses engraved with naturalistic flowers on the bowl, popular in the mid-18th cent.

Flower stand: see China-stand.

Flown blue decoration: a method of decorating porcelain with an under-glaze transfer-printed effect in which the design melts into the surrounding glaze with a kind of coloured halo, caused by firing in an atmosphere containing volatile chlorides. Flown blue effects were popular in mid-Victorian times. Other colours, such as brown, green and yellow are subject to the same treatment but have been little used.

Flute glass: a drinking glass with a tall, deep conical bowl, popular in the Netherlands in the 17th cent.

Fluting: a decorative form consisting of concave channels derived from a similar motif used on classical columns, used in close repeated formation as a border or body ornament. Found extensively on bodies of silver cups, tankards and other vessels in late 17th cent. alternating with gadroons (q.v.) to form corrugated surface. Also used as a decorative motif on furniture, particularly in the last quarter of the 18th cent. (See also Reeding.)

Foible: the portion of the sword blade near the point which is weak from the standpoint of leverage. Usually it comprises half to two-thirds of the length of the blade.

Foil: a thin sheet of metal placed behind a gem in a collet setting (q.v.) to strengthen its colour.

Fol. or **fo.** or **f.:** folio. See Book sizes.

Folded foot: the foot of a drinking glass where the rim has been folded under while hot, forming a selvage and giving extra strength to a part most likely to become chipped in use.

Folding table: "folding" tables appear in inventories of the 14th cent. but it is not known for what purpose they were used. The folding table had one fixed and one hinged leaf and when closed, the table had the hinged leaf resting on the fixed top. In modern "jargon" a folding table is sometimes incorrectly described as a credence table.

Foliot: the earliest form of controller in a mechanical clock. Always found with a verge escapement. The balance wheel and, especially later, the pendulum so improved time-keeping that it is very rare to find a clock with its original foliot.

Follis: the large Roman aes (q.v.) coin introduced by the reform of Diocletian in A.D. 296.

Folwell, John: Philadelphia master cabinet-maker of the Chippendale school (fl. 1775), whose works, according to Hornor, "are unsurpassed in historic appeal and artistic significance". Just before the Revolution, Folwell solicited subscriptions for his proposed book of American furniture drawings, entitled *The Gentleman and Cabinet-maker's Assistant*. In consequence, he is sometimes called "the Chippendale of America".

Fond chant: (*Fr.*), a term used to describe a six-pointed star lace ground found in so-called *point de Paris* lace (q.v.), English Midlands laces and trolly lace, Chantilly lace (qq.v.), etc.

Fond clair: (*Fr.*), a term used in lace-making, syn. with *fond simple*, to describe the mesh ground found in Lille lace (q.v.), with four sides formed of two twisted threads and two sides of crossed threads. This sometimes suggests diamond rather than hexagonal meshes, depending on the tightness of the work.

Fondeurs, Corporation des: (*Fr.*), the craft guild in France responsible for casting and chasing metal, either for sculpture, furniture or *bronzes d'ameublement* (q.v.). It was organized similarly to those of the *menuisiers-ébénistes* (q.v.) and *doreurs* (q.v.).

Food warmer: a composite article of pottery or porcelain, usually from 9 inches to 12 inches high, consisting of a hollow pedestal into which a covered bowl with a projecting flange nests

Within the pedestal, which has an arched opening at the bottom on one side, there is a cup or container (godet) which fits into a raised verge on the base. Food warmers were made in delftware, salt-glazed stoneware, and earthenware, at Leeds, Swansea and in Staffordshire, 18th and 19th cent.

Footing: upper edge of a piece of lace.

Footman: the name given to a four-legged trivet made to stand in front of the fire in the sitting-room or parlour. They were made of wrought-iron or brass, or partly of each, and commonly had front legs of cabriole design. The top was often pierced with a central hole so that it could be carried. The footman dates from the second half of the 18th cent. onwards.

Fore-edge painting: this term is most commonly used for an English technique originating in the 17th cent. and revived about 1785 by Edwards of Halifax, whereby the fore-edge of a book, very slightly fanned out and then held fast, is decorated with painted views or conversation pieces. The edges are then gilded in the ordinary way, so that the painting remains concealed (and protected) while the book is closed: fan out the edges, and it reappears.

Forestier, Étienne Jean and **Pierre Auguste:** (1755–1838), French sculptors, brothers, the sons of Étienne Forestier (c. 1712–68). All three were *fondeurs-ciseleurs* (bronze casters—see *Fondeurs, Corporation des*), and after the father's death his widow carried on the business with her two sons.

Their names constantly occur in the Royal accounts, and they are known to have worked at Versailles and Compiègne, and for the Prince de Condé. After the Revolution, Pierre Auguste established a successful workshop, supplying furniture, *bronzes d'ameublement* (q.v.), etc.

Form watch: a watch made in some form that departs from the standard of the period, e.g. book, cruciform, skull, dog, etc. These are found in the 17th cent. Later, at the end of the 18th, there are lyres, mandolines, baskets of flowers, fruit, etc.

Forsets, fossets, fosselets: terms defined by Bailey in 1730 as small chests or cabinets. They were smaller versions of the forser or fosser, an early form of strong box such as the Cockesden "waynscott fosser" (1610) and the "grete joyned forser" with two keys owned by the Pewterers' Company in 1488–89.

Forte: the strong portion of the sword blade, usually about one-third, nearest the hilt.

Fortin barometer: a type in which the level of the cistern is adjusted to a fixed pointer before a reading by difference is taken, thus eliminating capacity error.

Fortune-telling card packs: first issued in 1665. They consist of fifty-two cards with two others upon which complicated instructions are printed. In the upper left corner of each is a suit sign and the cards in each suit are numbered I to XIII, the odd numbers bearing a circle with signs of the zodiac, the even-numbered cards each holding answers.

Foules point d'or: see Piqué.

Foxed, foxing: of paper: discoloured, stained, usually with brownish-yellow spots.

Franc: French silver coin in 16th and early 17th cent. of testoon class with types, royal portrait and floreate cross. In 1795 established as the unit of the decimal system, and issued in one-, two-

and five-franc pieces. Types, head of Liberty or royal portrait and reverse, value in laurel wreath.

Franco-Burgundian tapestry: the great development of medieval tapestry seems to have taken place in the 14th cent., principally in France at Paris and Arras. But the Hundred Years War drove the French Court from Paris to the Loire, and it was the Dukes of Burgundy who patronized the 15th cent. florescence of tapestry. Apart from the *Apocalypse* tapestries at Angers, woven by Nicolas Bataille of Paris (c. 1375–80), and the *Nine Worthies* at the Cloisters, New York, scarcely a 14th cent. piece is known. Even 15th-cent. tapestries are rare, but the *Clovis* set at Rheims, the *Caesar* set at Berne, and *Alexander* in the Palazzo Doria, Rome, are eloquent remains of famous hangings which figured in inventories and chroniclers' accounts of marriages or court festivities. The Burgundian dukes fostered the arts and raised tapestry to the level of diplomatic gifts as highly prized as gold. Philip the Good inherited Flanders, Artois and Hainault (1384), which included Arras and Tournai, the two great tapestry cities of the 15th cent. With Charles the Bold's defeat and death in 1477, French and Flemish tapestries diverged as different schools.

Frankenthal porcelain: a factory was established at Frankenthal, near Mannheim in Germany in 1755 by Paul-Anton Hannong under the protection of the Elector Palatine. Hannong had made hard-paste porcelain at his factory at Strasbourg but the French authorities obliged him to cease his activities in view of the monopoly held by Vincennes (see Sèvres porcelain), and he consequently moved to Frankenthal. Frankenthal porcelain figures often have rich pierced, scrolled Rococo bases and sometimes include trellis work, a style which is connected with the modeller J. F. Luck (1758–64). Tablewares belonging to the period up to 1775, in which the best achievements of the factory were reached, are sometimes decorated in the Meissen (q.v.) manner and sometimes with elaborate figure subjects. Trellis and diaper

patterns were popular and cabaret sets (q.v.) were a favourite form. The factory closed in 1799. The marks varied, showing Hannong's initials until 1756 and thereafter a quartering from the arms of the Palatinate, occasionally also the lion from the same arms. The initials of the Elector Carl Theodor, with or without crown, appear after 1762, all in underglaze blue.

Franklin clock: a type of wooden movement shelf clock made (1825–30) by Silas Hoadley of Plymouth, Connecticut, and called by him "Franklin". It is perhaps the earliest instance that a clock was given a specific (model) name by a maker. This movement is practically an inverted form of the movement then being made by Terry and others.

Free blown glass: glass formed by blowing and manipulation with hand tools, without the aid of moulds; also called hand blown and off-hand blown.

Freedom box: small circular or oblong box, silver-gilt, when not gold, presented with a script conferring the freedom of a town. Particularly popular in Ireland from the late 18th to the early 19th cent.

Free endpapers: see Endpapers.

"French" chair: a high-backed, elaborately carved walnut arm chair which came into fashion shortly after the Restoration. These chairs were richly upholstered and were made en suite with stools. Although walnut was more usually employed, they were also made of beech and gilt. In the mid-18th cent. mahogany chairs in the Rococo (q.v.) taste, employing such forms as light cabriole legs (q.v.) and scroll feet, were described as French.

"French" scroll: see Scroll foot.

Fresco: a painting executed on the wet surface of a finely prepared mortar applied to the plaster of a ceiling or wall.

"Fretted square" mark: see Worcester porcelain.

Fretwork: two forms of fretwork were frequently used decoratively on mid-18th cent. furniture: (a) open fretted galleries appear on tea-tables or on stands made in the "Chinese" taste; (b) geometrical fretwork patterns were also used on chair legs or friezes, carved or applied, inspired by the "Chinese" or the "Gothic" taste.

Frieze: an architectural term describing the decorative band placed immediately below a cornice.

Also used to describe the band below the cornice on a piece of furniture.

Friggers: a colloquialism used to describe the innumerable minor articles made of glass, of which the principal purposes were to delight and surprise the recipient and beholder, and to exhibit the prowess of the maker. Into this category fall such objects as hand bells, flasks, rolling-pins, walking-sticks, tobacco pipes, swords, sceptres, crowns and hats.

Less common than the above are model ships with rigging and crew. birds on perches, fox-hunts with hounds in full cry, and similar tours de force. The latter were perhaps made as suitable table decorations at hunt breakfasts.

Friggers were made both at Bristol and at Nailsea, as they were at all the other glassworks in England. Unless such pieces bear a signature or other mark of identification, there is seldom any way by which the productions of one place can be distinguished from those of another.

Frog: a sleeve-like device, normally of leather, used to attach the sword to the belt. Usually the scabbard was thrust through the sleeve and a stud on its throat engaged in a hole in the frog.

"Frog" service: a celebrated service of cream-coloured earthenware manufactured by Josiah Wedgwood in 1773 for Empress Catherine of Russia. Each piece of this enormous service was painted at Chelsea with individual landscapes and mansions of England, and a leaf border with the crest of a green frog in purple black. The service was so named because it was intended for the Grenouille Palace.

There were more than 900 pieces: the ware cost £ 51 8s 4d: the decorations nearly £ 2,450: Josiah Wedgwood received for it £ 3,000.

It is now in the Hermitage, Leningrad.

Fromanteel family: London clock-makers of repute, the various members of the family being active between 1625 and 1725.

Frontis. or front.: frontispiece.

Frosting: a rough or matt white surface on silverware produced by acid fuming or scratch brushing. Not found before the early 19th cent., principally used on ornamental and figure work on silver centre-pieces (q.v.).

"Fruit" paperweight: glass paperweight (q.v.) containing canes so arranged to represent fruit.

Frye, Thomas: (1710–62), born in Ireland near Dublin, studied art and came to London about 1729. He painted portraits in oils and became proficient as a miniature painter. Became interested in the idea of manufacturing porcelain and in 1744 took out a patent with Edward Heylyn. Frye patented another porcelain formula in 1749 and in 1750, with the aid of two London merchants, established a factory at Bow.

Frye retired from the management of the Bow factory in 1759 when his health gave way. He toured in Wales for a time and then settled in London as a mezzotint engraver. (See also Bow porcelain.)

Fuddling-cup: a cup with 3, 5, 6 or more conjoined compartments communicating internally, made in *sgraffiato* (q.v.) slipware at Donyat and Crock Street, Somerset. Dates recorded from 1697 to 1770. Similar vessels were made in tin-glazed earthenware at Bristol. Earliest dated piece 1633.

Fude or **Hitsu:** Japanese term for a brush; also painted with a brush.

Fuh: another name for early Chinese copper coin known as a cash (q.v.).

Fukien porcelain: see Blanc-de-Chine.

Fulda porcelain: a factory was founded at Fulda in Germany in 1764 under a privilege from the Prince-Bishop of Fulda, Heinrich von Bibra, and continued until 1790. Examples of Fulda porcelain are rare and both the table wares and the figures are of high quality. The body is hard-paste. The mark varies. From about 1765 to 1780 a cross, taken from the arms of the city, was used, principally on figures, while again from 1765 to about 1788, two "Fs", linked to form an "H", below a crown, appear. Between 1788 and 1790 a crowned "A" is occasionally found.

Fulham carpets: Peter Parisot, an ex-Capuchin monk from Lorraine, procured the patronage of the Duke of Cumberland for a carpet-knotting factory in Fulham. He is supposed to have employed as many as a hundred workmen, many from the Savonnerie (q.v.), but owing to extravagances he was forced to sell up within five years (1755). A portrait of the Duke, dated 1755, is probably his work, and pile fire-screens are occasionally found.

Fulham stoneware: John Dwight of Fulham took out a patent in 1671 for the manufacture of "transparent earthen-ware" and stoneware, then sometimes known as Cologne ware. Dwight was followed by Margaret Dwight, and thereafter the works remained in the family for many years. In 1862 the factory came into the possession of Messrs MacIntosh & Clements: in 1864 it was disposed of to a Mr Bailey. It is still in existence as the Fulham Pottery and Cheavin Filter Co.

Marks:
<blockquote>

Fulham
Pottery
</blockquote>

This mark is found on a flask of brown-glazed stoneware decorated with a watch, c. 1811, in the British Museum. No other marks are known to have been used.

John Dwight contributed to the progress of pottery manufacture in England. He was the first maker of a semi-translucent stoneware, the link between earthenware and the fine porcelain produced later. He also made a successful copy of Cologne ware, a greyish durable earthenware used for pots, mugs, etc. imported from Germany in great quantities. Many such articles for domestic use, in various qualities, were made at Fulham in the 17th and 18th cent.

Some beautifully modelled statues and busts in salt-glazed stoneware were made by Dwight. Red ware of the Elers (q.v.) type was probably also made at Fulham. Between 1693 and 1696 Dwight instituted several law-suits to defend his patent rights for the manufacture of this and other types of ware. The brothers Elers were cited in one of these cases.

In the 18th cent. only the coarser wares were produced, beer jugs, tankards for the most part crudely decorated with reliefs of convivial and other subjects, and later marked with name of owner or inn for which they were intended. (See also Dwight, John.)

Fundame: a Japanese lacquer-work technique in which powdered gold is worked to a matt surface.

Funnel bowl: bowl shaped in the form of a funnel found on baluster-stemmed drinking glasses of the late 17th and 18th cent.

Fürstenberg porcelain: a factory was founded at Fürstenberg in Germany in 1747 by Duke Carl I of Brunswick, although porcelain was not made before 1753. Some of the early table-wares were modelled with Rococo patterns in relief in order to hide faults in the body and glaze. L. V. Gerverot, who had formerly worked with Wedgwood (q.v.), became manager in 1795. Classical figures after bronzes were produced, as well as copies of Wedgwood's jasper and black basaltes ware. The factory still exists. The mark used was an "F" in blue.

Fusee: a conically-shaped and spirally-grooved pulley which, utilizing the principle of the lever, equalizes the pull of the mainspring of a clock or watch on the train. This has generally been attributed to Jacob the Czech, of Prague, based on the earliest known survival in a clock by him, owned by the Society of Antiquaries of London, dated 1525.

g. or glt. or gt.: an abbreviation used in booksellers' catalogues meaning gilt; especially in the combinations g.e. for gilt edges, and g.t. for gilt top (q.v.).

Gadroon: a border ornament composed of radiating lobes of either curved or straight form. Used on oak furniture in the late Elizabethan and Jacobean period and on mahogany in the mid-18th cent. Also a familiar ornament on the rims and feet of silver cups and other vessels and on the borders of silver plates and dishes from the late 17th cent. onwards.

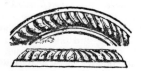

Gallé, Emile: (1846–1904), French glassmaker of Nancy whose glass reveals a Japanese inspiration in the use of natural floral motifs. Gallé abandoned symmetry and Classical proportions and sought an association with carved stone by means of using opaque coloured glass and crazings and irregularities in the material.

Gallipot: originally, pots brought in galleys; subsequently applied to pottery glazed with tin enamel, especially a small, glazed earthenware pot such as is used by apothecaries for ointments.

Galloons: the plain, ribbon-like outer border of a tapestry. The factory and weaver's mark, when used, are woven into the galloon.

Gally paving tiles: glazed tiles, usually earthenware covered with tin glaze used for wall decorations: the name was derived from imported wares brought from the Mediterranean in galleys.

Gaming table: folding top table made for card playing, often containing circular recesses at the corners for candlesticks and wells for counters. Early tables of this type date from about 1700 and during the course of the cent., a variety of forms were made.

Garde Meuble de la Couronne: (*Fr.*), the department which dealt with all matters connected with the furnishing of the Royal palaces in France. It was established by Louis XIV in 1663, and survived until the end of the monarchy. Very fortunately, its records exist more or less intact.

The first inventory of furniture belonging to the Crown was completed in 1673 and has been published in full by M. Emile Molinier, but the most important item among the records is the *Journal*, instituted in 1685 and continuing until 1784. In it every piece acquired for the Crown was scrupulously entered and given a number, with dates of delivery, the name of the maker, costs and measurements, eventual destination in the Royal palaces, and a full description. The numbers often correspond with those painted on the backs of existing pieces (see Inventory numbers), and these can be thus identified fairly closely from the descriptions and measurements.

The *Journal* consists in all of eighteen volumes and 3,600 pages, of which only a small proportion are missing, and is preserved in the *Archives Nationales* in Paris. After 1784 a new system of recording was introduced, but the same numbers were preserved, and these, in fact, continued to be used until well into the 19th cent.

Garden carpets: Persian carpets, showing formal designs with figures and animals.

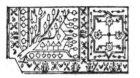

Gardner's porcelain: an Englishman named Gardner founded a factory in Moscow in 1758. His factory produced some well-known figures of Russian peasants. Some of Gardner's wares bear a mark resembling the Meissen mark of the Marcolini period. (See also Meissen porcelain.)

Garnish: a household set of plates and dishes.

Garniture de cheminée: set of five porcelain or faience vases consisting of two trumpet-shaped beakers and three covered vases, usually of baluster shape, a combination originating in China, whence it was adopted by most European faience and porcelain factories. Also made of silver in late 17th cent. England, France or Holland, but extremely few examples survive.

Gate-leg table: an oval or round table in oak or, more rarely, walnut, originally known as a "falling" table on

account of the two hinged leaves which hang down beside the frame and can be raised and supported on two, and sometimes four, gate supports. The leg turning used was very varied. These tables became particularly fashionable in the late 17th cent. when meals were eaten in dining rooms appointed for the purpose and served at smaller tables. Gate-leg tables made to fold completely flat are known but the more usual construction had a rigid central panel.

Gather: a blob of molten metal on the end of a glassblower's blowpipe ready for blowing.

Gaudreau, Antoine Robert: French cabinet-maker. One of the most celebrated of the known *ébénistes* (q.v.) of the Louis XV period. He was born c. 1680, and was in the Royal service from 1726.

Gaudy Dutch: the popular American name for a gaily decorated Staffordshire pottery produced c. 1810–30 for the American trade.

Gaudy Welsh: also known as Gaudy Ironstone. A popular American name for pottery wares (c. 1830–45 and 1850–65) made in England for the American trade.

Gauffrage: blind-printing, producing an embossed effect without colour, and used in Japan from the late 18th cent. as a technique in making prints.

Gauffred edges: many books have the edges of the leaves gilded. The gauffred edge is a pattern blocked or stamped on to the edges, so that a diamond or lozenge or some other decorative effect is produced.

Gemellion: this term describes one of a pair of basins used for the liturgical washing of the hands at the Mass. Though the ornament found on them is in most cases of secular character, their use seems to have been mainly ecclesiastical. One was provided with a spout at the side and served as an ewer for pouring water, while the other without spout received it. The gemellion was one of the standard

productions of the enamelling shops at Limoges, and the majority of those known are decorated with Limoges enamel. They date from the 13th and 14th cent.

Genoa lace: gold and silver plaited border laces were made at Genoa in the 16th cent. Pillow lace was perhaps developed here or alternatively in Flanders.

Genoa paper: a glazed paper, until the 1790s used exclusively for playing cards because of its silkiness and power of receiving colour freely. It took the glazing flint better than did the harsh English paper.

Genoese mandoline: see under Mandoline.

Genre painting: a painting representing a domestic scene of everyday life.

Genovino: gold coin issued in Genoa from 13th cent. with types of gateway and cross.

Georgette: popular name for a snuffbox made in the style of Jean George, the Paris mid-18th cent. goldsmith.

Georgian style: a style associated with works of art made during the reigns of the three Georges up to the time when the illness of George III made it necessary for the Prince of Wales to become Regent (1811).

Geographical playing cards: the earliest were issued in 1665 by H. Winstanley, Lothbury. Hearts represent Europe, diamonds Asia, spades Africa, clubs America. Packs illustrating the fifty-two counties of England and Wales were popular.

Gera porcelain: see under Limbach porcelain.

"German Flowers" (Deutsche Blumen): contemporary name for naturalistically painted flowers, introduced as porcelain decoration at Meissen about 1740. "Ombrierte Teutsche Blumen", flowers with shadows, are a variation. Later the treatment became freer, and smaller flowers, arranged in sprays or bouquets, were scattered over the whole surface until, under classical influence, they were confined between conventional rims and borders.

German silver: see Nickel silver.

Gesamtkatalog: a reference to the *Gesamtkatalog der Wiegendrucke*, an alphabetical listing of incunabula (q.v.), interrupted at the letter E by World War II and never resumed.

Gesso: a composition of parchment, size and whiting applied to furniture as a medium for carving and gilding. A pattern in low relief is carved in the thickness of the whiting ground and the background stamped or punched to give a mat effect, the whole surface being then gilded. Gesso work is found on table tops, mirror frames and stands dating from the late 17th and throughout the first half of the 18th cent.

Ghiordes knot: used in Oriental carpets from Djoshagan, Herez and Kurdistan, and sometimes from Tabriz, Shiraz and Herat. These last also use the Sehna knot (q.v.).

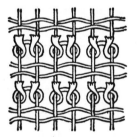

Ghiordes rugs: the finest of Turkish rugs. The knot is usually Turkish; yarns are very fine, warp and weft often being of silk. The colours are very varied, while the borders usually consist of bold conventional floral designs, beautifully treated.

Gibbons, Grinling: (1648–1720), carver and designer of Dutch birth and English domicile. He was "discovered" by the diarist John Evelyn. His work, of distinctive character, included the carving of picture frames with profuse and naturalistic foliage, fruit swags, birds and shells. Much of the work assigned to him is, in fact, by his contemporaries.

Gilding: various relatively impermanent forms of gilding were employed on salt-glazed stoneware, earthenware, porcelain and glass in the 18th cent., either by means of an emulsion composed of linseed oil and mastic, japanners' size, amber varnish, or honey. These were fixed by firing at an extremely low temperature. Honey gilding was used at the Chelsea and Worcester porcelain factories. It was rather dull in appearance but could be applied with enough thickness to allow for chasing. It was much more durable than size gilding.

Mercury gilding was introduced about 1785, raised gilding in 1802, liquid gold about 1855, bright burnished gold in 1860, and acid gilding in 1863.

Gold has been applied by pencilling, by transfer-printing, and with rubber stamps.

Giles, James: (1718–80), an enameller of Bow, Worcester and other porce'·ins from before 1760 until c. 1780. Many unusual styles of decoration came from his workshop. He was apprenticed to a jeweller, before becoming a ceramic artist. By 1760 he was well established and advertising that he was prepared to "procure and paint for any person Worcester porcelain to any or in any pattern", and in 1771 hired a room in Cockspur Street from which he advertised wares "curiously enamelled in figures, birds and flowers" and ornamented with mazarine blue, and gold.

He was financially embarrassed in 1777 and appealed to Duesbury (q.v.) for a loan, and when he ultimately failed Duesbury took on his premises and stock.

The gilding on wares decorated in Giles' workshop is said to have been thick and crudely chased.

Various styles of enamelling have been ascribed to him, the dishevelled birds, Chelsea landscapes drawn in black and coloured in green, some

Chelsea fruit painting, etc. O'Neale may have been employed by him.

Chaffers suggested that the red seal mark occurring over the Worcester crescent in underglaze blue may be an indication of his work. Honey suggested that the dagger and another mark on Bow was Giles' sign.

Gillow, Robert: an 18th cent. joiner of Lancaster to whom George Hepplewhite (q.v.) was apprenticed in his youth. Robert Gillow's firm opened a branch in Oxford St to which furniture from the workshops in Lancaster was sent. Some 18th cent. pieces made by Gillow and all those he made after 1820 were stamped "Gillow's" or "Gillow's, Lancaster". His son Richard, who died in 1811, became his father's partner in 1757.

Gilt tops or **top edges gilt:** interchangeable terms used in booksellers' catalogues meaning that the top edges only of a book have been gilded, and implying that the other edges have been cut smooth or at least trimmed. If they have not, the book is described as gilt tops, other edges uncut or simply t.e.g., uncut.

Ginette: see Dram glasses.

Gin glass: see Dram glasses.

Giobu: Japanese lacquer-work technique in which irregular pieces of foil are mixed with lacquer, giving a mottled effect.

Girandole: (1) a carved and gilt candle sconce (see Sconce) of asymmetrical design, sometimes enclosing a looking-glass as a back plate. About 1750 girandoles provided some of the most lively interpretations of the Rococo fashion. (2) a type of earring in which three pendent stones hang from a large central stone, worn in the late 17th and 18th cent. (3) a type of American wall clock designed by Lemuel Curtis dating from c. 1820.

Girdle-plate: a Scottish flat iron sheet on which oat-cakes were baked.

"Girl-in-a-swing" family: a group of porcelain figures manufactured at

Chelsea c. 1751; so-named from a figure of a girl in a swing in the Victoria and Albert Museum London. The figures are of primitive simplicity and show some affinity to Staffordshire wares of similar date.

Giulio: papal silver coin of gros (q.v.) class, originally issued by Julius II (1503–13) but continued into later centuries. Types, portrait of Pope and reverse figure of saint.

Glaive: see under Pole-arms.

Glass bottle seals: the circular glass seals found on glass bottles were almost certainly impressed with an original intaglio made of brass. This was made either by a professional engraver working on his own behalf or at the glassworks itself. No name of any craftsman connected with this particular branch of the art of die-sinking has been recorded, and the makers of these seals, as most of the makers of more elaborate desk seals, have remained anonymous.

Glass bottle seals fall into three categories, whether they bear dates or not, and may be conveniently classified as: armorial, name or initial, and "others", the last including merchant's marks, Masonic signs and the names of houses.

Glass pictures: see Back-painting, Under-glass painting, Mirror painting, Gold-glass engraving, Verre églomisé and Glass silhouettes.

Glass silhouettes: silhouettes painted on to glass by one of the following methods: (a) Verre églomisé (q.v.) and gold-glass engraving. Silhouettes of this kind were produced by the Parisian artist A. Forberger (1762–1865), who backed his portraits with gold leaf or blue wax and often gave them floral borders, and W. A. Spornberg, a Swede, who worked at the end of the 18th cent. in Bath, and whose profiles are backed with red pigment and usually surrounded by a geometrical border. (b) Painting on to the reverse side of flat or convex glass. This was a common form of silhouette painting, and one capable of giving very effective results, particularly on those painted

on convex glass, mounted over white backgrounds on to which their shadows could be thrown. Work of this kind was painted by Walter Jorden (late 18th cent.), Isabella Beetham, Charles Rosenberg (1745–1844), W. Rought (early 19th cent.), and many others.

Several silhouettists, among them John Miers, mounted their ordinary painted work beneath convex glass with églomisé borders and Mrs Beetham often combined églomisé mounts with portraits in plain black painted on the underside of the same glass. At least one silhouette in a glass millefiori paperweight (q.v.) is on record.

Glass walking-stick: chest-high shepherd's crook walking-sticks in pale green bottle-glass were made in the late 18th cent.: few remain. Early 19th cent. walking-sticks were tapered at the ferrule end: later examples appear to have been simply rounded off. Those with shepherd's crook heads, measuring about three feet in length were merely sheared off with a cold iron. These were intended for decorating the walls of cottage parlours. The majority are enriched with coloured spirals, those in red, white and blue being particularly numerous. These interior threads on genuine examples cause very slight ridges on the surface of the glass. In others the coloured threads are spiralled around the surface of the sticks.

Glastonbury chair: collectors' jargon for a type of chair with X-supports and elbowed arms linking seat and top of back. The name derives from an example at Wells, supposedly associated with the last Abbot of Glastonbury. Examples of similar construction have been made or embellished at various, including modern, periods. (See also X-chair.)

Glaze: the application of a glassy material to earthenware or porcelain renders it impervious to liquids and smooth to the touch. Glazes may be dull or matt or brilliant, translucent or opaque, or they may be shot through with brilliant colour. They may be hard and resistant to a knife edge or they may be soft and easily scratched.

Glaze has been applied by dusting powdered lead ore upon the ware, throwing common salt into the kiln so that it volatilizes and forms a thin film of salt-glaze, or by dipping in a liquid glaze solution.

Lead glazes were general until the end of the 19th cent. except for salt-glazed stoneware and hard-paste porcelain. John Rose invented a leadless glaze for porcelain in 1820 which was awarded the Isis gold medal of the Society of Arts, and Job Meigh a leadless glaze for red earthenware in 1822.

"G" mark: see Gotha porcelain, Gera porcelain (under Limbach porcelain) and Berlin porcelain.

"Goat and Bee" jug: a jug decorated in relief with goats and a bee, incised in the base with the word Chelsea, a triangle, and a date, generally 1745, which is regarded as an important documentary piece in respect of the Chelsea factory. A specimen dated 1743 has been recorded.

The shape is known in variations and unmarked, and was derived from a silver prototype. Goat and Bee jugs were made at Coalport, c. 1850.

Gobelins, Manufacture Royale des: (Fr.), the State-supported organization founded in 1667 by Letters Patent at Gobelins, France, through the inspiration of Colbert, Louis XIV's finance minister. It was designed to provide, apart from tapestry, all products of the luxury arts, including furniture, and its first great task was the equipment of the interior of the Palace of Versailles. It owed its success and great reputation to the energies of the first director, Charles Le Brun, who made it the foundation stone of the organized applied arts in France.

For the weaving of tapestries, there were ateliers of both high- and low-warp weavers; no expense was spared; and all the tapestry was the property of the King. Within twenty years Le Brun and his designers had created several new styles of tapestry and made the Gobelins renowned for sumptuous quality and originality. The different series of *Portières*, the *Seasons and Elements*, the *Months or Maison Royales* and the *History of the King* were novel and wonderful achievements. By 1694 one hundred sets (880 pieces) had been woven, mostly with gold. After Louis XIV's declining later years the Regency and Louis XV styles were reflected at the Gobelins. In 1730 Oudry became director, and though he over-emphasized pictorial effects, his *Chasses de Louis XV* was a masterpiece. As at Beauvais (q.v.), his style gave place to that of Boucher. In the latter part of the 18th cent. Neilson, who was Scotch by birth, was the most influential weaver. Until then no Gobelins tapestry could be bought from the factory, being reserved exclusively for royal and diplomatic use. France's financial embarrassments led to Neilson's taking special orders from abroad, and the sets of tapestry with furniture to match, as at Osterley, were the result. The classicism of the late 18th cent. did not interpret well in tapestry, and it is difficult to see the 19th cent. as anything but a steady decline.

Goblet: a drinking glass with the bowl supported on a tall stem.

Go-cart: a framework on wheels to support a toddler, also known as a baby cage.

Godet: a cup.

Goddard, John: (1723/4–85), the originator, perhaps together with his brother-in-law, John Townsend, of block-front (q.v.) and shell-carved cabinet furniture. Widely reckoned the foremost Rhode Island furniture-maker of his day. Apprenticed to Job Townsend, of Newport, whose daughter he married. His sons, Stephen and Thomas Goddard, became first-class cabinet-makers. (See Townsend, John.)

Gold anchor mark: see Chelsea porcelain.

Gold and silver lace: plaited border laces of gold and silver wire, exported from Genoa as early as the 16th cent.

Gold-glass engraving: a technique involving the engraving of a picture on the back of a piece of glass (usually a goblet or some similar container) through a layer of gold leaf previously attached to it. Sometimes colour was added from behind. Usually a second piece of glass was used to seal this engraving from behind although this was more often omitted in later work intended purely as pictures and not as incidental decorations for glass vessels. Many such pictures were made in Italy in the 14th cent. From this technique was developed verre églomisé and under-glass painting (qq.v.).

Gold leaf: gold beaten into very thin sheets.

Gold-tooled bindings: book bindings decorated by means of using small tools impressed in gold do not appear to have been introduced much before 1530. From the next twenty-five years quite a number of bindings have survived bearing the royal arms. Of Elizabethan fine bindings, the most typical are in the international style known as Lyonese, on which heavy centre- and corner-pieces were blocked in a press, and this style continued in use until about 1640. Very decorative leather bindings, elaborately tooled in gold belong to the later 17th cent. Of the English gold-tooled bindings of the 18th cent., among the finest are those designed by Robert Adam and "Athenian" Stuart for books intended to popularise their architectural styles and theories.

Gombron ware: in the early part of the 17th cent. the English East India Company established a factory at the port of Gombron, in the Persian Gulf. As a result of this, native Persian ware and Chinese porcelain imported into England from this source were referred to indiscriminately as Gombron ware. As late as the 1770s Horace Walpole wrote of "two basins of most ancient Gombron china", which may have been either Persian or Chinese. The modern name of the port is Bandar Abbas.

Gong: a spirally wound steel wire on which the hours are struck. First used instead of a bell in the last quarter of the 18th cent.

Goodison, Benjamin: a well-known 18th cent. cabinet-maker who supplied furniture to royal order and whose workshop was in Long Acre. D. 1767.

Goose-neck pediment: see Broken pediment.

Gotch: East Anglian word for a large stoneware jug.

Gotha porcelain: a factory was founded at Gotha in Thuringia in 1757. The finest wares date from 1772 when vases in the Classical taste, biscuit figures, etc. were produced. The first factory mark was an "R" (for Rotberg, the name of the original proprietor) which appears to have been used from c. 1770–83 or later, followed by "R – g" between 1783 and 1805, and then onwards a G or Gotha.

"Gothic" armour: a modern term for the style of plate armour, characterized by slender elegant lines, and decorated with cusped borders and shell-like rippling, developed particularly in Germany in the 15th cent. The term is extended to cover the 15th cent. Italian style, which was rounder in form than the German, and usually had smooth, plain surfaces.

"Gothic" harp: see Harp.

Gothic style: the word Gothic was first used by Italian art critics of the Renaissance (q.v.) to describe a style which they thought owed its origin to the Goths, the vanquishers of the Roman Empire. In fact the style was first developed in Northern France in the 12th cent., involving in architecture, the use of pointed arches, flying buttresses, rib-vaults and stone tracery in windows, arcading, canopies, etc. The new style quickly spread across Europe and remained dominant until the 15th cent. in the South and the 16th cent. in the North. Characteristic decorative motifs such as tracery, cusping, finials, trefoils, etc., all found in Gothic buildings, appear similarly on Medieval woodwork, metalwork, etc.

"Gothic" wallpapers: style of design favoured, if not innovated, by Horace Walpole for Strawberry Hill. Inspired by certain features of medieval architecture. Wallpapers of similar inspiration were also popular during the Gothic revival of the 19th cent.

Gotzkowsky, Johann Ernst: see under Berlin porcelain.

Gouache: a pigment used for painting composed of opaque colours and gum. The term is also used loosely to refer to the picture painted in this medium.

Gouge work: a form of decoration used extensively on oak furniture in the 17th cent. in which the pattern is scooped out by a semi-circular gouge.

Gourd cup: a tall silver cup made in the 16th and 17th cent. in a form reminiscent of a gourd, supported sometimes on a stem in the shape of twisted trees. Designs for gourd cups are to be found in the engraved pattern books of Hans Brosamer and Virgil Solis.

Gouthière, Pierre: French sculptor, the most celebrated of the later 18th cent. *fondeurs-ciseleurs-doreurs.* Born at Bar-sur-Aube in 1732, the son of a saddler. He is known to have been in Paris by 1758, where he became a *maître-doreur.* He was employed by the Crown between 1769 and 1777, but after the latter date his name disappears from the Royal accounts. Gouthière's signed works are exceedingly rare and can be supplemented by a few which can be identified by documents. Almost all bronzes of any quality of the Louis XVI period have been attributed to him, and it is only recently that the increased study of the Royal accounts have revealed the names of other *ciseleurs-doreurs,* who seem to have been his equals in many cases, even though we know little more than their names.

Grace-cup: another name for a small wine cup (q.v.).

Graham, George: London clockmaker who made an important contribution towards accurate timekeeping by his invention of the deadbeat

escapement (q.v.). Active between 1713–51.

Grandfather chair: see Wing chair.

Grandfather clock: properly known as a long-case clock. Came into existence directly after the invention of the anchor escapement (q.v.), 1670. The narrow arc of swing of this escapement made possible the enclosing of the weights and pendulum in a narrow trunk. When the term "grandfather clock" first came into use is uncertain, but Barham uses the term in his *Ingoldsby Legends,* which date from about 1835.

Grandmother clock: a small long-case clock, not exceeding 6 feet 6 inches in height.

Grand pianoforte: in England the grand piano was developed in the 1770s. In appearance instruments of this period are exactly like the contemporary harpsichord (q.v.) and seem to have been modelled on it. They are tricord throughout the five and a half octave compass (some early examples have five octaves only). They have two pedals, the damper lifter (loud, or sustaining pedal and the "soft" pedal, which slide the keyboard from left to right to engage only two of the three strings per note. When a small bolt on the right keyboard cheek is raised this pedal may be further depressed, to give the "una corda" (one string per note) pianissimo, which is marked in some of Beethoven's music.

Grand sonnerie: a system of clock striking whereby the hour and the quarter are struck at each quarter. The earliest known example is the movement with the silent escapement made by Tompion about 1676–80. This system of striking was rendered possible by the invention by Edward Barlow, in 1676, of the rack and snail method of striking (q.v.).

Grangerized: see Extra-illustrated books.

Granite ware: hard, durable and cheap white earthenware, made extensively for the American market in the middle of the 19th cent.

Graver: tool used to engrave a metal plate or to engrave silver with initials, coats of arms, etc. It is also used to sharpen the chased ornament on silver-wares (see also Engraving).

Grease-pan: the circular dish beneath the nozzle of a candlestick into which grease from the burning candle might drip. Grease-pans on glass chandeliers were of moulded pattern with plain edges in the early examples, but by 1750 were of extravagant shapes. The latter were elaborately cut and their pointed rims were drilled and hung with drops.

Greatbach, William: (1735–1813), modeller and potter, son of a farmer at Berryhill; worked for Whieldon and came into contact with Josiah Wedgwood; manufactured biscuit pottery, particularly fruit and pineapple wares to be sent to Wedgwood's factory to glaze, at Lane Delph 1760–70; his cream-coloured teapots decorated with black transfer prints of "The Prodigal Son" (engraved by Radford) are well known. He was ruined by a bad debt; worked for other potters, producing a good "china" glaze for the Baddeleys of Shelton; in 1788 employed by the Turners of Lane End; and from 1788–1807 worked for the Wedgwood factory receiving a pension for life on his retirement. A teapot in the British Museum bears his name. He also used the Chinese Seal mark.

"Grecian" harp: see Harp.

Grecian scroll: see Vitruvian scroll.

Greek fret: see Key pattern.

"Greek" lace: a name given to drawn and cut work embroidery (qq.v.), often combined with geometrical needle-point or pillow lace (qq.v.). When the British occupied the Ionian Isles they brought home great quantities, but much of it was imported from Italy while the Isles belonged to Venice.

"Greene" glasses: drinking glasses of the type ordered between 1666 and 1673 by the London firm of glass-sellers, John Greene and Michael Measey, from the Venetian maker, Morelli. The original drawings sent with the orders survive and provide a record of the taste of the period. Mainly illustrating simple shapes, they include short stemmed wine glasses with conical bowl, some with a flat base, tumblers and winged goblets.

Greenwich armour: armour made in the only English royal workshop, founded at Southwark by Henry VIII in 1511, and subsequently removed to Greenwich Palace, where it remained until closed in about 1637. It was staffed largely by foreign workmen, of whom one of the most important was Jacob Halder, master workman, 1576–1607. He was almost certainly responsible for an album of drawings of armours made at Greenwich, now in the Victoria & Albert Museum, which has made possible the identification of a number of surviving suits, several of which are in the Tower of London.

Grendy, Giles: (1693–1780): a successful joiner and chairmaker who exported much of his furniture. He became Master of the Worshipful Company of Joiners of the City of London in 1766.

Greybeard: a large earthenware spirit jar or jug; a Bellarmine (q.v.). Possibly named from the greyish stone-ware from which it was made and the fact that it usually was decorated with a bearded relief mask. "We will give a cup of distilled waters ... and ye may keep for the purpose the grounds of the last greybeard." – Sir Walter Scott (1771–1832) *The Monastery*, 1820.

Grey hen: stoneware liquor bottle.

"Greyhound" jugs: pottery jugs with greyhound handles and relief decorations of sporting subjects.

Grid-iron: a grid placed over the centre of the fire for cooking, comprising a number of parallel bars, on which meat, etc. rested during the process. Early grid-irons were of simple pattern and made of wrought-iron. Later ones sometimes had the bars channelled and leading to a trough at the front, which had a spout for pouring out the gravy and fat collected in it.

Gridiron pendulum: a type of pendulum invented about 1725 by John Harrison, a carpenter born in 1693 at Soulby in Yorks. Sometimes attributed jointly to him and his brother James. Harrison discovered that brass and steel have an expansion ratio of 3:2. This property is utilized in this pendulum, with its alternate rods of brass and steel. One side only is required, the other rods being put in for balance and symmetry.

"Griffin" mark: see Rockingham earthenware and porcelain.

Grisaille: a painting executed in varying tones of grey.

Groat: silver coin of value 4d. Issued commonly from Edward III to William IV with types similar to penny and, later, royal portrait and shield. Scottish groat from time of David II.

Gros: (groot, groschen, grosso), coins representing silver multiples of the denier (q.v.). Issued commonly throughout Western Europe from the 12th cent. onwards, with great variety of types. An example is the gros tournois of France, with representation of Tours and cross reverse.

Gros-point embroidery: a type of embroidery worked on a woven canvas in a cross-stitch.

Grossbreitenbach porcelain: see under Limbach porcelain.

Ground: a term used in lace-making, syn. with the French *fond* or *réseau*, and basically meaning any background to a lace pattern, but usually restricted to a mesh or net so that grounded laces (q.v.) are contrasted with those where brides (q.v.) support the pattern. Some grounds are best known by their French names. (See Fond chant, Fond clair.)

Ground-colours: areas of coloured glaze on porcelain or enamels, providing a background to painted or gilt decoration, often in reserved panels.

Grounded laces: laces with meshed backgrounds to their patterns, allowing more freedom of design than the alternative linking of brides (q.v.) found in early needlepoints (q.v.). The mesh might be made along with the pattern as in, for example, Valenciennes; it might be worked around the pattern afterwards as in Brussels *point d'Angleterre*; or worked first and the pattern put into it as in Alençon; or worked separately with completed pattern units attached to it as in Brussels *point plat appliqué*. The grounds are considerable aids in identifying old laces since in pillow laces the tiny hexagons or lozenges are composed of different numbers of threads variously twisted and plaited.

Grounded wallpapers: the overall application of colour to the paper before printing. A hand process up to within recent times, including various types, polished, lustred (with the use of mica), metallic, flock, etc.

Grubbe plates: four plates presented to the Victoria and Albert Museum London by Mrs Dora Grubbe, a descendant of James Giles (q.v.), the independent London porcelain decorator; used as a means of identifying wares decorated in Giles's workshop either by himself or his assistants.

Guard chain: a long chain hung round the neck to support keys or toilet requirements.

Gubbio maiolica: tin-glazed earthenware made at the workshop of Giorgio Andreoli at Gubbio, in the duchy of Urbino. This workshop was famous in the 16th cent. for its lustre wares and particularly for its ruby-coloured pigment.

Guéridon or **Guéridon table:** (*Fr.*), a small piece of furniture, usually circular, intended to support some form of light. In the 17th cent. in France it sometimes took the form of a negro figure holding a tray, and the name derives from that of a well-known Moorish galley-slave called Guéridon. Subsequently the term was extended to cover almost any form of small table on which candelabra, etc., might be placed. (See Candle-stand.)

Guernsey measure: a baluster-shaped pewter measure, encircled by two broad bands, and having a heart-shaped lid and twin acorn thumb-piece (q.v.); peculiar to Guernsey, C.I.

Guiennois: large gold coin of Edward III and the Black Prince, issued in their French possessions in Guienne. Types, prince in armour and elaborate cross reverse.

Guilder: silver coin of the United Provinces of the Netherlands in 17th and 18th cent., with types, provincial arms and personification of the Netherlands with hat on spear. Multiples of one and a half, two and three.

Guiliano, Carlo: (d. 1912), an outstanding 19th cent. Neapolitan jeweller who emigrated to London and established a reputation for his jewellery in the Renaissance style.

Guilloche: a border moulding composed of interlaced ribbon enclosing foliate rosettes. This form of ornament appears on furniture and metalwork, from the 16th to the 18th cent.

Guilloché: (*Fr.*), engine-turned (q.v.).

Guinea: gold coin of varying value, finally settling at 21s. Issued from 1670 to 1813. Types, royal portrait obverse and heraldic design on reverse. Multiples of five and two guineas and fractions also issued.

Guipure: confusing term for needle-point or pillow lace without grounds (q.v.) supported by brides (q.v.).

Guipure d'Art: a type of embroidery worked in white thread on a netted foundation in the manner of 16th cent. lacis (q.v.) and often classified as lace.

Guisarme: see under Pole-arms.

Guitar: the Spanish guitar is the finest of the plucked-string instruments. In its own country it has an unbroken record of continuous use for several hundreds of years, and its vogue elsewhere from about 1800 onwards has produced some superb instruments. Choice woods and inlays of mother-of-pearl and ivory were used with considerable delicacy and care, and no two guitars seem to be alike in decoration.

Gumley, John: (d. 1729), looking-glass maker at Lambeth and cabinet-maker to George I. Some knowledge of Gumley's activities has been gained from frequent notices in the press of his day. His glass-house was set up in 1705 and in the following year his showroom over the New Exchange received a commendation from the pen of Richard Steele. A looking-glass with the name *Gumley* carved on a small gilt plaque is at Hampton Court Palace and another with *John Gumley, 1703,* is at Chatsworth. He was in partnership with James Moore and would seem to have died some time prior to 1729, in which year accounts were rendered by Mrs Elizabeth Gumley & Co.

Gunner's stiletto: a stiletto (q.v.) with a scale on the blade for converting weight of gun-shot into diameter of bore.

Gwa: Japanese term meaning picture or drawing; drew (at the end of an artist's signature).

Gwafu: Japanese term for a book of sketches.

Gwajō: Japanese term for an album of folding pictures. (See also Japanese print.)

Gwim, James: originally a coach-painter in Kildare, who worked for Stephen Theodor Janssen (q.v.) at the Battersea enamel factory (q.v.). His designs for enamels included one of Britannia encouraging the Linen Manufacture in Ireland, engraved by Ravenet, and he was probably responsible for others in similar vein, such as Britannia encouraging the Arts and Sciences and Hibernia receiving the apple from Paris.

Gypcière: a medieval type of purse generally suspended from the girdle. The finest examples, dating from the 16th cent., had iron frames chiselled and damascened with gold and silver.

Hadley chest: an American type of chest found in and around Hadley, Massachusetts. A characteristic New England dower chest of 1690–1710. Its distinctive feature is the incised carving of tulips, vines and leaves which cover the entire front.

Hadley, H.: maker of fine quality holster pistols in the third quarter of the 18th cent. His productions were furnished with silver mounts of unusual richness. He followed the Hispanicising fashion in his barrel design.

Hague, The, porcelain: hard-paste porcelain was made at The Hague in Holland from about 1776 with the help of German workmen, while a certain amount of decorating of pieces made elsewhere was also done at the factory. A stork in blue, either under or over the glaze appears as a mark. Tournai porcelain (q.v.) was some-times decorated at The Hague and such pieces are found with the stork in blue over the glaze.

Haig, Thomas: cabinet-maker, in partnership with Thomas Chippendale (q.v.) from 1771 to 1779 and then with the latter's son, Thomas Chippendale the younger, (q.v.) until 1796.

Halberd: see under Pole-arms.

Half-armour: a light armour covering the whole body excepting the legs, and often also excluding the arms.

Half bound: this normally refers to a book of which the spine and outer corners are of leather, while the rest of the sides are covered with cloth or paper (often marbled). If there are no leather corners, the book is said to be quarter bound; if the leather corners are very wide, it is said to be three-quarter bound.

Halfpenny: silver coin with same types as penny, struck occasionally in the Saxon coinage and commonly in later Middle Ages. Copper halfpenny with royal portrait and Britannia reverse first issued in 1672 by Charles II.

Halfpenny, William and John: father and son who were both architects and designers and whose publications, such as *Rural Architecture in the Chinese taste* (1752) and *New Designs for Chinese Temples* (1750), disseminated the new light, exotic taste. Like other pattern books of this date produced by architects, they are concerned principally with building and garden architecture, but the latter includes some designs for chairs.

Half-seconds pendulum: a type of pendulum 9.8 inches in length, beating twice a second. This is the longest pendulum normally found on verge escapement (q.v.) clocks.

Half-tester: see under Tester.

Half-title: the leaf in front of the title page of a book (and of the frontispiece, if any) which carries on its recto the title (sometimes abbreviated) of the book, possibly a volume number or indication that it belongs to a series, and occasionally the price. The verso (q.v.) is often blank, but sometimes carries the printer's imprint (q.v.), or, in modern books, a list of other works by the same author or from the same publisher.

Hall, John: engraver, apprenticed in 1754 to Stephen Theodor Janssen (q.v.) at the Battersea enamel factory (q.v.).

Hall-mark: strictly speaking, the distinguishing mark of the Hall or Assay Office at which a piece of silver so marked is assayed, e.g. Leopard's head for London, Crown for Sheffield, etc. Used generally in the plural to denote the whole group of marks employed, viz. Hall, maker's, standard, and date-letter. There are no Hall-marks on American silver. (See also Date-letter.)

Hamadan rugs: Hamadan is the marketing centre for Kurdish rugs, and they are often known by this name. Heavy, long pile of great durability, rather coarse in stitch but well coloured, designs often embellished with animal figures. Hamadan rugs are frequently described as "Persian".

Hampshire, Isle of Wight: "lace" made in running stitch on machine-made net.

Hanap: the medieval name for "standing-cup" (q.v.).

Hancock, Robert: (1729/30–1817), engraver; son of John Hancock; apprenticed to George Anderton, Birmington 1746; working at York House, Battersea (q.v.), 1753 as engraver for enamels. Probably at Bow 1756 for a brief period before moving to Worcester where he served as engraver, becoming partner in the business 1772–74. Hancock joined Turner at the Caughley factory 1775. He was at Oldbury 1780 (and possibly did some engraving for Bilston enamels); Tividale, Nr Dudley 1781; Birmingham 1791; Bristol 1796; and London 1808. D. 14 October 1816 and was buried at Brislington, Bristol. Marks:

Hand blown glass: see Free blown.

Hand-coolers: semi-precious stones carved in the form of eggs, and of a similar size, for the purpose expressed in their name. Highly polished agates, marbles, and interesting pieces of bluejohn were favourite materials chosen for these attractive objects.

Hand gun: the earliest form of hand fire-arm, introduced early in the 14th cent. It consisted simply of a tubular barrel attached to a long wooden stock designed to be held under the arm, and ignited at the touch-hole by hand.

Handkerchief table: an American term for a single-leaf table with leaf and top triangular in shape. Closed, the table fits in a corner, opened it is a small square.

Han dynasty: dynasty of the Chinese Han Emperors covering the period 206 B.C. to A.D. 220. Earthenware found in Han tombs indicates that the skilful potter had mastered techniques of wide artistic possibilities, notably that of glazing. Vessels were still following metal forms, decorated with bands in moulded relief. A green or brown "lead" glaze was applied to a reddish earthenware, but some grey earthenwares were left unglazed. Even more important was the discovery at this time of felspathic-glazed stoneware. The hard impervious body with its semi-transparent olive-brown glaze, containing felspar rock, foreshadows the invention of porcelain.

Hanger: (1) a light, curved, single-edged civilian sword used by horsemen and sailors in the 17th and 18th cent. The term when first used appears to be synonymous with falchion and cutlass; (2) the triangular buckled sling attached to the belt, in which a rapier was carried in the late 16th and early 17th cent.

Hanoverian pattern spoons: see under Table-services.

Harache, Pierre: the first of the Huguenot goldsmiths seeking refuge in London from persecution to gain admittance to the Goldsmiths' Company (1682) and the right to have his wares assayed by the Company.

Hard-grain morocco: see Morocco.

Hardi: gold coin of the Black Prince struck in the French possessions with types, half-length figure of prince and elaborate cross.

Hard-paste porcelain: true porcelain manufactured from china clay and china stone, glazed with china stone made fusible with a flux. It shows a shining fracture when broken and is completely vitrified and dense. Chinese porcelain is hard-paste and much Continental but in England only three factories made it, Plymouth, Bristol, and New Hall in its early days. New Hall advertised its production as "Real China".

Harimaze: Japanese term for sheets printed with two or more irregularly-shaped subjects, to be divided up by the purchaser.

Harleian: a book bound in the manner of the 18th cent. bindings executed for the library of Robert Harley, Earl of Oxford, and his son, Edward. These were usually of red morocco, with a border made up of one or more rolls (or rows of single tools), and often had a large central lozenge made up with small tools. They were the work of several different binders, including the rival firms of Thomas Elliott and Christopher Chapman.

Harman, Barne: gunsmith, probably of German origin. He served with the Royalists during the Civil Wars as gunmaker to Prince Rupert. He was imprisoned during the Commonwealth, but was subsequently appointed gunmaker to Charles II at the Restoration. He died soon after. He produced screw-barrelled and breach-loading pistols at a time when such weapons were unfamiliar in England. He is associated with fine quality, practical weapons rather than *armes de grand luxe*.

Harp-lute: see Harps.

Harps: the largest and most familiar is the double-action harp used in modern orchestras, usually known as the "Gothic" harp. These instruments may have forty-seven strings or more, tuned diatonically, and seven pedals working in notched slots, each of which gives three positions. Numbers of smaller double-action harps, known as "Grecian" harps, were made by several makers in England and elsewhere following the invention of the double-action system in 1810, and are occasionally found. Before that date single-action harps, with only one notch for the pedals, are found.

A number of smaller harps and harp-like instruments also appeared in the early 19th cent. Among these may be mentioned the Royal Portable Irish Harp of Egan and the various inventions of Edward Light, of which the most commonly encountered is the harp-lute, virtually a small harp with additional strings on a fingerboard like a guitar. These instruments, though attractive in appearance, were practically domestic toys for the strumming of drawing-room ballads, and they died a natural death with the growing popularity of the pianoforte.

Harpsichords: have been known since the 15th cent., but the name suggests to most people the fine 18th cent. English instruments of Shudi, Kirkman, and their contemporaries. A few English and Netherlands instruments are known of the 17th cent. and before, but they are so excessively rare and valuable that the possibility of discovering an example is hardly worth considering.

The large English harpsichords from about 1730 onwards have two keyboards or "manuals", usually five hand-stops on the front board above the upper keyboard, and two pedals. There are three strings to each note, two "unisons" and one tuned to the octave, which can be used separately or together by means of the stops. On Shudi's instruments the right pedal works the "Venetian Swell", a louvred inner lid over the strings which can be opened by degrees to produce a crescendo. The invention was patented in 1769. The left pedal on most instruments operates the "machine" when a bolt in the left keyboard cheek is moved, and alters the arrangement of hand-stops in use, producing registration effects similar to that of an organ. Numerous single keyboard harpsichords are known.

Harrison, John: a carpenter's son, born in Yorkshire in 1693, who won a Government award, offered in 1714, for the invention of a marine chronometer. A London clockmaker of eminence, he invented the gridiron pendulum (q.v.).

Hash-dish: 18th or 19th cent. circular dish of silver or plate with straight sides, close-fitting cover and loop or drop-ring handles. Similar to, and probably used also as, a vegetable dish. Often found with open-frame stand and spirit-lamp.

Hasp: a hinged strap used with a pin or lock to secure a door or chest.

Hat badge: originally derived from medieval pilgrim signs, enamelled and jewelled badges were worn by men during the Renaissance. Antique cameos (q.v.), mounted in contemporary settings reveal the Humanist interests of the age. Many hat badges have mythological themes, while religious subjects usually include the figure of a patron saint.

Hausmaler: see Independent decorators.

Haystack: more properly Haycock, which it resembles. An Irish pewter tavern measure, made chiefly in Cork.

"H.C." mark: see Cassel porcelain.

"HD" mark: see Kelsterbach porcelain.

Heading sword: an executioner's sword, usually with a plain cruciform hilt long enough to be used with two hands, and a broad, straight, two-edged blade with a rounded or squared point. It was employed on the Continent, and especially in Germany, from the 16th to the early 19th cent.

Heart horse-brass: these brasses appear to have ornamented the check rein. One series of hearts was stamped in silhouette, sometimes in bold relief, perhaps more frequently with a flat surface. Plain hearts were cast within circular perforated frames, rayed piercing sometimes encircling closely spaced circular perforations: variations are numerous. A series of designs in which the heart is cast in the round has a secondary heart rising in relief from the centre. Rare is the heart within a heart, that is, a heart in relief with its centre pierced by a smaller heart. Three or six highly burnished small hearts arranged into the shape of a larger heart, was a popular design during the 1890s.

Hearty good fellow: toby jug in form of a swaggering standing figure clasping a jug.

Heller: from 17th to 19th cent. a copper coin of many German states, especially Cologne and Aachen. Multiples of two, four, eight and twelve, with variety of types.

Helm: a large headpiece or helmet, covering the entire head and face and reaching nearly to the shoulders, introduced at the end of the 12th cent. The top was at first flat but by the middle of the 13th cent. had become conical, giving an improved glancing surface. During the first half of the 14th cent. the helm was often worn over the bascinet (q.v.) in warfare, but was subsequently relegated to the tilt-yard, where it remained in use until well into the 16th cent. Later it was usually bolted to the breast and back.

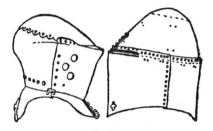

Hen and chickens: emblems of Providence, hence frequent use as adornments of money-boxes.

Hen dish: oval, basket-shaped egg-dish with cover in the form of a sitting hen.

Hepplewhite, George: (d. 1786), cabinet-maker, whose pattern book *The Cabinet-maker and Upholsterer's Guide* published after his death, in 1788, has made him known to posterity. Hepplewhite interpreted the new classical style inspired by Robert Adam (q.v.) and many of the designs in his pattern book are for inlaid furniture. As a working cabinet-maker he does not appear to have enjoyed any fame in his lifetime.

Herat carpets: fine quality Persian carpets. The design most closely associated with them is a close conventionalized all-over effect, with a recurring leaf or "fish" motif and small rosettes. This is copied throughout Persia; ground shade is usually dark blue, and a distinguishing feature of fine specimens is a soft green border. Knot: Ghiordes or Sehna (qq.v.).

Herculaneum: a potworks near the site of the present Herculaneum Dock in Liverpool was founded by Richard Abbey & Graham in 1793. It was sold to Worthington, Humble & Holland three years later. The company was enlarged in 1806 and continued to operate until 1833 when the partnership was dissolved and the property sold to Ambrose Lace and others for £25,000. Lace leased the premises to Thomas Case, gentleman, and John Mort, potter, who operated until 1836. Subsequently the firm traded as Mort and Simpson until the works were closed down in 1841. Apart from the Herculaneum Pottery the company was also in occupation of an earthenware factory on the Sankey Canal, St

Helens (1 biscuit, 2 gloss ovens). The advertisement of the sale of stock in the *Staffordshire Advertiser*, 14 November 1840, stated that the Herculaneum Pottery was "now about to be pulled down for the erection of docks". An "Unreserved sale of valuable copper-plate engravings Blocks and Cases, superior Figure Moulds" to be held at the Leopard Inn, Burslem, was advertised in the *North Staffordshire Mercury*, 23 January 1841. The products of the factory included blue-printed earthenware, cream-coloured stoneware jugs, drab stoneware, busts, earthenware figures, and from 1801, porcelain of the Staffordshire type.

Herold, Johann Gregor: (b. 1696), trained as a miniature and enamel painter, Herold was put in artistic direction of the Meissen porcelain factory (q.v.) in 1720 and was formally appointed director and arcanist (q.v.) in 1731, which he remained until his retirement in 1765. He himself decorated Meissen porcelain and was responsible for the introduction, about 1725, of scenes, painted in brilliant colours, containing pseudo-Chinese figures framed in scrollwork in gold and sometimes lustre.

Herring-bone banding: a decorative veneer (q.v.) border much used on walnut furniture of the late 17th and early 18th cent. consisting of two narrow strips of veneer laid together diagonally forming a pattern resembling a herring-bone or feather and contrasting in design with the surface veneer on the piece. Drawer fronts, table tops, bureau flaps and similar fields were frequently bordered with a herring-bone banding or cross banding (q.v.) or with both. Also known as feather banding.

Herring-bone fringe: see Blazes.

Hf.: half; an abbreviation found in book-sellers catalogues especially in the combinations hf. cf. for half calf, hf. mor. for half morocco. (See also Half-bound.)

"H" hinge: like the cock's head hinge, an early external type of hinge in the form of the letter "H" ex-

tensively used on cupboards of the 16th and 17th cent. Good quality hinges of these two varieties have stop-chamfered edges and were originally held fast by hand wrought nails, never by screws. (See also Cock's head hinge.)

Highboy or **high chest of drawers:** an American tall chest of drawers mounted on a commode or lowboy (q.v.) sometimes topped with a broken-arch pediment usually heightened with finials. Characteristically plain in New England; highly carved and ornamented in Philadelphia. The earlier examples are sometimes japanned (see Japan work) in a manner popular in England in the late 17th cent. Mid-18th cent. pieces are of mahogany, white walnut or walnut, while towards 1775 maple was also used.

High-warp tapestry: tapestry woven on an upright loom. In the Middle Ages such tapestry was considered superior. It is slower to make, but the work can be more exact and it allows for subtler effects of texture. The weaver sits at his upright loom, divides his warp with his left hand with the aid of leashes, and inserts his coloured wefts in accordance with his cartoon, which is placed behind

him. He works with the back side of the tapestry towards him and he can see the face by means of a mirror. For closer inspection he need only move round to the front of the loom. (See also Low-warp tapestry.)

Hila rugs: Caucasian rugs, frequently with a small centre medallion with matching corner-pieces, the subsidiary design being a clearly defined cone. Ice-blue is the distinguishing shade.

Hipped knee: an ornamental treatment of the knee of a cabriole leg sometimes found on good quality chairs and settees of the first half of the 18th cent. in which the carving on the knee is extended on to the seat rail above.

Hiramakiyé (*Japanese* = flat-sown picture), a Japanese lacquer-work technique involving a flat decoration on the lacquer surface.

Hiramé: (*Japanese* = flat aspect), a Japanese lacquer-work technique in which small pieces of gold or silver leaf are placed on the lacquered surface, fairly wide apart but evenly spread.

Hispano-Moresque maiolica: tin-glazed earthenware made in Spain by Moorish craftsmen first at Granada and later from about the end of the 14th cent. for some 300 years, in the workshops of the Manises in Valencia. The ware is decorated with metallic lustre pigments made from oxides of silver and copper, probably originally invented in Persia.

Hitchcock chair: an American adaptation of an English late 18th cent. painted and stencilled chair. It has round-turned legs, raked, and an oval-turned "pillow-back" top rail. Almost always painted black with stencillings of fruits and flowers in gold or colours. Named after Lambert Hitchcock, of Hitchcockville, Connecticut, who made this type of chair in quantity from 1820 to 1850.

Hitsu: see Fude.

Hob-nail cutting: a method of decorating glass vessels by cutting or grinding in deep relief to form a pattern of large diamonds, each with a flat point incised with a simple cross. Late 18th and early 19th cent. Irish and English glass vessels were frequently decorated with this doubly cut diamond pattern.

Hoechst porcelain: hard-paste porcelain was made at Hoechst-on-Main, Germany, from the year 1750, at a factory which had been founded four years earlier for the purpose of making faience. At first the new venture experienced financial difficulties but was subsidised by the Elector of Mainz in 1765. The factory closed in 1798. The early wares follow the Meissen example, a rich lilac being much favoured with gilding in the borders. Hoechst figures from about 1765 often have a grassy-mound base. J. P. Melchior became chief modeller in 1767, much of his work being in the classical style. The mark used is the wheel of Mainz, either incised or in colour, above or below the glaze.

Ho-ho bird : or *fêng-huang*, the phoenix.

Holdship, Richard and **Josiah:** engravers and part-proprietors of the original porcelain works at Worcester, from 1751 until 1759. Richard Holdship went to Derby, and in 1764 offered to impart information concerning the Worcester porcelain formula, and to teach "Printing in Enamell and Blew".

Some Worcester engravings carry a rebus design of R H in monogram and an anchor.

RH Worcester

RH Worcester

RH Worcester

These marks are traditionally regarded as those of Holdship who was believed to have been in charge of the printing department. This mark however may stand for Robert Hancock who later added his signature in full because the monogram was confused with that of Holdship. Much confusion has arisen from the initials of Hancock and R. Holdship being the same. The monogram with the reversed "R" has been described as RJH and believed to represent Richard and Josiah Holdship.

Holland, Henry: (1745–1806), an architect of influence whose work for the Prince of Wales at Carlton House and for Samuel Whitbread at Southill made him famous. He designed the interiors and the furniture at Southill in accordance with French Directoire (q.v.) taste.

Hollie-work: a type of white-work embroidery popular during the Georgian period, particularly for babies' clothes and bonnets. It was worked on fine linen, lawn or cambric in white thread. Delicate openwork patterns, worked without any foundation in the manner of needlepoint lace, were inserted into holes cut in the material, which were previously edged with buttonhole stitch. Alternatively, the threads of the ground material were drawn out one way only and the pattern worked on the remaining threads.

Hollins, Samuel: (1748–1820), son of Richard Hollins of Far Green, Hanley; manufacturer of earthenware and "red china" at a factory on the Caulden Canal, Vale Pleasant, Shelton, from c. 1780 until c. 1815. He was one of the original partners in the New Hall porcelain factory (q.v.) which traded as Hollins, Warburton & Co., and by a codicil to his will dated 27 April 1820 he left his interest in the Company (valued at his death £5,975), to his son Thomas Hollins of Cheetham Hill, Manchester.

About 1815 he must have made over his earthenware business to Matthew Mare, his son-in-law (who manufactured earthenware on the Cauldon Canal and is listed in Parson and Bradshaw's *Directory* 1818).

Samuel Hollins made excellent unglazed dark green and dark red stonewares with relief decoration.

Hollow cutting: a method of decorating glass vessels by means of cutting or grinding a pattern with a convex-edged wheel, producing shallow concavities in the glass.

A pattern of "hollow diamonds", consisting of intersecting cavities was much used on mid-18th cent. wares, but many variants of cut motifs were employed.

Hollow stem: a type of stem found on drinking glasses in the late 18th cent. in the form of a hollow cylinder, sometimes, though rarely, knopped.

Hollow-ware: a general term for vessels designed to hold liquids.

Holy-water bucket: the receptacle for the holy water sprinkled in the *asperges* at the beginning of the Mass. Early examples are normally straight sided, polygonal or cylindrical, and occasionally waisted; the bombé-vase shape came into fashion in the 17th cent. Handles were occasionally terminated with dragon heads.

Hon: Japanese term for a book.

Honan wares: black- and brown-glazed Chinese porcelain wares of the Sung dynasty (q.v.), probably made in Honan Province.

Honey gilding: see Gilding.

Honeysuckle motif: see Anthemion.

Honiton lace: pillow lace, the best and the first made in England, described as bone lace (q.v.) in about 1620 in Westcote's *View of Devonshire* and continuing until about 1725. Suggestive of *point d'Angleterre* (q.v.) with the ground worked round the pattern, but with less attractive pattern-shapes. Honiton net, made from costly Antwerp thread, and of excellent quality, was an important product in the 18th cent. Honiton *appliqué* lace was made with motifs of pillow lace (q.v.) applied to this net ground but the net was soon machine-made, with the flower motifs reduced to meaningless ugly shapes. Late in the 19th cent. Honiton made a tape pillow lace with brides (q.v.), sometimes in needlepoint, instead of a mesh ground, and also Devonia lace.

Hood: the upper removable portion of a long-case clock. In all, except very early cases, it draws forward.

Hoof foot: a foot in the form of a hoof appears on early examples of walnut chairs made with the cabriole leg between about 1695 and 1720. A simpler terminal, which retained its popularity for a longer period was the club foot (q.v.), introduced shortly after the first appearance of the hoof foot.

Hooped-back chair: see Windsor chair.

Hope chest: an American term used colloquially to describe a dowry chest, which itself is a misnomer, since a chest normally serves more purposes across the years than holding a trousseau (see also Dowry chest).

Hope, Thomas: (c. 1770–1831), a wealthy connoisseur and collector of antique sculpture and pottery, whose writings on architecture, furniture and costume are a guide to Regency taste. His book of designs, recording the furniture made for his house, Deepdene, in Surrey, entitled *Household Furniture and Decoration* was published in 1807.

Horae, or **Books of Hours:** manuscript or printed collections of prayers, etc., for private devotional use at the canonical offices of the Roman Church. Variations of detail between one diocese and another are indicated by such phrases as "Horae of the Use of Rouen", or "a Book of Hours of the Sarum Use".

Horn-book: "A leaf of paper containing the alphabet (often, also, the ten digits, some elements of spelling, and the Lord's Prayer) protected by a thin plate of translucent horn, and mounted on a tablet of wood with a handle" (SOED). Horn-books were used to teach children their rudiments from the 16th to early 18th cent.

Horn mark: a mark used on porcelain at the Chantilly factory and imitated at Worcester and Caughley.

Horse dressing glass: see Cheval-glass.

Horseshoe back chair: American name for a hoop back Windsor chair (q.v.).

Hoso-ye: small vertical narrow Japanese print about 12 × 6 inches.

Hounskull: see under Bascinet.

Hour circle: see Chapter ring.

Hsüan Tê period: (1426–35), classic reign for "blue-and-white" Chinese porcelains of very fine, richly-glazed material. A certain rhythmic vitality is found alike in the contours of vessels and in their painted lotus scrolls, flying dragons, etc. Blackish spots sometimes mottle the cobalt pigment. Underglaze copper-red painting, white wares with faint incised or slip designs (*an hua*), blue or red monochromes, and the use of yellow enamel grounds, are found. Later times (especially the 18th cent.) "borrowed" the reign-mark, and also made admirable copies of the wares.

Huchet: *Fr.* 17th cent. hunting horn.

Hull, Belle Vue Pottery: a potworks was started here in 1802 by James and Jeremiah Smith, Job Ridgway of Shelton and Josiah Hipwood. In 1806 the factory passed to Job and George Ridgway who, after working it for a few years, closed it down. In 1825 William Bell purchased the pottery and used it until 1840. Much creamware, usually painted or transfer-printed in blue or brown with landscapes, etc. was exported to Germany. The factory was a large one with a depot in Hamburg. The following marks were used:

Impressed

Transfer-printed

Hunting carpets: Persian carpets with elaborate hunting scenes, realistically depicted.

Hunting horn mark: see Chantilly porcelain.

Hunting sword: a short, light sabre with a straight or very slightly curved blade and usually no knuckle-bow. Originally designed to be worn while hunting, as its name implies; it was often affected by high-ranking officers during the 18th cent.

Husk ornament: an ornamental motif resembling the husk of a wheat ear used continually by architects and craftsmen during the Adam period. Festoons of husks and pendent husks in diminishing size appear for example, carved on chair backs of the period, as a decorative inlay on cabinet furniture, or applied and chased on silverware such as sugar vases or sauce boats. (See Bell flower ornament.)

Hutch: enclosed structure, often raised on uprights, or an enclosed structure of more than one tier. The name derives from Fr. *Huche*, a kneading-trough or metal-tub, but the significance of hutch was much wider. Food-hutch, often confused with dole-cupboard, is a name given to a hutch with perforated panels.

Ice glass: glass to which an appearance of cracked ice has been given by means of plunging the hot glass in water and later reheating it. This method of decorating glass was used in Venice in the 16th cent. and subsequently by Venetian workmen who set up glasshouses elsewhere.

Ice-pail: see Wine-cooler.

Ichimai-ye: single-sheet Japanese prints.

Icon: a religious painting which first appeared in Byzantium in early Christian times, and so quickly gained a foothold there that it soon became an integral and generally accepted feature of the Byzantine church, penetrating to the Balkans and Russia as Christianity spread into those lands from Byzantium. Icons can be regarded as the Greek-Orthodox equivalent of the religious pictures of the Italian Primitives, of which they were likewise the forerunners. They were originally developed from the tomb portraits of the Egyptians, and though the earliest took the form of presentations of single figures, especially Christ and the

Virgin, pictorial illustrations to the Gospels also became important.

Illuminated books: 19th cent. books in which the plates, and often part of the text, notably the initial letters of chapters, are not only coloured but gilded in imitation of the illuminated manuscripts of the Middle Ages.

Ilmenau porcelain: see under Limbach porcelain.

"Image toys": contemporary designation of mid-18th cent. Staffordshire pottery figures.

Imari porcelain: a familiar name for the porcelains exported by Japan from Arita in the province of Hizan during the first half of the 18th cent. "Brocaded Imari" in blue, red and gold were the inspiration of later English china and earthenware patterns made at Derby, Worcester, Spode, Mintons and Masons. These were generally known as "Japans".

"i" mark: see Limbach porcelain.

Imp.: short for impressit, impresserunt or imprimé, in which case it means printed by; or for imprimerie – printing establishment or works. The name of the printer is often found on a bird print, usually under the title.

Impasto: a term used in painting to describe the laying on of colour thickly.

Imperial paper copy: see Large paper copy.

Imperial Russian service: known also as the "Frog" service. Josiah Wedgwood received the order to make this enormous service of cream-coloured earthenware in March 1773. It was for the Empress Catherine of Russia, and was to be placed in her palace near St Petersburg (Leningrad), known as "La Grenouillière". The device of a green frog was painted in a shield in the border of each piece. The service numbered more than nine hundred pieces, each of which bore at least one painting of an English view, the obtaining of which caused a great deal of difficulty.

Impression: a term applied to any print made from a metal plate, wood block or stone.

Imprint: a notification to the reader (and to the legal authorities) of the person or persons responsible for the production of a book. Many of the earliest printed books bore no such note; but from about 1465 till late in the 16th cent. the printer's imprint was generally placed at the end of the book (and there properly called the colophon, q.v.). It normally comprised the place of printing, the name of the printer and the date.

With the development of the title-page during the 16th cent. the printer's imprint tended to be transferred thither (even if it was repeated at the end of the book); and from the latter half of the 16th to the middle of the 18th cent. it was often combined with the publisher's imprint, in such forms as *Printed by A.B. for P.Q.* Later, the lower half of the title-page came generally to be reserved for the publisher's imprint – again normally comprising place, name and date; the printer's name (and perhaps address) being relegated either to the back of the title or of the half-title or to the end of the book. Either type of imprint may be accompanied by the printer's or publisher's device or mark.

Ince and Mayhew: cabinet-makers, who published a series of some 300 furniture designs, entitled the *Universal System of Household Furniture*. They appeared between 1759 and 1763.

Incense boat: the vessel in which the incense is carried before it is placed in the censer to burn. Normally it is a fairly simple boat-shaped vessel, and it was occasionally made to match a censer. Made of precious or base metal, or of semi-precious stone mounted in metal.

Inc., incid., incidit: engraved.

Incise carving: see Scratch carving.

Incised decoration on pottery: decoration cut into the paste or body with a sharp pointed instrument. Much used by country potters for names, inscriptions and dates. (See also Sgraffiato.)

Incised stem: a type of stem found on drinking glasses in the late 17th and 18th cent. ornamented with spiral grooving.

Incunable, incunabula: The special use of *incunabula* (Latin for "things in the cradle") to mean books produced in the infancy of printing has for many years been further specialized to mean books printed in the 15th cent.

Incuse: a design or mark sunk into a coin; the opposite of relief (q.v.).

Independent decorators: in the 18th and early 19th cent. porcelain was often bought "in the white" for decoration by outside enamellers and gilders. This practice was much developed in Germany where these independent decorators were known as "Hausmaler". In England the most notable were Giles, Duesbury, Baxter (who embellished Coalport china), T. M. Randall & R. Robins (who from Spa Fields, London, decorated Swansea, Nantgarw and Coalport for London dealers).
Salt-glazed stoneware was similarly decorated by Duesbury, and cream-coloured ware by Mrs Warburton at Cobridge, Robinson & Rhodes at Leeds, and Absolon at Yarmouth.
Other English outside decorators were Fidèle Duvivier, Allen of Lowestoft, John Cutts & Sons of Shelton.

Indian mask: a mask with a plumed head-dress used as a decorative motif on crestings (q.v.), particularly of mirrors, at the end of the 17th cent., and more popularly, during the earlier years of the 18th cent.

"India" wallpapers: 18th cent. name given to many articles imported from the Far East, including paper-hangings specially made for the European market.

"India" ware: the term in general use in England during the 18th cent. for imported Chinese porcelain. It gained currency owing to the fact that the East India Company held a monopoly of trade with the East. It sold the goods it imported by auction at India House, London. This building in the City was demolished in 1861.

Inlaid book-bindings: bindings involving the use of coloured leather or leathers stuck, like mosaic, into the main skin. The term is also in two ways with reference to the leaves of a book: (a) the insertion of a leaf or a plate or a cut, in a larger and usually stouter leaf, to enlarge its margins, and thus its whole size (often in order to range with other larger leaves in a composite volume, when it is usually described as inlaid to size); (b) the laying down, or re-margining on all four edges, of a badly damaged leaf.

Inlaid furniture: furniture decorated with a surface ornament formed by insetting separate pieces of differently coloured woods, or bone, ivory, shell, etc., in a recessed ground. Inlay was popular as a decoration on chair-backs, chests, table friezes etc. between 1550 and 1650, and should not be confused with marquetry (q.v.).

Inlaid leaf: see under Inlaid book-bindings.

Inlaid tiles: a process of inlaying used by medieval potters for decorating paving tiles (Cleeve Abbey, Westminster Abbey) and by Sussex potters, c. 1790–1850, for useful and ornamental wares. The decoration was formed by impressing the body with punches or with printers' types, and filling in with clay of a contrasting colour, usually white on red.

Inscr.: inscribed.

Inscribed copy: unless specifically qualified, this term refers to the copy of a book which has been autographed or inscribed by the author. It often implies, further, that the copy has been inscribed to somebody or for somebody; but it is important to distinguish, were possible, between a presentation copy (q.v.), which is a spontaneous gift, and a copy inscribed by the author, often some while after publication, in response to an owner's request. The former naturally appeals much more strongly to the sentiment of collectors.

Inside dentelles: see Dentelle decoration.

Intaglio: a carved pattern or design hollowed out from the surface of a gem or of rock-crystal or glass.

Intarsia: see Tarsia.

Interlaced "Cs" mark: see Ludwigsburg and Niderviller porcelain.

Interlaced "Ls" mark: see Sèvres porcelain, Limbach porcelain and Longton Hall porcelain.

Inventory numbers: these are often found painted or branded on furniture made for the Crown or Royal Family of France. They frequently refer to the *Journal du Garde Meuble de la Couronne*, which has survived intact for some periods between the late 17th cent. and the Revolution. When accompanied by a Palace letter (q.v.), the numbers may refer to the inventories made of that particular Royal residence which may or may not be extant.

Inv., In., Invenit: invented, designed.

Iron red: a red pigment made from an oxide of iron; used to decorate ceramics.

Ironstone china: a hard, durable white earthenware alleged to contain slag of ironstone as one of its ingredients, patented by Charles James Mason in 1831. The patent specification was false and unworkable. Other firms have used the name, notably Ridgway & Morley and Geo. L. Ashworth & Bros.

Ishi-zuri: Japanese term for a stone-print.

Isleworth earthenware: pottery was made at a factory established about 1760 by Joseph Shore. It closed down about 1825.

"Welsh" wares, useful domestic articles decorated with zig-zag patterns in brown and yellow slip, were probably the main products of the factory.

Red, green and buff terra cotta teapots and ornamental pieces with relief decoration and of 19th cent. manufacture, marked "S. & G", have been wrongly ascribed to this factory. Its mark was:

S & G

Isnik pottery: Turkish earthenware made at Isnik in Anatolia. The industry flourished in the second half of the 16th cent. when the Ottoman Empire included Asia Minor, Syria, North Africa and a large part of southeastern Europe. The earthenware is white, covered with a clear alkaline glaze. Pigments used include rich blues, greens and reds. Designs are composed of formal flower motifs within scrolled borders. The name "Rhodian ware" is erroneously given to this pottery.

Ispahan carpets: Persian carpets or rugs, often employing medallion or vase designs (see Vase carpets) in a wide range of colours, the composition being very well balanced.

Issues and states: when alterations, corrections, additions or excisions are effected in a book during the process of manufacture, so that copies exhibiting variations go on sale on publication day indiscriminately, these variant copies are conveniently classified as belonging to different states of the edition. It may or may not be possible to determine priority of manufacture between them, but any priority of publication must be assumed to be accidental. When similar variations can be clearly shown to have originated in some action taken after the book was published, two (or more) issues are distinguishable.

Italian comedy figures: the Catalogue of the Chelsea porcelain factory (1755) refers to "Figures of the Italian Theatre". These subjects from the Italian *Commedia dell' Arte* were frequently copied by the porcelain modellers of Bow and Chelsea from Meissen adaptations of Callot and other designs in Luigi Riccoboni's *Histoire du Théâtre Italien*, (1728). Some became extremely popular; Pierrot, Harlequin and Columbine; Pantaloon; the Captain, the Doctor and the Advocate; Isabella and Cynthio.

The better known re-appeared in Staffordshire salt-glaze.

Italian quilting: see Quilts.

Jack: a mechanically-operated figure that strikes a bell on the outside of a clock. In the first instance jacks were of carved wood, a well-known example, dating probably from the 15th cent., being *Jack the Smiter* at Southwold, Suffolk. Jacks of a later date, on smaller portable clocks and on wall clocks, were made of metal.

In the 19th cent. a French writer carefully traced the origin of the word to its being a corruption of *Jacquemart:* the name of a 15th cent. clockmaker of Lille, France. Others have contended that it is an abbreviation of *Jacco-marchiadus:* a man in armour. In spite of this academic dispute, it seems hardly necessary to look farther than the still current and expressive name *Jack* for any man whose actual patronymic is unknown. These lifelike and nearly lifesize figures were doubtless the recipients of this commonly-used name, as they had none of their own.

Jack: see Brigandine.

Jackfield earthenware: earthenware is said to have been made at Jackfield in the 16th cent., but nothing is known with certainty until Richard Thursfield from Stoke began to manufacture there at the beginning of the 18th cent. He was succeeded by his son who carried on the business until about 1780, when it was taken over by John Rose from Coalport.

No marked examples are known, but there is reason to believe that a type of black-glazed red earthenware, usually decorated with oil-painting over the glaze, was made here from about 1760–75. But this kind of ware was produced in some quantity throughout Staffordshire at that time, so that no pieces can definitely be attributed to Jackfield.

Jacobean: term of convenience usually applicable to objects made in the reign of James I (1603–25), and perhaps, though unusually, to that of James II (1685–88). In general, loosely applied to furniture styles in direct descent from the Elizabethan tradition. It is thus employed of certain types of furniture covering virtually the whole of the 17th cent. and even later, though from the time of Charles II it is generally restricted to pieces of unmodish or traditional character. Jacobean is not now favoured as a descriptive label by scholarly writers, except in cases of uncertain dating, preference being given to a more precise system involving such approximations as "c. 1620" or "first quarter of the 17th cent.", etc.

Jacobean embroidery: see Crewel-work.

Jacob, Georges: French cabinetmaker. Was born in Burgundy in 1739 and died in Paris in 1814. Little is known of his early life, but he was the founder of a long line of makers of furniture who specialized in the production of chairs. He also made a number of beds, which show the same qualities. He worked extensively for the Crown and in consequence was denounced at the Revolution, in spite of his friendship with the painter Jacques Louis David. His own work is usually stamped:

G ♦ I A C O B

Jacobite glasses: propaganda glasses bearing emblems and mottoes of a cryptic character associated with the Jacobite cause. Most common is the six-petalled Jacobite rose with one or two buds: the rose is said to represent the House of Stuart, the small bud the Old Pretender, the large bud on the right being added later, either in honour of Prince Charles Edward's arrival in Scotland or after James's proposal to "abdicate" in favour of his son. Other Jacobite emblems include a stricken and burgeoning oak, oak leaf, bee, butterfly, sunflower, etc. (See also Jacobite pottery.)

Jacobite pottery: occasional inscriptions and emblems on salt-glazed stoneware, earthenware and Jackfield ware indicate Jacobite sympathies. Portraits of Bonnie Prince Charlie are not uncommon on salt-glazed stonewares. Inscriptions and emblems on contemporary glass such as "May the tenant be ready when the steward comes", a stricken and burgeoning oak, oak leaf, bee, butterfly, jay, Jacob's Ladder foliage, carnation, fritillary, thistle, triple ostrich plume, and the 6-petalled rose of the House of Stuart with one or two buds, all of which are considered Jacobite emblems have few echoes on pottery.

Jacquard loom: see Moquette.

Janssen, Stephen Theodore: Lord Mayor of London in 1754 and later City Chamberlain. A merchant stationer, considerable patron of the arts and friend of artists and engravers, he launched the painted enamel enterprise at York House, Battersea (q.v.), in 1753, his associates being the engraver John Brooks and the potter Henry Delamain. Was declared bankrupt in 1756, and there is no evidence of his having had any further connection with the painted enamel trade. Before he died in 1776 he had succeeded to his father's baronetcy and was again a wealthy and influential man. (See also Battersea enamel.)

Japanese inro: a seal-case worn with conventional dress in Japan at the other end of a cord to which various necessities were attached. It was convenient thus to carry everyday necessities as the dress included no pockets. The seal case was a small box of one or more sections fitted together, and lacquered or carved and held shut by a cord holder which could be slid down the cord. Early examples are of lacquered wood, sometimes with additions of ivory or shell. The shape is fairly constant but the number of compartments varies from one to five. Though intended at first for seals, these compartments came to be used for medicines and sundry needs. Slight variations of form and arrangement occur, as, for example, when the cases are enclosed in a surrounding sheath. Like netsuke, this art was described in a book known as the *Soken Kisho* of 1781. Inro was seldom signed in the 18th cent. but was increasingly signed in the 19th. The lacquer used is the natural gum of a sumach tree, mixed with various pigments and with gold and silver. Raised designs were produced by building up with gesso (q.v.) and other compositions. (See also Japanese netsuke.)

Japanese lacquer print: see Urushi-ye.

Japanese netsuke: the conventional dress of Japan had no pockets so it was convenient to carry necessities attached to a cord, at the end of which was a toggle to be pushed through the belt to hold the objects secure. This toggle was called a net-suke (= end attachment) and was carved to represent various subjects. The early history of netsuke is very obscure. The earliest book which discusses them seriously was the *Soken Kisho*, published in 1781. This book mentions about fifty carvers' names and discusses their work, with illustrations. Early examples are generally of ivory and are not signed by the maker. By the end of the 18th cent. more artists took up the profession of netsuke carving and then began the great era of this art, when artists became better known and took to signing their work. At first the netsuke were simple and bold in design, but towards the middle of the 19th cent. the designs became more naturalistic and intricate, while at the end of the century the simple rotundity of the piece was sometimes sacrificed to the fashion for detail. After the revolution of 1868, European dress gradually came into favour and the need for netsuke declined. They were then made for export to the European collector. There have been well over 2,000 makers who signed their works. Artists chose their own art-names of two syllables, sometimes followed by the name of the studio. The characters were written either in block letters (Kaisoh) or in cursory script (Sosho). A few artists are listed below, showing their names in Kaisho and in Sosho in order to illustrate the difference. (See also Japanese inro.)

KAISHO	SOSHO
玉山	
貫	
虎	
壽玉	
蘭亮	
忠利	
爲隆	

Japanese print: was "discovered" soon after the opening up of the country to foreign visitors in 1854, and considerable impetus was given to the formation of collections later in the century by the enthusiasm of the French Impressionists and their protagonists, who found much that appealed to their aesthetic senses, ever tuned to receive the new, the adventurous, the unacademic, in the calculated design and arbitrary use of form and colour, of the Japanese print designers. The most immediately attractive of these exotic engravings were the colour-prints of the late 18th cent., but in the methodical way of the European art-historian it was not long before the origin of these gay pictures were traced back to black outline prints of the 17th cent.

Indeed, the earliest wood-engravings made in Japan belong to a very remote period. Some can reliably be given to the 8th cent. and, as wood-engravings are still being published in Japan, the term "Japanese print" might conceivably embrace everything from the crude Buddhistic cuts of an almost legendary antiquity to the pseudo-Picasso abstractions of post-war Tokyo artists. Specifically, however, the term is usually held to apply to the productions of a certain school of mainly Yedo artists, the Ukiyo-ye, which arose in the mid-17th cent. and whose work was virtually ended by the time of the Restoration in 1868.

Book illustrations of great beauty and originality were designed during the Tokugawa or Yedo period (1615–1868) by painters of various other schools whose styles differ vastly from the Ukiyo-ye.

Japanned metal ware: see Pontypool.

"Japans": a loose term covering a wide variety of patterns and styles derived from oriental sources, employed in decorating English porcelain in the 18th and 19th cent., including Chinese *famille verte* and *famille rose* patterns (qq.v.); the Imari of Arita with showy floral or brocaded effects in underglaze blue and enamel colours with added gilding; and patterns in the Kakiemon style (q.v.) enamelled in turquoise, red, green, yellow and blue.

The "Japans" became very popular in the 1820s, and were extensively used at Derby, and in Staffordshire on bone china made by Spode, Minton and Davenport, as well as for decorating stone or ironstone china (Masons for example). (See also Imari and Kakiemon porcelain.)

Japan work: japanned or lacquered furniture began to enjoy a considerable vogue in the late 17th cent. As early as 1661 Pepys recorded seeing "two very fine chests covered with gold and Indian varnish". Lacquer work was originally imported from the East, and was known variously as Indian, Chinese or Japanese, but the best kind was made in Japan, and was called "fine" or "right" Japan, to distinguish it from substitutes. Most of the genuine Japanese work was brought to England by the Dutch, but the English East India Company handled Chinese and Indian varieties, which had a ready sale in the home market and went under the general name of "Indian" goods (and were sold in "Indian" shops). So great was the demands for these goods that some English merchants exported patterns and models of all kinds of furniture to be copied and lacquered by native workmen, who could thus manufacture English-style furniture. The completed goods were reimported and sold at home. But meanwhile an English japan industry had sprung up. In 1688 Stalker and Parker published their *Treatise of Japanning and Varnishing*, and in 1693 a company was formed with the title of "The Patentees for Lacquering after the Manner of Japan". Naturally, the home producers of japan disliked the practice of sending goods abroad to be lacquered, and so did other cabinet-makers, who looked upon it as unfair competition. In 1701 the London cabinet-makers, joiners and japanners petitioned Parliament to put a stop to it, and an Act was passed imposing heavier duties on all imported lacquer (12 & 13 William III, c. 11). Thus from that date nearly all japan work was home-made. It was very popular until about 1740, and much of it was exported. The

colours used were bright ones, often scarlet, yellow, etc., and carried out Eastern designs, but English work lacked the high quality of the true Oriental variety. In fact, inferior work was merely varnished. It was usually applied on a background of deal for carcases, or of beech for chairs. Good-class work often had a smooth-grained, veneered surface as a basis. Normally, designs were raised on the surface, but a rare form of lacquer work, known as Bantam work, used incised designs. Cabinets, chairs, bureaux, screens, clock cases and mirrors were among the more usual pieces for japanning. There was a revival of this fashion in the later 18th cent.

Jaquet-Droz, Pierre and **Henri:** father and son. Famous Swiss makers of automata. Pierre was born in 1721 and died in 1790 and Henri lived from 1752 to 1791. The two were joined ultimately by their apprentice, J. F. Leschot, and the firm was styled Jaquet-Droz et Leschot.

Jardinière: a container for flowers.

Jaseron chain: a thin Venetian gold chain from which a cross or a pendant was suspended, fashionable between 1804 and 1811.

Jasper: a fine close-grained stoneware body of unusual composition including in its ingredients barytes and barium-carbonate, dense and hard enough to stand polishing on a lapidary's wheel and capable of being stained throughout its substance with metallic oxides to fine shades of blue and lavender, sage and olive green, lilac, ochreous yellow (a rare tint) and a peculiarly velvety black. It was the culmination in 1774 of an extended series of experiments by Wedgwood "over a long period of time". Wedgwood himself described it as "white porcelain *bisque* of exquisite beauty and delicacy". To be distinguished from the less valuable "Jasper dip" (q.v.).

Jasper dip: coloured solution applied to white jasper body by dipping; name also of ware made of white jasper covered with a surface colouring.

Jaune jonquille: (*Fr.*), a daffodil yellow enamel ground used on Sèvres porcelain (q.v.) and introduced in

1753. The tone is deeper and warmer than that of the yellow ground porcelain made earlier at Meissen (q.v.).

Jelly glass: tall glass with a handle intended for jelly, custard or sillabub. Jelly glasses were much in use in the 18th cent. when it was customary to serve an elaborate dessert, the jelly-glasses set on glass salvers with baluster or moulded pedestal (q.v.) stems, arranged in tiers of two or three laden salvers.

Jennens and Bettridge: successors to Henry Clay's Birmingham factory in 1816, the largest manufacturers of paper ware with showrooms at No. 6 Hallam Street West, Belgrave Square, London. They advertised that "all goods impressed with our name are warranted". The firm closed in 1864.

Jensen, Gerreit: (known also as Garrett or Gerrard Johnson) cabinet-maker and "glasse-seller", who supplied much furniture to the Royal Household from 1680. A tall mirror at Hampton Court tallies with the description on his bill rendered in 1699, and it is assumed that Jensen had the monopoly of supplying overmantel mirrors and pier-glasses to the royal palaces during the reign of William and Mary. The date of his birth is unknown, but his will was dated 1715 and he retired from business in that year.

Jersey measure: a plain baluster-shaped pewter measure, with lid and thumbpiece as in a Guersney measure; peculiar to Jersey, C.I.

"Jesuit" china: Chinese porcelain wares of the first half of the 18th cent. painted with Christian subjects supplied by Jesuit missionaries, principally in black monochrome or *famille rose* (q.v.) enamels.

Jet-enamelled ware: one of the most celebrated productions of the Worcester porcelain factory in the 18th cent. consisting of wares transfer-printed in black. Giles purchased "jet-enamelled" services from Worcester in 1769.

Jewel ornament: ornament with raised devices distantly suggestive of gem-stones, often combined with raised mouldings arranged in geometrical designs. This type of ornament is found carved in relief or applied on early and mid 17th cent. furniture.

Jidai: (*Japanese* = ancient), period piece of Japanese lacquer-work, say 17th cent.

Joey: see Dram glass.

Johnson, Thomas: designer and wood-carver of London. He published a volume entitled *Twelve Girandoles* in 1755, and a more ambitious work, *One Hundred and Fifty New Designs*, between 1756 and 1758.

Joined furniture: term used in describing furniture made by a joiner.

Joiner: craftsman in early periods responsible for making house fitments as well as furniture. From the 15th cent., in the making of furniture, the joiner used the panel construction in place of thick boards, whereby the panel was held in position in a framework of stiles and rails (qq.v.). This rendered the furniture less cumbersome and more elegant in design. For the framing of the panels the joiner used the mortice and tenon joint. Throughout the 16th and for a large part of the 17th cent., the joiner remained the chief maker of furniture, to be replaced in the reign of Charles II by the cabinet-maker (q.v.). From this period the joiner confined himself to the making of bedsteads and "wainscot" furniture, so called as they were made from imported oak. Wainscot furniture was not veneered (q.v.) in the manner of the fashionable products of the cabinet-maker but in form followed the prevailing taste of the day.

Joney or joney grig: a dialect term for a pottery chimney ornament in the form of a dog. A well-known Burslem pottery in the 19th cent. was known as a "doll and jona" (figure and dog) works.

Jousting chests: a romantic name given to chests carved in high relief with naturalistic scenes of secular subjects, such as jousting and hunting. These may have been created as early as the 14th or 15th cent., but they have prompted many 19th and 20th cent. copies.

Juveniles: children's books. A jargon word but well established; borrowed from the publishing trade.

Juvenilia: a writer's youthful productions.

Ju ware: rare Chinese porcelain Imperial ware of the early 12th cent., with buff body and crackled lavender-blue glaze.

Kabistan rugs: considered the finest of the Caucasian rugs, are from the Baku district, and include the Kuba and Hila rugs. The design of the Kuba consists often of independent flower heads, palmettes and eight-pointed stars, with well-balanced borders carrying the same motifs. Some early examples show an elongated panel with interlocking tree forms.

Kabuki: popular plays produced in Japan. Towards the end of the 17th cent. prints began to be issued to record the Kabuki drama, depicting the most famous actors in their roles.

Kaendler, J. J.: appointed as chief modeller at the Meissen porcelain factory (q.v.) in 1731, was the first to recognize the sculptural possibilities of hard-paste porcelain, the secret of whose manufacture had so recently been discovered at the factory, and to exploit its inherent qualities. His Italian Comedy figures (q.v.) seem to dance on the shelves of china cabinets, and his fashionable ladies to swing their crinolines in rhythmic movements, anticipating Mozart's minuets. Even conventional tableware takes a share in plastic decoration, and the "Swan Service", which Kaendler modelled

for Count Bruehl (1737–41), reveals his creative genius in the many variations on the theme of swans. Kaendler's birds were all studied from nature, since Augustus the Strong kept a large collection of domestic and rare specimens at the Moritzburg. (See also Meissen porcelain.)

Kakemono: Japanese hanging picture, rolled up when stored.

Kakemono-ye: Japanese prints in the form of hanging pictures, usually about 26–28 × 10–12 inches.

Kakiemon style: a name given to a distinctive asymmetrical style of enamel decoration on Japanese porcelain, extensively imitated or copied in 18th cent. by German, French and English porcelain factories. In England porcelain painters at Bow, Chelsea and Worcester used the Kakiemon style, copied either directly from Japanese wares, or indirectly from Meissen copies or adaptations. Named after the Japanese potter Kakiemon (fl. c. 1650), who used enamel colours at Arita.

Kaltemail: (*Ger.*), literally cold enamel, although there is no English equivalent. A decorative technique used in the 16th and 17th cent. as a substitute for true fired enamelling on a surface which would be damaged by the heat of firing or was too large to be placed in the kiln. It was actually a form of hard-setting lacquer.

K'ang Hsi porcelain: Chinese porcelain made in the reign of the Emperor K'ang Hsi (1662–1722). The nobility and masculine elegance of the K'ang Hsi style is exemplified in Fig. A and in the forms of the "rouleau" and "trumpet" vases of Figs B and D. The ware now used was a most refined white porcelain, thinly and evenly glazed and with a meticulous finish, showing painted decoration to great advantage. For the best of the very numerous blue-and-white wares a brilliant sapphire blue was preferred, and designs, first drawn in outline and then washed in boldly in broad tones, are more precisely executed than hitherto. We find ambitious landscapes or figure subjects. On some pieces there is also painting in copper-red or a partial blue, celadon-green or golden-brown glaze. For enamelled wares, the brilliant *famille verte* (q.v.) palette soon replaced the Ming "five-colour" style (see Wu Ts'ai.) The rare vases with black or yellow ground (*famille noire, famille jaune*) are generally enamelled "on the biscuit" i.e. without intervening glaze, and this attractive technique distinguishes a whole *famille verte* group, which specially includes accessories for the tea table, study or studio. The third main group of K'ang Hsi wares are those with monochrome glazes, among them the sang-de-boeuf and peach-bloom red (see Copper-red porcelain glazes) and other high-temperature colours, blues, celadon-green, white, brown and mirror-black – as well as many others. The beautiful blanc-de-chine porcelain (q.v.) of Fukien and the unglazed red stoneware of Yi-hsing also flourished at this time.

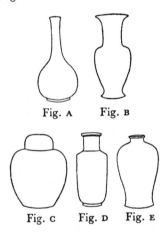

Fig. A   Fig. B

Fig. c   Fig. D   Fig. E

Kaolin: see China clay.

Kas: a Dutch form of wardrobe made in the Hudson and Delaware River valleys in America between about 1675–1750; a large clothes cupboard with panelled doors, large mouldings, overhanging cornice and, usually, ball-front feet. Often painted with decorative designs.

Kasak rugs: Caucasian rugs bearing panelled designs of bold character and in striking colours. They are deep pile rugs and have a masculine character entirely their own. Strong deep red, clear yellow and blue are the predominant shades. Woven with extra weft threads, the pile lies flat and is very strong.

Kat stitch: a term used in lace-making to describe a *fond chant* ground (q.v.) but frequently found in Bedfordshire lace and given legendary association with Katherine of Aragon.

Kauffman, Angelica: (1741–1807), painter, born in Switzerland. She worked in London between c. 1766 and 1782. In 1781 she married the Italian painter, Antonio Zucchi with whom she had worked while she was in England. She was employed by Robert Adam on interior decoration and also painted furniture.

Keeper ring: a rather heavy gold ring bearing chased decoration.

Kelsterbach porcelain: hard-paste porcelain was made at the factory of the Landgrave of Hesse-Darmstadt, Ludwig VIII, from 1761–68 by the arcanist (q.v.) C. D. Busch. The factory was later re-opened in 1789 with the help of another arcanist and remained in existence until 1802. The earlier wares were not marked, the crowned monogram "HD" appearing on the wares of 1799–1802 and occasionally on those of 1766 to 1768.

Kent, William: (1686–1748), an architect who also planned the land-scaping of gardens, painted pictures and was one of the first of his profession to lavish as much care on the interior of a house as he did on the building itself. He was an exponent of the Palladian style, and his name has been given to the mirrors with frames of "architectural" type that were fashionable in the years 1730–40.

Kerman rugs: this district of Persia has produced many rugs of merit, although they are usually of later manufacture. Medallion and tree designs are popular, introducing floral effects in graceful intertwining vines. The yarn used is rather soft. Fine examples are known as Kerman Laver rugs. The colours, beautifully toned, are particularly suitable for English furnishings. Knot: Sehna (q.v.).

Keshan carpets: Persian carpets in which medallion and prayer designs predominate, woven in wool or silk; they are orthodox in conception, and are notable for the use of ivory as a ground shade; the most favoured colours are rich tones of red or blue. The famous Polonaise rugs, remarkable for the use of gold and silver thread as a base and the unusual colour effects in pastel greens and browns, were probably woven in Keshan. It is thought that they were woven as gifts to foreign monarchs by the order of Shah Abbas. Fine Keshan carpets sometimes combine the medallion with the floral and tree motif. Knot: usually Sehna (q.v.).

Kettle-stand (also **urn-** and **teapot-stand**): a special stand which was introduced with tea-drinking in the later 17th cent., of two main kinds. (a) A small table, tripod or four-legged, with a gallery or raised edge round the top. Slender four-legged tables were common in the later part of the 18th cent., nearly always with a slide for the teapot. (b) A box-like arrangement set on four legs; the box was usually lined with metal, and had an opening in one side for the kettle spout, as well as a slide for the teapot. Another version of the box type had a three-sided enclosure with a metal-lined drawer. The two main types of stand persisted until the end of the 18th cent., when they were superseded by occasional tables.

Kettle-tilter: ("Idle-back", "Lazy-back", "Handy-maid"), a simple device of wrought-iron for tilting the kettle when water was wanted from it. Not only was there no need to soil the hand by touching a smoke-blackened kettle, but the handle of the tilter projected outside the fireplace, was cool and there would be no risk from scalding steam or water. The kettle was suspended over the fire in the tilter, which in turn hung from a pot-hook or crane.

Keyed bugle: see under Side-hole instruments.

Key pattern: repetitive pattern made up of straight lines joined at right angles and used as a border ornament by architects and craftsmen during the Classical revival in the late 18th and early 19th cent. Deriving from classical Greek architecture, it appears for example, as a decorative border on furniture, silver and porcelain. Also known as Greek fret.

Khorassan carpets: Persian carpets in which the yarn is generally softer; the stitch is fine and the general effect is more splendid than in Feraghan carpets, but they are not so durable. Knot: usually Sehna (q.v.).

Kick: the pyramidal dent found in the bases of many pre-1760 glass decanters, bowls, and bottles.

Kidderminster rugs: Kidderminster is probably the oldest centre of rug production in England, the early pieces being smooth-faced and without a true pile, that is to say, a cheap form of carpeting. Kidderminster carpets were often mentioned in inventories; for example, "4 carpetts of Kidderminster stuff", in the Countess of Leicester's inventory, 1634. Two-ply or double-cloth carpets were made there from 1735, when Pearsall and Brown built their factory. But in 1753 Brussels carpets or moquette (q.v.) were introduced by Brown in rivalry with Wilton (q.v.). A thousand looms were at work in 1807, rising to two thousand and twenty in 1838. Jacquard looms were introduced about 1825, and the use of jute rather earlier.

Kidney-dagger: a type of dagger with a guard formed by two lobate protuberances. It was probably from the kidney-dagger that the Scottish dirk (q.v.) developed in the 17th cent.

Kilmarnock carpets: double-cloth carpeting was made in Kilmarnock from 1778 and three-ply was perfected in 1824.

Kiln: oven used to fire body and glaze of hard-paste porcelain (q.v.) at about 1200–1400 C. (grand feu.)

Kiln waster: porcelain coming from the kiln spoilt, and therefore to be thrown away as useless. Kiln wasters discovered in excavation afford good evidence of factory production.

King's pattern spoons: see under Table-services.

Kinji: (*Japanese* = gold ground), a Japanese lacquer-work technique in which powdered gold is worked into the lacquer surface and then burnished.

"Kinuta" celadon ware: see Lung-chüan celadon ware.

Kirchner, Johann Gottlob: modeller at the Meissen porcelain factory from 1727–28 and 1730–33, where he was responsible for modelling some of the large figures and animals required by Augustus the Strong for the decoration of the Japanese Palace.

Kirikane: (*Japanese* = cut gold), a Japanese lacquer-work technique in which cut squares of gold leaf are embedded on the lacquer.

Kir-Shehr rugs: Turkish rugs with typical designs. The Mihrab is usually filled with a very angular tree, border and panel are conventional, while the colours are bright and virile, varying reds being a feature of the weave. Warp and weft are usually wool. (See also Turkish rugs.)

"Kit Cat glass": a baluster wine glass of the first quarter of the 18th cent. with tall stem and bowl curving outwards at the rim, known by this name on account of its appearance in a picture by Kneller of the members of the Kit Cat Club.

Kloster Veilsdorf porcelain: hard-paste porcelain was made at Kloster Veilsdorf in Thuringia from 1760, when a factory was set up under the protection of Prince Friedrich Wilhelm Eugen of Hilburghausen.
    The monogram "CV" (for Closter Veilsdorf) in underglaze blue was used in various forms as a mark. (See also under Limbach porcelain for other Thuringian factories.)

Knee-hole table: a table fitted with drawers and an arched apron-piece (q.v.) in the centre. Walnut tables of this type made at the end of the 17th and early 18th cent. could be used as dressing or writing tables, the arched apron allowing comfortable space for the knees of the sitter. Dressing tables of knee-hole form containing a row of small drawers on either side, on plain bracket feet (q.v.) and a recessed cupboard within the arched knee-hole were also popular in the early 18th cent. Some examples in mahogany dating from the mid-cent. have tops which can be raised to reveal a fitted interior. Library tables of knee-hole type with end pedestals containing drawers and a space in the centre were popular from the mid-18th cent.

Knibb, Joseph: a London clock-maker of fame active c. 1650–1711.

Knife-case: a container for knives, and other cutlery, introduced in the 17th cent. for use in dining-rooms. Two distinct varieties appeared; (a) until the later 18th cent. the usual shape was a box with a sloping top and convex front; the interior had divisions for the cutlery. Walnut, shagreen (untanned leather with a roughened surface) and later mahogany, sometimes inlaid, were the main materials; (b) this was succeeded by the graceful vase-shaped case the top of which was raised and lowered on a central stem around which the knife partitions were arranged; this type was designed to stand on pedestal or at each end of the sideboard. Straight-sided cases were favoured in the early 19th cent.

Knife-rest: a support for a knife at table used in the 18th cent. They were of two varieties: cross-ends joined from their centres by a short rod, and solid or pierced triangular ends joined from each angle by short rods.

Knop: swelling member on a shaft, pillar, or stem of cup or goblet; a knob. Many differently shaped knops are found on stemmed drinking glasses (see Ball, Cushion, Merese knop, etc.).

Knopped stem: a type of stem found on 18th cent. drinking glasses composed of a varying number of knops (q.v.) or knobs.

Knotted lace: made in 16th-cent. Italy with short lengths of thread or thin cord. When longer threads were introduced bobbins (q.v.) were developed to carry them, first of lead then of wood or bone and the threads were twisted and plaited.

Knotted pile carpets: when carpets first came to Europe from the Near East in the 15th and 16th cent. they were used as covers for tables, cupboards and chests, or were placed before the altar in church or chapel. Only kings and the higher nobility used floor carpets. A small number of knotted pile carpets in imitation of oriental ones were made in Europe. English examples date from the 16th and early 17th cent. Some of the patterns follow Turkish models, others are like contemporary English embroideries. In France, at the Savonnerie (q.v.), a Western style of carpet was created which was taken up by different countries when floor carpets became more general in the 18th cent.

Knulling: a short fluting of irregular outline used as a decoration on silver or plate in the mid-18th cent. for borders and on handles. Probably used in the past as synonymous with gadrooning.

Knurl toe: see Scroll foot.

Koban: thin, flat, oval gold coin of Japan issued from late 16th to early 19th cent. Plain surfaces except for stamps indicating value, etc.

Kōban: a Japanese print being a size smaller than the chūban (q.v.), about 8 × 7 inches.

Kopek: in 16th cent., Russian silver coin with type of Tsar on horseback. In 18th cent., a value, not token, copper coin with types Imperial arms and monogram of ruler within wreath. Variety of multiples and divisions.

Ko ware: crackled Sung celadon ware of Kuan type. (See also Celadon ware and Kuan ware.)

"KPM" mark: see Meissen porcelain.

Krater: two-handled Greek vessel of vase shape.

Kreuzer: billon coin of 16th and 17th cent. and copper in 18th cent. in many German states. Name derived from its cross design. Multiples in silver in later 18th cent. in Austria, Hungary and German states.

Kuan ware: rare Chinese celadon (q.v.) of the Sung dynasty, patronized by the Emperor, with dark grey porcellanous body and thick, often crackled glaze of pale greyish blue or greyish green colour, suggesting marble or jade; made at Hangchow (Chekiang Province) from the 12th cent. Creditable imitations were made during the 18th cent.

Kuba rugs: see Kabistan rugs.

Kula rugs: Turkish rugs, less varied in colour than other Turkish types, and the panels of the Mihrab are usually fully patterned. Borders are popular with repeating floral miniature motifs. (See also Turkish rugs.)

Kurdish rugs: Nomadic tribes wove these rugs. The virile designs are often bold and the colours limited. The yarns employed are generally coarse, but the effects are pleasing and the wearing quality excellent, often found in long runners. One of the outstanding types is the Bidjar, probably the heaviest of all Oriental rugs. Woven on a twofold warp, designs are various, often including a bold medallion and corner-pieces on a plain field, the borders in the Herat (q.v.) manner.

Kü Yüeh Hsüan ware: a group of 18th cent. Chinese porcelain wares of Imperial quality, carefully painted with flower and landscape subjects in coloured enamels, principally of the *famille rose* (q.v.), sometimes with coloured grounds. They are often inscribed with a poem. The title more properly belongs to some later painted glass vessels.

Kwachō: Japanese bird and flower pictures.

Label: (a) leather labels (or lettering-pieces) have been commonly used by book-binders since the 17th cent. They are generally of a different colour from that of the main skin, and almost always of morocco pared very thin (even if the book itself is bound, or half-bound, in calf). When two labels are used, sometimes of different colours, the conventional description is "double lettering-pieces"; (b) paper labels, printed from type or occasionally engraved, began to be used in the second half of the 18th cent. on the paper spines of boarded books. They must have been almost universal during the first quarter of the 19th cent., on books put up in this form; and they continued as the regular method of titling for boarded books even after this style was generally superseded by publisher's cloth. They were also used on the early cloth books, though with sharply decreasing frequency after 1832, when the process for applying titling and decoration directly on to the cloth was perfected; (c) library labels (see Ex-library).

Labelled furniture: furniture bearing the paper label of a cabinet-maker.

Lace glass: see Vetro de trina.

Lacis: French term for darned patterns on netting in vogue in 16th-cent. Italy, a direct preliminary to pillow lace (q.v.).

Lacquer work: see Japan work.

Lacy glass: American term for type of pressed glass made c. 1828–40 bearing intricate relief designs on a finely stippled, lace-like background. Lacy glass is brilliant and sparkling. Salts, dishes and plates, and more rarely, bases of lamps and candlesticks were made in this technique.

Ladder-back chair: a mid-18th cent. mahogany chair, the back composed of curved horizontal rails, frequently pierced. A similar type of back had been known in the late Stuart period.

Ladies' Amusement, The: extremely popular book of engravings, its full title being *The Ladies' Amusement; or, Whole Art of Japanning Made Easy*, by Jean Pillement and others. This contained upward of 1,500 patterns intended for commercial decorative work. Designs derived from this pattern book are to be noted on a number of painted enamel boxes, etc., which were made in South Staffordshire in the second half of the 18th cent.

Ladik box rugs: Turkish rugs which follow the Ghiordes (q.v.) design very closely, though the use of Rhodian lily motifs is a distinguishing feature.

Lalique, René: a modern French glass-maker producing moulded, pressed and engraved glass, often favouring massive bowls, vases, figures and panels for furniture, decorated with foliate and animal motifs in rich profusion.

Lambeth delftware: certain kinds of delftware and maiolica, the earliest known pieces being of the late 16th cent., are designated "Lambeth", although this type of pottery was made not only in the factories there but also at other works in Vauxhall, Aldgate and Southwark, and possibly in other riverside boroughs besides. Work from the various factories of this group cannot be assigned to individual potteries, and some is in fact difficult to distinguish from Dutch tin-glazed wares of the early period. Lambeth ware was produced over two centuries, and examples have principally come to light in excavations in the City of London.

In 1571 two potters from Antwerp, Andries and Janson, settled at Aldgate. Earliest examples of English tin-glazed ware date from about this time, not all these being derived from the Dutch tradition, although many potters from Holland certainly came to London in the late 16th and early 17th cent.

From the early 17th cent. Italian, Dutch and Chinese styles of decoration are common. Some are initialled for their owners, the letters usually being placed in triangle-form, and many bear the arms of London livery companies. Designs, usually in bright, thick maiolica colours include stylized fruit and foliage, star-shaped flowers, birds and sphinxes, and, towards the end of the 17th cent., portraits of kings, family groups, biblical subjects, inn signs and verses or inscriptions appear more frequently and colours become more various. Chinese subjects were copied from imported oriental wares and often greatly improved upon by simplification and freedom of treatment. Articles for domestic use formed a large part of the manufacture of the potteries; these included tiles, plates, mugs, jars, jugs, wine-bottles, posset-pots, punch-bowls, wall-pockets and plaques.

The Lambeth ware factories were still in existence at the beginning of the 19th cent. They were in decline, however, in 1800 and as regards work after that date no examples of decorated wares are known.

As no marks were used on these wares, their origin is ascertained by comparison with delftware known to be from Holland, inscriptions on various commemorative pieces, and names of owners sometimes incorporated in the design. In articles made at a later date, a more distinctively English form of decoration is apparent.

These later productions are sometimes difficult to distinguish from contemporary Liverpool and Bristol tin-glazed earthenware; in general, Lambeth potters produced a neatly-drawn design and more finished effect, but often lacked the vigour and individuality of the best examples from Bristol.

The glaze on early Lambeth pottery is usually white. In later pieces a blue-green tint becomes apparent, fairly easily distinguishable from the bluish-purple of Bristol (q.v.) glaze.

Lambrequin: (*Fr.*), a short piece of hanging drapery, often imitated in metal or wood for decorative purposes.

Lamerie, Paul de: the foremost member of the second generation of Huguenot goldsmiths working in London. Born in Liège in 1688, he was apprenticed to Pierre Platel. His earliest recorded work dates from 1711–12. He enjoyed the patronage of the leading nobility but not, curiously enough, of the Crown. One of the most prolific goldsmiths of his time,

his main achievement was the popularisation of the French Rococo (q.v.) manner in English silver. He died in 1751.

Lance: see under Pole-arms.

Lancet clock: design of late 18th and early 19th cent., in which a bracket clock has a pointed "gothic" top.

Langley, Batty and **Thomas:** two brothers who were authors of a pattern book, published in 1740 called !a *Treasury of Designs.* It included designs for furniture which could be treated in an architectural manner according to the precepts of Palladian taste although some of the designs indicate the acceptance of the new Rococo spirit which was shortly to become popular. (See also Palladian style and Rococo.)

Lang yao: see Copper red glazes.

Lantern clock: a clock of typically English design evolved in the early part of the 17th cent., and persisting, especially in the provinces, until well into the 18th cent. Erroneously called a Cromwellian clock. Much copied to-day. All original lantern clocks are weight driven and, with the rarest exceptions, never exceed a thirty-hour going period.

Large paper copy: a book, being one of a (usually small) number of copies printed on a larger size of paper than the main bulk of the edition; either for presentation, or for subscribers, or to be sold at higher price. The paper will often be superior quality; and, in the 18th cent. particularly, these were generally called fine or royal or imperial paper copies.

Larin: thin silver bars in shape of fish-hook, sometimes with stamp. Used as coins in coastal districts from Persian Gulf to Ceylon in 16th and 17th cent.

Latten: a yellow alloy of copper and zinc.

Lattice work: a form of decorative work popular on mahogany furniture of the mid-18th cent. Chippendale's

Director (1754) contained designs for a "Chinese Chair" and a "Gothick Chair" which include open lattice work on the legs and stretchers in the appropriate spirit. Chairs in the Chinese taste were also made with the back splat of lattice work, or with lattice work filling the space between the arm of the seat in the case of armchairs.

Latticinio decoration: a type of decoration on glass which came into use in the second quarter of the 16th cent. at Venice and remained long fashionable. It involved the use of opaque white or coloured threads of glass drawn together with tools into a network and melted into the surfaces of the clear glass vessel which was then blown and manipulated. Although the technique was of Venetian origin, it was also used by Italian workmen and their pupils at glasshouses set up elsewhere in Europe.

Laurel: gold coin of 20s, issued by James I. So called from obverse portrait crowned, in the Roman manner, with a laurel wreath.

Laver rugs: see Kerman rugs.

Lazulite: a blue-tinted parian ware (q.v.).

Lazy Susan: an American type of dumb waiter (q.v.) used for condiments in the early 19th cent.

Lead glass: glass containing lead as a flux. (See also Flint-glass).

Le Compte, Père Louis: a Jesuit missionary who published in Amsterdam in 1697 *Memoirs and Observations made in a late Journey through China*. The book was issued in translation in London in the same year. Le Compte devotes several pages to porcelain and mentions that blue-and-white was the principal product. He adds that the European merchants foolishly bought anything that the Chinese were willing to sell.

Leeds earthenware: the Old Pottery at Hunslet (as distinct from the later factories of Hunslet Hall and Rothwell in the same district) was established about 1760 by two brothers named Green. The factory was sold in 1825 to Samuel Wainwright and was known for a time as S. Wainwright & Co. Subsequently it was the Leeds Pottery Co. and Warburton, Britton & Co. It closed in 1878.

Marks:

Some comparatively modern Leeds productions are marked "Leeds Pottery" (impressed). The wares which sometimes make use of old patterns and old moulds are easily distinguishable from earlier pieces, for the mark is impressed in very even lettering and has none of the irregularity of the type used in marking earlier pieces.

Impressed

Impressed c. 1864

Early earthenware made at Leeds is notable for its colour, a rich cream with a deep fine glaze, sometimes of a slightly greenish tinge rather more hard and brilliant than Wedgwood but less even. Queen's ware of this sort was made in quantity in many Staffordshire potteries at about this time, but that made at Leeds has a particularly delicate and highly-finished appearance. From about 1780 until 1820 it formed the largest part of the production of the factory and was exported to several European countries. Pierced or basket-work was popular and made with great skill.

Plates bordered with interwoven twigs, all fashioned by hand; centrepieces of complex design and making use of figures; dishes with twisted handles; small, well-modelled figures; all these are characteristic subjects in Leeds cream-ware. Transfer-printing was also used to decorate some pieces. Red, black, lilac and green were colours most frequently used, together with the underglaze blue popular throughout Staffordshire at that time. Enamelled decoration was usually in subdued colours.

Certain types of agate wares were made, often having reserved panels painted with flowers.

At a later date, the factory also produced black Egyptian and lustred wares, and a white ware with a bluish glaze. (See also Wedgwood, Josiah.)

Leeds horse: large pottery model of a horse on a rectangular plinth made specially at Leeds, and probably used as the sign of a horse leech.

Left-hand dagger: a dagger used in conjunction with the sword in 16th and early 17th cent. fencing. It usually had quillons (q.v.), often strongly arched to entangle an opponents sword blade, and a side-ring, but a special form, with a triangular knuckle-guard, was used in Spain during the last three quarters of the 17th cent. in conjunction with the cup-hilt rapier (q.v.).

Legend: another term for inscription.

Lehr: the heated chamber or tunnel, sometimes known as a "leer", in which glass, whether hand-made or machine-made, has to be toughened by annealing (q.v.).

Leleu, Jean François: French cabinet-maker, born in Paris in 1729, and died there in 1807. Trained under J. F. Oeben (q.v.), after whose death in 1763 he hoped to be chosen to take over the direction of the workshop. Oeben's widow's choice, however, fell on Riesener (q.v.), whom she married, and Leleu never became reconciled to this. He used the stamp:

J·F·LELEU

Lenticle: the glass let into the door of a long-case clock to allow the motion of the pendulum bob to be seen.

Leontine chain: a long gold chain worn in the 19th cent., to which a watch was attached.

Lettering piece: see Label.

Lev. or **Levant morocco:** a high-quality coarse-grained goatskin, used in binding books; distinguished, for example, from another goatskin, Niger, which has a finer grain. It is usually highly polished and has been considered during the past hundred years to be the most elegant of the types of leathers used for book-binding.

Lever escapement: a type of watch escapement (q.v.) invented about 1758 by Thomas Mudge and incorporated in a watch given by George III to Queen Charlotte. Mudge only made one or two other examples and does not seem to have realized the importance of his invention, which lies in the fact that the balance is free from interference for the greater part of its swing, thus leaving it free to perform its true function as controller. From the commencement of the second quarter of the 19th cent., the lever escapement, in one of its many forms, became the standard escapement for watches and still is so to-day. Before that date, despite the appearance of the cylinder, duplex (qq.v.) and lever escapements, the standard watch escapement was the verge (q.v.).

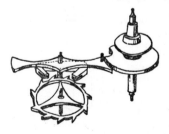

Lever lock: the earliest was patented in 1778 by Robert Barron, its mechanism a system of fixed wards in combination with two pivoting or lifting tumblers which he termed levers, held in position by a steel spring. Attached to the tumblers were stumps or studs which retained the bolt in its locked position. Only its own individually made key, cut in steps of different radii, corresponded with the varying lifts of the two tumblers, so that the latter were raised to the exact height to bring the studs into line with the slot in the bolt, and thus allow the top step of the key to act upon the stump and unlock it. Any attempt to pick the lock was frustrated by a number of upper transverse notches in the bolt. This rendered it impossible to tell when the tumblers had been lifted correctly. From this developed, in the early 1800s, the ordinary lever lock.

Library steps: found in libraries of large houses after about the middle of the 18th cent., and of two main kinds: (a) the fixed pair of steps, some with hand-rails, and (b) the folding steps, sometimes ingeniously fitted into other pieces of furniture, such as chairs, stools and tables.

Lighthouse clock: an American shelf or mantel clock designed by Simon Willard about 1800. The case is judged to have been modelled after the lighthouse on Eddystone Rock in the English Channel. Miller declares that "because of mechanical difficulties . . . very few were made".

Lille lace: pillow lace very popular in later 18th cent. England, made sometimes in black, but never as a dress lace. Its somewhat meagre patterns were heavily outlined in flat glossy trolly thread and set in a plain *fond clair* mesh.

Limbach porcelain: the Limbach porcelain factory in Thuringia was one of seven owned by members of the Greiner family, being founded by Gotthelf Greiner in 1772. The rather stiff, crude little figures modelled at Limbach, with scroll bases, are the most interesting of the factory's productions. Other Thuringian factories established or acquired by the Greiners include Wallendorf, founded in 1764 by Gotthelf Greiner and his cousin; Ilmenau, founded in 1777 and acquired by the Greiners in 1786; Grossbreitenbach, founded in 1778 and bought by Gotthelf Greiner in 1782; Gera, started in 1779 and taken over by the Greiners in the following year; and Rauenstein, founded by the Greiners in 1783. These Greiner factories and others in Thuringia produced utilitarian rather than decorative porcelain and were basically commercial enterprises, unlike the famous German factories which depended upon noble patronage. They used local china clay and sandstone containing quartz, and fuel was available cheaply from the Thuringian forests. The wares were inexpensive and intended for the country markets.

Between about 1772 and 1787 Limbach used a monogram formed by a "B" within an "L" or interlaced "Ls", and at the same period also interlaced "Ls" over a star in imitation of the Meissen mark of the Marcolini period (see Meissen porcelain). Wallendorf used a "W" written in two ways, one version, appearing between 1764 and 1787, closely approximating to the crossed swords of Meissen. Ilmenau, from about 1792 onwards used a dotted "i" in blue and Gera a "G" or the name Gera from about 1779. Rauenstein employed an "R" over a star or "R-n" from 1783 onwards. A clover-leaf mark was also used at the Greiners' factories from 1786 to 1792.

Limehouse: a London porcelain factory of short duration was situated here, near Dick Shore, as early as 1746 (*Daily Advertiser*, 1 January 1747), but was in difficulties in 1748 (*Daily Advertiser*, 3 June 1748) and probably wound up shortly after.

Limited edition: any edition of a book which is limited to a stated number of copies (books described as limited editions which fail to specify how many copies they are limited to should be regarded with scepticism).

Limmel: the early form of *lemail*, or scrapings or filings of metal.

Limoges enamel: the town of Limoges in France was a principal centre of enamelling (see Enamel) in the Middle Ages. The art of the 12th cent. goldsmith developed opaque *champlevé* enamel in place of the earlier translucent *cloisonné* in gold. Apart from the great centres on the Rhine and the Meuse, a regular industry, of which products were distributed all over Europe, was developed at Limoges. Numerous enamelled pieces used in the ritual of the Church were made and have been preserved in abbeys and cathedrals. Secular enamelled jewellery was also made in large quantities but little has survived. In the early 16th cent. the Limoges enamelling workshops regained their dominant position, using another technique, that of painted enamel on a copper base. No other Renaissance (q.v.) workshops could seriously rival those of Limoges in the production of sumptuously painted enamels in polychrome, often bright with gold. The sources of the designs used on these painted enamels were contemporary German, Italian and French engravings. (See also Enamel.)

Line-engraving: often called copperplate engraving; it was the favourite method of book illustration in the 17th and 18th cent. The design is incised by means of a burin, and a more formal effect than etching is produced. Colour could be added by selective inking of the one plate or by printing from several different plates, but neither method was as much used in books as hand-colouring.

Linenfold carving: a carved ornament suggested by folded linen, first found late in the 15th cent., very popular in the first half of the 16th, but not very often used in the later years of the century. Of Flemish origin, linenfold carving, sometimes described as parchment pattern, was used as a panel decoration principally on walls, but also on chests, chair-backs, etc. Sometimes the folds were ogee-shaped at top and bottom, or plain, and a later pattern includes carved tassels and other emblems.

Linen-press: a frame with a wooden spiral screw for pressing linen between two boards, dating from the 17th cent.

Ling lung: pierced openwork, as found on some 17th- to 18th-cent. Chinese blue-and-white porcelain bowls, and on elaborate vases of Ch'ien Lung (q.v.) and later date.

Lining papers: the 16th and 17th cent. saw a great variety of these papers, usually printed in black ink on self-coloured paper. Designs were floral, heraldic and conventional, and while generally produced specifically for lining boxes, coffers, etc., were sometimes used as wallpapers, particularly those designs capable of "repeat".

Linings: see Endpapers.

Linnell, John: cabinet-maker and carver, many of whose designs for mirrors and other furnishings have been preserved and are in the Victoria and Albert Museum. He worked in the period 1760–90, and his designs are mainly in the prevailing Chippendale style.

Lion (or **St Andrew**): Scottish gold coin issued from Robert III to Mary. Types, arms of Scotland and St Andrew on cross.

Lion mask: an ornamental motif of Classical inspiration used by furniture makers, silversmiths, etc. in the first half of the 18th cent. and during the Regency period.

Lion's paw foot: a foot carved in the form of a lion's paw sometimes found on carved and gilt armchairs of the late 17th cent. Lion's paw feet formed popular terminals to cabriole legs on early 18th cent. chairs and side tables but were not a feature of Rococo taste. The fashion returned during the Regency, when lion's paw feet appear sometimes on the front legs only, or on both front and back legs of chairs. Lion's paw feet were used also by silversmiths and appear, for example, as supports to late 17th cent. wine-cisterns.

Lip moulding: see Ovolo moulding.

Lith. or **Lit.:** means lithographed by. Follows the lithographer's name on the print. (See also Lithograph.)

Lithograph: a print made by what its inventor, A. Senefelder, c. 1797, called a "chemical process", based on the principle that oil and water do not mix. It was a single-plane process. The design was drawn with a special crayon on calcareous limestone, and a film of water passed over the surface. When greasy ink on the roller passed over the stone, the water repelled it, but the crayoned surface took it up, and an impression could be taken.

The process was first used for the production of ceramic transfers in 1839. Francis Morley, used this technique at Shelton, in the 1840s. Some of the lithographic stones have survived.

The first litho-transfers were made in 1863 and submitted to Josiah Wedgwood & Sons, Etruria, but they were extremely crude.

In the 1890s several firms experimented with litho-transfers, but little progress was made until the invention of Duplex paper.

Lithophane: a porcelain or bone china transparency moulded thinly in *intaglio* to produce monochrome illusionist pictures (portraits, figure groups, landscapes) by transmitted light. The process was invented in 1827 by Baron de Bourgoing, and used by Mintons, Copelands, and Grainger & Lee of Worcester. Lithophanes are sometimes called transparencies.

Lithotint: this was a development of the lithograph (q.v.) using the stone, by coating it with a resinous substance, as its predecessor used the aquatint. The resulting print was tinted and ranged in tones from brown to black. Charles Hullmandel was responsible for this new process, which he patented in 1840. A half-way house between the lithograph and the chromolithograph (q.v.), the lithotint, was used in a number of books between 1840 and 1860.

Littler, William: (1724-84), salt-glazed stoneware manufacturer, in partnership with Aaron Wedgwood at Brownhills, and porcelain manufacturer at Longton Hall trading as Littler and Co. from 1752 until 1760. Later manager to the firm of Baddeley & Fletcher at Shelton.

Liverpool delftware and porcelain: (1) Delftware: it is said that the manufacture of delftware in Liverpool began about 1710 when some potters from Southwark settled in the district, but potteries certainly existed in the city at an earlier date and some faience bowls painted with ships and inscriptions and made early in the 17th cent. are assigned to Liverpool. By 1780 the manufacture of delftware had almost ceased and many of the best potters had departed to work in Staffordshire.

Little is known of individual potteries in Liverpool, marks are rare, and only certain features common to wares from the district single them out for identification.

The date at which the manufacture of porcelain began in the Liverpool factories (of which there were about a dozen in 1760) is also uncertain; it is likely that potteries already producing delftware turned to porcelain manufacture to compete with the Staffordshire firms.

The industry in Liverpool was in decline in 1780–90, but some cream and white wares were produced after that period.

About 1750, John Sadler, another Liverpool potter, introduced (possibly invented) transfer-printing. In partnership with Guy Green he developed the process with such success that wares were imported from other parts of the country to be decorated at Liverpool in this way. A large export trade, mainly to America, grew up and by 1760 articles of all kinds both useful and decorative came in a steady flow from the factories.

Punch-bowls, made largely for ships and often bearing the name of the vessel and paintings of ships or marine subjects, form a large class of Liverpool ware. Many are very attractive, but some later examples are of enormous size and grotesque design. A characteristic example of the earlier type is in the Liverpool Museum, dated 1760 and inscribed "Success to the Monmouth".

Flower painting of a bold and rather crude type is seen at its most distinctive on a mug made for a man named Fazackerly in 1757, and this kind of decoration, making use of *bianco*, is known by his name.

Vases and jugs (especially ones of large size with curved sides), wall-pockets, trinket-trays, "bricks" (rectangular flower vases), were all made in quantity in Liverpool.

A large and attractive class of earthenware consists of tiles printed with such subjects as actors and actresses of the day etc., usually in black or red but occasionally in polychrome.

Chinese subjects popular in the 18th cent. were used at Liverpool as elsewhere, usually on a plain cream ware, painted or printed in blue under the glaze. In articles decorated in polychrome, a greyish-green, purple, bright blue and reddish-brown were much employed. The "Fazackerley" design of a flower in the shape of a Tudor rose, outlined in *bianco*, is distinguishable with certainty as Liverpool, and is found on a considerable number of plates and dishes. Armorial designs were often used, as were river-scenes and marine views. Flower decorations in reserved panels on a mottled ground of blue or purple were copied from imported oriental wares.

With the popularity of transfer-printing, a fashion grew up for reproducing illustrations from contemporary books, prints and paintings of the period. These are often well engraved and usually printed on plain cream wares in monochrome. Subjects from Hogarth and his school are characteristic.

Marks are almost unknown: a prunus blossom on the base of articles decorated in the Chinese manner is sometimes found, but this was also used at Bristol and, less frequently, at Lambeth. Numerals occur on various types of delftware; the numbers used are said to be higher at Liverpool than at either Bristol or Lambeth. A border of reddish-brown on plates is reputed to be a Liverpool characteristic.

(2) Porcelain: a considerable variety of porcelain is attributed to the Liverpool factories, some of which seems to have been experimental and some of good quality and pleasing design. None can be assigned to individual factories, and it is possible that some pieces attributed to Liverpool may have been of Staffordshire manufacture.

The paste used is soft, heavy and somewhat coarse, with a bluish glaze often deepening in colour at the base of the article. Some pieces are reminiscent of Worcester, especially in their shape. Tall jugs and coffee-pots, and barrel-shaped mugs, are especially characteristic.

The flower decoration used is similar to that found on Liverpool earthenware, and is usually in rather bright colours with the flowers outlined in black. Transfer-printing is of rather indifferent quality; it is often found in a dark shade of red which seems to be peculiar to Liverpool wares.

Livery cupboard: the cup-board was originally the board upon which the "cups" were displayed. In its early stages it was an open structure fitted with shelves normally two or three in number. Before the end of the 15th cent. the space on the central board or shelf was sometimes enclosed by panels at the side and doors in front. Contemporary inventories refer to livery cupboards and court cupboards (q.v.). Some modern authorities identify livery cupboards with those open structures not containing an enclosed compartment, and others with the type fitted with a doored enclosure. The term "livery" refers to the ration of food and drink dispensed in large households for the night and eaten in the bedchamber. For this reason livery cupboards are often listed in bedroom inventories. A form of hanging cupboard enclosed by two pierced doors, each with two rows of turned balusters, dating from the early 17th cent. is also known as a livery cupboard. By the 1660s the livery cupboard was outmoded.

"L" mark: see Worcester porcelain and Longton Hall porcelain.

Lobby chest: defined by Sheraton as "a kind of half chest of drawers, adapted for the use of a small study, lobby, etc.".

Lobing: see under Gadroon and Knulling.

"Lobster-tail" helmet: a modern term for a form of burgonet (q.v.) worn by cavalry in the 17th cent. It had a laminated tail, hinged cheek-pieces and a peak (often pivoted), with one or more bars extending from it over the face. The English form with three bars was the characteristic helmet of the Civil War.

Locking plate: a clock plate with notches set at increasing intervals around its circumference, which allows the striking train to sound the correct number of blows before the locking arm falls into a notch and stops the train.

Lock, Matthias: a designer who published a number of books of furniture designs between the years 1740 and 1769. He collaborated with H. Copland, and modern research has led to the conclusion that these two men were responsible for many of the plates in Thomas Chippendale's *Director* for which Chippendale earned so much fame. (See also Chippendale, Thomas.)

Lock-plate: (a) flat plate attached by screws, usually to the side of a firearm at the breech end of the barrel, to which the moving parts which provide ignition are attached; (b) the background to which all the pins and stumps of a lock are riveted and over which the cover is fixed; (c) plate protecting a key-hole or front-plate of a lock.

Loggerhead: a circular inkstand with a wide flat base, still used in banks.

Long-case clock: the correct horological term for a grandfather or grandmother clock.

"Long Elizas": curiously elongated renderings of Chinese women occurring upon Worcester porcelain in the 1760s. The name is an anglicized version from the Dutch *Lange Lyzen*.

Long pillow-covers: long pillow-covers, or "pillow beres", to give them their contemporary name, unlike the cushion-covers, were always worked on linen and were used in the bedroom. The most usual size for Elizabethan examples was about 35 by 20 inches, and the back of the cover, which was left plain, has rarely survived. All-over patterns of the coiling stem type were most popular and "black-work" was frequently employed. In the late 17th and early 18th cent. pillow-covers embroidered entirely in yellow silk are often found;

also examples quilted in white linen thread or cotton.

Longton Hall porcelain: little is known definitely of the history of Longton Hall, the first porcelain factory in Staffordshire. It is believed to have been established about 1750 and certainly before October 1751. It was first worked independently by William Jenkinson, but in 1751 in partnership with William Littler (q.v.) and Aaron Wedgwood. From 1752 until 1760 the style of the firm was Littler and Company. William Duesbury appears to have had some associations with the factory. Evidently the story of this factory is still far from complete.

Marks:

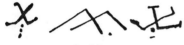

In blue

Crossed L's appear in several forms and these may stand for Littler, Longton. Marks are usually in blue under the glaze.

The name of Wm. Littler is associated with that of the factory almost from its foundation: his work there included much which seems to have been experimental. A deep blue glaze seen on some wares is supposed to have been his invention.

Two types of porcelain are attributable to Longton Hall. The more usual is a crude rather heavy porcelain of peculiar translucency for its thickness, the body appearing a pale green or blue with "moons" of white when seen by transmitted light. The basic colour is a rather cold glassy white in natural light.

The wares include leaf-dishes similar to those made in Staffordshire saltglazed stoneware, various articles in fruit and vegetable form often with twig-handles painted green, vases and basketwork dishes. Plates and dishes with moulded borders are frequent.

Decoration is in bright and rather crude colours, notably a deep underglaze blue, yellowish-green, dull pink and a rather thick red. Gilding was used sparingly.

The second Longton Hall type is a rather finer porcelain, in imitation of Meissen, often making use of the same subjects: vases decorated with applied double flowers, plates painted with birds, and bouquets of flowers, etc. There is some similarity to Chelsea in many of the pieces, but most are of inferior quality.

Figures were made at Longton Hall probably from the beginning. It is now known, as the result of recent excavations on the site, that the "Snow-man" type of figure was made here. Later figures have the merits of vigorous execution and individuality, but are usually roughly modelled and give the appearance of being unfinished. Scrolled bases picked out in red are a distinguishing characteristic of these figures, together with the Longton Hall palette of yellows, blues and paintlike deep red.

Loop-back chair: American term for a type of Windsor chair (q.v.).

Looped pile carpet: a carpet woven in loops, in the manner of velvet, which are afterwards cut.

Loopings or **draggings:** decorative device achieved by the glassblower in applying glass threads of contrasting colours to the body of the glassware, which are then dragged upward by a tool and embedded. The technique has been used since ancient times.

Lotus ornament: a decorative motif, intended to represent the lotus, inspired by the interest in Egyptian art prevalent during the Napoleonic wars. The campaign in Egypt provoked the general popularity of Egyptian forms and motifs and the lotus, as well as representations of the sphinx, etc.

appeared on furniture, silver, etc. in the first decade of the 19th cent.

Louis: French gold coin introduced by Louis XIII in 1640 with types, royal portrait and elaborate cross with *lis* in angles. Continued, with variations of type, up to the Republic.

Love bird thumbpiece: a thumbpiece (q.v.), representing twin birds, their beaks jointed, surmounted by a volute; found on pewter tankards.

Love-seat: an upholstered settee intended for two persons. (See Causeuse.)

Loving cup: a drinking vessel with two handles, originally used for toasting. General term for twin-handled cups.

Lowboy: a modern name for a piece of American furniture inspired by the English flat-top dressing table with drawers, yet in its final development, similar to a French commode. Low boys date from the 18th cent., New England examples being attractively simple and those from Philadelphia much carved and ornamented. Known in the 18th cent. as dressing tables, chamber tables or low chests of drawers, lowboys were often made as companion pieces to highboys (q.v.).

"Lowdin's" Bristol: see Bristol porcelain.

Lowestoft porcelain: a factory manufacturing soft paste porcelain was established in Bell Lane (now Crown Street), Lowestoft in 1757. The original partners were Robert Browne, Philip Walker, Obed. Aldred, and John Hickman. The firm lasted until 1802 and produced unpretentious coloured and blue-and-white ware of attractive quality. In spite of many ancient claims that it was, hard paste porcelain was never made here.

No mark was consistently used, but numerals up to 28 often in underglaze blue inside the footring are found on some pieces. Factory marks of Worcester, Meissen and other factories were sometimes imitated.

Many pieces made at this factory are dated or inscribed and a fairly complete sequence from the earliest to the last years of the factory can be established. Tea-caddies, inkstands, and other small pieces intended for visitors were often lettered "A Trifle from Lowestoft". Dates from 1761 until 1795.

The Lowestoft porcelain paste was very similar to that of Bow, although the glaze was generally thinner and rather absorbent. Patches of discoloration are to be found in Lowestoft tea cups.

Table wares and numerous small articles were most frequently decorated in underglaze blue, the colour being usually darker than that of Bow or Worcester. Porcelain moulded in relief was made in some quantity and can be identified from surviving moulds. A wicker-work design of rough character was much used. Openwork baskets and cabbage-leaf jugs were also made.

Oriental designs of figures in landscapes or flowers are common; marine views and inscriptions were popular, some being in distinctive colours, for the most part bright browns and reds. A similarity to Delft ware of the period is sometimes observable.

In the later articles the designs become more elaborate, Chinese influence being dominant. Commemorative pieces such as punch-bowls, jugs, and plaques, often inscribed and frequently painted with local views, were made. Amongst other pieces there are mugs with double-twisted handles; teapots of globular form and toy tea services. Recently a few figures have come to light, but no larger groups.

Low-warp tapestry: tapestry woven on a horizontal loom. The weaver controls his warp with treadles, leaving his hands free and is therefore able to work more quickly than the high-warp weaver. The cartoon is placed under the horizontal warp, requiring it to be drawn in reverse. At the Gobelins (q.v.) where both low-warp and high-warp weaving were employed, it was reckoned that at least a third more low-warp tapestry could be woven in a given time. (See also High-warp tapestry.)

Lozenge ornament: see Diamond ornament.

Ludwigsburg porcelain: hard-paste porcelain was made at the ducal factory at Ludwigsburg, near Stuttgart, in 1758–59 under Duke Carl Eugen. The factory itself had been founded at an earlier date for the manufacture of faience. The porcelain was brownish-grey in colour and consequently somewhat inferior for table-wares. The body was, however, admirable for figure modelling and the figures produced are the most sought after of the factory's productions. Of these, those modelled by the court-sculptor J. C. W. Beyer, appointed chief modeller in 1764, are masterly in their combination of Rococo elements and Classical tendencies. The factory was closed in 1824, but it had already begun to fail after the death of the Duke in 1793. The early mark consists of interlaced "Cs", with or without a crown, replaced by the stag's horns from the arms of Württemberg about 1793.

Lug: an ear (Scots); the handle of a quaich (q.v.).

Lunar clock dial: a dial which shows the lunar periods.

"Lund's" Bristol: see Bristol porcelain.

Lunette ornament: formal carving composed of semicircles, variously filled and embellished, frequently disposed in a repeat-band.

This type of ornament is frequently found on oak furniture of the first half of the 17th cent. The fan-shaped or lunette motif was also used on late 18th cent. furniture, either painted or inlaid.

Lung-chüan celadon ware: this centre for celadon wares (q.v.) in Chekiang Province, China, flourished during the Sung dynasty (q.v.). The greyish-white porcellanous body often appears brown where exposed raw to the fire. The characteristic glaze is thick, smooth and translucent, varying principally between a cool greyish and deep grassy green, the colour being derived from iron. Best known are the stoutly potted, large, heavy dishes, jars and vases exported in quantity throughout the Near and Far East. Finer wares are various in shape, often with freely carved or incised designs, or decoration impressed from moulds of fishes, dragons or plants, sometimes left unglazed and burnt an attractive red. The Kinuta celadon, a subdued bluish green in colour, is of outstanding quality. Another type with brown spots is the Japanese tobi seiji (q.v.). Early Ming celadons are similar, but often more elaborately decorated. Quality then declined rapidly.

Lustre: this term is now used to describe a vase with everted rim from which hang cut-glass drops. At one period it was used to describe a chandelier, and in 1739 Jerom Johnson the glass-seller, advertised for sale "the most magnificent lustre that was ever made in England".

The vase-lustre was made in pairs, and came into vogue in the middle of the 19th cent. The most esteemed were of ruby or green glass with an overlay of white, and decoration, in addition to the cutting, in the form of painted flowers or miniature portraits in colours, and gilding. They were made in Bohemia (now Czechoslovakia), but considerable numbers were manufactured in England, at Stourbridge and elsewhere. Wedgwood's (q.v.) jasper ware was used for embellishing lustres.

Lustre decoration: decoration on pottery or porcelain by means of thin films of metal. Josiah Wedgwood experimented with lustre decoration from about 1790 and his successors made commercial use of silver, pink (gold) and "moonlight" lustre from about 1805. John Hancock claimed to be the first to produce lustre effects in Staffordshire while employed by Henry Daniel & John Brown, enamellers of Hanley (*Staffordshire Mercury*, 1846). Hancock sold the recipe to various persons for small sums of money and its use soon became widespread. The earliest commercial use of silver lustre is stated to have taken place at Wolfe's factory in Stoke. Others had also had a hand in its early development and application. Various methods of application were used: pencilled, "resist", banded, or in conjunction with transfer-printing and enamelling. It enjoyed popularity in Staffordshire and the Out-Potteries from about 1805 until 1875. The export factors Burgess, Dale & Goddard did an extensive trade in lustre wares with the U.S.A. in the 1850s. The subjects used for lustre decoration cover the whole field of public and domestic life, religious, political, sporting, travel and sensational events, – the humours of every day life accompanied sometimes by pious quatrains, or sentimental and licentious doggerel.

Lutes: only very rarely will a specimen of the true lute be found, since few were made after the beginning of the 18th cent. The heyday of the instrument was the late 16th and early 17th cent. Nevertheless, it must be considered because of the growing attention it is receiving at the present day. The lute proper has a large pear-shaped body of the form now familiar in the mandoline, a wide, flat neck and a head or peg-box turned back almost at right angles. It may have anything from twelve to twenty-two strings arranged and tuned in pairs, and is intended to be played with gut frets on the neck, like the viols. The soundboard or table is ornamented with a "rose" of open fretwork which, in the earliest examples, is carved from the thin pinewood table itself. Instruments of approximately this form, but with only six single strings, were made in Germany during the 19th cent. in considerable numbers. They are not lutes as we understand the term, and are neither very old nor very valuable.

Lyonese binding: an international style of fine leather book-binding, on which heavy centre- and corner-pieces were blocked in a press. Characteristic of Elizabethan bindings, the style continued in use until about 1640. (See also Gold-tooled bindings.)

Lyre-back chair: a late 18th cent. chair of a design favoured by Robert Adam (q.v.). The splat contained in a square back, is carved in the shape of a lyre with metal strings.

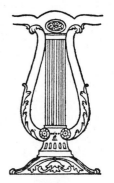

Mace: civic, university or state emblem of authority derived from medieval war weapon. Usually surmounted by Royal arms and crown. Silver examples date from 15th cent. onwards.

Machine-cut silhouette: silhouette produced by a mechanical profile machine, of which there were many forms. Such work may usually be distinguished by a certain hardness and lack of freedom in its outlines. There were, however, a few machine-cutters who produced commendable work. One such was Mrs Sarah Harrington (fl. 1775), whose shades are full of vivacity. On the whole machine-cutting is the most debased form of the art of the silhouette.

Machine-printed wallpaper: the first successful wallpaper printing machine was in operation in England about 1840. Based on calico-printing principles, it was dependent on the invention and supply of paper in "continuous" lengths.

Maculature: a weak impression. The copperplate or block from which prints are taken must be inked after each impression has been pulled; a maculature is a second impression taken without re-inking, usually to extract the remainder of the ink.

Made-up copies: a made-up copy of a book is one whose imperfections – the lack of a single leaf or more – have been made good from another copy of the same edition.

Maidenhead spoon: a spoon with a finial (q.v.) in the form of a female bust traditionally representing the Virgin Mary. Silver spoons of this type are described in a 15th-cent. inventory as "Cum jmaginibus Beatae Mariae in fine eorundum".

Mail: armour made of interlinked rings which, on most European examples, are riveted. It was known in Europe at least as early as the 2nd cent. B.C., and was the normal defence during the early Middle Ages. It was relegated to a subordinate role with the general adoption of plate armour in the 14th cent., but nevertheless remained in common use until well into the 17th. The extension of the term to cover all forms of defensive armour and the word chain-mail are both of comparatively recent date.

Main-gauche dagger: see Left-hand dagger.

Maintaining power: a device used in weight clocks and in clocks and watches fitted with a fusee (q.v.), whereby a subsidiary force is brought into play to keep the clock going while it is being wound. In early clocks the winding squares were often covered by shutters, which, when pulled aside, brought into operation the maintaining power, thus ensuring its use.

Maiolica (and **Majolica**): the name given to tin-glazed earthenware made in Spain and Italy from the 14th cent., being the Italian form of the place-name Majorca, whence ships engaged in transporting Valencian lustred pottery from Spain traded. First applied to Spanish lustred wares, the term was gradually extended to cover Italian lustred wares executed in the Spanish technique, and ultimately to any kind of earthenware with painted decoration on tin glaze. The technique of the Italian *maiolica* potter is described in *The Three Books of the Potters Art* by Cipriano Piccolpasso, c. 1556, translated by Bernard Rackham and A. van de Put. Should not be confused with MAJOLICA – the name absurdly given by Victorian potters to earthenware decorated with coloured glazes, introduced at Mintons about 1850, for decorative pottery, but applied extensively to domestic wares, to architectural pottery intended for facing pillars, walls, staircases, balconies, and to flower-pots and umbrella stands.

Maker's mark: the distinguishing mark of the individual goldsmith, device or initials struck on every piece of plate (q.v.) from his workshop. First enforced in London in 1363.

Malachite: a name given to a parian ware (q.v.), coloured to resemble the green of malachite stone.

"Malling" jugs: English tin-glazed pottery jugs splashed or mottled with metallic oxides in imitation of Rhenish "Tigerwares", and similarly mounted. Dates recorded from 1549 until 1618. Some of these wares have been attributed to a Sandwich-Maidstone potter, working c. 1582, and derive their name from a specimen formerly in West Malling church, Kent. Also called "Tigerware" or "Leopard-ware".

Maltese lace: pillow lace made from 1833, the designs including "wheat grains" grouped in fours to make Maltese crosses.

Manchette: a cuff-bracelet worn in the 19th cent.

Manchu dynasty: dynasty of the Ch'ing emperors in China (1644–1912).

"Mandarin" china: Chinese porcelain wares imported during the second half of the 18th cent. and later, with predominantly pink, red and gold enamelling of floral or figure subjects, often framed in underglaze blue scrollwork; frequently with undulating glaze.

Mandoline: a musical instrument with a deep pear-shaped body, of several types: the Milanese, with six single gut strings; the Paduan, with five pairs of strings; the Genoese, with five or six wire strings; and the Neapolitan, the most common in England, with four pairs of wire strings. All are played with a plectrum. Other types include the Portuguese guitar, with a flat, pear-shaped body, six double strings and a peculiar radial arrangement of screw pegs. The Spanish bandurria is a short, stubby guitar-like instrument with six double gut strings. In the 18th cent., the English guitar was popular, a small pear-shaped instrument with flat back and six pairs of wire strings played with the fingers and not with a plectrum. Many of these have a peculiar tuning device of small screw-nuts which are turned with a watch-key. The English guitar was an adaptation of the 16th and 17th cent. cittern of similar form, but with four double strings on ordinary violin-type pegs, a longer neck and a flat body which, however, tapered in thickness towards the lower end.

Manière criblée: prints in the *manière criblée*, sometimes called "dotted prints", are taken from a metal plate engraved in the same manner as a white-line wood-block. The name is derived from the groups of dots made on the plate with a punch to break up otherwise black areas of background. Prints of this type were made in the late 15th and early 16th cent., especially in Florence, and there are isolated examples of *manière criblée* prints by Giuseppe Scolari of Vicenza and Urs Graf. The method was revived in England towards the end of the 18th cent.

Mannerist style: an international style which emerged in the second decade of the 16th cent. as a reaction against the harmony and order of the Renaissance (q.v.). Embraced by the French court at Fontainebleau, where Italian artists were employed in the decoration of the Palace, the style spread throughout Europe as a Court art characterised by anti-naturalism and an intellectual approach to form. There were many local variations to suit local requirements but the same rejection of the Classical spirit, involving a disregard of naturalistic forms, is everywhere apparent.

Mannheim gold: an alloy of copper, zinc and tin.

Mansell, Sir Robert: a financier who organized the English glass industry in the first half of the 17th cent., and who eventually controlled glasshouses all over the country. He imported skilled workers from Murano, and successfully made mirror-glass.

Mantel clock: see Bracket clock.

Manton brothers: the foremost London gunmakers of the first quarter of the 19th cent. The two brothers, John and Joseph, vied with each other for supremacy. John, the elder, was more popular with the Royal family but Joseph was the greater. At the height of his career, he was unequalled and his name lives on as one of the most famous gunmakers of all time.

Manwaring, Robert: Cabinet and chair-maker. Published *The Cabinet and Chair-Makers' Real Friend and Companion* in 1765 and *The Chair-Maker's Guide* in 1766.

Marbled paper: "Coloured or stained with variegated patterns like those of marble, 1671", says SOED. Marbled paper: used since the latter part of the 17th cent. for the sides of binding and for endpapers, is made by lowering a sheet of paper on to a bath of gum or size, on the surface of which colours have been stirred with a stick or comb into a pattern; there was also a vogue during the late 17th and early 18th cent. for decorating the walls of halls and staircases with marbled papers painted by wood-blocks.

Marbled calf: introduced about the same time and also from Holland, is stained to a stylized pattern something like marble. **Marbled edges:** are executed by a modification of the technique used for marbling paper and are common on books bound since 1800.

Marbled ware: a slipware decorated by working together various coloured slips with a wire comb and sponge in emulation of marbled papers or natural stones. Common on Staffordshire, Swansea, Leeds and Don pottery in the 18th cent.

Marbled earthenwares had been made in China during the T'ang and Sung dynasties (q.v.), produced either by rolling together differently coloured clays or by manipulating a coloured "slip" on the surface.

Marcasite: iron pyrites, faceted in the manner of precious stones, made by mechanical process.

Marcolini, Count Camillo: appointed director of the Meissen porcelain factory in 1774, which he remained for forty years. The period of his directorship is known as the Marcolini period, the wares being marked during this time with crossed swords and a star between the hilts. (See also Meissen porcelain.)

Marieberg porcelain: porcelain was made at Marieberg, near Stockholm from about 1766. The factory was directed by a Frenchman who had previously worked at Mennecy (q.v.). It was closed in 1788. The mark was the monogram MB, either incised, in blue or in red.

Marine barometer: a type in which part of the bore in the vertical tube is constricted in order to minimize a movement of level in the vertical tube by reason of the ship's motion. This type must also be capable of plugging when not in use.

Markwick family: an eminent London family of clockmakers, the various members being active between 1666 and 1805.

Marlborough leg: a straight, tapered leg of square section, sometimes supported on a plinth, used by cabinet-makers in the second half of the 18th cent. The origin of the term is obscure but it may have been invented in compliment to the fourth Duke of Marlborough to whom Ince and Mayhew (q.v.) dedicated their *Universal System of Household Furniture.*

Marot, Daniel: a Huguenot refugee who became Minister of Works to William of Orange. He visited England from 1694 to 1697 and again in 1698. His designs for furniture and for the interiors of rooms interpreted the Louis XIV style.

Marouflage: a scarlet cloth backing to pierced lock plates.

Marquetry: (*Fr.*), *Marqueterie* from *Marqueter*, to spot, speckle, variegate. Ornamental veneer of wood or other materials in which veneers of various coloured woods were cut into delicate patterns and fitted together on to a prepared carcase. The practice of decorating case furniture and tables with marquetry was introduced from Holland in c. 1675. At first English cabinet-makers followed the Flemish fashion and used bird, flower and foliage designs, sometimes introducing bone and ivory. The colours toned to darker or golden shades by 1690 and later arabesques became popular. This phase of the fashion did not survive the early 18th cent. but marquetry once again enjoyed a period of favour in the last quarter of the cent.

Marquise: (*Fr.*), a small sofa also known as a causeuse (q.v.). English settees of this type are sometimes known as love-seats (q.v.).

Marquise ring: a ring of oval form, pointed at each extremity.

Marrow spoon: long, narrow-bowled spoon, usually double-ended with two widths of bowl for eating bone-marrow. Alternative version has normal tablespoon bowl and marrow-bowl in place of handle. Found from early 18th cent. onwards.

Marsh and Tatham: principal cabinet-makers to the Prince of Wales, future George IV, with whom the architect and designer Henry Holland (q.v.) was closely associated.

Martha Gunn: female toby jug modelled in the likeness of Martha Gunn (1727–1815), the Brighton bathing-woman.

Martha Washington chair: slender mid-18th cent. arm-chair with tapered outlines; a "lady's chair", with upholstered, low, shallow seat and high back, usually with serpentine cresting. So named in America because Martha Washington is supposed to have used a chair of this type at Mount Vernon.

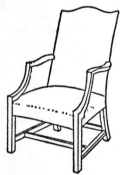

Martha Washington mirror: walnut or mahogany wall mirror, Georgian style, with handsome gilded mouldings, strings of leaves, fruits or flowers down the sides, a scroll top and a bird finial. The base is cut in a series of bold curves. Made in America from about 1760 to 1800, and known there by this name, because Martha Washington is supposed to have used one at Mount Vernon. (Also known in America as a Constitution mirror.)

Martha Washington sewing-table: oval box-form sewing-table with rounded ends and hinged top. Fitted with drawers and sewing material compartments, it is an American variant of an English late 18th cent. type. So named in America because Martha Washington is supposed to have used one at Mount Vernon.

Mason's bone china: Miles Mason, after some years of experimental potting in Liverpool and in Fenton started to make porcelain at a factory in Market Street, Fenton, in 1800. In 1807 he moved to the Minerva works, Fenton, where he continued to make porcelain and bone china in conjunction with his eldest son, William Mason. When he retired in 1813 the business was continued by G. M. and C. J. Mason, the other son, William, having taken over a separate factory. George Miles Mason withdrew from the business about 1829, leaving Charles James Mason to continue on his own account, or for a short period in partnership with Faraday until he became bankrupt in 1848. Charles James Mason started up again at the Daisy Bank, Longton in 1851, exhibited at the great Exhibition in that year but closed down in 1854. Marks:

Transfer-printed

Variations in crown

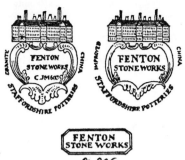

Transfer-printed

Early types of porcelain made by
Miles Mason were of an extremely
hard consistency and rather opaque;
a translucent bone paste was also
made. Blue printed decorations were
popular, and painted landscapes,
Chinese subjects, border patterns of
Regency type.

G. M. and C. J. Mason made showy
Imari (q.v.) patterns with massed
effects of colour and gold, often rather
crudely applied. Very large pieces
were made in ironstone china, including fire-places, bed-posts, vases
five feet high, some in a revived rococo
style, others with pseudo-Chinese
decorations. Blue-printed earthenware
was extensively made.

Mason's moulds and engravings
were acquired by Francis Morley.

Massachusetts shelf clock: a type
made by the Willards and others,
chiefly of Massachusetts. Also called
half-clock, box-on-box, or case-on-
case. Eight-day brass movements,
timepieces or occasionally striking
clocks. c. 1800–30. Rare.

Matapan: silver coin of Venice issued
from late 12th cent. onwards with types
similar to the ducat (q.v.).

Match-lock: the earliest form of
mechanical ignition for a gun, introduced late in the 15th cent., in which
an arm holding a lighted match (cord
made of tow soaked in a solution of
saltpetre) is brought into contact with
priming powder at the touch-hole by
pressure on a trigger. Despite the
invention of the wheel- and flint-locks,

it remained in use for military
purposes, on account of its cheapness,
until the end of the 17th cent.

Matt glaze: a glaze with a dull, non-
reflecting surface.

Matting: a dull, roughened surface
produced on silverware by repeated
punching with a burred tool. Much
used in mid-17th cent. on tankard and
cup bodies.

Maundy money: silver coins of 4d,
3d, 2d and 1d given by the sovereign
as alms on Maundy Thursday. In the
earlier reigns these were the ordinary
current coins, but from George II
were special issues with royal portrait
obverse and plain figure giving value
on reverse.

"Maximilian" armour: a modern
term for the style of fluted armour
which came into use in Italy and,
more particularly, in Germany during
the reign of the Emperor Maximilian I
(1494–1519). It is rarely found after
c. 1540, but examples dating from as
late as c. 1560–70 are occasionally
encountered. Modern writers sometimes use the rare 16th cent. English
term for fluted, "crested," to describe
this style.

Mayhew, Thomas: see Ince and
Mayhew.

Mazarine: pierced, flat silver straining
plate for use with fish dishes.

Mazarine blue: a dark rich blue
frequently used for the decoration of
porcelain, less frequently for earthenware. The origin of the name is unknown, but thought to be an attributed
use of the name Cardinal Giulio
Mazarine (1602–61) jurisprudent,
diplomat and Cardinal, or the
Duchesse de Mazarin (died 1699).
The name is mentioned in the 1756

catalogue of the Chelsea porcelain factory.

Mazer: medieval drinking bowl formed from a turned section of maple burr, mounted with silver rim and occasionally straps, usually gilt. Large standing examples on high feet found in Scotland and a few in England. Rare after the 16th cent.

"MB" mark: see Marieberg porcelain.

M.e.: marbled edges; i.e., a marble-veined multi-colouring of the fore-edge and perhaps one or more of the other edges of a book. (See Marbled paper.)

Meander ornament: a repetitive pattern consisting of straight lines intersecting at right angles used as a border ornament. Also known as a Greek fret or key pattern (q.v.).

Measure: a vessel of a standard liquid capacity, used in taverns for serving into drinking vessels.

Meat-fork: used at the fireside when cooking. It usually had two prongs and hardly differed from a toasting-fork.

Mechanical birds: among the most popular of all automata were birds, from the duck of Vaucanson (q.v.) onwards. Marie-Antoinette, Queen of France, possessed a life-sized canary in a cage, the underneath of which showed the dial of a clock. The bird sang realistically. Catherine II, Empress of Russia, was presented in 1780 with a large caged mechanical peacock made by James Cox (q.v.). On the smallest scale were the singing birds fitted into snuff-boxes. These were quite invisible until, on the pressure of a button, they sprang up, moved their heads, wings and tails and sang. They were, understandably, highly popular and expensive. Many were mounted in gold boxes, set with precious stones and contained a musical-box movement as well. The Jaquet-Droz (q.v.) and the Rochat brothers are among the best known makers of these remarkable tours-de-force, which date from the late 18th and early 19th cent. Even more remarkable are watches with singing birds and gold pistols from the mouths of which tiny birds emerge and sing when the triggers are pressed.

Mechanical draughtsmen: several automata that wrote words and sentences, or drew pictures, were constructed from 1750 onwards, notably by Friedrich von Knauss of Vienna (1742–89), Jaquet-Droz and Leschot, and Maillardet.

Mechanical pictures: framed pictures (landscapes, seascapes, etc.) in which figures, animals, windmills and water were all operated mechanically.

Mechlin lace: pillow lace, much imported to England, although it must be remembered that all Flemish laces until the 17th cent. were called Mechlin in England. Queen Anne, who prohibited imports of French lace, allowed those from the Low Countries. The earliest that can be identified, however, dates only to the 1720s. Handsome rococo patterns were used, outlined in a separate, heavier flat thread, the pattern and ground being made together in one operation. The ground was the familiar hexagonal mesh in which four sides were of two threads twisted and two sides were of four threads plaited three times. Structurally this was nearly the same as the Brussels ground but the effect was altogether less stiff and angular. Other grounds were sometimes used such as the *œil de perdrix* (q.v.). The spotted patterns of the 1770s onwards consisted of rows of small sprays and the mesh was also variously spotted, the whole effect being subdued and soft. Some lace in Mechlin style was made in Denmark in the 18th and early 19th cent.

Medallion design carpets: Persian carpets often included the medallion

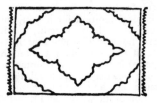

motif, common in all Eastern decoration. The Ardebil carpet in the Victoria and Albert Museum is considered the finest example of this type.

Medallion fans: fashionable from the 1770s to the 1790s. The mount of finely woven silk was painted all over with a light coloured ground. Upon this three medallion subjects were painted: the central one might be elliptical, rectangular or round, its smooth symmetry often emphasized by a flanking pair of small vignettes or medallions depicting associated subjects. These were the work of expert miniature decorators: the detail was displayed quite as finely as on the more costly chicken skin (q.v.). The background was ornamented with minor motifs, scrollwork, sequins, cut steel and other beads. The silk might be mounted on fine gauze.

Medallion fans with their narrower sticks of mother-of-pearl superseded mounts with all-over paintings, but although handsome they are not to be compared with the regal fans of the previous hundred years. Late in the period tiny Wedgwood jasper cameos were set in the sticks, many of which were richly overlaid with embossed gold or silver work, often in the form of a cartouche extending over six or eight sticks.

Medici porcelain: the first successful attempt to produce porcelain in Europe was made at Florence about 1560, under the patronage of Francesco de' Medici. Inspired by the contemporary blue-and-white Ming ware, an artificial porcelain was produced for a short time only, which contained some kaolin, the pure infusable clay used in China, mixed with powdered glass and frit.

Medici porcelain, proudly marked with the cupola of the cathedral and the "F" of Florence, is decorated in underglaze blue of varying intensity, which gently melts into the glaze.

Mei p'ing: Chinese porcelain "prunus" vase, with small mouth to hold one spray of plum-blossom.

Meisho-ki: Japanese term for guidebooks to famous places.

Meissen (or Dresden) porcelain: the foundation of the Meissen factory (near Dresden), 1710, marks the actual beginning of porcelain making in Europe, where its commercial value to an impecunious Court was immediately recognised. J. F. Boettger (q.v.), an alchemist in the service of August the Strong, Elector of Saxony and King of Poland, discovered, in 1710, a red stoneware "which surpasses the hardness of porphyry", as he reported to the King in March 1709. During the following year this red stoneware was offered for sale at the Leipzig Easter Fair. Almost immediately rival factories appeared, one at Plaue on the Havel, where a Prussian minister found red clay on his estate, another at Potsdam, encouraged by the King of Prussia himself. But neither of these factories was progressive, whereas Boettger succeeded in replacing the red clay with white kaolin (see China clay). Thus he produced the first real porcelain in Europe, called Boettger ware, after the inventor, and sold at the Leipzig Fair from 1713 onwards. Above the entrance to Boettger's laboratory, where the King had virtually kept him a prisoner, there is a significant inscription "God, our maker, has turned a goldmaker into a potter". The earliest tableware made at the Meissen factory followed the shape of contemporary silver and the first modeller, Johann Jacob Irminger, was a Court silversmith. Some of this porcelain is decorated with applied floral motives, some with enamel, gilding or lustre colour, which is a pale mother-of-pearl coating obtained from gold, the outcome of another of Boettger's experiments. The earliest figures show dependence upon ivory statuettes and ivory carvers are known to have found employment at the Meissen factory. A figure of the King himself, in heroic attitude, made first in red Boettger ware and later in white with enamel colouring, belongs to this period, and is attributed to the Saxon ivory carver, Johann Christoph von Luecke. With the rediscovery of underglaze blue at Meissen, the first factory marks were introduced. A pseudo-Chinese sign of square shape is the earliest mark recorded followed by the so-called Caduceus, in turn replaced by the letters K P M (Koenigliche Porzellan Manufaktur), until in 1724, the crossed swords, taken from the King's arms, were permanently adopted.

Special commissions executed for the King himself bear his initials A R (Augustus Rex) in underglaze blue. Incised signs are usually factory assembly marks for the convenience of workmen or repairers (q.v.). Meanwhile Johann Gregor Herold, a miniature and enamel painter, who had been in charge of the artistic direction of the factory in 1720, experimented with colours and, among others, produced a clear yellow ground which found the King's special favour, since it recalled the Imperial colour of China. Herold's chinoiserie subjects, based upon engravings, became an established fashion as a means of enamelled decoration, followed in the later 1730s by harbour views with figures which reveal the influence of Delft. In spite of the complete anonymity which Herold insisted upon, it is sometimes possible to trace a style of individual artists such as C. K. Hunger and A. F. von Loewenfinck since they were able to sign work done elsewhere, when visiting other factories. Such moving about by porcelain workers was often caused by financial gains resulting from the disclosure of technical secrets. Painted porcelain was more costly than whiteware and outside painters, called Hausmaler or independent decorators (q.v.) often executed private orders upon request. The Meissen factory suffered from such competition, and introduced measures to prevent the further sale of undecorated porcelain, unless imperfect or of a discontinued pattern. But we may be glad that the competition existed, for some of the Hausmaler, mainly those centred at Augsburg and Dresden, display an originality of design which would have been difficult to attain under the levelling influence of Herold's strong personality. With the employment at Meissen of Johann Gottlob Kirchner in 1727, the great period of porcelain sculpture begins. Misled at first by his ambitious royal patron, who commissioned large-scale statues for the Japanese Palace, Kirchner modelled figures which did not obey the innate laws of the new material. His powerful, fantastic animals, in white, are again more distinctive as remarkable tours de force rather than as cabinet pieces for the porcelain collector. J. J. Kaendler, who was appointed as chief modeller in 1731, was the first to recognise the possibilities of the new material, and to exploit its inherent qualities. His Italian Comedy figures seem to dance on the shelves of china cabinets. Even conventional tableware takes a share in plastic decoration, and the Swan Service which Kaendler modelled for Count Bruehl, reveals his creative genius in the many variations on the theme of swans. Kaendler's birds were all studied from nature, since Augustus the Strong kept a large collection of domestic and rare specimens at Dresden. Meissen figures and groups served often as table decoration, replacing earlier ones of wax or sugar. The themes are suggested by Court amusements, from theatrical characters performing with baroque exuberance, to disguised princesses and shepherds of sophisticated elegance. Mythological and allegorical subjects are never absent: river gods, seasons, continents or the arts, all richly endowed with the graces of 18th cent. society. Watteau scenes begin to appear on Meissen porcelain about 1738–40. At that time the King's daughter Maria Amalia Christina married Charles IV, King of Naples, and the famous service with green monochrome Watteau decoration, made as a wedding gift, established the new fashion. The increase demand for French engravings as sources of designs was satisfied by J. C. Huet, brother of the painter, who became the factory agent in Paris. Kaendler himself visited Paris in 1749, when French influence gained in intensity at Meissen. Elongated figures, painted in soft colours, turn into pleasing conservation pieces and an air of sentimentality prevails, replacing the whimsical mood and vigour of the earlier days. Kaendler was assisted by a few gifted modellers, and Peter Reinicke, as well as Johann Friedrich Eberlein deserve special credit. Friedrich Elias Meyer, appointed after Eberlein's serious illness in 1748, belonged to a younger generation. Meyer's figures are recognisable by their small heads and slender proportions, to which richly moulded and gilt scroll bases lend additional height. With the outbreak of the Seven Years' War in 1756, the Meissen factory suffered a heavy blow. The Prussians occupied the town and the King fled to Warsaw. Frederick the Great had thirty boxes of porcelain despatched to Potsdam and placed further orders for table services and snuff-boxes with the factory, some of which were copied later on at the Berlin factory (q.v.). After the war, Meissen never regained its former unchallenged lead. A neoclassical phase followed, known as the Academic period during which the wares were marked with the usual crossed swords with a small dot between the hilts (1763–74). During the directorship of Count Camillo Marcolini which immediately followed (1774–1814) the mark was the crossed swords with a star between the hilts. In the 19th cent. the factory made many debased versions of earlier wares. These are now commonly described as "Dresden" to differentiate them from the original wares, usually known as Meissen porcelain.

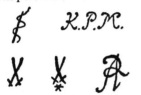

Melon-bulb: jargon and comparatively modern term for the swollen member on legs or posts of furniture. An exaggeration of the knop,

it attained full development in the Elizabethan period, becoming less globular in the early 17th cent.

Memento mori: see Mourning jewellery.

Mendlesham chair: a variety of Windsor chair (q.v.), being of stick construction, with turned legs and solid elm seats. This type of chair was traditionally first made by Daniel Day of Mendlesham in Suffolk. In examples of fine quality, the backs are decorated with inlay.

Mennecy porcelain: soft-paste porcelain was made at Mennecy, Île-de-France, between 1735 and 1785 (the factory being transferred to Bourg-la-Reine in 1773). The Mennecy factory imitated St Cloud and Chantilly (qq.v.) at first, soon attaining great technical skill. Kakiemon patterns (q.v.) were used in the early period but the mature style of Mennecy was chiefly inspired by that of Vincennes (see Sèvres porcelain). Tea-ware, coffee-pots, vases and flowers pots were made in quantity. Some figures were produced but soft paste did not lend itself easily to moulding in the round, and there was danger of collapse in the kiln during the firing. The mark "DV" appears on some pieces.

Menuisier: (Fr.), the term corresponds roughly to the English "carpenter" or "joiner". In France, as far as furniture was concerned, the menuisiers were responsible for making chairs, beds and other furniture made from plain or carved woods, as distinct from veneered pieces which were the province of the ébénistes (q.v.). Although permitted by guild regulations to work in both techniques, they seldom did so.

Menuisiers-Ébénistes, Corporation des: (Fr.), the craft guild in France which embraced all craftsmen engaged in making wood furniture. An apprentice began his training at the age of fourteen with a maître-ébéniste or maître-menuisier, lasting for six years. This period was followed by a further three to six years of training, known as compagnonage. During this latter time, the young man was paid for the work he did. After the *compagnonage*, he was ready to become a *maître* or master of the guild. After 1751, a *maître* was also required to stamp the furniture he sold. The maintenance of standards was in the hands of a *syndic* and six *jurés*. All pieces of furniture approved by the *jurés* were stamped with the monogram J.M.E. (*Juré* or *jurande des menuisiers-ébénistes*).

Mercury clock pendulum: a type of pendulum invented in 1726 by George Graham, who had previously experimented with brass and steel without conclusive results. The bob of the pendulum consists of a jar containing mercury. As the temperature changes the length of the pendulum rod, the level of the mercury in the jar alters in the inverse sense, thus keeping constant the centre of oscillation of the pendulum. Still in use to-day in high-grade clocks.

Mercury gilding: see Gilding.

Mercury-twist stem: a type of stem found on drinking glasses between about 1745 and 1765 containing air-twists of exceptionally large diameter spiralling down the centre in close coils, or a pair of corkscrew threads.

Merese knop: a knop or protuberance in the stem of a drinking glass or other glass vessel of sharp-edged, flattened form, resembling a button, and connecting bowl and stem or placed between the foot and the stem of a stemmed vessel. Also known as a collar knop.

Merline: see Bird-organ.

"Merryman" plates: an inscription, variously spelt, extended over a set of six plates made in tin-glazed earthenware in London from last quarter of 17th cent. until 1750 (dates recorded range from 1684–1742). The uncertain orthography was taken by W. B. Honey as an indication of manufacture by a Dutch potter working in England, if not of actual Dutch manufacture. Louis Gautier claimed the class for a Dutch potter working in England

named James de Pauw. Prof. F. H. Garner regards them as English. The rhyme reads (a) "What is a mery man, (b) Let him doe all what he kan (c) To entertayne his gess (d) With wyne and mery jests (e) But if his wyfe doth frown (f) All meryment goos downe." Other rhymes extended over a series of plates are recorded, such as the "Servant and Grace" series. The "Servant" series (dated examples 1711) has the following rhyme: (a) "I am a servant unto all, (b) Both rich and poor, grate and small, (c) Who uses me with diligence (d) Will be on me at small expense. (e) But when by servants I am ended, (f) My grate fault is I can't be mended". The "Grace" extended over a series of six plates, dated 1697, reads (a) "When thou sit down to meat, (b) Give thanks before thou eat, (c) Be sure that thou conceive (d) The mercies thou receive, (e) That such favours may be (f) Repeated unto thee".

Metal: the substance of glass, either molten or hard in the form of finished ware.

Metal spinning: a process by which a thin metal sheet is pressed against a wooden core in a spinning lathe to be forced into shape.

Metropolitan slipware: the name given to a class of red earthenware decorated with while trailed slip, most of which has been found in the London area and probably originated there; characterised by commonplace shapes and inexpertly applied inscriptions often of a puritan religious character. Examples dated from 1638 to 1659 are recorded. Articles made included jugs, mugs, bowls, chamber-pots. There are numerous examples in the British Museum. A chamber-pot in Hanley Museum is lettered, "Earth I am et tes most tru disdan me not for so are you."

Meuble à hauteur d'appui: (*Fr.*), a term used extensively at all periods in France to describe any low bookcase or cupboard, usually between three and four feet high.

Meuble d'entre deux: (*Fr.*), a term used in the 18th cent. in France to describe a type of furniture consisting of a cupboard or chest of drawers flanked at each side by a set of shelves. Sometimes these are enclosed by a curved door forming a small cupboard.

Mezzotint: engraving distinguished by dark tones, obtained by roughening the plate all over to produce a black and then smoothing where required for lighter tones. The engraver therefore works from black to white and in tone rather than line. This is the process par excellence for reproducing paintings in monochrome, and so it was used throughout the 18th cent. It is a process that lends itself to hand colouring, and it was often applied over an aquatint (q.v.) ground.

Midband: an American term to describe a moulded band slightly below centre of a silver tankard which strengthened and decorated it. Introduced in Boston in first quarter of 18th cent. Also used on large two-handled covered cups about 1740.

Midshipmen jug: an early variety of toby jug (q.v.), somewhat crude in potting and glazing. Jugs of this pattern are from six and a half to eight inches high and are thought to have been made by Astbury. (See Astbury type ware.) The fiddler jugs (q.v.) also belong to this early group.

Mihrab design: see Turkish rugs.

Milan lace: pillow lace. James I specifically prohibited the import of "all lace of Millan and of Millan fashion". In the later work identified today the pattern was worked first and the ground put round it at all angles.

Milanese mandoline: see under Mandoline.

Miliarense: silver coin equal to one-thousandth of the gold pound; introduced by Constantine the Great in the early 4th cent.

Milk glass: see Opaque glass.

Milk glass or **milk-white glass:** opaque white glass made in imitation of Chinese porcelain, produced by mixing oxide of tin with the body. This material was known to English glass-makers in the late 17th cent. and after a brief eclipse in the early 18th cent., seems to have regained popularity about 1730. From then until c. 1770, jars, beakers, tea-caddies, candlesticks etc. were decorated in fine enamel colours.

Millefiori glass: glass decorated by means of sections of rod bearing floral designs embedded in clear glass. The technique, employed at Venice in the 16th cent. was of Roman inspiration.

Millefiori paperweight: the first millefiori (Italian: thousand flowers) paperweights were made in Venice. The St Louis factory (q.v.) in Paris made them in 1845. In the next year they were made at Baccarat (q.v.), and before long they were produced at Clichy (q.v.).

Mille fleurs: decoration occurring on Chinese porcelain with panels of growing plants reserved on a flower-covered ground: employed from the Ch'ien Lung period (q.v.).

Mille fleurs field: a design used on Medieval and 16th cent. tapestries employing scattered flowers and leaves as a background to scenes of Medieval life.

Millegrain setting: a means of setting a gemstone whereby the stone is held in a mount ornamented with a band of very small beads of metal.

Ming dynasty: dynasty of the Chinese Ming Emperors covering the period 1368 to 1644. The dynasty, which began by overthrowing the Mongols, gave strong patronage to the porcelain industry, and in place of the variety of Sung wares (q.v.) and glazes, developed a more or less standardized porcelain body as a vehicle for brilliantly coloured decoration. Its animated character and lively forms may be seen in Figs. A–D. Ming glazes tend to be thick and "fat". Always popular, painting in underglaze blue was at its finest in the Hsüan Tê and Ch'êng Hua periods (qq.v.), since regarded as classic for perfection of material and harmonious proportion of forms and decoration. During the latter period painting in coloured enamels is found in the delicate *tou ts'ai* class (q.v.). In the 16th cent. the "red and green" family became conspicuous; but the Chia Ching and Wan Li (qq.v.) periods are further noted for many rich combinations of enamels, including those with yellow and turquoise. A rich violet blue distinguishes the best blue-and-white of Chia Ching (Fig. c). The Wan Li *wu ts'ai*, or five-colour decoration, remained prominent. In the decoration of Ming porcelain much use was made of scrolling floral designs, flying dragons and phoenixes taken from silk brocades and such pictorial subjects as landscapes with animals and garden terrace scenes with children. In later periods their execution becomes careless and little of note emerges after Wan Li. Exports of blue-and-white were very considerable, however, and the crisp porcelains brought to Europe from 1600 and boldly-painted "Transitional" wares may be very pleasing. These are not uncommon but the finer Ming wares are almost as rare as the Sung.

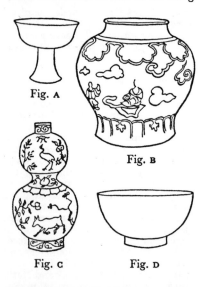

Fig. A

Fig. B

Fig. C   Fig. D

Miniature automata: not content with models a foot or so in height,

craftsmen, principally Swiss, set to work to make miniature automata. They made snuff-boxes and watches with disappearing singing birds; boxes with magicians who held up inscribed plaques with answers to questions that were put to them; and other boxes in which landscape and other scenes surprisingly came to life on pressing a button. Watches were made with miniature jacks that struck miniature bells; others showed moving figures that danced to the music of a minute musical-box within the case. One can only marvel at the ingenuity and skill of the designers and makers – and, at the same time, envy those fortunate possessors of these extreme rarities. (See Automata and Jacks.)

Minneteppich: German or Swiss term to describe 15th cent. tapestries depicting scenes of romantic love.

Mint condition: a term, found in booksellers' catalogues, borrowed from the numismatists, meaning as good as new. A book is sometimes described as a "mint copy", "dust-jacket defective, otherwise mint".

Mint-mark: the mark, in the form of a small symbol, letter or series of letters, placed on a coin to indicate the place where it was struck.

Mintons porcelain: founded by Thomas Minton in 1793, in partnership with William Pownall and Joseph Poulson. Minton had previously worked as an engraver, and for Spode. After Poulson's death in 1808 Thomas Minton continued the business on his own account and in 1817 he took his sons into partnership and traded as Thomas Minton & Sons. After Thomas Minton's death the firm was continued by Herbert Minton and John Boyle until 1841. During this period tiles and buttons were manufactured under patents of Samuel Wright 1830 and Richard Prosser 1840. Michael Daintry Hollins became a partner in 1845 and the style of the firm was Minton & Hollins, or Minton Hollins & Co., and so continued until the tile business was separated from the china and earthenware trade in 1868. Herbert Minton died in 1858 and his nephew Colin

Minton Campbell became head of the firm which was known as Minton & Co. In 1883 it became Mintons Ltd.

Early earthenware made at the Stoke factory is usually white decorated in blue, often in a pseudo-Chinese manner. These productions were of good quality and careful finish, owing much to Thomas Minton's early experience at Spode's. In 1798 porcelain manufacture was started but at first did not prove profitable, and was

Marks:

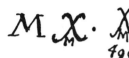

Transfer-printed
1800–36

Printed or impressed after 1851

MINTONS B B New Stone

Impressed
20th-century

Impressed

MINTON

Impressed 1861 onwards

1822–36

Transfer-printed
1860–80

Transfer-printed

Transfer-printed
M – 1822–30
M & Co – 1841–44
M & H – 1845–68

Transfer-printed

Transfer-printed
uranium glaze
1918

not made in any quantity until about 1825 when artists from the Derby factory brought new talent to Minton's. The body of the porcelain is from that time of a lighter and purer colour, and the glaze finer.

Some delightful patterns, evidently the work of one artist, are characterised by flecks, dots, circles, used to texture patterns of original and sometimes fantastic character.

Table wares figure largely among Minton's productions from the first. Early pieces have a mark which is sometimes confused with Sèvres. Dark blue grounds, medallions of flowers, Chinese landscapes and much gilding are all characteristics, but painting of finely engraved shells and similar subjects occur on early pieces.

Parian was made from 1845; majolica glazes were introduced in 1850 and used for table wares, toilet wares, figures and architectural faience. M. L. Solon brought to the factory the *pâte-sur-pâte* technique (q.v.).

MINTONS (DATE MARKS)

From 1824 onwards marks, as above impressed in the paste, were used on china and sometimes on earthenware to denote years of manufacture.

Minuet fan: see Brisé fan.

Miquelet: see Flint-lock gun.

Mirror cutting: see Table cutting.

Mirror-painting: a type of glass picture in which the glass was first coated at the back with an amalgam of tin and mercury to make it into a mirror. The parts to be painted were then scraped away and painted in as required. Such paintings were often made in China, where the technique is thought to have been introduced by Jesuit missionaries. Vauxhall bevelled plate glass was exported to China for this purpose in the 18th cent. (See also Under-painting.)

Mirror-stand: an adjustable mirror mounted on a shaft and tripod base, resembling a pole-screen; popular at the end of the 18th cent.

Misericord: in ecclesiastical woodwork, bracket on underside of hinged seat of stall, to support an occupant when nominally standing during certain offices. From a "monastic" usage of L. *Misericordia* (pity, compassion), in sense of "an indulgence or relaxation of the rule" (OED). Miserere is an incorrect alternative.

Mitre cutting: a method of decorating glass vessels by means of cutting or grinding a pattern with a V-edged grinding wheel of about 60 degrees. Many cut motifs were used on 18th cent. glass, based on panel, hollow (qq.v.) or mitre cutting. About 1800 the double-mitre wheel was introduced and cutting in deep relief in complicated diamond forms, etc. became fashionable.

Mitre joint: employed by joiners (q.v.) to unite the mouldings framing a panel in which the two edges are cut at an angle of 45 degrees.

Mixed-twist stem: a type of stem found on drinking glasses between about 1750 and 1770 including a combination of air-twist and opaque-white twist in a single stem.

"ML" mark: see Weesp porcelain.

"M" mark: see Mintons porcelain.

Mocha ware: a form of "dipped" pottery decorated with coloured bands into which tree, moss or fern-like effects have been introduced by means of a diffusing agent, a drop of which "ramifies" the coloured bands to produce the pattern. "Mocha" occurs under the heading "Dipped" pottery (q.v.) in the working-price list appended to *The Declaration . . . Chamber of Commerce* for the Potteries, June 1836. Undoubtedly many pottery firms whose names were appended to the list were making it.

The process was used from about 1780 until 1914, chiefly for ale, shrimp and nut measures, less frequently for kitchen and table wares.

Mock pendulum: a swinging bob attached to the escape arbor, which shows through a slot in the dial plate of a clock. Only used in clocks with the verge escapement. Sometimes called a false bob.

Modello: an oil sketch for a painting.

Modes: see Fillings.

Modillion: projecting brackets in the pediment or below the cornice found on furniture of architectural character.

Mohur: gold coin of the Mogul emperors in India, introduced by Akbar in 1563 and issued into 19th cent. Early examples were square but remainder round. Types, names of early Caliphs, and, reverse, Emperor's name and titles with date and mint. Jahangir (1605–28) struck some portrait types and designs illustrating the signs of the Zodiac.

Moiré wallpapers: printed or embossed wallpapers imitating watered-silk effects.

Mokumé: (*Japanese* = wood aspect). Japanese lacquer-work technique involving an imitation of wood graining.

Mon: Japanese term for badge or device serving as a sort of heraldic emblem for actors, courtesans, and others.

Monkey orchestra: "Monkies in different attitudes playing on musick" are listed in the 1756 catalogue of the Chelsea porcelain factory. They were copied from a series of Meissen porcelain (q.v.) figures modelled by Johann Joachim Kaendler, considered by some to be caricatures of the Court Orchestra of Saxony.

Monopodium: a solid three-sided pedestal table support mounted on claw feet. This type of pedestal base was used for drum or capstan tables (q.v.) during the early years of the 19th cent.

Monotype: plates painted with oil colour instead of ink yield a single impression which is called a monotype. This process was occasionally used by G. B. Castiglione (1616–70), William Blake (1757–1827) and Edgar Dégas (1834–1917). It has been further developed by a few modern artists.

Monstrance: vessel in which the Host is displayed, varying in size according to its use, i.e. whether it was primarily for use on an altar or intended to be carried in procession. Frequently enriched with enamelling and precious stones, they are among the most magnificent pieces of Church plate.

Monté à cage: a description of the elegant framework or cage, usually gold or silver, in which fine snuff-boxes, nécessaires, étuis (qq.v.) etc. were mounted.

Monteith: punch-bowl with indented rim. Introduced under Charles II. In silver examples, the rim at first part of the body, made detachable about 1690. The name is said to be derived from that of a Scottish adventurer with notched cloak.

Month clock: a clock that goes for a period of one month with one winding. The usual period is 32 days.

Moon dial: see Lunar dial.

"Moonlight" lustre: a marbled lustre effect, used as a decoration on earthenware, produced by mixing gold, pink, grey and other colouring stains, used by the Wedgwood factory (q.v.), early 19th cent., and the Turners of Lane End, Staffordshire.

"Moons": small areas of greater translucency observable by transmitted light in some early porcelains such as Chelsea, the cause of which is not known for certain.

Moore, James: (? 1670–1726), cabinet-maker in partnership with John Gumley from 1714. Moore is known to have made much furniture decorated with gilt gesso, on some of which his name is incised. He was concerned in the furnishing of Blenheim, and it is assumed that some gilt pier-glasses and tables there were made and supplied by him. (See also Gesso.)

Moorfields carpets: Thomas Moore, of Moorfields, successfully competed for a Royal Society of Arts award in 1757. An account of his workshop, where hand-knotted carpets of the highest quality were produced, was given by Lady Mary Coke in 1768. A carpet was then being woven for Lord Coventry, to cost 140 gns. Moore was extensively used by the architect Robert Adam (q.v.), and a number of his carpets have survived in beautiful condition, as well as Adam's designs for them at the Soane Museum. A carpet at Syon House is inscribed "by Thos. Moore 1769". There are two at Osterley, made about 1775 and 1778; and Chippendale (q.v.) recommended him to Sir Edward Knatchbull in 1778, who paid him £57 for a carpet for Mersham le Hatch. Moore's carpets in neo-classical designs were sumptuous additions to the houses they furnished.

Moquette: woven on the principle of velvet, but in coarser wool and linen materials, moquette is allied with plushes and Utrecht velvet as an upholstery or carpeting material. Tournai seems to have been its chief centre in the Middle Ages. It was much used in the 16th to 18th cent. Abbeville was the chief centre of production in France from 1667. Antwerp, Amsterdam, Utrecht and Leyden and Thuringia, in Germany, were other centres of production. Known as "Brussels carpet" in England, it was made at

Norwich and Bradford besides Kidder-minster and Wilton. The use of the Jacquard loom greatly increased and cheapened production in the early 19th cent.

Mor.: abbreviation used in book-sellers' catalogues meaning morocco (q.v.).

Moresque ornament: a linear orna-ment consisting of formal scrollwork and foliage, of Near Eastern deri-vation, found as a border decoration engraved on 16th cent. plate.

Morion: an open helmet much used by foot-soldiers in the second half of the 16th cent. Contemporary texts mention two forms: (a) the Spanish-morion, called a cabasset by many modern writers, with a pear-shaped, pointed skull and a narrow, flat brim; (b) the comb-morion, with high comb and a curved brim peaked before and behind. The modern term peaked-morion refers to an intermediate type with a curved brim, and a pointed apex terminating in a small stalk.

Morocco: originally leather made from the skin of North African or Moroccan goats, morocco today has no geographical significance, for most of it used for book-binding comes from other parts of the world; and the only common denominator among the numerous varieties of leather which go under the name is that they are all goatskin.

Of the various types of morocco commonly specified in catalogue de-scriptions, levant, hard-grain and niger refer to differences of grain, pattern or texture in the actual skin when tanned and dyed; straight-grain and crushed morocco refer to its treatment before it is put on the book; and morocco extra, super-extra or elegant (an old-fashioned term) refer to the degree of elaboration and the amount of gilt which have been lavished on it by the "finisher" in the bindery.

Morris carpets: the first carpets woven by William Morris were made about 1878 at Hammersmith (mark: hammer, river and letter M) and from 1881 at Merton Abbey. The later two-and three-ply carpets were woven for Morris & Co. at Heckmondwike, Yorks.

Morse: a clasp for fastening a cope, occasionally made of gold or silver and decorated with jewels.

Mortars: in Antiquity mortars were usually made of stone or heavy pottery; during the Middle Ages they were normally cast in bronze. Their use was widespread, both in the apoth-ecaries' laboratories for the grinding and pounding of chemicals and at home for the pounding of condiments and spices. In the painter's studio they might also have been found for the pulverization of pigments. From the 14th cent. onwards mortars survive in considerable numbers, especially from Flanders and England and later from Germany and Italy. With the ex-ception of Italy, they seem to be mainly the work of the bell foundries, and because the alloy used is so often close to that employed by these foundries, they are normally said to be made of "bell metal". They often bear in-scriptions in raised lettering, usually pious in intention or giving the owner's or maker's name as well as the date of production. Many 19th cent. after-casts were made, usually of very crude quality and slurred definition. Mortars of the 14th and 15th cent. are rare, the bulk being of the 16th and 17th cent. During the 18th cent. their manu-facture ceases.

Mortice and tenon joint: the mortice is a cavity, usually rectangular, and the tenon is shaped to fill the cavity exactly. The tenon was held fast by a peg. This was the principle joint used by the joiner in furniture making and was introduced in the 16th cent.

Mortice lock: a lock concealed from view by the use of a hole cut into the door edge. In most early mortice locks only the brass knob remained visible, the keyhole masked by a swinging escutcheon. Decoration might be added in the form of an ornamental end-piece matching the adjoining striking plate: this might be engraved, pierced, or cast and chased, often displaying the owner's coat of arms or cypher.

A new style of lock furniture associated with mortice locks was introduced during the mid-1760s. Robert Adam (q.v.), writing to Sir Rowland Wynn in 1767, observed that "Bent the locksmith is making lock furniture after a new pattern". This set consisted of an expansive back-plate of chased and gilt cast brass, in scrollwork designs symmetrically arranged with festoons of husks centering on the door knob and flanked with a keyhole escutcheon and a matching dummy escutcheon. The centre rosette and the escutcheon harmonized with the knob. In some instances the dummy was replaced by a small knob operating a night latch. Sets of such mortice locks with chased and gilt furniture in 1776 cost ten to twelve guineas.

Mortlake tapestry: Charles I, as Prince of Wales and later King, took an active interest in the Mortlake factory, which worked for the Court and rivalled the Paris factory set up by Henry IV, on whose charter it was modelled. Already active in 1620, Mortlake enjoyed a very high reputation in Europe until checked by the Civil Wars in the 1640s, which also caused the sale abroad of most of its finest works. Prince Charles' purchase of the seven extant cartoons of the *Acts of the Apostles* by Raphael for £ 300 in 1623 at Genoa undoubtedly did

much to enhance Mortlake's name. Other notable subjects woven were *The Months* and *Vulcan and Venus* (based on 16th cent. originals), *Playing Boys* and *Hero and Leander*, designed by Francis Cleyn, who was brought from Rostock as chief designer. Sir Francis Crane was in charge until 1636, and was succeeded by Sir Sackville Crowe at the Restoration. Rather later Verrio succeeded Cleyn. Among the fifty weavers from the Netherlands, Philippe de Maecht was the most notable. A few good sets were woven under Charles II from the old cartoons, but the more elaborate and beautiful borders were abandoned and a decline rapidly set in. Lord Ralph Montague became Master of the Great Wardrobe and acquired Mortlake in the 1670s. Soon the former, established at Hatton Garden in 1679, incorporated the best weavers from Mortlake. Francis Poyntz, last technical director of Mortlake, who wove the *Battle of Sole Bay*, (Hampton Court) worked there as manager (1667–85) as did Stephan Demay and Thomas Poyntz. The Mortlake mark, red cross on white shield, continued to be used, as it resembled the Arms of the City of London. Some weavers left Mortlake to set up independently, as William Benood in Lambeth (c. 1670), who signed a *Horses* set at the Victoria and Albert Museum. In 1685 the Great Wardrobe was moved to Soho (q.v.) and Mortlake was finally wound up about the year 1700.

"Mortuary" chair: a mid-17th cent. chair with scrolled back, the rails bearing in the centre a carved representation of a bearded head, traditionally thought to refer to Charles I.

Mosaic: this term is usually applied to the decoration of a wall or panel with a design made up of small fragments of stones or coloured glass fixed to the surface with cement or special adhesive. The best-known form of mosaic, usually called Roman or Byzantine mosaic, is formed of small cubes or *tesserae* of coloured stone and glass. The Romans also developed a second technique of mosaic, using, instead of cubes, various-sized segments cut into shapes so as to form a design or picture when joined together. This technique may be regarded as the forerunner of Florentine mosaic.

Mosaic binding: book-binding with polychrome decoration, produced by using: (a) paint; (b) onlays of very thinly pared leather applied on top of the leather of the covers; (c) genuine inlays of different-coloured leather inserted into the leather of the covers. Onlay is very much more common than inlay.

Moscow porcelain: see Gardner's porcelain.

Mould-blown glass: glass made by blowing a gather of metal into a mould, a technique known to the Romans who used clay moulds. Techniques introduced in the 19th cent. opened new possibilities. Of these, one-piece moulds were used during the earlier part of the cent. for shaping inexpensive hollow ware. A quick-setting flint glass was evolved as the molten glass solidified rapidly on the surface of the mould. Glass made by this process has a slightly pebbly appearance caused by contact with the mould. Two-piece open-and-shut moulds were invented in 1802 by Charles Chubsee of Stourbridge. Glass blown into such a mould could be shaped and decorated with diamonds and other motifs in deep relief. Patterns followed those worked on free-blown glass (q.v.) by the wheel-cutters. From 1825 the long accepted geometrical designs met active competition in the form of baroque scrolls, fan patterns and arch patterns. The three-pieced mould, with one fixed and two hinged sections, each cut with an intaglio pattern, dates from about 1830. When the glass was inflated within the mould, the blowing force caused the joints to open slightly, thus producing tiny ridges on the surface of the glass or a slight break in the pattern. Mould marks are no more than slightly convex swellings on the surface of the glass in no way resembling the hair lines or threads on pressed glass (q.v.), which are so sharply defined that they appear to have been applied. The number of marks indicates the number of pieces

forming the mould. From 1835 blown-moulded glass was finished by fire polishing.

Moulded glass: glass blown in a mould for pattern and given partial or final body shape by the mould; generally called blown moulded.

Moulded pedestal stem: a type of shouldered stem found on drinking glasses from about 1705 to 1750, also known erroneously as a "Silesian" stem. The earlier examples are four-sided and ribbed. Later the stem became reeded or polygonal and was often twisted spirally. Candlesticks, sweetmeats and dessert-salvers also were made with shouldered stems during the second half of the 18th cent.

Moulding: shaped member, such as used to enclose panels; or the shaped edge of a lid, cornice, etc.

Mount Mellick embroidery: a type of whitework, first introduced about 1830 at Mountmellick in Queen's County, Ireland, and revived as a local industry in the 1880s by a Mrs Millner. It was worked on a stout white satin jean in white knitting cotton which gave a raised effect to the work. The designs were naturalistic, passion-flowers, blackberry sprays, oak-leaves and acorns being the most favoured patterns. Many designs for this type of work were issued by Weldon's and other publishers in the late 1880s and 1890s.

Mourning fans: fans painted in black and grey overlaid with white. The ivory sticks were stained brown to unify the general tone and might be burnished with a simple design of silver blending with the grey of the mount. Solomon receiving the Queen of Sheba was a frequent subject late in the 15th cent.

Mourning jewellery: mourning jewellery became particularly fashionable in the second half of the 18th cent. Oval frames were favoured, of varying size according to the ultimate destination of the jewel, i.e. ring, pendant, locket or bracelet slide. These frames were set with enamels or miniature paintings of funerary urns on plinths, by which stood the bereaved under the shadow of weeping willow trees. The back of the frame was filled with an appropriate design, often a monogram of the deceased's initials executed in a lock of hair. Such jewellery was usually inexpensive; a thin gold frame was set with, at the most, seed-pearl or diamond sparks. Earlier mourning jewellery of the 16th and 17th cent. of which comparatively few examples remain, was of a more gloomy kind, including coffin-shaped pendants in gold or enamelled gold and enamelled jewels bearing such devices as skulls and cross-bones.

Moustache-cup: a cup with a screen or arrangement to protect the moustache from moisture when drinking, popular in Victorian times, introduced by Harvey Adams and Company, china and earthenware manufacturers, of Longton, Staffordshire.

Moustiers faience: Moustiers, in Provence, was a centre of the faience trade in the 18th cent. The best period, before 1750, saw the use of baroque ornamental designs in blue monochrome or in soft high-temperature colours.

Mouton: gold coin of France of 14th and 15th cent. with types of Lamb of God with cross and standard, and floreate cross reverse. Widely copied with variations of design in the Low Countries.

Movable books: these are books for children in which, by moving small flaps or ribbons which project below the level of the page, a transformation

of some kind is effected. At its simplest a dog will wave its tail, a parrot its beak; at its most elaborate, by a series of slats, a whole picture will transform itself, e.g. Indolence will become Industry. These started in the forties and continued through Queen Victoria's reign. By their nature these books were fragile, and it is hard to find any in perfect condition. See Percy Muir, *English Children's Books* (Batsford, 1954).

Movement: the "works" of a clock or watch.

"Mr and Mrs Caudle": relief decoration on brown stoneware spirit flasks, made about 1846 by Doulton of Lambeth (q.v.), and based upon Douglas Jerrold's *Punch* papers ("Mrs Caudle's Curtain Lectures"). One side shows "Mr and Mrs Caudle in Bed", the other "Miss Prettyman".

Ms. or mss.: manuscript or manuscripts. The expression is used arbitrarily about most documents other than letters, but may also refer to these. Thus the mss. of an author would include, say, the ms. of one of his novels, besides numerous a.d.s., a.l.s., t.l.s., etc. The ms. abbreviation is peculiarly confusing to autograph collectors having to do with German catalogues, since in German "MS" (for *Maschinenschrift*) is used to indicate that the ms. is not ms., but rather is type-written. The German refers to the ms. proper as an "HS" (for *Handschrift*) when it is hand-written.

Mudge, Thomas: London clockmaker who first invented the lever escapement about 1758. He was active between 1740 and 1794. (See also Lever escapement.)

Muffineer: alternative name for a caster (q.v.), usually given to those examples with low, slightly domed covers. The derivation presumably indicated their use for sprinkling salt on muffins.

Muffle kiln: kiln used for low-temperature porcelain or enamel firing (*petit feu*) of about 700–900° C. The porcelain piece is enclosed in an inner chamber "muffle", out of contact with flames or smoke, hence the name. It is used to fuse enamel painting into the glaze of faience and porcelain, and for the firing of soft-paste porcelain (q.v.) in general.

Mulberry spoon: see Straining spoon.

Mule chest: a mid-17th cent. chest, usually of oak or walnut, with a drawer, or two drawers side by side at the bottom. This type of chest was the forerunner of the chest of drawers.

Mulls: Scottish snuff mulls (the Highland pronunciation of "mill") vary a great deal within the limits imposed by their form. They are natural horns, sometimes twisted at the tapering end. The open aperture is surmounted by a decorative hinged lid often set with semi-precious stones. The local cairngorm, a pale topaz, is the most usually found. Dr Mott observes in his edition of *Dekker's Gull's Hornbook* that "The Scotch mull, or sneeshing mull, was often accompanied by a spoon and hare's foot attached by chain, the one for applying the snuff to the nose, the other for wiping the upper lip".

Multiple knops: knops or protuberances of a single shape repeated on the stem of a drinking glass or other glass vessel.

Muntin: upright (other than an outermost upright) connecting the upper and lower stretchers of a wooden framework. An instance is the bearer between the doors of the lower stage of a press-cupboard (q.v.); the number of muntins depend on the nature of the structure. (See also Stile.)

Mural clock: a clock made to hang on the wall.

Mushroom knop: a knop or protuberance on the stem of a drinking glass or other glass vessel of mushroom form, usually associated with incurved and funnel bowls.

Mushroom paperweight: a paperweight in which the canes are bunched together and raised in a sheaf from the bottom. Usually surrounded by a ring of lacework at the foot.

Musical clocks: the first mechanical music was performed upon cymbals or bells, and was a part of the display of some of the elaborate clocks made on the Continent of Europe from the 14th cent. and onwards. By the time of Queen Elizabeth I the mechanical principle had been extended to the operation of organs. There exists a description of a most complicated clock that was sent as a gift from the English sovereign to the Sultan of Turkey in 1593. This clock incorporated both carillon and organ, either of which could be played by hand or be set to operate when the clock struck the hour.

In the 18th cent. and later, large bracket-clocks and grandfather clocks were made with music on bells to be played each hour. They usually have a choice of tunes, which could be changed by moving a pointer on a dial on the face. A musical movement was constructed also that operated a small bellows and worked a miniature organ. With the introduction of the comb this, too, was adapted to become part of a clock.

Among the more prominent English makers of musical clocks were: Charles Clay, who exhibited a bell and organ clock to Queen Caroline in 1736; Markwick Markham; Christopher Pinchbeck, inventor of the gilt metal which bears his name and a famed clock-maker; and James Cox, who exhibited to the public musical clocks and watches, along with other mechanical *objets d'art*, in the last half of the 18th cent. The list of Continental makers should not omit Father Primitivus Niemecz, who made three famous clocks for the Hungarian Prince Esterhazy. These had music especially composed or arranged for them by Joseph Haydn.

Musical novelties: musical movements have been fitted, at one time or another, to almost everything. Tankards, jugs, fruit-dishes, and other objects play on being lifted. Fob-seals, watch-keys, rings and scent-bottles surprise the hearer by the emission of sound from such small articles and at the same time challenge the craftsman to make ever smaller objects. Even the handle of a decorative and useful fan, or of an umbrella or a walking-stick, might conceal a musical-box. Gold cases for sealing-wax are also known. One of these rarities contained a movement only an inch and three-quarters in length and little more than half an inch in width and height. It played a tune on five tiny bells. Albums of photographs render *Auld Lang Syne* on being opened; cigar- and cigarette-boxes play selections from comic operas and nearly forgotten musical comedies; and apparently normal chairs startle the weary who sit on them.

Perhaps the most novel of novelties was a bustle presented to Queen Victoria by an ardent patriot on the occasion of her Jubilee. This device emitted the strains of *God Save the Queen* whenever the wearer seated herself. It is not known that it was ever worn by the recipient, but had it been used the effect it caused must surely have been worthy of record.

Musical snuff-boxes: these were in the past, and are still, immensely popular when fitted as musical-boxes, and were made in great numbers. At first they were costly and elaborately cased in gold, silver-gilt or silver. Movements were of small size and light in weight. After the first decade of the 19th cent. horn, tortoiseshell and composition, as well as painted tin, were used for making the boxes, which were decorated with embossed designs, prints and other ornament. Gradually the movement became heavier and larger in size, and the space that remained in the box for containing snuff became smaller in relation to the size of the whole box. It would seem that the majority of the boxes made in the early part of the 19th cent., and later, were bought more as novelties than for any practical purpose.

Many of the snuff-boxes were made in Paris, and some of the horn and composition specimens have views of Paris landmarks in relief on their lids. London and provincial-made boxes are found with Swiss-made movements fitted in them.

Musical watches: the addition of the playing of music to the normal performance of a pocket time-keeper grew from the repeater mechanism, which was a necessity for telling the time in the dark before the use of luminous composition or the invention of electric light. The hour was repeated on one or more tiny bells upon pressing a button, and very little adaptation of the basic mechanism was needed. With more bells, and more pins to hit the hammers, more notes could be played to form a simple melody.

With the advent of the steel comb a much greater compass of notes could be achieved with no increase in the size of the apparatus.

Music-cover: the music-cover for sheet music, with a picture, in some way representing the song inside, came into its own with the invention of chromolithography (q.v.). During the entire Victorian period many thousands appeared, some very poorly, others well executed. Almost all were interesting or amusing. They appear to have been drawn, as are modern vulgar postcards, by a very small body of men who were otherwise practically unknown. Baxter allowed twenty-three of his prints to be reproduced after the ordinary publication as music-covers, but with this exception none of the names of the artists now mean anything to us. Music-covers, however, are a legitimate object for the collector. They express perfectly the many sides of the Victorian spirit; and in a minor key, but on a much larger scale, do for the period what the famous Currier and Ives lithographs did for the United States.

The authority on music-covers is Mr A. Hyatt King. An article written by him for the *Penrose Annual*, 1952, has been reproduced in pamphlet form with eight coloured reproductions in photolithography.

Musician (automata): many figures of musicians were made that performed with varying success on their chosen instrument, and several complete orchestras. (See also Automata and Jacks.)

Music-stand: see Canterbury.

Musket: a military match- or wheel-lock firearm introduced in the third quarter of the 16th cent. It was heavier than the arquebus (q.v.), and consequently was usually fired from a forked rest. After the introduction of the flint-lock (q.v.) the term was used loosely to describe any portable firearm larger than a pistol.

Musketoon: a short, heavy flint-lock (q.v.) gun with a large bore, generally used for discharging shot.

Mutchkin: a Scottish wine measure containing three quarters of an Imperial pint.

Naga-ye: see Kakemono-ye.

Nail-head decoration: a carved decoration in the form of a series of small squares, each containing a raised point resembling a nail head, used on furniture from the Middle Ages to the 17th cent.

Nailsea glass: the brownish-green glass speckled with white, with which the name of Nailsea, near Bristol, is associated, was used on occasions for the making of wine-bottles, and sealed examples exist. Some specimens are inscribed with initials, the date, and the name of a town. Glasses of this type were not exclusive to the West-country manufacture, and were probably also made in Scotland.

Name pallets: see under Signed bindings.

"Nankin" china: Chinese blue-and-white porcelain of the late 18th and 19th cent. which was shipped from Nanking.

"Nankin yellow": lustrous pale golden brown glaze used as a decoration on Chinese porcelain in association with K'ang Hsi (q.v.) underglaze blue painting, especially in export wares for the Near East.

Nantgarw porcelain: William Billingsley, who had been a well-known flower painter at Derby, founded the factory in November 1813, in partnership with his son-in-law, Samuel Walker. After exhausting his capital, William Weston Young advanced sums amounting to nearly £600 and eventually became partner in the venture. This proved inadequate and the three partners appealed for financial assistance to the Government with the result that their endeavours were brought to the notice of L. W. Dillwyn who arranged for the transference of the business to the Cambrian factory at Swansea.

Billingsley stayed at Swansea until 1816 when he returned to Nantgarw, there to be rejoined by Walker in 1817. With new capital supplied by W. W. Young and some country gentlemen, the Nantgarw concern was operated until the end of 1819, but, their capital exhausted, Billingsley and Walker were compelled to vacate Nantgarw in the spring of 1820. In November the moulds and plant, with some decorated and a lot of undecorated china, were offered for sale and taken over by Young, who became sole proprietor. No further ware was made, although much of the undecorated porcelain was painted by Pardoe (q.v.). Further sales took place in 1821 and 1822 when it was said that Rose of Coalport bought up the plant and moulds. Marks:

NANT GARW
G.W.

Billingsley himself decorated some of the Nantgarw products: he was assisted by his daughter and two other women. Billingsley also employed flower painters.

A much larger proportion of Nantgarw porcelain was sent undecorated to London to various independent enamellers. This was more ambitiously decorated and is usually fairly easily distinguishable from the simpler local designs used at Nantgarw.

During its short life the Nantgarw factory produced some fine porcelain of quite exceptional translucency. Billingsley himself compared it to that of Sèvres, and the decoration used was often in the French manner. Extremely white and at times almost glasslike, the porcelain unfortunately did not always stand firing and much was lost in the kiln. These losses led to the financial difficulties which eventually forced Billingsley to leave Nantgarw. He was never successful in finding a soft-paste of comparable quality which could be fired reliably.

Few shapes were made at Nantgarw and these are generally simple in character. Table wares comprising tea and dessert services were the chief productions of the factory. A distinguishing feature of the plates was a fine embossed scroll and flower pattern, although, of course, plain shaped plates were also used.

Less frequent are such decorative pieces as spill holders, taper stands, specimen and cabinet cups and saucers, pen trays and pot-pourri vases.

Nashiji: (*Japanese* = pear ground), a Japanese lacquer-work technique in which gold dust is sprinkled on the lacquer and then polished like aventurine (q.v.). Various forms, e.g. *Muranashiji* indicates that the gold is spread in irregular patches.

N.d.: an abbreviation used in booksellers' catalogues indicating that there is no date on the title page of a book.

Neale, James, Earthenware Manufactory: James Neale took over the factory in Hanley in 1778. Robert Wilson was made a partner in 1786 and for a time the firm was known as Neale & Wilson. In 1817, when John Wilson, a descendant of Robert Wilson, became bankrupt, the factory passed to other hands.
Marks:

Impressed

NEALE & WILSON

Impressed

The firm made good quality creamcoloured wares, blue-painted and lustred table ware, jasper, black Egyptian, marbled vases etc. many pieces in close imitation of Wedgwood. Designs from Wedgwood were not infrequently copied, and classical shapes and decoration figured largely in work from the pottery.

Figures are often of considerable merit. Usually small in size, they are modelled, and coloured in a neat restrained manner (a turquoise blue is notable for its frequent use) in fine, clear enamels. The figures were generally made for easy delivery from moulds, and were sometimes gilded. (See also Wedgwood, Josiah.)

Neapolitan mandoline: see under Mandoline.

Nécessaire: a container for miscellaneous small tools and instruments designed for various purposes. Included among 18th cent. toilet and household equipment, usually referred to in sales' catalogues as "implements", we find such engaging items as toothpicks, tweezers, ear-picks and tongue-scrapers. Queen Elizabeth was reputedly never without her ruby- and diamondstudded ear-pick on state occasions.

The more conventional implements to be found in nécessaires and étuis (q.v.) include snuffing-spoons, pencils, funnels for powders, scent-bottles, scissors and other sewing and manicure instruments, and very often ivory tablets for notes and prescriptions.

The nécessaires themselves are made in the same variety of materials as snuff-boxes.

Needlepoint lace: the ultimate development from cut work (q.v.) with threads tacked on to a parchment pattern as the basis for stitches worked with a needle and a single thread. An outline was drawn on parchment stitched to two thicknesses of linen and this outline covered with threads exactly tack-stitched in position about every quarter of an inch. This outline was buttonholed over closely to form the cordonnet (q.v.) and on this the lace was created, the solid areas of pattern – *toilé* (q.v.) – in close rows of buttonhole stitch and these linked and supported by connecting buttonholed brides (q.v.) or a regular mesh ground of buttonholed or looped stitches. It must be emphasized that a single thread on a needle was used throughout so that there could be no plaiting or weaving effects such as characterized pillow lace (q.v.). The lace was released from the parchment by cutting between the layers of linen.

Needlework cabinets: "A coffer maid in broderie upon reid satine" was listed among Elizabeth I's movables in 1561. This was a forerunner of innumerable examples characteristic of English needlework around the mid-17th cent. Every well-to-do young lady then embroidered a set of satin pieces for mounting on a little wooden cabinet fitted either with doors or with a fall-front to allow access to jewellery drawers and toilet compartments. In some examples the interior above the drawers consisted of a little well surrounded by lidded boxes for toilet accessories, and ornamented with pieces of the still-novel looking-glass and perhaps carpeted with a hand-coloured print. But the major work went into the exterior mountings, usually embroidered on the narrow rich satin, then newly available, that allowed the embroidery to break away from the customary ground-covering tent stitch into speedier ornament that left some of the ground visible.

Most often the main embroidery was scenic, such as one of a few favourite scriptural scenes – the story of Rebecca, or Jephthah and his daughter. Always the tendency was to crowd the scene with fascinating, disproportionate detail in the Elizabethan manner. Often some of the main figures were padded and stitched separately, their faces and hands of wood, silk covered, their clothes exquisitely wrought with minute lace stitches and decked out in all the trinket ornaments that age has rendered somewhat tawdry. Beads and coral, feathers and tinsel, were freely used in what was then termed raised work but has become known as stump work.

Needlework carpets: in the 16th and early 17th cent. Oriental carpets were much copied in Europe in cross- and tent-stitch on canvas. This was quite suitable for use on tables and cupboards, for which they were intended. There is a good collection in the National Museum, Zürich and some superb English examples in the Victoria and Albert Museum. In the 18th cent. they were again in favour, but the designs were now purely European, with lavish floral patterns for the floor of boudoir or drawing-room. Many of these carpets have survived in England, but they are rarely found in good condition, as they wear easily. Their beauty depends as much on the brilliant dyes used as on the design. The fashion continued into the 19th cent., but these pieces can be recognised by design and colour. Italian carpets embroidered entirely in silk are occasionally seen.

Nef: a vessel shaped like a ship and used in the later Middle Ages for the lord's napkin, knife and spoon. In 1392 a nef on wheels was recorded in the Papal collection. In the 16th cent. ornaments, jugs and cups were made in the same form, notably in Germany and Switzerland. Many were very elaborate and accurate models, richly enamelled and peopled with little figures of sailors.

Neuber, Johann Christian: (1736–1808), the maker of extremely beautiful and original snuff-boxes in hardstones. Usually round or oval, these boxes would consist entirely of small-shaped panels of different stones selected for their colour and translucence or opacity, held by a finely wrought gold webbing. The inlay work is of a uniformly high order, the whole surface being absolutely smooth, and the gentle harmonies of tone and colour combine happily with the different patterns, which almost invariably radiate boldly from the centre. Many boxes were composed of stones specially chosen for their local interest; numbers would be engraved on the slender gold skeleton mount, each referring to a particular little stone panel. Inside these boxes, which were known as *Stein Kabinetts Tabatieren*, a book serving as a key should be found listing in full the names of the various specimens numbered on the box.

Sometimes these numbered lists would be hidden within a secret compartment or drawer, which springs open when a particular part of the box is pressed. Miniatures or carved or engraved gem stones are usually set in the centre of the lids. He by no means restricted his expression to boxes alone, and the laborious technique, which was his life work, was used very successfully in the designing of *carnets*, *étuis*, *châtelaines* and centre-pieces, as well as a table and even an elaborate fireplace.

Nevers faience: the chief Nevers pottery was founded early in the 17th cent. by Italian potters. The decoration employed was akin to the pictorial style used rather earlier at Urbino (see Urbino maiolica). Chinese themes became popular later in the century, the wares often being painted in blue and manganese purple. At the same time a technique was adopted of painting in opaque white and colours on a deep blue enamel ground known as *bleu persan*. By the 18th cent., only cheap, popular wares were produced.

Nevers glass: see Verre de Nevers.

Neville, George: introduced the art of painting on papier mâché (q.v.) "on the black" (on a black ground) in 1831 whilst employed by Jennens and Bettridge (q.v.). His signature flower was a blue convolvulus, one petal turned over in contrasting colour. In 1846, he set up with a partner and died a wealthy man in 1887.

"New Canton": see Bow porcelain.

Newcastle-under-Lyme earthenware: famous for its clay pipes in the 17th cent., notably those made by Charles Riggs (d. 1676). From about 1730 until 1754 Samuel Bell (d. 1754) and Joseph Wilson made brown glazed Astbury-type (q.v.) teapots at a potworks in Lower Street. The names of thirty potters are given in the Newcastle Poll Lists between 1774 and 1792. In 1873 the names of forty potters are listed. In the closing years of the 18th cent. J. Bulkeley and William Bent manufactured in Newcastle, but dissolved partnership in November 1797. Robert Bath, variously described as earthenware manufacturer, saggar maker and licensed retailer of beer and tobacco, had a potworks at Halmerend near Newcastle but became bankrupt in 1840.

New England armchair: an American version of the hoop-back Windsor chair in which the hoop includes the arms so that one continuous binding encloses all the spindles of the back.

New Hall porcelain: in 1780 Richard Champion approached Josiah Wedgwood, seeking his advice and assistance in disposing of his patent for the manufacture of hard-paste porcelain. The outcome was the formation of a company comprising master potters of repute which operated first of all in Tunstall at the factory of Anthony Keeling, purchasing Champion's patent and commencing the manufacture of hardpaste porcelain in 1781.

A dispute arose among the partners shortly after the enterprise was launched, and Keeling and Turner withdrew. Champion also, having obtained the position of Deputy Paymaster of the Forces, went to London in 1782. The business was transferred to Shelton.

Samuel Hollins, Peter Warburton, John Daniel and William Clowes, who were their partners, purchased the New Hall Estate on behalf of the Company.

Samuel Hollins died in 1820 and John Daniel in 1821. Daniel's place as manager was taken by John Tittensor who managed the business until it finally closed down in 1835. In 1831 the estate and factory were offered for sale. In 1832 they were announced to be let, but the business was not finally wound up until the sale of manufactured stock in 1835.

As well as earthenware, two grades of porcelain were made at this factory: hard-paste porcelain until about 1810, and bone china subsequently. The firm also traded in potters' materials, being able to supply Cornish clay and Cornish stone for local use.

The "Sprigged muslin" type of pattern is chiefly associated with New Hall, but elaborate painted and gilded wares were produced, with chinoiseries and picturesque printed landscapes washed over in crude bright colours. Fancy jugs with relief hunting scenes were made as well as chimney ornaments, although the latter have never been identified. The Neo-Classic mode is evident in some of the handles, but not stressed. A distinctive silver-shape teapot is peculiar to this factory.

Little has been recorded about the personnel of this factory.

Marks:

Pattern numbers prefaced by a letter "N" or "No" in cursive style occur on hard-paste porcelain: a double circle enclosing the words "New Hall" on bone china. Earthenware is usually unmarked.

Initials and pattern number printed before 1812; circular mark transfer-printed 1812–35.

Nickel silver: silver plated on white alloy. (Also known as German silver.)

Niderviller porcelain: hard-paste porcelain was first produced at Niderviller in 1765 at a factory established in 1754 for the manufacture of faience. In 1770 the factory passed to the Comte de Custine and in the early 19th cent. changed hands again. It has continued working to the present day. Niderviller figures are of a quality to rival Sèvres (q.v.) and include such genre subjects as the *Cries of Paris.* Porcelain flowers were made. The monogram of the Comte de Custine, formed by interlaced "Cs" was used as a mark between 1770 and 1793.

Niello: a black alloy containing lead inlaid decoratively on silver. Much practised in the 19th cent. in Tula, Russia. (See also Tula work.)

Niger morocco: see under Morocco.

Night clock: a clock that shows the time by night, usually by means of a light shining through a pierced dial.

Night-table: a pot cupboard which replaced the close-chair (q.v.) after 1750; sometimes also fitted as a washing-stand (q.v.). Among the features commonly found on these pieces may be noted a drawer under the cupboard, a tambour front and a tray top. Some night-tables were given a triangular shape to fit into a corner.

"Night-Watchman" jug: a variety of toby jug (q.v.) representing a seated figure holding a hat and a lantern.

Nip: see Dram glass.

Nishiki-ye: Japanese brocade pictures, colour-prints.

"N" mark: see New Hall porcelain.

Noble: large gold coin first issued by Edward III in 1344 of value 6s 8d with obverse, king standing in ship and reverse an ornate cross. A Scottish noble appeared under David II.

Nock, Henry: London gunmaker of the late 18th cent., best known as the maker of a seven-barrelled carbine, intended for use in the tops of ships. He received the Royal Warrant of George III and was a large scale manufacturer of service arms.

Noggin: a small drinking vessel. Noggin-bottle, a small bottle holding a quantity of liquor, usually a ¼ pint. "The Ingenious John Dwight . . . hath discovered the Mystery of the Stone or Cologne Wares (such as D'Alva Bottles, Jugs, Noggins)".

Nomisma: the gold coin of the later Byzantine Empire. Usually scyphate in form with types of the Emperor, Christ, the Virgin and saints.

Nonesuch chest: chest, dating from the second half of the 16th cent., decorated with an inlaid design representing an ideal building resembling the Palace of Nonesuch, near Cheam, built for Henry VIII. Such architectural motifs were, however, much favoured by Renaissance taste and many such chests were made in Germany.

Northern celadon: Chinese Sung wares probably from Honan Province, with grey porcellanous body burnt brown where exposed, and usually glazed base. The glaze is often glassy and olive-green to brown in tone. They include beautifully shaped bowls, pear-shaped vases, and small shallow dishes superbly carved with plant forms or free designs incised with a comb.

Norwich carpets: Norwich carpets are mentioned in 17th-cent. inventories. Possibly Turkey-work (q.v.) was made there as well as cloth carpeting and moquette (q.v.).

Nottingham alabaster: figures, plaques and altar pieces carved in alabaster in certain districts of England, notably Nottingham, Lincoln and York. The craft flourished in the 14th and 15th cent. and was one of the first to achieve commercial success.

Nottingham earthenware: pottery was made in Nottingham from the 13th cent. and its production continued along characteristic lines until about 1800. The manufactories making Nottingham wares are unidentified, but occasionally the name of the potter appears on the article. James Morley, one of the defendants in the action for protection of his patents brought by Dwight of Fulham (q.v.) late in the 17th cent., certainly worked here as did other members of the Morley family. The name of William Lockett is found on pieces made about 1755, and William Woodward is listed as a maker of slipware in the 18th cent. As Nottingham began to decline as a centre for pottery, neighbouring towns (Denby, Chesterfield and Swinton amongst others) began to produce wares similar in style. The last authenticated piece from Nottingham is dated 1799.

Earliest pieces made in Nottingham were of lead-glazed earthenware. Many-handled tygs (q.v.) date from the 16th cent. It is believed that stoneware began to be made in the second half of the 17th cent. About 1690 the most productive period in Nottingham began. The ferruginous clay which overlaid a very hard body gave a rich brown colour and a faint metallic lustre to the surface of the wares. The grain of this surface is much finer than that of other stonewares of the period, and the pieces are light and usually very thin. Posset-pots, some teapots (now rarely seen), mugs and small jugs were made in Nottingham. The decoration often consists only of lines incised round the piece; formal flowers, sometimes reserved in a lighter colour, or alternately painted in slip of a darker colour, bands of roughened clay, small stamped patterns and, more ambitiously, the piercing of an outer layer of clay (called "carving") were all common forms of decoration. Inscriptions were often incised. Very much later some designs in relief were produced in the Fulham manner, but these entirely lack the charm of the simpler designs.

Nottingham wares are nearly always distinguishable from other stonewares made at rival factories by their superior design and finish. Nowhere at this period were salt-glazed articles made with such precision and sureness of touch.

"Nottingham" is sometimes marked, often as part of an inscription or in shortened form – a jug in the Victoria and Albert Museum is marked "Nott". 1703.

Novelty clock: any of many types which, in addition to indicating time, has some unusual feature or that indicates time in a peculiar way. Most clocks in this group were made after 1850; many are now rare and are of interest to collectors for their peculiar features. Most were inexpensive when originally manufactured; some were made to be sold as souvenirs, or to be used for advertising purposes and might be made in the shape of flowers, animals or globes. Many sorts of novelty alarm clocks were made – some that lighted a lamp or fired a powder charge at the pre-set time. Other novelties had the conventional pendulum replaced by swinging figures or flying balls.

Nove porcelain: soft-paste porcelain was made from about 1752 at the Nove factory, Venice, which had originally been established about 1728 for the purpose of manufacturing faience. The factory remained in existence until about 1835, the mark being an eight-pointed star in red and gold.

Nozzle: the socket in which the candle is held on candlesticks, wall-lights and chandeliers.

N.p.: an abbreviation used in book-sellers' catalogues to indicate that there is no place of publication (or perhaps publisher's or printer's name), given on the title page of a book. In America the abbreviation is also used by professional cataloguers to mean a book for which there is no prospect of getting a Library of Congress card.

"NS" mark: see Ottweiler porcelain.

Nulling: see Knulling.

Nummus: generic term for coin but commonly applied to the multiple bronze coins of the Byzantine Empire with emperor's portrait and Greek numeral of value.

Nuremberg egg: a misnomer applied to early South German watches. Arose from the misreading and mistranslation of "Uhrlein" into "Eierlein" (little clocks into little eggs). These early watches were usually drum shaped.

Nymphenburg porcelain: hard-paste porcelain was first made with the assistance of the arcanist (q.v.) J. J. Ringler in 1753. The factory at that time was situated at Neudeck but was moved in 1761 to a building in the palace grounds of Nymphenburg. From 1755 to 1767 the factory was under the patronage of Prince Max III Joseph of Bavaria and Count Sigismund von Haimhausen. It was during this early period that the most famous wares of the factory were produced. Later in the century it became the property of the Elector Palatine and ultimately of the State. In the latter part of the 19th cent. it was leased to a private company and still exists to-day. The table-wares of the early period are decorated in an imaginative Rococo (q.v.) style, or with flowers, fruit, or landscapes in the manner of Meissen (q.v.). The most renowned wares of the factory are the figures modelled by Franz Anton Bustelli who was chief modeller at the factory from 1754 until his death in 1763. His figures capture the playful mood of the rococo period, sometimes rendered in pure white and sometimes in restrained colours, exploiting to the full a capricious and lively spirit. His work is closely akin to that of the contemporary Bavarian wood sculptors and displays a masterly linear rythm. Some of Bustelli's models seem to have been reassembled by a "repairer" (P. A. Seefried) after his death, while the modern factory has made copies in pure white porcelain of some of the early models. Bustelli's successor, D. Auliczek, continued along established lines, but showed his originality by modelling animal groups of a type not hitherto attempted. In 1797, J. P. Melchior, formerly at Hoechst (q.v.) and Frankenthal (q.v.), came to Nymphenburg, where, following the taste of the time, he modelled his sensitive portrait busts and medallions in biscuit (q.v.). The Nymphenburg mark, the shield from the arms of Bavaria, is usually shown upon the base, impressed as part of the decoration.

Nyon porcelain: a factory was founded at Nyon, near Geneva in 1780 and existed until 1813. Current French fashions were closely adhered to and many of the wares bear floral decoration.

Oban: an oriental coin; multiple of ten of the Koban (q.v.) with similar types.

Oban: Japanese print of full-size, 15 × 10 inches.

Obol: generally small silver Greek coin, one-sixth of a drachm (q.v.). Various multiples also issued.

Obsidian: a dark-coloured volcanic rock of glassy consistency, usually containing dark green flecks. Parian ware (q.v.), by 1850 made by many firms in Staffordshire and generally referred to as Statuary Porcelain, imitated obsidian.

Obverse: the principal side of a coin or medal ("heads") on which the more important design appears. From Hellenistic times the obverse of a coin has usually been reserved for the ruler's portrait.

Occasional table: modern term to describe the small table, intended to serve various purposes, first introduced shortly after the Restoration and popular, in different forms, throughout the 18th cent.

8vo (octavo): see Book sizes.

Oeben, Jean François: French cabinetmaker, born c. 1720, the son of a postmaster at Ebern in Franconia. He married in Paris in 1749, but we do not know the date of his arrival there from Germany. He entered the workshop of C. J. Boulle (q.v.) in 1751, and on the latter's death in 1754 Oeben succeeded him as *ébéniste du Roi* and was granted lodgings at the Gobelins (q.v.), whence he moved in 1756 to the Arsenal.

While working for Boulle, he was also employed by Madame de Pompadour and others, and after his move to the Gobelins he began in 1760 his most celebrated work – the monumental *Bureau du Roi Louis XV*, which, however, was not completed until after his death. Riesener (q.v.) who was one of his assistants, succeeding him at the Arsenal, together with Leleu (q.v.).

Oeben also collaborated with Carlin (q.v.) and with P. Caffieri (q.v.). He died bankrupt in Paris in 1763, where his widow carried on the business until 1767, when she married Riesener, who then carried on the business in his own name.

Oeben only became a *maître-ébéniste* in 1761 under special circumstances, having worked for the Crown for so long. His stamp on furniture is therefore rare, and when found it is more probable that the piece was made by Riesener before he took over the business, as Madame Oeben continued her husband's stamp while running the workshop herself.

After Cressent (q.v.) and Gaudreau (q.v.) Oeben is the most celebrated *ébéniste* of Louis XV's reign. He specialized in elaborately-planned pieces, fitted with secret drawers and complicated locking devices, but, owing to the amount of furniture which must necessarily have left his workshop unstamped, his work cannot easily be identified.

Oeil-de-Perdrix: (*Fr.*), literally, partridge eye: (1) a decoration in enamel colours, used on porcelain, consisting of an even ground of small circles usually upon a coloured background; (2) a term used in lace-making, synonymous with *réseau rosacé* and *fond de neige* or snowflake ground, to describe the most effective of the grounds used in Argentella needlepoint lace and the pillow laces of Valenciennes and some Binche and early Mechlin (qq.v.).

Each of the irregular spidery meshes had a dot in it.

Offprint: a separate printing of a section of a larger publication (generally of composite authorship) made from the same setting of type.

Offset: in a book, the accidental transfer of ink from a printed page or illustration to an adjacent page. This may be caused either from the sheets having been folded, or the book bound, before the ink was properly dry, or from the book being subsequently exposed to damp.

Ogee: in the shape of a double curve, the lower part being concave and the upper convex.

Ogee bowl: a popular shape of bowl found on mid- to late 18th cent. drinking glasses in which the bowl rises from the stem in a gentle "S" curve. Double- and triple-ogee bowls, formed by two or three curves, were particularly favoured for sweetmeat glasses.

Ogee pattern wallpapers: geometrical device based on circles much favoured by wallpaper designers.

Oil-colour printed playing cards: this process was patented by the firm of De la Rue in 1832, a quick-drying printing ink not liable to rub off in glazing being applied by metal or wooden blocks. This method gave a sharper impression, and colours were more vivid than formerly.

Oil-gilding: gilding on porcelain or glass applied by means of japanner's size, used in the 18th cent. before the method of firing gold became known.

"Oilspot" glaze: some of the Chinese wares bearing so-called Honan brown and black glazes of the Sung dynasty bear attractive silvery spots, caused by precipitated iron crystals.

Old English pattern spoons: see under Table services.

Oleograph: a reproduction of a painting in oils, in which the colours

of the original are copied by a process resembling chromolithography. (See also Chromolithograph.)

Olive button: see Bullet knop.

Onlaid bindings: see Mosaic binding.

O'Neale, Jeffrey Hamet: (1734–1801). O'Neale, miniaturist, book illustrator and ceramic artist, was born in Ireland, worked at Chelsea soon after 1752 and later for Worcester and Josiah Wedgwood as an outside decorator. From the latter he received three guineas a week which Wedgwood considered excessive, although he acknowledged that "O'Neale works quick" (1771). In 1765 he was a member of the Incorporated Society of Artists. O'Neale's signature, O.N.P. is found on Worcester and Chelsea porcelain. Animals, illustrations from the Fables of Aesop, figures in landscape were among the subjects he used. It has been suggested that he also worked for James Giles (q.v.) of Kentish Town, London. Signed Worcester pieces are to be found in the British Museum.

O.N.P

One and a quarter seconds clock pendulum: a type of pendulum 5 feet 1 inch in length. When the improved performance of the seconds pendulum (q.v.) and anchor escapement (q.v.) were realized, attempts were made to increase this by using longer pendulums. William Clement first made clocks with $1\frac{1}{4}$ seconds pendulums. The seconds dial of a clock originally so made should have four divisions between each 5-second interval on the seconds dial. Sometimes clocks have their escapements and pendulums altered from 1 second to $1\frac{1}{4}$ seconds in order to enhance their value. These will generally have their old seconds dials with five divisions. The base of a $1\frac{1}{4}$ seconds clock should have a door to allow access to the bob.

On-glaze decoration: decoration applied to glazed pottery or porcelain after the ware has been glazed and fired, literally decorated on top of the glaze.

Onslow pattern spoons: see under Table-services.

"Onyx" glass: glass of several colours mingled before the formation of the vessel in imitation of onyx. A Roman technique, revived in Renaissance (q.v.) times, particularly in Venice and Germany.

Onza: Spanish gold coin of eight escudos (q.v.).

O.p.: an abbreviation used in book-sellers' catalogues to indicate that a publication is out of print.

Opalescent enamel: see Enamel.

Opaque china: trade name for a fine white porcellanous earthenware used by Swansea, Ridgway & Morley and others.

Opaque enamel: see Enamel.

Opaque glass: glass rendered opaque-white by the addition of tin oxide, or arsenic or the ashes of calcined bones. Venetian Renaissance glass vessels were decorated with threads of opaque-white, known as latticinio (q.v.) work, while opaque-white glass alone is also known to have been made in Venice in the latter part of the 15th cent. Opaque-white glass aroused particular interest on account of its resemblance to porcelain and it is recorded that this type of glass was included in orders placed by English merchants with Venetian glassblowers in the second half of the 17th cent. At this period there was in England, as else-where, an enthusiasm for Chinese porcelain. It is possible that some surviving examples of this date may have been made in England. In general, however, English opaque-white glass belongs in date to the second half of the 18th cent. and was made not only at Bristol, as is so commonly thought, but at many other glasshouses in the country. The wares, which include sets of vases, tea caddies, candlesticks, etc. and snuff-boxes and other "toys", were de-corated with enamel painting in the manner of porcelain, which was now being made for the first time in Eng-land, and doubtless the close simi-larity of the two materials encouraged the making of opaque-white glass. (See Bristol glass and Edkins, Michael.)

Opaque-twist stem: a type of stem found on drinking glasses in the second half of the 18th cent. containing spirals of dense-textured white enamel, vary-ing from fine hairs to broad solid tapes; single or compound in more than a hundred variations; (a) straight stem with single twist; (b) with shoulder or central knop and single twist, usually multiple spiral; (c) straight stem with compound-twist (q.v.) – the most common type – from 1760; (d) with knops in various positions, shoulder, central, base, or any two or all three, with compound-twist, from 1760.

"Opal" glass: glass rendered semi-opaque or of an opalescent "milk-and-water" colour, an effect which could be obtained by the addition of the ashes of calcined bones. Late and early 19th cent. country-market glass table wares included sugar-basins, milk-jugs and vases of opal white glass, often painted in unfired colours.

Ophicleide: see under Side-hole in-struments.

Opus Anglicanum: the name given to English ecclesiastical embroidery of the 13th and 14th cent. The art of embroidery had flourished in England from Saxon times, but it reached its highest peak of excellence in the 13th cent., and was known all over Europe as *opus anglicanum*. The figures and other details are mostly worked in fine split-stitch with backgrounds of couched-work. A great deal of *opus anglicanum* was exported to the Continent, where some of it still remains. Towards the middle of the 14th cent. the standard of both design and execution began to decline.

"Orange-jumper": local subject on Yorkshire cream-coloured earthen-ware made at the Don pottery, c. 1808, depicting a coarse-featured local horsebreaker who acted as messenger for Lord Milton in the 1807 election. He is clothed in orange, the "colour" of Lord Milton. Orange-tawny was considered the colour appropriate to the lower classes.

Original state or **original condition:** as used – and very widely used – by cataloguers and collectors of books, this almost always refers to the book's exterior; and it will be found applied to books in cloth, boards, wrappers, leather or indeed any other covering for which the quality of originality can be claimed.

That it is claimed more often, especially of leather-bound books, than can in fact be substantiated, is an index of the steadily increasing importance attached to it since the last quarter of the 19th cent.; and indeed it is accepted doctrine with most collectors today that, to a copy in a fine binding or an appropriate binding, must be preferred (other things being equal) a copy in original binding.

Ormolu: the term "ormolu" (from the Fr. *moulu*) is used to describe decorative objects and furniture mounts of the 18th and 19th cent., cast in bronze or brass and gilt. Though cast and gilt bronze was by no means an innovation in the 18th cent., it was used in France to an extent that could not be paralleled in previous epochs. Ormolu was not by any means an exclusively French production, similar work was done in Germany, England, and elsewhere, but the fineness of design and perfection of finish of the French artists was never equalled. The main volume of production was of furniture mounts, but vases, candlesticks, chandeliers, andirons, inkstands and clock-cases were also made.

These objects were cast, chiselled, and finally fire-gilt. True ormolu should be distinguished from cheaper objects cast in the same moulds and from the same metal, which were roughly finished and lacquered instead of being chiselled and fire-gilt. Ormolu of the Régence and Louis XV periods was never so finely finished as that of the Louis XVI and Empire periods. During the first half of the cent. French

furniture was very lavishly decorated with ormolu, and the effect was achieved by mass of ornament rather than by detail. Later, when marquetry and parquetry were going out of fashion, we find less florid mounts against a background of figured mahogany, a setting which showed them off to the maximum advantage. In the Empire period the ormolu mounts played, if possible, an even more important role, and furniture was constructed as a vehicle for the display of fine ormolu. Such was the detail of the chiselling put into good work, that it was hardly less expensive than similar articles made of silver-gilt.

After the Restoration in France we find a deterioration in standards of production, and the large-scale reproduction of earlier styles, but throughout the 19th cent. there were still craftsmen who could turn out very fine work in this medium, and it is extremely difficult to distinguish between 18th-cent. ormolu and the best of the 19th cent. reproductions.

In England the Birmingham firm of Boulton & Fothergill produced ormolu vases, candlesticks and perfume-burners during the 1760s and '70s. The finish was never up to the highest French standards but the designs, furnished by the Adam Brothers, were of great elegance and fitness for purpose. There was no great demand for furniture mounts in England, but many houses of the second half of the 18th cent. still retain their ormolu door furniture made by Boulton after Adam designs.

Orris lace: see Arras lace.

Orrery: see Planetarium.

Ostensory: see Monstrance.

Ostrich egg cup: sometime supposed to be the eggs of griffins or phoenixes, ostrich eggs were often mounted as cups (and occasionally made into flasks) in the 16th cent. and later. Many surviving specimens are German.

Ottweiler porcelain: a factory was started at Ottweiler, Nassau-Saarbruecken in 1763 for Prince Wilhelm

Heinrich of Nassau-Saarbruecken. It existed until 1797, making hard-paste porcelain in its earlier years and latterly only earthenware. The table-wares are sometimes decorated with mythological or figure subjects framed in rococo scroll-work, and pear-shaped jugs reflect a taste for French forms. Figures were made, and the French modeller Paul-Louis Cyfflé worked here about 1765. The mark in use from 1763 to about 1775 is the "NS" of Nassau-Saarbruecken in blue or gold and occasionally incised.

Oude Amstel porcelain: see under Weesp porcelain.

Oude Loosdrecht porcelain: see under Weesp porcelain.

Overdoors: (supraporte), furnishing paintings on wood or canvas or painted or printed papers suitable for the decoration of the space between the top of a door and cornice. A speciality of the wallpaper maker in England, France and America during the 18th cent. Similar decorative panels were made to fit empty chimney-places in summer months.

Overglaze: decoration applied to porcelain or pottery above the glaze.

Overlay paperweight: the coating of the exposed surfaces of a paper-weight with one or more layers of white or coloured glass. The finish is then cut to leave windows (see Punty mark), through which the interior of the paperweight is visible. Very rarely, after the above process, the weight is further encased in clear glass. Such a paperweight is known as an enclosed overlay.

Overmantel: an ornamental mirror over a mantelpiece.

Overstuffed seat: a chair seat in which the upholstery is carried over the seat rail and secured beneath it.

Ovolo base: hollow ware (q.v.) having a base formed by a plain projecting quarter-curve or moulding. Pewter flagons of the 17th cent. are found with this type of base.

Ovolo moulding: (1) a small oval convex moulding chiefly used in repetition, sometimes with egg and dart enrichment, as 16th cent. border ornament. Some use also made of the ornament on plate (q.v.). Some use also made of the device in late 18th to early 19th cent. (2) a continuous moulding of convex profile, also known as a lip moulding, applied by the cabinet-maker in the early 18th cent. to the top edges of chests of drawers, stands, tables, etc.

Owl jugs: jugs with detachable heads made in slipware in Staffordshire in the late 17th and early 18th cent., and white salt-glazed stoneware from 1730 to 1770, sometimes with brown slip enrichment.

Ox-blood glaze: see Copper-red glazes.

Oxbow, oxbow front: an American term used to describe the curved form, resembling a bow, and the reverse of a serpentine curve, often employed by Boston and other New England cabinet-makers in the late 18th cent. Chests of drawers and other types of case furniture of the finest quality were designed with oxbow fronts.

Oyster veneer: a type of veneer (q.v.) in which the wood is cut from small branches and laid together to form a surface pattern resembling a series of oysters placed next to each other. This oyster veneering was used on cabinet doors and drawer fronts during the late 17th cent. and derives from a Dutch fashion. The woods used included walnut, olive, laburnum and kingwood.

Pad foot: a simple terminal to a cabriole (q.v.) leg used on chairs, settees and tables from about 1705, resembling in shape the club foot (q.v.) but resting on a small disc.

Paduan mandoline: see under Mandoline.

Pagoda: small gold coin issued in great number of states in South India from 17th to 18th cent. Great variety of types, often representation of a god.

Pagoda wallpapers: Chinese wallpapers.

Paillons: small decorative spangles in gold, silver or colours cut into formal shapes and set in translucent enamel on boxes, étuis (q.v.) etc.

Painted silhouettes: these were produced in a number of techniques on various materials, ranging from paper to glass. (See under Glass silhouettes.)

Painted wallpapers: probably used in England as early as the end of the 15th cent., though few if any of these have survived. Painting of "perspectives" was undertaken by 18th cent. paperhanging makers, frequently after the plain paper and been hung.

Paktong: an alloy of copper, nickel and zinc, of whitish colour, resembling silver when polished. Grates, candlesticks and other domestic appliances were made of this metal in the last third of the 18th cent. The name is derived from the Chinese, who used the metal for hinges and furniture mounts. It is also known as tutenag, which, properly speaking, is zinc without admixture of other metals.

Palace letters: these, with inventory numbers (q.v.), are often painted or branded on French furniture and occasionally stamped on *bronzes d'ameublement* (q.v.), made for the French Crown. On veneered furniture they are usually to be found on the carcase at the back or under marble slabs, but in the case of chairs and joined furniture generally, they are often in the under parts and sometimes on the bottom of the upholstered seats. They almost always take the form of the initial letter or letters of the palace concerned beneath a crown. Thus F = Fontainebleau; C.T. = Château de Trianon; W (two Vs) = Versailles; S.C. = Saint Cloud, etc. Like inventory numbers, their existence on furniture of any date is worth careful investigation.

Palissy ware: lead-glazed pottery made by Bernard Palissy (d. 1590), born at Agen and long resident at Saintes in France, consisting of dishes either decorated with casts from nature or fishes, reptiles and other creatures, moulded with Renaissance ornament or figure subjects, covered with coloured glazes. His methods were adopted by other potters, particularly at Avon, near Fontainebleau. In England, lead-glazed earthenware dishes were made in imitation of Palissy ware and examples dated between 1633 and 1697 are known.

Palladian style: a style of architecture based upon the principles followed by the Italian architect Palladio in Italy in the 16th cent. In England, a small group of connoisseurs, led by the Earl of Burlington and the architect William Kent (qq.v.) encouraged a revival of this style in the first half of the 18th cent. The rigid principles of Classical proportion, involving the use of Classical forms and motifs, were applied not only to buildings but to their interior decoration and to furniture. The type of furniture was consequently of architectural character, lavishly carved and frequently gilded, making use of pediments, heavy cornices, swags of fruit or flowers, masks, lions' paws, etc.

Pallet: a tool with a short strip of decoration designed primarily for decorating the panels of the back of a book-binding. Specialized kinds can be used for lettering or signed bindings.

Pallets: the parts of the escapement of a clock against which the teeth of the escape wheel push, giving impulse to the pendulum or balance.

Palmette: see Anthemium.

Panakin: apparently the word now reduced to pipkin (q.v.). A small saucepan with a wooden handle held in a horizontal socket.

Pancheon: a large shallow bowl with sloping sides used for settling milk.

Panel: compartment usually rectangular, and sunk or raised from the surface of its framework. Panel is the filling of such framework, whereas panelling refers to the framework and its filling.

Panel cutting: a method of decorating glass vessels by means of cutting or grinding a pattern on the flat edge of a grinding wheel. Also known as flat cutting, many variants of cut motifs are found on 18th cent. glass.

Panelled chests: typified joiners' as distinct from carpenters' furniture. The horizontal rails and vertical stiles and muntins (q.v.) that formed the framework to the loose panels of the chest were held together by mortice and tenon joints (q.v.), allowing the wood to respond to atmospheric changes. Joiners' work in 1632 was defined to include dovetail joints (q.v.), and the wide early style of dovetail may be noted down the corners of some chests in walnut, cypress and other woods that could be undercut in a manner impossible with oak. Plat in 1594 made reference to a "foure square chest . . . close the sides well with dovetails or cement". But corner dovetails in view on the outside of a chest are usually taken to indicate Continental work.

Panelled construction: until the 15th cent., furniture in England was made of heavy boards. A new method was then introduced by the joiners involving the use of panels held in a framework of stiles and rails (qq.v.). Panelled construction rendered furniture less clumsy and provided new possibilities for design.

Panel, panelled binding: a term used in the description of book-bindings, having a rectangle, formed of single, double or triple fillets (q.v.), whether gilt or blind (plain), either on the sides or between the bands on the spine of a book.

Panharmonicon: a mechanical orchestra which reproduced the sound of many instruments, constructed by J. N. Maelzel (1772–1838) and for which Beethoven wrote an overture, *The Battle of Victoria,* in 1813.

Panorama: these are sheets which either roll up round some central drum or fold up, and which in either case can be extended to their full length, when they display a picture, more or less complete, of some historical event or of some extended scene, e.g. *Queen Victoria's Grand Tour of the Thames from Source to Mouth.* They are coloured or uncoloured. The Victorian Age was the age of panoramas; although they existed much earlier and much later. Until comparatively recently street vendors used to sell panoramas of *The Lord Mayor's Show* which rolled up inside a brass case. *The Coronation, and The Wedding of Queen Victoria* and the *Duke of Wellington's Funeral* were the subjects of fine panoramas. *The Position on the Alma* and *A Bengal Infantry Regiment on the March* are other subjects. The Great Exhibition produced a heavy crop. Some are: *The House that Paxton Built* (7 feet 8 inches long), by George Augustus Sala; *The Great Exhibition "Wot is to Be"*, a "comic" also by Sala; *The Great Exhibition of Doings in London for* 1851 (published by Ackermann & Co.); *The Overland Journey to the Great Exhibition,* by Richard (Dicky) Doyle. (See also *Life in England in Aquatint and Lithography* 1770–1860, Curwen Press, 1953, from the library of J. R. Abbey.)

Papal roses: golden roses were sent by the Popes to princes who had rendered signal service to the Roman Church and, later, to important ecclesiastical bodies. Of the many made in the 14th and 15th cent. few survive; one of the most notable, the gift of Pius II, is at Siena. All were made by goldsmiths working in Rome.

Pap-boat: small, shallow oval bowl with tapering lip or spout at one end for feeding infants. Surviving silver examples date from early 18th cent. onwards, but they were also made of other materials. Sometimes known as a pap-dish.

Paperhanging maker: 17th and 18th cent. term describing the maker of wallpaper, superseded by "paper-stainer" until "wallpaper manufacturer" became generally used within the present century.

Paperweight: heavy bun-shaped piece of clear glass containing within a pattern or design of coloured glass representing flowers, fruit, butterflies, etc. Cone-shaped examples of light green glass sometimes contain vases of flowers. Originating in Venice in the 19th cent., the art of making glass paperweights was perfected at the St Louis glassworks in France and at the French factories at Baccarat and Clichy. French paperweights were copied widely in England. The glass-making centres of Stourbridge and Bristol produced examples. The White-friars Glassworks in London and George Bacchus and Son in Birmingham also made paperweights. The successful sale of French paperweights imported into America induced manufacturers there to produce their own wares. The factories of Deeming Jarves at Sandwich, Cape Cod, opened in 1825, and at East Cambridge and South Boston, in Massachusetts, opened in 1818 and 1837, produced designs in the French manner and evolved original models.

Papier-mâché: a material composed of paper, reduced to a fibrous pulp, with chalk and sand and shaped by being pressed into boxwood moulds, was made in England in the mid-18th cent. An improved composition of ground rags, glue, flour and water was patented in 1786 by Obadiah West-wood of Birmingham. A real advance in technique was made by Henry Clay of Birmingham, who, in 1772, patented a process for making a tough, heat- and moisture-resisting material which could be oven-japanned to acquire a surface finish as lustrous as oriental lacquer. It was made from sheets of paper having a porous texture, saturated with a solution of flour and glue. Any number of sheets of paper could be applied, attached by glue and dried between each addition. When the correct thickness was reached, the shape was taken from the mould and planed and filed. Decoration was painted in colour, gold or bronze over the dried and varnished object and covered with a coat of shellac. The piece was then hardened in a japanning oven and rubbed with oil to obtain a polish. Trays, boxes, tea-caddies and coasters were among the many objects made.

"Pappenheimer": a heavy rapier with a form of swept hilt (q.v.) in-corporating two large perforated shells. It was used during the first half of the 17th cent. and was named after the celebrated Imperialist general of the Thirty Years' War, Gottfried Heinrich, Count von Pappenheim (d. 1632). Sometimes referred to as a Walloon sword.

Papworth, John Buonarotti: (1775–1847), an architect whose popularity and versatility were such that he did not confine his attention solely to buildings. He painted in water-colours, and designed book illustrations, furniture, silverware and gardens. He designed a glass throne for the Shah of Persia, and is considered to have been responsible for the introduction of chandeliers composed of long "prism" drops arranged in concentric rings. Many of these were made by John Blades, of 5 Ludgate Hill, London, for whose business premises Papworth designed the front.

Parcel-gilt: descriptive of plate (q.v.) decorated by the partial application of gilding (see also Silver-gilt).

Pardoe, Thomas: (1770–1823), an artist who worked for the Derby, Worcester and Swansea porcelain factories from about 1785 until 1809, when he removed to Bristol and worked as an independent enameller until 1821. Thereafter he decorated porcelain at Nantgarw. Principally a flower painter, much of his work is found on all the above porcelains and also on Coalport. Plates copied from botanical magazines were seen in his earliest work. Later his painting is inclined to be careless. His signature in gold is quite often found on various pieces.

Pardoe, Fecit Bristol.

His son, W. H. Pardoe, opened the earthenware manufactory at Nantgarw in 1833.

Parian ware: a special kind of biscuit porcelain (q.v.) used for statuary and intended to replace the famous Derby biscuit porcelain, and stated in the *Art Union*, Vol 10, 1848, to have been invented at Copeland & Garretts, Stoke-on-Trent, about 1845, with the active encouragement of Thomas Battam (1810–64) who was art director. Elsewhere Spencer Garrett is credited with its invention, which was disputed, however, by John Mountford, by Minton, and by T.&R. Boote. John Mountford stated (*Staffordshire Advertiser*, 20 September 1851) "I am prepared to prove that in the latter part of 1845 I discovered that material known as 'statuary porcelain', that I gave to Mr S. Garrett (then of the firm of Messrs Copeland & Garrett) the receipt for its production". John Mountford was then employed at the Copeland factory. T. &. R Boote claimed that Thomas L. Boote first made the body in 1841, "when learning the art of pottery with Mr E. Jones, and he produced a further specimen from the same receipt in the year 1842 when with Mr Maddock". Mintons claimed they produced it in 1845. By 1846 it was in commercial production and by 1850 numerous firms were making the body. Wedgwoods called their parian Carrara. Until about 1849–50 the body was generally known in the trade as Statuary Porcelain. Parian tinted to various shades was popular in 1870s and 1880s.

Parison: a glassblower's term for an inflated, unformed gather (q.v.) of metal.

Parquetry: (*Fr. Parqueterie*, from *Parqueter*, to inlay), a form of decorative veneer in which the pattern formed is geometrical. Parquetry was first used in England in the second half of the 17th cent. It was not popular in the earlier 18th cent. but returned to fashion for case furniture made in the French manner in the second half of the cent.

"Parson and Clerk": a figure group produced in earthenware showing a drunken parson being conducted home by his clerk, after a night's carousal; first made by Enoch Wood (q.v.) c. 1790 as a sequel to the "Vicar and Moses". This popular satire on the squarson type of incumbent was also used with appropriate verses as a transfer-print on cream-coloured earthenware in Staffordshire and Leeds. The design was possibly suggested by the fourth plate, "Night", in Hogarth's series "Four Times of Day" (engraved and dated 25 March 1738) which shows a reveller being led home after celebrating Restoration Day.

Parting-shards: bits of fired pottery used to separate pots after they have been glazed to prevent them sticking together: "Their flat ware though it be leaded, having only parting-shards i.e thin bits of old pots put between them to keep them from *sticking* together.' (R. Plot, *Natural History of Staffordshire* 1686.)

Partizan: see under Pole-arms.

Parts, part-issues: to most collectors parts means first and foremost the best-selling fiction published in this style from *Pickwick*, which started the vogue in 1836–37, to *Daniel Deronda* (1874–76), which was a late example. During this period most novels continued to be published in three volumes and borrowed by their readers from the circulating libraries. But a number of books by popular writers were published (usually with illustrations by a popular artist) in paper-covered parts, to be bought in instalments – monthly, fortnightly or weekly – and bound up when complete. These part-issues were mostly of large octavo size and usually sold for a shilling. The final part, which contained the title-page and other preliminaries, would often be a double number, when the complete set is described as "in the original 13/12 parts."

The Victorian novels so issued are mostly not nearly as uncommon as might be supposed from their fragile character and intentionally impermanent coverings. But it is true that they have very seldom survived in fine unrestored condition.

Parure: a full set of matching jewellery including a necklace, brooch, earrings and bracelet.

Passglas: (*Ger.*), a German glass beaker encircled by a notched spiral thread dividing it into equal parts so that the glass could be passed from guest to guest allowing each his allotted share.

Paste-down: see Endpapers.

Paste jewellery: jewellery made with coloured glass, used to reproduce precious stones. Paste gems have been known since Roman times, usually with coloured foil placed beneath in order to enhance their appearance. Colourless paste is practically a modern invention, worn as a substitute rather than an imitation of precious stones.

Pastel: a dry flaky crayon made of pigments and gum-water. The term is also used to describe a picture in this medium.

Paste print: paste prints were made in the 15th cent. from metal plates, similar to those used in the *manière criblée* process (q.v.), on which a glutinous ink or paste was used; so that gold leaf or tints of colour could be added to the impression.

Pastiche: an inferior version of a work of art by a copyist.

Pastille-burners: box-like containers, often made in the shape of cottages, summer-houses and churches, with detachable perforated lids for burning cassolette perfumes, made in china and earthenware in the 18th and 19th cent. but very popular 1820–50. Cassolette perfumes consist of finely powdered willow-wood charcoal, benzoin, fragrant oils and gum arabic.

"Patch" family: porcelain figures made at Chelsea and Derby (qq.v.), so named from the presence of three or four dark unglazed patches left on the under surface by the pads or wads of clay upon which the wares were rested during the glost-firing.

Patchwork quilts: in England patchwork quilts did not originate until the 18th cent., and most surviving examples date from the end of the 18th or the early 19th cent. Most patchwork patterns were geometrical or formal, such as the "Honey-comb", which was composed entirely of hexagons, and was the most popular design. Other patterns, such as the "Shell" and various "Feather" patterns, were taken from traditional quilting designs. True patchwork consists of a mosaic of fragments of materials sewn edge to edge, but some so-called "patchwork" quilts are, in fact, applied work (q.v.), as, for example, are those quilts where floral motifs are cut out from chintzes and applied to the ground of the quilt. American patchwork quilts of the 18th and 19th cent. show an amazing variety of patterns of much greater elaboration than English examples. There are over three hundred named designs, many of them with a religious origin. One of the most striking and commonest traditional patterns is the "Star of Bethlehem", an eight-pointed star worked either as a single central motif surrounded by smaller stars, or as a number of small stars of equal size regularly arranged on a white ground. Other quilts were made with applied coloured patches on white grounds elaborately quilted with geometrical, feather or floral designs.

Pâte-de-verre: *(Fr.)*, moulded glass made of actual glass of various colours, powdered and mixed and re-fired. The technique was used in ancient Egypt and has been adopted in modern times in France.

Paten: small circular plate for the wafer or Protestant Communion bread, made of silver, silver-gilt or even gold. Medieval examples have a shaped central depression and a broad flat rim. The depression is engraved with appropriate religious subjects and, in the case of the finest examples, also enriched with translucent enamel. Elizabethan paten covers fit the cup and have a flat seal foot. Later examples follow this pattern until the Gothic revival. Small circular footed waiters or "tazze" (q.v.) should not be confused with ecclesiastical pieces.

Patera: an ornamental motif, of Classical origin, based on the saucer used in sacrificial libations, of round or oval form. The patera was frequently used for decorative purposes on furniture of the Adam (q.v.) period and during the early years of the 19th cent., either carved or painted. It also appears on contemporary metalwork.

Pâte-sur-pâte: *(Fr.)*, literally clay-on-clay. A French technique known as *pâtes d'application*, involving the building up of translucent white or tinted

reliefs on coloured parian (q.v.) or porcelain by means or modelling and painting. First employed at Sèvres, and introduced into England at Mintons in 1870 by Marc Louis Solon (1835–1912), the ceramic craftsman and historian. Solon never repeated any of his subjects which were all entirely hand-done. His pupils, Frederick Alfred Rhead and Alboin Birks (1861–1941) exploited the process, the last named carrying on the technique with modifications until his retirement in 1937, particularly on service plates. But nearly all the pieces which he decorated in this process were mould-made repetitions of a stock design, extensively touched up by hand. Birks' designs were continued for a short period by his assistant, Richard Bradbury, whose signature occurs on late examples. The process was discontinued in 1939.

Patina (and **colour**): of furniture, woodwork and metalwork, patina is the undisturbed surface, heightened by centuries of polishing and usage, or by the presence of oxide produced naturally on the surface of metal. Patination and colour pose problems to a faker. To some extent they can be simulated, but deteriorate when artificially produced (see also Fake).

"Paul Pry": model for pottery figures and toby jugs based upon the meddlesome hero of John Poole's comedy of that name, 1825.

Pavé setting: a means of setting jewellery, popular in the late 18th and 19th cent., in which the ornament is paved with clusters of stones touching each other and held in position by grains of metal.

Pavillon: gold coin issued by Philip VI of France (1328–50) with obverse type of king seated under canopy. Imitated by the Black Prince in his possessions in France.

Paw foot: a terminal to a cabriole leg (q.v.) carved in the form of a lion's paw used on tables and chairs in the mid-18th cent. and particularly on those pieces inspired by the designs of William Kent (q.v.).

Pawn: the name is the old English form of peon or day labourer, and in old English chess-sets pawns were carved to represent eight occupations: the king's pawn, a banker-merchant; the queen's pawn, a physician-apothecary; bishops' pawns, notaries, inn-keepers or provision dealers; knights' pawns, keepers of the king's highway or workers in stone, iron or wood; rooks' pawns, letter-carriers and farm labourers.

Not until the later 18th cent. was it usual to carve eight identical pawns for a cabinet set of chessmen. (See also Chessmen.)

Pax: a tablet with a projecting handle behind, used in the Eucharist when it is kissed by the celebrant, the other priests and, very occasionally, the communicants. It is usually decorated on the front with a sacred symbol, a scene from the Gospel (usually the Crucifixion) or the lives of the saints, engraved, nielloed or enamelled.

Paysage wallpapers: see "Scenic" wallpapers.

"Peachbloom" glazes: see Copper-red porcelain glazes.

Peaked morion: see Morion.

Pea-pod designs: a series of engraved designs, the most important dating from the second quarter of the 17th cent., intended for the use of goldsmiths in making enamelled gold miniature cases, cameo frames etc., using stylised, leaf-shapes resembling pea-pods.

Pear-drop moulding: a moulding, found below a plain cornice on late 18th cent. bookcases, carved in a repetitive design of inverted pear-shaped forms.

"Pearl" ware: white earthenware containing a larger proportion of flint and white clay than cream-coloured earthenware; made by Josiah Wedgwood 1779 but not much used by him. Also a dry body made by Chetham & Woolley, Lane End, c. 1795 and used like jasper for the manufacture of ornaments.

Pear shape: a term used to describe a curved or pyriform shape in hollowware.

"Pebbled" vases: vases with marbled surface (see "Agate-ware").

Péché mortel: (*Fr.*), a couch made up of a stool and an easy chair, similar to a duchesse (q.v.). Chippendale (q.v.) illustrated designs for these couches in the third edition of his *Director*.

Pedestal table: a round-topped table supported by a central pillar on a tripod base, the legs being of cabriole form (q.v.), ending in club or claw-and-ball feet (qq.v.). Pedestal tables were used for general purposes and varied in the degree of carving applied to the base and legs. They were first introduced about 1730 and remained popular throughout the cent.

Pediment: architecturally, the triangular end to a roof. During the 18th cent. pediments sometimes surmounted the cornices of bookcases, cabinets, etc. (See also Broken pediment.)

Peepshow: a peepshow derives from a cabinet carried round in the 17th and 18th cent. by peepshow men, into which the spectator could peer for a small sum, seeing something like a more modern stereoscopic view, where the scene was made up of various pieces cut out and graduated at different lengths from the viewer. The Victorian peepshow folded up, then pulled out again with two eye-pieces through which the perspective view could be seen. Almost always coloured, it stretched to a convenient length between eyes and outspread hand.

Peever: a piece of slate or stone used in the game of hopscotch; also a disc of pottery, so used, coloured and lettered with the name of the owner. Made at Alloa and elsewhere in Scotland in the 19th cent.

Pegged chests: occasionally a chest is noted which can be dismantled for travelling or store by removing wooden pegs in the manner of many early table trestles. Some are authentic, but obviously the design was very much in the mood of the 19th cent. pseudo-medievalism.

Pegged construction: furniture made by joiners constructed with mortice and tenon (q.v.) joints, the tenon being held in the mortice by a square peg, riven or split from green wood.

"Peggy Plumper": crude decoration sometimes appearing on earthenware, showing Peggy Plumper sparring with Sammy Spar for mastership of bed and board, accompanied by a long rhyme "about wearing the breeches".

Peg tankard: rare form of 17th cent. silver tankard, the interior fitted with a vertical row of small studs to measure drinking.

Peking bowls: Chinese porcelain bowls of Ch'ien Lung (q.v.) or later date, with painted *famille rose* (q.v.) medallions reserved on a single-coloured ground covered with engraved scrollwork; said to have been sent as yearly tribute to the Emperor at Peking.

Pellatt, Apsley: (1791–1823), glass-maker, whose father of the same name founded the Falcon Glasshouse in Southwark, London in the late 18th cent. Apsley Pellat patented a novel form of cameo, being a relief moulded in a porcellaneous material enclosed in deeply cut glass, which he called "crystallo-ceramie" (q.v.) or "cameo incrustations".

Pembroke table: a small table with short drop leaves supported on swinging wooden brackets. The term Pembroke is first used in England in the 1760s. Although Chippendale lists tables of this description as "breakfast tables" in the *Director*, he used the term on bills. Sheraton popularized the type of table and claimed that it was named after the lady who first ordered it. It was particularly popular in the late 18th cent. period and Hepplewhite also suggested designs for it.

Pencilling: 18th-cent. term for painting with a brush.

Pendeloque: a gemstone of drop-shape, faceted and used as a pendant.

Pendent husks: see Husk ornament.

Pennsylvania Dutch: the name applied to German settlers in Pennsylvania. Their furniture and crafts have many distinctive qualities since they assimilate English and German peasant styles. Their cabinet-makers worked in soft woods which they painted and often decorated with floral patterns and other motifs from the vocabulary of peasant design.

Penny: the standard silver coin from 8th to 14th cent. In the early Saxon kingdoms the obverse bore the king's name and the reverse that of the moneyer; types, usually, cross motif. An occasional portrait type was used for obverse and became common after the unification of the kingdom when the place of minting also appeared on the reverse. Types with variations of cross reverse continued under the Normans and Plantagenets. Similar pennies were struck in Scotland and Ireland. The familiar types of copper penny were first issued in 1797.

Penny bank: earthenware money-box in the form of a house or chest of drawers.

Pentimenti: traces in an oil painting of an earlier composition abandoned or altered by the artist in the course of his work.

Percussion lock: the latest form of ignition for a firearm, involving the use of a detonating compound. The first patent for a lock of this type was taken out in 1807 by the Rev. Alexander Forsyth (d. 1843). As put on the market, this had a small, flask-shaped magazine which could be rotated on a central spindle, and which contained detonating powder in the lower end and a spring-loaded striker in the upper. By turning the magazine through 180 degrees a small amount of powder was deposited in a recess in the central spindle, connecting through a channel to the touch-hole; when the magazine was returned to the normal position this powder was detonated by the striker, which was itself struck by a hammerlike cock.

Improvements made on the Forsyth lock included the pellet- or pill-lock, in which the detonating powder was replaced by a pellet, sometimes enclosed in a paper cap; and the tube-lock, which used a tubular metal primer held by a spring clip. All types were superseded by the percussion-cap system, apparently invented between 1818 and 1820, in which a thimble-shaped copper cap containing detonating powder was placed on a hollow nipple communicating with the chamber, and fired by the action of the cock. Many flint-lock guns were converted to this system, which remained in use until the second half of the 19th cent.

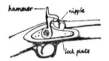

Perfume-burner: pierced baluster-form metal vase on scroll feet of late 17th cent. date. Rare.

Pergolesi, Michele Angelo: Italian painter employed by Robert Adam. He was in England from c. 1758. Between 1777 and 1801 he published his *Original Designs* for painted furniture.

Perpetual calendar clock: clock including a calendar, which corrects itself for the short months, and more exceptionally, for leap year. The mechanism consists of a slotted wheel revolving once a year (or four years) with slots of varying length which control the movement of a lever, allowing it to pass one or more teeth of the calendar wheel at a time.

Perry, Edward: an important manufacturer of papier-maché (q.v.) who started in Queen Street, Wolverhampton, later moving to Paul Street. The Wolverhampton *Directory*, 1829, described him as "Manufacturer of Fine Paper Goods and Fancy Pontypool Work".

Persian carpets: the Persian carpet at its best is worthy to be ranked among the great examples of creative art. Springing naturally from a luxury-loving and refined civilization, and finding at hand an unsurpassed quality of wool from the highlands of Persia, combined with a natural feeling for colour and form in all classes of its people, it is not surprising that many of these lovely pieces are so beautiful. There are secrets of dyeing: the ability to use brilliant colours impervious to strong sunlight and time alike, yet applied without damage to the sometimes delicate fabric. The apogee of Persian craftmanship seems to have been reached during the reigns of Tashmak (1524–77) and Shah Abbas (1588–1629), and it is in this period that a number of the most famous carpets now existing were woven, usually under royal decree or patronage, and irrespective of cost. The famous Ardebil carpet from the Mosque of Sheik Safi in the Victoria and Albert Museum, London, for instance, was largely the work of one man, who commenced his labours on this one carpet as a young weaver and finished it as an old man of over seventy, weaving into the cartouche:

"I have no refuge in the world,
    other than thy threshold,
My head no protection other than
    this porchway.
The Work of the slave of the Holy
    Place, Maksud of Kashan in the
    year 946."

Peso: Spanish silver coin of four or eight reales (piece of eight) struck from late 15th cent. Types, originally Spanish arms with value VIII and arms of Castille and Leon. From

Charles III royal portrait on one side. Pillars of Hercules type on peso struck in Latin American mints.

Petit-point embroidery: a type of embroidery worked on a woven canvas in a tent stitch or slanting stitch. The technique, which combined rich and pictorial effects, had rarely been used in the Middle Ages but was characteristic of post-Renaissance secular embroidery all over Europe. It was much used for cushion and chair covers.

Petits patrons: see Cartoons.

Petronel: a large pistol, or short arquebus (q.v.), fitted with a match- or wheel-lock (q.v.) and used in the late 16th and early 17th cent. It had a curved stock, which was rested against the chest when fired.

Petuntse: fusible feldspathic ingredient of hard-paste porcelain. (See China-stone.)

"Pew" group: figure group representing a man and woman (more rarely two men and a woman) seated upon a high-backed settle; made in white salt-glazed stoneware, Staffordshire, about 1730–40; more rarely in earthenware. The name was probably derived from Sir Arthur Church's description in *English Earthenware* 1884 – "a man and a woman . . . are seated on a high-backed bench or pew".

Pewter: an alloy, chiefly, of tin, with varying proportions of copper, lead, antimony or bismuth.

"PH" and "PHF" mark: see Frankenthal porcelain.

Phyfe, Duncan: New York master cabinet-maker (1768–1854). Born in Scotland, he went in his early 'teens to Albany, New York, and there became apprenticed to a cabinet-maker. In 1790, aged twenty-one, he arrived in New York City, where shortly he set up a shop and made fine quality furniture in the Sheraton and Directoire styles. Phyfe's work possesses grace of line, refinement of proportion and delicacy of ornament – reeding, fluting, cameo-carving – which lend it both elegance and distinction. Among his chairs, sofas and tables he produced so many little masterpieces incorporating the lyre motif that he is now considered the chief American exponent of this decorative form. Phyfe's individuality again stands out in his Empire-style furniture. He was so successful, that at one time he employed a hundred workmen; eventually his work suffered from his success. He retired from business in 1847. Fine collections of Phyfe furniture are owned by the Museum of the City of New York; the Metropolitan Museum, New York; the Taft Museum, Cincinnati, Ohio; and Henry Ford's Edison Institute, Dearborn, Michigan.

Pianoforte: see under Clavichords and pianofortes.

Picot: (*Fr.*), a term used in lace-making to describe the purl or tiny loop ornamenting bride or cordonnet (qq.v.).

Pictorial lace: made in the mid-17th cent. and resembling the raised embroidery now known as stump-work (q.v.) and with similar use of raised canopies, loose hangings, beads, seed pearls, and disproportionate details to fill in the background.

Piece of eight: see Peso.

Pie-crust table: a round tilt-top table on a tripod base popular in the mid-18th cent. The top has a scalloped edge finished with a carved moulding which is suggestive of the notched rim of a pie crust. The tripod consists of three cabriole legs terminating generally in claw and ball feet.

Pie-crust ware: pottery pie dishes of buff stoneware with covers simulating pastry were made during the flour tax by the firms of Wedgwood, Turner, etc. ("After Brummel's retirement, viz., in July 1800, the scarcity was so great that the consumption of flour for pastry was prohibited in the Royal Household, rice being used instead; the distiller left off malting, hackney coach fares were raised 25 per cent, and Wedgwood made dishes to represent pie-crust." Capt. Jeffs, *Life of George Brummel* Esq. 1844, Vol 1, p. 49.) "About 1780 he (Turner) discovered a vein of fine clay ... at Green Dock ... From this he obtained all his supplies for manufacturing his ... *Stone Ware Pottery* of a cane colour ... some of them represent different kinds of pastry ..." (Simeon Shaw, *History of the Staffordshire Potteries*, 1829, pp. 172–73).

Pied de biche (hind's hoof spoon): also known as split end. See Trefid spoon.

Pierced earthenware: earthenware decorated by hand-piercing the walls in the leather-hard state with punches shaped like leaves, hearts, trefoils, quatrefoils, etc., arranged to form intricated lacelike designs. It was extensively employed at Leeds, where the designs were executed with remarkable precision and delicacy. The process was also used by Wedgwood and others in Staffordshire.

Pier glasses: tall, narrow mirrors, usually made in pairs, to hang on the wall space between windows, in elaborately carved and gilded frames, popular throughout the 18th cent.

Pier table: a table designed to stand against the pier, the part of the wall between the windows. The pier table was often placed below a looking glass (or pier glass). Early 18th cent. examples were often of gesso while those designed in the latter part of the cent. were lightly constructed, sometimes with marble tops or veneered in satinwood. At this period they were often semi-elliptical or D-shaped.

Pietre dure: the Italian term for those stones (literally "hard stones") which are roughly classed as semiprecious in English: i.e. such stones as are composed mainly of silicates in contrast to "soft" stones, such as limestone and most marbles, which have a large proportion of calcium in their composition. Much used for table tops, altar frontals, and decorative cabinets from the 16th cent.

Pig-faced visor: see under Bascinet.

Piggin: a small milk pail. A pig-wife is a woman who sells crockery.

Pike: see under Pole-arms.

Pilaster wallpaper: a richly patterned paper suitable for use in elaborate schemes of panelling. Sets of papers containing units of the complete scheme were made in France and in England during the early part of the 19th cent.

Pilchard pots: earthenware pots made in North Devon, South Wales, and Cornwall for the West Country fishermen, and known by size as "gallons", "bussas", and "great crocks", etc.

Pilgrim bottle: in Middle Ages a leather bottle, sometimes with metal mounts, used for carrying water. It was of flattened form with loop on each side through which suspension cords were passed. A few early examples have survived in silver (e.g. French bottle in All Souls College Oxford) but many more in earthenware. The type is also known in the rare Medici porcelain (q.v.). Pilgrim bottles of exceptionally large size were made of silver in the late 17th and early 18th cent. These seem to have been intended for display as sideboard plate only.

Pilgrim furniture: a general term used in America to describe the New England furniture made during the 17th cent. for the Puritans, the "Pilgrims". Exceptionally fine collections may be found at the Wadsworth Atheneum, Hartford, Conn., and the American Antiquarian Society, Worcester, Mass.

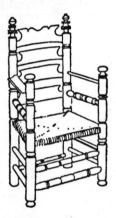

Pilgrims' badges: cast from lead, these badges were distributed at the shrines of medieval Europe to pilgrims, and were worn in the hat or on the person as evidence that the pilgrimage had been completed. These little objects, worthless in themselves, usually bore some allusion to the saint at whose shrine they were received. The best-known pilgrims' sign is the shell of St John of Compostella in Spain. The most popular English shrine was that of St Thomas at Canterbury. Pilgrims' signs, being made of lead, bear a superficial resemblance to the notorious class of fake lead medallions and amulets of the Middle Ages, made in London about the end of the 19th cent., and commonly known after their inventors as "Billies and Charlies" (q.v.). The lettering of any inscription on a putative pilgrims' sign should be examined

with care, as it is in this feature that the fakers betrayed themselves.

Pillar and scroll clock: an American shelf or mantel clock by Eli Terry. The wooden works are housed in a vertical rectangular case with a scrolled-arch top, small, round pillars at the sides, and delicately small feet. Also known as a "Terry" clock.

Pillow lace: the most usual name for laces made with bobbins (q.v.) as distinct from needlepoint laces (q.v.) although those too were worked on cushions. Padded boards were used at first.

Pill-slabs: apothecaries' pill-slabs were made in tin-glazed earthenware at Lambeth, and were decorated frequently with the arms of the Apothecaries' Company, or those of the City of London.

Pinchbeck: an alloy of copper and zinc similar to brass but containing a higher percentage of copper. Invented by the London watchmaker, Christopher Pinchbeck (d. 1732). Finished with gilding, it was much used in the 18th cent. for watch-cases, étuis, etc. and had the advantage that when the gilding was worn, the metal did not show a different colour.

Pinchbeck, Christopher Snr. and Jnr.: London clockmakers, the father being active between 1695 and 1732 and the son between 1735 and 1783.

Pineapple cups: standing covered cups in the shape of stylized pine-

apples, were distinctive products of Germany (called *ananaspokal*), where they were made in the 16th and 17th cent. Some stand as much as 30 inches in height.

"Pineapple" ware: see "Cauliflower" ware.

Pin-hinge: method of hinging, as found on 13th cent. chests, the lid being pinned through the rear stiles (q.v.) and pendent side-rails of the lid.

Pin locks: these were usually in oak, the flat bolt passing completely through the locks, one end expanded to engage in the jamb socket, the other shaped to form a handle. Three recesses were sunk into the top edge into which loose pins fell from above when the key was removed, thus holding the pin immovable. Pin locks were opened by inserting a wooden key into an aperture immediately above the bolt handle, and lifting it slightly. Projections on its upper surface raised the locking pins so that the bolt might be withdrawn from its socket.

Pinprick picture: see under Transparencies.

Pinx.: short for pinxit or pinxerunt. Means painted by. Found after the artist's name.

Pinxton porcelain: a small porcelain factory was established at Pinxton about 1796 by William Billingsley and John Coke. Billingsley left the concern in 1801 and his partner Coke carried on the works until they were sold to a landscape painter named John Cutts in 1804. The factory is believed to have been closed about 1812. Marks:

Billingsley himself decorated some of the wares. He brought to Pinxton from Derby a staff of workmen, and the soft-paste porcelain produced while the factory was under his man-

agement was made to his own formula: it is of that peculiarly translucent quality characteristic of Swansea and Nantgarw. Simple shapes were decorated in the Derby manner, not, however, making use of the raised flowers and leaves characteristic of Derby. The best known designs from Pinxton are those using only a small sprig – a cornflower or forget-me-not – on a white ground. Plates and dishes were most often edged with gold, or with a dark red or blue.

Landscapes washed with a yellow-green colour are fairly common. Ground colours are exceedingly rare on most flower decorated pieces, but occasionally a canary-yellow is seen.

Billingsley left the factory, taking his recipes for soft-paste porcelains with him; and there-after a much coarser and more opaque type of ware was made, not unlike Derby of a poor quality.

Pipe-clay: a fine white clay used in the manufacture of tobacco-pipes. According to Dr Pococke, pipe-clay was imported to Staffordshire from Poole, Dorset, but earlier local white firing clays were used by the Newcastle-under-Lyme pipe-makers.

Pipe-kiln: a tubular wrought-iron frame with a handle at the top and feet at each end. Clay "churchwarden" pipes were placed in the kiln in order to clean them when they had become foul, and the pipe-kiln and its contents were then put into an oven. It is said that in country districts the local baker performed this task.

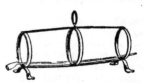

Pipe-rack: a stand for clay pipes. Of the various wooden kinds in use in the 18th cent. one can distinguish (a) the stand of candlestick form with a tiny circular tray on the stem, pierced with holes for holding the pipes, and (b) the wall rack, either an open frame with notched sides so that the pipes could lie across or a board with shelves from which the pipes hung down. In addition to these, metal pipe-kilns were widely used from the 17th cent. – iron frames on which the pipes rested, deriving their name from the fact that they could be baked in an oven to clean the pipes.

Pipe-tray: a long and narrow wooden tray with partitions for "churchwarden" pipes, in use throughout the Georgian period.

Pipkin: small metal earthenware vessel, like a saucepan with spout and turned wooden handle, for warming brandy.

Piqué: tortoiseshell inlaid or overlaid with cut sheet or pinhead in gold or silver. Boxes of all descriptions, fans, bodkin-cases, games counters, étuis, shuttles and many such small articles of tortoiseshell are found, decorated with gold or silver piqué. The gold points, or clous d'or, as they are called, are known as piqué point, and the inlaid strips piqué posé. Tiny points tracing the design are described as foules point d'or.

Piraube, Bertrand: one of the foremost gunmakers at the Court of Louis XIV. He was granted a *logement* in the Galerie du Louvre in 1670 and produced some of the finest presentation firearms for the French king.

Pirlie-pig: earthenware money-box. "Pig" is a North Country word for an earthen jar: "pirlie" is a diminutive indicating something of slight value.

"Pisan" armour: a misleading modern term for a type of late 16th-cent. armour, apparently produced chiefly in Milan and Brescia. Its chief characteristic consists of bands of coarsely etched decoration of confused design.

Pistole: Spanish gold coin, a double escudo (q.v.), introduced by Philip II. Type and standard copied in most West European states.

"Pistol" handle: the characteristic 18th cent. knife handle was of pistol

shape. Porcelain or stoneware were fashionable materials but silver remained usual for all except the cheaper grades made of horn or wood.

Pl. or **plts.:** plates.

Planetarium: a representation of the chief celestial bodies, sun, moon, earth and planets, which, when put into action, usually by turning a handle (although some are driven by clocks), shows the relative motion of these bodies. More usually called "Orreries" after Richard Boyle, 4th Earl of Orrery, in the mistaken belief that the first of these was made for him. The first was made by Tompion and Graham for Prince Eugene in about 1705.

Planishing: giving a smooth surface to a sheet of metal by hammering with an oval-faced punch, originally called a planishing teast.

"Planter" jug: see Sailor jug.

Plaquettes: plaquettes are found cast in lead and silver as well as in bronze, and were used to decorate household utensils and furniture from the 15th cent. onwards. They have also been collected for their own sakes by connoisseurs since the 16th cent., and formed part of collectors' cabinets, together with medals, intaglios and cameos. It is not always easy to distinguish between medals and plaquettes, but basically the medal has an obverse and a reverse and is circular, whereas the plaquette is one-sided and square, oblong or oval. More precisely, the medal is commemorative or historical in character, bearing on its obverse the portrait of a notable personage, usually surrounded by an inscription, while plaquettes are purely decorative in intention, with mythological, historical or religious subjects depicted. Plaquettes belong to the category of reproducible objects, and one may almost speak of different "states", as in the case of prints. In each reproduction it tends to lose some of its definition, and poorer, often modern, copies show little of the sharpness and individual chasing that characterize the first few to leave the artist's workshop. Plaquettes are more closely connected with painting than with sculpture, and their composition can be related to the various Renaissance schools of painting – and especially to the engravings which gained in popularity during the 16th cent. They were mostly issued from the schools of bronze casters, beginning with Donatello's in the 15th cent.

Plaquettes of religious subjects were made north of the Alps from the 15th cent. onwards, and in the early 16th cent., under Italian influence, secular subjects began to be produced in southern Germany, especially Nuremberg, in the Vischer school and by Peter Flötner, who is not known to have worked in the round at all. Plaquettes never attained the popularity in the Netherlands and in France which they enjoyed in Italy and Germany.

Plaster silhouette: silhouette (q.v.) painted on slabs of plaster, often with beer as a medium. Plaster was at one time a common background, its snowy depth giving the greatest possible contrast and sharpness to the black of the shade or silhouette. Probably the greatest master of this type of silhouette was John Miers (1758–1821).

Plate: the generic term for wrought silver or gold. Later applied by transference to the imitative wares of Sheffield and to electroplate.

Plateau: a flat plinth or stand for a centrepiece, usually of silver, with mirror centre. Principally of early 19th cent. date. Large examples are sometimes many feet in length and consist of numerous sections in order to run the full length of a dining table.

Plate lock: lock in which the working parts are exposed and riveted to a heavy hatchet-shaped plate of wrought iron fixed flat against the door. The iron bolt worked in slides and engaged in a striking plate fitted to the door jamb. The visible working parts might display some decoration. By utilizing only the minimum number of parts, at a time when iron and steel were highly expensive, plate locks were made at comparatively low cost. Antique plate locks are of iron, made close-textured by hammering: the Victorian type have cast or rolled iron plates.

Plate mark: the name given to the indentation made by the edges of the plate on a print. This mark forms the frame of an etching or line-engraving (qq.v.) but is rarely visible on woodcuts or lithographs (qq.v.). Impressions of etchings or engravings cut within the plate mark are said to be clipped and are of considerably less value than those on which the mark is to be seen.

Plate money: large flat squares of copper with mark of value in each corner and centre, issued in Sweden in the 17th and 18th cent.

Plate-pail: a mahogany container with handle for carrying plates from kitchen to dining-room, often a long journey, in large houses in the 18th cent.; of various shapes, generally circular with one section left open for ease of access.

Plate-warmer: this stood before the fire in kitchen, living-room, or dining-room, to heat the plates preparatory to the serving of a meal. Several types of plate-warmer have been recorded; all date from the 18th and 19th cent., and the surviving examples are not numerous. One variety is in the form of a wrought-iron revolving stand on a tripod base with upright bars to hold the plates in position. Another kind is similar to a Dutch-oven (q.v.), and has a handle so that the whole apparatus, complete with warmed plates, might be brought from the fireside to the table. A third type is the cat: an ingenious arrangement of three turned wood or metal rods, arranged cross-wise to form a double-ended tripod that could stand either way up.

Plinth: architecturally, the square base of a column. Also the base or foundation supporting a piece of sculpture, a porcelain figure, a piece of cabinet furniture, etc.

Plique à jour enamel: see Enamel.

Plymouth earthenware: coarse earthenware (brown and yellow) was manufactured here in the 18th cent., but gave way about 1810 to the production of painted or printed cream colour. In 1815 three factories were operating in Plymouth.

The Plymouth Pottery Company founded by William Alsop made common blue transfer-printed white earthenware.

Jewitt gaves its mark as "P. P. Coy. L, Stone China" with the addition of the Royal Arms.

Plymouth porcelain: this, the first English factory to make hard-paste porcelain (q.v.) was established in 1768 by William Cookworthy, who in that year patented his formula for the manufacture of hard-paste. He was aided in the founding of the works in Coxside, Plymouth, by a company of Quakers: in 1770 the factory was

moved to Bristol, and in 1773 the patent rights were sold to Champion who assumed control of the business. The factory was known as the Bristol China Manufactory. In 1775, in the face of intense opposition from potters in Staffordshire under Wedgwood's leadership, Champion obtained a modified renewal of the patent, but crippled financially was compelled to sell out to a company of potters in Staffordshire in 1781.

Marks: A number of different marks were used, and some of these were certainly employed after the factory had been moved to Bristol.

$$2\!\!\!\!\!4$$

Tablewares, figures and statuettes, vases and other ornamental pieces were made at Plymouth. Early porcelain was often decorated in Oriental styles in underglaze blue. Applied decoration in relief was used for shell and rock-work pieces such as salt-cellars, small dishes etc., these proving very popular. Sets of the "Seasons" and the well-known "Continents" are typical of the figures produced at Plymouth and later at Bristol.

Much of the early porcelain made at Plymouth is clearly of an experimental nature. Flaws, firecracks and discolourations are common, and a smoky tint affects nearly all the colours used. The glaze is rather thick and dull in appearance. In pieces decorated in underglaze blue the blue is of a greyish tone, often according pleasantly with the body of the ware which is semi-translucent and has a grey, faintly brown tint by transmitted light.

Figures made at an early date at Longton Hall clearly served as models for those made later at Plymouth. The resemblance is so marked that it has been suggested that Cookworthy acquired some of the actual moulds used there when the Longton Hall factory closed down.

Generally there is little originality in forms of decoration, and most designs are derivative, Derby and Worcester influences being apparent in many cases. Work in the Sèvres style by Soqui is of a higher quality, some of his birds and landscapes being very well executed. (See also Soqui.)

Figures have scrolled, hollow bases, picked out in dull crimson.

Transfer-printing is extremely rare and does not seem to have been used with any success.
(See also Cookworthy and Bristol.)

Point d'Angleterre à brides: (*Fr.*), pillow lace, variant of point d'Angleterre (q.v.), the meshed ground supplemented by *brides picotées* (see Brides and Picot).

Point d'Angleterre lace: this is not an English lace but is a pillow lace made in Brussels. English dealers so named it in 1662 when the import of Flemish lace into England and France was prohibited. It is the loveliest of Brussels laces, distinguished by the raised rib of plaited threads outlining leaves, etc., in a pattern which was loosely woven and edged elsewhere with rows of open stitches. The ground was worked after the pattern and was the Brussels hexagonal mesh, sometimes accompanied by the snowflake ground associated with Valenciennes lace (q.v.).

Point de France lace: a needlepoint lace. Some collectors limit the term to French raised bride-linked (see Brides) laces in contrast to grounded needlepoints made in the 18th cent. Designs were more flowing than in the raised Venetian needlepoints (q.v.). The term is more usually accepted in its original usage for the lace made at a number of towns in France where the craft was established in 1665 with state support, under Venetian tutelage, including especially Alençon.

Point de Paris lace: pillow lace believed to be the first made in France, but there is no proof that this had any association with a coarse type of lace now sold by that name.

Pointillé: a tool, or the impression of a tool, on a book-binding, leaving a dotted and not a solid outline, first introduced in France c. 1640.

Point lace: all French laces, including pillow laces (q.v.) so that it is impossi-ble to reserve the term for needle-points (q.v.).

Points: a point is any peculiarity in a book whose presence in or absence from a particular copy calls for note. It is most often used of bibliographical peculiarities: the evidence (or alleged evidence) for priority of issue, binding variants, misprints, variant advertisements, cancels, textual changes, etc.

Points d'esprit: (*Fr.*), a term used in lace-making to describe small square dots scattered over a mesh ground, as in Lille lace (q.v.).

Poissardes: (*Fr.*), long earrings fashionable about 1800 in France.

Pole-arms: a modern term connoting any type of cutting or thrusting weapon mounted on a long handle.

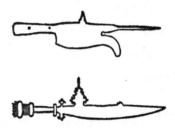

They can be divided into the following classes: (a) thrusting weapons, including the spear in all its forms; the houseman's lance, at first simply a long spear, but later fitted with a large metal guard for the hand (vamplate); the pike, a long spear, often measuring as much as 22 feet in the 16th and 17th cent., when it was used by the infantry to form a "hedge" against cavalry; the partizan, which had a long triangular head, usually with two pointed lugs at the base; (b) percussion weapons, consisting mainly of the various forms of club (including the horseman's mace), the axe and the hammer, the last two often having a sharply pointed fluke at the rear of the head; (c) weapons designed for cutting and for thrusting, including the halberd, which had a flat axe blade balanced by a fluke and a long, sharp spike above; the bill and the guisarme each with a cutting edge curving up to form a short hook, a fluke at the rear and a spike above; and the glaive, with a large cleaver- or scythe-shaped blade.

Pole-screen: see Fire-screen.

Pomander: from the French "pomme d'ambre". Small box usually of precious metal for sweet-smelling spices carried to ward off infections. Formed as segmented spheres, skulls, fruits or other fancies. Used up till the 17th cent. Partially superseded by vinaigrettes (q.v.).

Pompadours: the name given to fine fans dating to the reigns of the first two Georges (1714–60). These were radiant with burnished gilding, set with flashing jewels and glowed with paintings copied from or resembling the works of Boucher and Watteau. The cost of such a fan ranged between £12 and £15.

Pontil: see Punty.

Pontil mark: see Punty mark.

Pontipool: the industrial japanners of Birmingham and South Staffordshire found it convenient to market their japanned metal under the name of "Fancy Pontipool Ware", the spelling serving to distinguish it from the Allgood japanned ware. (See also Pontypool and Allgood family.)

Pontypool ware: the name given to japanned ware made by the Allgood family (q.v.) at Pontypool, Monmouth-shire. Their many agents sold Allgood productions as "Pontypool Japan" and their London agent, Edward Binyon, Fenchurch Street, London, advertised in 1783 that his was "The Original Warehouse for the Real Ponty-Pool Japann'd Ware". The terms "Ponty-pool" and Pontipool (q.v.) distinguish-ed japanning on metal from japanned wood and Clay's japanned paper ware dating from 1772. (See Papier-mâché.)

The craft of japanning, or lacquering was first practised in England during the reign of Charles II, when the in-creasing demand for Oriental lacquer stimulated efforts at imitation, at first on wood, then on metal. Japanners on

metal are recorded at Bilston in Staffordshire whence the trade spread to Wolverhampton. The Pontypool workshop was founded in 1730. (See also Japan work.)

Pope and Devil cup: reversible bell-shaped cup showing the Pope in his triple tiara when held one way up, and the Devil when reversed. Sometimes inscribed "When Pope absolves, the Devil smiles". Late 18th cent.

Poppy- (popey-) head: decorative finial of a bench- or desk-end, as in Medieval ecclesiastical woodwork. Plant and floral forms are numerous; human heads, figures, birds, beasts and other devices are found.

Porcelain: a word loosely applied in the 17th and 18th cent. to white wares with oriental designs attempting to simulate imported oriental porcelain, such as delftware, stoneware, etc. Imported Chinese red teapots were called red porcelain, a name which clung to Elers-type red teapots and other wares throughout the 18th cent.

The term has been used more narrowly and correctly since the 18th cent. to describe translucent wares made in emulation of Chinese and Continental porcelain, but only three factories certainly made true (that is' hard-paste) porcelain in England, namely Plymouth, Bristol and New Hall.

The fine porcelains of the 18th cent. were soft-paste, either glass, or bone, or soapstone.

The standard bone china, produced since the time of Spode, is a hybrid porcelain with heavy percentage of bone ash in the ingredients. (See Soft-paste and hard-paste porcelain.)

Porcelain transparencies: see Lith-ophane.

Porphyry ware: a red-stained parian ware (q.v.) said to resemble porphyry.

Porringer: two-handled bowl with or without cover for porridge, caudle, posset or other concoctions. Surviving examples date from the first half of the 17th cent. and last into the 19th. Shallow bowls with flat handles commonly called cupping- or bleeding-bowls (q.v.), were in fact small porringers.

Portable barometer: a type in which the cistern or siphon can be entirely enclosed, and in which the mercury can be plugged in the vertical tube.

Portland House: Wedgwood (q.v.) and Bentley's showroom in Greek Street (No. 12) was given this name. It was opened in June 1774, and the cream-ware service made for the Empress of Russia was placed on exhibition. In 1791 one of the best copies of the Portland vase (q.v.), after having been shown to Queen Charlotte, was p'aced on view there.

Portland vase: a cameo glass vase traditionally but erroneously stated to have contained the ashes of Alexander Severus and his mother, and to have come from his sepulchre at Monte del Grano; probably made at Alexandria c. 50 B.C. Before 1642 it passed into the possession of the Barberini family from whom it was purchased by Sir William Hamilton in 1770, who sold it to the Duchess of Portland. Lent to the British Museum in 1810 but smashed by an "inebriated neurotic" named Lloyd in 1845 and restored with the aid of Wedgwood's copy. Put up for sale at Christie's 1929 but withdrawn when the bidding reached £29,000. Purchased by the British Museum in 1946.
Josiah Wedgwood copied the Portland Vase 1786–90, his copy being pronounced accurate in effect and detail by Sir Joshua Reynolds P.R.A. The first edition comprised 29 specimens. William Webber was chiefly responsible for the modelling. There were several subsequent editions, the 1839 being notable because the nude figures are "decently" draped; the Bellows edition was issued for an American firm in 1909; an ordinary jasper Portland Vase has been issued from 1880 onwards. The finest 19th cent. edition is that undercut and polished by John Northwood of Stourbridge for Wedgwood's in 1877–80, limited to 15 copies, cipher signed N above the Wedgwood impress mark.

Portmanteaux: a term introduced about the mid-16th cent., applied to cases specifically for horse travel yet large enough for bulky clothing. In the 1620s, for instance, the Howard Accounts refer to a leather portmanteau priced 10s 1d, and in 1611 Cotgrave noted " a portmantue with chaine and locke". There are numerous references to portmanteau saddles, even to portmanteau horses, in the 17th and 18th cent. Thus the *London Gazette* referred to "a coloured leather Portmantle Saddle". Such a saddle, according to Randall Holme, had "a Cantle behind the seat to keep the Portmantle . . . off the Rider's back".

"Portobello" ware: pottery made at Tunstall, Staffordshire, c. 1830, in imitation of banded and "Pratt" type pottery made at Portobello in Scotland.

Portrait-miniature: a small scale portrait in oil or water-colour, usually on vellum or ivory.

Portuguese bulb: a simple, baluster turned chair leg in the form of an inverted pear, used on late 17th cent. chairs, when the Restoration fashion for more elaborately turned legs had abated.

Portuguese guitar: see under Mandolines.

Posset-pot: straight-sided or bell-shaped vessel with multiple loop handles and spouts, generally covered with a slanting or dome-shaped lid, and occasionally "crowned" with an elaborate knob and series of handles. Used for carrying or drinking posset, made in the 17th and 18th cent. in slipwares, delftware, stoneware, etc. A favourite inscription on Staffordshire slipware specimens was "The best is not too good for you". Two-handled bowls of silver are also known as posset-pots. Also called a spout-spot. (See also Porringer.)

Post horn: see Coach and post horns.

Posy ring: a ring with a motto engraved on the inside.

Pot: a term used in the 17th cent. apparently to designate any type of open helmet. Modern writers usually confine it to the large, wide-brimmed variety used by 17th cent. pikemen.

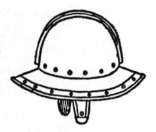

Potato ring: see Dish ring.

Pot belly measure: a Scottish pewter tavern measure with broad belly and narrowing neck.

Pot board: an open shelf or board forming the lower stage of a 17th cent. court or livery cupboard (qq.v.).

Pot-hook: (cottrall, jib-crook, hanger, tramelle, hake) a wrought-iron device that was in use from medieval times for suspending a pot over the fire. By means of a ratchet it could be adjusted for height. In Scotland the same means was attained

by using a chain and hook, known as a "jumping rope".

Potiche: large, broad-mouthed Chinese porcelain jar of "baluster" shape, with cover; favoured from Ming (q.v.) times.

Pot lace: see Antwerp lace.

Pottery: opaque fired earthenware.

Pottery moulds: the introduction of porous plaster-of-Paris moulds as a means of making pottery, made possible a wide variety of shapes of irregular form and decoration.

Some form of mould had been in use in Staffordshire for a long period, probably "formers" made of wood, fired clay (pitcher moulds) or alabaster. Metal moulds were used for fine sprig decorations.

The porous plaster mould was adopted c. 1745, and the process was to cut a model or block in alabaster (Aaron Wood was described as a "block-cutter") make impressions from it in clay, assemble them and fire them to form "pitcher" moulds from which working moulds in plaster could be run off as required. Later a model was made in clay, "blocked and cased" by the mould-maker from which working moulds were prepared.

Many old moulds exist, some dated and inscribed, thus affording valuable evidence of factory or individual style.

Pottle-pot: quart pot.

Poudre d'écaille: a composition of powdered tortoise-shell coloured to the required tint by a dye.

Pouncebox or **pot:** baluster or vase-shaped bottle for sprinkling powdered pumice (pounce) on writing-paper. Indistinguishable from a sandbox (q.v.).

Pouncing: producing a powdered effect on a metal surface.

Powder blue glaze: a mottled glaze used on Chinese porcelain of the K'ang Hsi (q.v.) period, when it was sometimes enriched with gilded designs (often since restored) or used as a surround for underglaze painting. A rich blue, granulated ground-colour was also used by the Worcester porcelain factory (q.v.). The effect was achieved by blowing powdered pigment onto the surface of the ware, prepared with a coating of oil.

Powder-flask: flask for carrying the black powder used for charging muzzle-loading guns. It was made in a variety of different shapes and was usually fitted with some kind of measuring device. A smaller flask was often carried for the finer powder used in priming. The more elaborate example was customarily made en suite with a firearm and was decorated with inlaid bone or silver, corresponding to the decoration on the gun. Powder flasks were also made of metal.

"Pratt" ware: earthenwares made at the end of the 18th and beginning of the 19th cent., decorated with a distinctive palette of high temperature colours, including a drab blue, yellow, ochre, dirty orange, dull green, brown, etc. Relief decorations are common. Figures also were decorated in this range of pigments. This type of ware is usually associated with Felix Pratt of Fenton, and the name "Pratt" is occasionally found on them, but it is unlikely that the earlier pieces were made by Felix Pratt, who was not born until 1780 and died in 1859. William Pratt (1753–99) and his wife Ellen Edwards (1760–1815) who succeeded him, may have been responsible for some of these wares which are, however, known to have been made by potters in other parts of England and Scotland over a long period of time.

Prayer rugs: oriental rugs, bearing as central feature the "Mihrab", a design derived from the traditional form of altar of the Mohammedan mosque.

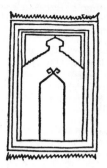

Preissler, Daniel: see under Schwarzlot decoration.

Prelims or **p.l.:** preliminary leaves of a book.

Première partie: (*Fr.*), see Boulle marquetry.

Presentation copy: when used without qualification, this may always be taken to refer to the copy of a book which was the gift of the author. But only a book spontaneously presented properly qualifies for the description; one merely signed in response to an owner's request is called an inscribed copy (q.v.).

The pre-eminent quality in any presentation copy will always be that of its association – the interest or importance of the recipient, his connection with the author or other such special recommendation. This will override most of the niceties distinguishable in the wording of the presentation inscription.

Présentoir: a serving knife with a thin broad blade, with the edges either parallel or widening slightly towards the point, which was either cut off square or slightly rounded. The présentoir first makes its appearance in the 15th cent.

Press books: a jargon term, but a useful one, covering the books produced by (a) private printing-presses, e.g. Strawberry Hill, Lee Priory,

Eragny, Gregynog; (b) concerns which, though not printing houses, call themselves "presses" because they specialize in fine book-production, e.g. Vale, Nonesuch; and sometimes (c) printers whose work is collected for its own sake, whether it was executed for a commercial publisher, e.g. Bulmer, Chiswick, Curwen, Bruce Rogers, or issued over their own imprint, e.g. Aldus, Estienne, Plantin, Baskerville.

Press cupboard: during the 16th cent. there were several kinds of cupboard. A press cupboard was entirely closed, with small cupboards in the upper stage and a large cupboard below. (See also Court cupboard.)

Pressed glass: glass pressed mechanically in moulds; molten glass is dropped into a patterned mould, a plunger is rammed into the mould, forcing the glass into all parts and impressing the pattern upon it. The plunger has a smooth surface so that the inside of the piece is smooth in contrast to blown moulded glass. The method originated in the United States in about 1827 and

is sometimes wrongly known in America as "Sandwich glass" from the famous factory at Sandwich, Massachusetts where it was first produced on a large scale. By 1829, many American glasshouses were producing pressed glass which also formed an important part of English production of the second quarter of the cent.

Pricket candlestick: the earliest form of candlestick in which the candle was stuck on a metal spike, usually iron, projecting from the wax-pan.

The socket type, in which the candle was held in a cup or socket, did not become usual until the 14th cent., though it was certainly known much earlier.

Pricking: delicate needle-point engraving used principally for decorating silver with armorials and inscriptions in 16th to 17th cent. and also to a limited extent with naturalistic decoration on small scale.

Prie Dieu: (*Fr.*), a chair with a tall back and low seat intended for prayer.

Priming: basic preparation of a canvas before a picture is painted.

"Prince Hal" jug: a variety of toby jug (q.v.), being one of Ralph Wood's later models, dating from c. 1775.

Princes' metal: a brass alloy evolved in the 1670s and tinged to the colour of gold. The metal was heated until slightly red and laid to pickle in a diluted spirit of vitriol. After removing dirt and scale by washing, it was immersed for a moment in *aquafortis*, dried, and burnished with a bloodstone.

Printer's blanks: see Blank leaves.

Printer's imprint: see Imprint.

Printer's waste: see Waste.

Printies: circular or oval concavities cut into glass vessels to form a decorative motif. Sometimes they cover the entire surface of the vessel, or two or three rows encircle the body of a decanter, jug, rummer (q.v.) or bowl.

Print rooms: rooms decorated by means of pasting prints on to the wallpaper, framed in paper. This type of mural decoration became fashionable in the Regency and the Duke of Wellington made his own print room at Stratfield Saye.

Prints: a print is an individual impression taken from any form of plate or block which has been worked on either by hand or by mechanical means or by a combination, so that the final impression will produce some design. Mr Basil Gray, in *The English Print* (Faber, 1937), says: "The art of the print may be justly defined as the art of multiplying a design in such a way that each impression is, at least approximately, as good as any other".

Prismatic cutting: a method of cutting glass vessels in deep relief in a pattern of horizontal prisms adapted to curved surfaces. Popular as a means of decorative cutting in the first half of the 19th cent. and sometimes known as step cutting.

Priv. pr.: privately printed.

"Privy Council" ware: see Shu fu.

Prodd: see under Cross-bow.

Profile silhouette: a silhouette portrait in which features other than the outline are drawn, sometimes in great detail. Silhouettes in which features and hair are drawn in gold paint on a black ground come into this category. Some profiles are merely miniatures painted in sharp outline. Edward Foster of Derby (1761–1865) painted many portraits of this type.

Proof before letters: an impression of a print taken before title, publisher's line, etc., have been added.

Provenance: the ownership pedigree of an object.

Prunts: applied blobs of glass tooled or moulded into various forms and

applied to the stem or bowl of a drinking vessel.

Pseud.: pseudonym; an assumed name, as Mark Twain or O. Henry.

Pu: early Chinese bronze coin of the type imitating, in miniature, original objects of barter such as knives and spades. In circulation in last half of the first millenium B.C.

Publisher's binding: a term used to differentiate the binding of a book as it was issued by the publishers, whether in boards, cloth or leather, from a binding commissioned later by the purchaser or any other binding put on after publication.

Many elaborate leather bindings were issued by the publishers on fine books during the Victorian period. Examples are McIan, *Clans of the Scottish Highlands*, 2 vols. (1845–47); Wyatt, *Industrial Arts of the Nineteenth Century at the Great Exhibition*, 2 vols. (1853); Waring, *Art Treasures of the United Kingdom* (1858); Heath, *Beauties of the Opera and Ballet* (1841).

Publisher's cloth: the use of cloth for edition-binding of books by the publisher dates from about 1823. For the collector this meant the establishment of a uniform original binding functionally inseparable from the book within it and readily identifiable, if not on sight at least by comparison with other copies of the same edition. And it has become an established convention that no book issued in publisher's cloth should be admitted to the fastidious collector's library in any other dress. Exception would be made for presentation or association copies (q.v.), and (by any except fanatics) for books so rare that even a rebound copy may present the only chance of a lifetime. But the exceptions are few.

Publisher's imprint: see Imprint.

Pulse watch: see Stop watch.

Punch: a die for striking the maker's touch or other identification or decorative designs into metal.

Punch-bowl: large circular bowl made in silver, tin-enamelled earthenware, salt-glazed stoneware or porcelain, ranging in size from half-pint to twelve quarts, used for serving punch. Silver examples are with or without drop-ring handles and were used contemporaneously with Monteiths (q.v.) from the 17th cent. onwards.

Punched work: elementary form of embossing metal, struck with blunt punches grouped to form primitive floral designs, principally used on mid-17th cent. silver.

Punch kettle: a vessel like a gigantic tea-pot used c. 1750 for blending, carrying and serving hot punch.

Punch-marked coins: flat, square silver coins of India of the last few centuries B.C. Surfaces covered with small punch marks of natural objects, animals and symbols, probably the marks of merchants and states guaranteeing the pieces.

Punto in aria embroidery: Italian term meaning stitch in the air, and used to describe a very early form of lace, the cutwork (q.v.) fabric reduced to a strip supporting the needlepoint (q.v.) work. The transformation was complete when the line of fabric was replaced by threads laid over the pattern drawn on parchment. The earliest work consisted of simple little vandykes worked in buttonhole stitch.

Punty or **pontil:** a long iron rod attached to one end of blown glass during the finishing processes after removal from the blowpipe.

Punty mark or **pontil mark:** a scar left on blown glass when the punty (q.v.) is broken off. Generally found on the base of a glass. From about 1750 these marks were usually ground and polished into a smooth depression and this was invariably the case on fine glass from about 1780.

Puritan furniture: a term sometimes used in America to describe the simple, functional, 17th cent. New England furniture of the early Puritans (see Pilgrim furniture).

Puritan spoon: a mid-17th cent. spoon with flat stem, straight top edge and nearly oval bowl, the earliest form of English flat-stemmed spoon.

Purled ornament: all-over diaper moulding with small round or oval compartments found on glass vessels.

Puzzle fans: evolved in the mid-18th cent. by John Cock, London. Instead of two subjects back and front, four pictures were displayed according to the way in which the fan was manipulated. These fans had more blades than was usual as they needed to be strung in such a way that only half of each was visible at one time.

Puzzle jug: a pitcher or jug made in earthenware, stoneware or delftware usually with a capacious globular body and pierced, cylindrical neck offering a challenge to the uninitiated drinker. "From Mother Earth I take my birth/ Am made a joke for man;/ And am here filled with good cheer/ Come taste it if you can", or "Here gentlemen come try your skill/ I'll hold a wager if you will;/ That you drink not this liquor all/ Without you spill or let some fall". The rim of the neck

usually consisted of a hollow tube connected with the inside by the hollow tubular handle, and this rim tube generally issued into a number of spouts or apertures, frequently three but sometimes five or even seven. Almost invariably there was a hidden hole underneath the top of the handle. To meet the challenge the drinker had to block all the openings excepting the one from which he intended to imbibe the contents, and drain the jug by suction. Commonly made in the 17th and 18th cent., particularly at Liverpool. Prof. Garner points out that the perforations and proportion of neck to body in delftware offers a clue to origin; those made at Liverpool generally being pierced with 4 hearts and ellipses arranged circularly; those of Bristol with intersecting circles; and those of Lambeth with narrow necks.

Pyx: a small vessel, usually a cylindrical silver box, in which the sacrament is carried to the sick. They were frequently richly decorated. Many Medieval examples survive of Limoges enamel. Only one English silver pyx of medieval date is known to exist: the 14th cent. example in the Victoria and Albert Museum.

Quadrans: a Roman coin; quarter of the as (q.v.). In the Republican aes grave types are head of Hercules on obverse and prow on reverse with mark of value • • • . The quadrans is found only occasionally as a small bronze coin in the early Empire.

Quadrigatus: the commonest of the Roman Republican silver didrachms (q.v.) with types, young Janus head on obverse and, on reverse, Jupiter in a four-horse chariot.

Quaich: Scottish drinking-bowl, originally of wood in stave formation, later silver-mounted and then entirely of silver and also of pewter. Shallow circular form on rim foot with two or three flat handles or lugs (q.v.). Found from early 17th cent. onwards.

Quail patterns: sometimes called partridge patterns. A pattern used for the decoration of porcelain on the Continent and in England based on the example of Japanese Kakiemon (q.v.) porcelain, incorporating, with foliage and rocks, a pair of quails. In England, used on Bow, Chelsea and Worcester porcelain, on Delftware of the 18th cent. and on earthenware of the 20th cent., where it has been adapted as an underglaze transferprint in blue.

Quare, Daniel: London clockmaker active between 1674 and 1724.

Quarter bound book: see under Half bound book.

Quarter clock: a clock striking at the quarters as well as at the hour.

4to (quarto): see Book sizes.

Quatrecouleurs: the art of combining various colours of carved gold in a decorative scheme. The colour of gold is determined by the nature of the alloy. If copper is added to the pure gold, the result will be a red gold, if silver is added a green gold is obtained, and so on. Many subtle effects are possible as the balance of the alloy is varied.

Quatrefoil knop: a knop or protuberance on the stem of a drinking glass or other glass vessel of short form, pressed into four wings by vertical depressions, the metal being drawn out with pincers.

Queen Anne style: during the reign of Queen Anne (1702–14) and until the 1720s English taste in the decorative arts favoured simplicity of form and ornament. Attention was given to line and proportion. Furniture relied for its beauty on effective use of figured walnut veneers with little reliance on wood carving, while silverware also displayed simple glowing surfaces in place of the heavy embossing so recently in favour. Gently curving forms and restrained elegance characterise the style of the period.

Queen's pattern: a counterchanging pattern consisting of alternate radiating whirling bands of red-on-white and white-on-blue ornament with gilded embellishments used at the Worcester porcelain factory from c. 1770 onwards, and continued into the Flight and Barr, and Chamberlain periods.

Also known as the "Catherine wheel", "Whorl", or "Spiral" pattern.

Queen's pattern spoons: see under Table-services.

Queen's ware: the name given by Josiah Wedgwood (q.v.) to his perfected cream-coloured earthenware, after he had obtained for it the royal patronage and title "Potter to the Queen"; subsequently adopted for this staple product of the earthenware industry throughout Staffordshire.

Quilling: an American term for a ribbon of glass applied decoratively to glassware and pinched into pleats; also called "pinched trailing".

Quillon dagger: a type of dagger with a simple cross-guard.

Quillons: the cross-guard of a sword or dagger.

Quillwork or paper filigree: this is made of paper strips about an eighth of an inch wide, fluted, twisted, or rolled into tight little scrolls which are then arranged in designs closely resembling mosaic work. Coloured paper is used, or white may be painted or gilded at the edge; when gilding is used the effect is that of gold filigree; sometimes motifs are outlined in silver wire, and the work resembles silver filigree. The flutes and scrolls are pasted by one edge to a background of paper, silk or wood, and are combined with other substances to form elaborate designs.

Quilts: coverlets with a layer of wool, flock, or down between two pieces of material with lines of stitching, usually back-stitch passing through the three layers. In England quilting is a traditional craft, and it reached the height of popularity and excellence in the 17th and 18th cent. During the first half of the 17th cent. quilted doublets and breeches were worn, and during the 18th cent. quilted satin petticoats were fashionable. Quilted bed coverlets were made in great numbers from the late 17th cent. onwards. In addition to the pattern formed by the quilting stitch, which was sometimes purely geometrical, sometimes of elaborate floral arabesques, the quilts were often further ornamented by embroidery in coloured silks. In the late 17th and early 18th cent. coverlets and pillow-cases were often quilted entirely in yellow silk. Others had a small quilted diaper background with floral or "chinoiserie" motifs embroidered in coloured silks.

Another type is "corded" quilting (often known as Italian quilting, although there is no evidence to support an Italian origin). This type of quilting, employed for decorative rather than utilitarian purposes, was extremely popular in England during the 18th cent. Two layers of material, usually fine white linen, were sewn together in an elaborate design, often of scrolled arabesques (q.v.), worked by means of two parallel rows of stitching about a quarter of an inch apart. A cord was then inserted between the two rows of stitching through small holes cut in the back of the material. Quilting was also practised in most European countries, notably Sicily and Portugal, and in Oriental countries, particularly India and Persia. (See also Patchwork quilts.)

Quinarius: a Roman coin; the half-denarius (q.v.), a rare issue, both in the Republic and Empire. Types usually identical with the denarius. Early quinarii have mark of value V.

Quizzing fans: an amusing notion dating from the mid-18th cent. These fans were provided with peep-holes covered with transparent material: when open the fan showed a series of perforations around its upper border. Behind such a fan a woman could present a modest pose, yet miss nothing of the risqué plays of the time. In late examples a quizzing glass was fitted above the pivot.

Rabbet: a groove cut lengthwise in a piece of wood into which the edge of a board can fit. In furniture made by a joiner (q.v.), the bottom boards of drawers were nailed to the sides whereas cabinet-makers (q.v.) used the method of fitting bottom boards into a rabbet cut into the drawer sides.

Rack and snail striking: a system of clock striking invented in 1676 by Edward Barlow which, except for turret clocks, has practically superseded the locking plate in this country. This type of striking made repeating clocks possible.

Rail: the horizontal section of a framework holding a panel. Joined furniture of the 16th and 17th cent. was constructed on the panel system, involving the use of rails as horizontal members and stiles as vertical members of the framework. (See also Panelled construction.)

Raised work: see Stump work.

Raising: the normal technique of forming a hollow vessel from sheet silver by successive rows of hammering on a wood block, stretching and curving the metal. The silver, hardened by the hammering, is annealed (q.v.) or softened by repeatedly being raised to red-hot heat as required.

Ramponneau: (*Fr.*), *Tabatière à la ramponneau* indicates a box designed in the form of a barrel.

Ramsey, David: an Edinburgh and London clockmaker and the first Master of the Clock Makers' Company. Active between 1590 and 1655.

Ram's head motif: a decorative form representing a ram's head mask, of Classical derivation and much used by Robert Adam (q.v.), both as an architectural motif and in his designs for furniture and metalwork. With the

general adoption of forms and motifs inspired by the Classical revival, the ram's head mask was used on silverware, porcelain etc.

Randolph, Benjamin: an American cabinet-maker who shares with Thomas Affleck (q.v.) the reputation of being the leading exponent of the Philadelphia Chippendale school (fl. 1762, d. 1792). He owned considerable property and is believed to have had the largest cabinet-making shop in Philadelphia. Of him Nagel says: "No other American cabinet-maker mastered the true spirit of the rococo more completely or came closer to the English tradition than Randolph."

Rapier: a sword with a long, straight blade, introduced in the 16th cent. It was at first designed for thrusting and cutting, but as the science of fencing developed, emphasis was laid increasingly on the former. It was primarily a civilian weapon and in the 16th and 17th cent. was usually used in conjunction with a dagger or a cloak held in the left hand.

Rappen: small Swiss copper coin of late 18th and early 19th cent. with types of shield in wreath and value and date.

Rasp: a grater. Ivory tobacco-rasps are quite common.

Ratafia glass: a cordial glass of flute form, dating from the second half of the 18th cent.

Rat-tail spoon: the principal form of the late 17th to early 18th cent. spoon, distinguished by a tapering rib running down the back of the bowl.

Rauenstein porcelain: see under Limbach porcelain.

Ravenet, Simon François: (1706–74), French engraver who was a pupil of Jacques-Philippe le Bas. From le Bas he learned the technique of first etching his subject and then afterwards deepening the lines with a graver. This was precisely what was required for perfecting the method of decorating enamels by means of transfer printing invented by John Brooks at the enamel factory at York House, Battersea (q.v.). Ravenet came to London before 1750 and at once attracted notice. Over forty plates, besides smaller pieces representing cupids, decorative borders, etc. used on Battersea enamels, can be ascribed to Ravenet on the evidence of a peculiarly flowing line and graceful rendering of drapery. The subjects include royal portraits and others of famous contemporary figures, Classical and mythological subjects.

Raven, Samuel: a Birmingham decorator of japanned table snuff-box lids, cigar cases, and card cases from about 1818 until the early 1840s. His pictures were copied from well-known engravings such as *The Blind Fiddler, Rent Day, The Cut Finger, Village Politicians* by Wilkie; *The Young Bird* by Burnet and *Beeswing* by Kidd were favourites. Harlow's *The Proposal* and *Congratulations* were repeated times without number. (See also Papier-mâché.)

Ravenscroft, George: (1618–81), a glass-maker employed in 1673 by the Glass-Sellers' Company to start researches into an improved means of making glass. It appears that Ravenscroft used ground silica from English flints, replacing the imported Venetian pebbles, and alkali in the form of potash. Early experiments indicated that too great a quantity of potash was included, as the vessels made revealed a fine network of cracks, known as "crisselling" (q.v.). As a remedy, a proportion of oxide of lead replaced the excessive admixture of alkali. The new material came to be known as "glass-of-lead" or "flint glass". It was heavier and more brilliant in light-dispersing qualities than the thin Venetian crystal which had hitherto been made in England or imported from Venice and made possible decoration by means of cutting and engraving which became popular in the 18th cent. Ravenscroft was granted a patent for his invention in 1673 and became official glass-maker to the Glass-Sellers' Company in the following year, there being two glasshouses, one at Henley-on-Thames, intended for experiment, and the other in the Savoy in London. The defect causing crisselling had been remedied by 1676, when Ravenscroft arranged with the Company that his glasses should bear as his seal a raven's head.

Raven's head seal: see Ravenscroft, George.

Real: silver coin of gros (q.v.) class, issued in Spain from 14th cent. onward, with types the crowned royal initial and arms of Castille and Leon.

Re-backed binding: this means that the binding of a book has been given a new backstrip or spine. It is mostly used of leather-bound or boarded or wrappered books, for this often necessary but usually unsightly form of repair is seldom resorted to for publisher's cloth. Unless otherwise stated, it is assumed that the new back is of similar material to the old.

Re-cased book: a book which, being shaken or loose, has been taken out of its covers and resettled in them more firmly.

Recessed carving: a type of carving on furniture much used by provincial joiners (q.v.) in the 17th cent. in which the background is removed, leaving the pattern raised and exposed. The background was usually stippled or punched to give it an even surface and to create a contrast with the plain pattern. This method of decoration is also known as sunk carving.

Recoil escapement: see Anchor escapement.

Recto: the front, or obverse, side of the leaf; i.e. the right-hand page of an open book. Its complement is the verso (q.v.).

Red anchor mark: see Chelsea porcelain.

Red china: fine red stoneware of the type introduced into Staffordshire by Elers (q.v.), made from about 1693 until end of 18th cent. A similar body was made by Josiah Wedgwood which he called Rosso Antico, but Wedgwood was aware that it differed little from wares then in current production in Staffordshire. He wrote to Bentley, 3 March 1776, "I am afraid we shall never be able to make the Rosso Antico otherwise than to put you in mind of a red-Pot-Teapot".

Reed-and-tie moulding: an ornament composed of contiguous parallel convex mouldings bound together by straps simulating ribbons. (See also Reeding and Fluting.)

Reeding: similar to fluting (q.v.) but with the ornament in relief. A decorative motif used by furniture makers and silversmiths as well as architects, derived from the classical column similarly fluted or reeded.

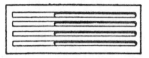

Reed top writing-box: whereas a large desk might open with a solid cylinder lid, a writing-box might have the space-saving opening associated with tambour tables. In this the rounded top could be pushed out of sight inside the box, being constructed of lengths of thin moulded beading glued side by side on to a back of strong canvas, pliable enough to move in curved runners.

Refectory table: popular modern term for a long table of the type in use in the second half of the 16th cent. until the Restoration.

Reform flasks: brown salt-glazed stoneware spirit flasks made by

DANIEL O'CONNELL

Doulton (Lambeth), Stephen Green (Lambeth), Oldfield (Chesterfield),

and Joseph Thompson (Wooden Box Pottery, Hartshorne), in the form of prominent politicians and royalty, at the time of the Reform Bill, 1832. Personalities portrayed included William IV, Queen Adelaide, Lord Grey, O'Connell, Brougham, Richard Cobden, and Lord John Russell.

Regard ring: 19th cent. ring set with jewels of varying types, whose initial letters spell a word.

Regence: (*Fr.*), Philippe d'Orleans was Regent during the minority of Louis XV from 1715 to 1723. It was during this period that the Regence style, a transitional phase between baroque and rococo, was developed.

"Regent china": a very translucent china body, resembling that of Nantgarw, but harder, introduced in 1811 for occasional use during the Regency at Chamberlain's Worcester factory and marked specially:

Chamberlains
Regent China
Worcester
E 155
New Bond Street
London

Reggivaso: (*Ital.*), a vase stand, a purely decorative piece of furniture which enjoyed wide-spread popularity in the 18th cent. Reggivasi were made in the form of putti, satyrs, chained negro slaves or blackamoor page-boys and are often minor works of sculpture of great charm. A superb example by Andrea Brustolon in the Palazzo Rezzonico at Venice is made in the form of a group of river gods holding trays for the porcelain vases.

Registry mark: appearing on English earthenwares in two cycles, 1842–67 and 1868–83. A lozenge with code-letters and numerals assigned by the "Registration of Designs" Office.

Regulator: a high-grade long-case clock with compensation pendulum (q.v.) and possibly other refinements, such as roller bearings and jewelling. The hour is frequently read off a disc revolving behind the dial proper, and showing through an aperture.

Re-jointed book: when the outside joints of a book have deteriorated through the stages of *rubbed, tender* and *weak*, to being more than merely "slightly" defective, its owner may decide to have it re-jointed. If the damage has not gone too far and if the binder is skilful, this can be done so neatly as to be hardly perceptible on the shelf – and occasionally even in the hand.

Relief: a design or ornamentation is said to be in relief when it is raised above the surface of the surrounding ground.

Relief decoration on porcelain or pottery: there are various ways of producing relief decoration: by free-hand modelling, free-incising or piercing or, more frequently, by pressing soft clay in plaster moulds; also by impressing the surface of soft clay objects with cut metal stamps. Occasionally separately moulded low reliefs are applied to the surface.

Reliquary: the vessel in which a relic or relics of the saints are kept. Reliquaries have been made in a great variety of patterns, offering the maximum scope for the invention of the goldsmith. Early examples were generally of architectural design, like the reliquary of Pepin d'Acquitain in the treasury of Ste Foy at Conques, which dates from the 9th cent. and, with its high roof and round-headed niches, resembles a shrine. Some made in the Rhineland in the 12th cent. (one is in the Victoria and Albert Museum and another at the Schlossmuseum, Berlin) were made as model romanesque churches. Church-shaped reliquaries followed, a little tardily, the changes in architectural taste, and the shrine of St Elizabeth at Marburg (1236–39) is decorated with a mixture of romanesque and early Gothic ornaments. Reliquaries in the form of limbs and busts were also made as early as the 11th cent., and held their popularity for some five hundred years. They were frequently enriched with precious stones, which have in some instances (the bust of St Agatha at Catania) been so richly augmented by the offerings of the pious that the original work is now practically obscured.

Re-margined: when one or more of the three outer margins of the leaf of a book has been restored, it is said to be re-margined. If it is the inner margin only, the proper term is extended. If all four margins have had to be renewed, the leaf is described as inlaid. (See also Inlaid book-binding.)

Remarque proof: a print on which the engraver or etcher has added a little sketch or token in the margin as a sign of state (q.v.). This practice of marking prints was fashionable in the late 19th cent.

Remboîtage: the transference of a book from one binding to another or the result of this nefarious practice.

Renaissance: a revival in Europe of Classical ideals in literature, painting and architecture, which marked the end of the Middle Ages and the abandon of Gothic forms. The movement began in Italy in the 15th cent., spreading quickly throughout Western Europe and making itself felt in England by the early 16th cent.

Rent table: see Capstan table.

Repairer: (or *bossierer*), workman responsible for assembling the porcelain clay impressions of figures from moulds, attaching heads, limbs, etc., and finishing the figure which was usually modelled by another artist. Incised and impressed marks on figures and groups often refer to these repairers.

Repeat design: a characteristic of most wallpaper designs which enables these to be repeated when the sheets or lengths are placed in juxtaposition. English makers well understood this principle as early as the 16th cent., and the idea goes back probably farther than this in textile production.

Repeater: a clock or watch on which the hours, and generally also the quarters, and in rare cases the five minutes and even the minute, can be made to strike at will by the pulling of a cord, the pressing of a knob, etc. Repeating clocks were common until the end of the first quarter of the 19th cent.

Repoussé: (*Fr.*), a term much used in 19th cent. auction sale catalogues to describe embossed work. It refers to the technique of producing a design in relief on a ductile material, such as silver, copper or iron, by hammering the reverse side. A block of pitch was used to support the metal while it was being hammered.

Réseau: (*Fr.*), see Ground.

Re-set: (1) when a leaf or leaves, or a whole section of a book, has come loose from the binding and has been stuck back again, usually with paste or glue, it is said to be re-set; (2) if the whole book is so shaken and loose as to be unserviceable, it may be re-set in its binding (see also Re-cased book); (3) a printer resets type for a new edition.

Resht patchwork: a type of mosaic patchwork (q.v.) produced at Resht, Persia, during the 18th and 19th cent. for covers and prayer-rugs. The designs are inlaid in coloured felts with outlines and details worked in coloured silks in chain-stitch and couched-work. In-

ferior examples are often not true patchwork, as the small pieces are applied to the ground and not inlaid. A similar type of work was produced in Ispahan.

Resist printing: (1) an ancient "dyed" style of printing textiles in which the fabric is printed in the desired design with a substance which protects those areas of the cloth from the action of the dye. The patterns are usually white on a dyed ground, often indigo blue. (2) Pottery was also decorated by a resist process, a method generally used with silver lustre. The decoration is painted upon the glazed surface of the ware in a "resist", covered with metallic solution and fired, the infusible resist portion firing away during the process leaving a white decoration reserved against a bright metallic background.

Restoration: (1) a proper renewal of a piece by a candid replacement of hopelessly damaged or missing parts; (2) restored is sometimes used to indicate either that a piece has been over-restored, or that the extent of its restoration is dubious.

Restoration furniture: term applied to certain elaborately carved and scrolled chairs, etc., their backs surmounted by crowns or boys and crowns (q.v.). It was said that such pieces recorded the restoration of King Charles II (1660), but many so-called Restoration chairs are now known to date from late in his reign when not from a subsequent period. Such chairs may be of mixed woods, and other than oak.

Reticella: a type of Italian needle-point lace. Many English white-work samplers of the second half of the 17th cent. are of cut and open-work with designs taken from Italian *reticella*.

Reticulated pattern: a pattern in diamond-like formation or resembling network. Glassware decorated with a moulded pattern of this form is said to be reticulated.

Revere, Paul: (1735–1818), a Boston, Massachusetts silversmith in whose work the rococo and neo-classical styles found noteworthy expression.

Reverse: the less important side of a coin or medal ("tails").

Rhenish stoneware: German salt-glazed stoneware frequently imported into England in the 16th cent., many pieces being mounted with Elizabethan silver or silver-gilt neckbands, covers, handles and footrims.

Rhenish "tigerware": mottled brown salt-glazed stoneware made in Germany and imported into England in the 16th cent. German jugs of this material were mounted in England in silver-gilt.

Rhinoceros vase: a large, ungainly, covered porcelain case surmounted by a rhinoceros, made for Earl Fitz-william, Marquis of Rockingham, at Swinton, c. 1826. The original is preserved at Wentworth House; a companion is in the Victoria and Albert Museum. It was painted by Edwin Steele.

Rhodian ware: see Isnik pottery.

"Ribband-back" chair: a mahogany chair, the splat carved in the form of knotted ribbons and bows in a manner highly expressive of rococo (q.v.) taste. Ornament inspired by ribbons

had been used on chair backs in France earlier in the 18th cent. Chippendale (q.v.) included designs for "ribband-

back" chairs in *The Gentleman and Cabinet-Maker's Director* which he published in 1754.

Ribbon work: embroidery in fine, narrow silk ribbons often combined with chenille thread and aerophane, a kind of muslin gauze. This type of work originated in the third quarter of the 18th cent. and was popular in both England and France, particularly for dress trimmings, bags, hand-screens and other small articles.

Rib or diamond moulding: a pattern consisting of straight or twisted lines forming diamonds or ribs impressed upon the surface of a glass vessel or dish.

Rib-twist stem: see Incised stem.

"Rice-grain" decoration: a decoration used on Chinese porcelain in which small perforations in the body are filled with transparent glaze; a technique adopted from Persian pottery, popular during the 18th cent.

Ricketts glassworks: wine-bottles with seals are sometimes found bearing the mark shown in Fig. A in raised letters round the base.

Fig. A

The Ricketts family were prominent in the business life of the city of Bristol between 1750 and 1850, and one or another of them was connected with such varied occupations as porter-brewing, tobacco, banking, and the manufacture of glass. Jacob Wilcox Ricketts and his brother, Richard Ricketts, were partners with John

Wadham and David Evans, successively, in the Phoenix Glasshouse, Temple Gate, which was renowned for good quality cut glass comparable with that made in London and Stourbridge.

In 1811, Jacob Wilcox Ricketts and his third son, Henry, together with two partners, purchased a glassworks known as the Soapboilers' Glasshouse, in Cheese Lane, St Philip's, Bristol. They continued to make cut glass at the Phoenix factory, and made bottles in their newly acquired premises, both trading under the name of Henry Ricketts and Co. After various changes in the structure of the business, it was closed finally in 1923.

Rider: (or rijder), gold coin also called the Phillipus, struck by Philip le Bon for Brabant in 1435 with obverse type of prince on horseback and reverse elaborate cross.

Ridgway earthenware and porcelain: the family of Ridgway had extensive connections in the potteries from the end of the 18th cent. In 1792 Job Ridgway and his brother George acquired the Bell Bank Works at Hanley, Staffordshire, and the partnership continued until 1802, when Job Ridgway established a separate factory at Cauldon Place. Job's two sons, John and William Ridgway, succeeded their uncle at the Bell Bank. In 1830 John

Ridgway left to follow his father at the Cauldon works, while his brother William carried on and extended the Bell Bank.

Several other firms came under Wm. Ridgway's, and his son E. J. Ridgway's, ownership, including those formerly owned by Geo. and Thomas Taylor, Elijah Mayer, Palmer and Wilson, Toft and May, and Hicks, Meigh and Johnson. The whole concern, known as W. Ridgway & Son, was dissolved in 1854, and shortly afterwards the Bell works were purchased by Joseph Clementson.

John Ridgway owned the Cauldon works until 1859; later they were taken over by Brown, Westhead, Moore & Co.

Marks:

Transfer-printed
1814–30

In the various factories owned by the Ridgways all kinds of pottery and porcelain were made. In the time of Job Ridgway, blue-printed wares were produced, and also a type of porcelain akin to Swansea. Bone china of excellent quality was made at the Cauldon factory in the first half of the 19th cent.; designs used at the end of this period are very similar to those of Minton with whom Ridgway's seem to have been in competition.

Wm. Ridgway's son, E. J. Ridgway, is noted for his introduction of jasper (q.v.) wares which were manufactured with considerable success in the early and mid-19th cent. Stoneware articles of excellent design and finish were also made. The Ridgways pioneered several decorative processes, including the application of photography.

Riesener, Jean Henri: French cabinetmaker. The most famous *ébéniste* (q.v.) of the 18th cent. in France. Born at Gladbeck, near Essen, in 1734, but it is not known when he came to Paris. He entered Oeben's workshop at the Gobelins about 1754, and moved with him to the Arsenal. At Oeben's death he was selected by the widow to take over the workshop, and he married her in 1768, the year when he became a *maître-ébéniste*. In 1769 Riesener completed the great *Bureau du Roi Louis XV*, which his predecessor had left unfinished (see under Oeben). In 1774 he succeeded Joubert as *ébéniste du Roi*, and for ten years enjoyed the patronage of the Crown to a hitherto unprecedented degree, as expenditure during that decade was higher than it had ever been. His wife died in 1776, and seven years later he remarried, but unhappily.

After 1784 his prosperity began to decline and he was made drastically to reduce his prices by the Treasury. It was at this time that Beneman (q.v.) to a certain extent succeeded him in the favour of the Court. Queen Marie Antoinette, however, seems to have remained faithful to Riesener throughout, for she continued to order furniture from him right up to the Revolution.

He continued in business during and after the Revolution but never actually reinstated himself. He seems to have retired in 1801 and died in Paris in 1806.

J·H·RIESENER

Riesener's stamp appears frequently on furniture of all kinds in the Louis XVI period, but it is probable that works bearing Oeben's stamp may also be by him, and made while he was working for Madame Oeben before their marriage (see Oeben).

He was the most versatile, and became the most accomplished *ébéniste* of the time, and certainly deserved the success he obtained. His work covers nearly all types of furniture in use, and he specialized in highly elaborate marquetry, mostly in geometrical designs.

Rigaree trail: a process of glassblowing in which applied threads of glass are attached to a vessel and melted in to give a more or less smooth surface; such threads can be tooled in parallel vertical lines to form tiny contiguous ribs, which are produced by the edge of a small metal wheel.

Rim lock: the mechanism is entirely closed within a rectangular metal case and attached to the inner surface of a door. In addition to the locking bolt, such a lock might have an independent smaller knob operating a spring catch to prevent the lock from being opened from the outside. Both of these entered the striking plate screwed upon the jamb.

Rising hood long-case clocks: the earliest form of long-case clock with a rising hood, made before the door was introduced in the front. The hood slides up on grooves in the back-board and is held in place by a catch, thus allowing access to the dial. As clocks increased in height, the rising hood became impracticable, and the draw-forward type of door was introduced.

Rising sun ornament: a fan-shaped ornament of semi-circular form, carved to suggest the rays of a rising sun, used as a decorative motif on late 18th cent. American case furniture. The term "setting sun" is also sometimes used. It was so often the only decoration on New England highboys that its presence generally indicates the New England origin of the piece. James (later President) Madison recalled that when the Constitution of the United States was finally adopted after much contention, Benjamin Franklin pointed to a decoration of this type painted on the back of the chairman's chair and said he had looked at it many times during the sessions "without being able to tell whether it was rising or setting, but now I . . . know that it is a rising . . . sun".

Riven wood: this was much used in early strong chests, saving labour although wasting wood, and ensuring enduring work, little subject to warping and splitting that would render a plate chest useless. The tree trunk was split or riven along the natural growth lines of dense, non-cellular tissue radiating from the tree centre. These rays show a relief on old, weathered, riven timber, and probably suggested the early linenfold (q.v.) patterns.

Rivière: a long necklace consisting of gemstones, very often of diamonds, worn in the first quarter of the 19th cent.

"R" mark: see Gotha porcelain, Rauenstein porcelain (under Limbach) and Volkstedt porcelain.

Roan: a thin, soft kind of sheepskin used by book-binders as a cheap substitute for morocco from about 1790 onwards. Not at all durable, and seldom elegant, even when well preserved.

Rocaille: see under Rococo.

Rockingham earthenware and porcelain: the Swinton Old Works or the Rockingham Works was founded at Swinton in Yorkshire about 1745 by Edward Butler. William Malpas made white and brown wares here in 1765 and later, in the early 1780s, Thomas Bingley and Co. made various types of earthenware. From 1787 until 1806 the factory was linked to Leeds, first as Greens, Bingley and Co. (1787–1800) and then as Greens, Hartley & Co. (1800–06). Its wares are probably inseparable from those of Leeds or Staffordshire. In 1806 William Brameld took over, trading as Brameld & Co. and when he died in 1813, his three sons continued the factory, producing earthenware of all kinds, including the well-known manganese-brown Rockingham glaze and the equally celebrated "Cadogan" type teapot. About 1820 they started to make bone china (q.v.) of the Staffordshire type, got into financial difficulties, and in 1826 became bankrupt. An appeal was made to Earl Fitzwilliam who granted financial resources and the right to use the griffin passant crest as a trade mark. From 1820 until 1842 excellent china was made, usually in a florid, rococo (q.v.) taste. Marks:

Impressed

Brameld

Painted in red

None of the earthenware known to have been made at Rockingham before 1765 has been identified but after that date a brown stoneware, often indistinguishable from that made at Nottingham, was produced. Wares manufactured in the early years of the Brameld family's ownership are similar to Leeds; creamware, stonewares including black basaltes, marbled and "tortoiseshell" articles, were all made. From 1820 the characteristic types of Rockingham porcelain were manufactured. Decoration is often extravagant, including much gilding and flowers modelled in full relief. The simpler wares include some biscuit figures and table wares decorated with flowers on a pale green ground. Dinner and dessert services were made to order and in 1832 a most ambitious dinner service was made for William IV, decorated with views of castles and country seats.

"Rockingham" glaze: a lustrous, purple-brown lead glaze (stained with manganese) made at the Rockingham factory, Swinton, early 19th cent., and in Staffordshire.

Rococo: the word derives from the French *rocaille*, a term used to describe a style of decorative art first evolved in France about 1700. Shortly before the middle of the 18th cent. the fashion for rococo was adopted in England. An imaginative and vivacious style, it combined with fantasy and charm motifs based on shell and rock forms, foliage and flowers, "C" scrolls and tortuous curves.

Roemer: a drinking vessel usually of pale green glass, consisting of a hemispherical bowl and a hollow conical foot. The roemer is of German medieval derivation and became the traditional Rhenish wine glass, which is still made to-day. The form was adopted both in England and the Netherlands in the last quarter of the 17th cent.

Roentgen, David: French cabinet-maker. Born near Frankfurt in 1743, the son of the cabinet-maker Abraham Roentgen, whose workshop at Neuwied on the Rhine he took over in 1772 and developed considerably. He first came to Paris in 1774 and received patronage from Queen Marie Antoinette. This established his reputation which, by the time of his second visit in 1779, had increased considerably, and he established a depot in Paris for selling furniture, as he did also in Berlin and Vienna. He travelled widely and visited Italy, Flanders and Russia, where he sold a great deal of furniture to the Empress Catherine II.

In 1780 he was compelled to become a *maître-ébéniste* in Paris, using the stamp: DAVID, and in 1791 was made Court furnisher to King Frederick William II at Berlin. He was ruined by the Revolution and his depot in Paris was confiscated. His workshop at Neuwied was also overrun by Republican troops. He returned there in 1802, however, and died in 1807.

Roentgen specialized in furniture veneered with extremely elaborate pictorial marquetry and fitted with complicated mechanical devices, concealing secret drawers and multiple locks. His furniture was mostly made outside France and is seldom stamped.

Rogin: a Japanese lacquer-work technique, involving the use of powdered silver, burnished, on a lacquer ground.

Roiro: a Japanese lacquer-work technique. A black lacquer with a high polish. Also called "mirror black".

Roll: a book-binder's tool in the form of a wheel bearing an engraved "repeat" or continuous design, with which a pattern is impressed on the binding. The term also refers to the impression made by the tool.

Rolling-pins: the glass rolling-pins that have survived are sufficient in number to prove they must have been made in quantity. Popular opinion is that they all emanated from the Bristol or the Nailsea glassworks, and that they all date from the first years of the 19th cent. or earlier. There is no doubt that a proportion of them actually did come from the west country, but in the majority of instances it is impossible to say where they were made or at what date. They were made usually to be sold cheaply at markets and fairs, and others, engraved or painted with amorous pledges, were intended for personal presentation.

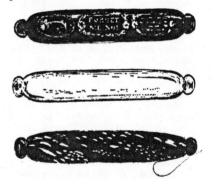

There would seem to be little doubt that these articles were designed for use as rolling-pins, although it is doubtful if many of them were actually put to use in pastry-making. It is much more likely that they were hung on a farmhouse or cottage wall for decoration or as a reminder of the giver.

Roll or **piece of wallpaper:** early paper-hangings consisted of a number of sheets (generally a dozen) joined together end to end. Each sheet was roughly 22½ inches wide by 35 inches long (double demy), giving a length of about 12 yards. Today the British Standards Institution length of a piece of wallpaper is 11½ yards.

Roll-top desk: (*Fr. bureau à cylindre*); similar to a cylinder-top desk (q.v.) but the writing-table and fittings are enclosed by a curved slatted panel. The French term is the same for both types of desk.

Roman strike: a system of clock striking devised by Joseph Knibb in the latter part of the 17th cent. to reduce the power needed, in spring-driven clocks especially, to drive the striking train. The hours are struck on two different-toned bells, one striking up to III and the other once for V, and twice for X. In clocks so made the IIII is usually marked IV. Sometimes found also in long-case clocks.

Romayne work: old term for Renaissance carving with heads in roundels, scroll-work, vases, etc., some few heads being portraits, but most purely formal. The taste was widespread in Europe, and traditional traces survived in Brittany until quite a late period. The vogue for romayne work in England was under Henry VIII (1509–47), thereafter dwindling.

Rondel-dagger: a type of dagger with a disc-shaped guard and pommel.

Rörstrand pottery: produced at Rörstrand in Sweden at the factory founded in 1726 and still in existence.

Rose cutting: a method of cutting gemstones, used from the mid-17th cent., in which the stone has a flat base and is pointed on top, with usually twenty-four facets.

Rose du Barry: a popular misnomer for the coloured ground used on Sèvres porcelain and properly known as rose Pompadour.

Rose-engine-turning: basketwork patterns produced on pottery and porcelain on the engine-lathe.

Rose, John: (d. 1841), founder of the Coalport porcelain factory. Rose purchased the Caughley factory in 1799, and the moulds and stocks of Swansea and Nantgarw 1822–23. He was awarded the "Isis" Gold Medal of the Society of Arts for a leadless felspathic glaze in 1820 which was commemorated by one of the Coalport factory marks. The business was continued after his death by his nephew, William F. Rose (d. 1864).

Rose-noble: (or Ryal); large gold coin of value 10s issued by Edward IV in 1465 to replace the noble. Designs similar to those of noble but with rose on ship's side. This coin with variations in design was struck by the Tudor and Stuart monarchs.

Rose Pompadour: a ground colour introduced on Sèvres porcelain (q.v.) in 1757. The claret ground found in Chelsea porcelain (q.v.) is believed to have been an imitation, introduced in 1760. An advertisement of 1768 cited by J. E. Nightingale (*Contributions towards the History of Early English Porcelain from Contemporary Sources*, Salisbury, 1881), mentioning "Mazareau and Pompadour Sets" probably refers to this colour. Coalport (q.v.) produced a rose Pompadour in the 19th cent.

Rosette: see Patea.

Rosewater ewer and dish or **basin:** used for finger-washing at table. Extant examples of silver from early 16th cent. onwards. Dishes were made usually circular or occasionally oval. Ewers were of various form, chiefly vase- or helmet-shape. Important pieces of decorative plate displayed the highest standards of ornament and design of their periods. Less important examples were made in other materials.

Rosso Antico: the name given by Josiah Wedgwood to his red stoneware, which was a variation on the "red porcelain" introduced into Staffordshire by Elers (q.v.): "We shall never be able to make the Rosso Antico otherwise than to put you in mind of a red-Pot-Teapot." (Wedgwood to Bentley, 3 March 1776). (*Letters of Wedgwood*, 1903.)

Roubiliac, Louis-François: (1695–1762), son of a banker in Lyons: studied under the sculptor to the King of Saxony, Balthasar Permoser: returned to France and worked with Nicholas Coustou in Paris: came to England in 1720 and worked here for the rest of his life, leaving only for a brief visit to Rome in 1752. He enjoyed the esteem of Walpole and became the most celebrated sculptor in England, his statue of Handel making him popular. Other and perhaps better works are his George I in Golden Square, and the Nightingale monument in Westminster Abbey.

His connection with the Chelsea porcelain factory has been the subject of considerable speculation. He belonged to the Soho circle of French expatriates, and Nicholas Sprimont (see Chelsea) was godfather of his

daughter. The white royal busts have been attributed to him, as also have three large figures representing the senses of "Sight", "Smell" and "Truth". Roubiliac died in 1762.

Rouble: large Russian silver coin of thaler or crown class, issued from time of Peter the Great with types, Imperial portrait and Russian double-headed eagle.

Rouen faience: tin-glazed earthenware made at Rouen. This type of earthenware was made in France as early as the 14th cent., but the technique did not enjoy a wide use until Italian potters migrated to France in the 16th cent. and set up maiolica potteries at Rouen and elsewhere. The Rouen potteries achieved fame in the reign of Louis XIV, when faience was produced, decorated in blue or in blue with red or orange, with formal scrollwork designs. 18th cent. wares have a wider range of colours and show the influence of Chinese *famille verte* porcelain (q.v.).

Rouen porcelain: Louis Poterat, a faience manufacturer, was granted a monopoly for the making of porcelain in 1673. Few pieces are known. The body is a white vitreous frit porcelain with a yellowish surface, similar to that made somewhat later at St Cloud (q.v.). Porcelain was made only on a very small scale at Rouen and the factory does not appear to have continued after 1700.

Rouge de fer: (*Fr.*), iron-red enamel colour used on Chinese porcelain, particularly in Ming times, while it is also prominent on K'ang Hsi *famille verte* (q.v.) pieces and appears on *famille rose* wares, and as a monochrome glaze from Yung Chêng (q.v.).

Roundabout chair: see Corner chair.

Roundel: circular ornament enclosing sundry formal devices on medieval and later woodwork; also human heads as in romayne work (see also Whorl).

Round-funnel bowl: bowl of a drinking glass in the form of a round funnel, popular in the later 17th cent.

Until about 1690 the bowl was long in proportion to the stem but by the early 18th cent. the bowl was less deep.

Round Glass House: the first flint glasshouse to be established in Ireland during the early 1690s by Captain Philip Roche. It continued to operate until 1755. The Round House appears to have been a highly flourishing business until the export of glass from Ireland was prohibited under the Excise Act of 1745. This prohibition was directly responsible for the glasshouse closing down ten years later and from then until 1764 no fine flint glass appears to have been made in Ireland. Then an already existing bottle-house at Marlborough Green, Dublin, was enlarged to produce flint glass. When, in 1780, import restrictions were removed, several well-equipped glasshouses were established in Ireland, notably at Waterford, Belfast, Dublin and Cork. (see also Waterford glass and Cork Glasshouse.)

Royal binding: any binding blocked with the royal arms. Very often these do not denote royal ownership, but are used purely decoratively, e.g. the blind-stamped panels of Henry VIII's reign or the calf bindings, c. 1600, with Queen Elizabeth I's crowned falcon badge; both of these groups are trade bindings. Bibles and Prayer Books with the royal arms are very unlikely to have been personal possessions of the sovereign. They may have been part of the chapel furniture issued to all English ambassadors abroad; they may have come from a royal chapel; or they may even come from a parish church. Even books in an elaborate binding with the royal arms and a dedication to the king may never have been in royal possession, for sometimes an author seems to have had identical bindings made for his presentation copies. The dedication copy of Robert Adam's *Ruins of the Palace of the Emperor Diocletian at Spalato*, 1764, is one of six copies known bearing the royal arms.

Royal clock pendulum: see Seconds clock pendulum.

Royal paper copy: see Large paper copy.

Royal portable Irish harp: see Harps.

"Ruby-back" decoration: see under *Famille rose*.

Rummer: a short-stemmed drinking glass with capacious thinly blown ovoid bowl and small foot, popular in the late 18th and early 19th cent. Later examples are of heavier metal and stand on a square base. They were used in particular for hot toddy which was a fashionable drink in the Regency.

Runner: alternative term, used in America, for the rocker of a rocking chair.

Rupee: Indian silver coin, first commonly issued by Mogul emperor, Akbar (1556–1605) and continued until 19th cent. Types as for mohur (q.v.). Often square in shape.

Russia leather: cowhide tanned by a special process, giving it a very rich, smooth effect; and originally scented. It was particularly popular with English book-binders between about 1780 and 1830, often being decorated with a diced or lozenge pattern in blind. But it is apt to fail at the joints, and it is not much used today. (See also Blind-tooled binding.)

Ryijy rugs: Finnish rugs made in the old Norse tradition of knotted pile technique, which may go back to the Danish Bronze Age quite independently of Near Eastern influence. Although derived from Norway and Sweden, in the 16th cent. Finnish pile weaving already enjoyed a special reputation. Made primarily for bed coverings, sleigh-rugs, or horse cloths, they have a very long knotted pile, but the ground texture of wool or linen is not thick and there are usually ten to twenty shoots of weft between the rows of knots. The knotting technique is also curious and varied. Made on a narrow loom, two widths were joined together, but a wide loom was also used. Patterns vary from plain-colour weavings and geometric motives to simple floral patterns. It was customary for a girl to make a rug for her dowry and many such pieces are dated, though few after 1860. The making of these exceptionally attractive rugs has been revived in the present cent.

Sabeji: (*Japanese* = rust ground), Japanese lacquer-work technique intended to produce a surface in imitation of old iron, etc.

Sabre: a heavy, curved, single-edged sword used chiefly by cavalry from the late 16th cent. onwards.

Sabre leg: a term used to describe a sharply curving chair or settee leg in the classical style which prevailed in the late 18th and early 19th cent.

Sackbut: a 17th cent. trombone.

Saddle seat: some late 18th cent. chairs have a gently curving seat sloping down in the centre which is described colloquially as a saddle seat. A slightly different form is found on Windsor chairs where the centre of the wooden seat is shaped to resemble a saddle.

Sadler & Green: John Sadler, b. 1720 (son of Adam Sadler, a printer in New Market, Liverpool) invented a process by means of which pottery, already glazed, could be decorated with designs first engraved on copper plates, thence transferred to paper and finally on to the wares. The colours were then fired in a muffle kiln (q.v.) for fixing. This method of transfer-printing made possible the accurate reproduction of complex designs. Guy Green was Sadler's partner in an extensive business carried on in Harrington Street from the middle of the 18th cent.

It is said that the process was actually invented by Sadler about 1750; not until 1756 was a form of patent contemplated (but never finalised) as Sadler and Green decided to keep the invention secret.

The firm is believed to have manufactured pottery, but its wares have not been identified with certainty. They decorated large quantities of Staffordshire and Liverpool earthenware; Wedgwood's Queen's ware was sent regularly to them for printing. Oriental patterns, portraits, illustrations from Aesop, tiles showing figures of actors and actresses – all these were printed at the factory. Much of the earlier work was in black, or black and red.

Sadler retired about 1770, and Green continued the business until 1799. Marks:

SADLER   1756
          SADLER & GREEN

Sadware: pewterers' term for plates, dishes and chargers.

"Sailor" jug: a variety of toby jug (q.v.) representing a Jack Tar of the period seated on a sea chest with the usual jug, glass and pipe, and on some models, an anchor at his feet.

Salamander: a bar of wrought-iron with a thick round or oblong piece at one end; somewhat like a long-handled shovel in appearance. The larger end was heated until it became red-hot, and then held near bread, cake, etc., in order to brown it.

Salem rocker: a type of rocking chair made at Salem, Massachusetts in the early 19th cent. It is similar to the Boston rocker (q.v.) but with a lower back.

Salem secretary: an American classical style bureau with a china cabinet as the upper part. There is generally a double-doored centre part with a drawer that pulls out to serve as desk and flanking single-door sections.

Salem snowflake: an American term for a six-pointed punched decoration resembling a star or a snowflake found as background carving on Salem furniture.

Sallet: the characteristic helmet of the 15th cent., usually worn with a deep chin-piece (bevor). Its form generally follows that of the modern sou'wester, although it comes well down over the face, either having a movable visor, or a vision slit in its forward edge. The German type usually has a long, graceful, pointed tail, often laminated. The barbute (q.v.) is one of the forms of this helmet.

Salopian: mark used at the Caughley porcelain factory. (See also Caughley porcelain.)

Salor rugs: Turkestan rugs similar in texture to Bokhara rugs (q.v.), but the octagonal gule (see Turkoman rugs) is more pronounced and the red is usually slightly brighter than in the Tekke.

Salt-glazed stoneware: stoneware in which the glaze is formed by throwing salt into the kiln when it reaches the maximum temperature. The salt decomposes, forming sodium oxide and hydrochloric acid, the former combining with the alumina and silica of the surface of the wares to form a thin coating of glaze.

Chief centres of salt-glazed stoneware manufacture were Fulham and Lambeth, Nottingham and Staffordshire.

Salt kit: dome-topped ovoid jar surmounted by a knob and loop-handle with a wide circular aperture at one side; used for storing salt, etc.

Salute: gold coin of Charles VI of France (1380-1422) and Henry V and VI in the English possessions in France. Types as *carlino* (q.v.).

Salver: a flat, circular plate for presenting other vessels. Early examples of silver have a central spreading foot and are often erroneously called tazzas. From about 1725 salvers were supported on small feet. Oval and polygonal forms are also found, with chased or plain centres. Early pieces have plain moulded borders, followed by shell and scroll, pierced, beaded or gadrooned patterns.

Samarkand rugs: see under Chinese Turkestan rugs.

Samenuri: Japanese term to describe the decorative use on inro (q.v.) etc. of fish-skin applied to the object after staining Shagreen.

Sampler: an embroidered panel originally intended as a reference sheet of stitches and patterns and later as an exercise for a beginner. The earliest surviving English samplers date from the first half of the 17th cent. and are worked on loosely woven linen in coloured silks and metal thread. They are generally shorter than those of the second half of the cent. Geometrical designs were used, together with animals, birds and floral motifs. In the second half of the cent., the samplers are long and narrow, on finer linen and the patterns formally arranged in horizontal rows, worked in pale-coloured silks. Another common type is the white-work sampler of cut and open-work. By the 18th cent. the sampler had become a child's exercise. They are generally squarer in shape and are usually signed and dated. The alphabet, texts and mottoes are commonly included and the colours are generally brighter.

Samson porcelain: this Paris porcelain factory is well known for clever copies of old armorial Chinese porcelain, which have been made there for more than half a cent. The coats of arms are often those of Great Britain or of France, or of some famous person.

Examined closely, these copies should not deceive the collector. Samson's productions sometimes bear a simulated Chinese "seal" mark or a disguised "S" beneath the base in red. The factory specializes in reproductions of old porcelain of almost every kind.

Samt-teigdrucke: known in French as *empreintes veloutées* and occasionally referred to in English as "flock prints". They were printed from ordinary black-line wood-blocks on which a glutinous ink or paste had been used, Before the ink dried the impression was sprinkled with powdered colour which gave it a velvety surface. Such prints were executed only in the 15th cent. and are very rare indeed.

Sand-blast: a method of obtaining a matt finish on a metal by directing a jet of sand by means of compressed air or steam.

Sandbox: baluster or vase-shaped pot used for sprinkling sand on wet ink. Found as part of inkstands or separately (see also Pouncebox).

Sand-dredger: see Sandbox.

Sand glass: an early form of measuring time by the period required for a given quantity of fine sand to pass from one bulb of the glass to the other, through a fine neck. Usually found in sets of four, the glasses recording the four quarters of the hour. In genuine early examples the two bowls are separate and joined by an applied band.

"S & G" mark: see Isleworth.

Sand-grain aquatint: a sand-grain aquatint is obtained from a plate which has been pulled through the press with a piece of sand paper to roughen its surface.

Sang-de-boeuf glaze: see Copper-red porcelain glazes.

Saruk carpets: these Persian carpets follow closely the tradition of the Keshan carpets (q.v.), often using the Herat motifs and medallion designs.

The construction is sturdy, closely knotted deep pile. Knot: Sehna (q.v.).

Saryk rugs: Turkestan rugs, generally not so fine in texture as Bokhara rugs (q.v.), but bearing a similar design.
    These Bokhara types are all woven in prayer rugs and also in fine camel bags.

Satsuma ware: pottery made at Satsuma, on the island of Kyu shu, Japan. The wares date back to the early part of the 17th cent. Late 18th cent. Satsuma includes cream-coloured wares decorated with enamel colours and gilding. Much was produced for export in the 19th cent. very elaborately decorated.

Sautoir: a long gold necklace often consisting of linked chains set with semi-precious stones or plaques of enamelled gold.

Savery, William: renowned cabinetmaker of Philadelphia (1721–87) hoswe work ranged from simple rushbottom chairs to elegantly carved highboys (q.v.).

Savona maiolica: tin-glazed earthenware made in the 17th and 18th cent. at Savona, Italy. The 17th wares were largely decorated in blue and white which had become the contemporary fashion, reflecting the interest in Chinese blue and white porcelain.

Savonnerie carpets: knotted pile carpets in the Turkish manner were first successfully made in France by Pierre Dupont, whom Henry IV installed in the Louvre in 1606. In 1627 the old soap works on the Quai de Chaillot, called the Savonnerie, were acquired and Dupont's partner, Simon Lourdet, began work there with orphan children as apprentices. The Louvre and Savonnerie workshops flourished, particularly under Louis XIV. Pierre Dupont died in 1644 (he wrote a treatise on carpet-making, *La Stromatourgie*) and was succeeded by his son, who removed to the Savonnerie in 1672. During the 18th cent. work continued steadily at the Savonnerie, although many of the workmen emigrated. Not till 1768 were Savonnerie carpets available to private individuals, but prices were very high and few pieces sold. Under Napoleon the looms were kept busy. The Savonnerie was amalgamated with the Gobelins in 1825, where some looms are still at work. It was the Savonnerie which set the standard for European hand-knotted carpets and created a style which was copied far afield. The drawing shows the method of knotting used for a line of knots of the same colour; the Turkish knot was used.

Sawbuck table: an American table with an X-shaped frame, either plain or scrolled. Often found in rural New England and Pennsylvania German examples are common.

Scagliola: *(It.)* a technique used for the imitation of marble and especially of Florentine mosaic. The term *scagliola* derives from the name of the special plaster or gesso (q.v.), made of pulverized selenite, which is of extremely fine quality, and takes a very high polish. Two processes were developed for the imitation of Florentine mosaic. The first consisted in painting on the wet gesso ground, fixing the colours by heat and then polishing the surface until it resembled a mosaic of *pietre dure* (q.v.). The second consisted in inlaying coloured plasters in the surface of the *scagliola* panel. This latter process was first developed in Northern Italy during the 16th cent. and reached its apogee at Florence in the mid-18th cent.

"Scale" ground: a distinctive Worcester porcelain decoration, sometimes referred to as "fish-scale" design, but possibly derived from Meissen "Mosaik" border. Used at Worcester as early as 1761 in pink, and in 1763 in blue. The Chelsea *Catalogue* 1756 frequently cites wares decorated with "Mosaic Border".

Scalloping: a rim outline formed by a series of semi-circles. Sweetmeat glasses of mid-18th cent. date were cut round the rim in this manner and were described in contemporary references as "scaloped" and "corner'd trim".

Sceatta: small British silver coin issued in 7th and 8th cent. with developments of types and designs copied from late Roman coins.

Sceaux porcelain: a factory at Sceaux (Seine) was founded about 1748 but production was very limited in the early years on account of the monopoly held by the royal factory of Sèvres (q.v.). In 1775 the Duc de Penthièvre, High Admiral of France, became the patron of the factory and porcelain was produced with greater freedom – by now in the Louis Seize style. The factory closed in 1794. Rare pieces bear an anchor mark.

"Scenic" wallpapers: exemplified in their most attractive form by the French panoramic types sometimes known as paysage or landscape papers. Among the first of these to be produced was *Vues de Suisse*, by Jean Zuber, Rixheim, in 1804.

Schaper, Johann: (1621–70), a German painter of stained window-glass who worked at Nuremberg and finding insufficient opportunity for decorating window-glass, turned his attention to the decoration of pottery and glass vessels. He painted mainly in black, known as schwarzlot (q.v.), sometimes using touches of red and gold. Glass beakers and goblets were painted in a similar manner by his followers.

Schiavona: a basket-hilted sword with a straight, two-edged blade, used during the late 16th and early 17th cent. by the Dalmatian troops (*stradiots*) in the employ of Venice. It is often erroneously described as the prototype of the Scottish basket-hilted broadsword.

Schmelzglas: (*Ger.*), see "Agate" glass.

Schwarzlot: (*Ger.*), black monochrome decoration, sometimes heightened with iron-red or gold. This technique, originating with Dutch glass-decorators and Nuremberg glass and faience painters, was probably first applied to porcelain by Daniel Preissler (q.v., 1636–1733), of Bohemia, whence it became characteristic for the decoration of Du Paquier porcelain, executed by Jacobus Helchis and others. (See Vienna porcelain.)

"Scimitar" blade: 18th cent. knife blades were frequently curved in a so-called "scimitar" form, both the knife and the fork being mounted on "pistol" handles (q.v.).

Scissor-work silhouette: silhouettes cut freehand from paper. Although this technique is not capable of giving such great refinements of finish as any of the painting methods employed, it is nevertheless capable of giving very striking effects of a different kind. Its most notable quality is the uncompromising sharpness given to the outlines of its subjects. It is possible for a cutter, by holding several thicknesses of paper together, to cut as many duplicates at the same time, thus giving several "originals". The most prolific cutter of all was A. Edouart. Other noteworthy cutters were Francis Torond, "Master"

William James Hubard (1807–62), who achieved fame as a prodigy, and the ill-fated Major John André (1751–80), who was hanged by the Americans as a spy in the Civil War. One method of cutting was to cut out the portrait as a hollow from a piece of white paper and then mount it over a piece of black paper or material.

Scole chair: see Mendlesham chair.

Sconce: a general name for a wall-light consisting of a back-plate and either a tray or branched candle-holders. Metal seems to have been the chief material from later medieval times until the end of the 17th cent. when looking-glass became fashionable for back-plates (and when "girandole" was another name for these pieces). The use of looking glass meant that sconces tended to follow the same decorative trends as contemporary mirrors but metal back-plates continued to be made and for a period after 1725 there was a preference for carved and gilt wood and gesso-work, often without looking-glass. About 1750 sconces provided some of the freest interpretations of the asymmetrical rococo mode, either with looking-glass in a scrolled frame or in carved and gilt wood only; Chinese features were often blended with the rococo. In contrast, the sconces of the Adam (q.v.) period had delicate classical ornament in gilt wood or in composition, built up round a wire frame. Cut-glass sconces were in vogue at the end of the 18th cent.

Scoop pattern: popular term for a band or other disposition of fluted ornament, gouged in the wood, the

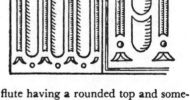

flute having a rounded top and sometimes base. A motif of renaissance origin, its use was widespread (see also Fluting).

Scorper: small chisel for engraving silver with blades of various shapes.

Scotch carpets: double-cloth or ply weavings for the floor, also known as Kidderminster or Ingrain.

Scotia moulding: concave moulding of half round section, being the reverse of an astragal (q.v.).

Scottish dirk: a broad-bladed dagger with root-wood grip, usually carved with Celtic interlace. 19th cent. examples have pommels set with a cairngorm.

Scraped lithograph: a lithograph (q.v.) executed by a reverse process which gives the impression the appearance of a mezzotint (q.v.). The whole surface of the stone is covered with lithographic chalk which the artist scrapes away to bring out high lights and on which he draws with a point to obtain white lines.

"Scratch blue" ware: a class of white salt-glazed stoneware decorated with free floral, bird or other ornament and inscriptions incised upon the wares in the unfired "green state"; into which a mixture of clay and cobalt, (the exact proportions of which were determined by experiments made by Gordon Forsyth c. 1922), was rubbed. Specimens dated from 1724–76 recorded. The majority of the dated pieces were made from 1745-55.

"Scratch brown" ware: a type of salt-glazed stoneware decorated with incisions into which brown pigment or clay was introduced: Specimens dated 1723–24. Used on settles of "Pew" Groups (q.v.) c. 1730–40. Superseded by "scratch blue" (q.v.).

Scratch carving: a cheap method of carving used on 16th and 17th cent. joined furniture in which the design is formed by a single outline scratched on the surface of the wood. Also known as incise carving. Chip and recessed carving (qq.v.) were other contemporary methods of carving on furniture.

"Scratch cross" family: a group of porcelain wares, marked with an incised cross or one or two knife incisions on the inner surface of the footring, including pear-shaped jugs and cylindrical mugs, regarded by Bernard Rackham as indications of an experimental early Worcester paste (*Catalogue, Herbert Allen Collection of English Porcelain*, 1923). George Savage says they are probably workmen's marks and states that they also occur on "indubitable Bow mugs" (*18th century English Porcelain*, 1952). F. A. Barrett records them as occurring possibly on Liverpool and Bristol porcelain also (*Worcester Porcelain*, 1953).

Screen writing-tables: late 18th cent. devices by Gillow and others with adjustable screens of pleated silk.

Scriptor: see Scrutoire.

Scroll foot: a fashionable terminal to a chair leg in the mid-18th cent., in which the foot is in the form of a carved scroll. Designs for chairs with scroll feet were included in the third edition of Chippendale's (q.v.) *Director* where they were described as "French" chairs. Also known as a knurl toe.

Scroll salt: a form of salt-cellar popular in Lambeth delftware (q.v.) of the 17th cent. based upon a silver proto-type. F. H. Garner says the three projecting arms were used "to support a napkin". Penzer (discussing silver) says the arms were used to "provide a stand for a flat porcelain fruit bowl".

Scrutoire or **escritoire:** an early writing cabinet consisting of an upper part of drawers and pigeon-holes, enclosed by a let-down front which provided a writing surface when lowered, and a lower part formed by either a chest of drawers or a stand with legs and stretchers. This type of writing cabinet, also known as a scriptor, was made in the late 17th cent., usually of walnut. The disadvantage of having to remove the writing materials before the front could be closed led to the introduction of the bureau writing cabinet or bureau bookcase, as it is now termed. This had a shallow cupboard enclosed by two doors for the upper stage and a bureau for the lower. The bureau bookcase became fashionable during the reign of William III and has never lost its popularity.

Sc., sculp., sculpt, sculpsit, sculpebat: engraved.

Scudo: large silver coin in Italy, particularly in Papal states from 16th cent. onwards with types of ruler's portrait and various reverses – eagle on globe, shield, etc. *Scudo d'oro* with similar types.

Sculpture d'appartement: (*Fr.*) a term often applied to the pairs, or groups, of figures, usually rather larger than small bronzes and made for the decoration of the great French *salons* and galleries of the time of Louis XIV. They were normally enriched by much gilding and the use of coloured marbles.

Scumbling: a term used in painting to describe a method of softening passages or rendering them less brilliant by means of spreading a thin layer of opaque or semi-opaque colour over the relevant portion of the picture.

Scutcheon: shield on which are armorial bearings or other devices, and, by extension, sundry shield-shaped ornaments and fitments (see also Lock-plate).

Sealed glasses: George Ravenscroft (q.v.) who invented a new type of flint glass in 1673, obtained permission from the Glass-Sellers' Company in 1676 to mark his vessels with a seal bearing his device, a raven's head. Shortly afterwards other glasshouses also began using seals on their glasses and this practice seems to have been common until about 1684, even on glasses containing no lead.

Seal-top spoon: the most common surviving form of early spoon with flat seal-like finial placed on a short turned baluster of oval, circular or polygonal section, and with hexagonal stem. Examples range from the 15th to the late 17th cent.

Seat rails: the horizontal members framing the seat of a chair.

Seaweed marquetry: a form of marquetry (q.v.) employing a complicated foliate design resembling flowing sprays of seaweed. This type of marquetry was used particularly on clock cases but also on cabinets and table tops about 1700. In the early 18th cent. the popularity of marquetry declined.

Second-hand card packs: the reissue of second-hand packs of playing cards was common, enabling once-used packs to become servants' perquisites. They were then sold to the original vendors, resulting in the production of forged aces, now collectors' prizes.

Seconds clock pendulum: a type of pendulum 39.14 inches in length. Those of longer length were made practical by the invention of the anchor escapement (q.v.). The vastly improved timekeeping resulting from the adoption of the seconds pendulum and the anchor escapement in the early 1760s caused it to be called the Royal pendulum.

Secretaire bookcase: a piece of furniture which came into use in the mid-18th cent. It consists of an upper stage with shelves, usually with glazed doors, and below a desk closed by a drop front which falls down to reveal a writing table and small drawers. The drop-front is usually supported in its horizontal position by counterweights within the carcase, but occasionally by struts. Beneath is a cupboard with shelves or long drawers.

Secretary: a modern term used in America for an enclosed writing desk with a cabinet section above that can be used for the storage of books or china. (See Bureau bookcase.)

"Secret" decoration: see An hua.

Sedan clock: a large-dialled watch some 4 to 6 inches in diameter, with bow for hanging in a conveyance. Usually has a small watch type of movement behind the much larger dial.

Seeds: a term used to describe the minute air bubbles sometimes found in glass, indicating that the glass-house could not raise the furnace temperature high enough to eliminate all air bubbles trapped among the raw materials.

Sehna or **Sennah rugs:** the Sehna knot (q.v.), generally described as Persian, is named after this weave. Finely woven Persian rugs in small Herat (q.v.) and cone designs, although lighter in colouring and general effect. These rugs are of real merit and can be distinguished by the very short upstanding pile.

Sehna knot: a knot used in Persian carpets from Sehna, Ispahan, Tabriz (also the Ghiordes knot), Saruk, Serebend, Feraghan, Kerman, Shiraz and Herat.

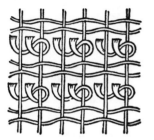

Self-winding watch: see Automatic winding watch.

Semi-china, semi-porcelain: durable porcellanous earthenware: stone-china (q.v.).

Semis: (a) a Roman coin; the half as piece of the Republican aes grave with prow reverse and obverse, laureate head of Saturn with mark of value S. In the late Empire the semis was the half solidus and of similar types. (b) a repeating pattern of small ornaments used by book-binders, "sown" over the covers of books.

Sen: cast copper coin of Japan from 8th to 10th cent., similar to Chinese cash (q.v.). Issue resumed in 16th cent.

Sepia aquatint: an aquatint (q.v.) printed in brownish ink.

Septre mark: see Berlin porcelain.

Sequin: a Turkish coin; popular name, derived from Venetian zecchino (see Ducat), for Turkish gold altun (q.v.).

Serebend rugs: Persian rugs bearing a cone design usually on red or blue field, the border following Herat (q.v.) influence; the sehna knot (q.v.) is used. Fine examples are known as Mir.

Serinette: see under Bird-organ.

Serpent: see under Side-hole instruments.

Serpentine-fronted: cabinet furniture, such as sideboards or chests of drawers, of the second half of the 18th cent., was sometimes constructed with the front of undulating form, consisting of a convex, flanked by two concave curves.

Serre-papier: (*Fr.*), see Cartonnier.

Sestertius: in early Roman Republic a small silver coin, the quarter of the denarius (q.v.) with identical types. In the Imperial coinage the sestertius was the major bronze piece, equal to four asses. The types after the first two emperors are, consistently, an Imperial portrait and titles on the obverse and a personification or scene on the reverse with the letters SC.

Settle: long, backed seat with boxed base, or on legs, and at each end side-pieces or arms. Fixed or movable, the settle represents a stage preceding the settee, a derivative of the chair. Some quite late settles have one end scrolled like a sofa-head. Some, mostly country-made, settles have a storage press in the back, such being loosely known as a bacon-cupboard.

Sévigné bow: a brooch in the form of a bow, worn in front of the bodice, popular in the 18th cent. Sometimes several bows of graduated size were worn on the corsage, in which case they were known as Brandenbourgs.

Sèvres porcelain: soft-paste porcelain was first made in 1738 at a factory at Vincennes, installed in an abandoned royal palace. In 1756, the factory was transferred to Sèvres where it flourishes to this day. A monopoly protecting the factory from competition, allowed Vincennes exclusive rights in the making of porcelain and in decorating it with figure subjects and gilding. This monopoly forbade the engagement of Vincennes workmen elsewhere and provided for the punishment of deserters. As further protection, a factory mark, consisting of the royal cypher, two crosses "Ls", was introduced in 1753 and a date letter added at the same time. Thereafter the name *Manufacture Royale de Porcelaine*, was assumed, well before the time (1759) when the King finally bought the concern.

A new hard-paste porcelain, made concurrently with soft-paste, was made from 1769, marked with a crowned version of the crossed "L's" and named *Porcelaine Royale* to distinguish it from the *Porcelaine de France*.

The earliest Vincennes, unmarked as yet, includes jardinières (q.v.), jugs, ice-pails and trays of simple shape. Among the factory's first achievements are decorations in blue monochrome with flesh tones added, and the earliest of the many famous ground colours, a dark and sometimes mottled *gros bleu*. Occasionally gold decoration is used alone, but more frequently in combination with *gros bleu* grounds and reserved panels, which are painted with figures and birds in landscapes or with silhouetted birds among blossoms. As yet, there are few figures, but the modelling of naturalistic flowers proved to be the factory's greatest success.

Biscuit porcelain, as a medium for figure modelling, was first mentioned in 1753, and soon began to displace glazed and coloured figures. The influence of Boucher upon early biscuit groups of children and pastorals is felt strongly until the sculptor E. M. Falconet entered the factory. During his nine years at Sèvres, Falconet created models which were entirely original and belong to the best in the factory's history. The most characteristic of all Sèvres wares are those decorated with paintings enclosed in panels, reserved upon various coloured grounds, each shade in succession a triumph: turquoise in 1752, yellow the following year, pea-green in 1756 and the pink known as rose Pompadour a year later.

Finally, the strong, even *bleu de roi*, of such unequalled brilliance that an all-over pattern called *oeil-de-perdrix*, consisting of tiny gilt dots within rings and white circlets, was often applied to soften the effect. Festoons of flowers were also popular. Landscape and figure decorations, which are frequently signed at Sèvres, tend to become more sumptuous than they had been on early Vincennes porcelain.

The Revolution of 1789 finally put an end to any restrictions on the production of other factories, but Sèvres survived in spite of the financial difficulties. The 19th cent. saw the introduction of new colours and technical innovations such as *pâte-sur-pâte* (q.v.), but artistically there was a rapid decline. The factory is still working.

Sewing table: a small table with drawers and, frequently, a cloth bag to hold the sewing. This type of table was introduced in the late 18th cent. (See also Work-table.)

Sgraffiato: a means of decorating pottery by cutting away, incising or scratching through a coating of slip to expose the colour of the underlying body. A technique popularly used in Devonshire, Somerset, South Wales, Staffordshire and Sussex, 17th to 19th cent.

Shade silhouette: a silhouette portrait in which the face is painted in black. Ideally, the whole portrait should be in black, but sometimes clothes, nosegays or other details are inserted in colour, but the face itself must have no detail at all apart from that of its outline. J. Buncombe, who practised from c. 1745 to c. 1825 at Newport, Isle of Wight, painted fine shades of soldiers in which the uniforms are shown in colour and in great detail. Edward Foster of Derby often painted faces in brown, blue or some other colour, and unless details are shown in the faces, such may also be termed shades.

"Shadowy blue" ware: see Ying ch'ing.

Shagreen: shark-skin often dyed green. Used from the 17th cent. onwards for covering cases for cutlery, scientific and medical instruments and domestic articles, especially tea-caddies.

Shaker furniture: a whole range of furniture – chairs, tables, chests of drawers – made in America by early 19th cent. Shakers, a celibate sect. This furniture while provincial, is so simple, well proportioned and soundly constructed, that it is much prized today. Usually in pine, maple, walnut or fruit woods.

Shearer, George: English furniture designer, contemporary of Hepplewhite and Sheraton, whose work first appeared in the 1788 *Cabinet-Maker's London Book of Prices*. The sideboard, as usually made in the classical style, appeared first in his book of designs.

Sheepshead clock: a lantern clock in which the chapter ring extends appreciably beyond the rectangular frame of the front dial plate.

Sheepskin binding: a soft leather, with little grain. Good sheepskin, well handled, can make a not despicable book-binding. It was a popular trade binding for 17th cent. poetry and other small books. But it has mostly been used for the commoner and cheaper sort of work; and it is all too liable to loss of surface on the covers, weakness at the joints and tearing off in long strips.

Sheffield plate: the earliest and most effective substitute for wrought silver. Invented by Thomas Bolsover about 1743. Composed of copper ingot fused to a thinner one of silver and rolled to requisite thickness, the metals remaining in the same relative proportions when rolled. First used for buttons and other small articles, but from about 1765 onwards a serious rival to silver in every type of vessel.

Until the 1790s copper was silver-plated in the actual factories in which the ware was fabricated. Afterwards plating became a specialist trade, being made and stocked in three standard qualities, according to the thickness of the silver. This was sold to the plate-workers.

An eight-pound copper ingot alloyed with about one-fifth its weight in brass, and measuring eight to ten inches long by about three inches wide and two inches thick, was smoothed and cleaned on the upper and lower surfaces. At first this was done by hand-filing; from about 1820 by steam-driven planing machines.

An ingot of silver was rolled to the required thickness, as needed for varying qualities of metal, the lowest weighing sixteen pennyweights, to cover one face of the copper. This was increased to as much as eight ounces for the very rich plating used before the introduction of silver mountings and for the lavishly engraved work from 1820. The coating of silver required to be more than a mere film, otherwise it discoloured when heated by the soldering iron. A rectangle of silver plate, flawless in texture and unpitted, measuring about one-eighth of an inch less each way than the surface of the copper ingot, was cleaned on one side. The two bright surfaces were then placed together and bedded by placing a heavy iron upon the silver and striking it with a sledge-hammer until every part of the two surfaces was in close contact.

A heavily whitewashed piece of thick sheet copper was placed over the silver and firmly bound to the ingot with iron wires, burnt borax and water being applied to the edges of the silver to act as a flux. The ingot was now placed in an oven containing a charcoal fire and its door pierced with a small hole through which the plater could observe its progress. A bright line encircling the edges of the silver told him when fusion had taken place. He immediately removed the ingot and plunged it into diluted spirits of salt. After cutting the wires the ingot was compressed in a rolling machine, repeated annealing being required as it was gradually converted into sheets of specified width and gauge. These sheets, of perfectly united silver and copper were not silvered on both sides until the early 1770s.

Shekel: Jewish silver coin issued in the two revolts against the Romans in 132 B.C.–A.D. 5 and A.D. 66–70. Types, chalice, screen of Tabernacle, etc.

Sheldon tapestry: tapestry weaving was undoubtedly practised in England in medieval times, but mostly on a small scale for armorial pieces or coarse *verdures* (q.v.). Finer pieces may have been worked but cannot now be identified. The weavers' main occupation was certainly repairing the innumerable tapestries which were in constant use, and in need of cleaning and restoration. Flemish, Dutch and French weavers settled in England in the 16th cent. William Sheldon claimed his factory, set up under Richard Hyckes in about 1560, as the first in England. This cannot be strictly accurate, but Sheldon's workshops at Barcheston in Warwickshire and Bordesley in Worcestershire are certainly the first about which anything definite is known and whose productions can be identified. The tapestry maps of local counties are known from fragments bought from his house at Weston by Horace Walpole in 1781; they bear a date 1588. These and another set woven at least a generation later can be seen at the Victoria and Albert Museum. Other hangings are known as well as cushion covers, which were much used in the days of hard oak benches; also small cushions, book-bindings and glove gauntlets. Sheldon tapestry is rather coarse and shows analogies in style with the carved wooden fireplaces of Elizabethan and Jacobean country houses. To furnish these it was singularly appropriate and this little weaving enterprise flourished until the founding of Mortlake (q.v.).

Shell ornament: a motif in general decorative use during the first three quarters of the 18th cent. A simple shell is sometimes found carved on the knees of early 18th cent. chairs, while more elaborate forms appear on furniture of the second quarter of the cent. Freer and more imaginative versions of the shell motif were used on silverware, furniture, porcelain, metalwork, etc. during the mid-18th cent. (See also Rococo.)

Shell thumbpiece: a thumbpiece (q.v.) formed of a ribbed or plain escallop shell, found on tankards, etc.

Shepherd's crook arm: chair or settee arm of elegantly curving shape, the end in the form of a shepherd's crook, fashionable during the first three decades of the 18th cent.

Sheraton, Thomas: (1751–1806), a drawing-master and designer who supplied designs to cabinet-makers. Sheraton was a journeyman cabinet-maker in his youth but does not appear to have owned a workshop in London or to have been a practical cabinet-maker. He published *The Cabinet-Maker's and Upholsterer's Drawing Book* in four parts between 1701 and 1794. He favoured light, delicate furniture, including painted work and for his finest pieces he recommended satinwood. He also advised other tropical woods, popular about 1800, for the best apartments of the house. His designs were more inventive than those of Hepplewhite (q.v.).

Sherratt, Obadiah and **Martha:** started to manufacture pottery figures and toys in Hot Lane, Burslem about 1815, but moved to Waterloo Road in 1828. On Sherratt's death the business was continued by his son Hamlet about 1846, and subsequently by his widow Martha (née Vernon, b. 1784). The firm closed down between 1851 and 1860.

Sherratt's figures are never marked.

Shield-back chair: a late 18th cent. chair, the uprights and cresting carved in form of a shield, containing a carved and pierced splat (q.v.). Chairs of this type were included in

Hepplewhite's (q.v.) *Cabinet-makers and Upholsterers Guide* published in 1788.

Shield mark: see Vienna porcelain and Nymphenburg porcelain.

"Shield toby" jug: an early variety of toby jug (q.v.), so called because a shield is found at the left-hand side with the words impressed "It's all out then fill him again". Probably made by Ralph Wood (q.v.), there are perhaps not more than a dozen examples of this model known. They are well potted, with fine thin glazing and invariably have a Roman nose.

Shilling: silver coin first issued by Edward VI with types of profile portrait and shield on cross. With minor variations in design this remained a standard denomination.

Shiraz rugs: Persian rugs woven by Kashkai nomads, bearing designs of a conventional Moslem character, related in style to Caucasian types. Diamond medallions predominate, while cone designs and latch hooks are also used. The term Mecca is often used to describe pieces of outstanding merit. Knot: Ghiordes or Sehna (qq.v.).

Shirvan rugs: Caucasian rugs, similar in design to the Hila rugs (q.v.) but generally coarser in quality and lacking the detail of the former. Crude animal forms are often introduced.

Shouldered stem: see Moulded pedestal stem.

Shrinkage: the contracting of porcelain after firing by about one-seventh of the size of the mould.

Shu: rectangular silver coin of Japan, issued from 17th to early 19th cent. Types, normally Japanese characters indicating value.

Shu fu ("Privy Council") ware: Chinese Yüan dynasty (q.v.) porcelain of Ching-tê-chên with slightly opaque, bluish-tinged glaze covering moulded relief designs of flying cranes, lotus sprays, and the characters "*shu fu*".

Side-hole instruments: the most curious "brass" musical instruments for the general collector are those with side finger-holes to obtain the scale. This very old device is found at its most typical in the serpent, an eight-foot-long wooden instrument wrapped into the peculiar shape that gives it its name. Many of these instruments were made in England in the early 19th cent., although, in fact, the serpent was invented at the end of the 16th cent. English examples usually have brass mounts at each end, six ivory-bushed finger-holes and from three to thirteen keys. There should also be a brass right-angled "crook" and an ivory mouthpiece. Other instruments on this principle, which had a vogue in the first half of the 19th cent., are the keyed bugle and the ophicleide. The first of these was a treble instrument made of copper, with from five to ten brass keys. The ophicleide is a bass instrument, usually of brass but sometimes partly of wood, with from nine to eleven keys.

Side-rails: the two vertical members, also known as uprights, forming the back of a chair and enclosing the splat (q.v.).

Siegburg stoneware: stoneware, made of creamy white clay, usually unglazed but sometimes covered with a colourless salt-glaze, made at Siegburg, near Bonn in Germany from the Middle Ages. The potteries came to an end with the sack of the town by the Swedes in 1632.

Signature letters: the letters (or, in some modern books, numerals) printed in the tail margin of the first leaf (at least) of each gathering or section of a book, as a guide to the binder in assembling them correctly. Signatures normally run from A to Z (omitting, by convention, J and U, which in earlier days were capitalized as I and V, and also W). If the whole alphabet has been run through, they usually proceed to AA, BB, or Aa, Bb, etc.

The term signature is also used, by extension, to mean the gathering or section itself; e.g. "last signature stained", or "two signatures missing", or "lacks first leaf of sig. F".

Signed binding: the binder's name will usually be given in a catalogue description if a binding is of any quality or interest, and if its executant or designer can be identified. Bindings can be positively attributed on several kinds of evidence; (a) by the printed or engraved label, known as a binder's ticket, such as have been in use since the 18th cent.; (b) by the binder's name, letter-stamped in gilt or blind inside the front or back cover; or by French binders of the late 18th and early 19th cent., at the foot of the spine; or sometimes in ink at the edge of one of the endpapers. These are known as name-pallets; (c) by a manuscript note of the owner for whom it was bound; (d) very occasionally, by some external documentary evidence, such as the binder's bill or a reference in correspondence.

Often, however, no such evidence is available; and then the cataloguer must fall back on an inferential attribution, based on stylistic grounds. The degree of credence to be accorded to such an attribution will depend on one's confidence in the person who makes it: confidence first in his knowledge and judgement; secondly, in his integrity.

Sign-post barometer: see Diagonal barometer.

"Silesian" stem: see Moulded pedestal stem.

Silhouette: the name usually given collectively to shades and profiles. It is derived from that of Étienne de Silhouette (1709–67), the parsimonious finance minister of Louis XV. He was an amateur cutter of shades. As such portraits were cheap, they were dubbed

à la Silhouette, as indeed at the time were all cheap objects. He was not the originator of the art.

Siliqua: small silver Roman coin of the 4th and early 5th cent. Types, diademed imperial head on obverse and reverse commonly a seated figure of Roma.

Silver-gilt: silver with an applied surface of gold. Traditional technique known as fire, water, mercury or wash gilding consists of painting on an amalgam of mercury and gold. The former is driven off with heat and the gold combines with the silver. Modern method of electro-gilding employs the use of electric current in a bath of gold solution, producing a deposition of the latter as in electro-silver-plating.

Simple clock pendulum: a theoretical conception consisting of a weight or mass suspended by a weightless thread.

Single rope turning: see Twist turning.

Single-twist stem: a type of stem found on drinking glasses in the second half of the 18th cent. containing air, enamel, or coloured thread spiralling around a clear glass centre, or a pair of reciprocal spirals.

Siphon barometer: a type in which the reservoir is situated in the return portion of a J-shaped tube.

Skeleton clock dial: one in which the metal is cut away from the applied chapter ring, leaving only the numerals, minutes and interhorary marks.

Skillet: (posnet, pipkin) medieval skillets were shaped like cauldrons, and it was not until the 16th cent. that this ancestor of the modern saucepan became recognizable. These later skillets had no feet, but were made with the sides sloping outwards so that the circumference of the top was greater than that of the base. The handle was popularly used for advertising the name of the maker or for the spreading of texts such as "Ye Wages of Sin is Death". They were of earthenware or sometimes bronze. Examples in silver, supported on three feet for heating gruel or other liquids date from the 17th cent. They have covers of flat cap form with flat pierced handles resembling cupping-bowls.

Skirt base: a wide, spreading base sometimes found on late 17th cent. pewter flagons.

Slat-back chair: a simple, late 17th cent. chair with a back of horizontal slats. This type of chair is said to be a precursor of the late 18th cent. ladder-back chair (q.v.).

Sleigh bed: an American 19th cent. bed in late classical style with high front and back, generally terminating in scroll-shaped rails that make it look a little like a sleigh.

Slider: see Coaster.

Slip: clay reduced to a liquid batter, used for making, coating, or decorating pottery; "these (clays) mixed with water they make into a consistence thinner than a syrup, so that being put into a bucket it will run out through a quill; this they call slip, and is a substance wherewith they paint their wares".

Slip-top spoon: early form with hexagonal stem with sloping or bevelled end. Examples occur from medieval period until mid-17th cent.

Slipware: earthenware decorated with white or coloured slip (q.v.). (See also Combed ware and Sgraffiato.)

"SL" mark: see St Louis glassworks.

Smallsword: a light civilian sword with a simple hilt, often richly decorated, which succeeded the rapier (q.v.) in the third quarter of the 17th cent., with the beginnings of fencing as it is known today. The slender blade, although designed principally for thrusting, was at first double-edged, but from c. 1700 one of hollow triangular section became almost universal. The modern term *colichemarde* is often used to designate a blade which is wide near the hilt and narrows

suddenly half-way along. The small-sword remained in active use until the end of the 18th cent., and still survives in the sword worn with modern court dress.

Smalt (smalts): the deep blue of cobalt oxide, also sometimes known as smales. Used in the preparation of enamel colours for the decoration of pottery and porcelain.

"S" mark: see Caughley porcelain.

Smith, George: early 19th cent. cabinet-maker and designer. Published *The Cabinet-maker and Upholsterer's Guide* in 1826.

Snaphaunce: the earliest form of the flint-lock (q.v.), introduced apparently in the middle of the 16th cent. It is regarded by many writers as a distinct type, its chief difference from the flint-lock being that the pan is fitted with a separate sliding cover opened, when the steel is knocked back by the cock, by the action of a cam. Most surviving examples date within the 17th cent.

„Snowman" figures: porcelain figures heavily glazed with a thick, opaque, glassy glaze, obscuring the modelling, sometimes identified as the production of an experimental porcelain factory at Newcastle-under-Lyme, but now known to be the production of Longton Hall.

Snuff-box: a box to contain snuff found in great variety of forms from late 17th cent. onwards, in solid gold, silver and wood, tortoiseshell and other materials mounted with silver, enamels, etc.

Snuffers: scissor-like implement for trimming candlewicks. When closed, the cutting blade fits into a shallow box which is intended to hold the snuffed wick. The box is of pricket form for removing candle-ends. Survivals common from late 17th cent.

Snuffer-stand: upright container on stem and moulded base into which snuffers (q.v.) fit. Introduced in late 17th cent., but superseded by trays in the early 18th.

Snuffer-tray: oblong or oval tray with or without small feet and scroll or ring handle at side for holding snuffers (q.v.). Not to be confused with spoon-trays (q.v.).

Snufftaker: standing toby jug formed as an ugly man taking a pinch of snuff, usually with a deep purple-brown lustrous "Rockingham" glaze (q.v.).

Soap-box: spherical box of silver, pewter or brass for soap-ball, standing on moulded base with screw-on or hinged pierced or plain cover. Can be mistaken for pounce- or sand-box (q.v.), but the spherical form appears to have been peculiar to soap-box.

Soapstone (soaprock): soapstone or steatite was first used as an ingredient of the English soft-paste porcelain paste at a Bristol factory, and was adopted as the basis of early Worcester porcelain. Benjamin Lund, the Bristol Quaker brass-founder, was licensed to quarry soaprock or soapstone at Gew Graze near Mullion, 7 March 1748.

Sofa table: a rectangular table, sometimes with two front drawers in the apron and hinged leaves at each end; the under-frame of two legs at each end, or graceful bracket supports connected by a stretcher. This type of table was made in the late 18th cent. and was extremely popular in the Regency period. It was intended for the use of ladies seated at a sofa.

Soft-ground etching: an etching (q.v.) which relies on the softening of the ground of the plate by grease. Over this is laid a sheet of paper on which the drawing is made. When the paper is removed the ground adheres where the pencil has done its work.

Soft-paste porcelain: porcelain which is both softer as a material than true or hard-paste porcelain, and less refractory and therefore requiring a less intense heat to fuse it. It differs also from hard-paste in that the glaze of hard-paste is closely allied to the nature of the body and may be fired with it, whereas soft-paste porcelain is given a lead glaze which is fired at a second (glost) firing at a lower temperature in the glost-oven.

Soho tapestry: when the Great Wardrobe moved to Great Queen Street, Soho, in 1685, the tapestry factory at Mortlake (q.v.) was virtually abandoned and Soho became the centre of production, most workshops apparently having some connection with the Wardrobe. From 1689–1727 the leading figure was John Vanderbank. *Chinoiserie* tapestries "in the Indian manner" on brown grounds were very much in vogue. He was succeeded by Paul Saunders (active as late as 1758), known for his romantic landscapes. Joshua Morris wove Arabesques (or grotesque) sets designed by Adrian de Clermont, a French immigrant. These tapestries, entirely in keeping with early 18th cent. taste, are perhaps the most distinguished contribution of the period. Bradshaw, who was connected with Morris at Soho, wove tapestries after pictures by Watteau and Pater. In general, a great deal of tapestry seems to have been woven under William and Mary, Queen Anne, and George I and II.

Solidus: (1) the lighter gold Roman coin introduced by Constantine the Great about 312 A.D. Obverse type a diademed Imperial portrait. Reverse types limited to Victory types and a few personifications of Imperial qualities; (2) gold coin of the Byzantine Empire with obverse type, usually the Imperial portrait (see also Nomisma).

Solitaire: (a) tea set for one person; (b) a game introduced in the 18th cent. and then known as the "solitary game". It was played on a thick circular board drilled with fifty or sixty holes half an inch apart, each being fitted with a turned peg, often in ivory or ebony and other woods. Alternatively, in the 19th cent. the holes were made saucer-shaped and each contained an ornamental glass marble. The men were removed one at a time by jumping as in draughts.

Sombre binding: book-binding of black leather, tooled in blind and often with black edges. The style (no doubt connected with mourning observances) was much in use on devotional books between 1675 and 1725. Such bindings were produced by all the important binders.

Soqui (Saqui): Monsieur Soqui, a bird-painter alleged to have come from the Sèvres porcelain factory (q.v.), was described as an "excellent painter and enameller". He worked at Plymouth and Bristol porcelain factories.

Soufflé dish: silver or plated cylindrical bowl with liner, usually two-handled, to hold soufflés, introduced in early 19th cent.

Soumac rugs: Caucasian rugs in a tapestry weave with conventional designs. Large octagonal and star panels; colourings are mainly a deep copper and blue.

South Staffordshire enamels: painted enamels appear to have been produced in South Staffordshire shortly after the establishment of the enamel factory at Battersea (q.v.) in 1753 and at a rather later date, in Birmingham. Snuff-boxes, scent bottles, étuis, wine labels, candlesticks and tapersticks, etc. were produced in large quantities, the examples from the mid-18th cent. decorated with pastoral scenes, portraits or flowers and insects on a white ground. From about 1760, coloured grounds were introduced. Towards the end of the cent. and until about 1830, when the industry appears to have died out, cheaper wares such as buttons, summararily painted patchboxes and similar small articles were made.

Southwark delftware: see under Lambeth delftware.

Sovereign: large gold coin of value 20s introduced by Henry VII in 1489 with types of king enthroned and Tudor rose on shield. Continued under the Tudors with variations of portrait. The modern sovereign with reverse type of St George and the dragon was introduced in 1820.

Soy frame: silver or plated oblong or oval stand with ring frame for holding soy or sauce bottles. Introduced in late 18th cent. Found *en suite* with larger cruet (q.v.) frames.

Spade foot: a rectangular foot of tapered form found on late 18th cent. furniture.

Spandrel: space between the curve of an arch and the frame in which it is contained.

Spängler, Jean Jacques: son of the director of the Zürich porcelain factory, at which factory he learnt the craft of ceramic modelling. In 1790 Spängler signed an agreement to work at Derby for three years, but appears to have been of a restless temperament, and after attempting to return to the Continent in 1792 was arrested and imprisoned at Ramsgate. He returned for a short time to Derby afterwards, but little more is known of him. A few Derby models can be attributed to Spängler with certainty.

Spanish calf binding: a method, originating in Spain, of decorating the sides of a calf book-binding by bold dashes, or large flecks of red and green acid dye.

Spanish foot: a scroll form with curving vertical ribs, often used as the

terminal for a chair or settee in the late 17th cent.

Spanish morion: see Morion.

Spanish point lace: the name Spanish point was variously applied to loosely woven gold and silver lace, much imported from Italy; to a raised needlepoint lace (q.v.) resembling the Venetian, similarly imported, and to silk laces mainly from Chantilly and Bayeux, until Spain made her own.

Spatter: a cheerful range of pottery, with sponged colour and painted designs, made c. 1820–50 in Staffordshire for the American market.

Spelter: a base metal used in the 19th cent. for producing cheap and inferior decorative objects.

Spice-box: a general name for caskets of indeterminate purpose of the early 17th cent., usually of shell outline with scallop lid and shell or snail feet. Later applied to oval caskets of the Charles II period which may also have served as tobacco boxes. An 18th cent. version has centrally-hinged twin lids with or without a detachable nutmeg-grater in the centre.

Spinario: figure of boy made in pottery and porcelain, extracting a thorn from his foot, copied from a statue in the Capitoline Museum, Rome.

Spinet: see under Virginals.

Spit: a metal bar with which meat was pierced and placed on cobirons before the fire for roasting; as the bar was rotated, all sides of the meat received the heat equally. The spit had prongs in the centre, and a grooved pulley at one end to connect by chain or rope to some sort of motive power, human, animal or mechanical. This motive power, if human or animal, was termed a "turnspit", and if mechanical a "jack". Illustrations in early manuscripts show that boys were employed as turnspits, and by the 16th cent. spit-jacks were in use. These latter were made of brass and iron, and were driven by large weights of stone or metal, which descended slowly into pits dug for the purpose to increase the length of fall. Like the weights of a clock, once they had completely run down they were wound up again. Another mechanical method of turning the spit was by a fan fitted in the mouth of the chimney, which was operated by the rising draught. A further method was the employment of dogs, specially trained for the purpose, which were confined in a small treadmill fixed to the wall of the kitchen. At the end of the 18th cent., spring-driven jacks were in use, and culminated in the neat bottle-jack, brass-cased and driven by clockwork.

When not in use the spits were kept in the spit-rack: a row of hooks at either end of the space above the fireplace.

Splat: the vertical central section contained within the uprights of a chair back.

Splayed leg: outward sloping leg. The back legs of chairs are frequently splayed to increase stability.

Splint: an American term for a seat made of thin interlaced hickory or oak strips. Much used in early American chairs, stools and settees of simple type. Still popular today in the kitchen.

Split-turned ornament: oak furniture of the mid-17th cent. was often ornamented with simply turned balusters, split in half and applied. Split balusters applied in this manner were frequently used decoratively in conjunction with applied jewel or lozenge ornament (see Diamond ornament).

Spode, Josiah: the Spode factory was founded by Josiah Spode (1733–97) in 1770; first apprenticed to Whieldon of Fenton in 1749, he became manager of the works owned by Turner and Banks at Stoke at the age of twenty-nine. On the death of Banks in 1770, Spode took over the factory on mortgage. By 1776 he was making earthenware in his own name, trade was increasing, and he was engaged on extensive pioneer work to improve his productions. He died in 1797, leaving a prosperous business to his son, Josiah Spode II (1754–1827). A grandson of the founder, Josiah Spode III, succeeded him, and the factory was carried on under his ownership until his death in 1829. The firm was bought from his executors in 1833 by Wm. Taylor Copeland, already a partner in the business in the time of the third Josiah Spode. During the period 1833–1847 the title was Copeland & Garrett. Thereafter, and up to the present day, the firm has been known by Copeland's name alone – sometimes as Copeland, late Spode – and is still owned by descendants of Wm. Taylor Copeland.
Marks:

Printed in purple

SPODE

Printed in blue   in red

COPELAND & GARRETT

The first Josiah Spode inherited a tradition of earthenware manufacture to which he adhered in the early years of his ownership of the factory; the favourite oriental designs were used and improved, the transfer-printing in blue underglaze being especially successful. His work to improve the quality of transfer-printing greatly affected the future use of this process. In later patterns much of the transfer-print is left unpainted, only small portions of the design being enamelled afterwards. He also made jasper, black Egyptian and black-printed wares of good quality.

Josiah Spode soon turned to the manufacture of porcelain. After the expiry date of Cookworthy's (q.v.) patent for making porcelain from Cornish china-clay and china-stone, Spode took this basic recipe (on which he had been experimenting for several years), adding to it calcinated bone, which combination of ingredients produced a bone-china of fine quality, transparent and durable. This bone-china was to become the basic formula for china made by future generations of potters, and still remains a standard for present-day manufacturers. His son is credited with the introduction of Spode felspar and stone-china, the former akin to porcelain in its hard transparent body.

In the first half of the 19th cent. the Spode and Minton factories were rivals in both artistry and output.

Early earthenware is usually easily distinguishable, as is most Spode work, and pieces were almost invariably marked from 1800 onwards. Some reproductions of Meissen and early Worcester have had their marks removed by grinding, but identification is still possible: Spode's paste was considerably softer than that of Meissen, and the colours used in Worcester reproductions are on the whole brighter than those of the originals. Chelsea colours and types of design were used from time to time.

In the early years, the most popular Spode pieces were in the Chinese style. The peacock pattern and other designs originating in *famille rose* (q.v.) porcelains were also highly successful.

In porcelain, plates and dishes of unusual form were made as a departure from the circular and oval shapes traditionally used. Ground colours – dark blues, reds, yellow, green and lavender amongst others – of very rich appearance are characteristic, and most often found in conjunction with motifs of flowers and fruit, birds, etc. Designs became more ambitious and the demand for extravagant decoration grew. Gilding was profuse and stippled or solid gold grounds were frequent. Designs reminiscent of Sèvres and other continental porcelain were much used.

At the same time a form of decoration traditionally English is found; landscapes were painted in panels surrounded by coloured borders, garlands of flowers etc., some of these pieces being extremely effective.

"Sponged" ware: a crude, easily-recognised, peasant style of decoration on pottery achieved by free painting and by dabbing the ware with a sponge impregnated with pigment.

Spool salt: a salt-cellar resembling a flattened hour-glass.

Spool turning: an American term for ornamental turning resembling a row of knobs or spools. Often used for American Empire table legs and early to mid-19th cent. head- and foot-boards of beds. Very popular today.

Spoon-back chair: an American colloquial description of a Queen Anne chair with a back, curved like a spoon, conforming to the human back.

Spoon-tray: small oval or oblong dish of early 18th cent. date used for holding teaspoons in the absence of saucers.

Sporting prints: the great day of the sporting print was from the end of the 18th cent. to, perhaps, 1850. But all the best-known artists were at work well before 1837, and most of their best work had been done by that date. The principal artists are: Henry Alken (1784–1851), who produced an immense body of work, including the illustrations for R. S. Surtees's *Jorrocks' Jaunts and Jollities* (1837) (2nd edition 1843), and for Surtees's *Analysis of the Hunting Field* (1846) (2nd edition 1847); Charles Hancock (1795–1868); Charles Cooper Henderson (1803–77); John F. Herring (1795–1865), whose aquatints (q.v.) of race-horses are perhaps the best known of all sporting prints. Of these, only a very small number were published after 1837; James Pollard (1797–1867); and Dean Wolstenholme Junior (1798–1882). John Leech (1817–64) can be added to this, since he illustrated the best known of Surtees's works, *Handley Cross, Mr Sponge's Sporting Tour*, etc. But he is better known as a humorous illustrator in *Punch*. Many of his large drawings were reproduced as hand-coloured lithographs, but although some portray hunting and riding, they are basically comic pictures.

Spout-cup: popular in the early 18th cent. and later; a feeding-cup, generally with bulbous body and domed cover; handle generally at right angle to spout, and spout of duck-neck shape, close to body; for feeding children and invalids.

Spr.: an abbreviation used in book-sellers' catalogues to mean sprinkled. If the edges of the leaves of a book are sprinkled, they have been brush-spattered with colour. If the leather of the binding has been sprinkled, which is sometimes the case with calf bindings, it has been carried out with a liquid, such as copperas, to give it a characteristic speckled or mottled appearance. Thus Spr. cf.

Sprayed leaf thumbpiece: a thin, wide fan-shaped thumbpiece (q.v.) with deeply-gouged lines radiating from the foot in a leaf pattern.

Sprigged decoration: application of relief ornament to pottery or porcelain, often in a contrasting colour by "sprigging" from a metal or hard-plaster mould, as on jasper ware (q.v.).

Sprimont, Nicholas: (1716–71), born at Liège, nephew of the silversmith Nicholas Joseph Sprimont, to whom he served an apprenticeship. Came to England where he appears to have worked as a silversmith. In 1745 became factory manager and part proprietor with Charles Gouyn and Thomas Briand (d. 1784) of the Chelsea porcelain factory. After breaking with his partners he obtained for Chelsea the secret patronage of William Augustus, Duke of Cumberland, second son of George II. He was ill in 1758 and again in 1763. In 1769 the factory equipment was sold, and in 1771 he died.

Spur marks: rough marks formed by spurs or stilts upon which glazed pottery or porcelain wares are supported during the firing process. These are distinct from and smaller than the marks left by the bit-stones used earlier.

Sprinkled: a term used to describe (1) certain calf book-bindings and (2) the edges of the leaves of a book, and meaning coloured with small specks or spots. In sprinkled (or speckled) calf, these are normally of a darker brown than the natural leather (stained calf is very rarely sprinkled). For edges the commonest colour is a dull red. (See also Spr.)

"Square" piano: see under Clavichord.

"Squire" jug: a variety of toby jug (q.v.) representing a country squire, seated corner-wise in an armchair, usually with a green or blue coat and brown hat and breeches.

"S" reversed mark: see St Louis glasshouse.

"S" scroll: see Flemish scroll.

Stackfreed: an early South German device of unknown origin to be found in very early watches, whereby a roller attached to a strong spring bears against a shaped snail or cam, the radius of which decreases. The friction on the pivots of the snail and roller decreases as the spring is allowed to approach the centre of revolution of the snail; as the main spring is unwound and loses power the braking action of the roller decreases, tending to keep constant the force exerted by the spring on the watch movement. The principle of the lever underlies this as in the fusee. Both methods are found in the early 16th cent., but the fusee ultimately supplanted the stackfreed everywhere. (See also Fusee.)

Stake: an iron tongue or anvil, on which a piece of silverware is formed. Many kinds of stakes are used, shaped for certain purposes, such as to give an inward curve, a flat surface, etc.

Stalker and Parker: The authors of a treatise on japanning, published in 1688, which did much to encourage the art among amateur enthusiasts, known as the *Treatise of Japanning and Varnishing, Being a compleat Discovery of those Arts. With the best way of making all sorts of Varnish for Japan . . . The Method of Guilding, Burnishing, and Lackering . . . Also Rules for Counterfeiting Tortoise-shell, and Marble . . . Together with Above an Hundred distinct Patterns of Japan-work, in Imitation of the Indians, for Tables, Stands, Frames, Cabinets, Boxes, etc.* (See also Japan work.)

Stamped gold: thin gold sheet stamped into a required form and used for making cheap jewellery mounts towards the end of the 18th and in the 19th cent.

Stamped work: relief ornament produced on metal by hammering from reverse of the sheet into an intaglio-cut die. Commonly used in 16th cent. for strapwork and ovolo borders on silverware, and occasionally for larger surface patterns. In late 18th cent. developed on a commercial scale with large dies at Sheffield and Birmingham for candlesticks, dish-borders, etc.

Stamps on French furniture: various names and letters are often found stamped on French furniture made in the 18th cent. or later. The most important of these is the stamp (*estampille*), giving the name and often the initials of the *ébéniste* (q.v.) who made the piece of furniture. After 1751, it was compulsory according to guild regulations to strike a stamp on all work, unless the craftsman happened to be working for the Crown. Before 1751 *estampilles* are very rarely found.

These stamps are a most important means of identifying the makers of individual pieces of furniture, but it must be borne in mind that sometimes they only refer to the repairer of a piece as distinct from its original maker. Thus some pieces bear more than one *estampille*, and it is often doubtful which *ébéniste* was the actual maker.

The *estampille* is of roughly uniform size and format, usually incorporating the *ébéniste*'s name and initials, but sometimes the surname only. They are usually found in an inconspicuous place on the carcase of the piece, on the bottom or top rails, front or back, under marble tops, etc. Very occasionally they appear on the surface of the veneer and sometimes panels of marquetry are signed in full by their makers.

Another important stamp to be found on French furniture after 1751 is that of the *jurés*. It consists of a monogram incorporating the letters JME (*juré* or *jurande des menuisiers-ébénistes*), and its presence implies that the piece concerned has passed the standard required by the *jurés* of the guild (see *Menuisiers-Ébénistes, Corporation des*).

In addition to the *estampille* and the *juré*'s stamp, furniture made for the Crown sometimes, though by no means always, bears the stamp of the *Garde Meuble de la Couronne* (q.v.). Inventory numbers and palace letters (q.v.) are usually painted or branded, but seldom stamped, on furniture.

In the 18th cent. *bronzes d'ameublement* (q.v.) are very rarely stamped, but sometimes they do bear signatures. Jacques Caffiéri frequently signed his work with his surname. Inventory numbers and palace letters are even rarer, but they do occasionally occur on bronzes, and where they can be checked with existing documents they are found to be of 18th cent. origin.

Standing cup: large ceremonial or decorative cup on high stem and foot,

found in every variety of style and decoration down to the end of the 17th cent., after which it is replaced by the two handled cup on low foot without stem. Examples without covers have probably lost them in the past.

Standing salt: a standing salt of precious metal was the focal point of the medieval banquet high table. Many forms have survived. Elizabethan examples of pedestal- or bellform are richly decorated. Early 17th cent. models have "steeple" finials to cover. A later cylindrical type has scroll supports on the upper rim.

Standish: an inkstand formed by a rectangular flat plate standing upon four feet, and having a curved edge. Upon the plate stand ink-well, dredger, etc., and there is usually a drawer beneath for quills.

Star mark: see Doccia porcelain and Nove porcelain.

State: a term used with reference to prints. Each time there is any addition made to a plate, or lithographic stone, between printings, the new form becomes a new "state" of the print.

Stater: (1) gold coin of the Ancient Britons of 1st cent. B.C. imitating the stater of Philip II of Macedon. Of original types of laureate head of Apollo and horse-drawn chariot, little survived after successive copying across Europe except the wreath on obverse and disjointed horse on reverse; (2) a Greek coin and generically a piece of a given weight. Sometimes applied to the principal silver coin of each city but more commonly denotes a gold or electrum coin.

States: see Issues and States.

Statuary porcelain: the original name of Parian ware (q.v.).

Staunton chess-men: these very popular chess-men were designed by the Hon. Howard Staunton, son of the Earl of Carlisle, and registered by him at the Patent Office in 1849. Their makers then, as now, were Messrs John Jacques & Son, London. The conventional king and queen are crowned, the bishop mitred and the rook a castellated tower. They are found in boxwood, natural colour and dyed red or black.

St Cloud porcelain: faience had been made at St Cloud, near Versailles, before the 1670s, by Pierre Chicanneau, who is thought to have invented a type of soft-paste porcelain. Little is known of the discovery but the porcelain factory was said to be safely established by 1700, the early wares being of excellent quality with a clear, warm glaze. Oriental shapes were eagerly copied and many pieces were decorated in the "Kakiemon" style (q.v.). The factory closed in 1773.

Steatite: see Soapstone.

Steel engraving: a process of engraving, starting soon after 1800, upon steel rather than on copper plates. More impressions could be taken from a steel than from a copper plate. This was, however, such a mechanical process. where the actual engravers were treated merely as hands, that it quickly fell into disfavour, not before it had produced some fine books, such as Turner's *Rivers of England* (1833–36). But it continued through the early Victorian years, though never as a serious force.

Collectors of steel engravings should note that it is highly unlikely that any book illustrated by this method was issued coloured. Many seem to have undergone a transformation since. (See B. Gray, *The English Print*, 1937).

Steele, Thomas: (1772–1850), a porcelain decorator who worked at the Derby factory in a careful, highly coloured style. He painted fruit and for a time appears to have worked at Swinton (Rockingham factory), later in Staffordshire for Davenports and from 1825 to 1843 for Mintons.

Steen: originally an earthen vessel with two ears to hold liquids, later used for bread, meat or fish.

Steeple cup: a popular term for a particular form of standing cup, surmounted by an obelisk or pyramid finial, found in the reign of James I and early years of Charles I.

Stencilled playing cards: from the late 17th cent. to the 1830s the majority of cards were stencilled. Court-card outlines were printed from two pear-wood blocks, the designs so arranged that the figures on the one block were coloured red, yellow, blue, grey (a dilute blue) and black; the figures in the second block contained no black. These produced court cards for ten packs. The pips had a printing block for each suit, each containing cards for two packs. The colours were applied to the blocks by means of a paper stencil stiffened by painting each side with several coats of oil paint. The cards were then well dried, aired and rubbed with Castile soap, which enabled the glazing flint to be operated without damaging the card.

Stencilled wallpaper: one of the earliest forms of wallpaper and a ready means of repeating the design automatically over large surfaces. Stencilling was common during the 17th cent. as a means of adding colours to a block-printed outline.

Stencilling: a technique of applying colour with a brush through openings cut in heavy waterproof paper, used in the decoration of furniture, tôle (q.v.) and textiles. Most surviving examples date from the first half of the 19th cent.

Step: a term used to describe a flattened glass button connecting the stem of a rummer (q.v.) with its foot.

Step cutting: see Prismatic cutting.

Stepped lid: term indicating the elevations on the lid of a vessel, e.g. a tankard, as "single-stepped" or "double-stepped".

"Step" toby jug: probably the first toby jug (q.v.) to be modelled at a date not later than 1750. It is thought that this variety of toby jug, representing a seated figure holding a pipe may have been modelled by Aaron Wood (see Enoch Wood). It is sometimes known as a "Twyford" jug and the potting and glazing is rather more crude than is the case with later models.

Sterling Standard: the normal standard for wrought plate in the British Isles. Established in London in 1300 and in force till 1696. Then replaced by Britannia Standard (q.v.) till 1720, when Sterling was restored as legal. Consists of 11 oz 2 dwts of fine silver in every pound Troy (12 oz) of wrought metal, or 925 parts in 1,000.

"Stick" chair: see Windsor chair.

Stickwork: known as inlaid turnery from the 1830s, although no inlay was used. This type of ornamental woodwork appears to have been evolved at Tonbridge early in the 18th cent. Fillets of various softly coloured native woods were coated with adhesive and pressed together longitudinally, to build up a variegated block. At first such blocks were shaped by the turner into chessmen, backgammon men and table skittles, all favourite indoor games of the period. Stickwork continued as a substantial manufacture until mid-Victorian days, and was made also in London.

Stiegel type glassware: glassware produced in America at Stiegel's Manheim glasshouses. H. W. Stiegel (1729–85) was born in Cologne and his family settled in America in 1750. In 1763, having visited Europe, he brought back English and German glass-makers and set up his factory in Pennsylvania.

He produced vessels in lead metal, especially cylindrical tumblers engraved in the German manner and much coloured glass moulded with network.

Stile: in construction the outermost upright section of a framing as a muntin is the inner section.

Stiletto: a variant of the quillon-dagger (q.v.), first introduced in the 16th cent., with a stiff, narrow blade designed for stabbing only.

Stipple engraving: an engraving technique simulating tone, the design being engraved by means of grouped and graded dots. The invention of stipple engraving with a diamond point on glass vessels is attributed to Frans Greenwood (1680–1761), a native of Rotterdam who used it as a medium of pictorial work. Many of his stipple designs on wine glasses bear his signature and dates ranging from 1722 to 1755.

Stirrup-cup: handleless and footless drinking cup in the form of a fox's or greyhound's mask, based on the classical rhyton and introduced in the second half of the 18th cent. for sporting prizes and commemorative trophies. Made in silver and also in earthenware by Whieldon (q.v.) and others and in soft-paste or bone porcelain at Chelsea, Derby, Rockingham and Coalport.

Stirrup guard: a form of knuckle-bow on a sword which resembles half of a stirrup.

St Louis glassworks: the St Louis glassworks in France was founded in the second half of the 18th cent. and became a close competitor of the Baccarat (q.v.) factory. The first dated paperweights were made at the St Louis works in 1845. They were of millefiori pattern. Paperweights are known with the letters "SL"; sometimes with the "S" reversed.

Stock lock: a plate lock (q.v.) let into a rectangular block of oak and thereby attached to the door by bolts or rivets, later by screws. The mechanism in some stock locks was covered with an iron plate decorated with pierced designs, usually trefoil or cinque foil, with a matching plate covering the wooden block. From the mid-18th cent. the mechanism was almost invariably covered with a solid iron plate.

Stomacher: the breast-piece of 15th to 18th cent. European female dress which was usually embroidered or jewelled. In some cases the stomacher formed part of the corset, when laced at the back, but when the corset was laced at the front the stomacher was made as a separate piece and pinned over the corset lacing. Few stomachers earlier than the 18th cent. have survived. The basic V-shape of the stomacher, tapering to a point at the bottom, varied with successive changes in fashion until it died out with the introduction of the Empire style of dress. Continental examples are often elaborately shaped at the lower end and French examples are usually more ornate than those of English origin.

Stone-bow: see under Cross-bow.

Stone china: a hard white earthenware containing china-stone, made as a cheap substitute for porcelain in Staffordshire from c. 1805 and said to have been introduced by Josiah Spode II (see Spode, Josiah).

Stones: red and black specks within the fabric of early flint-glass, the result of imperfect fushion between oxide of lead and silica.

Stoneware: opaque, dense, intensely hard and completely vitrified pottery.

Stoning: polishing silver with an emery-stone.

Stop watch: one in which the seconds hand can be stopped or restarted at will without stopping the whole movement. In the earliest stop watches, c. 1680–90, the stop stopped the whole movement. They were used by doctors and were called "pulse watches".

Stork mark: see The Hague porcelain.

Storr, Paul: a London goldsmith working between 1797 and 1821, who is generally considered to be the creator of the Regency style in silver. Working for Benjamin Smith and subsequently for the Royal goldsmiths, Rundell, Bridge and Rundell, he is believed to have been responsible for the design and execution of the great series of silver vessels ordered by the Prince Regent and known as the Grand Service. In 1819 he set up on his own account but did not succeed in retaining the royal custom.

St Petersburg porcelain: St Petersburg was the Russian Imperial factory, and although experiments appear to have been undertaken earlier in the cent., no examples of porcelain made before 1762 exist.

Straight-funnel bowl: the bowl of a drinking glass of straight-sided form shaped like the frustum of an inverted cone.

Straight-grain morocco: see Morocco.

Straining spoon: spoon with pierced bowl, found either in large sizes for gravy or similar use or in teaspoon size with thin, tapering stem and pricket top, used for skimming leaves from teacups. These latter have been called mulberry or olive spoons but have no possibly explicable function for such fruits. Their purpose as tea-strainers is exemplified by their conjunction with teaspoons in fitted tea-caddy caskets.

Strapwork ornament: an arrangement of interlaced ribbon and scroll-work, sometimes mixed with foliage and flowers. This type of ornament became popular in the second half of the 16th and early 17th cent. It appears carved on oak furniture of the period and engraved or repoussé on silver. In the late 17th cent., a more delicate form of foliate strapwork, based on the designs of the French engraver, Jean Bérain was included in the characteristic repertoire of Baroque (q.v.) ornament.

Strasbourg faience: the Strasbourg factory was founded in 1721 by Charles-François Hannong, the earliest productions being blue and white, with baroque borders. Paul-Anton Hannong took over the factory from his father and experimented successfully in the manufacture of porcelain. The monopoly granted to Vincennes (see Sèvres porcelain) compelled him to cease and in 1755 he started a porcelain factory at Frankenthal (q.v.). The faience factory at Strasbourg was continued by his son, Joseph-Adam Hannong.

Strass: a form of white paste, closely resembling a diamond in effect, called after the inventor, Joseph Strass, a Viennese, who came to Paris as a jeweller in the middle of the 18th cent. It contains a high percentage of lead, hence more closely resembling a natural diamond when faceted.

Strawberry diamond cutting: a method of decorating glass vessels by cutting or grinding in deep relief to form a pattern of large diamonds, each flattened at the point and cut with numerous very fine relief diamonds. A type of decoration appearing on Irish and English glass in the late 18th and early 19th cent.

Strawberry-dish: a name given to small saucer-like silver dishes of 17th and early 18th cent. date, the early examples with punched decoration, the latter with fluted scalloped borders. Probably used for a variety of purposes.

Straw-work: a method of decorating furniture, particularly smaller pieces, such as mirror frames, with tiny strips of bleached and coloured straws to form landscapes, geometrical patterns, etc. This craft came to England from the Continent towards the end of the 17th cent. and was centred at Dunstable.

Stretcher: a horizontal member of various forms connecting chair or table legs. Stretchers on late 17th cent. chairs were often elaborately carved, while those on mid-18th cent. examples in the Chinese taste were sometimes of lattice work.

Striae: undulating markings sometimes apparent in glass, perfectly vitrified and transparent, showing the metal to be of uneven composition because it has been insufficiently molten before working.

Strike-silent: any mechanism that stops at will the striking or chiming of a clock. The early forms had a pin showing through the dial, attached to a lever, and had the dial marked "N" and "S" (Not and Strike). Later a subsidiary dial appeared for this purpose.

Striking plate: the metal plate fixed to a door frame into which the bolt of a lock is shot by the key. The plate has a lip on which the bolt strikes.

Stringing: a line or lines of inlay used as a decorative border on furniture. In the late 18th cent. it was the practice to apply stringing of contrasting woods or, in the early 19th cent. of brass.

Stripping: furniture whose original surface has been removed and which has been reduced to the wood is said to have been stripped. Though stripping can be properly used, it should never be lightly indulged, for the warm glow of the patina (q.v.) is lost.

Struck: the term applied to coins produced from dies (q.v.). The surface of a struck coin is characteristically smooth.

"Stucco" wallpaper: wallpaper imitating the effect of stone or plaster. During the 18th cent. the term was generally descriptive of papier-mâché (q.v.) with which industry the paperhanging maker was then closely associated.

Stuck shank: a stem of a glass vessel made from a separate gather of metal welded to the base of the bowl.

Stump: a circular pin within the case of a lock to guide the different working parts. In lever locks (q.v.) it works in the gating, that is, a slot cut in the lever.

Stump legs: plain turned legs of "stump" shape, common as the back legs of North Country chairs from c. 1725 until the end of the cent. This type of leg was found to increase the strength of the chair.

Stump-top spoon: 17th-cent. form with octagonal stem swelling at the end and diminishing to a flattened point. Rare.

Stump-work or **raised-work:** raised embroidery, in which portions of the design were padded to give a three-dimensional effect, was widely used in England from about 1625 to the end of the cent. to decorate caskets, mirror-frames and book-bindings and for embroidered pictures. The type of work originated from the raised ecclesiastical embroideries of the 15th and 16th cent. in Italy and Germany, and was used earlier for church work in England. Scenes from the Old Testament, the Judgment of Paris, and other mythological subjects, or representations of a King and a Queen were most popular. The interspaces of the designs were filled with quaint beasts, birds and sprigs of flowers.

Sucket-fork: silver two-pronged fork with flat handle, a spoon at other end, used for eating fruit.

Suffolk lace: pillow lace (q.v.), simple and less expert than the Midlands lace and with similar indications of Lille inspiration. Coloured worsted lace was also made.

Sugar basket: pierced or plain silver vases or boat-shaped baskets were made from about 1760 onwards. The pierced examples usually have a swing handle and glass liner and were often made with matching cream basket.

Sulphides: the earliest glass paper-weights to achieve notice were the type known as sulphides, or encrusted cameos. They comprise a plaque, made of unglazed white china with modelling in relief, embedded in glass. The process resulted in the china plaque appearing to be silver in colour. They were made at all three of the French paperweight factories and in England, with success, by Apsley Pellatt (q.v.).

Sulphur-tint aquatint: sulphur-tint aquatints are produced by dusting powdered sulphur above a layer of oil on the surface of the aquatint plate. Particles of the sulphur corrode the plate in a delicate grain which gives the appearance of a colour wash to the prints.

Sumi-ye: Japanese ink-pictures, i.e. printed in black only.

Sumpter trunks: a usual term for the pairs of travelling chests carried by sumpter- or baggage-horses or mules, or in the late 18th cent. sumpter cars. Lady Grisell Baillie paid four pounds for a pair in 1715. Sumpter-horses were comparable with pack-horses. Bailey, in 1730, defined a pack as a horse-load of wool – about 240 pounds. Sumpter-cloths frequently bore the crest or cipher of their owner.

Sunderland ware: several manufactories of a coarse type of cream-coloured earthenware, for the most part transfer-printed (q.v.) and frequently pink-lustred, existed in the Sunderland area in the late 18th and the 19th cent. The following are the best known of these firms:

NORTH HYLTON POTTERY, Sunderland: founded by Christopher Thompson and John Maling in 1762. Later the firm was known as Dixon, Austin & Co., and subsequently as Dixon, Phillips & Co. (owners of the Garrison Pottery in the same district). Marks:

DIXON & CO.
DIXON, AUSTIN & CO.
SUNDERLAND
(Impressed)

Wares decorated with transfer-prints (Wear Bridge), sentimental inscriptions and splashes of pink lustre were popular.

FORD POTTERY, South Hylton, Sunderland: the pottery was founded in 1800 and was owned by John Dawson & Co. The Dawson family worked it until 1864 when it closed down. Mark:

DAWSON (impressed)

WEAR POTTERY, Sunderland: founded in 1803 by Brunton & Co., and known soon after by the name of Samuel Moore and Co. Popular subjects – views, commemorative inscriptions etc. – decorate their wares. Marks:

MOORE & CO.
SOUTHWICK
MOORE & CO. (impressed)

SOUTHWICK POTTERY, Sunderland: in 1789 the pottery was owned by Anthony Scott, owner of another pottery at Newbottle. Combed slip-ware was included in the productions of this factory. Mark:

SCOTT (impressed)
(See also Lustre decoration.)

Sun flash horse brass: a face piece, extremely popular in Kent, was originally a disc of latten (q.v.) with its centre hand-raised into a high dome or boss and encircled with a wide, flat rim. This extended almost across the horse's face and weighed about six ounces. In rolled brass the outer rim might be serrated. In some examples of the 1850s–80s the flat rim was pierced with twelve triangular rays extending outward to the rim which, from the early 1870s, might be encircled with drilled perforations. The entire brass, including dome and perforations, might be stamped from 1880. Sometimes the dome might be surrounded by a series of concentric circles in relief, number and width varying. A splash of colour might be given from the mid-1890s by fitting into the raised centre a boss of coloured glass or enamelled china: colours noted include yellow, green, dark blue, red, ringed red, white, blue. A series of uncommon rectangular sun flashes had incurved clipped corners and a central dome against a plain ground: others were shield-shape. Some late cast examples display the sun flash against a wide and elaborately patterned rim.

Sung dynasty: dynasty of the Chinese Sung Emperors covering the period 960 to 1279. During this period, pottery of some of the most beautiful shapes and glazes was produced. It excelled particularly in felspathic stonewares of a more or less porcellaneous nature, characteristic of which are the Lung-Chüan and Northern celadons (qq.v.) with their serene forms and soft jade-green depths of colour. Also of this kind are the rare Imperial Kuan or Ko (Fig. c) and Ju wares (qq.v.) and the opalescent blue and purple Chün (q.v.). Very attractive, too, are the brown and black glazes of Honan and Tz'ŭ Chou in the north (qq.v.) and the Chien ware (q.v.) tea bowls from southerly Fukien. All the above owe their colour principally to the presence of iron under varied kiln conditions. Among the vigorously shaped stonewares of Tz'ŭ Chou are those with skilfully carved decoration relieving white, brown or green glazes (Fig. A); and

on others bold floral painting in brown now makes its appearance. Delightful incised designs of plants and animals are also a feature of much Sung pottery and especially of the superb creamy-white Ting (q.v.) and bluish ying ch'ing porcelains (q.v.). Typical of Sung forms are the small-footed bowl, two-handled jar, mei p'ing vase (q.v.) and graceful bottle shown in Figs. A, B and D. Large dishes, jars and bowls are found especially among the celadons exported in quantity throughout the Near and Far East.

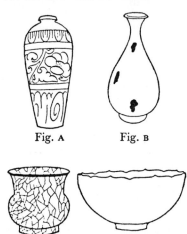

Fig. A   Fig. B

Fig. c   Fig. D

Sunk carving: see Recessed carving

Sunray clock: a type developed in the late 17th cent. at the time of the cult of the "Roi Soleil", Louis XIV. A central circular dial with carved wooden sun's rays emanating therefrom. Much copied today. Original clocks have the rays of hand-carved wood.

Supper-set: a series of four open dishes, which fit into each other around a central circular covered tureen or dish. Made of silver, Sheffield plate or porcelain. Mrs Philip Lybbe Powys, who carefully recorded the events of her daily life in a series of Diaries covering the years from 1755 to 1809, entered under the year 1797: "August 31st.–In the morning we went to London a-shopping, and at

Wedgwood's, as usual, were highly entertain'd, as I think no shop affords so great a variety. I there, among other things, purchas'd one of the newly-invented *petit soupée* trays, which I think equally clever, elegant, and convenient when alone or a small party, as so much less trouble to ourselves and servants."

Sur fond reservé enamel: see Enamel.

Surimono: a Japanese term meaning literally "printed things", especially prints used for greetings or to mark special occasions.

"Surrey" enamel: see under Enamelled brassware.

Suspension: technical term referring to the method by which the pendulum of a clock is supported.

Sussex pig: pottery jug with a loose head used as a cup, enabling the user to drink a hogshead of liquor without disquieting after effects. Peculiar to the Sussex factory of Cadborough, Rye, 19th cent.

Sussex slipware: crude types of slipware were made at various places in Sussex – Brede, Chailey, Rye, Winston, Dicker and Burgess Hill amongst them – in the late 18th and early 19th cent. Articles for domestic use such as jugs, plates and flasks formed the chief of their productions.

A better-finished and more interesting variety of slipware was produced at this period in Rye, Chailey and Brede, and also at Bethersden in Kent. This was made by inlaying with white clay incised or stamped designs (often inscriptions first impressed with printer's type) on the body of the ware. Formal patterns, foliage, stars, etc., are found on articles made in this way. At Burgess Hill an agate ware (q.v.) was made.

Sussex wares are often distinctive by reason of a streaked glaze used with pleasant effect on many pieces. A glaze speckled with manganese is also common. Jugs in the form of a pig, the head forming a lid or cover, and flat pocket flasks, seem to be peculiar to the Sussex potteries.

The Rye pottery, still in existence at the present time, made some interesting pieces in a red ware in the 19th cent. These were experimental and not made commercially.

Swag: a festoon of flowers, fruits and leaves used as a decorative motif in the late 17th and early 18th cent. During the neo-classical period of the late 18th cent., swags of husks or drapery were used.

Swagger sticks: short canes, slender, varnished and decorated with cords and tassels, carried during the early Georgian period, continuing until early in the 19th cent. An eyelet hole was bored through the stick and threaded with a woven silk cord looped so that it could be swung from the wrist.

Swan-necked pediment: see Broken pediment.

Swansea earthenware and porcelain: the Cambrian Pottery at Swansea was founded about 1764. William Coles is believed to have been the proprietor during the early period. Coles died c. 1778–79 leaving the pottery to his three sons. Coarse red wares were manufactured in the early days. By 1790 John Coles was joined by George Haynes and the firm became Coles & Haynes.

In 1802 William Dillwyn purchased the lease of the pottery on behalf of his son Lewis Weston Dillwyn. Haynes remained as manager, the firm being Haynes, Dillwyn & Co. In 1817 another company was formed which rented the Cambrian Works from Dillwyn, and traded as T. & J. Bevington & Co. Their lease expired in 1824 when the potworks reverted to Dillwyn, who in 1831 took his son Lewis L. Dillwyn into partnership.

David Evans and a man named Glasson took over the pottery in 1850. The works were closed down in 1870 and later dismantled.

Marks:

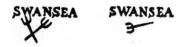

The Swansea factory in its early years made wares similar to those produced in Staffordshire at the period – cream-wares, blue-printed, black basaltes, marbled wares and articles decorated with enamels and with lustre.

In 1814 Billingsley and Walker, then occupying the factory at Nantgarw, joined Dillwyn at Swansea with the intention of collaborating in the production of a porcelain stronger in body and less subject to flaws in firing than that previously made at Nantgarw to Billingsley's formula. After experiments lasting nearly two years, a more stable composition was produced and manufactured commercially until September 1817. There are at least three distinct varieties of this paste, the most successful being that known as "duck-egg" because of its greenish translucency by transmitted light. Later a more opaque type of porcelain was made; this had a yellowish tinge and a thin, rather dull, glaze. A third type is much harder, white and glassy in appearance.

After 1817 a porcelain incorporating soapstone and much inferior to the earlier kinds was made.

Porcelain made during Billingsley's period at Swansea is sometimes hard to distinguish from Nantgarw. The shapes and designs used at Swansea were often more ambitious, and in the period 1814–17 many of the productions owe much to French porcelain of the period. Designs taken from natural history, particularly flowers reproduced from rather stiff botanical prints or in sprays or scattered groups, are characteristic of Swansea. Thomas Pardoe and Wm. Pollard were probably the most influential decorators at the factory.

Table ware, and especially plates, form the largest part of existing Swansea pieces.

Fakes are not uncommon – some marked with a Swansea mark – and were usually made in France.

(See also Nantgarw porcelain and Billingsley, William.)

"Swatow" ware: porcelains with thick, "fat" glaze and roughly-finished, glazed, gritty base, made in S. China and probably exported from Swatow, especially to Japan. Dishes, with wild, powerful painting in red, green and turquoise enamels and similar underglaze blue wares date from the late 16th to 17th cent.; also celadon, light brown and pale blue monochromes with white slip flowers.

Sweetmeat basket: small oval or circular silver basket introduced about 1740, found separately or on epergne (q.v.) branches. Early examples mostly pierced with cast floral borders. Later ones solid and decorated with engraving.

Sweetmeat glass: glass supported on a stem with a shallow bowl, examples from the second quarter of the 18th cent. often being decorated with shallow cutting or slicing. Referred to in the 18th cent. as "desart glasses", they were intended, with jelly glasses, to be served on glass salvers arranged in a tier, thus providing the elaborate display required for dessert. (See also Jelly glass.)

Swelling knop: a slight protuberance on the stem of a drinking glass, containing an air tear.

Swept-hilt rapier: a modern term for the type of rapier hilt, introduced in the 16th cent., in which the guard consists of a complicated series of curved bars.

Swing-leg table: a term used in America to describe a hinged-leaf table with a swinging rather than a gate leg. Handsome examples, some of them cabriole, survive. (See also Drop-leaf table.)

Swinton: see Rockingham porcelain.

Swirl paperweight: familiar name for a paperweight composed of coloured canes radiating spirally from the top.

Sword stick: a walking-stick concealing a sharp, rapier-like steel blade. Sword sticks date from the 1730s and continued in production until the late 19th cent.

"Sympathetic" strings: see under Viola d'amore.

Tabernacle mirror: an American term generally applied to the late 18th cent. mirror with flat cornice under which is a row of gilt balls above a scene painted on glass; columns at sides.

Table-chair, -bench: correct term for the absurdly misnamed monk's chair, or bench. Chair-table is also used. Convertible chair, the back pivoted to form a table-top when dropped across the uprights. Though the type existed in pre-Reformation times, most surviving examples date from the 17th cent. and can have no monastic association in England. The device was convenient in saving space and furniture.

Table clock: a clock with a horizontal dial, designed to be placed on a table and viewed from above.

Table cutting: a method of cutting gemstones in common use before the invention of rose cutting in the mid-17th cent., whereby the stone was ground to have a flat horizontal facet on top. Also known as mirror-cutting.

Table-services: matching sets of spoons, forks and other table ware. Complete extant services of silver are very rare before the end of the 17th cent. and are not common until the

mid-18th. The main patterns are:

Feather-edged: found in the second half of the 18th cent. The stems bear a narrow border fluting, resembling the edge of a feather.

Fiddle pattern: the stems are shaped with a broad upper section and notched shoulders at the bowl end, resembling slightly the basic form of a violin. This pattern was introduced in the early 19th cent. Sometimes they are found plain, or with threaded edges, and sometimes with stamped shells on the top.

Hanoverian: the stems have a central longitudinal ridge on the front and upcurved ends. This pattern was the most usual from c. 1720-40.

King's pattern: an early 19th cent. pattern, with shaped stems and waisted hourglass tops, decorated with scrolls shells and foliage.

Old English pattern: a perfectly plain form with flat stems spreading slightly to the rounded ends. This pattern was in common use from the mid-18th cent. onwards. Scottish and Irish varieties often have more pointed stems.

Onslow pattern: a rare mid-18th design in which the upper third of the stems are decorated with radiating fluting and cast and applied corkscrew-like scroll tops.

Queen's pattern: this is a less elaborate form of King's pattern, the decoration struck only on the upper surface of the stem and without a shell on the bowl.

Tabouret: (*Fr.*), a stool.

Tabriz carpets: Tabriz, the capital of ancient Persia, was one of the principal centres of carpet weaving. Both the carpets and rugs bear more realistic types of decoration than those characteristic of Ispahan (q.v.). The greatest of the "Hunting" carpets (q.v.) were woven at Tabriz, while other motifs include court figures and animals and birds, although the medallion motif on a plain ground was also popular. Silk is sometimes used in fine specimens, either for contrasting effect with wool, or sometimes alone.

Takamakiyé: (*Japanese* = raised sown picture). A Japanese lacquer-work technique whereby the design is in high relief, modelled in composition, and is then lacquered in the desired colours.

Talavera maiolica: tin-glazed earthenware made at Talavera in Spain. Towards the end of the 16th cent., the pottery at Talavera began to replace those of Valencia (see Hispano-Moresque maiolica). Blue and white and polychrome wares were made, closely influenced by the Italian potteries.

Tale-glass: a second-quality metal (q.v.) taken from the top of the pot, and sold more cheaply than the lower, finer metal.

Tallboy: a double chest of drawers, also known in the 18th cent. as a "chest-upon-chest". This piece of cabinet furniture was first made early in the 18th cent. and derived from Dutch example. Early tallboys stand on plain bracket feet, while the ogee bracket foot became popular towards the mid-cent. The tallboy was a development from the earlier chest on stand and continued in use throughout the cent., to be gradually replaced by the wardrobe.

Tallow cutting: a method of cutting gemstones in which the stones are rounded in form with a flat top.

Tambour front: a curved sliding top fitted to writing desks, fashionable in the late 18th cent.

Tambour-work: a form of chain-stitch embroidery worked with a steel hook, popular in England and France during the late 18th and early 19th cent. The name originated from the way the fabric to be embroidered was stretched over a round frame in the manner of a drum-skin.

Tandem horn: see under Coach horns and post horns.

"T" and "T°" marks: see Tebo, also Bow, Bristol and Plymouth porcelain.

Tang: the narrow portion of the sword blade which passes into the hilt.

T'ang dynasty: dynasty of the Chinese T'ang Emperors covering the period 618 to 906. This period was the golden age of China, great in literature and painting, and receptive and fertile in its contacts with the outside world. T'ang pottery conveys an unmistakable vitality and refinement, expressed in beautifully proportioned forms and a disciplined use of rich colour. The lead glaze was now revived, and applied over a fine white earthenware in green, golden-yellow and blue colourings of great brilliance, which were often splashed on or mottled together or used to enliven designs incised into the surface. Designs were also impressed from moulds. Favoured subjects were stylized flowers and birds, and others – the palmette and vine – which, like some forms, were derived from Hellenistic sources. Among the tomb figures of the time are models of calm, smiling ladies, dancers, ferocious warriors and mythical monsters, and horses and camels with their riders and attendants, showing the most sensitive observation in their modelling. Some unglazed earthenwares were painted "cold", usually over a white "slip" of clay, which enhanced the colours. Apart from these, and the refined pale-green Yüeh ware (q.v.) the chief glory of T'ang potters was their invention of translucent white porcelain. This material, composed of refined china-clay and china-stone fused at a high temperature, is found chiefly in small bowls. General indications of T'ang date are flat bases, and glazes which stop well short of the foot.

Tan-ye: Japanese prints coloured by hand with tan, a red-lead pigment.

Tanzaku: Japanese narrow vertical prints, inscribed with verses, about 14 × 6 inches.

Tao Kuang period: (1821–50), characteristic Chinese porcelain wares of this reign are those minutely painted in *famille rose* (q.v.) style, employing low-toned enamels, and *graviata*, coloured grounds. *Tou ts'ai* decoration was also popular. The body is coarser than in 18th cent. wares, and the glaze has an oily sheen.

Taper-box: small cylindrical box with handle and hole in lid to contain coiled sealing-wax taper. Found from about 1700 onwards (see also Waxjack).

Taperstick: small version of contemporary candlestick to hold sealing taper. Found both in vertical form and with flat base similar to chamber candlestick (q.v.). Extant from late 17th cent. onwards. In 18th cent. found as central fitting to inkstands.

Tappit hen: a Scottish pewter measure, i.e. a "hen with a top to it" (fanciful). The true tappit hen holds 1 pint Scots (equals 3 pints English), but the term is usually applied to all capacities.

Tari: silver coin, principally of Knights of St John in Malta. Multiples of eight, twelve, sixteen and thirty. Types, bust of Master of the Order with reverse, shield or St John's cross.

Tarsia: (*It.*), a form of wood inlay or marquetry widely used in Italy but most notably in Lombardy and Tuscany. Tarsia or intarsia decoration made up of polygonal tessere of wood, bone, metal and mother-of-pearl arranged in geometrical patterns, was very popular in Lombardy and Venetia in the 15th cent. and much used for the decoration of cassoni (q.v.). The art of pictorial tarsia was brought to a high level of excellence at Florence in the 15th cent. by a number of craftsmen, of whom Francesco di Giovanni, called il Francione, was, according to Vasari, the most highly esteemed. In the 15th and subsequent cent. tarsia was much used for the decoration of both ecclesiastical and domestic furniture. Panels representing views of real or imaginary architecture were popular on cassoni

in the late 15th and 16th cent., but during the 17th cent. abstract designs seem to have been preferred. In the 18th cent. tarsia was applied to tables and chests of drawers, usually in patterns of flowers and ribbons.

Tassies: (1) replicas of intaglios (q.v.) or glass paste impressions worn as jewellery and named after James Tassie, who settled in London in 1766, where he became famous for these cast gems. (2) Scots for a drinking cup. (*Fr. tasse.*)

Tate-ye: Japanese prints; upright pictures.

Taws: small balls or marbles made of earthenware or stoneware used in game of carpet bowls, made in Staffordshire, Yorkshire and Scotland.

Tazza: (*It. Cf. Fr. tasse; Scottish tassie*); wine-cup with shallow circular bowl. The name, correctly applied to such pieces of 16th to 17th cent., has become erroneously extended to cover flat dishes and salvers on central foot. Its derivation is clear, however, and can have no connotation with the latter pieces.

Tea-caddy: a container for storing tea. "Caddy" is a corruption of *kati*, a Malay measure of weight of just over one pound. The custom of locking up the family's tea in a box continued long after tea had ceased to be an expensive luxury; caddies, therefore, were invariably provided with locks, and were either divided into small compartments or were fitted with tea canisters (q.v.) for the different kinds of tea. A great variety of materials was used in their construction, in-

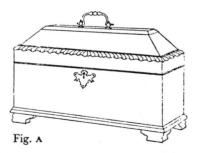

Fig. A

Fig. B

Fig. C

cluding woods of all kinds and papier-mâché (q.v.). There was also considerable diversity in shape, from rectangular (Fig. A) to square and octagonal (Fig. B); while vase and pear (Fig. C) forms were introduced after 1750.

Tea-canister: the container for tea in the caddy (if the latter were not already divided into compartments); made of glass, metal or earthenware; usually bottle-shaped until c. 1750, and vase-shaped later.

Teapot-stand: see Kettle-stand.

Tea-poy: until early in the 19th cent. the tea chest stood loosely upon a small tripod table with an octagonal tray top. *Simmonds' Dictionary of Trade,*

1850, defined tea-poy as "an ornamental pedestal table with lifting top, for holding tea". The tea-canister (q.v.) is often wrongly termed a tea-poy.

Tear-drop handle: see Drop handle.

Tears: bubbles of air enclosed within the stems of drinking vessels for decorative purposes. From 1715 to about 1760 clusters of spherical or comma-shaped tears appeared in bowl-base, knop and finial.

Tebo: probably the French name Thibaud anglicised. Very little is known about this craftsman who has been the subject of speculation. A "Mr Teboe, jeweller" is recorded as living at Fetter Lane, London, in 1747, (*Daily Advertiser*, 13 November 1747). There is evidence of a repairer (q.v.) at the Bow porcelain factory from about 1750 who signed his work T°. Sometime between 1760 and 1768 the same workman was at Worcester, and his mark also occurs on Plymouth porcelain of the Cookworthy period. From about 1775 Mr Tebo was working for Josiah Wedgwood who formed a poor opinion of his ability, (Josiah Wedgwood to T. Bentley 3 July 1775, 11 July 1775, and 28 October 1775). Subsequently he went to Dublin and passed into obscurity.

T.e.g.: an abbreviation used in booksellers' catalogues meaning top edge gilt. This refers to the gilding by the book-binder of the trimmed top edges of the folded sheets.

Tê-Hua porcelain: see Blanc-de-Chine.

Temmoku: Japanese name for porcelanous wares with lustrous brown glazes, especially Sung Chien wares.

Tempera: a method of painting in pigments composed of some glutinous substance soluble in water, as egg yolk, usually executed on a ground of chalk or plaster.

Templet: see Bezel.

Tenon: see Mortice and tenon joint.

Terra cotta: red biscuit earthenware varying in colours according to firing, from pink to purple-red.

Terrestrial globe: a spherical model of the earth. The suggestion that the world was, in fact, round was expressed in world models at an early date and a famous example is the globe made in 1492 by Martin Behaim. In the 18th cent., globes were considered a valuable addition to a library. They were sometimes made in pairs consisting of a terrestrial globe and a celestial globe, showing a spherical map of the heavens. The parts of the globe are, first, the sphere, constructed of wood or lathe and plaster or of metal, such as copper or brass. The meridian is a flat graduated hoop of metal or wood which encircles the orb and into which the poles of the axis are set, permitting rotation. This meridian, borne on a short column, can be turned to raise or lower the poles. The framework of the stand carries on its upper surface, surrounding the globe, the horizon, on which is presented a perpetual calendar with day of the month, the sun's place in the zodiac, the points of the compass and fixed feasts and winds. A mariner's compass was often introduced on the stand. The surface details were printed on paper, pasted on to the orb. While a pillared stand, with the globe set into the encircling horizon, was the chief method of presentation, the sickle-shaped support, consisting of a brass half circle mounted on a turned column and base, was later common, especially for small globes. The style of the stand varied with furniture fashions.

Terret: these, more correctly termed fly terrets, are also known as swingers and flyers. The terret is a vertical ring set between the horse's ears and in which swings a horse brass with both faces finished and polished. Such brasses are smaller in diameter than the ordinary horse brass.

Tester: a wooden canopy over a four-poster bed. In the late 17th cent. posts, back and tester were covered with costly material and the corners of the tester were sometimes surmounted by plumes of feathers. At this period a new type of bedstead without footposts was introduced, known as a "half-tester". Mid-18th cent. mahogany four-posters allow the posts and carved cornice of the tester to be exposed, while Regency fashions encouraged the French taste for high-domed canopies.

Thaler: large silver coin of crown (q.v.) class. Name derived from original coins struck from silver from Joachimsthal in Bohemia in 1518. This quickly became the pattern for large silver coins throughout Western Europe and was struck in most countries under variety of names and with many types, latterly with rulers portrait obverse and armorial shield reverse.

"Thin man" toby jug: a variety of early toby jug (q.v.), perhaps made by Whieldon (q.v.) or perhaps by Ralph Wood Senior (q.v.). The figure represents a thin man holding a pipe and mug of beer and the glazing and modelling are not entirely assured.

Thistle bowl: bowl of a drinking glass of thistle form in which the bottom or lower part is a solid or a hollow sphere of glass.

"Thistle" cup: an exclusively Scottish silver cup, dating from c. 1690 to the early 18th cent., rather like a teacup, with single S-shaped handle, and everted lip. Principal decoration is calyx-like arrangement of *appliqué* lobes rising from foot towards waist, and waist is also encircled by fillet. The handle is sometimes enhanced with beaded ornament.

Thomire, Pierre Philippe: French bronze caster. Born 1751, the son of a *ciseleur.* Worked under the sculptors

Pajou and Houdon. In 1783 entered the service of the Sèvres porcelain factory. From 1784 onwards he was frequently employed by the Crown to make mounts for furniture, and often collaborated with G. Beneman (q.v.).

Thread circuit: a thin trail of applied glass encircling a bowl rim or decorating the neck of a glass vessel.

Threading: one or two narrow lines engraved as a border on silver spoon and fork stems and other small pieces.

Thread setting: the setting of a gemstone in which the stone is surrounded by a thin strip of gold.

Three-decker novel: the popular term for the novel issued in three volumes, an almost universal practice until the very end of the Victorian age.

Three-piece glasses: drinking glasses in which the bowl, stem, and foot are made separately and welded together.

Three-quarter bound: see under Half bound.

Thrymsa: small gold British coin struck in 17th and 18th cent. with types imitating the tremissis (q.v.) of the late Roman Empire, usually obverse portrait and cross motif reverse.

Thumbpiece or **billet:** the projecting part above the hinge of a covered vessel whereby the cover might easily be opened with the thumb. Found in a great variety of forms on flagons and tankards of silver, pewter, etc.

Thuringian porcelain: see under Limbach porcelain.

Tical: silver coin of Siam. Small silver bars bent inwards in bullet shape. Plain, except for punch-mark, usually on inside and outside of bend. Issued from 14th to 19th cent.

Tic-tac escapement: a type of escapement (q.v.) found in some early clocks and a modified form of the anchor escapement (q.v.).

Tidal clock dial: a dial that indicates daily the time of high tide at any given port. Not found on Continental clocks. The earliest English dials were made for London, and show high tide at noon and full moon at 3 o'clock. Since the 24-hour cycle is completed each lunation, by having two circles, one fixed and marked 1–29½ (the days of the lunation) and the other movable, marked 1–12 twice over, the daily times of high tide for that port will be shown.

"Tigerware" jug: a big-bellied pitcher with a cylindrical neck made in German salt-glazed stoneware, imported into this country in the 16th cent. Examples are found mounted with Elizabethan silver or gilt embossed and engraved neckbands, covers, handles and footrims. Imitated in English tin-enamelled earthenware. (See "Malling" jug, also called "Leopard" ware.)

Tills: forerunners of the fitted tray in a modern trunk. Inside many 17th cent. chests a small tray was fitted on the right near the lid. Sometimes it was itself lidded, the lid hingeing into the framework of the chest; sometimes it was locked and occasionally had a false-bottomed hiding place. Catharine of Aragon in 1534 had "one cofar having four tilles therein, the fore-front of every one of them gilte". The lidded box-like tills in a chest might be called drawing chests or drawers, although the chest-of-drawers, as a considerable piece of bedroom furniture and as distinct from a cabinet of tiny drawers, was evolved only in the 17th cent. Thus, in 1599, Minshen referred to "a great chest or standard with drawing chests or boxes in it."

Ting: the small three-footed Chinese cauldron used as an incense-burner.

Tin glaze: a lead glaze, used as a decoration on pottery and made opaque by the addition of tin ashes. Sometimes called tin-enamel. Used in England from c. 1570 until the early 19th cent.

Ting ware: light, fine-grained, creamy-white porcelain of the Sung dynasty (q.v.), with ivory-toned glaze often running into gummy drops; from Ting Chou (Chihli Province). Common forms are shallow-lobed bowls and rimless dishes. The finest examples have decoration of plants or flowers, fish, swimming ducks, etc., freely incised under the glaze. Designs were also impressed from moulds. Ting type wares were also made elsewhere, and at later dates – for example, the "Kiangnan Ting" of South China, with softer, sandy body and crackled glaze, probably of the Ming dynasty and later. 18th-cent. imitations of Ting at Ching-tê-Chên do not resemble it in quality.

Tint: a residual colour tinge apparent in glass and inherent in the ingredients from which the metal is composed.

Tinted aquatint: an aquatint (q.v.) washed over by hand with a water-colour tint.

Tinted lithograph: a lithograph (q.v.) which has undergone two printings, the key in black, followed by a printed tint.

Tinted lithograph coloured: a lithograph (q.v.), printed in black with a monochrome mechanical print, other colours being applied by hand.

Tipped in: a term used of books to describe a leaf lightly attached, by gum or paste, usually at the inner edge. Plates, *errata* slips or a single inserted leaf will sometimes be described as being tipped in, as distinct from being sewn in. But the term is much more frequently used of something originally alien to the book which has been put with it by an earlier owner; e.g. an autograph letter from the author, or some similar associated document.

"Tithe pig": figure subject in porcelain and earthenware, also used as decoration of mugs and jugs accompanied by such rhymes as "In Country Village lives a Vicar Fond as all are of Tithes and Liquor". A well-known toby jug is inscribed "I will have no child to the X pig". The collection of tithe in kind was abolished by the Tithe Commutation Act, 1836.

Toad mugs: commonly made in the North Country in the 19th cent., but also more rarely elsewhere. They consisted of drinking mugs with a large toad inside which can be seen only when the pot is emptied, causing surprise and consternation because of folk superstitions concerning the use of toad poison. The inscription "Tho' malt and venom seem united . . ." is not uncommon.

Toaster: these were either in the form of standing toasters or the familiar fork, and were used for the toasting of both bread and meat. The fork almost always has three prongs. A variation of it is the toastholder, which has two short upcurved arms at the end of a long handle.

Standing toasters are rare and vary much in design. Some have simple tripod bases and central pillars with turned finials. On each pillar is a bell-shaped fitting with three prongs for holding the food to be toasted, and these are adjustable for height. Others are either in the form of a circular trivet (q.v.) with a three-pronged fork, or stand on the ground like a table toastrack.

Toasting glass: a drinking glass with a tall stem drawn to a diameter of one-eighth to one quarter of an inch.

Toastmaster's glass: a drinking glass with a thick bowl designed to magnify its capacity, on a tall stem. Short, deceptive glasses, known as sham drams, were used by tavern-keepers in the late 18th and first half of the 19th cent.

Tobi seiji ("buckwheat celadon"): Japanese name for brown-spotted Sung celadon wares of Lung-chüan (q.v.).

Toby Fillpot: nickname of a noted toper, Harry Elwes, who, through contemporary engravings, served as model for the original toby jug (q.v.).

Toby jug: a jug in the form of a man holding a mug of beer and a clay pipe, adapted from an engraving issued by Carrington Bowles with the verses of a song *The Metamorphosis*, or *Toby Reduc'd*, said to have been translated from the Italian by the Rev. Francis Fawkes. The brim of the three-cornered hat formed the lip of the jug, and the crown a detachable cover or cup. Female toby jugs are known, as well as other variants.

Made by Ralph Wood, James Neale, Lakin & Poole, Spode, Davenport and others in Staffordshire, Yorkshire and other areas.

Variants include:
Toby Fillpot
Admiral Howe
The Black Man
Martha Gunn
The Gin Woman
The Parson
The Welsh Country
   Gentleman
The Convict
The Hearty Good Fellow
The Snuff Taker
The Planter
Punch (19th cent.)
John Bull (19th cent.)
Pickwick (19th cent.)
Shield Toby
Bluff King Hal
The Collier
The Thin Man
The Farrier
The Unfrocked Parson
   (sometimes called
   Dr Johnson)
The Night Watchman
The Sailor

Paul Pry (19th cent.)
The Royal Bargeman
The Fiddler
Judy (19th cent.)
The Woodman (19th cent.)

Toddy-lifter: a pipette with bulbous or decanter-shaped body for lifting hot toddy from bowl to drinking glass, used in the first half of the 19th cent.

Toft, Thomas: a name occurring on numerous large round slipware dishes and more rarely on hollow-wares. It is not known for certain whether the name is that of maker or recipient, but it would seem that the traditional view that Thomas Toft made these pieces is justified for it is unlikely that any collector would have wished to have 35 or more such outsize dishes, some even decorated with the same subjects. The Royal Arms occur on Toft dishes at least five times.

Variations in letter A
in Toft signature

There are numerous references to Thomas Toft in Stoke-on-Trent Parish Registers. He died a pauper in 1689. 35 large dishes, 2 jugs and a posset-pot are recorded with Thomas Toft's name. They are decorated with "trailed slip", the dishes having trellis rim borders interrupted by panels enclosing the name. More rarely a border of fleur-de-lis or heads was used. The centre decorations comprised Royal Arms, (incorrectly rendered), Arms of the Cordwainers' Company, the Boscobel Oak, Pelican-in-her-Piety, lions rampant, double-headed eagles, figures of cavaliers and ladies, a man smoking, and foliage. Dated examples are known – 1671, 1674, 1677, and 1689.

Togidashi: (*Japanese* = polishing out), Japanese lacquer work technique in which the design is made in colours and then rubbed down to an absolutely even surface, which gives a water-colour effect.

Toilé: (*Fr.*), a term used in lace-making, in preference to the English clothwork or mat, to describe the solid part of the pattern. In needlepoint lace (q.v.) it was composed of rows of stitches, buttonhole or loop. In pillow lace (q.v.) the multiple threads achieved an effect of weaving.

Toilet mirror or **dressing-glass:** a small mirror designed to stand on a table or, in early examples, to hang on the wall. This kind of mirror was a luxury in the medieval and Tudor periods, and did not begin to come into wider use until the late 17th cent. Post-Restoration mirrors were usually square in shape, and frequently had their frames decorated with stump-work; they stood by means of a strut or hung by a ring. By about 1700 oblong mirrors with arched tops, in narrower moulded frames, veneered or japanned, had begun to replace the square shape. In the 18th cent. several changes occurred. Shortly after 1700 appeared the mirror supported by screws in uprights mounted on a box stand; the box was often in the form of a flap or desk above a drawer which contained the many toilet requisites of the time; the mirror had a pronounced arched heading at first, and the front of the box was sometimes serpentine in form. The older type of strut support, without the box stand, continued to be made, however, and occasionally a stand with small trestle feet was found. By 1750 mahogany was in general use for toilet mirrors, though some in the Chinese style were gilt or japanned. Simpler designs were introduced in the neo-classical period; mirror frames, in mahogany or satin-

wood, were often of oval or shield shape, and the uprights were curved to correspond. The stand was also a simpler arrangement, as toilet articles were now placed in the table on which

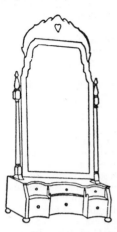

the mirror stood. At the very end of the cent. and later, a wide oblong mirror was fashionable, and was usually swung on turned uprights. Mahogany and rosewood, often deco-rated with stringing, were the chief woods for such mirrors at this time.

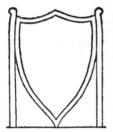

Toilet service: silver, or silver-mounted ebony or tortoise-shell sets of toilet-boxes, vases, mirror, candlesticks, brushes, etc., of great magnificence introduced after the Restoration and lasting into the late 18th cent. Later replaced by wooden dressing chests with silver-mounted glass fittings.

Toison: gold coin of Philippe le Beau (1496–1505), issued in Brabant with obverse type crowned shield with, below, insignia of Order of the Golden Fleece. Also a silver piece of similar types.

Tôle: (*Fr.*), sheet iron. A term now in common use for any painted tinware, although *tôle peinte* is the complete form.

Tombac: a white alloy of copper used in Germany in the 18th cent. for snuff-boxes and toys (q.v.).

Tompion, Thomas: the most famous of Restoration clockmakers, described by a contemporary as "a person deservedly famous for his excellent skill in making watches and clocks, and not less curious and dexterous in constructing and handworking of other nice mechanical instruments". He introduced into his clocks many refinements such as perpetual calendar (q.v.) work and elaborate repeating and astronomical work. He was active as a clockmaker between 1671 and his death in 1713, when he was buried in Westminster Abbey.

Tooling: the process of decorating a leather book binding or a vellum binding by means of a metal tool. (See also Gold-tooled bindings.)

Torchère: see Candle-stand.

Tortoiseshell ware: cream earthenware covered with a lead glaze stained with mottlings of blue, brown and green from oxides of cobalt, manganese, and copper. Made by Whieldon (q.v.) and other potters, c. 1750.

Torus moulding: a large convex moulding of semi-circular section.

Touch: the pewterer's trade mark. From the late Middle Ages it was obligatory for a London pewterer to mark his wares with a mark or touch which he had registered at Pewterers' Hall. The Great Fire of 1666 destroyed Pewterers' Hall and with it the touch-plates. The system was revived in 1668 when all pewterers were required to restrike upon a new plate, and it continued into the beginning of the 19th cent. No date letter appears on pewter, but other marks, including quality marks, excise marks etc., and

what are erroneously called "hall-marks" were applied. The latter were small punches, usually four, resembling those used on silver. One usually contained the maker's initials. These marks had no authority in law or craft regulations.

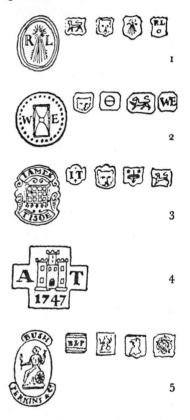

1. Robert Lucas, London, c. 1640
2. William Eden, London, 1690
3. James Tisoe, London, 1734
4. Adam Tait, Edinburgh, 1747
5. Bush & Perkins, Bristol, c. 1775

Touch-plate: a flat sheet of soft pewter for recording pewterers' touches. (See also Touch.)

Touchstone: a piece of polished "stone" on which a piece of silver of known quality could be rubbed to compare its mark with that of a piece being assayed.

Tourbillon: a watch in which the escapement is mounted on a revolving carriage, which carries it round. Invented by A. L. Breguet in 1801 to avoid positional error.

Tournai porcelain: soft-paste porcelain was made at Tournai in Belgium from 1751 and the following year the factory became known as the *Manufacture Imperiale et Royale*. Wares were made in the manner of Sèvres (q.v.) and principally biscuit figures were produced, some of which were copied at Derby (q.v.). In the 19th cent. much early Sèvres, Chelsea and Worcester porcelain was copied. The mark of crossed swords with four small crosses, one in each angle, is found in various colours.

Tou ts'ai ("contrasting colour") enamels: delicate, sparing designs on Chinese porcelain in underglaze blue, set off by transparent enamel colours, chiefly red, yellow and green; their jewel-like quality was perfected under Ch'êng Hua (1465–87). Deceptive imitations and new-style wares were made under Yung Chêng and Ch'ien Lung; and again revived under Tao Kuang (1821–50).

Townsend, John: renowned cabinet-maker of Newport, R.I. (b. 1733). He made excellent block-front (q.v.) furniture and is believed to have been associated with his brother-in-law, John Goddard, in originating this form. Outstanding member of a famous furniture-making family, which included his father, Job, several brothers, sons and nephews. Some scholars think the Townsends deserve most of the credit now given to John Goddard for originating block-front furniture (q.v.).

Toys: an 18th cent. term to describe small objects of metal, enamel, porcelain, etc. such as scent bottles, patch boxes, étuis (q.v.) châtelaines or seals.

Toy theatres: the Toy Theatre or Juvenile Drama started before the Victorian period but achieved its greatest popularity after 1837. It developed from individual portraits of famous actors and actresses sold at a penny plain and twopence coloured at the beginning of the 19th cent. These portraits had a flavour of their own about them, showing the performers in a highly histrionic manner and being crude but not unpleasant, a flavour which was never lost as these portraits developed into the Juvenile Drama. This development took the form of a series of sheets which showed popular plays, giving not only the whole cast but the scenery, and with a book of words included. The figures on these sheets could be cut out and pasted on to cardboard, so that the juvenile producer could make them perform while reading aloud their various parts. During the 'thirties a further refinement was added, in that ready-cut tinsel made from coloured metal sheets could be bought to put on the figures.

By the 'fifties publishers of these sheets had ready-made wooden stages for the performers. The characters fitted into slides which moved through grooves across the stage, and later there were, instead, tin stands with wires attached. By the 'seventies the real craze for the toy theatre was over.

Tr.: transcript. Used indiscriminately of manuscript copies without regard to the period of transcription unless specified.

Trade binding: a book-binding executed for a retail or wholesale bookseller prior to the development of publishers' bindings in the 19th cent. Before 1820 ready-bound books formed only a small proportion of a bookseller's stock, much of which would be in sheets or, after 1770, in paper-covered boards, uncut, ready for binding to the customer's order.

Trade card: 18th cent. trade cards were usually printed from an engraved or etched copper plate with a highly ornamental border, enclosing the tradesman's name and address and a list of his chief productions. The border might also display a selection of fashionable goods then in demand. Cleverly designed and skilfully engraved by etching or line-engraving on improved copper, the majority were the work of specialists who, like Matthias

Darly, and William and Cluer Dicey, advertised themselves as "Engravers of Shopkeepers Bills" who made "Shop-keepers Bills curiously engrav'd on Copper Plates".

Trail ornament: a border pattern consisting of formal leaf spray or tendril in a running design. Carved vine trails appear, for example, on 17th cent. oak furniture, while the early 19th cent. goldsmiths favoured bands of chased ivy trails as a decorative motif. It was, in fact, an ornamental form used in various ways at widely different periods.

Trailed ornament: a technique of the glassblower in which looped threads of glass are attached to the surface of a glass vessel and melted in. Ribbed surfaces may be produced by means of trailed threads melted in the body of the metal.

Trailed slip: a clay slip used for coating or decorating pottery and applied by trailing it from a spouted or tubular vessel.

Trailing, pinched: a technique of the glassblower in which applied threads of glass, melted into the body of a vessel, are pinched into a wavy formation.

Train: a series of wheel and pinions geared together, forming the mechanism of a clock or watch. They are going, striking, chiming, musical, astronomical trains, etc.

Transfer-printing: the application of decorations from engraved copper plates to pottery, porcelain or enamels by means of bats of gelatine (bat-printing) or later (c. 1800) by paper tissues, first practised on enamel wares at Battersea (q.v.); was effected overglaze at the Bow (1756) and Worcester (1756–57) porcelain factories by Robert Hancock, and at Liverpool by J. Sadler c. 1756. Printing in blue underglaze was practised at Worcester c. 1759 and popularized during Hancock's employment at Caughley 1775, and adopted soon after at Liverpool, Lowestoft, Bristol and in Staffordshire. Other colours were used during the 19th cent. including pink, puce, orange-brown and green. Gold-printing was patented by Peter Warburton in 1810. Multi-colour and block-printing were used from the 1840s in Staffordshire. (See also Black printing.)

Transformation: see Transparencies.

Transformation playing cards: first issued in London, 1808. In these pictures the requisite number of suit signs served as prominent features, such as hearts for men's faces, diamonds as parts of feminine dress, clubs and spades as carved motifs in pseudo-Gothic furniture. Making transformation cards from ordinary packs became a fashionable pastime, pen and ink converting cards into designs of topical or personal association.

Translucent enamel: see Enamel.

Transparencies, pinprick pictures, etc.: a coloured print mounted on a board and pasted over a transformation scene which will show through when the print is held before a strong light. The best-known Victorian series of Transparencies are Spooner's *Transformations* and Morgan's *Improved Protean Scenery*, both of which appeared in the late 1830s and the 1840s.

Pinprick pictures were a more simple form of transformation, since a coloured print was perforated with a number of small holes and, hence, when held to the light the print would appear to be illuminated. Coloured paper would sometimes be fastened behind the print to change, for instance, sunlight into moonlight, or to show a church in the daytime illuminated at night when held up to the light. An elaboration of this was the making of small transparent slides, which were placed in a box and viewed through peepholes. By raising lids in the box at the top or at the back, the print could be transformed.

The Transparency is not a Victorian invention but, like so many other peculiarities, achieved its greatest popularity in Victorian times. The classic book on the subject is *An Essay on Transparent Prints* by Edward Orme

(1807). This is illustrated and tells how to construct a transparency.

Treasury inkstand: a four-footed oblong box, with double lid centrally hinged, containing four compartments for writing accessories. So called from an example in the Government department of that name.

Tree calf binding: a calf bookbinding (popular in the 19th cent., less common today), the sides of which have been stained by the interaction of copperas and pearl-ash to a design resembling a tree, and then highly polished.

Treen: old adjectival form of tree meaning wooden. Now used of a variety of wooden articles, mainly small and of almost any period, such as· bowls, Welsh love-spoons, staybusks, boxes, pepper-mills, etc.

Trefid or **trifid spoon:** also known by the French term, *Pied de biche.* Late 17th-cent. spoon with flat stem widening to a lobed outline at the top, split by two cuts forming three sections suggestive of a cleft hoof. The ends sometimes curve upwards. Normally found with rat-tailed (q.v.) bowls.

Tremissis: (1) small gold Roman coin, equal to a third of the solidus (q.v.) and of similar types; (2) small gold Medieval coin, the third of the solidus. Widely copied throughout Western Europe from 6th to 8th cent., particularly by the Merovingians in France. Favourite types, obverse portrait and cross reverse.

Trenails or **treenails:** the old term for cylindrical pins of hardwood used for fastening timber together, mentioned, for example, in an inventory of 1571 "iij hounrethe treenales". Square wooden pins might be used green, driven into round holes for greater firmness.

Trencher salt: small individual saltcellar with solid sides lying flat on the table. Earliest examples date from about 1630. The standard form of table salt till about 1725. Of circular, oval, square or polygonal form with oval or circular well.

Trestle table: a long table supported on free-standing trestles. This type of table was in use for dining in the Middle Ages until well into the 16th cent., when a table supported on a joined frame was used.

Triangle mark: see Chelsea porcelain.

Tricoteuse: (*Fr.*), a term probably of 19th-cent. origin, applied to a small work-table surrounded by a gallery, part of which can be lowered to contain sewing materials.

Tric-trac: a game representing a complicated form of back-gammon, so-called from the clicking sound made by the pieces during play. Boards intended for tric-trac are distinguished by a shallow gallery surrounding each of the two playing areas, a feature found in most games tables from the late 1760s.

Tridarn: a Welsh variety of the press cupboard (q.v.) made in three stages, the two lower enclosed and the top open.

Triens: a Roman coin; third of the Republican as (q.v.). Obverse type, head of Minerva in crested helmet and mark of value • • • •

Triple reed dish: having a rim with multiple mouldings around the edge.

Tripod table: see Pedestal table.

Triptych: a picture or carving consisting of three sections, the outer two forming hinged doors which could be closed. A characteristic form for an altar piece.

Trivet: (Brandis(e)), strictly a three-legged stand on which utensils might rest before the fire, but the word is used to cover many types of stand. The trivets of the 17th and 18th cent. were usually circular and of wrought-iron; sometimes they had a projecting handle. Later versions, also on three legs, were of an oblong shape with one end curved and fitted with a handle, while the far end had curved projections to fit over the fire-bar of a grate. Others dispensed with legs, and were made to hang on the front of a stove; of this last type many were made in the 19th cent. of cast-iron with pierced brass tops.

Trolly lace: pillow lace, coarse, made especially in the 18th cent. in Devonshire, with heavily out'ined patterns in a *fond chant* ground (q.v.).

Trolly thread: gimp outlining the pattern in Lille lace (q.v.).

Trumpet bowl: bowl of a drinking glass of waisted incurving form, merging into a drawn stem (q.v.).

Trussing coffers: a frequent term for leather-covered travelling chests, usually implying smaller articles than standards; as, for instance, was indicated in a reference of 1622: "Commodities packt up in Bundels, Trusses, Cases, Coffers or Packes."

Tschinke: a light wheel-lock gun, generally rifled, used for bird-shooting in the area of Germanic culture during the 17th cent. The butt usually takes a sharp downward curve while the lock has an external mainspring.

Tsuikoku: (*Japanese* = heap black), a Japanese lacquer-work technique in which a deep surface of solid black lacquer is prepared. The design is then carved in the lacquer.

Tsuishu: (*Japanese* = heap red), a Japanese lacquer-work technique in which a deep surface of solid red lacquer is made, of several layers, and the design is carved in the lacquer.

Tuckaway table: an American hinged-leaf gate-leg table with cross legs which fold into each other as compactly as if tucked away.

Tudor style: the Tudor dynasty lasted from 1485–1603; during this period, both architecture and the decorative arts gradually discarded the Gothic tradition of the Middle Ages and adopted the new modes of expression fashionable in Renaissance Italy.

Tula work: a particular type of silverwork, decorated with niello (q.v.) and sometimes partly gilt, to which the town of Tula in central Russia has given its name, although, in fact, such work was not only made at Tula. Snuff-boxes and similar small articles were decorated in this manner with figure subjects, floral or geometrical ornament. Most examples are of no earlier date than the beginning of the 19th cent., although the art of decorating in silver with niello has a longer history in Russia. Tula was also a centre of the iron and steel industry and Peter the Great established a Small Arms factory there in 1705. (See also Chiselled steel.)

Tulip ornament: a formal ornament which appeared frequently in the second half of the 17th cent. in a variety of forms. Tulips were painted on tin-glazed earthenware, carved on oak furniture and both chased and embossed on silverware. An intense interest in horticulture, which had already developed in the late 16th cent., was encouraged by the introduction of new plants from the East. The tulip is first recorded in Europe in 1559 and in seventy-five years became the rage. 1634 was the year of tulipomania in Holland, when huge sums were paid for rare bulbs.

Tulip (pear): a pewter tankard or mug with body of bulbous form.

Tumbler cup: small, plain drinking-bowl with rounded base and straight sides. Extant from mid-17th cent. onwards.

Tumblers: units in a lock mechanism to retain the bolt. These are immovable to any but the right key which lifts them to predetermined heights and shoots the bolt.

Tunbridge ware: although the term acquired a wider meaning it was first applied to the simple, well finished marquetry and parquetry work (q.v.), the "ornamental woodwork" – that made the Spa shops celebrated as gift emporiums. This work was introduced in the mid-1680s by the master wood-worker named Jordan and at first consisted of patterned veneers using various coloured native woods. The designs were mainly geometrical but included borders of heavy scrollwork and, in the 18th cent., representations of flowers and foliage, animals and so on. Large quantities of games boards were sold. When the Games Act (1739) came into operation many indoor games were prohibited. The Tunbridge ware men set about evolving new games to evade the law and some of these are noted by Hoyle.

The furze, holly, yew and cherry, abundant in the Tunbridge Wells district, were used, as well as any wood of unusual colour or grain that gardeners at the numerous large residences might find. Other woods came from London merchants of native and foreign hard woods. The marquetry work of Tunbridge Wells achieved such fame that the term Tunbridge ware was adopted by London specialists, who took the opportunity of exploiting the fashion.

Rows of elongated triangles known as vandykes were a feature of Tunbridge ware, arranged alternately in light and dark woods. These appear to have been derived from the pattern on backgammon and tric-trac boards which were among the first manufactures. Vandykes might border parquetry designs composed of various diamond and parallelogram shapes, so arranged as to produce effects of solid cubes viewed in perspective. Handles and spindles might be of lathe-turned stickwork (q.v.).

By the early 19th cent. Tunbridge ware had become a specialized branch of the small cabinet-making trade. This ware usually possessed a pine-wood base with kingwood, rosewood or walnut veneer as a setting for ornament in a wide variety of colourful woods.

Robert Russell was a late worker in the Tunbridge style. He is known to have made dressing-cases, work-boxes and portable desks in the late 18th cent. and the catalogue of the Great Exhibition records him as having sent a "Tunbridge ware marquetrie inlaid lady's work-box fitted with a till, etc. Made in the Gothic style from native woods".

Turkey work: this was the name generally given to carpets, cushions and upholstery, knotted in the manner of Near Eastern rugs, in 16th and 17th-cent. inventories. Apart from larger carpets and rugs, Turkey-work cushions appear to have been made in not inconsiderable numbers in England, though they are now rare. Examples can be dated throughout the 17th cent., and armorial cushions are noteworthy. In the 18th cent. cross-stitch embroidery took the place of knotted pile for upholstery.

Turkish rugs: the most numerous to be found in Europe are those from Anatolia and Asia Minor. Many were imported from the 18th cent. onwards, and due to their distinctive designs and fine quality, were not used on floors but as wall hangings and more often as table coverings, a custom which is still in general use in Holland. They came from Ladik, Kuba, Ghiordes and Kir-Shehr; the main design is usually what is called the Mihrab, a representation of the Mosque arch, often embellished by a hanging lamp between the pillars. Some were intended as prayer rugs. During the 14th and 15th cent. the Ottoman Turks invaded Persia on several occasions and enriched their own carpet and rug industries by importing skilled Persian craftsmen. The influence on these carpet weavers is most marked and a tradition of design and quality was established. The greatest period was during the reigns of Selim the Great and Sulliman the Magnificent, when Persian carpet weaving was at it enith. Contemporary specimens ar a marked resemblance to Persian rugs, but the national characteristics are clearly apparent. The flowing lines familiar in the finest products of Tabriz and

Ispahan (qq.v.) have become bold and angular. The use of stronger colours and realistic flowers are other distinguishing features.

Turkoman rugs: throughout Turkestan, rugs are woven in traditional variations of the same motif, the octagonal gules, known as the "elephant's foot", and generally dyed in deep, glowing Turanian red, with dark blue and black.

Turlutaine: see under Bird-organ.

Turner: maker of turned wooden members. Furniture with turned supports was made in the Middle Ages. Turners were themselves chair-makers, and there are examples of early chairs consisting only of turned members, held together by a dowel joint, instead of the mortice and tenon joint of the joiner (qq.v.). In the 17th cent., turners were still the makers of cheap chairs with rush or wooden seats, of which the Windsor chair (q.v.) is an example and they continued to be so, producing a variety of simple forms, until well into the 19th cent.

Turner, John: (1738–87), potter at Stoke from about 1756; then at Lane

End from 1762–87; continued by his sons John and William Turner until 1803, when the company was enlarged. John Turner withdrew in 1804, and the company was wound up in 1806 when both the younger Turners were declared bankrupt.
Marks:

TURNER   TURNER & CO.
Impressed   Impressed

Turner's Patent

In red

This mark was adopted for the firm's stoneware, usually painted in red, from 1800–05.

John Turner was, Josiah Wedgwood apart, the most famous Staffordshire potter of his time. Skilful, enterprising and successful in business, much of his work is equal in quality and similar in style to Wedgwood's.

Turner manufactured white stoneware in partnership with R. Bankes at the works of Josiah Spode in Stoke till 1762 when he moved to Lane End to manufacture on his own account, largely cream-coloured wares, stoneware, dry bodies and jasper.

In 1775 Turner was involved with Wedgwood in the opposition of the Staffordshire potters to the extension of Cookworthy's (q.v.) patent, which Champion tried to effect.

John Turner was a member of the New Hall porcelain (q.v.) company from 1781–82. He died in 1787.

William and John Turner succeeded their father, continuing successfully all the styles he had manufactured. But their prosperous business was ruined through its dependence on the Continental trade which was lost to them as a result of the French Revolution and the Napoleonic Wars. Their two factories closed in 1806, John Turner joining Thomas Minton as manager.

Turning: until about 1700 turning was one of the outstanding features of the legs of chairs, tables and stands, and of the uprights of chairs. It was carried out on the foot-operated pole lathe which rotated the wood while the turner's chisel cut the required shape. (See also Twist turning, Bobbin turning and Baluster turning.)

Turret clock: a clock for use in a church tower or other building.

Tutenag: see Paktong.

12mo (twelvemo): see Book sizes.

Twin acorn thumbpiece: a thumbpiece (q.v.) in the form of two acorns rising from a wedge attached to the lid of pewter measures, etc.

Twin cusped thumbpiece: a thumbpiece (q.v.) in the form of two semi-spheres rising from a broad base found on pewter flagons, etc.

Twist turning: a variety of turning used by English furniture makers for the decoration of chair and table legs, etc. in the late 17th cent. It came to England from the Continent shortly after the Restoration and replaced the earlier bobbin turning (q.v.). At first the Flemish "single rope" style was used, but this was followed by the English double rope or "barley sugar" twist, finished by hand and sometimes pierced. The design was becoming less popular on chairs by 1685 but persisted on tables for some time longer.

Two-handled cup: introduced in the late 17th cent., developing from porringer form and gradually re-placing the earlier standing cup on a high stem. It is normally found with cover but is of great variety of size and decoration. Used for "loving cup" ceremonies, race prizes and display generally.

Two-piece glasses: drinking glasses in which the stem is drawn in a piece from the bowl and a foot is added.

Two seconds clock pendulum: 13 feet 0½ inches. When making the first two clocks for Greenwich Observatory, in 1676, Thomas Tompion introduced 2-seconds pendulums and year movements, in an attempt to secure the greatest accuracy. These are thought to be the first clocks so designed in England. When the clocks were removed from Greenwich they were converted to movements with 1-second pendulums. 2-second pendulums are now only found in some turret clocks.

"Twyford" toby jug: see "Step" toby jug.

Tyg: a word of obscure origin used to describe cylindrical drinking vessels with from one to twelve handles: a multiple-handled beaker.

Type: the design, whether in relief or incuse, on either side of a coin or medal.

Tz'ŭ Chou ware: The Tz'ŭ Chou neighbourhood of China (Chihli Province) has made stonewares from the Sung dynasty until the present day. The characteristic body is hard and greyish white, covered with slips and glazes of creamy-white, brown or black and occasionally green colour, often ingeniously combined. The Sung wares are remarkable for bold sensitive shapes – especially tall, swelling vases and jars with loop-handles at the shoulder. Plates and dishes are rare. One type of decoration has leafy floral designs strongly incised or carved through the glaze to reveal another colour beneath. Another is bold painting in brown or black. Black painting under a turquoise glaze was popular about the 14th cent. Red, green and yellow enamel painting is sometimes of Sung date. Ming wares employed similar techniques, and elaborate landscape and figure subjects became more common; but there is a marked decline in their vitality.

Uchiwa-ye: Japanese prints; fan-shaped pictures.

Uki-ye: Japanese "perspective" prints.

Unaker: china clay. It is mentioned in the patent specification of Heylyn and Frye, (1744) as "the produce of the Chirokee nation of America called by the natives Unaker" (specification of patents No. 610, 6 December 1744). It was used with a frit to make early Bow porcelain (q.v.).

American china clay was known to

Cookworthy (q.v.) by 1745. Richard Champion received from his brother-in-law, Caleb Lloyd of Charleston, S. Carolina, in 1765 a consignment of china clay, but the discovery of the fine clays of Cornwall released English potters from any necessity to import the ingredients of their wares.

Unct. or unc.: an abbreviation used in book-sellers' catalogues meaning uncut (q.v.).

Uncut, cut (of edges): collectors have always, and rightly, cherished books with ample margins; for it has been the habit of book-binders from earliest times to trim off more rather than less of the rough edges of the leaves than was intended by those who designed the printed page; and every time a book is rebound it is liable to lose more. Of books published before the age of edition-binding, therefore, a tall copy is preferable (other things being equal) to a short one.

With the adoption (1825-35) of publisher's cloth as the original and intentionally permanent covering of the majority of books published in England and America, the collector's attitude to their edges is radically changed. For if he is in pursuit, as he usually is, of a copy in its original condition as issued to the public, he will require that its edges (whether uncut, rough-trimmed or cut smooth) shall conform to a now standardized margin. All that he needs, therefore, in this particular respect, is an assurance that the edges have not been cut down by a re-binder or repairer.

Under-glass painting: early examples of painting under glass belong to Antiquity. In these examples, the technique by which they were produced consisted of engraving the picture on the back of a piece of glass (usually a goblet or similar container) through a layer of gold leaf which had previously been attached to it. Sometimes colour was added from behind. Usually a second piece of glass was used to seal this engraving from behind, although this was more often omitted in later work intended purely as pictures and not as incidental decorations for glass vessels. Many such

pictures were made in Italy in the 14th cent. and the method is known as gold-glass engraving. From this method was developed that known as *verre eglomisé*, in which the technique consisted of painting a picture in reverse directly on to the underside of a piece of glass and then backing the whole of the glass with either metal foil, wax or some other coloured pigment. From this to ordinary under-glass painting was but another step, and instead of the foil or pigment, realistic or decorative backgrounds could be painted in or, on the other hand, especially in the case of silhouettes produced by this method, the unpainted portion of the glass could be left perfectly clear.

Another method of under-painting was mirror painting. This was similar to the old-glass engraving process, excepting that an amalgam of tin and mercury, to make it into a mirror, was applied to the glass. The parts to be painted were then scraped away and painted in as required. Such paintings were often made in China, where the technique is thought to have been introduced from Europe by Jesuit missionaries. Vauxhall bevelled plate glass was exported to China for this purpose in the 18th cent.

Underglaze decoration: decoration (painting or printing) applied to pottery or porcelain in the biscuit condition before the application of glaze.

The colours are absolutely permanent.

Union pin: a pin made up of two sections so that the point of the pin on one part fits into a hole in the other part and is thus sheathed.

Unite: gold coin of value of 20s first struck by James I. So named from the allusion of the inscription to the Union of the Crowns. Types, a profile portrait and an heraldic design. Charles I also issued this denomination together with some triple unites struck at provincial mints during the Civil War.

Universal table: a type of small dining table with draw leaves to extend the top, made in the late 18th cent.

Unopened: this means that the leaves of a book issued entirely untrimmed (and therefore having the folding of its component sections still intact at the top and fore-edges) have not been severed from their neighbours with the paper-knife. It must not be confused, with uncut (q.v.).

Uprights: the outer, vertical members of a chair back.

Urbino maiolica: tin-glazed earthenware made in the city of Urbino in Italy. At Urbino and Castel Durante (q.v.) during the course of the 16th cent. the decorative designs previously employed gave way to pictorial designs in a warmer palette. (See also Castel Durante.)

Urn: a decorative, two-handled vase with domed lid, of classical derivation. Urns as decorative adjuncts were used architecturally from the Renaissance (q.v.) onwards. They also appear as finials (q.v.) on furniture, metalwork, etc. during the 18th cent. and were particularly favoured as a decorative form by late 18th cent. architects, designers and craftsmen, such as Robert Adam, Matthew Boulton, Josiah Wedgwood, etc. (qq.v.).

Urn-stand: see Kettle-stand.

Urushi-ye: Japanese lacquer prints which involved the application of metal dusts.

Usk japanned ware: a break-away factory, manufacturing japanned ware (q.v.), established by two of the Allgood brothers (q.v.) in 1761, seven miles from Pontypool (q.v.) and operated by them until early in the 19th cent. Maintaining that they were the original makers of Pontypool japan they marketed their ware under that name.

Valenciennes lace: pillow lace. True Valenciennes is reputed to have been made in the town and false Valenciennes in the region around, the countrywomen continuing the older style of ground (q.v.) when the townswomen developed a new one early in the 18th cent. although both were "true" in that they were worked pattern and ground in one operation. False Valenciennes included lace with mixed grounds while true Valenciennes had a clear open diamond mesh worked with four – later three – plaited threads. Patterns were mostly the old Flemish scrolls and conventional flowers without a cordonnet (q.v.) and worked with such exactitude that it became important, and rare, for one worker to complete a whole piece. Around the mid-18th cent. the four pieces for a lady's cap and lappets might cost £45 and represent two or three years' work. Since the early 19th cent. this lace has been made largely in Belgium.

Valentines: valentines take their name from St Valentine, who was martyred in Rome by the Emperor Claudius the Second on what is supposed to have been 14th February, A.D. 270, for helping the early Christians. Further, and more legendary still, on the night before his death he sent a last message to his gaoler's daughter, whose sight he had miraculously restored, signed "Your Valentine". Early valentines were just written messages.

The commercial valentine, or the valentine as we now know it, started in the early part of the 19th cent., and was a hand-coloured engraving, varying much in quality, with a motto in verse. The drawings of quite well-known artists, such as George Heath or George Cruikshank, were used for valentines.

The real age of the Valentine was from 1840 until around the turn of the cent., lithography and chromolithography replacing the earlier methods of production and a great elaboration of design being introduced. The best period was from 1840–60. After 1860 they became mass-produced and over-elaborate, though this is admired by some collectors.

Borders of embossed lace and later of perforated lace were often used, with, occasionally, embossed envelopes to match. Silk was sometimes used in the middle of the design. Valentines could also be mechanical, i.e. by moving a tab protruding from the bottom of the card a lady's skirts could be raised or a gentleman's whiskers moved. There were valentines of an elaborate cut-out pattern, which, when raised, disclosed a romantic scene. There were puzzles, acrostics and cryptograms, and there where valentines showing dolls with real material stuck on to make the clothes. Others had layers of cloth, wax, dried flowers, seaweed or shells. In addition, velvet, net, plush, looking-glass, cork, feathers and imitation jewellery were used. A rare form of valentine was the musical, where the front page lifts to show a musical quotation.

Vamplate: see under Pole-arms.

Vargueño: see Bargueño.

Variant: a general-purpose term used to describe a copy or copies of an edition of a book exhibiting some variation, whether of text, title-page, illustrations, paper or binding, from another copy or copies of the same edition. Its use does not necessarily imply that the copy or copies in question are abnormal; in fact, it is most frequently and properly used when doubts exist as to the priority, or even the precise relationship, between the two or more observed variants, and where in consequence no norm has been established. (See also Binding variants.)

Vase carpets: Oriental carpets bearing a design representing a stylized vase of flowers. Chinese in influence,

the design is made up of graceful interlocking palmettes and floral

designs, developing from a central motif.

Vaucanson, Jacques de: (1709–82), one of the earliest makers of automata of which records survive. Three of his figures were exhibited in Paris in 1738, and later in London, St Petersburg and in Germany. On the occasion of the London exhibition, a booklet was published, of which the title page reads: "An account of the Mechanism of an Automaton or Image playing on the German Flute; As it was presented in a Memoire to the Gentlemen of the Royal Academy of Sciences at Paris. By M. Vaucanson, Inventor and Maker of the said Machine: Together with a Description of an artificial Duck, eating, drinking, macerating the Food, and voiding Excrements; pluming her wings, picking her feathers, and performing several operations in Imitation of a living Duck....". Vaucanson's figures caused sensations wherever they were shown and were the commencement of a long series of exhibition pieces.

Vauxhall Glasshouse: a manufactory of plate-glass was commenced here about 1665 by George Villiers, second Duke of Buckingham. John Bellingham approached the Duke with a secret process for making mirrors, and as a result the Vauxhall factory was started and Bellingham was given the post of manager. Glasshouses continued to operate in Vauxhall until the end of the 18th cent., and old mirror-plates are often referred to today as "Vauxhall".

Veneer: veneering was the chief decorative feature of walnut furniture introduced by cabinet-makers in the second half of the 17th cent. Since that period veneers of many other woods, such as yew, elm, mulberry, mahogany, rosewood, zebrawood etc. have been used to achieve decorative effect by the cabinet-maker. Thin layers of wood, cut by hand-saw, perhaps one-eighth of an inch thick, are glued to the carefully prepared carcase. Cut from the part of the tree which would show a delicate figuring, the veneer was applied to drawer fronts, door panels, table tops, etc. in such a way that the figure on the various parts would match. (See also "Curl" veneer, "Burr" veneer and Carcase.)

Venetian flat point lace: needlepoint with a solid *toilé* (q.v.), the fillings few and simple and the brides (q.v.) numerous and decked with picots (q.v.).

Venetian glass: thinly blown sodaglass, worked at a low temperature, cooling quickly, and requiring great speed of manipulation. The Venetian glassmakers, perhaps before the 15th cent., rediscovered the processes of decolorizing glass with manganese. The resulting "cristallo" became the admiration of Europe and established a Venetian supremacy in the art of glassblowing which lasted until the late 17th cent.

Venetian grounded point lace: needlepoint meshed lace introduced to follow the 18th cent. French fashion and much resembling Alençon (q.v.). The lace patterns were in the rococo mood of their time and somewhat florid.

Venetian pillow lace: a minor product dating to the early days of pillow lace (q.v.) and much resembling early needlepoint (q.v.).

Venetian raised point lace: needlepoint. This had a distinctively thick multi-thread cordonnet (q.v.) and no mesh ground (q.v.). It was used on the ends of men's cravats in the 17th and early 18th cent. and had a sumptuous effect of carved ivory.

Venetian rose point lace: needlepoint, lighter than raised point (q.v.). The cordonnet (q.v.) might have two or three rows of picots (q.v.) and more picots were introduced on the many brides (q.v.) which were dotted with tiny roses suggesting a powdering of snowflakes – hence its alternative name *point de neige*. Popular in England in the 17th and early 18th cent. for men's falling collars, ruffles, etc.

Venice porcelain: hard-paste porcelain was made at a factory in Venice started in 1720 by Francesco Vezzi with the help of an arcanist (q.v.) C. K. Hunger, who had previously been at the Du Paquier (q.v.) factory in Vienna. Both in form and decoration Vezzi porcelain resembles that made by Du Paquier. The wares are marked va vena or venezia in underglaze blue or underglaze red. Another factory was started by Geminiano Cozzi in 1765, but in this case a variety of soft-paste was made, the wares largely imitating Meissen (q.v.). The factory existed until 1812, the mark used being an anchor in red.

Venisons: bowls "made to fit into one another . . . in capacity ranging from a pint to a peck" (George Bourne), made at Frimley, Cove, and Farnborough, c. 1800–50.

"Verditure" or **verditer** (*verd de terre*) **wallpapers:** 18th-cent. name for plain blue-grey wallpapers.

Verdure: a tapestry with a design based principally on floral and plant forms. 16th-cent. verdures with wonderful scrolling foliage are especially noteworthy. In the second half of the 17th cent. formal verdure patterns changed into landscape-verdures. The many styles of verdure have always been favourite furnishing tapestries. Oudenarde, Enghien, Lille, Aubusson and Felletin specialized in verdures.

Verge escapement: the original escapement (q.v.) for mechanical clocks. Date of invention unknown but perhaps the 13th cent. Although it is an escapement in its worst form, in that it never leaves the pendulum or balance free for an instant, nevertheless it was in its day as revolutionary an invention as was, later, the anchor escapement (q.v.). It held the field unchallenged for about four hundred years; even thereafter it remained in use for clocks and watches, along with better types, for another one hundred and fifty years. It was used in bracket clocks as long as there were only one or two in a house, and they were carried from room to room, since it does not need any very careful levelling.

Vermeil: (*Fr.*), silver-gilt (q.v.).

Vermicelli ground: a ground, usually of gold, used as a decoration on porcelain, formed by covering the surface with a continuous wriggling line. The name is adapted from the long threads of vermicelli.

Vermicular collar: a wavy trail of glass encircling the stem of a glass vessel or decanter neck.

Vernis Martin: a term applied generically to all varnishes and lacquers used for furniture and interior decoration in France during the 18th cent. It derives from the brothers Martin, who in 1730 were granted a monopoly to copy Chinese and Japanese lacquer. They also evolved a special kind of coloured varnish, which was applied in a large number of coats and then rubbed down to give it lustre. It was available in various colours, including grey, lilac, yellow and blue, but the most famous was the green, which was often applied to furniture. Vernis Martin was also used to decorate woodwork, carriages, fans and small boxes. The Martin family were much patronized by the Court and by Madame de Pompadour (see also Japan work).

Verre de fougère: (*Fr.*), Glass made in inland districts in France from potash obtained by burning bracken from the forests, known in France as *verre de fougère* and in Germany as *Waldglas.*

Verre de Nevers: (*Fr.*), Nevers glass. This small French town became a centre of glass-making in the 16th cent., when Lodovico Gonzaga, by his marriage with Henriette of Cleves, became Duke of Nevers and brought Italian glassmakers from L'Altare to settle in the town. Glass in the Italian manner was made here until the 18th cent. In particular, small figures and "toys", made of portions of glass rod, blown or manipulated, are ascribed to Nevers and appear to have been made throughout the period.

Verre églomisé: (*Fr.*), glass decorated at the back with designs in colour and gold and silver foils. It is a method that has been practised for many hundreds of years, but for some reason is named after an art-collector, J. B. Glomy, who died in France in 1786. Borders of *verre églomisé* in arabesque patterns and with coats-of-arms were used to frame mirrors c. 1695.

Verso: the back, or reverse, side of the leaf of a book; i.e. the left-hand page of an open book.

Verzelini, Giacomo: (1522–1606), a Venetian glass maker, believed to have come to England from Antwerp in 1571 and perhaps to have worked for Jean Carré (q.v.). In 1575 he obtained a privilege from Queen Elizabeth I for twenty-one years to make Venetian glass in London and to teach the art to Englishmen. He set up a glasshouse in Broad Street in London and the tradition which he founded was to dominate glass making in England until the last quarter of the 17th cent.

Vetro di trina: (*It.*), glass decorated with intricate patterns formed by threads of white glass embedded in the clear glass. Of Roman inspiration, this type of decoration was used in Venice in the 16th cent., the technique involving the arrangement of rods containing threads of white glass round a cylindrical pot which were taken up on a gathering of clear glass, the pattern being formed by twisting the gathering as required. Subsequently the shape was obtained by blowing and manipulating. This type of glass is also known as lace glass.

Vezzi: see Venice porcelain.

Vicar and Moses: a popular subject with the Staffordshire figure makers during the second half of the 18th cent. first made by Ralph Wood. It shows a parson in the pulpit asleep, with the parish clerk at the desk below conducting the service. Recorded with Ralph Wood glazes, as a "white" figure group, and in enamel colours. Extensively pirated. The marks

R. WOOD   Ra Wood
                 Burslem

occur occasionally. The incised mark

has been noted on a number of examples, some spurious.

Victoriate: early Roman Republican silver coin, normally with head of Jupiter on obverse and Victory crowning a trophy on the reverse.

Vienna porcelain: Claudius Innocentius Du Paquier, assisted by Christoph Conrad Hunger, an enameller and goldworker who had worked at St Cloud and at Meissen (qq.v.) and Samuel Stoelzel, an arcanist (q.v.) from Meissen, founded a factory at Vienna in 1717. He started by producing tableware derived from silver shapes, decorated with Chinese motives and exotic flowers. About 1725 German flowers and European subjects were introduced in colours and in *schwarzlot* (q.v.), a black monochrome heightened with gold. Du Paquier figures formed at first parts of vessels only, supports, handles or finials, but gained independence about 1730 and came into their own. The mingling of rustic pottery tradition with the urbanity of Meissen models gives these figures an air of wondering surprise. Financial difficulties forced Du Paquier to sell his factory to the State in 1744, when a complete reorganisation took place. At that time the Vienna mark, a shield incised or, more often, in underglaze blue, was first introduced. New findings of kaolin (q.v.) in Hungary (1749) and sound management finally brought prosperity to the factory. L. Dannhauser and J. J. Niedermeyer modelled figures of great charm. During the latter part of the cent. the transition to Classicism took place under the direction of Konrad von Sorgenthal (1784–1805). Table wares in the manner of Sèvres (q.v.) have coloured grounds and gold decoration of restrained design, including medallions with portraits or landscapes. Figures of the period are often biscuit, to reproduce the effect of antique marble statues. These figures are clad in stylized Greek gowns, and their timid character seems due to a certain slackening of creative power. However, the factory carried on until 1864.

Vignette: an ornamental design or picture, not framed in a border, the edges being sometimes shaded off into the surrounding paper, used as a means of decoration in a book.

Vinaigrette: small box fitted with a hinged inner lid or grille, sometimes simply perforated or, more often, pierced in elaborate and attractive designs. A perfumed sponge is secreted underneath this grille and the aroma escapes through it when the box is opened. Introduced in the late 18th cent., they were made to represent books, purses, eggs, etc. Usually in silver or gold, vinaigrettes are often beautifully engraved or chased.

Vincennes porcelain: see under Sèvres porcelain.

Vinovo porcelain: a variety of soft-paste porcelain was made at Vinovo (Turin) between 1776 and 1820. The mark used consisted of several variations of the letter "V" containing a cross.

Viola da gamba: see under Viols.

Viola d'amore: a musical instrument standing on its own between a viol (q.v.) and a violin, notable for its system of "sympathetic" strings, a duplicate set of wires passing under the fingerboard and through the bridge. Although out of reach of the bow and fingers, these strings vibrate freely in sympathy with the notes played and produce a peculiarly ethereal effect. There are seven bowed (gut) strings and seven (steel) sympathetic strings, and since all terminate on separate tuning pegs in the head, this is of extraordinary length. A fair number of these instruments were mad in Italy, France and Germany during the 18th and 19th cent. The instrument usually has a viol-type body, the top is traditionally decorated with a carved head of a blindfold cupid, and the soundholes are of an unusual "flame" pattern. The broad neck is not fretted.

Viols: six-stringed musical instruments (some of the larger have seven), similar in general appearance to the violin family, of which they are the forerunners. Unlike violins, viols have sloping shoulders, flat backs, long flat necks with short fingerboards and C-shaped soundholes. They were made in five or six sizes from a small treble (pardessus) to a great bass (violone). Not many genuine old specimens survive. The most characteristic is the viola da gamba, approximating in size and pitch to the 'cello, though rather smaller in body. A fair number of English gambas are known, many of them made by or attributed to Barak Norman. Viols are sometimes found which have been converted for modern use as violas or 'cellos by being renecked and having the shoulders cut down.

Virginals: the virginals and the spinet are both small domestic musical instruments with only one string to each note and one row of jacks or plectra, one for each string. Like the harpsichord, they both have keys which work a plucking device. The virginals proper is a rectangular instrument, the whole interior of which is covered by the soundboard. Through this the jacks protrude to reach the strings. These pass diagonally over the soundboard on two bridges. The form belongs peculiarly to the 16th and 17th cent. and many examples are known. They are usually finely decorated within and without. The spinet is a little more common, as it continued to be made until a rather later date. The shape is that of a harp on its side, with the keyboard along the shorter of the straight lines which converge on the left of the player. They are united on the right by the curved side of the "harp". These instruments sometimes date from the 17th cent. and reflect Jacobean tastes with their oak casework and stands. Later instruments in walnut or mahogany with bandings of other woods are more numerous.

Visor: that part of the helmet which protects the face and is pierced with slits to allow vision.

Vitruvian scroll: a border ornament consisting of a band of repeating scrolls resembling waves, much used as an architectural motif and on furniture during the 18th cent. During the classical revival of the latter part of the cent. this type of border ornament appears consistently upon carpets, ceramics, metalwork etc.

Volkstedt porcelain: originally a soft-paste porcelain was made at Volkstedt in Thuringia about 1760, but later the factory secured a privilege from the Prince of Schwarzburg-Rudolstadt and acquired the secret of making hard-paste. The body was greyish and of uncertain quality, frequently imitating the Meissen mark. From about 1799 onwards an "R" for Rudolstadt was used.

Volute: a scroll form, as on an Ionic capital.

Voyding dish or **voyder:** large dish for collecting broken meats and table remnants. A medieval term. The only known surviving example in silver is a 17th-cent. replacement of an earlier dish, belonging to the Drapers' Company.

Voyez, John: (1735–1800), modeller and manufacturer of French extraction, brought to Staffordshire by Wedgwood 1768 but quarrelled with him. Issued catalogue of seals and intaglios 1773 and did an extensive trade, undermining that of Wedgwood 1773–76; probably modelled for the Ralph Woods, of Burslem; "Fair Hebe" jug 1788 made for Richard Meir Astbury; in London 1791; disappears from record.

J VOYEZ 1788

Vulliamy family: a London family of clockmakers. The eldest, Justin, was active between 1730 and 1790, his son

Benjamin from 1775 to 1820, and Benjamin Lewis, one of the last of the old school of London clock and watchmakers, from 1809 to 1854.

Wager cup: a double cup formed as a skirted woman holding a swinging cup above her head, the skirt also forms a cup, both to be emptied without a spill. Made on the Continent from the 16th cent., a few rare examples survive in England from Charles II period and other copies made in late 18th and early 19th cent. Wager cups were also made in the form of a windmill, so that when they were inverted, the body of the mill acted as the bowl.

Wainscot chair: modern jargon for a panel-back joined chair of the late 16th and early 17th cent.

Waiter: small tray for handing wine-glass, letters, etc. Conforms generally to salver form (q.v.). In 18th cent. silver waiters were often found in pairs *en suite* with a larger salver. The small early, footed form often misnamed "tazza" (q.v.).

Waldglas: (*Ger.*), glass made in inland districts from potash obtained by burning bracken from the forests.

Wall-bracket: the detachable wall-bracket, as distinct from the fixed architectural feature, appeared towards the end of the 17th cent., and seems to have been used at first for displaying china. Its prominent position in the room singled it out for special decorative treatment in carving or gilding. In the early Georgian period the bracket was often used to support a bust or vase, and as a result it tended to become larger in size and more heavily ornamented; but with the return of the fashion for displaying china about 1750 and the growing use of the bracket for supporting lights, it became altogether more delicate in appearance, and was adapted to the various styles of the Chippendale and Adam (qq.v.) periods. The wall-bracket supporting a clock was a popular form of decoration in the later 18th cent.

Wallendorf porcelain: see under Limbach porcelain.

Wall, John: (1708–76), Dr John Wall was the son of a one-time Mayor of Worcester and a successful local tradesman. He was the ward of Lord Sandys and married Lord Sandys's cousin. Well-educated locally, he went to Oxford, became a Fellow of Merton, studied medicine at St Thomas's Hospital, London, and did some competent amateur painting. He was one of the original shareholders in the Worcester factory formed in 1751 for the manufacture of soapstone porcelain. He died in 1776. The first period of Worcester porcelain is known among collectors as the "Dr Wall period" and is used to cover wares produced up to the year 1783, seven years after his death.

Wall-lights or **sconce:** (*Fr.*) *bras de lumière, appliques,* a lighting appliance usually of more than one light which can be fixed flat to the surface of a wall. In France they were very popular in the Louis XV and Louis XVI periods and large numbers were made, usually of ormolu and often in pairs or sets of four or six. The *ciselure* and gilding on many of them are often of very high quality.

Wall-lights for candles were extant from the Restoration into the 18th cent. The wall-plate was usually of cartouche form with embossed decoration and branches for one or more candles. A plain form with rounded top to wall-plate and flat pan with single low socket also occurs. The name was also used in the past for the normal candlestick.

Walloon sword: see "Pappenheimer".

Wall pocket: flower or spill vase shaped as a mask, fish, or cornucopia, made in Staffordshire salt-glaze, and in Liverpool and Lambeth delft, 18th cent.

Walton, John, pottery figures: made from first decade of the 19th cent. until 1835, with tree backgrounds decorated with bright enamel colours, and Egyptian black (q.v.).

Often there is a large blue scroll on the base of the figures, which are sometimes marked within a scroll at the back. Occasionally the mark is underneath.

Wan Li period: (1573–1619), a period in which Chinese porcelain continued to be made in many of the Chia Ching styles (q.v.). Porcelain with enamels and underglaze blue painting (the *wu ts'ai*) are especially characteristic. The numerous blue-and-white export wares are very variable in quality, often with poor blue and careless drawing. Pieces expressly intended for Europe become common.

Ward: a fixed projection in a lock to prevent a key from entering or turning unless correctly shaped.

Warming-pan: an enclosed metal pan, often with pierced or engraved cover and a long handle, used for warming beds, usually made of copper. Examples in silver are rare, but one or two late 17th cent. versions survive.

Washing-stand or **basin-stand:** specially adapted for bedroom use after 1750, and of two main kinds. A tripod stand with three uprights, a circular top fitted with a basin, and a central triangular shelf with a drawer (or drawers) and receptacle for soap A four-legged version of this type was also made. A cupboard or chest of drawers on four legs with a basin sunk in the top, the latter covered by a lid or folding flaps.

Wassail bowl: two-handled loving cup passed clockwise around the company on convivial occasions.

Waste: spoiled or surplus sheets of printed matter, often used before 1650 by book-binders for lining the back of a book, making boards of compressed layers of paper or as endleaves. Book-seller's waste – surplus quires of recent books or discarded fragments of old ones – is of little value in localizing a binding. Printer's waste, however – proofs, trial sheets, overprintings, etc. – is not so likely to travel as sheets from a completed book, and may give a clue to the place of binding.

Water clock: a contrivance used in Egyptian, Greek and Roman times for measuring time by the regular flow of a stream of water changing the level in a container, on the surface of which floated a means of indication on a fixed scale. Water clocks in the 17th and 18th cent. were drums with internal pierced sloping divisions, causing the water to pass slowly from one to the other, making the drum revolve and its axis roll down a graduated framework. Very few genuine examples exist.

Waterford glass: the earliest record of flint-glass making at Waterford was discovered by Westropp in *The Dublin Journal*, 1729: "a glasshouse near Waterford now producing all sorts of flint-glass, double and single . . . sold at reasonable rates by Joseph Harris at Waterford, merchant". This glass-house was at Gurteens, three miles from the city, and operated until 1739, producing a negligible quantity of glass. The now celebrated Waterford glasshouse started production in 1784, financed with a capital of £10,000 by George and William Penrose, merchants. The Irish Parliament, however, granted the Penroses a subsidy to cover the expense of building and equipping their glasshouse. As works manager they employed John Hill, member of a family operating at the important Goalbournhill Glasshouse near Stourbridge. In evidence given before a committee examining commercial relations between Great Britain and Ireland in 1785, John Blades, a leading cut-glass manufacturer in London, stated that "Mr. Hill, a great manufacturer of Stourbridge has lately gone to Waterford, and has taken the best set of Workmen he could get in the County of Worcester". The Penrose glasshouse was bought in 1799 by Ramsey, Gatchell and Borcroft, who built a new factory in Old Tan Yard, advertising the old premises to be let. Gatchell had become the sole proprietor by 1811 and with successive partners, the firm remained in the family. At the Great Exhibition of 1851, Gatchell exhibited a magnificent "Etagere or ornamental centre for a banqueting table, consisting of forty pieces of cut-glass, so fitted to each other as to require no connecting sockets of other material; quart and pint decanters cut in hollow prisms. Centre vase or bowl on detached tripod stand. Vases and covers. Designed and executed at the Waterford Glass Works". This was Gatchell's swan song; his final effort to compete with England was a failure, and he closed the glasshouse later in the same year. It is difficult to distinguish Waterford glass from that made at other Irish glasshouses. Irish glass was said to display a slightly dusky tint although that from Waterford, by the first decades of the 19th cent., was claimed to be clear and colourless. No excise duty hampered the development of the Irish glass houses in the 1780s and the glass produced was ideal for cutting in deep relief which became so popular. Much deep cut glassware was sent to England, where the Excise Duty, imposed under the Glass Excise Act of 1745 and increased later in the cent., discouraged heavy glass-making. The first Irish glass excise duty was imposed in 1825.

Water-leaf ornament: an ornament found on late 18th and early 19th cent. plate consisting of a large, unribbed leaf.

Waterloo Glasshouse Company, Cork: established in 1815 by Daniel Foley, a glass and china seller of Hanover Street, who set up as a specialist in extensive table-services in cut-glass for military messes, particularly for regiments occupying France. By the end of 1816 he employed about a hundred men and women, many experienced workers deserting from the Cork Glasshouse Company under the lure of higher wages. Glass trumpets were made for sale. A steam engine was installed to operate the cutting wheels and other machinery, thus drastically reducing costs.

Geoffrey O'Connell was taken into partnership during 1825, the firm operating as Foley and O'Connell, Waterloo Glass Works Company. They advertised that they had introduced a new annealing process which enabled them to guarantee their flint-glass to withstand hot water without breaking. The excise duty was too heavy a burden, and in mid-1830 the firm ceased operating. Fifteen months or so later it was reopened by O'Connell, who introduced up-to-date methods of blown-moulding and advertised that he had "restored one hundred families to employment".

The venture could not compete with English prices, however, and in 1835 he was made bankrupt owing to his failure to pay excise duties.

Watermark: a distinguishing mark, sometimes including the maker's initials, name or device, and occasionally the date, impressed in the pulp during the process of papermaking, and visible in the finished product when held against the light. They have been indexed, and approximately dated, in such works as Briquet's *Les Filigranes* (1282–1600), 1923, and Heawood's *Watermarks mainly of the Seventeenth and Eighteenth Centuries*, 1950.

Wauters family: tapestry weavers of Antwerp, Michael and Philip Wauters worked specially for the export trade in the latter part of the 17th cent. Apart from connections in Vienna, Paris, Lisbon and Rome, they studied the English market carefully and produced for it *pièces de petites dimensions à la mode d'Angleterre*. They imitated popular English tapestry sets, such as *Hero and Leander*, *Playing Boys*, *Metamorphoses*, and the Duke of Newcastle's *Horsemanship* series. Their mark is distinctive and their work can nearly always be distinguished from English weaving. Peter Wauters was also connected with them.

Wave pattern: see Vitruvian scroll.

Wax-flower modelling: groups of wax flowers and fruit in glass cases were a particular Victorian feature of decoration. At their best they are fascinating, although it is difficult to find specimens in perfect condition with the colours unfaded. Several Victorian books deal with the subject, notably Mrs Peachey's (artist to Her Majesty) *The Royal Guide to Wax Flower Modelling* (1851) (with four coloured groups of flowers to help the budding modeller).

Waxjack: open-frame stand for coil of sealing wax taper threaded on central pin and led through nozzle above. Found from the mid-18th cent. onwards.

Webber, Henry: a modeller employed by Josiah Wedgwood (q.v.) between the years 1782 and 1794 both at Etruria and at Rome with John Flaxman.

He was engaged in the copying of the Portland vase.

Web foot: see Duck foot.

Wedge thumbpiece: a thumbpiece (q.v.) formed by the extension of the lid attachment upwards to a point.

Wedgwood, Josiah: (1730–95), Josiah Wedgwood was born in 1730 at Burslem. He left his brother's pottery, where he had been apprenticed in 1752 to go into partnership at Stoke with John Harrison and where he made agate, tortoise-shell and other staple wares until, desiring greater experimental opportunities, he joined Thomas Whieldon (q.v.) for a five-year partnership in 1754.

On leaving Whieldon in 1759 Wedgwood took over the Ivy House Works, which he retained until 1773 for the manufacture of useful pottery wares. In 1764 he rented the Brick House (or Bell Works). In 1766 he bought the Ridge House Estate where he proceeded to erect a factory which he named Etruria. The same year he proposed a partnership to Thomas Bentley, a Liverpool merchant whose taste for classical art accorded with his own. In 1769 Bentley joined him, the partnership lasting until Bentley's death in 1780. The Wedgwood & Bentley Etruria period was responsible for the finest products of the factory.

He died in 1795, when the factory was inherited by his second son Josiah.

WHIELDON/WEDGWOOD partnership, 1754–59:

Wedgwood improved coloured glazes generally, and in the course of his experimental work devised "a green glaze to be laid on common white (or cream-colour) biscuit ware". He described this glaze as "the result of many experiments that I made in order to introduce a new species of coloured ware to be fired along with the tortoise-shell or agate ware in our common glass ovens, to be of an even self-colour, and laid upon the ware in the form of a coloured glaze".

IVY HOUSE, 1759–64:

Wedgwood continued the production of staple and Whieldon style wares but added green and, after 1760, yellow glaze, devising such shapes as the cauliflower and the pineapple to use the new colours to advantage.

Cream-ware was probably perfected by Wedgwood in 1762 when he presented Queen Charlotte with a caudle and breakfast set. After 1765, in which year Wedgwood was first styled "Potter to the Queen", the product was known as Queen's ware. The best examples are pale in shade, light in weight, often decorated in coloured enamels, with border patterns often of neo-classical design. Most cream-ware and all Queen's ware items are impress marked, the earlier in upper and lower case, the later in upper case only. Manufacture has continued to the present day.

BRICK HOUSE or BELL WORKS, 1764–69:

Wedgwood concentrated on increasing out-put of useful wares in Queen's ware, though many items, both useful and decorative, were made in basaltes. Items are impressed in upper and lower case, or in upper case; quality is high.

ETRURIA, opened June 13th 1769:

The first day's production consisted of six Etruscan ware vases thrown by Wedgwood while Bentley turned the wheel. They were painted with red classical figures and inscribed "Artes Etruriae Renascuntur" ("The Arts of Etruria are re-born"), a clear indication of the ambitions and tastes of the partnership and the style which was to dominate its period.

Before 1780 basaltes had been developed as a decorative body applied with endless variation to the manufacture of chimney ornaments, vases and decorative useful ware of the finest quality. The seal and wafer marks were used on vases and larger pieces, and the upper and lower case or upper case. Wedgwood & Bentley mark impressed on smaller items. Encaustic and enamel decoration, finely finished and enamel decoration typify the basaltes of this period.

Creamware was developed decoratively, the "surface agates" and other styles emulating polished stone, garnitures or suites of chimney ornaments being the most successful. These are often found with basaltes bases with the wafer or seal mark, or are otherwise impressed Wedgwood & Bentley.

It was also during the partnership that Wedgwood developed his most successful decorative ware. Called at first "the white body", Wedgwood's intention was to to devise a body with lapidary imitative possibilities, one capable of emulating Graeco-Roman objects in coloured glass or polished natural stone. Through 1773 to 1774 he experimented with "white spars and earths", many of which had never been used before. By the end of 1774 he had developed a "fine white terracotta of great beauty and delicacy" with a "waxen" finish. By 1776 he had improved the body, which he then described as "a fine white artificial jasper of exquisite beauty and delicacy, proper for cameos, portraits and bas-reliefs".

Jasper was used with conspicuous success as a decorative body, a vast range of items being produced in it of great fineness and finish, including tea and chocolate ware, vases, plaques, bas-reliefs, and cameos in all sizes, in light and dark blues, green, black, lilac or lavender, and a peach-pink, usually with white reliefs. The jasper product of the partnership period is, however, largely blue-and-white or solid white, and is usually marked Wedgwood & Bentley, impressed though many smaller items are found unmarked, being units of sets and sold as such.

While basaltes, jasper and Queen's ware are the most successful of Wedgwood wares, other "dry" or unglazed bodies enjoyed a considerable market

in both decorative and useful applications. These were all made from local marls to which various "ochrous" earths were added to produce colour. There are many variations of colour due to the quantity of admixture and the degree of firing. These wares were described by Wedgwood as
(a) Rosso antico; dark red to chocolate
(b) Cane ware; buff
(c) Terra cotta; light red
(d) Drab ware; olive grey
(e) White stone ware: pure white.

JOSIAH WEDGWOOD
Feb. 2nd 1805

wedgwood WEDGWOOD

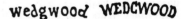

Wedgwood & Bentley: Etruria

WEDGWOOD
WEDGWOOD

Wedgwood

W. & B.

Wedgwood & Bentley 356

WEDGWOOD & SONS   WEDGWOOD

E. Lysore

Wedgwood & Bentley

Wedgwood
Wedgwood

WEDGWOOD

WEDGWOOD

Josiah Wedgwood II's conduct of the factory was unsuccessful due to his lack of interest coupled with the damage to trade caused by the Napoleonic Wars – so much so, that in 1811 he wrote "the business is not worth carrying on, and if I could withdraw my capital from it, I would tomorrow". Nevertheless, the period is distinguished by ten years of experiment in and production of bone-china (1812–22). The ware found no great success.

By 1828 Wedgwood's trade had so declined that the London showrooms were closed, the stock of wares and old moulds and models being sold for £16,000, a considerable disaster to the firm and one from which it was unable to recover for many years.

In 1875 a London showroom was opened again and in 1778 the making of bone-china revived. With the opening of the modern Wedgwood factory at Barlaston (started before and completed just after the 1939 War) the firm regained its eminent position.

Wednesbury: a South Staffordshire centre of the enamelling trade from 1776, when Samuel Yardley started there, and highly praised for its products in the early 19th cent. The last enameller, Yardley's grandson, gave up the trade in 1840.

Weesp porcelain: hard-paste porcelain was made at Weesp in Holland from about 1764, the factory moving first to Oude Loosdrecht in 1771 and then to Oude Amstel in 1784. The mark of crossed swords with a dot at the pommel of each hilt and three dots at the outside angles formed by the intersecting blades was in use while the factory was at Weesp. During the Oude Loosdrecht period an "M.L" was used, either incised, in underglaze blue or in enamel colours, while at Oude Amstel the word "Amstel" was employed, either in blue or black.

Weisweiler, Adam: French cabinet-maker. Born c. 1750 at Neuwied and trained in the workshop of Roentgen (q.v.). Established in Paris before 1777. Became a *maître-ébéniste* in 1778. He worked for the dealer Daguerre and, through him, supplied a large amount of furniture for the Royal palaces, and particularly for Queen Marie Antoinette at St Cloud. He was a good business man, and in consequence survived the Revolution safely, and was employed under the Empire, during which time he executed commissions for Queen Hortense. He was still in business in 1810. He used the stamp:

A·WEISWEILER

Wellington chest: a tall narrow chest containing about a dozen drawers which can be locked by a single hinged flap securing all the drawers.

Welsh dresser: a cupboard intended for the display of plate, usually of oak, consisting of enclosed section with one or two doors below three drawers, and a superstructure holding shelves.

"Welsh" ware: shallow meat dishes with feathered slip decoration, in form like a gardener's trug, commonly made in Staffordshire, Sunderland (Scott's "Superior Fireproof") and Isleworth, under this name.

"Welshman" toby jug: a rare model of toby jug (q.v.), the figure being seated on a chair with the Welsh goat between his knees.

West Country measure: a tavern measure (q.v.) with bulging body tapering to a narrow spouted neck. Of West Country origin. Examples of copper measures of this type are more frequently found than those of pewter.

What-not: a portable stand with four uprights enclosing shelves, in use after about 1800 for books, ornaments, etc.

Wheat-ear ornament: carved ornament in the form of a wheat ear, frequently used on late 18th chair backs of shield-shape design. Chair backs of this type were included in Hepplewhite's (q.v.) *Cabinet Maker and Upholsterer's Guide.*

Wheel barometer: a siphon-type in which the variation of the mercury level is magnified and registered on a circular dial.

Wheel engraving: glass, rock crystal and semi-precious stones can be decorated by means of the lapidary's wheel, which is in principle a grindstone, fed by water and abrasive and mounted with metal or stone discs of various sizes according to the pattern desired. Engraving on glass is the same process as cutting, the surface of the material being afterwards polished, although sometimes a matt surface is used to contrast with a polished surface. The technique of wheel engraving was used by the Romans and in modern times, was first employed as a means of decorating glass at the Court of Rudolf II in Prague in the late 16th cent. English wheel engraved glass vessels date from the first quarter of the 18th cent., wine glasses bearing simple borders of scroll work and formal flowers being characteristic.

Wheel-lock: mechanism for igniting a gun, in which a piece of pyrites, fixed between the jaws of a cock, is pressed against the grooved edge of a wheel projecting through the bottom of the priming pan. The wheel is forced to rotate by a spring, released by the trigger, and rubs against the pyrites, causing a shower of sparks which ignite the powder. The lock is usually wound by means of a spanner, but on rare examples this is effected automatically, when the cock is drawn back.

The earliest known illustration of a wheel-lock mechanism is that in the Codex Atlanticus of Leonardo da Vinci (d. 1519). There is, however, no evidence to show that this was ever made, the first practical wheel-lock apparently having been produced in Germany in c. 1520. It is rarely found on military weapons, probably on account of the expense of manufacture, but it was much used for sporting and target guns until well into the 18th cent.

Wheel mark: see Hoechst porcelain.

Whieldon, Thomas: (1719-1795), a potter who founded his factory in 1740. From 1754 until 1759 Josiah Wedgwood (q.v.) was his partner. He built up an extensive business and made a fortune estimated at £10,000 from his trade. He declined potting about 1780, and became High Sheriff of Staffordshire in 1786. No marks were used at his pottery.

Whieldon, one of the best-known of English potters, had a strong and lasting influence on the tastes of his time and on the work of craftsmen to follow him.

He gave his name to a highly developed type of earthenware distinctive for its wide range of colours made possible by the use of coloured clays in the body and also by means of staining oxides in the glaze. Starting from the agate ware (q.v.) made at an earlier date, Whieldon revived and improved the methods formerly used, producing marbled wares of considerable merit. Simple shapes were customary in plates, dishes and other articles, the pieces relying mainly on colour for their appeal. "Tortoiseshell" ware (q.v.) was amongst Whieldon's most successful productions. For decoration, applied reliefs often in paler clay are characteristic. Spouts and handles were often made in a lighter-coloured clay, and lead glazes were used.

Josiah Wedgwood became Whieldon's partner in 1754; he was certainly in a great measure responsible for many of the improvements and developments which gave Whieldon his leading place amongst potters of his time. It was Wedgwood who revived the use of a brilliant green glaze, almost unused since the 16th cent., and put it to service in the making of "pineapple" and "cauliflower" pieces which were later to achieve great popularity.

Pieces made of black ware with gilt decoration were also made by Whieldon from about 1750. A similar body was used by potters at Jackfield (q.v.) in Shropshire at about this time, and the two are often indistinguishable.

Salt-glazed stoneware and earthenware were often made in the same shapes and from the same moulds. The formula for cream-coloured earthenware which formed the basis for many of Whieldon's productions was taken up by Wedgwood when he established his own factory and developed to become the Queen's ware on which his early reputation rested.

About the middle of the 18th cent. Whieldon engaged in making figures, both in salt-glaze and earthenware. The subjects were those familiar to a rural community; musicians, equestrian figures of extremely lively conception, soldiers, gamekeepers etc., all rendered in a simple manner and again relying on colour for their immediate effect.

The makers of such various kinds of Staffordshire wares of the time cannot usually be named with certainty. Many pieces are ascribed to Whieldon or Astbury. Whieldon made almost every type of ware in common use at this period, and added his knowledge and craftsmanship to the development of many of them. His pupils extended his influence, many becoming potters of repute.

Whistle tankard: see Blowhole.

Whorl: circular ornament on medieval (and later) furniture. The varying geometrical patterns employed were chip carved with the aid of a compass and set square. The general sense of the word seems to approximate whirl. The terms whorl and roundel are both used to describe this type of ornament.

Wilkes, John: a well-known locksmith of Birmingham responsible for a series of signed locks, most of them in latten (q.v.), some in blue steel serving as a background to applied brasswork, or in engraved steel. Wilkes became celebrated for his Detector lock of which many examples exist *in situ* in England and on the Continent. This lock is ornamented with the figure of a late Caroline soldier in relief. The left leg is extended by pushing a secret catch and this reveals the keyhole. The toe-cap of the boot then points to a number on the dial, by which the number of times the door has been opened is registered, as each turn of the key causes the number to change. The lock bolt is released by pushing back the hat.

Williamite glasses: wine glasses dating from after the Rising of 1745 engraved with portraits of William III, the Orange Tree or suitable inscriptions.

Willow pattern: a popular pseudo-Chinese design used as a decoration on porcelain and first engraved by Thomas Minton, and known in numerous variants. Mintons (q.v.), Spode, Turner, Davenport, Adams and others in Staffordshire used a version of the pattern, as did the factories of Leeds, Swansea, Liverpool and Sunderland. Dated examples are rare: a plate with this design in

Hanley Museum, Stoke-on-Trent is lettered "THOMASINE WILLEY, 1818".

Wilton carpets: although a charter for clothiers was granted in 1701, it is doubtful whether carpets were then made there. Lord Pembroke introduced Brussels carpet or moquette (q.v.) looms in 1740. From that date Wilton was in keen rivalry with Kidderminstser. The cutting of the looped velvet pile was probably an early speciality of Wilton, a type of carpeting subsequently called by its name. Wilson carpets, made on velvet or moquette looms in narrow strips with simple geometrical patterns, were certainly much used in 18th-cent. houses, as well as the costlier knotted pile carpets. The Brighton Pavilion accounts, for example, record orders for both. It is unlikely that knotted pile carpets were made at Wilton until the acquisition of the Axminster looms (q.v.) in 1835, since when they have continued to work.

Wincanton pottery: a pottery at Wincanton worked by Thomas Lindslee (who came from the Limekiln Lane Works, Bristol) and Nathaniel Ireson, made tin-glazed earthenware in the second quarter of the 18th cent. Pieces dated 1737 to 1748 are known. A typical decoration includes motifs within panels reserved against a speckled manganese ground.

Windmills, Joseph: a London clockmaker of repute, active between 1671 and 1725.

Windsor chair: a simple chair of traditional design, the back consisting of turned spindles, the legs turned and splayed. Both the back spindles and the legs are fixed to the solid wooden seat by dowel joints. Also known as "stick" chairs, existing examples date from the 18th and 19th cent., the basic form yielding little to the pressure of fashion. Early 18th cent. types include the fan- or comb-back, with a horizontal cresting rail and sometimes a central vase-shaped splat, flanked by turned spindles. Later examples have bow- or hoop-backs. The materials are beech, elm,

ash or yew, the seat usually being of elm or ash and saddle-shaped in form. American Windsor chairs have no central splat, the back being formed entirely of spindles. They appear to have been first made about 1725. A type fitted with rockers, known as the Windsor rocker, is also found.

Wine bottles: tin-enamelled globular bottles were made at Lambeth (specimens dated 1629 to 1672) with initials, date, and name of wine in blue such as Sack, "Whit", Claret, or "Rhenish".

Rackham and Read adopted the suggestion put forward by Frank Falkner that these were made for wine samples, being too small for use in such hard-drinking days, (*English Pottery*, 1924) but they may have been intended for what appears, from contemporary diaries, to have been a customary gift, on January 1st, of a bottle of wine (F. H. Garner, *English Delftware*, 1948).

Wine-bottle stand: a silver oval bowl on moulded base for holding the early form of glass wine-bottle with rounded base dating from the early 18th cent. The very rare examples that survive are sometimes mistaken for sugar-bowls.

Wine-cistern: large oval vessel on base or separate feet for keeping bottles in cold water or ice. Wooden wine-cisterns were lined with lead and came into wide use after c. 1730. Silver survivals date from Charles II to the mid-18th cent. These can be regarded as important decorative pieces of a high standard of design and ornament.

Wine-coaster: see Coaster.

Wine-cooler: (also known as ice-pail) a silver or plated vessel for keeping a single bottle in cold water or ice. A few survivals from early 18th cent. but not common till about 1780. Vase or tub shape, and occasionally of double oval form. Occur in pairs or sets of four or more. Usually fitted with liner and flat rim.

Wine cup: small, individual silver goblet on high stem, common in the late 16th and 17th cent. but revived in the Regency period. Also known as grace cup. Very small examples of mid-17th cent. have a small, trumpet-shaped foot in place of a stem.

Wine-fountain: large vase-shaped silver urn with tap in body. Made in second half of 17th and early 18th cent., often en suite with wine-cisterns (q.v.). They were used to keep wine, but were also used for the more humble purpose of holding water for washing up silver vessels. Numerous English examples survive, but very few from other European countries.

Wine-funnel: tapering funnel with detachable strainer for decanting. Circular stands of saucer form with domed centres were used with the funnels.

Wine-glass cooler: a glass vessel resembling a finger-bowl but with one or two lips in the rim.

Wine-label: pierced or chased label with the name of the wine hung by chain round decanter neck. A rarer form has neck ring in place of chain. Made in silver and enamelled copper in many varieties of form and name, including plain initials (see also Bottle tickets), occuring from mid-18th cent. onwards.

Wine-taster: silver small shallow, circular bowl with one, two or no handles and slightly domed centre. The handleless form with plain spreading sides when reversed is occasionally mistaken for a trencher salt. Examples occur from the mid-17th cent. onwards.

Wing bookcase: see Break-front bookcase.

Wing chair: upholstered arm chair with a high back, stuffed arms, and

wings. This type of armchair was introduced towards the end of Charles II's reign, and the form soon became standardized, remaining popular until after the middle years of the 18th cent. It was also known as a Grandfather chair.

Wing lantern clock: a type, popular for about a quarter of a cent. at the end of the 17th cent., where the pendulum was placed between the going and striking trains, and took the form of an anchor, the flukes of which appeared each side of the main framework, and were protected by wings.

Wire work: among the rarest pieces of Sheffield plate are those constructed from plated wires, dating chiefly between 1785 and 1815. They were a direct result of George Whateley's patented invention of 1768, by which copper rods, round, flat, square, and triangular, could be silver-plated. Not until after the expiry of the patent in 1782 was this work carried out on a considerable scale, the demand being chiefly for a wide range of inexpensive table baskets, toast-racks, and epergnes. The wires at first were cut into short lengths, fitted into holes drilled into rim and base, and soldered into position. Early in the 19th cent. less expensive wire ware was made by bending lengths of wire into continuous curves forming patterns. These were soldered to rim and base, thus saving the cost of drilling. Ball handles might consist of flat wire curved and spaced with balls or other ornament, or of twisted wire of various sections.

Witch balls: glass globes of 19th cent. date made probably at Nailsea, Bristol (qq.v.) and elsewhere. They exist in many sizes, from a few inches to a foot and a half in diameter and in several types, some with colours roughly painted on the interior of clear glass, others silvered or of coloured glass and with coloured pictures stuck to the inside of a clear globe.

Witch bottles: bellarmines have been so named, because they have been found frequently under the thresholds or hearths of old houses, or in ditches or river beds, usually filled with such things as pieces of cloth pierced with pins, twists of human hair, hand-made nails, finger-nail parings, and bones.

These charms were either intended to ward off the evil effects of witch-craft, or to inflict some injury upon another person by magical processes.

"W" mark: see Berlin and Wallendorf (under Limbach) porcelain. For "W***" mark, see Wood, Enoch.

Wolverhampton lock: the finest English locks have been made here from early in the 17th cent. In 1660 Wolverhampton paid a hearth tax on 84 locksmiths' hearths and there were 97 in nearby Willenhall. The Georgian locksmiths of Wolverhampton maintained their high reputation and, when George III equipped the Queen's House, now Buckingham Palace, he specified that certain locks should be made in Wolverhampton.

Woodcut: a relief process, or black line process, obtained by cutting the plank of the wood with a knife.

Wood engraving: a very large number of engravings and, in particular, of book illustrations of the Victorian era were from wood blocks, the artists and engravers (often one and the same person) following after the great tradition started by Thomas Bewick (1753–1828). The illustrations of the 1860s were largely reproduced by wood-engravings.

Wood, Enoch: (1759–1840), Enoch Wood was the son of Aaron Wood, the celebrated block-cutter and modeller; He started to manufacture pottery in partnership with Ralph Wood about 1784, making useful earthenware, cane ware (q.v.), Egyptian black, coloured bodies, and seals and cyphers. In 1790 he took into partnership James Caldwell of Linley Wood, and traded as Wood & Caldwell until 1818. Subsequently he took his sons into the business, who continued it under the style Enoch Wood & Sons until 1846 (six years after his death).
Marks:

E. WOOD

ENOCH WOOD
SCULPSIT
(impressed or incised)

WOOD & CALDWELL

There are several variations.

Impressed

Enoch Wood was an accomplished modeller who did portraits of John Wesley from life, which became famous. Other busts were executed by him, notably Whitefield, Handel, King William IV, Emperor Alexander of Russia. Large figure groups such as the "Ariadne & Bacchus" after a sculpture by Houdon are characteristic. Toby jugs, groups representing "The Night Watchman" or "Parson & Clerk" are more attractive. Many tree background pieces were made by him. These are usually enamelled over glaze, sometimes with the addition of touches of silver lustre.

Excellent blue-printed earthenware was made for the American market. Over sixty American views were produced, usually with an elaborate "shell" border. English and French views were also made, and religious subjects.

Jasper wares and black basaltes in the style popularised by Wedgwood were made, and some experimental porcelain.

Wood, Ephraim: (b. 1773 d. after 1830), cousin of Enoch Wood (q.v.) and the younger Ralph Wood; enameller, gilder and lusterer of earthenware, and manufacturer of pottery figures.

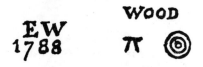

Wood, Ralph: there were three generations of potters of this name; Ralph Wood the elder (1715–72), was the son of a miller. He commenced to manufacture salt-glazed stoneware, "Whieldon" ware, figures and toby jugs in Burslem in 1754 and built up a successful business which was continued by his son, Ralph Wood II (1748–95) and grandson, Ralph Wood III (1781–1801) until 1801. Marks:

R. WOOD
(impressed)

Ra Wood   Ra Wood
(impressed)   Burslem

1770 Ralph Wood

Incised

A rebus mark in the form of a miniature representation of trees occurs on some Wood figures. Many Wood figures were impressed with mould numbers which have been tabulated and identified.

Ralph Wood figures and toby jugs of the early period are characterised by skilful modelling in relation to the glaze effects which the elder Ralph Wood introduced. These stained glazes, applied with a brush, were generally rather grey and washy in appearance but richer and deeper where the modelling or tooling was sharp.

Black basaltes figures were made and a number of excellent toby jugs. John Voyez (q.v.) is believed to have modelled for Ralph Wood. The younger Ralph Woods decorated their figures with bright on-glaze enamel colours.

Worcester porcelain: the Worcester manufactory was established in 1751 by a company of subscribers including Dr John Wall, physician, William Davis, apothecary, Richard and Josiah Holdship, and Edward Cave whose association with the *Gentleman's Magazine* gave the factory products considerable free publicity.

Porcelain manufacture was commenced at Warmstry House, from a formula used at Bristol.

In 1772 the original company was reconstituted and Robert Hancock held for two years shares in the business. After the death of Wall in 1776 and Davis in 1783 (end of "Dr Wall" period) the concern was bought by the London agent Thomas Flight for his two sons, Joseph and John, and Robert Chamberlain left the factory to form a rival company.

John Flight died in 1791, and in the following year Martin Barr joined the company, the successive partnerships being

Flight & Barr   1792–07
Barr, Flight & Barr   1807–13
Flight, Barr & Barr   1813–40

In 1840 Chamberlain's concern was amalgamated with the original business and from 1847 his premises used, in place of Warmstry House, as the porcelain manufactory.

Walter Chamberlain and John Lilly became owners of the business in 1848, and in 1850 were joined by W. H. Kerr. From 1852 the style was Kerr & Binns and from 1862 the Royal Worcester Porcelain Company.

A third Worcester factory for porcelain, started by Thomas Grainger in 1801, was absorbed by Royal Worcester in 1889, while a fourth, founded by James Hadley in 1896, experienced a like fate in 1905. The Royal Worcester Company continues.

About 1755–65

1760

1760–95   1755–83   1780

In blue 1783–89

In red 1789–92

In red 1792–1807

1800   1820

B.F.B. Incised   F.B.B.

Barr, Flight & Barr 1807–13

Flight, Barr & Barr 1813–40

Printed Kerr & Binns

Impressed 1852–62

Printed James Hadley & Sons 1896–1903

James Hadley & Sons 1896–1903

Since 1862 Impressed

Early Worcester porcelain was a soapstone paste, almost indistinguishable from that of Bristol of preceding years, thin and hard-looking, at first a creamy white, but soon somewhat greyish in tint, and finished with glaze which tended to shrink or recede from the foot-rings. Useful wares were made, teapots, cream jugs, cups and saucers, as well as other items; shapes were often derived from silver. Underglaze blue chinoiseries (q.v.) in imitation of imported "Nankin" china were among the earliest decorations. Sometimes the underglaze blue of early Worcester is blurred. Other pseudo-Chinese decorations were done in a brilliant palette of enamels, with delicate drawing.

In the Dr Wall period (1752–83) the settled conditions of productions resulted in a much wider range of wares and decorations, marked by excellent potting. Shapes of useful wares are generally dominated by silver forms. A thin glaze tending to shrink from the footring is still characteristic; it is never crazed. Landscape and figure subjects in the European style; fantastic crimson landscapes in reserved panels against yellow grounds; red landscapes painted upon relief scrolls super-imposed on leaf dishes; flower painting in the style of Meissen (q.v.); transfer-printing in black, brown, purple or red, occasionally washed over in colour; all these may be found in the early Wall period. After Chelsea (q.v.) artists had been taken on at the factory about 1768, decoration became more elaborate and Meissen influence gave place to Sèvres (q.v.). Workmanship was always of the highest quality although decorations tended to hide the quality of the paste. The looser Kakiemon (q.v.) patterns were replaced with brocaded Imari (q.v.) all-over designs, panelled with fan-shaped and circular patches. Coloured grounds were extensively used in combination with reserved panels enclosing exotic birds, or foliage and figure subjects framed in gold. Sometimes grounds were diapered with patterns, such as the imbricated dark-blue ground generally known as "scale blue". A powder-blue ground was also used. Gilding was generally lace-like in quality and of excellent workmanship. Much Worcester porcelain in this period was outside decorated at James Giles's (q.v.) workshop in London. Vases with large reserved panels were supplied to John Donaldson (q.v.) to be filled with figure subjects, such as *Leda and the Swan* after Boucher, or to J. H. O'Neale (q.v.) to be painted with animals or long-limbed graceful mythological figures. Fluted jugs with rococo handles, "cabbage-leaf" jugs, elegant candlesticks, rococo flower holders, jugs with mask or foliated lips, flanged bottles and leaf dishes of many kinds were made from the 1760s.

Black-pencilled Chinese subjects of a rather attenuated kind contrast with precise imitations of the oriental in colour. Transfer-printing at Worcester was extensively used. From 1760, blue-and-white decoration, transfer-printed or painted, was characterized by a deep strong tone almost like indigo blue. Figures in Worcester porcelain have a certain rarity value but are lacking in accomplishment. The poses are awkward and stiff. Interest in paste diminishes towards the end of the 18th cent., and decoration becomes of supreme importance. Landscapes of a topographical kind were adapted from contemporary engravings usually of local or near-local subjects in the finished style popularized at Derby. Classical subjects, shells, feathers, portraits, are typical of the neo-classic phase of Worcester production. Armorial services, in this as in earlier periods were extensively produced.

In the 19th cent. "Japans" in the style of Derby or Spode (qq.v.) became common; new ground colours were brought into use, covered with sea-weed and vermicelli patterns in bright mercury gilding. (See Gilding.) Later Worcester porcelain of the 19th cent. has often distinctive, if not aesthetically satisfying qualities. The almost miraculous pierced wares of George Owen, emulating Japanese ivory carving, or the styles derived from Japanese export Satsuma (q.v.) are typical.

Work-table: the name usually applied to the special table made in the second half of the 18th cent. for ladies' needle-work, etc.

In Sheraton's time these tables were of several kinds; some, mounted on four tapered and reeded legs or on trestle feet, might include, in addition to a drawer, such fittings as a pouch for the work materials, an adjustable fire-screen and a writing-board or slide. Another type, the "French Work-table", was a tray on trestle feet with a shelf or shelves below.

Wormed stem: see Air-twist stem.

Wrappers, wrappered: paper covers, plain, marbled or printed. A wrappered book, in antiquarian parlance, is what would ordinarily be called a paper-back, and it has nothing to do with dust-wrappers or dust-jackets.

"Wreathing": spiral marks appearing as a defect in thrown porcelain wares. Some examples of Bristol hard-paste porcelain show "wreathing".

Wrigglework: a form of engraved decoration on pewter and silver, employing a zig-zag line cut by rocking a gouge from side to side in its progress. Used in conjunction with line engraving at certain periods, principally late in the 17th cent., for filling in spaces between engraved lines.

Writing-box stands: the post-Restoration writing-box might be placed on a stand instead of a table. This had gate-legs and the fall-down flap of the box opened on to them for writing.

Even towards the end of the 17th cent. box and stand might be separate, although the box was acquiring the characteristic shape of the more elaborate desk, with the writing portion based on a chest of drawers. The simplest stands were without drawers, and resembled some of the first toilet looking-glass boxes. Early legs were turned and tapering, linked by flat, waved stretchers. By about 1705 simple cabriole legs were coming into use.

Writing-table: many varieties of small writing-tables can be found dating from the end of the 17th cent., when they were first introduced. Early examples were made with turned baluster legs and folding tops, and were frequently used also as side- and card-tables. Gate-legs were usual, and some were fitted with a drawer. Decoration with marquetry is often found. In the early 18th cent. small knee-hole writing-tables were popular, with tiers of narrow drawers on each side of the central recess. Similar tables, it may be noted, were also used as dressing-tables, and it is not always possible to determine their exact purpose. After the introduction of mahogany, when the fashion arose for larger pedestal tables in libraries, many versions of the convenient lighter table continued to be made. It was at the end of the cent. that perhaps the most elegant kinds of these smaller tables were seen, frequently of satin-wood. Some closely resembled contemporary secretaires and cheverets; others were fitted with an adjustable board for writing and with a screen.

Wrotham pottery: slipware (q.v.) was made at Wrotham and in the neighbourhood in the 17th and 18th cent., when the pottery there was extensive. A Wrotham pottery was in existence in 1612; no dated pieces are known after 1739. Owners are unknown, but it is suggested that Thomas Jull, whose initials appear on some Wrotham pieces, may have been one of them. Similar wares were being made in Staffordshire at this period making identification difficult in some cases, but many pieces are marked "WROTHAM", often in conjunction with the initials of potter or eventual owner.

Wares for domestic use formed a large part of the production of Wrotham. Cups, jugs, tygs and posset-pots were all made there, though dishes seem to have been comparatively rare. The body of the ware was usually of lead-glazed red clay, decorated with white or yellow slip in simple patterns; these were inscriptions in either applied or trailed slip, pads of white clay bearing initials or designs in relief. Some applied decoration is edged with an imitation of stitching, and other types of ornament derived from embroidery are used. Handles often bear a groove through their length which is filled with a twisted cord of white and red clay. Stars, masks and rosettes occur frequently as motifs. Many of the jugs are reminiscent of Rhenish stoneware (q.v.).

Wrought iron: literally iron which has been worked or formed by a blacksmith. The term has also come to mean a type of iron which contains practically no carbon but a considerable amount of slag which often gives it a grainy appearance. Wrought iron is readily worked and welded in the forge and is characterized by great toughness and ductility.

Wrythening: diagonally twisted or swirled ribbing or fluting on the bowl or stem of a glass vessel.

Wrythen-top spoon: a rare medieval form of spoon in which the stem is surmounted by a spirally-fluted ovoid finial.

Wu ts'ai (five-colour) wares: this generally implies the characteristic Wan Li period Chinese porcelain wares, painted in underglaze blue and enamel colours (red, green, yellow and purple). Some, however, date from Chia Ching (q.v.), and they cont'nue into K'ang Hsi's (q.v.) reign, when the *famille verte* was introduced.

X-chair: chairs covered all over with fabric, supported on an X frame date from the Middle Ages. The frames and legs were usually of softwood. Early 17th cent. examples survive. The X frame was used for stools in the second quarter of the 18th cent. and returned to popularity during the Regency.

Yard-arm barometer: see Diagonal barometer.

Yard-of-ale: a drinking glass measuring some three feet or so in length. There is a record of one dating from as early as the year 1685.

Considering their fragile nature it is not surprising that surviving yards-of-ale are seldom above a cent. old. The greater number of such survivors are not straightforward drinking vessels, but trick glasses. In them, the flared mouth tapers at length to a bulb at the foot, which ensures that the drinker cannot rest the vessel, and once started the glass must be drained completely or the contents will be spilled. The trick about these glasses is that when the liquid has been nearly all consumed and the glass is raised above the horizontal to finish the remainder, the air trapped in the bulb by the action of lifting the glass forces the residuum

violently into the face of the unlucky victim.

Quite a number of the glasses must have been produced in the glasshouses of Bristol and Nailsea, but it is not possible to distinguish them from others that were made elsewhere.

Yasuriko: (*Japanese* = file powder), a Japanese lacquer-work technique in which metal filings are sprinkled on the surface of the lacquer, often graduated in size but not deeply laid like *nashiji* (q.v.).

Year clock: a clock designed to go for one year with one winding.

Ye-goyomi: Japanese pictorial calendars.

Yehon: Japanese term for picture book. (See Japanese print.)

Yellowback: the term applied to a series of cheap reprinted books, mostly fiction, because of the colour of the binding, which was basically yellow. Cloth was not used but boards with a pictorial design, sometimes of a very striking nature. Many very famous books have appeared as yellowbacks: most of Trollope, some of Thomas Hardy, even Jane Austen. Collecting yellowbacks is amusing and does' not cost much money, but unless space is no object considerable selectivity should be employed. Most yellowbacks are in an atrocious condition, and it is well in this, as in all other forms of collecting, to refuse all but fine copies.

The inventor of the yellowback was Edmund Evans, who prepared an illustrated coloured cover as a novelty for a series of "railway" novels, to be read on train journeys. The basic colour was originally white, but this was found not to wear and yellow was substituted. (See Michael Sadleir, *Nineteenth Century Fiction*, 2 vols., 1951.)

Yi-hsing stoneware: unglazed red and brown Chinese stoneware teapots which accompanied the new drink to late 17th-cent. Europe. They are often beautifully shaped, rounded or faceted, with incised or moulded relief decoration. Less pleasing are over-naturalistic forms of tree-trunks or fruit. Signatures of Ming potters are too common for credence; dating is difficult, but later pieces are generally of poorer quality. Crudely enamelled pieces are probably 19th cent. Glazed imitations of Sung Chün ware are spoken of.

Ying ch'ing ("shadowy blue") ware: Chinese porcelain with brilliant transparent glaze of a pale bluish or greenish tinge, made in Kiangsi and other provinces chiefly during the Sung dynasty (q.v.). The best examples are of a sugary fracture, thinly and delicately potted: lobed bowls, cups or vases. Freely incised or moulded designs often resemble those of Ting ware.

Yoko-ye: Japanese prints; horizontal pictures.

Yomud rugs: Turkestan rugs which usually have diamond-shaped motifs, often composed of latch hooks and cloud-band borders.

York House: the factory engaged in making painted enamels, Battersea, London, owned by Stephen Theodore Janssen, 1753–56. (See also Battersea enamel.)

Yorkshire chair: see under Derbyshire chair.

Yorkshire clock: a broad and ill-proportioned long-case clock made for some years towards the end of the 18th cent. and early 19th.

Youghal lace: needlepoint, reproducing the Venetian flat point lace and rose point (q.v.). This lovely lace was developed in Co. Cork in the late 1840s, but later was largely replaced by crochets.

Yüan dynasty: dynasty of the Mongol Emperors in China, covering the period 1279 to 1368. The irresistible onslaught of Genghis Khan resulted in the establishment of the Yüan dynasty in China by his famous descendant Kublai. During this period, porcelain decorated in low relief known as *shu fu* (q.v.) or "Privy Council" ware became important. With the adoption

of painting in underglaze blue and the rise of the porcelain factories of Ching-tê-chên (q.v.), a radical change in taste took place.

Yüeh ware: celadon ware (q.v.) with grey porcellanous body and thin, pale, greyish green or buff glaze, made in Chekiang Province in China from about the 3rd to 11th cent. Early examples often borrowed forms and moulded decoration from bronze work. Later pieces may be delicately potted, with lobed sides, and delicately incised designs.

Yung Chêng porcelain: porcelain made in the reign of the Chinese Emperor Yung Chêng (1725–35). This short reign brought a taste for softer colouring and somewhat feminine refinement, the *famille verte* enamels giving way to those of the *famille rose* (qq.v.) with their prominent rose-pink (introduced from Europe) and other semi-opaque colours. Thin "egg-shell" plates and bowls were adorned with delicately drawn flowers or ladies. Elegance of shape also distinguishes the monochromes, again expanded in range of colour. The classic Sung and Ming styles, e.g. the Kuan and Ko ware (qq.v.), and the delicate *tou ts'ai* (q.v.) enamels were revived and imitated and, indeed, most underglaze blue or red wares of the Yung Chêng and Ch'ien Lung (q.v.) periods reflect the 15th cent. (Hsüan Tê or Ch'êng Hua) style. From this time, too, wares with designs copied from European prints or with coats of arms supplied to order were much exported.

Zecchino: see Ducat.

"Z" mark: see Zürich porcelain.

Zucchi, Antonio: (1726–95), Italian painter who made the acquaintance of Robert Adam in Italy and was later employed by him in England. Married Angelica Kauffman (q.v.).

Zürich porcelain: the early porcelain made at Zürich at a factory founded in 1763 and directed by Adam Spängler; soft-paste was produced, but some two years after the foundation of the factory, hard-paste was introduced. In spite of the artistic excellence of its work, the financial difficulties were such that the factory closed soon after 1800. Some of the Zürich figures, in particular, are much sought after. The mark was a "Z" in blue.

Zwischengoldgläser: (*Ger.*), German glasses of the 18th cent. decorated with gold-leaf applied and engraved. The tumbler thus decorated had been ground down for the greater part of its height so that a second, outer glass without a bottom could be fitted over it in order to protect the gilding.

For Further Reading

GENERAL WORKS

COMSTOCK, HELEN. *The Concise Encyclopedia of American Antiques.* 2 vols. The Connoisseur, London. 1958; Hawthorn Books, Inc, New York. 1958; McClelland and Stewart, Toronto. 1958

EDWARDS, RALPH and RAMSAY, L. G. G. *The Connoisseur Period Guides.* 6 vols. The Connoisseur, London. 1956–58

PRATT, RICHARD and DOROTHY. *Treasury of Early American Homes.* Rev. ed., Hawthorn Books, Inc, New York. 1959. *The Second Treasury of Early American Homes,* Hawthorn Books, Inc, New York. 1954, 1959.

RAMSEY, L. G. G. *The Concise Encyclopedia of Antiques.* 5 vols. The Connoisseur, London. 1955–60; Hawthorn Books, Inc, New York. 1955–60

ARMS AND ARMOUR

BLAIR, CLAUDE. *European Armour.* Batsford, London. 1958

HAYWARD, J. F. *Armour.* Victoria and Albert Museum, London. 1951

HAYWARD, J. F. *Swords and Daggers.* Victoria and Albert Museum, London. 1951

HAYWARD, J. F. *European Firearms.* Victoria and Albert Museum, London. 1955

HELD, ROBERT. *The Age of Firearms.* Harper Bros., New York. 1957

PETERSON, HAROLD L. *Arms and Armor in Colonial America 1526–1783.* Harrisburg, Pennsylvania. 1956

BOOKS, PRINTS AND SILHOUETTES

CARTER, JOHN. *ABC for Book-Collectors.* Hart–Davis, London. 1952

CARTER, JOHN. *Books and Book Collectors.* Hart–Davis, London. 1956

COMSTOCK, HELEN. *American Lithographs.* Barrows, New York, 1950

GRAY, BASIL. *The English Print.* Black, London. 1937

HILLIER, J. *Japanese Masters of the Colour Print.* Phaidon, London. 1954

HIND, A. M. *The Processes and Schools of Engraving.* 4th ed. British Museum, London. 1952

JACKSON, E. NEVILLE. *Silhouette-Notes and Dictionary.* Methuen, London. 1938

LEHMANN–HAUPT, H., WROTH, L. C. and SILVER, R. G. *The Book in America.* 2nd ed. Bowker, New York. 1951

MUIR, P. H. *Book-Collecting as a Hobby.* Gramol Publications, London. 1944

RUFFY, A. W. *Japanese Colour Prints.* Victoria and Albert Museum, London. 1952

TOOLEY, R. V. *English Books with Coloured Plates 1790–1860.* Batsford, London. 1954

CLOCKS AND WATCHES

BAILLIE, G. H. *Watchmakers and Clockmakers of the World.* 2nd ed. N.A.G. Press, London. 1947

BRITTEN, F. J. *Old Clocks and Watches and their Makers.* 7th ed. Dutton, London. 1956

DREPPERD, CARL W. *American Clocks and Clockmakers.* Branford, New York, 1955

LLOYD, ALAN. *The English Domestic Clock.* Privately printed. 1938

LLOYD, ALAN. *Chats on Old Clocks.* 2nd ed. Benn, London 1951

PALMER, BROOKS. *The Book of American Clocks.* Macmillan, New York. 1950

Symonds, R. W. *A History of English Clocks*. Penguin, London. 1947

FURNITURE

Downs, Joseph. *American Furniture*. Macmillan, New York. 1952

Edwards, Ralph. *English Chairs*. 2nd ed. Victoria and Albert Museum, London. 1957

Edwards, Ralph. *Georgian Furniture*. 2nd ed. Victoria and Albert Museum, London. 1958

Edwards, Ralph and Jourdain Margaret. *Georgian Cabinet-makers*, Country Life, London. 1946

Fastnedge, Raplh. *English Furniture Styles from 1500 to 1830*. Penguin, London. 1955

Gloag, John. *A Short Dictionary of Furniture*. Allen and Unwin, London. 1954

Gloag, John and Hackfnbroch, Yvonne. *English Furniture with some furniture from other countries in the Irwin Untermyer Collection*. Thames and Hudson, London. 1958

Heal, Sir Ambrose. *The London Furniture Makers (1660-1840)*. Batsford, London. 1953

Iverson, Marion Day. *The American Chair: 1630-1890*. Hastings House, New York. 1957

Kimball, Fiske. *The Creation of the Rococo*. Philadelphia Museum of Art. 1943

Macquoid, Percy and Edwards, Ralph. *The Dictionary of English Furniture*. Rev. ed. by Ralph Edwards. Country Life, London. 1954.

Nutting, Wallace. *Furniture Treasury*. 3 vols. Macmillan, New York. 1948-49

Pinto, Edward H. *Treen*. Batsford, London. 1949

Strange, T. A. *A Historical Guide to French Interiors*. 3rd imp. McCorquodale, London. 1950

Symonds, R. W. *Furniture Making in the Seventeenth and Eighteenth Century in England*. The Connoisseur, London. 1955

Victoria and Albert Museum.
A History of English Furniture. London. 1955

Ward-Jackson, Peter. *English Furniture Designs of the Eighteenth Century*. Victoria and Albert Museum, London. 1959

Watson, F. J. B. Wallace Collection Catalogues: *Furniture*. London. 1956

GLASS

Buckley, W. *European Glass*. Benn, London. 1926

Buckley, W. *The Art of Glass*. Allen and Unwin, London. 1939

Elville, E. M. *Paperweights and other Glass Curiosities*. Country Life, London. 1954

Haynes, E. B. *Glass through the Ages*. Rev. ed. Penguin, London. 1959

Hughes, G. Bernard. *Old English, Irish and Scottish Table Glass*. Batsford, London. 1956

McKearin, G. S. and H. *Two Hundred Years of American Blown Glass*. Crown Publishers, Inc, New York. 1950

Thorpe, W. A. *English and Irish Glass*. Medici, London and Boston. 1927

Thorpe, W. A. *A History of English and Irish Glass*. 2 vols. Medici, London. 1929

Thorpe, W. A. *English Glass*. Black, London. 1935

JEWELLERY AND ENAMELS

Evans, J. *A History of Jewellery 1100-1870*. Faber, London. 1953

Flower, Margaret. *Victorian Jewellery*. Cassell, London. 1951

Hughes, Therle and Bernard. *English Painted Enamels*. Country Life, London. 1951

Steingräber, E. *Antique Jewellery. Its History in Europe from 800 to 1900*. Thames and Hudson, London. 1957

MUSICAL INSTRUMENTS AND BOXES

Carse, Adam. *Catalogue of the Adam Carse Collection*. Horniman Museum, London. 1951

CLARKE, J. E. T. *Musical Boxes.* Fountain Press, London. 1952

DONINGTON, ROBERT. *The Instruments of Music.* 3rd ed. London. 1953

GALPIN, F. W. *A Textbook of European Instruments.* Sweet, London. 1937

GALPIN SOCIETY, THE. *British Musical Instruments.* London. 1951

GEIRINGER, KARL. *Musical Instruments.* Allen and Unwin, London. 1943

HOKE, HELEN and JOHN. *Music Boxes: Their Lore and Lure.* Hawthorn Books, Inc, New York. 1957

POTTERY AND PORCELAIN

BARRET, F. A. *Worcester Porcelain.* Faber, London. 1953

BEMROSE, GEOFFREY. *Nineteenth Century English Pottery and Porcelain.* Faber, London. 1952

BUSHNELL and DIGBY. *Ancient American Pottery.* Faber, London. 1955

COOPER, RONALD. *Pottery of Thomas Toft.* Leeds Art Gallery. 1952

CHARLESTON, R. J. *Roman Pottery.* Faber, London. 1955

CUSHION, J. P. and HONEY, W. B. *Handbook of Pottery and Porcelain Marks.* Faber, London. 1956

DIXON, J. L. *English Porcelain of the Eighteenth Century.* Faber, London. 1952

GARNER, F. H *English Delftware.* Faber, London. 1948

GRAY, BASIL. *Early Chinese Pottery and Porcelain.* Faber, London. 1953

HACKENBROCH, YVONNE. *Chelsea and other English Porcelain, Pottery and Enamel in the Irwin Untermyer Collection.* Thames and Hudson, London. 1957

HAGGAR, REGINALD G. *English Country Pottery.* Phoenix House, London. 1950

HAGGAR, REGINALD G. *The Concise Encyclopedia of Continental Pottery and Porcelain.* Deutsch, London. 1960; Hawthorn Books, Inc, New York. 1960

HAYWARD, J. F. *Vienna Porcelain of the du Paquier period.* Rockliff, London. 1952

HONEY, W. B. *The Ceramic Art of China and other countries of the Far East.* Faber, London. 1945

HONEY, W. B. *Corean Pottery.* Faber, London. 1947

HONEY, W. B. *Dresden China.* Faber, London. 1947

HONEY, W. B. *German Porcelain.* Faber, London. 1947

HONEY, W. B. *French Porcelain of the Eighteenth Century.* Faber, London. 1950

HONEY, W. B. *A Dictionary of European Ceramic Art.* 2 vols. Faber, London. 1952

HYDE, J. A. LLOYD. *Oriental Lowestoft. (Chinese Export Porcelain).* 2nd ed. Ceramic, Newport, Mon. 1954

JENYNS, SOAME. *Later Chinese Porcelain.* Faber, London. 1952

JENYNS, SOAME. *Ming Pottery and Porcelain.* Faber, London. 1953

JOHN, W. D. and BAKER, WARREN. *Old English, Lustre Pottery.* Ceramic, Newport, Mon. 1951

LANE, ARTHUR. *Early Islamic Pottery.* Faber, London. 1947

LANE, ARTHUR. *French Faience.* Faber, London. 1948

LANE, ARTHUR. *Greek Pottery.* Faber, London. 1948

LANE, ARTHUR. *Italian Porcelain.* Faber, London. 1956

LANE, ARTHUR. *Later Islamic Pottery.* Faber, London. 1957

MACKINTOSH, SIR HAROLD. *Early English Figure Pottery.* London, 1938

MANKOWITZ, WOLF. *Wedgwood.* Batsford, London. 1953

MANKOWITZ, WOLF and HAGGAR, REGINALD G. *The Concise Encyclopedia of English Pottery and Porcelain.* Deutsch, London. 1957; Hawthorn Books, Inc, New York. 1957

PRICE, R. K. *Astbury, Whieldon and Ralph Wood Figures and Toby Jugs.* Lane, London. 1922

RACKHAM, BERNARD. *Medieval English Pottery.* Faber, London. 1948

RACKHAM, BERNARD. *Early Stafford shire Pottery.* Faber, London. 1951

RACKHAM, BERNARD. *Italian Maiolica.* Faber, London. 1952

RACKHAM, BERNARD and JEREMY, P. *Animals in Staffordshire*. Penguin, London. 1953

SAVAGE, GEORGE. *Porcelain through the Ages*. Penguin, London. 1954.

SAVAGE, GEORGE. *18th Century English Porcelain*. Rockliff, London. 1952

SAVAGE, GEORGE. *Pottery through the Ages*. Penguin, London. 1959

TOWNER, DONALD. *English Cream-coloured Earthenware*. Faber, London. 1957

WATNEY, BERNARD. *Longton Hall Porcelain*. Faber, London. 1957

SILVER AND PEWTER

HAYWARD, J. F. *Huguenot Silver in England 1688–1727*. Faber, London. 1959

MICHAELIS, R. F. *Antique Pewter of the British Isles*. G. Bell and Sons, Ltd., London. 1955

OMAN, CHARLES. *English Domestic Silver*. 4th ed. Black, London. 1959

PHILLIPS, JOHN MARSHALL. *American Silver*. Parish, London. 1949; Chanticleer Press, New York. 1949; Clarke Irwin, Toronto. 1949

TAYLOR, GERALD. *Silver*. Penguin, London. 1956

VICTORIA and ALBERT MUSEUM. *Tudor Domestic Silver*, 1948. *Early Stuart Silver*, 1950. *Queen Anne Domestic Silver*, 1951. *English Medieval Silver*, 1952. *Mid-Georgian Domestic Silver*, 1952. *Regency Domestic Silver*, 1952. *Charles II Domestic Silver*, 1958. *Bottle-tickets*, 1958. London

TEXTILES

KENDRICK, A. F. *English Embroidery*. Newnes, London. 1905

KENDRICK, A. F. *English Needlework*. Black, London. 1933

KENDRICK, A. F. and TATTERSALL, C. E. C. *Handwoven Carpets, Oriental and European*. 2 vols. London. 1922

PETO, FLORENCE. *American Quilts and Coverlets*. Parish, London. 1949; Chanticleer Press, New York. 1949; Clarke Irwin, Toronto. 1949

THOMSON, W. G. *A History of Tapestry*. Rev. ed. Hodder and Stoughton, London. 1930

VICTORIA and ALBERT MUSEUM. *Notes on Quilting*, rept. 1949. *Notes on Applied Work and Patchwork*, rept. 1949. *Catalogue of English Domestic Embroidery*, 1950. *Indian Embroidery*, 1951